Private and Confidential

Private and Confidential

Letters from British Ministers
in Washington
to The Foreign Secretaries
in London, 1844–67

James J. Barnes
and
Patience P. Barnes

SUP

Selinsgrove: Susquehanna University Press
London and Toronto: Associated University Presses

Associated University Presses
440 Forsgate Drive
Cranbury, NJ 08512

Associated University Presses
25 Sicilian Avenue
London WC1A 2QH, England

Associated University Presses
P.O. Box 338, Port Credit
Mississauga, Ontario
Canada L5G 4L8

The paper used in this publication meets the requirements
of the American National Standard for Permanence of Paper
for Printed Library Materials Z39.48-1984.

Library of Congress Cataloging-in-Publication Data

Barnes, James J.
    Private and confidential: letters from British Ministers in Washington to the foreign secretaries in London, 1844-67 / James J. Barnes and Patience P. Barnes.
        p.   cm.
    Includes bibliographical references (p.   ) and index.
    ISBN 0-945636-33-4 (alk. paper)
    1. United States—Foreign relations—Great Britain. 2. Great Britain—Foreign relations—United States. 3. Diplomats—Great Britain—Correspondence. 4. United States—Foreign relations—1815–1861. 5. United States—Foreign relations—1861–1865. 6. Great Britain—Foreign relations—1837–1901. I. Barnes, Patience P. II. Title.
E183.8.G7B218 1993
327.73041—dc20   91-50101
                                                                          CIP

PRINTED IN THE UNITED STATES OF AMERICA

Contents

Acknowledgments

One of the greatest pleasures in undertaking this project was the opportunity to correspond with, or in some instances to meet personally, the heirs of those whose letters we have reprinted. Permission to reprint, or access to materials was kindly granted by: the Duke of Norfolk (Pakenham papers); the Earl of Clarendon; the Earl of Derby; the Earl of Elgin (Bruce papers); the Earl of Malmesbury; Baron Napier and Ettrick; Lady Hermione Cobbold (Bulwer papers).

Libraries were equally cooperative in providing access to the correspondence we sought, and in granting us permission to quote from their holdings. The Bodleian Library of Oxford University houses the Clarendon and Crampton papers, while the Public Record Office contains the Russell papers as well as the official dispatches of the British Foreign Office. The Foreign and Commonwealth Office in London was most helpful in interpreting the intricacies of diplomatic procedure and the drafting of dispatches. The Historical Manuscripts Commission readily made available the files relating to Lord Malmesbury and Lord Palmerston. Likewise the Liverpool Record Office graciously furnished the Derby papers. Finally the resources of the British Library and the Library of Congress were invaluable.

Of the many individuals who assisted us, special mention should be made of Patricia Radinger Pratt, Jennifer Chase Barnes, and Geoffrey Prescott Barnes, for their unfailing help with the reading and deciphering of handwritten letters; Richard Edgar-Wilson who proofread the entire manuscript before publication; Wabash College students David Feeback, Thomas Ristine, and Robert Vega, who devoted hours of painstaking effort to make sure our transcription of correspondence was accurate; and the staff of the Wabash College Library, especially John Swan, Mark Tucker, Ann Lebedeff, and Bruce Brinkley.

Much-needed and appreciated financial support was given by Wabash College, the American Philosophical Society, and the Fulbright International Exchange of Scholars program.

Finally we are most indebted to Elaine Greenlee, who has assisted with the book since its inception, aiding in the research and faithfully transcribing countless versions of the text.

Private and Confidential

Introduction

British diplomatic correspondence of the nineteenth century usually took the form of official or "public" dispatches. These were labeled "public" because Parliament had the right to call for, debate, and eventually publish them in the diplomatic Blue Books. At the beginning of each calendar year, diplomatic missions abroad began a new series of dispatches, numbering them in sequence. During the 1840s, 1850s, and 1860s British ministers in Washington sent two hundred to three hundred such dispatches each year. It was the chief task of unpaid diplomatic attachés to copy these in "black ink, in a large, legible, round, and distinct hand, with a sufficient interval between the Lines, on Folio Paper, and one quarter of the page is to be left on the inner side as a margin."[1] They were then placed in the Foreign Office Archives and eventually bound into stout leather volumes, now housed in the Public Record Office. These comprise the essential documents of any diplomatic history.

In addition to the "public" dispatches, there were several classifications of semiprivate correspondence that normally were not made available on request to either Parliament or the public at large. A Foreign Office circular letter of 1874 reiterated this distinction for the benefit of consuls stationed abroad.[2]

> In drafting your ordinary Despatches upon current affairs, . . . you will insert nothing which, in your opinion, it would be unwise to publish, or which could not be published without serious injury to your own usefulness as a Public Officer.
>
> Any information which is of a confidential nature should be reserved for Despatches marked "Confidential" or "Secret"; and from these you should carefully exclude any matter which could properly be published.
>
> I should wish you to understand that in future, when Despatches are received at the Foreign Office which are not marked "Confidential" or "Secret", it will be assumed that all that is contained in them is, in the writer's view, proper for immediate publication, and may be published without detriment, in his own judgment, either to his own position or to the public service, if Her Majesty's Government think it desirable.
>
> On the other hand, it will be assumed that, in Despatches which are marked "Confidential" or "Secret", the contents are of a character which, for the reasons above mentioned, makes it inexpedient that *any* portion of the Despatch should be published.

Still a third classification of dispatches passed between the foreign secretary and selected agents abroad. The use of the designation "Private and Confidential" was usually reserved for heads of mission, as distinct from consuls. Most of the letters in this volume were so categorized by the British ministers in Washington who served during the years 1845–67. At this time, Great Britain was represented not by an embassy but by a legation,[3] and there were six gentlemen who filled the post of envoy extraordinary and minister plenipotentiary to the United States: Richard Pakenham (1844–47); Henry Bulwer (1850–51); John F. T. Crampton (1852–56); Lord Napier (1857–59); Lord Lyons (1859–64); and Frederick Bruce (1865–67). Each was invited to correspond "privately" with the foreign secretary in London. "Confidential" or "Secret" dispatches automatically became a part of the Foreign Office Archives and were "placed on record," even though they were rarely published in a Blue Book. By contrast, "Private and Confidential" letters did not become part of the official archives unless specifically "placed on record" by the foreign secretary. Thus, the bulk of "Private and Confidential" letters are not to be found in the Public Record Office but among the personal papers of the various foreign secretaries who received them and usually retained them when leaving office.

During these years seven members of Parliament served as foreign secretary: Lord Aberdeen (1841–46); Lord Palmerston (1846–51); Lord Granville (1851–52); Lord Malmesbury (1852); Lord John Russell (1852–53); Lord Clarendon (1853–58); Lord Malmesbury (1858–59); Lord John Russell (1859–65); Lord Clarendon (1865–66); and Lord Edward Stanley (1866–68). Each of these men handled his "Private and Confidential" correspondence differently. Of the seven, Lord Palmerston was most inclined to place his incoming "private" letters on record, so that fully half of Henry Bulwer's correspondence can be found among the public dispatches at the Public Record Office. On the other hand, Lord Clarendon rarely recorded his "private" letters, although he undoubtedly shared some of them with the prime minister and other cabinet members. Foreign secretaries also differed in their willingness to invite private communications from those who were not heads of missions. For instance, John Crampton was secretary of the legation and chargé d'affaires in Washington from 1846 to 1851, but as far as can be determined, he was never asked to communicate privately with Lord Palmerston. Yet Lord Clarendon did not hesitate to correspond privately with the British chargé d'affaires between the time Crampton left Washington and Lord Napier arrived to replace him. An envoy extraordinary and minister plenipotentiary could not take such private exchanges for granted, as we see from Crampton's letter to Lord Granville shortly after Crampton was designated minister to the United States in 1852: "I am much gratified by your permission to put myself on a footing of confidential correspondence with you upon such matters as it may be advisable to treat in that manner."[4]

Ministers to Washington also differed in the number of "Private and

Confidential'' letters they penned each year, although the average was generally between thirty and fifty, each varying in length from a few pages to more than a dozen. Crises naturally generated more frequent writing, and so it is not surprising that far more private letters were written during the American Civil War than at any other comparable period.

Contemporary critics accused Victorian diplomats of using two sets of dispatches: public ones to mislead or even deceive the nation, and private ones to implement policy and protect reputations. Allegations of secret diplomacy were stoutly denied by several expert witnesses before Parliament in 1861.[5] Lord Clarendon characterized the charges as ''very incorrect'' and ''utterly and entirely without foundation.'' Earl Cowley, for years British ambassador to France, assured the investigating committee that ''there is no secret diplomacy, properly so called,'' while Lord John Russell echoed, ''there is none such carried on; anything that is agreed upon is a matter of public despatch.''[6]

The veteran diplomat, Viscount Stratford de Redcliffe, was a bit more cautious in dismissing the possible, if unintended, conflicts between public dispatches and private letters: ''anything which has the effect of contradicting in private what is made matter of instruction in the public correspondence, or anything that produces an action in public affairs, of which there is no trace in the public correspondence, is open to objection, as it is liable to abuse.''[7] As we shall see in chapter 1, there was also some confusion in the mind of Richard Pakenham, arising from what he perceived to be differences between Lord Aberdeen's official and private instructions.

Nevertheless, private correspondence was held to play a vital role. Lord Clarendon was emphatic: ''I consider that it is totally impossible to carry on the business of the Foreign Office with our foreign ministers unless by writing private letters.'' Lord Cowley agreed: ''It would be impossible to carry on the business between Paris and London without a great deal of private correspondence.''[8] Perhaps the most eloquent spokesman supporting the existing practice was Lord Wodehouse.[9]

> I think that it is indispensible that there should be a private correspondence between the Secretary of State for Foreign Affairs and the heads of missions abroad, but all matters of public importance should be recorded in despatches, and a private letter should only be supplemental to a public despatch; for instance, in recounting an interview with a minister, there may be some small personal details which it might not be altogether proper to put in a public letter, but everything that is of public importance should be recorded. Then, a private letter may contain a good deal of gossip, and many stories which may be more or less worth recounting, but for the precise accuracy of which a minister could not vouch, so as to make them the subject of public despatches.

Sir George H. Seymour expanded on this theme: ''Supposing that a particular person gave me a piece of intelligence of a secret nature, I should be sorry that that person's name should be quoted in a public Despatch, although I should have no objection to put it into a private letter, as it might give weight to the testimony."[10]

The practice of publishing extracts from diplomatic correspondence was always a delicate one. What seemed innocuous enough at the time might come home to haunt an envoy five years later. While some witnesses before the 1861 Select Committee felt they had never been embarrassed or annoyed by subsequent publication of some of their dispatches, others, like Seymour, were more fearful. "I think that it is apt to give offence, and causes apprehension and trepidation. The approach of a Blue Book is always looked to with great anxiety; there is no doubt about that."[11] In Washington in 1850, Henry Bulwer expressed some of the same concern over Parliament's scrutiny of what was to be called the Clayton-Bulwer Treaty.[12]

> I would beg you in the publication of any documents which you judge necessary to lay before the House of Commons with the Convention of April 19, to pay what I will venture to term "an exaggerated attention" to the possibility of any word or passage of any communication of mine exciting the susceptibility of this over-susceptible people.
>
> I should not deem it necessary to trouble you on such a subject did I not think that the propensity to be offended is at times stronger here, or at least parties make it appear stronger, than any reasonable person at any distance could imagine, and as I am sure that certain parties are more or less jealous of my supposed popularity (I will here include my French colleague) I am anxious to avoid, as far as I can, giving them any opportunity of the kind they look for.

By making Bulwer's "Private and Confidential" letter "official," Palmerston would merely have been placing it on record and filing it with the public dispatches. He would not have been authorizing its publication—quite the contrary—but rather indicating that it should be made available to future officials of the Foreign Office instead of disappearing with him when he left the cabinet.

There were certain ministers, however, who genuinely relished the prospect of their dispatches, both public and private, appearing in print. Crampton was one. As he silently endured vicious attacks by the American press and his political opponents, he explained to Lord Clarendon, "I have embodied all I had to say in a despatch to you which if ever necessary may come out through the proper official channels by being laid before Parliament. . . . I shall therefore pass over with perfect equanimity all their attacks in Congress or the papers and never reply to them except through the official channel of a despatch to my Government."[13]

Perhaps the American historian and diplomat John Lothrop Motley best summed up the predicament confronting envoys on both sides of the Atlantic. Writing to James Russell Lowell in 1864, he lamented:[14]

> Since [Secretary of State] Seward instituted this system, (which between you and me I don't at all fancy) of publishing annually the despatches to and from the State Department, one is obliged to write the most perfectly circumspect and idiotic trash—if I have any facts or comments at all worth reading to make, the letters containing them are always marked "private and confidential" and very often written on note paper like this.

Motley's allusion to the type of paper on which "Private and Confidential" letters were written raises yet another complication. There were in fact two sizes of paper on which a head of mission could communicate privately with his superior, as Viscount Stratford de Redcliffe pointed out in 1861. "Letters marked Private and Confidential written in regular form on large paper" were given a semiofficial status and might be occasionally published at the "discretion of the Secretary of State." Alternatively, communiqués written on ordinary notepaper and marked with the single word "private" were treated as "correspondence between individuals, although relating to public subjects." Stratford de Redcliffe readily acknowledged that he would feel distinctly ill-used if such a private letter ever found its way into a government publication.[15] Bulwer expressed a similar ambivalence when sending Lord Palmerston both a private note and a "Private and Confidential" letter in the same mailing. "I have marked my long communication on Cuban affairs as Private and Confidential in order that you may make it official or not as you may deem best. I am fully aware of one's tendency to exaggerate the importance of matters passing under one's especial observation and am therefore only distrustful in this instance of my own judgment."[16]

In this volume we have not sought to distinguish between letters marked "Private" and letters marked "Private and Confidential." Of those that are included, the majority were labeled "Private and Confidential," but only a few were placed on record, and these we have cited as "P.R.O. F.O. 5," indicating that they are in the Public Record Office as part of the Foreign Office 5 series dealing with the United States.

In choosing which letters to reprint, we were confronted by widely divergent letter-writing habits. Some ministers like Palmerston wrote relatively few private letters, while Crampton and Lyons were voluminous correspondents, and here we had to be highly selective. Even then, the arrangement of these letters presented a difficult problem. Should they be organized chronologically, regardless of the issues dominating a given time, or would a topical framework be preferable, at the expense of continuity? In the end, we opted for a chronological order so that the style and temperament of each minister would emerge within a chapter.

The primary emphasis throughout this book is on the ways in which six British ministers perceived American politics and society, and how they conveyed their understanding to London. This is a one-sided correspondence to be sure, but our purpose is to focus on the implementation of British policy in Washington and not on its formation in London.

Certain other considerations governed the editing of these letters. Most of them appear in print here for the first time, but where a portion has been published elsewhere, we have indicated accordingly. Minor alterations in punctuation and abbreviation have been introduced in the interest of readability.

Perhaps the single most distinctive characteristic of the "Private and Confidential" letters was their candor. Not only did this give them vitality and a sense of immediacy, but at the same time, it posed awkward security problems for their delivery. Ordinarily, dispatches were sent in a sealed diplomatic pouch that accompanied the regular United States post from Washington to New York. There it was claimed by an agent of the British government and placed aboard a British vessel bound for Liverpool. It was generally felt that the weakest link in this system was the American post office, and so, whenever possible, all "Private and Confidential" communications were entrusted to a special courier traveling between Washington and the ports of New York and Boston. In February 1853, Crampton tried to explain to the new foreign secretary, Lord Clarendon, the inhibitions imposed by the absence of such a courier.[17]

This is however not my "messenger week" and I therefore cannot launch out as freely into the realms of truth as I could do when I have a sure conveyance. I do not mean to insinuate by this that the U.S. Post Office is sufficiently advanced or "smart" as to possess a "cabinet noir" for the benefit of the Government. Letters are however subject to a risk much more disagreeable to the writer, of being lost, and found, and making their first appearance in the columns of some enterprising newspaper under the heading of a "rich treat to our readers" or "diplomatic scheming divulged", as happened to Bulwer's first Private and Confidential letter to Mr. Chatfield in Central America.

Bulwer and Crampton never quite knew how the *New York Herald* got hold of such a private communication, but the episode was later told by the newspaper's managing editor, Frederick Hudson.[18]

A gentleman travelling from the interior of Honduras to Omoa, on his way to Havana, found by the road-side portions of a mail which had been examined and rifled by robbers. He gathered up some of the letters, among which was the above free and easy note [from Bulwer to Chatfield]. It was carried to Havana and shown to a number of Spanish merchants, and obtained by the correspondent of the *Herald* in that city. It created a sensation in diplomatic circles in Washington and London.

Crampton wrote a "Private and Confidential" letter almost every week, but the need for a prompt response varied considerably. On 9 April 1854 he began his letter to Lord Clarendon, "I have thought it right to send this letter by messenger to Boston, as you will thus receive it a week earlier," and a month later he reiterated:

> I have thought that the subjects treated of in this letter, as well as the importance of a safe arrival of Mr. Marcy's answer to our note in regard to neutrals, would justify me in sending my correspondence by special messenger to Boston instead of giving it to the American Post Office, which is getting worse and worse in regard to regularity and safety.

Two years later, however, he reported, "Nothing has occurred here of sufficient importance to render it necessary for me to send a special messenger to Boston, so that I only employ the American Post Office."[19]

The status of shipping agents and special messengers is usually so modest as to make them almost invisible when it comes to historical reconstruction. In one instance, however, a lasting relationship developed between the British legation in Washington and the family of Thomas William Moore, a Nova Scotia loyalist who became agent for British packets as early as 1800. During the War of 1812 and for a few years thereafter, he was also assigned to a variety of other duties, including the consulship of the Port of New York. In 1827 the British decided to discontinue packet service from Liverpool to New York and to send all official business henceforth via Halifax to Boston. Moore accordingly established a new agency in Boston, while retaining a New York office under the management of his nephew, T. W. Charles Moore. It was Charles who eventually became the "special messenger" previously alluded to. He agreed to carry private parcels along with official diplomatic communications and to expedite private British claims against the United States government. Invariably, he was also entrusted with a wide range of secret undertakings, such as dispersements of cash to unofficial agents and delivering letters by discreet means. Typical of his reports was one to Crampton on 14 November 1855: "I arrived here [New York] in good time, your Despatches were in charge of the Sardinian Secretary of Legation, the letter for Bartlett was delivered to him at his place and the other communication was postpaid and sent forward."[20] In 1866, Charles Moore completed fifty years of messenger service for the British government and retired to his home on Staten Island with a pension equal to two-thirds of his £250 salary.

During the first half of the nineteenth century, two other factors influenced the conveyance of diplomatic correspondence between London and Washington: frequency of sailings and type of ships. Prior to 1840, the typical sailing time across the Atlantic took six weeks, and there was generally one government packet per month carrying British dispatches either to or from

America. Thus, three or four months could elapse between the time a British minister in Washington sent a letter and received a response from the foreign secretary in London.

This timetable changed dramatically in 1840. On 19 July of that year the first regular Cunard steam packet sailed from Liverpool, reducing the crossing to ten or twelve days. This made it possible for a letter written at the beginning of a month to secure a reply by the end of that same month. The expanding Cunard line, with its large subsidies from the British government, soon made possible more frequent communication between Washington and London.

In response to the competition, Congress enacted legislation in 1845 and 1848 that subsidized American shipowners. The E. K. Collins line acquired the New York to Liverpool route, and by June 1850 had five new steamships ready for service that were faster than anything owned by Cunard.

During the next decade, rivalry between the British and American lines grew so keen that at least one or two ships sailed from New York to Liverpool each week. Although Her Majesty's dispatches always had to travel on British ships, frequent sailings meant greatly improved transatlantic communication.

The extra care taken with the sending and receiving of private letters testifies to their importance for contemporary diplomats. Composed amidst the confusion and bustle of daily routine, their style is often hasty, sometimes breezy, but always refreshingly candid. Invaluable as sources of fresh historical insight, they reflect the shrewd observations of career diplomats who felt unconstrained, knowing their views would be held private and confidential.

A word about the Appendix, which takes the form of a biographical directory: since many of the same names keep cropping up in the letters and throughout our text, we have thought it more efficient to provide basic biographical information about the more important of these in the directory. Thus, if one wishes to be reminded about the details of a prominent United States senator like James M. Mason or an American diplomat and politician like James Buchanan, it is only necessary to turn to the end of this volume. In addition to these more prominent individuals, we have also included within the directory a number of lesser-known persons, for the very reason that background on them is hard to come by. In such cases, we have noted the names in the text and specifically referred the reader to the Appendix. Finally, some names are omitted from this compilation either because they are so briefly alluded to in the letters or else because we have failed to discover more about them.

Although the letters that follow often seem detailed and highly specialized, they are integral to a fuller understanding of Anglo-American relations in particular and American society in general during the middle decades of the nineteenth century. North American affairs were transformed during the decade of the 1840s by the war between the United States and Mexico. Almost overnight, American territory was vastly augmented by the acquisition of California, Arizona, and New Mexico. The United States emerged as a Pacific

Ocean power, with potential designs upon the Hawaiian Islands, Japan, and the mainland of China. In the eyes of the British, this was confirmed in 1853 by Admiral Perry's forceful opening up of Japan to international relations and trade. They had recently fought China in the so-called Opium War of 1839–42, had acquired the island of Hong Kong trading rights at Canton, and viewed with suspicion growing American activity in the region.

During the years 1844–67, the British often thought that their Canadian provinces were at risk from American encroachment. Should serious disturbances break out again in British North America, such as happened in the 1830s, it was likely that the Americans might exploit their proximity by either persuasion or force. Many Americans were convinced that a majority of Canadians wished to rid themselves of British imperial rule and perhaps become incorporated into an expanded United States. Commercial or fishing disputes along the Canadian-American frontiers might just provoke the spark, and if these pretexts were lacking, then Irish revolutionaries in North America might provoke a crisis. These latter reckoned that an Anglo-American conflict might prove to be Ireland's opportunity for home rule.

In addition to Canada, Britain had commercial and diplomatic interests in Central and South America. To be sure, she was having second thoughts about the value of such protectorates or colonies by the 1850s, but one thing was certain: she did not wish to see these areas come under American domination. The United States kept denying such aggressive intentions, and yet scarcely a year went by without some band of American adventurers interfering in the internal affairs of Nicaragua, Panama, Cuba, or Mexico. Central America was no longer a primitive tropical backwater but a vital isthmus linking the East and West coasts of the United States by means of oceangoing vessels. It was only a matter of time until a canal would be constructed across some portion of this isthmus, and the Americans were determined to control that transit route.

To many Europeans, the Americans seemed to be the apostles of republicanism and revolution. American values were deemed to be contagious, a threat to established monarchical institutions and traditions. In effect, the Americans were viewed as dangerous subversives, not unlike the way the Soviet Union appeared to many Western nations following World War II. In this sense, the Europeans often thought they must adopt a kind of containment policy or else see the United States pursue unlimited expansion. Similarly, many Americans truly believed in their democratic ideology and saw no reason why they should not be allowed to spread the blessings of liberty throughout the globe. Of course, American Manifest Destiny was limited by geography and a modest military and naval establishment. There were also other Americans who thought that their nation had quite enough domestic problems to cope with, without inviting additional ones abroad.

The middle decades of the nineteenth century witnessed the growing conflict over states' rights and slavery that culminated in the American Civil War. British observers were often struck by how many internal American issues usually resolved themselves into some aspect of Northern and Southern sectionalism. This might take the form of whether the Kansas and Nebraska territories would be admitted to statehood with or without slavery. Southerners were thought to be especially imperialistic if it meant adding slave territories, such as Cuba or portions of Central America, to the United States. By the same token, some Northerners were accused of wanting to annex some part of Canada, since that would provide another free-soil state and help tip the balance of power in the Senate.

It will also be seen in what follows in this volume that British diplomats could not get over certain American idiosyncracies. These included the level of venality and corruption in American politics. Violence not only characterized elections but pervaded all of society. The image of the gun-toting American was not just reserved for the wild West but was endemic in the nation's capital. Fistfights or worse in the halls of Congress were not uncommon.

To be sure, British visitors to the United States delighted in finding fault with the local inhabitants, their customs, manners, and institutions. However, such spiteful comments contained more than a grain of truth, and there is nothing like coming to terms with how others see one. That is why we feel that these private diplomatic letters are so valuable, since they provide the peculiar insights of intelligent outsiders.

The latter half of this volume is preoccupied with the coming of the Civil War, its various stages, and its immediate aftermath. Americans often lose sight of the fact that the North never thought of the conflict as a civil war but insisted upon referring to it as the War of the Great Rebellion. Southerners were thus in arms against their lawful federal government and were not to be treated as independent freedom fighters. It became crucial for the North to convince other nations, especially Great Britain, that they should not recognize the independence of the Confederacy. It was equally the goal of the South to secure such diplomatic recognition. The following letters provide us with a sense of immediacy as Her Majesty's minister in Washington watched the ebb and flow of war and tried to make sense of it all for the benefit of his superiors back in London.

Letters, even diplomatic ones, always place the reader in the midst of things. There is not the hindsight of later interpretation, and one is caught up in the moment, not knowing what next week or month will bring. We have tried to retain as much of this contemporaneity as possible so that the reader can relive the experiences and share the perspectives of the various letter writers. However, should the reader not wish to proceed chronologically, it will be easy to browse thematically. A quick reference to the index will reveal portions of letters dealing with such topics as we have intimated above. This, then, is a volume for the edification of both the specialist and the generalist. Most important of all, it is a collection of letters to be sampled and enjoyed.

1

Sir Richard Pakenham and the Oregon Question, 1843–1846

During the latter decades of the eighteenth century, both Britain and the United States began to lay claim to the Northwest coast of North America. The third voyage of Captain James Cook initially established the British position, buttressed by the explorations of Alexander Mackenzie and George Vancouver, along with the trade of the Hudson's Bay Company. The American rights to the Oregon Territory were based, first of all, on Captain Robert Gray's discovery of the mouth of the Columbia River, followed by Lewis and Clark's tracing of the river's course, and later reinforced by the commercial energy of John Jacob Astor.

The peace settlement after the War of 1812 left much of the frontier between the United States and Canada indefinite. Not until 1818 was the boundary between the two countries more or less settled. Then, by means of a treaty, the United States acquired an area bounded on the north by the forty-ninth parallel extending eastward as far as the Lake of the Woods (northern tip of present-day Minnesota), and on the west by the Rocky Mountains. Left unresolved, however, was the vast territory between the Rockies and the Pacific Ocean—the so-called Oregon Territory. Consequently, both countries continued to explore and settle this half-million square miles of wilderness during the next ten years.

In 1827 another effort was made to settle the Oregon boundary, but to little avail, so the earlier treaty was essentially renewed indefinitely. To abrogate, one party or the other needed to give only a year's notice.

This was the state of things when a special British negotiator, Lord Ashburton, sailed to America in 1842 to seek further clarification from the secretary of state, Daniel Webster.[1] By this time, it had become clear that the United States wanted to extend her northern frontier along the forty-ninth parallel from the Rockies all the way to the Pacific. Forewarned, Her Majesty's government was prepared to concede most of the present-day states of Oregon, Washington, Idaho, Montana, and Wyoming—over a quarter of a million square miles—provided that the boundary would angle south from the forty-ninth parallel at the Columbia River and follow its course to the sea. The Hudson's Bay Company had become well established in this area, and Britain was determined to protect its interests there. Both countries could then have equal access to the river, which was deemed absolutely necessary. Extremists on each side pushed for far more, including many Americans who coveted all of British Columbia to north latitude 54°40'! Not surprisingly, nothing came of Ashburton's overtures.

The following October, the British decided to make fresh efforts toward a negotiated settlement of the Oregon Territory by sending Richard Pakenham to Washington. At this time there was no ambassadorial relationship between the two countries, and Pakenham's formal title was therefore envoy extraordinary and minister plenipotentiary. He had spent the previous eight years representing Great Britain in Mexico, and in view of growing Mexican-American frontier tensions over a newly independent Texas, he was a particularly appropriate choice for the assignment. Before his departure from England, his superior at the Foreign Office, the secretary of state for foreign affairs, Lord Aberdeen, gave him explicit instructions[2] concerning Oregon: he was empowered to negotiate a treaty provided that the Columbia River constituted part of the boundary; as a concession to the United States, he could offer access to any port, a so-called free port, between the mouth of the Columbia and the forty-ninth parallel; or, if the Americans preferred, they could establish a free port somewhere on Vancouver Island south of latitude 49°. Failing this, he could guarantee more than one free port, provided that all of Vancouver Island remained in British hands. Finally, if these terms met with rejection, he was to propose that the issues in dispute should be submitted to the arbitration of a friendly sovereign.

Pakenham reached New York on 13 February 1844 and presented his credentials in Washington to Secretary of State Abel Upshur on 21 February. Six days later he had a promising conversation with the secretary, and it seemed as though many of the Oregon problems could be ironed out. The very next day Upshur was killed by an accidental explosion aboard a warship on the Potomac River, and so followed months of frustrating delay.

In the meantime, Lord Aberdeen gave further thought to his official instructions to Pakenham, deciding to supplement them with what he regarded as far-reaching concessions. These he conveyed in a private letter instead of in a formal dispatch.[3] As we shall later see, Pakenham understood them to take precedence over his previous directive, which led to great discomfort and confusion all around.

Lord Aberdeen's proposal almost reversed the initial policy, clearly reflecting the growing British feeling that a reasonable settlement with America was preferable to a military showdown. When all else failed, Pakenham was authorized to hint at Britain's willingness to yield the Columbia River boundary line provided that she had free access to the river and to all ports northward to the forty-ninth parallel. This latitude would then be accepted as the frontier, but none of Vancouver Island would come into American possession. The

Hudson's Bay Company would also continue to have certain privileges in the previously disputed triangular-shaped territory.

On 28 March 1844, Pakenham addressed his first private letter[4] to Aberdeen since reaching Washington. By this time it was known that the American president, John Tyler, had appointed a new secretary of state, John C. Calhoun, who was to assume his duties at the beginning of April.

> I had the honour, on the 24th of this month, to receive Your Lordship's very kind and private letter of the 4th.
>
> I had not forgotten Your Lordship's parting directions respecting the alternate proposal which it might be desirable to draw from the American negotiator, supposing the concessions which I am officially instructed to offer should fail to lead to an arrangement of the Oregon question. But I am not the less pleased to have in my possession a more detailed explanation of Your Lordship's views on that particular point. You may be sure, My Lord, that I shall act in this delicate matter with all the discretion that the case requires.
>
> Since my arrival in this country I have begun to think better of our prospects respecting the Oregon affair, and I believe that I may venture to promise Your Lordship one thing, which is that if we cannot definitely settle the question there will be no quarrel—no scandal—to alarm the public in England or otherwise seriously to embarrass Her Majesty's Government.
>
> The fact is the Americans are much more afraid of a rupture than we are, and I am convinced that the bare probability of such a result would cause such demonstration on the part of the leading interests in this country in favour of peace as would speedily lead to the removal of all difficulties.
>
> Nor are mischievous declamations in Congress which at a distance appear to argue so warlike a disposition to be taken at their literal import. A great deal of all this is nothing more than an electioneering manoeuvre, to make what they call Political Capital in this country. Even in this sense the subject appears to have become nearly exhausted, and the becoming attitude assumed by the Senate has put an end to all apprehension of any violent proceedings, at least while the negotiation is in progress.

April and May 1844 found President Tyler and his new secretary of state, Calhoun, far too preoccupied with the annexation of Texas and the forthcoming Democratic party convention to give much thought to Oregon. Although Texas had declared her independence from Mexico in 1836 and been formally recognized by the United States a year later, she could not prevail upon the American government to incorporate her into the Union. In general, the South wanted to acquire the Texas territory on the assumption that one or more new slave states could be created. Calhoun signed a treaty of annexation on 12 April and submitted it to the Senate for ratification. Northern senators were reluctant to strengthen the hand of the South in Congress, however, and, spurred on by antislavery constituents, defeated the treaty.

Early in 1844 Tyler realized that the Democratic party would not support his aspiration for a second term as president, so he decided to use the annexation issue to split the party and allow him to forge a third party coalition. However, most Democrats ignored him, and at their national convention in Baltimore at the end of May, they fastened on the "dark horse" candidacy of James K. Polk. Undaunted, Tyler also announced his candidacy. Pakenham's next private letter[5] of 13 June reflects on these events.

> In a letter marked Private, which I had the honour to write to Your Lordship on 28 March, I ventured to express the opinion that even if we should fail to effect a settlement of the Oregon question there would be no quarrel, nor no scandal to alarm the public in England or otherwise to cause serious embarrassment to Her Majesty's Government.
>
> I am sorry to say that recent events in this country have tended to diminish in some degree the confidence which I then felt in the continuance of a good understanding with the American Government.
>
> It is true that in the course of a few days the Congress will adjourn, without, as may now be hoped, any violent or irritating measure having been adopted by either House on the subject of Oregon. The Negotiation will accordingly be carried on without the apprehension of annoyance or interruption from that source. I am also happy to say that my intercourse with Mr. Calhoun continues to be of the most friendly character, notwithstanding our mortifying failure of his operations on that question.
>
> The quarter from which I think that mischief is to be feared is Mr. President Tyler. The failure of his Texan treaty, and the check which he had received in his electioneering schemes by the appointment of another candidate on the annexation interest, have reduced him to the situation of a desperate man, without sense of shame or principles to control him. He still clings with reckless pertinacity to the hope of being re-elected; and Your Lordship may depend upon it that if he thought that by bringing about a War with England, on the Oregon question, or by any other manoeuvre equally desperate and condemnable, he would add to his prospects of success, he would resort to it at a moment's notice.
>
> As far then as he is concerned, Your Lordship must not be surprised at anything that may happen until the question of his election is set at rest.
>
> I suppose that immediately after the adjournment of Congress, Mr. Calhoun will be ready to enter on the Oregon negotiation. We shall then perhaps discover what has been the motive of his late rather mysterious silence and inaction on that subject.

Once President Tyler abandoned his hopes for a second term, it presumably became easier and more pressing for him to think of his long-term reputation as a statesman. A successful resolution of the Oregon dispute might enhance his image. For the first time since becoming secretary of state, Calhoun was authorized to explore the topic with Pakenham. After two conferences in August, Pakenham summarized the alternatives open to Great Britain.[6]

> Your Lordship will see that we are at length at work upon the Oregon question.
>
> It is already quite clear that none of the concessions which I am authorized to make will be sufficient to induce the American Government to accede to the line of boundary claimed by us—viz. The Columbia River. On the contrary Your Lordship may be sure they will cling to the 49th Parallel of Latitude with more tenacity than ever, if indeed they do not claim something beyond it in order the better to strengthen their position as an "ultimatum".
>
> Nor do I think that Mr. Calhoun will easily be brought to accede to the proposition for an arbitration.

Before the close of the session of Congress, two Senators, Mr. Archer of Virginia, a moderate and good man,—and Mr. Buchanan, our constant enemy and reviler—both of them members of the Committee on Foreign Relations, asked me of their own accord why England should not consent to submit the Oregon question to the arbitration of some friendly Power, rather than to allow it to become the subject of serious misunderstanding with this country. This circumstance I mentioned to Mr. Calhoun in the way of conversation, but he spoke of the plan suggested as a recourse to be made use of only when every other attempt to effect a settlement should have failed. The truth is they will first try to obtain what they want either by negotiation or by bullying, and they will submit to arbitration only as a last extremity.

I come now, My Lord, to the case foreseen by Your Lordship's private letter of 4 March, relative to an arrangement for making the 49th degree of Latitude the Boundary with the proviso that all ports to the south of that parallel to the Columbia inclusive, should be free ports to Great Britain.

In my conversations with Mr. Calhoun when he spoke of the 49th degree of Latitude as a position which this country was not disposed to recede from, I asked him how it was that the Americans expected that all the concessions were to come from Great Britain, while they constantly decline to make any sacrifice or abatement from their original pretensions, for the sake of effecting a compromise. He said that if we agreed to make Latitude 49 the Boundary as far as the Sea or Inlet, the United States might perhaps be willing to make over the whole of Vancouver's Island to Great Britain, leaving the Strait [of Juan de Fuca] free to both Nations. This is more I believe than any American negotiator had yet offered, and if to it were added the freedom of the Columbia River, the case anticipated by Your Lordship's letter of 4 March could have arisen. I think it not impossible that Mr. Calhoun in his anxiety to obtain the 49th degree of Latitude as a Boundary may come to this at last. I have therefore alluded to such a possibility in my Despatch[7] of this date; but I do not think, My Lord, that enough has yet been ascertained of what is likely to happen in that sense to make it worthwhile to deliberate on the case beforehand. If Mr. Calhoun should make the proposal, I will refer it to Your Lordship without in any way committing myself as to its reference, and then it will be time enough to send out Instructions. As yet Mr. Calhoun has behaved with great appearance of fairness and good humour. What he may have in reserve we shall know more about when we see his written argument.

In the meantime he shows no disposition that I can discover to hurry matters to a precipitate issue, as I at one time feared might be the case, vis-a-vis to some electioneering manoeuvre. If such an idea should now occur to him, I shall be able I think to defeat it by referring his statement to Your Lordship and thus keep the Question open until after the elections.

During the autumn and winter of 1844–45, Calhoun continued to insist on the forty-ninth parallel and rejected Pakenham's counterproposal to arbitrate the disputed frontier. Nevertheless, the American posture was still one of cautious amicability, as exemplified in President Tyler's annual message to Congress on 3 December 1844: "It will afford me the greatest pleasure to witness a happy and favorable termination to the existing negotiation upon terms compatible with the public honor, and the best efforts of the Government will continue to be directed to this end."[8] Tyler's moderation may have masked an ulterior motive with respect to Texas. He did not wish to worsen relations with Britain at a time when, in the same speech, he was urging a new scheme to annex Texas. Instead of a formal treaty requiring two-thirds of the senators to ratify, he invited both houses to sponsor a joint resolution that allowed a simple majority in each house to decide the matter. The vote in the Senate at the end of February 1845 was narrow but favorable, 27 to 25, while the House gave Tyler a more resounding 132 to 76. Now it was up to Texas, and the congressional resolution made it clear that if Texas acquiesced, it could forego the transitional status of "territory" and be admitted immediately into equal statehood.

Within a few days of the Texas resolution, President Tyler stepped down from office and James K. Polk took his place. By almost any standards, Polk's inaugural address of 4 March 1845 was a flamboyant and expansionist one. Although not dwelling at length upon Oregon, he made it clear that America was obliged to protect her citizens in the disputed regions. "The world beholds the peaceful triumphs of the industry of our emigrants. To us belongs the duty of protecting them adequately wherever they may be upon our soil."[9] And Polk had no doubt that American "soil" extended at least to the forty-ninth degree of latitude, if not beyond, by virtue not only of prior discovery but also of international treaties with France and Spain. This confidence in America's right to the Oregon Territory, combined with a sense of Manifest Destiny, greatly alarmed the British government. All of a sudden, the United States seemed to have no intention of negotiating a settlement and, moreover, virtually challenged Britain to do anything from six thousand miles away.

On 2 April 1845 Aberdeen wrote from London and declared that Her Majesty's government was prepared to resist American pretensions.[10] "Judging from the language of Mr. Polk, I presume we will expect that the American Government will denounce the Treaty without delay. In this case, unless the question be settled in the course of the year, a local collision must speedily take place, which may too probably involve the countries in the most serious difficulty, and finally lead to war itself." He assured Pakenham that "our naval force in the Pacific is ample" and indicated that the Hudson's Bay Company had been authorized to take whatever steps "as may be thought useful and necessary." While hoping for a compromise, Her Majesty's government had also taken the additional precaution of requesting from Parliament an expansion of naval and maritime recruitment.

The appointment of James Buchanan as Polk's secretary of state increased British anxiety. As a former senator from the state of Pennsylvania, he was an outspoken critic of Britain. However, in the spring of 1845 Sir Robert Peel's position as prime minister seemed unassailable, and the famine in Ireland had not yet begun to undermine his majority in Parliament.

Texas continued to occupy the attention of the American government, while Great Britain maneuvered to assure Texan independence from both Mexico and the United States. Knowing that Mexico's Santa Anna had said that

America's annexation of Texas would be tantamount to a declaration of war against Mexico, Britain concurrently urged Mexican recognition of the republic of Texas, something that Mexico had continually refused to do, hoping that improved Mexican-Texan relations would combine to thwart the American annexationists. By the time of Pakenham's next private letter, 28 April, annexation still hung in the balance.[11]

> I had the honour on the 24th of this month to receive Your Lordship's private letter of 2 April, which was delivered to me by Sir George Simpson [chief agent for the Hudson's Bay Company].
>
> The declarations of Her Majesty's Ministers in Parliament on the Oregon question have made Mr. President Polk look very foolish. He is afraid to go forward, and ashamed to go back. But when the first smarting of the rebuke has passed away, I think the good effects of what has happened will become more apparent. In the meantime all reasonable people blame him as they did before for those words so foolishly introduced into his Inaugural Address; although I feel bound to say that notwithstanding their obvious impropriety, it was never imagined here that they could attract as much attention as has been created by them in England.
>
> There has not yet been time to hear of the effect produced in the more distant parts of the country by Your Lordship's and Sir Robert Peel's declarations—but except in the remote Western districts, which are beyond the reach of warlike operations, I have no doubt that the result will be the same as it has been at Boston, New York and Philadelphia; that of salutary alarm and apprehension.
>
> Luckily, Congress is not sitting, or on the spur of the moment something disagreeable might have occurred which could not be afterwards so easily remedied. It is most devoutly to be wished that affairs with Mexico may not take such a turn as to render an extra session necessary: for a meeting of Congress convoked especially for warlike purposes could scarcely fail to lead to mischief. Your Lordship will see in the extracts from the newspapers which I forward by this packet that recourse to arbitration is strongly recommended as the simplest and most honorable way to get out of the difficulty; I mean with respect to Oregon. If it were happily to occur to some of the leading Powers of Europe, interested in preserving the peace of the world, to say a few words to the Government of the United States in that sense, in the way of friendly advice and admonition, I think they would gladly avail themselves of such an excuse to accede to our proposal.
>
> As Your Lordship desired, I have conversed fully with Sir George Simpson on the plan to be adopted in the Oregon territory. He is so well acquainted with this country and has such ample opportunities of judging of what is likely to happen, that in that way he requires no advice from me for his guidance. He talked of erecting a fort at the Mouth of the Columbia on the Company's account, but he finally agreed that in the present state of the question anything having the appearance of forceable occupation had better be avoided—that such a course of proceeding would in a manner justify corresponding arrangements on the part of the Americans and thus render collision more probable.
>
> It will be time enough to do things of that sort after notice has been given of an intention to abrogate the existing Convention, if unfortunately events should take that turn.
>
> Mr. Buchanan pretends that he has not had time yet to look into the state of the negotiation and he has not alluded in the least remote degree to any intention to break off the treaty. I think the American Government are far more anxious at this

moment about the fate of Texas than they are about Oregon. If the combination now in progress should be consummated, we must be prepared for a violent burst of indignation from the annexation party, which they could try perhaps to make us feel in the other business—but that cannot be helped.

Texas still had not responded to the invitation to join the Union when Pakenham next wrote to Aberdeen on 13 May 1845.[12]

> I had the honour on the 8th of this month to receive Your Lordship's private letter of 18 April.
> Things in this country bear upon the whole a more quiet appearance than, under all the circumstances, of the case might have been expected. As far as the Government are concerned, I attribute this in a great measure to the apprehension of serious difficulties with Mexico in the event of annexation being consummated, and to a desire not to aggravate those difficulties by getting into trouble with Great Britain.
> Should matters go off quietly with Mexico, or if what I now think scarce likely to happen, the annexation scheme should be knocked on the head by the recognition of the independence of Texas by Mexico, perhaps they may become more saucy.

Six weeks later, Texas finally announced her intention to become an American state, referring it to a popular vote of the electorate later in October and claiming statehood at the end of December 1845. It remained to be seen whether Mexico would take military action or not.

Meanwhile, in June the United States replaced Edward Everett with Louis McLane as American minister to the Court of St. James. When McLane sailed for England on 16 June he carried with him an unofficial copy of Buchanan's latest proposal on the Oregon question. The official copy, dated 12 July, was delivered to Pakenham.[13] In it, the secretary of state reiterated America's claim to all of the territory in dispute, pointing out the logic of extending the American frontier along the forty-ninth parallel from the Rockies to the Pacific Ocean. At the same time, he offered "to make free to Great Britain any port or ports on Vancouver's Island, south of this parallel, which the British government may desire."

Pakenham's reply politely but firmly noted that Buchanan was offering less in 1845 than the British had turned down in 1826.[14] Besides the refusal of access to the Columbia River, there seemed to be a calculated misunderstanding about Vancouver Island. The British regarded all of the island as belonging to Her Britannic Majesty, and so it was no favor to concede free ports south of latitude 49°. This being so, Pakenham declined to "refer" Buchanan's proposal to Lord Aberdeen on the grounds that it was doomed to rejection and suggested that Buchanan spend his time formulating a more realistic set of alternatives. In effect, Pakenham was implying, as he had so often before, that if Britain conceded all the land between the Columbia River and the forty-ninth parallel, America could at least give free access to navigation plus other meaningful concessions.

Polk was particularly incensed by Pakenham's action and ordered Buchanan to withdraw the proposal and offer nothing in its stead.[15] When Lord Aberdeen learned what had transpired, he addressed a stern reprimand to Pakenham in an official dispatch of 3 October 1845, agreeing that the American proposal was intolerable but at the same time insisting that the door should have been left open for further negotiation.[16]

In his "official response"[17] to Lord Aberdeen on 28 October, Pakenham sought to justify his rejection of Buchanan's proposal, reserving comments on his true predicament for the pages of his private letter of the same day.[18]

Nothing has ever half so much distressed me as the tenor of Your Lordship's communications by the last packet—respecting the Oregon negotiations. In my despatch no. 114 of this date I venture to submit some remarks in explanation of the motives which guided my conduct, which I am sure will receive Your Lordship's indulgent attention; and I now beg leave, in answer to Your Lordship's private letter, to mention another consideration derived from previous private letters of Your Lordship's which went far in determining the course pursued by me, to my sorrow I find erroneously. Premising that your private letter goes farther than the official Despatch, inasmuch as it says that I ought to have accepted Mr. Buchanan's proposal for the purpose of reference, while the Despatch says that I did right in not accepting it, but that I should have added that I could send it home for consideration.

In Your Lordship's private letter of 4 March 1844 you direct me under certain supposed circumstances to endeavour "without committing myself or my Government to draw from the American negotiation a proposal to make the 49th degree of Latitude the boundary. . . ." And in another letter dated 18 April 1845[19] you say as follows: "If Mr. Buchanan should propose an extension of the 49th parallel *to the sea*, as the line of boundary, . . . *I think it should be clearly understood that the navigation of the Columbia should be common to both Parties and that the Ports within the Straits of Juan de Fuca* and south of Latitude 49 should be free ports, by whomever they might be occupied."

Now see My Lord how immeasurably Mr. Buchanan's late offer, which I am blamed for not accepting for consideration, falls short of the case supposed by these instructions. In part it embraces not a single one of the conditions set forth as necessary to justify a reference to Her Majesty's Government—and even the case then supposed—Your Lordship seemed to me to treat as rather an extreme one.

How then My Lord could I imagine that I should act in conformity with Your Lordship's wishes, in accepting Mr. Buchanan's late unbecoming proposal for the purpose of reference? Even now I am convinced that if I had followed that course I should have caused more embarrassment to Her Majesty's Government than has been caused by the course which I did adopt—and I think that the obvious and simple remedy for such embarrassment could, in that case, have been a disavowal of my conduct and a reproof more severe than that which I am now smarting under. In truth I think that if ever there was a case in which a summary and indignant rejection could have been justifiable, it is the case now before us—and yet I went no farther than to say that "I did not feel at liberty to accept it." . . .

For God's sake remove me from this country, in which nothing but pain and mortification can henceforth tend my course. Since I have had the misfortune to act contrary to Your Lordship's wishes in a matter of such importance, and even I must add, to misunderstand the views and intentions of Her Majesty's Government as to the manner of dealing with the Oregon question, of which facts the American Government cannot be ignorant, I am sure that I can no longer carry on the business of the Mission with the least prospect of advantage to the public service. Besides which, the little confidence that I ever possessed in my own judgment is now so completely shattered that I shall no longer be able to proceed with that decision and firmness of purpose necessary to carry a man with safety, even through the most trifling difficulties. I entreat Your Lordship to believe that I do not take this step through any unworthy feeling of pique or mortification, at what has happened, but from a motive superior to all personal considerations and honest regard for the interests of Her Majesty's service.

Having administered an official rebuke, Aberdeen hastened to reassure Pakenham in a private letter[20] dated 3 December 1845.

It was with very great concern that I perceived from your private letter of the 28th of October how deeply you had felt the remarks made in my Despatch respecting your rejection of Mr. Buchanan's proposal. For the pain which you have experienced, I really think there was no sufficient reason. No censure was expressed, and none was intended; but had you acted at variance with your instructions, or taken a step without any instructions, the case might have been different. You were perfectly aware that you could not assent to Mr. Buchanan's proposal, and you might naturally feel convinced that your Government would not agree to it. But although under such circumstances I find no ground for censure, I do not the less regret that it had not occurred to you to deal with it in the manner suggested. . . .

To tell you the truth, I am much more disposed to censure your suggestion of recall, as a *wrong-headed* proceeding, and as a much greater imputation on your judgment and good sense. Notwithstanding the unpromising appearance of the present state of the negotiation, I feel satisfied that we are now nearer a settlement than ever. If we press arbitration, they must either accept it, or give us facilities for reopening the direct negotiations. If they do neither, they will be so manifestly in the wrong that I greatly doubt their receiving the necessary support, even from the most hostile portion of the American public. I expect a strong declaration from the President in his annual message, and even a recommendation to terminate the treaty. I shall not at all regret this; for as the crisis becomes more imminent the chance of settlement improves. I imagine the President and his Government are more afraid of the Senate than they are of us, and much management is required to accomplish what they really desire. Mr. Polk may well doubt his power of obtaining the sanction of two thirds of the Senate, to any convention which he could conclude with us. But many things may shortly occur to improve the prospect of affairs very considerably. The access of Indian corn to our markets would go far to pacify the warriors of the Western States.[21]

On 29 December 1845, Pakenham responded with gratitude and resilience.[22]

I am very grateful for Your Lordship's kind and considerate letter of 3rd December. Your Lordship may now call me "wrong-headed," or anything else you like. Perhaps the less I say about what has passed, the better; but if you knew what it was to be pitied by such a man as Mr. Buchanan, you would understand that I could not but take the thing a little to heart.

The fact is, the United States Government went to work under the impression,—an impression, I firmly believe, derived from Mr. Everett's correspondence,—that Her Majesty's Government were so anxious for a settlement that they would consent to almost any terms. Under this impression, they were astonished at the coolness with which I received their proposal; they thought that I would not be countenanced in what I did by Her Majesty's Government, and they flattered themselves that, by appearing to hang back, they would frighten us, and end by having it all their own way. They now begin to find out that they were rather mistaken. But they had so far deluded themselves that reports were circulated in every direction that I was to be recalled; and Mr. Buchanan, in his clemency, actually went so far as to say that he would write to Mr. McLane to tell him how well disposed the President and all the Members of the Government were towards me, and how sorry they should be to lose me;—in fact, almost offering to intercede for me. If Your Lordship had seen how I retained my composure and self-possession under this trial, you would have formed rather a high opinion of what I am capable of enduring in the case of good humour and conciliation.

Aberdeen was quite right in predicting "a strong declaration from the President in his annual message, and even a recommendation to terminate the treaty." On 2 December, Polk urged Congress to give the requisite twelve months notice prior to ending the treaty of 1827 and scoffed at the British reasons for rejecting Buchanan's proposal of 12 July. He claimed that Pakenham had allowed "the negotiation on his part to drop" and asserted the right of the United States "to the whole Oregon territory, and . . . over our citizens . . . the protection of our laws and jurisdictions, civil and military."[23]

For the next few months, Pakenham had no alternative but to propose arbitration, since the Polk administration refused to make any fresh proposals. Toward the end of January 1846 the American government became uncomfortably aware that Britain was increasing her military expenditures.[24] In London, Lord Aberdeen assured McLane that such preparations were not directed against the United States, but their implication was perfectly clear: if the stalemate over Oregon led to hostilities, the British were prepared. Consequently, Buchanan hastily authorized McLane to approach Lord Aberdeen in a spirit of friendliness and conciliation. By February, Pakenham felt the responsive repercussions in Washington.[25]

I have had the honor to receive your Lordship's private letter of 3rd February. I had yesterday a conversation with Mr. Buchanan, in the course of which he told me a good deal of what had passed at the interview between your Lordship and Mr. McLane on 29th January. His account, as far as it went, corresponds with what is stated in your Lordship's letter. He added, however, that you had intimated to Mr. McLane that a fleet of thirty sail of the line and a large force of steam vessels were about to be fitted out as a preparation for anything that might happen. "The appearance of such a force on our coast," he proceeded to say, "or any other menacing demonstration would play the very devil." I use his own words. I agree with Mr. Buchanan in thinking that any active demonstration at this moment would have a bad effect, but, on the other hand, I have no doubt that an attitude of dignified and imposing preparation, which shall prove to the American people that England is determined to "stand no nonsense," will be attended with the best results, and be sufficient, with a little patience and forbearance, to bring matters to a favourable conclusion.

I am happy, meanwhile, to be able most conscientiously to assure your Lordship that my language and deportment have never ceased to be such as you desire me to observe. A single word of anger or menace has not, up to this moment, escaped my lips; and I continue my friendly intercourse with the members of the Government and everybody else, just as if nothing about Oregon was going forward. The most that I have ever said in the way of warning, and this only in quarters where it might be said with safety, has been that I feared that the course of the United States Government in rejecting everything offered or proposed on our part, might, in the end, wear out the patience of the people of England, and lead to such an expression of opinion as Her Majesty's Government might be unable to control.

The House of Representatives responded to President Polk's desire to terminate the 1827 treaty by passing a resolution to this effect in February. However, the Senate took until April to support a similar measure, and the resulting document was couched in markedly moderate terms. Since Aberdeen had made it clear to the American minister in London that no further British initiative would be forthcoming until the Senate's views were known, he seemed well satisfied when writing officially to Pakenham on 18 May 1846.[26]

In complying with the recommendation of the President to terminate the Convention under which the Oregon Territory is at present occupied, the Legislature of the United States have accompanied their decision by Resolutions of a pacific and conciliatory character; and have clearly signified to the Executive Government their desire that this step should not lead to the rupture of amicable negotiations for the settlement of the question. I can scarcely doubt that the Government of the United States will be duly influenced by the desire thus unequivocably expressed by Congress; and it is in this hope and belief that I now proceed to instruct you to make another, and I trust final, proposition to the American Secretary of State, for the solution of these long-existing difficulties.

On that same day Aberdeen enclosed a draft treaty which was strikingly similar to his 4 March 1844 private instructions and which included the things that he had been angling for all along.[27] Britain proposed to acknowledge the forty-ninth degree of latitude as constituting the American boundary to the Pacific Ocean, but all of Vancouver Island would remain in British hands. The Hudson's Bay Company would retain certain trading privileges between the Columbia River and the forty-ninth parallel until the year 1859. Employees of the company and British subjects trading with the company would also enjoy a permanent right to navigate the Columbia River, comparable to that of American citizens. This last point of a "permanent" rather than a temporary right threatened to create a problem for Pakenham because he was not empowered to make any substantive changes in the treaty, only minor alterations in wording.

Aberdeen expanded his views in an accompanying private letter to Pakenham, but it was the postscript, not the body of the letter, that was of particular interest.[28] Mindful of his having reproved Pakenham seven months earlier for not correctly interpreting his instructions, he now wanted to avoid tying Pakenham's hands too tightly. There was always room in diplomacy for intelligent disobedience, he said.

> It has occurred, as being barely possible, that some state of things may have arisen in the United States, which, in your judgment, would render it desirable for you to withhold our proposals from being made to the Government. I cannot conceive this; but still, if you should be conscientiously convinced that, if I possessed a knowledge of the same facts, it would not be my desire that the proposals should be made, I beg that you will exercise your own discretion, and suspend them accordingly.
>
> I repeat, that I think it in the highest degree improbable that such should be the case; at the same time, as you may feel reluctant not to comply with precise instructions, I wish to give you full liberty on the subject.

While he thus wrote, the United States had slowly drifted into war with Mexico. This came about because the Mexicans would not sell part or all of present-day New Mexico and California. Skirmishes regularly took place along the Texas-Mexican border, and by May Congress, and then the president, declared a state of war. While Pakenham waited for the draft treaty to arrive from England, he tried to assess the impact that the Mexican War would have on the Oregon negotiations.[29]

> I think there is no fear that Congress will adjourn before the end of August. They have not yet begun the discussion on the Tariff, and this War with Mexico will give rise to a great deal of talk and legislation. It seems to me that the Americans greatly underrate the difficulty and expense of a war with Mexico. Unless the Mexican character has undergone a great change since I left that country, I think the Americans will meet if not with a gallant resistance at least with a sullen and dogged resolution to protract the struggle to the utmost, were it only for the sake of the expense and embarrassment which such contest must occasion to this country.

When the draft treaty arrived, Pakenham lost no time presenting it to Buchanan. His private letter of 7 June shares his high optimism.[30]

> I have not time to answer by this opportunity, as fully as I should wish, Your Lordship's private letter of 18th May, which I had the honor to receive on the 3rd instant. I hope and believe that we are going on well. This seems to be also Mr. Buchanan's opinion. He said yesterday, and also in a previous informal conversation, that the two Governments were now so far agreed as to make it impossible that the Oregon question should give rise to any serious misunderstanding between them. I think Your Lordship's instructions reached Washington at a very favourable moment. Your Lordship may depend upon it that the war with Mexico has its effect in the Councils of the American Government, and will make them

very anxious to get rid of the Oregon difficulty before they get deeper into the mud with Mexico.

While speaking on this point, I trust that I have not committed a mistake in supposing that the postscript to Your Lordship's letter was not intended to apply to the case of a war with Mexico.

It seemed to me that it would be neither politic nor worthy of a country like England to make any difference in our manner of dealing with the Oregon question on account of the existing state of things between Mexico and this country. Not politic, because, as we can never calculate with anything like certainty on what may be likely to happen in such a contest, any further success which may attend the operations of the invading force would, under such circumstances, tend to make the American Government more impracticable than ever on the Oregon question, particularly as the motive for any suspension of our negotiation on that account would have been too palpable to escape their penetration for a moment. It would have irritated the whole community beyond endurance, and alienated from the cause of peace and good-will towards England those who have hitherto laboured most zealously in our favour.

Unworthy of us I think it would have been, because England is, and ought to appear to the world to be, able to defend her own rights and interests without the assistance of any such complication.

Furthermore, should Her Majesty's Government determine to interfere in any way between this country and Mexico, such an interference will be far more dignified, and I should say effective, if disengaged altogether from considerations affecting our own immediate interests.

Once the president had a concrete proposal from the British in his hands, he was inclined to seek the advice of the Senate before taking any official action. Proceeding in this way was distinctly unorthodox. Ordinarily, the executive branch would sign a treaty first, then submit it to the Senate for its "advice and consent." However, Polk had indicated, as far back as October 1845, that he would reverse this order because he was convinced that the Senate would reject any British proposal, and if he could be sure of this, he could confidently oppose any treaty that did not suit him. Thus, Polk's cabinet considered the draft treaty for several days, and then on 10 June sent it to the Senate. On 12 June the Senate advised the president to accept its terms, except for the provision allowing the British perpetually free navigation of the Columbia River. They amended this to coterminate with the Hudson's Bay Company's privileges in 1859. Pakenham describes his subsequent encounter with Buchanan in a private letter dated 13 June.[31]

After a few hours' deliberation in each of the three days,—Wednesday, Thursday, and Friday,—the Senate, by a majority of thirty-eight votes to twelve, adopted yesterday evening a resolution advising the President to accept the terms proposed by Her Majesty's Government. The President did not hesitate to act on this advice, and Mr. Buchanan accordingly sent for me this morning, and informed me that the conditions offered by Her Majesty's Government were accepted by the Government of the United States, without the addition or alteration of a single word. At the beginning of our conversation, Mr. Buchanan observed to me, that the privilege of navigating the Columbia River, which, by the second article of the Convention, is secured to the Hudson's Bay Company, and to British subjects trading with the same, was understood by the Senate to be limited to the duration of the license under which the Company now carry on their operations in the country west of the Rocky Mountains, to which I replied that the article proposed by Her Majesty's Government spoke for itself; that any alteration from the precise wording of that article which the United States Government might wish to introduce would involve the necessity of a reference to England, and consequently, to say the least of it, some delay in the termination of the business. This he seemed to think, under all the circumstances of the case, had better be avoided, and it was finally agreed that fair copies of the Convention should be prepared, and the signature take place on Monday next.

On Tuesday, probably, the Convention will be submitted to the Senate, where its approval may now be considered as a matter of course; so that the treaty, with the President's ratification, may be forwarded to England by the Great Western Steam Packet appointed to sail from New York on the 25th of this month.

Also on 13 June,[32] Pakenham reiterated his great satisfaction with the way things had turned out.

The Oregon question is settled at last, and I for one am heartily glad of it.

The positive impatience shown by Mr. Buchanan, to sign and conclude, convinces me that the fear lest any complication should arise out of the Mexican war has done a great deal in inducing the American Government to accept Your Lordship's proposal without alteration. The bare suggestion of a reference to England was sufficient to overcome every difficulty that was talked of. If it had not been for this circumstance, I am far from being satisfied that the matter would have been so promptly and easily settled.

I am now most anxious to hear that I have correctly interpreted the postscript to Your Lordship's letter of 18th May. The more I think of it, the more I become confirmed in the opinion, that to have suspended the negotiation or tried to create delay by reason of, or on account of, the difficulties with Mexico, would have been a most dangerous experiment, and might have spoiled everything. I think that the fortuitous assistance which we have derived from that cause, as above alluded to, is as much as we have a right to expect from that quarter.

Buchanan and Pakenham duly signed the treaty on 15 June, and it was officially communicated to the Senate the following day. Two days later the Senate gave its approval, and it was ratified by the government of the United States on the nineteenth.

News of the ratification reached England just as the Peel ministry was forced out of office. Whether anticipation of this affected America's acceptance of the treaty is conjectured by Aberdeen in a letter to Pakenham on 30 June.[33]

The intelligence of the conclusion of the Oregon affair arrived most opportunely yesterday morning. In announcing the resignation of Ministers, and the dissolution of his Government, it afforded Sir R. Peel the most valuable means of completing his picture of the state of our foreign relations. It was warmly responded to by the House, and I think the Convention has given universal satisfaction. On our retirement, therefore, from office, I am not aware that we leave any question behind us which is likely to grow up into a serious cause of quarrel with the United States.

I think the President took the most prudent course in referring the matter to the Senate; and the Government have acted wisely and well in promptly adopting the advice of that body.

I entertain no doubt that it was not the apprehension of any embarrassment in consequence of the Mexican War which led to this decision; but that it was entirely owing to the impending change of the administration in this country, and a desire to settle the whole affair with us before our departure. Mr. McLane told me he had informed his Government, we should not be in office on the 1st July, and that, if they desired to bring the negotiation with us to a successful conclusion, no time was to be lost. The conduct of my predecessor and expected successor, with regard to the Ashburton Treaty, had filled Mr. McLane with the greatest alarm, which, I presume, was shared by the Government of the United States. Be the cause of their decision what it may, it is a most fortunate and happy event.

You were perfectly right in not permitting the Mexican War to exercise the least influence on your proceedings. Successful or unsuccessful, it would not have made the slightest difference in the terms proposed. The postscript to my letter, to which you refer, had no reference whatever to Mexico, or indeed, to anything else in particular, but was merely intended to give you full discretion to act as you might think best under any unforeseen contingency.

Having concluded this difficult and threatening affair, I should have been glad, at no distant time, to have removed you, according to my promise, to some post more agreeable to yourself; but this must now be left undone. Lord Palmerston, however, I know to be fully sensible of your merits and claims, and I cannot doubt that you will meet with due attention from him. So far as I am concerned, I fear that you must be contented with my good wishes, which I beg very sincerely to assure you that you will always command.

Pakenham wrote his last private letter to his former superior at the Foreign Office on 27 July 1846.[34]

I have had the honour to receive Your Lordship's private letter of 30 June.

I sincerely rejoice to find that the intelligence of the conclusion of the Oregon affair arrived in time to grace the closing scene of the late Administration.

As Your Lordship may perhaps like to see the terms of the President's message communicating our late proposition to the Senate for their opinion, and also Mr. McLane's account to his own Government of what passed between Your Lordship and him in relation to that proposition, I take the liberty to enclose a paper in which both these documents will be found.

Mr. McLane appears to have entertained no expectation that the terms offered by Your Lordship would be accepted here, and to have been prepared for some modification of them as a matter of course. Your Lordship will I daresay recollect that in various despatches (no. 138 of 29 December last; Separate and Confidential for the same date; and Separate and Confidential for 26 February)[35] I took occasion to convey to Your Lordship the assurance derived from sources of unquestionable authority, that terms similar to those which were ultimately offered would be accepted and ratified here. My satisfaction at finding in the end that I had not been deceived in that expectation was great indeed—and hence the exultation with which I announced to Your Lordship in my Despatch of 13 June that the terms offered by Her Majesty's

Government were accepted "without the alteration or addition of a single word".

I am very thankful for the kind expression contained in the concluding part of Your Lordship's letter. Indeed, I hope Your Lordship will believe that I am deeply sensible of the kindness and indulgence which I have uniformly experienced at Your Lordship's hands.

For the better part of a year, Pakenham continued to serve as British minister to Washington under the veteran foreign secretary, Lord Palmerston. Then, in May 1847, he took a leave of absence while awaiting reassignment. Having spent the past twenty years in the Western Hemisphere, he was anxious to return to Europe, but no new appointment was forthcoming, and instead of returning to the United States, he went into early retirement. The secretary of the legation in Washington, John F. T. Crampton, became chargé d'affaires pending the designation of a new minister. Several years elapsed before Lord Palmerston named Henry Lytton Bulwer envoy extraordinary and minister plenipotentiary to the United States.

2

Henry Bulwer and Central America, 1850–1851

The years 1845–49 witnessed an extraordinary expansion of United States territory. A vast new state of Texas was added to the Union, and clear title to the Oregon Territory was acquired. A subsequent war with Mexico also secured most of present-day California, Arizona, and New Mexico. All of a sudden, so it seemed, the United States had become not only an Atlantic seaboard and Gulf of Mexico power but also a Pacific Ocean titan as well. The discovery of gold in California in 1849 served to accelerate the normal process of westward migration by land and sea.

Britain's interests in the Caribbean, Central America, and the Pacific were therefore simultaneously threatened by strident American expansionism. If the Americans also succeeded in constructing an interoceanic canal across Central America, that would presumably further jeopardize Britain's maritime position. Lord Palmerston, British foreign secretary since 1846, was already viewing events in the Western Hemisphere with growing alarm. He had never been a great admirer of the Yankees and was convinced that they would take all they could grab. He was adamant that Britain should not in any way facilitate the augmentation of American power. British presence in Central America had long been a dubious blessing anyway. It was a destitute region, plagued by disease, ignorance, and civil war. Keeping political and commercial agents there was questionable at best, since it was a favorite area for so-called filibustering expeditions by foreign adventurers who sought to exploit indigenous strife to their own private advantage. Often the British found themselves in the midst of internal squabbles in Guatemala, San Salvador, Honduras, Nicaragua, or Costa Rica, with little assurance that their long-term interests were being served. Thus, even though she was of two minds as to whether to remain in Central America, Britain was steadfastly sure that she did not want America to independently take over part or all of that extended isthmus on the pretext of fostering interoceanic communication.

The United States was equally ambivalent. Although an American company had negotiated the right to build a railroad across Panama in the mid-1840s, the government showed surprisingly little interest in Central American affairs.

As late as 1849, two envoys, Hise[1] and Squier,[2] negotiated separate treaties with one or more Central American states, but the American secretaries of state were inclined to repudiate such treaties. Within the Democratic party there were those who regarded America's Manifest Destiny as extending to the Caribbean and Central America, but when a Whig president, Zachary Taylor, was inaugurated in March 1849, the new administration was far less jingoistic than that of James K. Polk.

President Taylor chose as his new secretary of state the experienced Delaware politician John M. Clayton, who had long been intrigued by the idea of an isthmian canal. As he wrote to a member of the United States Corps of Engineers in 1849, "The subject is one which attracted my attention twenty years ago, since which time it has never ceased to occupy my mind; and I have neglected no occasion of seeking from well-informed persons, accurate, reliable and useful information in regard to it."[3] Consequently, Clayton made it clear to the British chargé d'affaires in Washington, John Crampton, that the United States government was keenly interested in cooperating with Her Majesty's government in order to build a canal. Crampton relayed this intimation to Lord Palmerston, who found himself faced with the choice of pursuing the issue with the American minister in London, Abbott Lawrence, or of entrusting the preliminary negotiations to the newly designated British envoy to Washington, Henry Bulwer. By the time the latter sailed to America, Palmerston made up his mind to ask Bulwer to proceed formulating some sort of treaty with the United States for the joint protection and use of an isthmian canal. Abbott Lawrence had very much hoped that he would be able to undertake the challenge of negotiating such a treaty with the wily and flamboyant Palmerston, but Lawrence's protracted illness at the end of 1849 and beginning of 1850 reinforced the choice of Bulwer.

When Bulwer reached Washington in late December, Secretary of State Clayton had become aware of two facts unknown to him when he first broached the canal isue with Crampton. First, the American Atlantic and Pacific Ship Canal Company, partly owned by Cornelius Vanderbilt, had already contracted with the Nicaraguan government to undertake the eventual construction of a canal.[4] Although the Nicaraguan route was longer than some of the others projected, it had certain distinct advantages: it was several hundred miles north of Panama, thus saving the additional three to five days of oceangoing travel; about four-fifths of the distance across Nicaragua could be navigated by steamboats using preexisting arteries; from the Atlantic side, ships could sail up the San Juan River, transfer passengers and baggage around several rapids to other steamers, and then link up with boats already crossing Lake Nicaragua, leaving only about eleven miles of foothills through which a canal would have to be cut. Provided that Vanderbilt's company could accomplish this engineering feat within twelve years, its steamers would be given exclusive rights on the route for ninety-seven years. Prior to the canal's completion, the company was authorized to convey passengers by steamer as far as possible, and then by mule trains or, later, by railroad the remaining distance to the Pacific.

There was one almost insurmountable obstacle confronting the ship Canal Company: the estimated costs were so high that not only was the company unable to finance the undertaking from its own resources, but even potential American investment capital would not be enough. Over half the amount necessary would have to be raised abroad, especially from British investors, and this was why the company staunchly supported an Anglo-American isthmian treaty rather than unilateral treaties such as those negotiated with Nicaragua by Hise and Squier. The company's chief lobbyist in Washington was Joseph L. White,[5] whose brother had signed the contract in Nicaragua. Joseph White favorably impressed Secretary of State Clayton, and Bulwer came to have considerable confidence in him as well.

In addition to the Canal Company's contract, Clayton now also presented Bulwer with the fait accompli of Squier's treaty with Nicaragua, signed on 3 September 1849. This gave exclusive control over a future canal to America in return for its guarantee to protect Nicaraguan independence. By the late 1840s, Nicaragua was clearly pro-American in its foreign relations, while its neighbor, Costa Rica, was regarded as little more than a British protectorate. Even Clayton was somewhat reluctant to support a treaty that might involve the American government in rescuing the Nicaraguans from the machinations of either the Costa Ricans or the British, so he had not yet submitted the Squier treaty to the Senate's Foreign Relations Committee. In the back of his mind, Clayton hoped that he and Bulwer could come up with an alternative which would satisfy the Ship Canal Company as well as the Nicaraguans while minimizing, if not eliminating, the likelihood of an Anglo-American confrontation. Such an Anglo-American treaty would also be the wedge by which the United States could force Britain out of Central America. Like many other Americans, Clayton resented Great Britain's maritime strength and saw no reason why she should continue to meddle in an area that was clearly in the American sphere of influence. What particularly rankled was the high-handed way in which the British asserted their so-called protectorate over the enfeebled tribe of Mosquito Indians along the Atlantic coast of Nicaragua and Honduras. Although the British had had trading rights with the Mosquito coast dating back to the sixteenth century, that had been acknowledged by Spain in the eighteenth century, the situation had drastically changed, according to the United States, after the dissolution of the Spanish Empire in the early 1820s. Nicaragua and Honduras then became sovereign states with independent jurisdiction over the Mosquito Indians. Yet, as late as the mid-1840s, the British were still forcibly propping up and defending the regime of a Mosquito kingdom, claiming that were it not for their protection, the Nicaraguans would subjugate the Indians. Until the territory was safeguarded by some sort of international guarantee, they would not consent to withdraw their support. True to their word, between October 1847 and March 1848 they resorted to gunboat diplomacy, forced the Nicaraguans to back down, and secured recognition of the Mosquito king in return for the withdrawal of British arms.

The capital of Mosquitia was the village of San Juan at the mouth of the San Juan River. The British renamed it Greytown, while the Americans continued to recognize it only by its older Spanish name. Both countries realized that this modest collection of huts and warehouses stood astride the Atlantic terminus of a future interoceanic canal, and so there is little wonder that America suspected that Britain's protection was motivated less from humanitarian concern for the Indians than from a desire to superintend America's advance into Central America.

On 6 January 1850, Bulwer wrote his first private letter to Lord Palmerston, explaining the situation as he understood it.[6]

I have endeavoured since being here to ascertain the real springs of this Nicaraguan and Mosquito commotion without knowing which it is difficult to know precisely what will set such commotion at rest.

Here is the pith of the matter. The Company formed at New York for the projected Canal has contrived in one way or the other to obtain considerable influence in the Senate, the representative Assembly, the Press and even the Gov't.

This was the origin of the various proceedings with the State of Nicaragua by which the United States have in a certain degree compromised their policy; of the loud clamour as to the unfortunate protectorate of Mosquitos which the Company at first thought stood in their way, and of the position in which matters now are.

It is undoubtedly the wish of the Gov't. after all its coquetting with the Nicaraguans to get something for them. And it would be a feather in their cap if they could annihilate our Savage friend's[7] dominion; but this, whatever Lawrence[8] may make of it, is a secondary point. The real and principal one is that the design of the New York Company should succeed as that at all events it would look well in the market.

What I have wanted has been to get all question as to the several rights of the Mosquitos and Nicaraguans put on one side, to get the question of the Canal placed on its own.

The way in which this in my opinion can best be done is by our refusing altogether to enter in the first—viz. the rights or cession of the rights of the Mosquitos, but offering at the same time a direct convention with the United States in respect to the second viz. the forming and protecting a water passage of communication across the isthmus.

This would have moreover the great advantage of catching the public mind here, and destroying at once, without entering into, their millions of prejudices which now exist.

In the position in which the U.S. and G. Brit. stand towards each other it is difficult if we do not cement this union to prevent at no distant time their rupture. Such a treaty as I suggest would greatly tend to effect this union.

I should have preferred a treaty for the purpose of 1st. exploring and deciding upon the best passage and then undertaking to protect it, and I send you privately such a rough draft of a scheme of this kind as I think would be generally acceptable here unless a particular interest shows against it. But unfortunately the U.S. Company has such an interest and it would represent the question of exploration as an artifice used for the purpose of delay, and Mr. Clayton also would not enter heartily into any scheme which did not give the preference to a Society, in which in some way or other, it does not matter how, I believe and indeed know he is particularly interested. I should strongly recommend therefore settling the matter at once by some such a treaty as I send you for the protection of the Canal of the U.S. Company.

It would not only quiet matters at once but engage all those who have been noisy in hushing up their own clamour: and if you give me instructions to make such a treaty on the understanding that it stops all further discussion as to Mosquitos I think I can undertake to succeed. I should add that I am only in favour of the spirit and sense of the said project, not of its wording, since I only made up my mind after seeing certain parties last night upon the matter and of course have written very hastily.

The Company will be willing to make any regulations you desire, and will abandon such pretensions as you deem unadvisable. I saw the headman[9] in it, in short, a few hours ago; he was brought here by *Clayton's* headman; in a confidential interview he made quite clear to me what I before suspected. No treaty, even making one with the United States, would be absolutely necessary, as it appears to me, with the Nicaraguans: the Canal would construct itself; the Company deriving from Nicaragua such rights as it can offer and obtaining through us the facilities which the Mosquitos can afford.

What was further done therefore with respect to the Mosquito dominion would be an affair of future convenience and not at this time of contract or discussion.

I hope I have made myself clear but I have no further time to save the packet, which I have ordered the messenger, in case of any accident of snow, to use every means of attaining, since I think it may be important for you to get this letter as soon as possible.

I only wish that I could venture to send you the project already agreed to since it might be useful at the opening of Parl. but not knowing what you are about with Lawrence I have not dared to do this.

On 20 January 1850 Bulwer again wrote, but this time he was chiefly preoccupied with trade between Britain and her colonies on the one hand, and the United States on the other. During the latter 1840s, Canada had suffered especially from a decline in the market price for her agricultural produce and natural resources. If the United States could be prevailed upon to lower her tariff on imports from Canada, then such produce would return a better price. There were many interest groups in the American states that balked at the idea of lowering specific tariffs. Both the British and their colonists wondered what was the best way to promote a "reciprocal" reduction of duties in the interest of expanded trade. It could take the form of a treaty between the mother country and the United States, or the American Congress might be persuaded to act unilaterally to foster freer trade.

Great Britain was steadily removing impediments to commerce and shipping at this time, and sought to encourage other nations to do likewise. Causing particular frustration were the American registration acts that regulated the coastal trade of the continental United States.[10] Goods coming from abroad could be unloaded at any American port, but thereafter a ship registered in a foreign country could not stop at other American ports. Only ships built and registered in an American state could trade from one American harbor to another, including the vast new coast of California.

As compared with the canal negotiations, Bulwer was far less sanguine about the passage of a reciprocity bill or a modification of the registration acts.[11]

> You will read a letter of mine respecting the personal character of Clayton. The fact is that I hardly ever find him precisely in the same mind or holding the same language.
>
> At one time he told Crampton he disapproved of a reciprocity bill for the Canadas, and preferred a general treaty for all the Colonies; then he told me that he would have nothing to do with a Treaty, but had become upon the whole favorable to the Canada reciprocity bill; a day or two ago he took up again tho' loosely the question of a Treaty, and said that he had quite forgotten the communication I had made him luckily in Crampton's presence that I was ready and authorized to enter into the discussion of one with him. In one conversation I understood him to say that many persons would be opposed to an alteration in the United States registration act, but that he and the Govt. should be quite neutral on the matter and more lately he has repeated that the Govt. would be neutral but added that he himself was personally opposed. In regard to excepting California from the coasting trade he spoke in one interview so as to make me think that he was not only favorable to this view but that he conceived Congress would be so, and indeed again with some modification he has used this language; but at the same time, now that I can see my way a little clearer into these affairs, it appears to me almost impossible to obtain such an exception, since every Senator of note considers that to place any State in an exceptional position from other states would be a violation of the Constitution and there is almost a certainty that California will be accepted as a State.
>
> When I arrived he was in a state of desperation about Nicaragua; and would have settled the question in almost any way that I had been authorized to propose, stating at the same time he should lay no papers or treaties respecting it before Congress until he saw his way clearly to a termination of that affair. Now he appears to take the matter quite calmly and coolly, to be almost indifferent about its prompt solution, and is going to lay Squier's Treaty before the Senate. At the same time we are on the best of terms and he really seems well intentioned; but I never saw any person with whom it is more difficult to negotiate a business and more necessary to bring matters at once to a point in writing.
>
> As to the Canada bill we have had the committee on commerce in the Representatives assembly sounded and it will go with us. We have to get a patron[12] for it in the Senate and are looking out for one. If I see Clayton in earnest as to a general treaty, I shall discuss it with him without stopping the progress of the bill, but as he merely wanted me to tell him all we would grant without in the least saying what he would accept, I deemed it best to tell him that if he would tell me that the President was really disposed to agree to a general treaty on the basis of reciprocal exchange of natural produce between this country and the North American colonies, we would then discuss the matter fully and see what exceptions or additions would be made to the grounds we started upon, but that unless there was some serious desire of the kind it would have no success and which by confusing men's minds as to what was really wanted would interfere with the progress of the especial measure affecting the Canadas. He is to think over the affair. . . .
>
> I fear in this session we shall not succeed with the Register, tho' I believe ere long

the Free Trade Party will prevail here and then very probably give us what we ask in this matter, and menace us with war on some other.

As to Nicaragua, Mosquitos, Canal, etc.—Clayton seems to me in what they call here—a fix. Lawrence has promised him, I imagine, that you will give up the Indian Claim and cede the territory of our wild Sovereign to the greater Nicaraguans, and this Cabinet has so compromised itself with these latter that it clings to Lawrence's assurance; but at the same time all the leading men of Clayton's party would be quite satisfied with turning the question of Nicaragua and Mosquitia altogether by such a convention as I've tried to suggest, and if this were proposed to Clayton he would not dare to refuse it, unless some new tempest then blows. I should like something of this kind moreover to satisfy certain parties in England. One of the leading members of the Democratic Party here has, I understand, been corresponding with Hume and Cobden on the subject: and was very violent upon it, but this man whom I happen to know would consider a downright proposition from us to deal with the great question at issue as a complete scuttle to all the smaller ones.

I shall be much obliged to you not to let out in any way to Lawrence what I say of Clayton, since it is very important that I should keep well with him, and now that I know him and this place better the disagreeable peculiarity I have mentioned will not so much signify.

By the beginning of February 1850, Clayton and Bulwer were able to agree on the draft of a canal treaty, which the latter hastily sent off to Lord Palmerston for this approval. In his private letter of 3 February, Bulwer wearily but triumphantly described what had happened.[13]

I sincerely trust that the projet[14] of a convention which I send herewith will meet with your approval. I understood you to say when we last discussed the subject of the Mosquito question that it was one which you would be glad to get out of, if any creditable mode for doing so presented itself; this, and your letter to Lawrence, have principally guided me in the business. I say principally, because I have also been influenced by the feeling that, with this question of Canada pending, you would be particularly anxious to avoid any great anti-Anglican excitement.

The Mosquito claim, moreover, seems to me just one of those things which one cannot give up and yet would not wish to fight about; especially if it would seem that we are defending a sort of semibarbarous potentate on the one hand and that the Americans are for extending a great benefit to civilization on the other. If we come to a quarrel on any matter I think it advisable not to do so on this, and at all events to make it clear that we on our side, were willing to do everything that the advantage of mankind required and our own honor allowed. But this is not all. The convention in question appears to me not merely to get rid of a difficulty, but to turn what was a difficulty into a cause for credit and congratulation. I have endeavored in it to bring together all the elements of difference between us and this Country which were abroad in those hotbeds of discord, the Central American states, and reduce them together into a basis of peace and good understanding.

It has been however I assure you with the greatest difficulty that I brought things to this point and prevented them from shaping themselves into a very different result. Clayton at one time had determined to aim for popularity by violence on this very Mosquito question. Not only did the President write his letter to the President of Nicaragua under these auspices, and Squier make his Treaty, but I found a large book[15] compiled by him and a man in the State Dept. which was about to see the light and has not: that would have blown this trifle into an affair of the gravest importance. You will have seen that since my arrival the matter has been kept pretty quiet, but the demands for papers in the two assemblies and the articles in the press that have lately accompanied these demands, had already disturbed the equanimity of Clayton's mind and made him fearful that he should neither get credit for settling the business, nor embroiling it, when the news of Lawrence's serious illness arrived. He thought it necessary that he should instantly come to a decision, and either produce his papers and stand by his Nicaraguans—"America for the Americans"—or lock up his Treaties and correspondence and embrace us. As he changes his mind, as often as he looks into it, I hardly know which line he would at last have taken, but for the aid I have derived from some people about him and from the head man (I must say also) of the American Canal company.

Having convinced him that the only chance for a canal was in our agreement with his Govt., he has labored hard for us. At his instigation (this is a secret) the Nicaraguan Chargé d'Affaires,[16] was induced to write to Clayton saying that his Govt. did not acknowledge Hise's treaty, and he has also, by sending to be altered a certain portion of his contract, on which Mr. Squier depends, rendered it possible to prevent any discussion upon this last until your answer arrives. It is however most urgent on this ground that such answer should come *as soon as possible*, Clayton begs for it a fortnight earlier than the time stated in our arrangement; it being his wish, if he has a favorable answer and can present our treaty to the Senate to make Squier fit into it and to refuse all other papers and correspondence, saying that as the matter is terminated by the documents produced, no others are necessary. . . .

If this project of [a] treaty is approved of he may be depended upon; he will build his fame upon it, and upon the principle of amity and alliance with us which it establishes: General Taylor is I know aware of the project and approves of it, but Clayton does not formally admit this as your sanction is uncertain. I really on reading over the document think, that as we wish for nothing that we abandon and get the U.S. to abandon everything that we give up, and establish in the clearest manner principles which must destroy all jealousy where so much has always hitherto existed, the present arrangement (every other consideration apart) is one desirable. It annoys me to have been obliged to enter into it however before getting your answer to a somewhat similar plan which I had thought of and transmitted to you, but I had no choice. This is better and fuller. Whatever I hear from you before your reply to this reaches me, I shall wait before stirring further in this matter until such reply comes. I am getting on with the Canada affair and have got an unanimously favorable report from the Committee on Commerce. I should like to write to you on general American politics, but cannot at this time attempt it.

On 18 February, Bulwer again wrote.[17]

It is lucky that I pinned Clayton, who is the most variable of men, at the time I did so. Had this not been the case the first note would now be smelling of a new Oregon affair. No time would suffice to go into all the details of this business, more especially as the Secretary of State talks each time one sees him of honour and generally talks the next time in a different strain from that of the last interview. I do not believe him a bad fellow, but it is impossible to describe or follow his mind's fancy. He is now however heart and soul in a peaceful arrangement of this question, and it is our interest if possible to sustain him, for were he to go, I really see no peaceful or at least no quiet termination of it—such is the foolish way in which it would be treated. It seems to me impossible that Lawrence, with such a Master as Clayton, and such a Senate as there is here, could even settle it; or venture on any palatable mode of doing so. He will probably, if he lives and continues to take part in the business, begin if he had not already begun a Mosquito controversy, and thus furnish new papers for Congress, rendering final arrangements more difficult.

I have here at present Clayton, the Company, Clay, Webster, Benton, and the Editor of the great Whig newspaper,[18] all for the arrangement as it stands: and my notion is that as it is, it would do. Nevertheless, if we could make it fuller by clearing up that misty Mosquito protectorate it doubtless would be better. There cannot be any denial given to the fact that the Mosquito monarch surrounded by Johnsons and Walkers and Smiths[19] and what not, is a queer affair, and that there is some difficulty in declaring that England will not do this, that, and the other, if Englishmen with a Mosquito mask on, and England to back them, can. It might be well moreover, if a good expedient turned up, for settling this Mosquito business altogether, to take advantage of it; and this cannot be denied, but Nicaraguans, Hondurans, and Salvadorians all want to be citizens under the stripes, and that when we get the U.S. solemnly to declare against annexation of these parts, and grant exclusive appropriation of any canal or communication we settle matters a good deal therein. I understand that if our business goes on smoothly, Squier is to be at once recalled, which in itself would be no inconsiderable blessing. However, I would do nothing that surrendered, on any consideration, the Mosquitos to the Nicaraguans, or that could be considered by the higher order of men here "shabby" because in such case we should lose more than we should gain. Indeed, looking at the whole matter, if we had taken this Mosquito territory in our own name, and that it was of use to us, I should stand by it—*Conte qui Conte*, but in reading over our papers, and knowing what is got upon the matter here, I think that there is something which looks rather unsound and in these days untenable in the Indian Chief, with the Jamaica Crown and the English Council. I fear it would not be parliamentary, and then there would be all the philosophers who are ever for canals and never for cuffs, and who would give up not only the Mosquito territory but all Asia, Africa, America and Europe sooner than fight about either especially with friendly, go ahead, Republicans. For these reasons my dear Lord Palmerston, tho' tolerably bellicose in my way, I'm here all for peace if it can now be secured on decent conditions. You may be sure that if we lose the present opportunity there will be on this side of the water at least a tremendous clatter. You will be obliged in England to make preparations for war in order to avoid it, and I am so afraid, pardon me these fears for they are connected with my respect, affection, and regard for you, that then, at the critical moment you may be left in the lurch, and some composition cooked up here worse than any that might now be concocted.

If therefore, you would either take this matter in hand at once yourself, or give it to me with tolerable latitude to settle it, supported as I am by Clayton's own declaration which he cannot decently cast off, I would earnestly recommend one of these courses.

I should carry into the affair, for my own part, a strong desire it is true to bring it to an amicable conclusion, because I really think a great thing may be made out of it, but at the same time I would rather cut off my hand than sign or agree to any thing which I thought could in any way be derogatory to you or to my country.

Toward the end of March Bulwer received permission from Lord Palmerston to proceed with negotiations for a canal treaty based on the *projet* sent to the Foreign Office on 3 February. However, without informing Bulwer, Clayton sent Squier's treaty of 3 September 1849 to the Senate Foreign Relations Committee on 25 March. Six days later, Bulwer learned of this and was predictably annoyed. His letter to Lord Palmerston expanded on his frustration.[20]

> With reference to my despatch #56[21] I should mention that I have learnt from a source, which leaves me no room to doubt of the accuracy of my information, that Mr. Clayton on receiving a despatch from Mr. Lawrence inclosing one from Your Lordship relative to the temporary occupation of Tigre Island, sent the Treaty of Mr. Squier with the state of Nicaragua to the Senate—a fact of which he never informed me, though I think after what has passed, he should have done so.
>
> This conduct is the more surprising since I had every reason to believe not only from what Mr. Clayton, had told me, but from what I know he also told the chargé d'affaires from Nicaragua himself; that the aforesaid Treaty would not and could not in its present form be laid before Congress.
>
> It appears however that the Secretary of State would persist, notwithstanding all I told him to the contrary in considering Your Lordship's note to Mr. Lawrence a declaration that the British Government would seize and occupy, and claim dominion over any parts of Central America that it thought proper, and then consequently Your Lordship would not agree to the great principle of the Treaty which was sent home to be submitted to you, or give me such instructions as would enable me to carry it out.
>
> I think there is fair ground for complaint against Mr. Clayton in this particular. But I take it as the better principle to avoid complaints as to past conduct, when a friendly feeling in the future can remedy the mischief of previous error.
>
> I have not therefore made any reproaches to Mr. Clayton on account of the inconveniences which he has doubtless placed in the way of our negotiations by communicating Mr. Squier's Treaty to the Senate previous to ascertaining fully Your Lordship's views, since I found that the expression of those views as it has now reached me has dispelled the erroneous ideas as to English policy which the Government here for a moment entertained.
>
> Moreover, as Mr. Squier's Treaty is yet only in the hands of the Secret Committee of Foreign Affairs in the Senate, and not publicly known, to Congress, it is by no means difficult to make alterations therein as may be necessary to prevent its clashing with the more important convention which may be concluded with Great Britain. Thus upon the whole though I never wish to be sanguine with respect to a government the action of which has so many difficulties to encounter as that of this country, nor in respect to a Minister who is in his resolutions so variable as Mr. Clayton, I am inclined to think I shall be able to announce to Your Lordship by the next packet that as far as Mr. Clayton and the United States Government are concerned the business in question is settled.
>
> In regard to the Senate some opposition is to be expected from those who are desirous that the United States Government should profess the doctrines of Conquest rather than those of Peace, but I nevertheless believe that the consent of this body will not be unreasonably withheld from an arrangement which is not only fair and equitable in itself, but highly honourable to the character, and highly advantageous to the real interests of the Government's subscribing to it.

On 19 April 1850, Clayton and Bulwer signed the treaty destined to bear their respective names. Both nations agreed not to acquire territory in Central

America not to erect fortifications or in any other way intervene militarily in the region. Once a canal was built, each nation would have equal access to it. The language of the treaty was intentionally broad and somewhat vague in order to gain the widest possible support in both countries. Thorny issues such as the Mosquito Indians and the disposition of Greytown were ignored because both signatories wanted nothing to stand in the way of Anglo-American cooperation. These ambiguities or unresolved questions eventually came home to roost, but for the moment Clayton and Bulwer each thought he had got the better of the bargain: Clayton, because he assumed that Britain would now no longer want to maintain her minor possessions or protectorates in Central America, thus paving the way for American diplomatic and commercial domination; Bulwer, because he trusted that he had finally put a stop to American expansionism in Central America.

Bulwer dispatched the treaty to Lord Palmerston on 28 April, together with lengthy explanations as to the changes made in the final draft.[22] He also wrote privately, seeking advice about the Mosquito Indians and Greytown.[23]

> The treaty made for the construction of the Canal, abandoning nothing contrary to our honor, secures some advantages and takes away, as I have already said, all cause for immediate or disagreeable dispute between Great Britain and this country. However the whole subject is not disposed of without going somewhat farther.
>
> Now, as I consider the matter (and I beg for Your Lordship's advice and opinion therefore) the case stands thus.
>
> We have no longer any interest in maintaining the Mosquitos where they are, nor our protection over them, in that locality. Upon the whole we should have a good deal of trouble and no advantage from such a course; but still though the protectorate in question is but a shadow, and of no avail to us, even rather a burden, we could neither withdraw it, nor alter the condition of things on which it rests, if pressed to do so in any disagreeable or hostile way, or even if a conflicting claim was put up directly by the power with which we were discussing the matter in direct opposition to that claim for which we have long since declared ourselves. On the other hand— we might perhaps terminate and settle this point, if it were considered and discussed between ourselves and a friendly power in general and on friendly grounds.
>
> If the notion I thus entertain is correct, it would follow that should our treaty and the treaty between this country and Nicaragua be settled without any assertion of the right of Nicaragua over the Mosquito territory, we might then in amicable arrangement with the United States, arrive at some plan for withdrawing the Mosquitos from the vicinity of the Canal, and thereby remove at once all grounds of future discord.
>
> I remember that Your Lordship did not seem altogether adverse to a plan frequently put forward of purchasing the Indian title. Something of this kind might perhaps be settled. A sort of recognition of the Mosquitos in a particular district might also be obtained from the Central American States, on certain conditions and the nature of their position be in this way—(if it were desirable,) benefitted by the sphere of their pretensions being contracted.
>
> An agreement might become to, as to the land thus vacated, favorable to the purposes of commerce and the construction of the Canal; and conditions imposed as to the nature of the Government therein to be established. The Mosquitos being

withdrawn the cession of the disputed territory to any particular Central American State comes by the terms of our treaty art. VI, one of friendly adjustment between us and the United States.

In short the ground seems in this way clear. I shall however be exceedingly glad to know either publickly or privately what are Your Lordship's views as to these matters, and if they coincide in the main with mine, or differ as to any essential point; since it might be well now that we are occupied with this affair to settle it completely and at once.

It would also greatly interest me to learn what has passed between Your Lordship and the Nicaraguan Agent in London, if I were not intruding making such a request.[24]

During April and May 1850, the United States Senate had two distinct but potentially overlapping treaties to ponder: that of Squier signed on 3 September 1849 and the Clayton-Bulwer Treaty of 19 April 1850. Neither Clayton nor Bulwer wished to have the Senate vote upon the Squier Treaty until their own had been ratified, and they had reason to hope that the desired order would come about because the Nicaraguan chargé d'affaires in Washington, Eduardo Carache, had not yet received full powers to modify Squier's treaty so that it would conform with the provisions of the Clayton-Bulwer Treaty. Nonetheless, Bulwer worried lest anti-British feeling among some senators, especially Democrats, be used to bring forth the Squier Treaty as a way of blocking theirs. In his private letter of 6 May, Bulwer felt moderately optimistic.[25]

I mentioned to Your Lordship, in my despatch marked Private and Confidential of 28 April, that there were some Senators who were disposed to maintain, in Squier's treaty with Nicaragua, the recognition of the right of that state over the proposed line of the Canal, on the ground that this recognition was now merely a barren step which would be satisfactory to Nicaragua and could not be obnoxious to us, since we were both to enjoy the privileges on the Canal, and both to guarantee its security. I had however on Thursday last a long conversation with Mr. Clayton on the subject, calling to his recollection the various circumstances in our negotiation that would show that such recognition had never been contemplated by either of us when the treaty was signed; and that although its effects could not be productive, after the arrangement we had entered into, of any serious and hostile consequences, yet it would destroy that perfect harmony and air of good feeling and cordial understanding which it was so important, as one of the main consequences of our treaty, to preserve; the more especially as the faith of Capitalists in the success of the enterprise would almost, if not entirely, depend on their belief that Great Britain and the United States were linked together in a complete spirit of union and amity, to protect it.

Mr. Clayton and myself have sometimes differed on this point: but I am happy to say that the above mentioned remarks were on this occasion fairly considered by him, and that he expressed the earnest desire to stamp the whole of our arrangement with the character of friendship, and to remove therefrom anything which might tend to weaken such impression. I have also found other members of the Government and Senate in the same disposition, and I likewise hear that the Nicaraguan Chargé d'Affaires, who is expecting full powers to make a new treaty, has declared that he considers our treaty so important to this state, both on account of the joint protection thus afforded to the Canal, and also on account of the great advantage which his country will obtain by the two great maritime nations renouncing all schemes of ever establishing their power therein, that he will be willing to solicit this Government when the above mentioned powers arrive, to make such alterations in Squier's convention with Nicaragua as may tend to secure the stability of that signed by myself and Mr. Clayton.

During his first year as minister to Washington, Bulwer's private and confidential correspondence dealt mostly with the topic of Central America, with occasional letters about Canadian reciprocity or American filibustering activity against Cuba. However, the following letter was a departure of sorts. His long experience in diplomacy entitled him to provide Lord Palmerston with a realistic appraisal of the American diplomatic service.[26]

As a Committee of the House of Commons is appointed in England to consider the expenses of Her Majesty's Diplomatic Service, and I see references are being constantly made to the American Diplomacy, respecting which rather erroneous notions seem to prevail, I have deemed that it might be interesting to Your Lordship, and not without interest to the Committee to receive certain particulars on this subject, though my statement written in haste, lest it should arrive too late for the object which calls it forth, will not be so complete as I could desire.

It will perhaps somewhat startle Your Lordship when I say that there are no Diplomatic Servants in Europe so well paid considering the circumstances under which they are employed as those of the United States, and that there is no system so recognized as defective throughout this country as that which sometimes receives encomiums in our own.

Your Lordship is aware that those who enter the Diplomatic Service in Europe, serve in most countries, and certainly in ours, a very long apprenticeship before they attain any stature of much emolument. Few get to be ministers before twenty years service; five, six or seven of which are generally passed without any salary at all.

The American Diplomatist goes through no such apprenticeship. Diplomatic appointments in America are made according to the distribution of patronage belonging to the states which have contributed to the ruling President's election. Such a state having a right to such an extent of patronage, a Diplomatist is chosen from it. He is usually a lawyer or member of Congress. The Gentleman selected moreover is one who wishes on account of business, or with a view to pleasure and information, to visit Europe; he would not give up his position at home for such employment, but a short absence on foreign service will rather strengthen it; and therefore without abandoning his calling, whatever it may be, he consents to go ahead for a brief space of time.

He thus arrives at the head of the Diplomatic Profession at once, whether as Chargé d'Affaires or Minister, according to the Court to which he is sent.

His salary as Minister is £1,800 per annum [$9,000]; but he has £1,800 allowed him as a budget, and £450 as a return allowance.

These salaries are alike at all Missions, but the contingent expenses (which are additional for House Rent, etc.) differ.

It is to be observed by a glance at this system of payment, that the shorter time the Diplomatist stays at the place he is appointed to the greater his salary is. No one stays long, unless it be a Gentleman who has a good fortune of his own, and some particular motive for being abroad.

From 1845 to 1850 there have been the following American Agents at St. Petersburg: Mr. Todd, Minister who left in 1845, Mr. Clay, Chargé d'Affaires, being removed thereto from Vienna. Mr. Ingersoll, Minister—Mr. Bagby, Minister, Mr. Brown, Minister, giving an average of £4000 a year.[27]

The American Minister's pay commences in most instances, not ten days before proceeding to his Post, as with us, but at the time of his appointment. He can when abroad, quit his Post, and travel to other countries without any deduction of salary. If he is moved, even during the same year, from one mission to another, he has a double budget, and return allowance.

Mr. Donelson,[28] lately returned from Berlin to Frankfurt, received in one year $30,000 or something more than £6,000.

Mr. Clifford,[29] first sent on special Mission to Mexico, and then named as Minister, received in one year the same sum. I believe he is not coming home.

It is to be stated that the American Minister never lives at any expense, unless he is a man of great private fortune, his purpose being so transitory. It not infrequently happens that he is named when Congress is not sitting by the President, and though disapproved of by the Senate when it meets, he has received his budget and received his return allowance, and a salary during the time that has elapsed since the President's nomination. Mr. Webb[30] lately named to Vienna, and now disapproved of by the Senate, is in this position. A rapid glance over this general statement will show how much it varies from the general notions reflecting it.

I am bound moreover to say that the general opinions in the Senate, and amongst persons at all qualified to judge of the matter, is that the usual American Salaries are too low; and although the Governments of the States are always jealous of the expenses and patronage of the Central Government, for this is a peculiarity in the American System, some alterations in respect to them will ere long very probably take place.[31]

The economy of the American Service being thus questionable, the position of the American Agents being thus shown to have many advantages, I come to the consideration which is never to be lost sight of,—viz: their efficiency.

It must be at once stated that nearly all the American gentlemen chosen for diplomatic situations abroad, are Gentlemen of a certain station and ability.

Their capacity however in almost all European Countries is of little avail to them. They neither know the language nor usages of Foreign Countries; and if they succeed in their Missions (this is far from being said disparagingly) it is simply because the American Government having an object in view, such object being generally a claim, demands it clearly and boldly with the not disguised threat, which it knows its whole people will heartily support, that if the demand is not complied with the most energetic means will be adopted to enforce it.

Here lies the strength of the American Diplomacy: the policy on which it rests however, though generally a successful one, might not, in a multiplied series of cases, be a cheap one, and is at all events not accordant with the language held in our country on such matters. But whilst I assert without fear of contradiction from anyone, even such Agents themselves, that the Representatives of the United States in most courts in Europe, though able and clever men, are not adapted to their situations; I must make an exception with respect to our own country. There such Agents have the advantage of the language. They understand the laws and customs. Their ability has fair play, and it must also be stated that America never omits to choose one of her very best men (such men always preferring England to every other Mission) to represent her at St. James.

I ought here perhaps to bring under Your Lordship's notice a general theory adopted in this Country as to official appointments, and which has exercised a great influence over the social and political systems that prevail throughout the American Continent.

It is agreed that the rate of Salaries, and the social system of the State go together. It is said that where the law and custom of primogeniture prevails, higher salaries are to be given; and that where low salaries are adopted, there the law of primogeniture ought not to exist. In one case, fortunes it is contended, being divided, are moderate and general; and consequently few persons expect to derive more from a profession or calling than is the ordinary income derived from inheritance by those who are amongst the wealthier and better classes in the Country:—incomes in the United States rarely exceed £2000 to £2500. Furthermore it is stated that persons in professions (where property is thus partitioned out) who have not risen from the very lowest rank, have all a competency, either in enjoyment or expectation to add to what their exertions procure them.

On the other side, public speakers and writers have held that where the style of living and expense which forms the criterion of a certain class and station in life is much higher, there men who hold a high position under Government expect more, and that moreover as the whole hereditary patrimony is generally taken by the eldest in the family, the younger have frequently little of their own to add to the gains of their profession. Under these views, the cheapness of the Central Government being admitted as the rule of the United States, the several states themselves have all one by one done away with the law and custom of primogeniture.

This particularly may be worth noticing, because if it really be true that the systems of society and government move together as wholes, and cannot be moved separately as parts, it may then become a question with those who desire to introduce great changes into the one whether they are equally prepared to witness the introduction of great changes into the other.

The Senate approved the Clayton-Bulwer Treaty in June 1850, and the coauthors of the document exchanged ratifications on 4 July. Several days later President Zachary Taylor died, and his vice president, Millard Fillmore, assumed office. At the State Department, Daniel Webster replaced John M. Clayton as secretary of state. One of Webster's early decisions was to terminate Squier's appointment as American envoy to Central America, but his pending treaty still had to be dealt with. It is a measure of Webster's confidence in Bulwer that he asked the British minister to draw up a private memorandum on how best to modify Squier's treaty.[32] Meanwhile, having been dismissed, Squier felt free to attack Bulwer and the Fillmore administration publicly in the press. This behavior confirmed British suspicions that the Mosquito Indian problem could have been solved long since had it not been for incendiary American agents in the area. Now Joseph W. Livingston, the American consul at Leon, capital of Nicaragua, continued to stir up trouble, giving rise to complaints by Lord Palmerston. Bulwer tried to reassure his superior in a letter of 7 October.[33]

In reference to Your Lordship's communication No. 117 of September 11[34] in regard to the conduct of Mr. Livingston who styles himself United States Consul at Leon, and also United States Consul for the Port of San Juan de Nicaragua, I informed Mr. Webster this morning of the same, and of Your Lordship's remarks thereupon together with such other reasons for stopping this Agent in the course he seems to be pursuing, as occurred to me. Mr. Webster entered entirely into the spirit of my observations and informed me that Mr. Livingston should instantly receive orders to keep quiet, and if he' were not so that he should be removed.

In order that Mr. Webster should not forget this promise before leaving Washington which he is about to quit for a few weeks, I have written to him a private note upon the same subject, enclosing him a copy of Mr. Livingston's communication and of Your Lordship's opinion thereupon.

I understand that though Mr. Livingston speaks of Instructions from his Government he received no such instructions from his Government; and I trust that the dismissal of Mr. Squier will have a salutary effect upon other United States Agents of the same stamp in Central America.

The problem of finding a suitable replacement for Livingston, should that become necessary, was not easy, as Bulwer related to Lord Palmerston.[35]

As the advantages and disadvantages of the system of Salaries adopted in this Country and the efficiency of the Government Agents which that system procures is frequently under discussion in England, I cannot refrain from relating to Your Lordship what occurred to me this very morning at two separate Departments, my communication to Your Lordship being of course confidential.

I was speaking to Mr. Webster about the advisability of sending forthwith a suitable Agent to Nicaragua in order that some course to settling its disputes with Costa Rica, and also as to the alterations to be adopted in Mr. Squier's Treaty might as soon as possible be taken.

Mr. Webster said to me he would at once send to Nicaragua such an Agent, but that he actually found it impossible to lay his hands upon any person who would come to his office, study the subject, and then go to Nicaragua with the intention and ability to carry out his Instructions discreetly and quietly. He added he had been consulting some Members of the Foreign Affairs Committee in the Senate if they knew such a person, and they had said they did not.

I went afterwards to the Secretary of the Treasury[36] about some other business. He was complaining about the manner in which he was overworked by details. I have, said he, the authority from the Legislature to appoint an Assistant who would take a great deal of this business off my hands, but this permission is useless. I cannot find any competent person to undertake the office for the advantages it affords.

On 27 January 1851, Bulwer returned to a discussion of American representation abroad, this time focusing on the situation in the consular as distinct from the diplomatic service.[37]

Although I deem it right that Your Lordship should be acquainted with the facts that have come to my knowledge with respect to the Consular service of the United States, I should feel considerable objection to such facts as I am about to state being presented in any way to the public.

The truth however is that the state of the Consular service of the United States instead of being a fit object of imitation to our Government is a subject of shame to this Country itself.

The practice of paying by fees, and almost in every situation by fees alone, has established a variety of abuses; I say nothing of the inequality of the remuneration which such a system produces, some of the Consuls receiving,—as at Liverpool for instance £3,000 or £4,000 a year, and others little or nothing. But the fact is that as no state money accompanies this species of patronage it is usually disposed of without much observation or much thought as to the persons who receive it.

I happen to know that no longer ago than last year, a French cook was appointed United States Consul at the important town of Lyons.

In many places small shopkeepers perform the Consular functions; and I know on very good authority of one instance of an arrangement made between the director of a public Hospital and the American Consul at that place to the effect that he should have one half of all the money he paid on behalf of distressed American seamen.

I have also heard on equally good authority of other and similar instances of venality.

It signifies little what rules are laid down by the State Department for its servants when they are frequently of so inferior a description: and though at times an able man may for some special object be selected, whose reports correspond with his ability, it is evident that the general quality of the reports of the American Consuls must bear a due relation to the class of men from whom they proceed.

By late February 1851, both Nicaragua and Costa Rica had new representatives in Washington. The opportunity for compromise seemed to be at hand. In the early summer the United States and Nicaragua had a commercial treaty ready to sign. This, incidentally, gave great satisfaction to Bulwer, since the treaty eliminated the objectionable features that Squier had previously introduced. On the eve of Bulwer's return to Great Britain, however, the treaty was indefinitely postponed because Marcoleta, Nicaragua's chargé d'affaires, felt that the status of Greytown was still unsatisfactory. A fortnight before his departure for London, Bulwer reviewed his tour of duty in America.[38]

> I have now done here pretty nearly all I can do for sometime to come.
>
> With respect to reciprocity with Canada I have Webster's promise that the matter shall be recommended to Congress and altho' he has not confirmed that promise in writing as he said he would, and that some difficulty exists on the part of the President, who comes from the Canadian frontier, on the subject, I am still disposed to think that Mr. W will finally make his own views prevail and at all events this Legation cannot do more just now upon the subject.
>
> In regard to Central America the main objects are effected—by Mr. Webster expunging from his offer of a commercial treaty with Nicaragua all the objectionable portions of that commercial treaty entered into by Mr. Squier and by his defining clearly in my presence and in that of Molina[39] and Marcoleta the position of the U.S. Govt. with respect to the differences between us and Nicaragua.
>
> The winding up of this affair I still deem of great importance, but it must await Mr. Marcoleta's new instructions.

The problem of the Mosquito Indians and their "capital" of Greytown was almost irreconcilable, given the assumptions of the different parties involved. The British were inclined to be highly pragmatic. If it suited their overall purpose to defend the territorial rights of the Indians, they would do so. If, on the other hand, it was necessary to dispossess the Mosquitos of Greytown or some other portion of their coastline, that would be done, provided some face-saving compensation was made to the "savages." The Nicaraguans and the Americans were more dogmatic. They would not admit that indigenous natives had property rights in a legal or international sense. Perhaps John M. Clayton best summed up this view in a letter to Abbott Lawrence of 2 May 1850.[40]

As to the Mosquito title, the United States could not possibly recognize that, without abandoning a principle as old as their existence, for you know, we never acknowledge any right in an Indian in any part of America, except a mere right of occupancy, always liable to be extinguished (that's our technical word for it) at the will of the discoverers. We could not recognize such a title in any case without admitting the illegality of the tenure by which we hold all the lands in our country.

Bulwer sailed from New York on 13 August 1851. He hoped to be given either a leave of absence or a reassignment to a European post. His short stay in Washington was the result of a number of personal concerns that haunted him during his tenure there, and in fact he was not to return to the United States again.

The nineteenth-century American diplomat John Bigelow has left us a particularly striking portrait of Bulwer. Bigelow observed him occasionally during his tour of duty in 1850–51 and got better acquainted with him in Paris in 1864.[41]

He was a singularly fascinating man; fascinating without being lovable. I never heard him utter a sentence of which I should not have regretted missing a word. His talk was always well informed without being in the least pedantic or intensive. Every word was most skillfully adapted to his purpose, whatever that purpose might be. The wish to please and win you was most artfully concealed under a languid, tired-out, valetudinarian manner which conveyed an impression of the most perfect indifference about the effect he was all the while trying to produce. This was the wooden horse in which he entered the citadels he wished to hold. You needed to know him long and pretty well to detect under the disguise of this lazy, languid, shuffling, exhausted manner of his, the designs he had upon you, for he was never without a design of some sort. He was *bavard*; he never talked apparently to gratify his vanity, nor did wine or stimulants of any kind, in the use of which he was anything but abstemious, seem to increase his loquacity a particle. Silence with him was not infrequently as effective an instrument as speech. It would not do to put too much trust in his sincerity, nor any at all in his sentimental professions. He was an Epicurean from head to foot; the world was his oyster, which, with any weapon that would best serve his purpose, he would open.

During the middle decades of the nineteenth century, no British minister to Washington was more highly respected or cordially mistrusted than Bulwer. It was a mark of respect that many American politicians resented him for having got the better of Clayton in the canal treaty of 1850. Both men genuinely thought they had contributed considerably to a lessening of tensions, but within a year or two the Clayton-Bulwer Treaty inflamed Anglo-American relations more than ever.

3

John F. T. Crampton and the American Political System, 1852–1853

During the nineteenth century there were few British diplomats in Washington who equaled John F. T. Crampton in length of tenure in office and keenness of insight. Following tours of duty at Turin, St. Petersburg, Brussels, Vienna, and Bern, he was appointed in July 1845 as secretary of the legation at Washington; and when Pakenham returned to Britain late in the spring of 1847, he assumed the duties of chargé d'affaires. It was thought that a new envoy extraordinary and minister plenipotentiary would soon be dispatched to Washington, but as it turned out, Crampton remained the head of the legation until Bulwer took over in December 1849. Upon the latter's departure in August 1851, Crampton again took charge, and was rewarded for his performance of duty by being designated the British minister to Washington the following February.

During most of this time, Crampton served under Lord Palmerston and, as previously mentioned, the foreign secretary did not honor Crampton with an invitation to communicate privately. However, when Lord Malmesbury became foreign secretary in 1852, he encouraged Crampton to write to him personally, as shown by the opening letters of this chapter. There is another gap in the private correspondence due to further changes in the ministry in London. However, by February 1853 Crampton realized that Lord Clarendon would soon become foreign secretary, signaling what became an unbroken three years of lengthy private and confidential letters.

Although Crampton was not well known outside diplomatic circles, he proved to be one of the most astute observers of the American scene. This was due in part to his length of stay in Washington, but it was also a result of his being a bachelor with few family ties to distract him and of his natural love of intrigue. He seems to have gotten on especially well with Secretary of State Daniel Webster, as the opening letters imply. Webster's death was, therefore, a great blow to Crampton's aspirations, as he was on rather cool terms with Webster's immediate successor, Edward Everett, and cultivated only mild intimacy with Everett's successor, William L. Marcy.

The first letter written by Crampton in this collection was dated 9 August

1852, just one year after Bulwer left Washington. Central America still preoccupied the attention of British and American statesmen. Nicaragua was still dependent on America, while Costa Rica looked to the British for support. The Mosquito Indians perpetuated the fiction that they ruled over a thousand miles of coastline, whereas the truth was that they were being propped up by British gunboats. At the mouth of the San Juan River, Greytown governed itself precariously, always subject to bands of immigrants and renegades from many nations trying to exploit the transisthmian route to the Pacific Ocean.

The year 1852 also witnessed renewed friction between Canadian and American fishermen over their respective rights to the coastal waters of North America. The Webster-Ashburton Treaty of 1842 was supposed to have clarified these rights by prohibiting American fishermen from coming within three miles of the Canadian coast except for temporary landings for the purpose of drying fish. However, the Americans interpreted the three-mile limit as applying to bays and inlets, especially the vast Bay of Fundy, whereas the Canadians insisted upon drawing the coastline across the mouth of such bays. Threats and reprisals were thus inevitable.

The fisheries dispute greatly complicated the British and Canadian quest for a reciprocity treaty with the United States. How could the American Congress be expected to lower its tariffs on Canadian crops and raw materials while tempers flared over the harassment of Yankee fishing vessels?

Eighteen hundred fifty-two was also a presidential election year; Millard Fillmore was not expected to seek reelection, and by August the campaign was in full swing. The Democrats nominated the dark horse New Hampshire lawyer Franklin Pierce, while the Whigs went in the opposite direction and selected a hero who fought in the war against Mexico, General Winfield Scott. Crampton's first private letter to Lord Malmesbury dealt with many of these protracted concerns.[1]

During my visit at Marshfield,[2] Mr. Webster conversed very freely with me regarding his own political and personal position and expressed himself thoroughly disgusted with the conduct of a great majority of his own [the Whig] Party. So much so that he said that staunch a Whig as he was, he was of opinion that it would be better for the Country that the Democratic Candidate for the Presidency should succeed, than that the man the Whigs have put forward on the low ground of our appeal to the ignorance and vanity of the Mob. It was now, he said, the object of the Scott Whigs to persuade the Country that it was on the eve of a War with Great Britain and consequently ought to have a Military President—Hence the baseness of their allying themselves with the "Young America" Party and the Ultra-Democrats in a War Cry about the Fisheries. He particularly alluded to Mr. Davis of Massachusetts and to his affected indignation at the idea of treating with Great Britain about reciprocity of Trade "under duress"; this, said Mr. Webster is a mere manoeuvre to carry the decision of the Question on to the next Administration. Mr. Webster is, I believe, particularly hurt by the line taken by Mr. Davis,[3] who is a Whig and Senator from Mr. Webster's State, at the Baltimore Convention where he supported

General Scott's claim to the candidature for the Presidency against those of Mr. Webster and Mr. Fillmore. Mr. Webster evidently apprehends that there is a disposition on the part of this section of the Whig party to impede the Administration in their endeavours to settle the present difficulties both as regards the Fisheries—Reciprocity of Trade with the British Colonies, and the Nicaraguan Question, with a view to the advantage they might derive from the state of uncertainty which would prevail as to the Foreign Relations of the Country for the purpose of carrying the Election of General Scott—a man totally unfit, he remarked, to get the Country out of the embarrassments they will have created. Of General Scott I should not speak, said Mr. Webster, but you know what he is—a coxcomb—a man of "fuss and feathers"— without bad intentions or feelings perhaps, but liable to be carried away by others into any sort of folly which might promise food for his vanity.

I rather imagine that the President feels somewhat hurt by Mr. Webster's absenting himself so continually from Washington at times when his presence was very essential to the Administration, the main pillar of which he certainly must be considered. He had at one time contemplated resigning rather than returning to the seat of Government to which, since the result of the Baltimore Convention, he seems to have taken a strong dislike, and which the delicate state of his health has increased. I am happy to say however that he has now made up his mind to continue in office till the end of the Presidential Term. Were he to quit the Administration, its weakness would be such that we might despair of concluding any of the matters now pending between the two governments, and I did not therefore fail to exert any little influence I possess with Mr. Webster to confirm him in his resolution to remain in the Cabinet. He is, I think, sincerely well disposed towards England (his partiality towards us has indeed often been made a ground of attack against him). On the other hand although his popularity is not of that universal description which was enjoyed by Mr. Clay, there is no statesman in America who has so strong a hold on the minds of the People of this Country, or whose proceedings in regard to transactions with Foreign Nations are regarded with greater confidence. In the admiration felt for Mr. Webster there is perhaps some mixture of fear on the part of some, and of dislike on the part of others, but there is no difference of opinion as to his capacity, and few political men like to get into a contest with him upon any subject to which he has directed the powers of his mind. Few indeed have tried the experiment without getting the worst of it.

A week later the dispute over fishing rights still monopolized the attention of American politicians.[4]

The excitement on the Fishery Question has been very much enhanced by the particular circumstances under which it has arisen. Congress is about to separate for the purpose of proceeding at once to the work of what they call "Campaign" for the Presidential election. You may therefore imagine that the leaders of the violent and warlike parties are glad to take the opportunity afforded of making noisy demonstrations of standing up for American interests and bidding defiance to Foreign Powers and especially to Great Britain immediately before they appear before the people. Those who are better disposed are unwilling to be held up as luke warm supporters of American rights, so that we can scarcely expect any frank expressions of opinion even on the part of those who are convinced of the extravagance of the pretensions set up by American fishermen to be allowed to take our fish upon our own coasts without any sort of equivalent, and the unsoundness of the arguments by which the plain sense of the provisions of the Convention of 1818 is thought to be invalidated.

On 12 September Crampton forwarded a copy of a letter he had written almost a year before to Lord Elgin, the governor-general of Canada.[5] In it he attempts to explain to Lord Malmesbury how the American political system worked. It is a kind of whimsical as well as cynical exposé of how Congress functioned.

> I will only add to the long official despatch with which I have troubled you today,[6] that my impression is that Mr. Fillmore is perfectly sincere in his wish to settle all our Commercial Questions, and that he will make an honest endeavour to do so, but I could not but observe at the same time that he did not seem as sanguine of success as I could have desired. The Babel-like state to which the Congress of the United States has been reduced by the continued infusion of new elements of the lowest and worst description from the Western States—the disappearance of all the Political Leaders who used to exercise any influence, or give the least unity or order to their proceedings, and above all the almost universal absence of common honesty, both political and pecuniary, which prevails, go very much to justify his apprehension. It has been over and over again intimated to me from quarters which admit of no doubt of the reality of the fact, that without the application of a round sum of money, we shall do nothing: that all our measures will be "killed off", as they call it, and regular engagements are offered for ensuring success on certain pecuniary conditions. Such things will, no doubt, sound strange to you but I would not allude to them without positive evidence of their reality.

Crampton's lengthy letter to Lord Elgin then followed.

> A proposition has been made to me with regard to the "Reciprocity Bill" of so extraordinary a nature that used as I am to the ways and means by which things are carried on here, I did not believe it to be serious until I ascertained beyond the possibility of doubt the source from which it came, and the power of those who made it to fulfill their Engagement should we agree to their terms.
> The proposition is simple enough, and is this: that certain persons engage to carry or procure to be carried through both Houses of Congress, during the next session, the Reciprocity bill upon the payment by me to them or their agent of the sum of 20,000 Pounds, to be divided and used by them for the purpose:—twenty or thirty percent of the same as a sort of retaining fee; the rest to be paid after the bill shall have finally passed.
> I communicate this to you much more with a view of giving you a specimen of the "style" of Politics at Washington, than with a view to any practical use that could be made of the information. Even if our Government could dispose of such a sum for such a purpose, I am quite aware that I should scarcely succeed in persuading them that I had not been completely humbugged by whoever brought me the proposal. Indeed I was disposed to look upon it myself as mere nonsense until, to my infinite surprise, I found that it was a perfectly practical proposal, and well considered by those who made it. The worst feature of the case however is that it is accompanied by an intimation that a non compliance with the terms will ensure the *opposition* of the "Organization" as it is called, who made the offer, and they are unfortunately quite powerful enough to cause it to be rejected.[7]

I was always aware that a great deal was done in Congress in this way, and thought that something might be done in regard to the Reciprocity Bill by such means, though I imagined at the same time that we should have peculiar difficulties in implying that it were ever thought expedient to have recourse to them. I was therefore little prepared to have the affair proposed to me "en block" with everything foreseen and prepared, and nothing to be supplied but the moving power—but the truth is that what they call the "Organization" has within the last five or six years been brought to such a system that what may be called the outside Congress is more powerful than the Congress itself, and that there is scarcely a measure the passage or obstruction of which is not previously arranged by mutual compact long before it comes before that body and even before the session begins.

It would be very difficult for me in the compass of a letter to explain to you the nature of the "Organization" which has made the present overture to me a very reason for knowing the proposal to be seriously intended: it would besides oblige me to mention names which I would not like to trust to the accidents or risks of post offices etc. I will only say that knowing who they are, and what are the means at their disposal, I am fully convinced that they can pass this bill if they choose, and they can secure its rejection if they choose. Indeed even their inaction would ensure that. In short, as things now stand I fear that we have not the smallest chance of getting this question settled by fair means. This has been intimated to me by the only person[8] on whom I have to depend for managing and bringing forward this bill in Congress, in a way which I could not misunderstand, and this makes me anxious to put you in possession of the whole state of the case this early, in order that the Canadian Government may not, under the notion that the recommendation of the Measure in the President's Message at the next session will ensure its success, be unprepared for what I cannot but think certain, viz. that it will meet this session exactly the same fate as it did on every previous occasion.

The gentleman to whom I allude is the same who had charge of the Reciprocity Bill in Congress last session: he is the rising man of the rising Party in the United States, and has by far the best chance of being placed at the head of affairs at the next Presidential election. At all events as majorities now stand, he is by far the most powerful person in Congress. He is just come to Washington, and I of course took the earliest opportunity of calling upon him, and it was suggested that I should do so by the Parties of whom I have spoken above, in order to see how the land lay with regard to the Reciprocity Bill. We had a very long conversation on the matter, the substance of which it may be interesting to you to know. He began by expressing himself and thought, more strongly than he had ever done before, in favour of the Measure, the mutual advantages of which he set forth in the clearest manner. The next question therefore which arose was how the Measure was to be got through Congress. He then went into detail into the obstacles which were to be overcome and the means of overcoming them, and in so doing displayed an acuteness and a knowledge of the politics of this country which, although I had a high opinion of his talents, surprised me. This is a measure, he said, for or against which there can not be got up any National or Party feeling. We cannot therefore hope to carry it by a hurrah. It is one which requires great study to understand it and its advantages or even its bearing on the different Interests of the Country; its supporters are friendly to it, not on any general principle, but from various local and peculiar considerations; the opposition to it is of the same varied character; the only means of getting it is therefore one which involves great knowledge of men's characters, of their local and personal interests and prejudices—great knowledge of the question in its bearing on each of these Interests—great tact in the manner of approaching the subject with different men—and above all great *labour* in keeping account of the "ayes and noes" etc. And when we are assured of a majority keeping it up to the mark at the moment required. I have, he said, carried measures in this way myself, and I know the hard work it requires. With regard to the present Bill, much as I desire its success, I have too much on my hands to render it possible for me to undertake much of that sort of work. With respect to what you yourself could do, it would no doubt be useful that you should speak to some of our People with regard to certain political bearings of the measure, particularly as regards its bearing on annexation; but your attempting to do more than this would, from your position, do more harm than good. An agent from Canada, particularly if a man of any prominence in the Canadian Government, would also do more harm than good—although if some Gentleman well acquainted with the details of the Question should *happen* to be in Washington at the time, it would be useful.

This of course brought me straight up to the Question—whom then are we to employ? To whom are we to apply? This is the difficult part of the business. It is difficult to fix upon one person:—one man may be good to influence a particular set of men, who, if he attempted to act upon another set, would, although he should use the proper arguments, do more harm than good. We then ran over some names—I seemed to find objection to them on some account or other: but at length, after several minutes leaning his head on his hand in apparently profound reflection, he said there is a man, who, if we could get him to act—with the assistance of some others whom he could command—might do what we want better than any others in the U.S., and who, if he would take up these things in earnest, I think would ensure our carrying the Bill. He then, to my surprise I confess, though I was somewhat previously prepared for it, named the very *person* from whom the proposal stated at the beginning of my letter was brought to me.[9] Now this man I also know to be the great "faiseur" for the person I was talking to, in his capacity of Candidate for the Presidency and also to be chief mover of the sort of secret "Organization" I have previously mentioned by which almost any measure whatever, unless it happen to have a decided National Character can be carried. I leave you to draw your own conclusion as to the way things hang together here, but I have even much more direct evidence of the means which are employed to bring about measures in this great Republic.

I fear I have troubled you with rather a long epistle on the subject without any more practical result than a little insight as to the blessing of Democratic Republics and their superior purity.

In October 1852 Webster was in a serious carriage accident, and his imminent demise prompted Crampton to reflect upon its probable consequences. With him alive, Crampton stood a good chance of concluding the reciprocity, Anglo-American literary copyright, and Central American treaties, whereas his death would doubtless cause the Fillmore administration to be even more timorous than usual. Admittedly, as noted by Crampton in this next letter, Webster was clearly no longer the man he used to be.[10]

It is true that Mr. Webster's powers had latterly been much impaired; it was difficult to rouse his attention to matters of business, and after even a moderate degree of mental exertion he was liable to relapse into a state of languor which it was painful to witness. A great deal of the business of this Department has consequently, during the latter months, been entrusted to certain political hangers-on of Mr. Webster's.

At all events the information upon which he has acted has been supplied by them, and has not been sifted and examined by him with the acuteness for which he was formerly so remarkable. To this cause I attribute some grievous mistakes which he has lately fallen into as well in regard to his own political position at home as to international questions. Among these latter must be placed as well the Lobos Islands affairs.[11] Had he not taken what was told to him about these matters on trust, he never would have committed himself in the way he did.

Crampton's final letter to Lord Malmesbury of 6 November 1852 was written soon after the Democratic Party routed the Whigs at the polls.[12] Playing a key role in the election victory had been the so-called Young America movement, according to Crampton, and unfortunately for Britain, this was the element of the Democratic Party which was most xenophobic and expansionist. Young America originally backed Senator Stephen A. Douglas for president, but when the "Little Giant" failed to secure the nomination, they threw their support to Franklin Pierce.

The Presidential Election has terminated in a most signal defeat of the Whig Party; so much so, that taken together with the recent loss of their two Great Leaders, Mr. Clay[13] and Mr. Webster, I do not see how they are to take the field as a Party again. Add to this that all the Measures which they advocated have become obsolete, and that during their four years of office they have not been able even to bring one of them forward. This is a state of things not without its danger to the victorious Party, as well as to the Union; for the absence of questions which divide the Country into two parties pretty equally balanced in each State, as well as over the whole Union, always had a tendency to make parties run into the natural division of North and South—free state and slave state parties. This has been the rock which the best American statesmen have always exerted themselves to steer clear of; for it is evident that if to the discordant element resulting from the natural difference of habits and opinions in the free and slave states were added divergent political opinions on other subjects which should aggravate this difference instead of counteracting it, as it has hitherto generally done, it would be difficult for the Confederation to hold together.

The worst feature connected with the success of the Democratic Candidate, who, I believe, is personally moderate in his principles, and who Mr. Webster, not long before his death, assured me, confidentially, that he preferred to General Scott as regards the safety of the Foreign Relations of the Country—is that it is so much owing to the "Young America Party". The force of this party lies in the Irish and German emigrants and in those who want their votes for their own purposes. Hatred of Great Britain and a wish to interfere in the affairs of every other nation in support of rebellion and revolution is the great characteristic of this section of the Democrats. Whoever swaggers, threatens, and uses the most insolent language toward Foreign Governments, is sure to have their support, and I need not say that there is no want of orators and writers who indulge them in this taste to the utmost extent. The nature of the American People, however, is generally so practical, that I am convinced that a Government which should be driven by the violent party I have mentioned into some difficulty with a Foreign Government, which, while it deranged the commercial and monetary affairs of the Country, did not promise to lead to some immediate tangible profit to the whole Union, would rapidly lose its popularity. If the Whigs, therefore, were to have courage and foresight enough now to take decided ground against this aggressive spirit, although they would no doubt at present be subjected to great abuse and unpopularity, they would lay the ground for returning to power on the first occasion when the other Party should have run the Government into some quarrel which might threaten to affect injuriously any of the great Interests of the Country, and such a contingency is, I think, not at all unlikely to occur.

Several months passed. Then, on 5 February 1853,[14] Crampton addressed his first private letter to Lord Clarendon. The Fillmore administration had one more month in office before the inauguration of a new president. Congress would be continuing in session a bit longer than this, but Crampton did not expect much to happen.

I am sorry to say that there seems to be no probability of our concluding the Convention respecting the Fisheries and Reciprocity of Trade with the present Administration of the United States. They seem to come to a decision that it is better policy for them, as a Party, to leave these questions to be settled by their successors in office. I ventured, in a private letter to Lord Malmesbury, to express some apprehension that such a wish existed on the part of President Fillmore, and I regret to find that my suspicions were well founded. Their motives, I imagine, to have been two-fold. 1st, being Protectionists in commercial Policy they are, although in a Minority, averse to lose popularity among the adherents who still remain attached to them in considerable numbers, *particularly in the states to which they themselves belong*, by bringing forward a Measure which is generally looked upon as a fresh inroad upon Protection, or at least as one naturally adding to its still further development of Free Trade Principles. 2nd, they are in a decided minority in Congress, and they apprehend that, even if they were to make up their minds to redirect the measure to the Legislature, it would have to be so treated by their adversaries as to redound little to their credit with the majority of the Country on the one hand, while they would forfeit the confidence of their own particular adherents on the other. Mr. Abbot Lawrence, who is the great Representative of the Protectionist Interests in the North, is now here and has, I think, exercised a very decisive influence in bringing about the adverse decision of the Cabinet.[15] He has been in confidential communication with me at Mr. Everett's request and he told me very frankly that he had advised the President not to sign the Treaty. He gave a number of reasons for this, which I confess did not appear to me very conclusive, but he summed up what I believe to be the real one by saying "in fact, take it all in all, I don't think it would do him [Mr. Fillmore] *any credit* to do so." Now as I know that Mr. Fillmore and Mr. Lawrence are generally looked upon as the Candidates whom the Whigs hope (altho' with very little chance of success, as it appears to me) to bring forward at the next Presidential Election. . . .

The step which has been taken in Congress of bringing forward a Bill for admitting British-caught fish onto the American Market free, conditionally on the admission of American Citizens to the full use of the British Fisheries, is one which I regret. It will not satisfy the Colonies, and yet it will be represented here as a fair and liberal offer; and their not responding thereto will be made a sort of justification for encroachment on the part of the United States.

Two days later, Crampton provided Lord Clarendon with an extensive review of the American political scene and the growing American appetite for overseas involvement.[16]

First then in regard to Mr. Pierce. I know him not, nor have I met anybody at Washington who seems to be intimately acquainted with him. He is by profession a Lawyer, and was some years ago a Senator of the United States. It is evident that he cut no figure in the Senate, good or bad: he retired to a small town in his own state (New Hampshire) and practiced Law. His success does not seem to have been great, for in 1847 he started, as a Volunteer, to the Mexican War with the rank of a General (which rank, by a strange anomaly, the President can confer on whom he pleases; and it has often pleased him to bestow it absurdly). This is the least sensible thing I know of him, for he was old enough to know better, and I need not say had ''never set a squadron in the field or the division of a battle knew'' more than any other village Attorney. He kept on a line with his companions of arms however as far as bread and water were concerned, and was looked upon, I hear, as a good natured, jovial fellow. This at least is in his favour, that his name never appeared as mixed up with ungentlemanly squabbles which took place between General Scott and almost all the other officers under his command—particularly the volunteers. . . .

With regard to his political principles, he has kept them pretty close: he is a Democrat of course, but I believe that he is not one of the Go-ahead Manifest destiny School, or as they are now called, the ''Filibusters''. . . . It is due to Mr. Pierce to say that during the period of his being President-elect, which is perhaps the most trying period of the whole term, he has not done anything which has committed him.

With regard to the composition of Mr. Pierce's Cabinet, it is, I think, a good sign that he has succeeded in keeping his counsel on the matter. He could have no object in this did he intend to have a red hot Young American administration. There is a great struggle going on on the subject among the different sections of the Democrats, and the filibusters as you will have seen by the late Debates in the Senate, are preferring their Claims by blowing the Coals to the utmost extent on the various pairs of bellows which they can bring to bear on the ''Manifest Destiny'' question. To anybody unacquainted with the domestic party contests going on here, such an outbreak would be inexplicable and alarming, for they would seem like a drunken Irishman at a fair trying to pick a quarrel with everybody they meet. . . . Notwithstanding all this I received ''the most satisfactory assurances'', which I believe too, from the very foremost of the agitators, General Cass[17] for instance, that ''none of this is going to lead to any trouble between us'', and that all will be quiet after the 4th of March. . . .

With regard to the probability of Mr. Pierce's seeking popularity by picking a quarrel with us, I may be wrong, but I do *not* then think he will do so. Nor do I think that such a quarrel, if it really threatened to be a serious one, would be popular but quite the reverse. Too many vital interests would be affected by it. . . . Nothing but the most wanton attack by us upon some point in which either the Interests of all the States were involved or which should enlist the general pride of the Country could possibly in my opinion keep them together in a War with us.

2ndly, your second inquiry regards the influence of the defeat of the Whig Party on the Protective System. I think it is plainly clear from the experience of the last four years that there is very little chance of Protection being revived. Certainly not as a general principle. The Whigs have had possession of office during a whole Presidential Term, and yet every effort that they have made, either directly or indirectly, to modify the Tariff in a Protective sense has signally failed. . . . On the other hand, I do not think that we have much to expect in the way of a partial lowering of the present Tariff which should afford considerable incidental protection to American Manufacturers. We may however expect a freer system of commercial intercourse as regards our North American Colonies, for although the measure we are now at work on may be obstructed in Congress this session, from a wish to take it out of the hands of the present administration, or from their own timidity, I think we shall obtain it from their Successors. There is certainly a free Trade majority in Congress, but there are certain points connected with local interests, and which do not affect the general question very sensibly, upon which it is very difficult to bring the majority to bear.

3rd., as regards the increase of American Manufacturers, I will set myself to get you accurate information, but my general impression is that they have done so to such a degree as to be seriously detrimental to us. The increase of Population and the sudden demand *from* California have however no doubt given them considerable impetus.

4th., the Cuban question does not seem to me to present so immediately threatening an aspect as it did some months ago. "Filibustering" Expeditions are just now a little at a discount, and the excitement on the subject seems to have taken the direction of speechifying in the Senate. However, I still hold the opinion that there is a permanent conspiracy for the acquisition of the Island here, and that there is an understanding between the Conspirators here and part of the Creole Population. I should rather say the more educated part of the Population than the Mass of the small Planters who are illiterate and bigotted and have all that hatred of Strangers which is general in the Spanish Race. I don't think the Americans could count upon much assistance from the Creoles unless the Americans were themselves very successful against the Spanish Authorities in the first instance and, were the Invaders to fail, they might be certain that their supposed Allies would be the first to join the Spaniards in hunting them down. The Yankees are, I think, aware of this, and so long as the Spaniards keep a large force on the Island, and that the idea prevails that our Naval forces will interfere, piratical private expeditions will not, I think be attempted.

However, this matter of Cuba is one which involves very serious considerations for us, and one which I think is now come to such a point that we can no longer avoid looking it in the face and making up our minds as to what we are to do or not do about it. The question, as you truly observe, involves Peace or War or, at all events, a risk of War. The step we have already taken in proposing the Tripartite Convention puts us, as it seems to me, in a dilemma from which there is no escape[18]—namely, that we must either take a step further in the same direction, by making, in conjunction with France, a declaration to the United States similar to that which the United States has made to us, that we cannot allow them to take Cuba; or that we must take a step backward or rather out of the whole business, and tacitly admit (for our silence will be deemed equivalent to this) Mr. Everett's Manifest Destiny Doctrine. . . .

There is another point of view, however, in which I think the question of Cuba is to be looked upon: This is as a part of the more general question of aggression and domination of the United States on every part of this Continent; and in this regard it may be worthwhile to consider whether if the attempt to check this is to be made at all, whether the point of Cuba is not as good a point to make a stand upon as any other. As an illustration of what I mean I would call your attention to the case of the Sandwich Islands.[19] I am not sufficiently versed in such matters to know how far the neutrality of those Islands is essential to our Commercial Interests in the Pacific, but I know that the Americans have an eye upon them, and that they will lie more exposed to a coup de main than even Cuba. The United States have now a strong point at San Francisco, and California is rapidly developing. I am convinced that the Japan Expedition is intended to result in the acquisition of some permanent establishment there.[20]

An American exploring Expedition has also been despatched to go up the River

Amur which runs from the Russian Possessions to the Sea through the Northern part of China, a point of curiosity which I have reason to know the Russian Government by no means approves of, so much so, that the Government which is now beginning to turn its attention to the commerce of the Pacific, has made a sort of semi-overture to me, thro' an agent they have just appointed to the Sandwich Islands, as to the expediency of their joining us and France in an agreement to maintain their neutrality.[21] With regards to these islands, you will recollect that the United States has held to us exactly the same language as with regards to Cuba, viz. that they will *not allow us* to become possessed of them, declining to make any renunciation of them on their own part. These things are, I think, worthy of consideration, and the point of time seems to me to have come when it behooves us to come to a determination as to whether these aggressive Plans are of such vital importance to our Interests as to oblige us to resist them, or whether it would be more prudent to let things take their own course rather than pre-engage ourselves on any particular course in regard to them.

In connection with this subject comes the consideration of what is called the "Monroe Doctrine", which the Democratic Politicians here are so busy in preaching and in inculcating, and which it is now the fashion to *assume* as an admitted principle of Public Law from which the rights of aggression and domination on the part of the United States on all parts of the Hemisphere is deduced as a sort of corollary. The annunciation of this doctrine amounts to nothing less than an attempt to establish a principle of Public Law applicable to this Quarter of the World analogous to that prevailing to a certain extent in Europe with this difference however, that while in Europe such principles were established with the consent and by the agreement of all the Parties concerned, and consigned in solemn Treaties, here the attempt is made to lay down a Law of a much more sweeping nature by the *ipse dixit* of a single Power over two whole Continents and the adjacent Islands, not only without the agreement of the other Powers who hold them, but notoriously counter to their wishes and Interests, and also in a manner inconsistent with their Independence. By eternal repetition this so-called doctrine is gradually becoming, in the minds of the Democracy here, one of those habitual maxims which are no longer reasoned upon but felt, and any imagined "violation of the Monroe Doctrine" is now vehemently taken up as a just reason for a preemptory demand for satisfaction from any Foreign Power who may have committed it. Now altho' I know that a great deal of this language is held for *home* political purposes, each party out-bidding the other in its offer of "Americanism", still it cannot be denied that a very dangerous effect is produced upon the Masses by such doctrines, and it becomes a very grave question what position Foreign Powers ought to adopt in regard to them. It seems to me quite clear that if carried out to their full effect, we should be forced to resist them *somewhere*, and the question remains as to the point at which it would be advisable to make a stand.

All these considerations would give an impression of a very dangerous state of things, but I think nevertheless that there are two checks upon which we may generally count as preventing the aggressive spirit of this People being carried to extremes. The one is the inextinguishable struggle between North and South—Free States and Slave States. It insinuates itself into every part of their proceedings; discussions begun upon subjects apparently the most remote, invariably degenerate into Northern and Southern Squabbles. The subject once set going, everything else becomes indifferent—all unity of action is paralyzed. Foreign Relations are forgotten or made subservient to the paramount question of the maintenance or dissolution of the Union. The other is the real injury to the material and commercial interest of a practical and money-making people, which they are perfectly aware would result from a serious quarrel with England, or even from the risk or expectation of such a quarrel. Their preparations for war are small, and they know that they could not begin one in a hurry.

I find that I have written you a very long letter without having answered half your questions; but I will not inflict any more of my lucubrations upon you till next Packet, when I shall take up the other subjects of your letter.

A fortnight later Crampton resumed his discussion of American politics.[22]

The great excitement now to come on . . . is what is called the "division of the Spoils", in other words the turning out of every man, woman, or child who hold a place under Government, and the putting in their places all those who were concerned in the invention of Mr. Pierce, and in "running" him, "campaigning" him and "platforming" him, and finally housing him in the "Executive Mansion" [White House]. As there are fifty applicants for every place this will give that Gentleman full occupation for a considerable time, and as all the newspapers, telegraphs, public meetings, Stump Speeches, etc., etc., will be put into requisition for that purpose, Cuba, Honduras, the "Monroe Doctrine", and Manifest destiny will be allowed to go asleep tho' not to die. I am, nevertheless, inclined to think on the whole, and to say in answer to the 8th Inquiry in your letter of the 5th Ultimo, that the language of the Politicians of the Democratic Party does not truly represent the feeling of the American People towards England or in regard to War. If they do not altogether misrepresent them, they certainly grossly exaggerate them, and I think from all I can collect, that the feeling of hostility to us is rapidly on the *decrease*. . . .

With regard to your questions as to the Irish Emigrants abandoning the Catholic Religion. The last Census proves that it must be true to a great extent that they do so. There has been a great deal of exaggeration in regard to the success of the Catholics in the United States in proselytizing and in the spread of their religion. It appears that of the present population about one *thirty-seventh* is Catholic, and it is calculated that the descendants of the Irish Settlers and other Catholics who came to the Colonies before the Revolution, ought to have produced a larger proportion. Popery in the United States has not the same character as it has in Ireland. The thunders of the Church or the curses of a Priest have no terrors here, and the conversion of anybody from one religion to another scarcely excites a remark, and it would be impossible for a priest to visit it with social pains and penalties as at home. If an Irishman here does not like his priest, or takes the fancy, he has nothing to do but walk out of the Chapel into the Methodist Meetinghouse on the other side of the Street, where he finds people of his own Class and condition, and nobody would dream of attempting to deter him by a threat, or even remarks, upon the matter. The consequence is that "Mother Church" does not deal in anathemas here, and that the soothing and seductive system alone is employed.

With regard to the Slavery Question neither General Pierce nor anybody who is President or ever hopes to be President or hold any office in the Federal Government, will ever attempt to meddle with it: the slightest suspicion that a man has even a bias either one way or the other on this subject *finishes* him as an *aspirant to office*. It is the great rock upon which all political men have split. It is in vain that devotion to the Union, the whole Union, nothing but the Union is protested by a candidate; if an inadvertent letter is produced, written ten years ago, or an old speech collected in which the cloven foot of the abolitionist can be even inferred much less shown, there is an end of his hopes of official position in the Federal Government and vice versa; a Southern Man who has "gone for extending the area of Slavery" may also give up all ideas of Federal Office. He may be a great man in his own States, but not at Washington. You are quite right in what you say as to the inexpediency of our meddling with this subject. We can only do harm by it, and if I was to think of anything more particularly which would serve as an answer to your inquiry as to what we can do to conciliate the good will of people here I should say—let them alone on this subject. We do not conciliate the North by agitating it—for their social prejudice against negroes is just as strong as that of the South, and their hatred of Southern Slavery rests upon other grounds than ours. It is a political party feeling and not one of philanthropy. They think the Southerners are aristocratic and that the votes they exercise in virtue of their negroes give them a political importance and a power of wielding it which the Free States do not possess. On the other hand the South *feel* the deepest resentment, mixed with fear, of *foreign* Interference, and are morbidly suspicious and jealous of it. I think that I must now have tired your patience and will therefore reserve my further American lucubrations for another time.

In his letter of 27 February Crampton reflected the prevailing mood of expectancy as Americans speculated about the makeup of the forthcoming Pierce cabinet.[23]

Altho' the Curtain is about to rise, the Playbill of the Names of the performers in the new Administration of the United States has not yet been authoritatively published; but altho' the distribution of office is not announced or perhaps completed, we know pretty well among whom the spoils will be divided, and it is satisfactory to be assured that none of the names of those who have made themselves conspicuous by advocating violent courses, are included in any of the Lists of those who are to hold office. The President-Elect is here, and seems to be on good personal terms with Mr. Fillmore and Mr. Everett. Mr. Cushing is talked of as the most probable to be Secretary of State; and Mr. Everett tells me that being, as himself, a Boston man with whom he is on very good terms he will be able, on delivering him the Seals of the "State Department" to converse with him very freely about all the subjects pending between our two Governments.

On 7 March Crampton was able to report upon Pierce's inaugural address and the composition of the cabinet.[24]

I send you today with my despatches Mr. Pierce's Inaugural Address and a list of the new Administration. Both these are much what I expected they would be. Mr. Pierce had of course to "go for Cuba and the Monroe Doctrine", but he has qualified the one with expressions of decent respect for the Law of Nations, and has not accompanied the other with offensive remarks on Monarchy and British tyranny: the rest of the address consists of commonplaces including the glorious principle of rotation in office or the division of the spoils for the sole benefit of "Self and Partners" for the next four years. I do not envy him this part of his power however, for after a battle every regiment thinks the victory depended upon it alone, so after a Presidential election, every separate State claims to have turned the scale and to be entitled to the largest share of the reward.

    With regard to the Administration Mr. Marcy, the Secretary of State, is by no means an ultra-democrat, and he was chosen by Mr. Pierce in preference to Mr. Cushing (who is a "filibuster") who fought hard for the Office: this seems to be a good symptom.

Congress, after a great deal of speechifying, has separated without doing anything. The Senate however remains in Session for a month or so for what is called appointments, consideration of treaties, etc., which is conducted in Secret Session and does not require the presence of the other House of Congress.

A week later the new administration was hopelessly bogged down with governmental reorganization and patronage appointments.[25]

The new President and Administration have, as I expected, been so besieged by "office seekers" and occupied by the "division of the Spoils" that I have not yet had an opportunity of touching upon any of the subjects of interest pending between the two countries. . . .

Mr. Clayton has made a good Speech on the Foreign Policy of the country in the course of which he had courage enough to attack the "Monroe Doctrine" and to give its true history showing conclusively that although often put forward by individual Presidents and made the subject of resolutions and Motions in both Houses on many occasions for the last twenty-five years, it has never been adopted by Congress; and consequently that the attack made upon him for not embodying this doctrine in the Treaty of 1850 [signed by him and Bulwer] is altogether groundless.

During the opening months of 1853, many observers ascribed the slowness of the Pierce administration to organize the machinery of government not simply to the extreme pressure exerted on it for appointments but rather to a personal tragedy that struck the family. On 6 January the president-elect's eleven-year-old son Benjamin was killed in a railway accident from which the rest of the family escaped unharmed. In his letter of 21 March Crampton describes the universal sympathy shown at the time.[26]

We, that is the Corps Diplomatique, have been at length received by the new President and his Administration. I was agreeably disappointed by Mr. Pierce's appearance and address, which were much superior to what I expected. He looks *clean*, has not an unpleasant countenance, and has an evident wish to please those he speaks to by comporting himself to the best of his abilities like a gentleman. These may seem small matters, but in this country they are almost infallible indications of political tendencies. "Manifest Destiny" men almost universally affect the reverse of all this—let their hair grow long—don't brush their coats—look sallow and sour and, in general, aim rather at the low French and German than the Anglo-Saxon type in their dress and appearance. The "Administration" who were ranged by Mr. Pierce's side at the reception produced by no means so favourable an impression; they may be very worthy men and distinguished citizens, but a more uncommonly common and unprepossessing set of fellows I seldom saw.

Mr. Pierce, alluding to the sympathy which had been expressed by the Queen in regard to the death of his son, expressed himself with great good taste and showed by his manner that he felt *really* touched by the kindness of Her Majesty's remarks, which I am very glad were conveyed to him.

I endeavoured to have some conversations yesterday with Mr. Marcy on Central American Affairs, in regard to which I wished to set him right upon some points of importance before he answered a Resolution of the Senate calling for documents on the subject. He thanked me for this and seemed generally well disposed, but honestly confessed that he had not been able since his accession to office to look at a single paper connected with the Question, with which he said he had a very slight acquaintance. The appearance of the Staircase and Passages of the State Department, which were more like those of a theatre on a benefit night than those of a Public Office, from the crowds of office seekers and others which beset them, was, I am sorry to say, by no means encouraging as respects the rapid solution of the various complicated affairs on hand. . . . "Young America", under the leadership of Mr. Douglas, wishes to show Mr. Pierce that he cannot pass over its claims with impunity: Mr. Douglas consequently makes violent Speeches and people who have come up to Washington under his wing to get places, fill the galleries of the Senate and applaud whatever he says. The effect however is not the less injurious on important matters of business between the two Countries as is exemplifed by the case of the Treaty for the settlement of mutual Claim,[27] which, Mr. Clayton tells me, would have been lost, had he not run forward at the exact moment with two of his friends and saved it by a single vote, and also in the delay, not defeat, of the Copyright Treaty which the Committee did not venture to risk by reporting it on the same day.[28]

One of the issues that periodically plagued Anglo-American relations was what the British referred to as the "Coloured Seaman" question. According to the laws of most Southern states, free blacks, including British sailors, could not remain at large for any length of time. From the South's point of view, they set a bad example for slaves and might even incite slaves to violence. If a British ship put in at a Southern port, it had to see that its black crew members either remained aboard ship or, in some instances, stayed in the local jail until the vessel was prepared to sail. Occasionally this resulted in their being illegally detained or, worse yet, kidnapped and sold into slavery. In the spring of 1853 the British consul at Charleston, George Mathew, became so involved in one such case that he was regarded as persona non grata in South Carolina, and it was recommended that he be transferred to Philadelphia.[29]

I have received your kind letter of the 11th and I am sure I need not say that I am infinitely gratified that you have found anything to interest you in my attempts to give you any useful notions on American affairs; or more especially that I am deeply sensible of my good fortune in their having met the notice and approval of Her Majesty. The notion of the more experienced Part of the Conservative Party here is, and I believe they are right, that the great Mass of the Democratic Party, tho' they seem to encourage the more violent members of it, are in reality, by no means in earnest in wishing to run the Country into a serious difficulty—that they do not care much if the house is set on fire as long as they know that the Conservatives will come up in time to extinguish the flames: the Whigs have therefore, on more than one occasion, and particularly in the Oregon affair,[30] found it the better plan not to oppose the violent proceedings of their opponents in the beginning, when their opposition would only increase the clamour, but to stand aloof until the dangerous consequences of Democratic Violence begin to make themselves evident, and that in the better part of that Party itself begin to think it time to "call for water" and *then*, and not until then, to come to the rescue with the general approbation of the Country. This succeeded perfectly in regard to the Oregon question: the Whigs then actually to the disappointment of the Democrats, voted in support of the celebrated motion to "give notice" to Great Britain to leave the Territory, from which moment dated the ignominious course of backing out which Mr. Polk found it necessary to resort to, and which ended by Peace being decided on by a triumphant majority . . . .

I am glad to hear that Mr. Bunch[31] has been promoted: he is well fitted for the post and a very good person. I have written to ascertain his views as to an exchange between him and Mr. Mathew who, to say the truth, I should be glad to see in some other place than Charleston. We have a very disagreeable question in South Carolina in regard to which Mr. Mathew has perhaps got into a false position. I have lately had some serious conversation with some of the South Carolinians on the matter, particularly with Mr. Aiken formerly Governor of the State and a man of great influence and intelligence. He seems very well disposed to bringing the thing to a practical settlement, but is decidedly of opinion that it never can be done by the course Mr. Mathew has adopted.

A week later the ramifications of the problem were continuing to grow, further increasing Crampton's concern.[32]

I also enclose Mr. Bunch's answer to the enquiry you desired me to make as to whether he would be disposed to take the Consulate at Charleston instead of that at Philadelphia, to which he has been lately appointed. I think he is right as to the fact of the Consulate at Charleston being rather the less desirable of the two as regards Environment and Climate. He is much more likely to get the South Carolinians to make some modification in their inhospitable Slave Laws as they affect our free coloured Seamen from the West Indies than Mr. Mathew, whose zeal carried him a little too far in that matter. The plan to prove the Law of South Carolina on the subject unconstitutional by an appeal on some particular case to the Supreme Court of the *United States* is, I fear, altho' it was at one time encouraged by Mr. Webster, not likely to succeed—and if it did not succeed, it would leave the question in a worse position than before. A Case of this sort would involve the whole of the delicate and difficult limitations of Federal and State jurisdiction and the Supreme Court, if the case came up to them, would have recourse to every possible legal dodge to get rid of such a Question. . . . The whole of the exasperating topics of discussion between the North and South would also be revived however the matter ended, and Great Britain would be accused of having invoked it from a Machiavellian desire to sow dissension between the Northern and Southern States. The Question too might, as the best lawyers here inform me, last for years and get into a sort of "Jarndyce v. Jarndyce"[33] case, as it would turn upon the limits of Jurisdiction of different Courts, and might be argued ad infinitum without reference to the merits of the case, we remaining, in the meantime, without any redress of the evil complained of. Under these circumstances it appears to me to be more prudent to endeavour to procure such a modification of the Law of South Carolina as has been made by Louisiana, which, though it does not cover the whole abstract ground of our grievance, relieves us from it practically. This I am inclined to think, from the conversations I have had with Mr. Butler and Mr. Aiken of South Carolina, might be effected if Mr. Mathew was removed, and the proceedings for testing the *Constitutionality* of the law of South Carolina in question allowed to drop. . . .[34]

. . . The Senate are still in session, occupied with confirming appointments which are the absorbing topics of the day. Mr. Marcy still professes that he has not had time to look into a single state paper since he came into office. A good many of the

Senators have dispersed and can now barely make up a "quorum". . . . I hope so soon as the Senate goes, to be able to ascertain the real views of the Government of the United States upon the various questions pending between the two countries, and I really cannot see what object they can have in evading a consideration and settlement of them.

By mid-April Crampton was able to report on two important diplomatic appointments: former Senator James Buchanan as American minister to London and Pierre Soulé as minister to Madrid.[35]

I mentioned in my last letter that Mr. Buchanan was talked of as Minister to England: he has now been nominated and confirmed by the Senate. All things considered, they might have made a worse appointment. He belongs to the older School of Democrats, and I think only became a Democrat at all from some personal disgust to the Whigs to the extreme section of which he formerly belonged. You will find him of the bland and pompous school than of that which seeks to shine by swaggering and showing contempt of the usages of Society. When you see him you will not want to be informed that he is shrewd and even cunning for this is written in his countenance, and he enjoys a very well-earned reputation in that way here. He is more timid about committing himself than Americans generally are, and, on the other hand, it is well to be pretty cautious in communication with him. In other respects you will find him good humoured and tolerably civilised. He has amassed what in this country is a large private fortune; some three thousand pounds a year; and is, I guess by no means as sincere a Democrat in the usual sense of the word as he pretends. As regards his views respecting Cuba, "are they not written" in his despatch to Mr. Saunders at the 42nd page of the Executive Document no. 121 enclosed in my despatch no. 197 of 1852 to which I would refer you, for his despatch is worth reading and very characteristic of him.[36] He was very angry with Mr. Fillmore for sending a copy of it to Congress.

This brings me to the appointment of Monsieur Pierre Soulé to be American Minister at Madrid, an appointment of a very exceptional character I think, and which connected as it is thought to be with the declared opinion of Mr. Buchanan in the above-named despatch, and of Mr. Pierce himself in his Inaugural Address, presents rather an ominous aspect. M. Soulé is, as his name imparts, a Frenchman,— and, what is worse, a French Political Refugee—and what is still worse, he has not only committed himself to the fullest possible extent, and in the most ostentatious manner, on the subject of the acquisition of Cuba, but has adopted all of the extreme opinions of his adopted Country upon every other point. As Representative of Louisiana he is, of course, an out-and-outer on the subject of Slavery, and as a European Liberal, he claims to be the great advocate and an expounder of the cause of the oppressed Nations of that quarter of the World. All of the refugees from all parts of the world flock around him here: he associates with Pulszky from Hungary, Gonzalez, the companion of Lopez , and with Mr. Law, the great filibuster leader of all Cuba Annexation Plans.[37] I was sorry to hear by the by that M. Soulé, M. Pulszky, and this Mr. Law, whom I look upon as a Desperado of the worst sort, were invited to dine with the President the other day at "a select party"—Mr. Cushing of course assisting.

Calderon,[38] as you may imagine, is rather in an uneasy frame of mind at all this, and I can scarcely blame him, for it evidently portends *some movement* or *other* in regard to Cuba. The first thing of course will be a renewal of the offer to purchase it from Spain, and I understand that M. Soulé, who is full of vanity and not very prudent, says that he can supply Spain with very good motives, "of the *most friendly* sort", for consenting to the arrangement. The offer will, of course be refused—and my fear is that, as it will not at all suit M. Soulé's political book here to come back with a pure and simple failure of his Mission, both his interest and vanity will require him to seek éclat by becoming the cause of some quarrel between the two Governments either on that or some other subject. To you who know Madrid, I need not expatiate on the ways and means by which this may be brought about; and he will be as obnoxious to some of the other Foreign Missions there as to the Spanish Government, for he is in known correspondence with the French and other Refugees in England and in the Island of Jersey. . . .

The only antidote I know of to M. Soulé's mischievous designs is his own extreme vanity. Altho' no longer young, he prides himself on his seductive powers, and would be likely to sacrifice a great deal to obtain "des succes de salon" at Madrid. He is not disagreeable in manner and if he goes by way of England, I will give him an introduction to you. I understand that in conversation he is much more moderate than he was, and from several articles in the paper (I enclose two), probably written by himself, I perceive "qu'il met l'eau dans son vin", fearing probably that the Spanish Government may refuse to receive him.

Not many weeks could elapse without Central American affairs intruding upon the notice of Britain and America. On 2 May Crampton reported the appointment of a special American envoy that seemed calculated to enhance the potential for conflict.[39]

The only event which has occurred here which affects us is the nomination of a Gentleman who rejoices in the name of Solon Borland to the newly created Post of Minister to the five Central American States. This is, I am sorry to say, a bad appointment. Mr. Solon Borland is an ultra-Western Democrat. He was Senator for Arkansas, and particularly distinguished himself last session by his violent conduct, which you will admit not to be an exaggerated account of him when I tell you that having made some statements in a Speech upon the subject of the Census, not, one would imagine, a very exciting topic, which were objected to in the mildest manner by Mr. Kennedy, a very inoffensive person, who is at the head of the Census Commission, Mr. Solon Borland made no other reply than by flattening poor Mr. Kennedy's nose to his face by a blow of his fist, and this in the Senate Chamber itself. The bone of Mr. Kennedy's nose had to be extracted by a very severe surgical operation, so that you may judge of the earnestness of Mr. Solon Borland's manner of doing business. I fear that if he carries the same energy into his diplomacy in Central America we shall be in a bad way there. His other "title" to the post is his having been one of the small minority who voted against the Clayton-Bulwer Treaty in 1850. Mr. Borland's appointment however, I have good reason to believe, is not made with a view to embroil matters with us in Central America, but as a requital for political services at the Presidential Election, and I am assured that he holds moderate language in regard to Central American affairs, and in reality cares for nothing about the matter but the Salary and outfit which he is to receive. That such an appointment should be made however shows how every consideration is postponed in this Country to local electioneering claims. This it is which makes this Government so difficult to deal with.

Although I always make great allowance for the violence of the abuse of England and lay a great deal of it down to the account of making political Capital by singing upon an old note which like the "No Popery" cry in England is sure to find a response in feelings which have become habitual, altho' less intense than formerly, I nevertheless entirely agree with you as to the dangerous and ticklish nature of our relations with the United States. Even where there is a friendly feeling to England there is a hatred of the English Government at least, and, as I was able to judge in 1848,[40] there would be a general satisfaction at its overthrow. So long as they think we are strong and can hold our own, they will be friendly enough, but I fear that in our "dark hour" we should have little sympathy to expect except from those who should suffer pecuniary loss by a political convulsion in England or a disastrous war, and this sympathy would not be very loudly expressed. If we were engaged in a war in which the more absolute Governments of Europe seemed to be leagued against us, we might have the popular sympathy of the United States, but in no other, and any outbreak in Ireland would be sympathised with and encouraged to the utmost.

Two months after the cabinet was installed, Secretary of State Marcy still avoided dealing with diplomatic business.[41]

This want of energy in grappling with the question at issue has been my great difficulty with the present Administration. Mr. Marcy assures me that it has really and truly been for want of time to become acquainted with the elements of them, and having seen the way in which he is beset and persecuted for offices, I can easily believe that there is great truth in what he says. He told me the day I had my conversation with him, that on the day before the Cabinet sat for five consecutive hours discussing one appointment, namely, the Marshalship of the United States at Washington—an office about the calibre of that of a Stipendiary Magistrate in Ireland. . . .

The great difficulty of the Central America and Mosquito question is to know how to lay hold of it, or in what form to put it into a Convention with the United States without the concurrence of Nicaragua, who, with the mixture of indolence and obstinacy and total indifference to prosperity or progress which characterise the wretched Cross between Aztecs, Negroes, and Spaniards of which its population consists, refuses all our proposals. It is difficult for the Government of the United States to enter into a Convention with us to dispose of territory to which they have declared in their opinion Nicaragua has the best title. They have fortunately not yet bound themselves to enforce this title for Nicaragua, and could therefore consistently advise her to come to terms with the parties by whom it is disputed.

On 5 June 1853 Crampton reiterated his concern regarding one of the issues that most plagued Anglo-American relations prior to the Civil War. Although the United States was duty bound by treaty to prohibit the slave trade between the West Coast of Africa and North America, its expenditure of money and resources was, in Crampton's view, totally inadequate.[42]

I send you today a reply to my note about the abuse of the United States Flags in the Slave Trade. It is a more civil one than we have generally got in answer to this often repeated complaint. The Government, I fear, has little power to take effective measures to prevent it. The United States Naval Officers are zealous enough in capturing Slavers, but the force is so small, particularly now that they have sent the greater part of it to Japan, that little is to be done. The difficulty of getting Slavers condemned by Admiralty Courts when captured and brought into American Ports is another encouragement to Slave Traders, and this difficulty, strange as it may seem, is much greater in the Northern States which profess Abolitionism, than in the South where Slavery exists. This arises from the Shipbuilders of the North being interested in the prosperity of the Trade for which they furnish by far the greatest part of the vessels under whatever Flag they afterwards sail. With regard to the smallness of the Naval force of the United States, it is characteristc of their reliance on the power of swagger to observe the threatening tone they hold to all the world when, in reality, a sudden rupture, even with a Second-rate Power, would expose their Coasts and Commerce in an almost defenceless condition to an enterprising enemy.

It will be recalled that Crampton had concluded in his letter to Lord Elgin of 3 November 1851 that nothing of interest to Britain could get through the American Congress without the support of a secret lobby such as the Organization. Although the following letter to Lord Clarendon of 19 June 1853 does not spell things out explicitly, it contains clear evidence of Crampton's willingness to explore such clandestine tactics. Crampton probably knew, although Lord Clarendon did not, that Secretary of State Marcy was a former member of the Organization. So was Robert J. Walker, whom Marcy recommended to Crampton as someone well able to assist the British and Canadians in securing a reciprocity treaty.[43]

I have had a long conversation with Mr. Marcy on the subject of the commercial Negotiation, and also, at Mr. Marcy's suggestion, with Mr. Walker, formerly Secretary of the Treasury in Mr. Polk's administration. The fact of my being referred to Mr. Walker seems to me to augur well as to the disposition of the present Government to make liberal commercial arrangements with us; for if they adopt Mr. Walker's views, they will adopt those of the sincerest as well as the ablest and most indefatigable advocate of Free Trade in this Country. Mr. Walker, as you may perhaps be aware, is the author of the American Tariff of 1846—the greatest step in the direction of Free Trade which has ever been made by this Country, and which would have been much greater if he had had his way more completely. However he succeeded in establishing the *principle* that the United States Tariff was to be adjusted with a view to Revenue alone, without any regard to Protection. The difficulty which he experienced in carrying this through Congress was great, and nothing but the most indefatigable labour and energy on his part could have done it. He is consequently thoroughly acquainted with all the commercial questions of the Country not only in themselves but as regards their position in public opinion in each State of the Union, in Congress generally, and even in the minds of each important Member of that Body, and he is on watch for every fluctuation of feeling which may take place on the subject. His opinion therefore as to the difficult questions of what can or cannot be done upon any commercial question, is extremely valuable, and as he is one of the very few sincere advocates of the general principle of Free Trade in this Country, I place great reliance on his honesty. Mr. Walker is besides, and in this he is an exception in his political party, well disposed towards England, partly from his appreciation of the immense importance of the commercial relations of the two Countries, and partly "I guess" owing to a very well timed eulogism which was pronounced upon his great commercial Report in 1846 by Sir Robert Peel in a Speech in Parliament at a time when the Report was very fiercely attacked here . . . .

Both Mr. Marcy and Mr. Walker are decidedly of opinion that it would *not be expedient* to include in the present negotiation other matters than those which have already been brought under consideration, viz. the Fisheries, Reciprocity of Trade with the Colonies and the questions obviously connected with those objects. This objection does not, they state, arise from an unwillingness on their part to extend freedom of Commerce between the two Countries . . . but from the conviction that an attempt now to introduce such provisions into a Treaty would defeat the object in view. Mr. Walker said that he understands the President intends to recommend to Congress a further modification of the Tariff in a liberal sense, and that he is decidedly of opinion that as Parties now stand the recommendation would be acted upon; but he is as decidedly of opinion that if such modifications were brought forward in a Treaty with Great Britain, it would not in the present composition of the Senate obtain the necessary "two-thirds" vote. . . . I fear however that if in this Negotiation we are to wait till we get a reasonable balanced arrangement, we can never expect to bring it to a conclusion. There are two main reasons for this, exclusive of the characteristic sharp dealing of this People in all matters of bargain—the first is that in this arrangement all or at least by far the most important advantages or valuable considerations which we had in our power are already granted; and the Americans feel perfectly assured that we are not going to withdraw them which would be the only course by which we could force equivalents. This is the case in regard to the Coasting trade of our Colonies and the East Indies which we have given them, and the privilege of British Registry to American built ships. Again in regard to Reciprocity of Trade in natural productions with the Colonies, the real equivalents by which we could have obtained this, we have ceded long ago: these are the admission of American corn to the British Market free of duty by our own Legislature in the change of our Corn Laws, and of the consequent abolition by the Canadian Legislature of the discriminating duty in favour of British Manufacturers in the Provincial Market where American Manufacturers now meet them on equal terms. Now the principal object of the Canadians in pressing for reciprocity is to get their wheat, which is charged with a duty of 25% on importation into the U.S., received on the same terms as American wheat is received in Great Britain—this being evidently a very fair piece of reciprocity. Had the concession of our own markets been made conditional on this at the time, it of course would have been granted, but as the Americans know very well that we are not going to rescind our Corn Laws in order to obtain it, they do not look upon our measure as a concession to them, but as one adopted for our own sake; and the same in regard to the changes of our Navigation Laws, as they affect Registry and the Coasting Trade.

I do not mean to infer from this that we ought to have adopted another course, but only that the course we have adopted makes it very difficult for a Negotiator now to obtain anything like an evenly balanced arrangement.

The second reason is, and this regards more particularly the Colonial part of the arrangement, that although the advantages of this proposed arrangement considered in itself, are certainly on the side of the U.S. in amount of commercial gain, those advantages are, or are thought by the colonies to be, very essential to their welfare, whereas by far the greater portion of the U.S. are very indifferent or very little alive to them—while many doubt that there would be any advantage at all to the U.S.

A week later Crampton had to report the disappointing news that Robert J. Walker had accepted an appointment to China and would soon be on his way. Meanwhile, a serious episode had arisen in Louisiana in which a black man who claimed to be a British subject was accused of fomenting a slave uprising.[44]

> I have myself had several long conversations with Mr. Pierce and I must say that they have left a very favourable impression, both as to his personal character and his disposition to be on friendly terms with us. He has placed our intercourse on a very satisfactory footing by begging of me to visit him as I would a personal friend without any previous application for an interview, and saying that the oftener I did so the better he would be pleased.
>
> Mr. Walker, my conversations with whom I told you of in my last letter, is going to China as Minister from the United States. I have had a conversation with him on this subject which was quite satisfactory as regards his disposition to act in concert with us on availing ourselves of any opportunity which may offer itself for opening the trade of China to the Commerce of the World without any attempt to obtain exclusive advantages. He told me that he had not accepted the Mission without "carte blanche" as to his proceedings to effect this object. Mr. Walker will pass thro' London on his way to his post, I hope [he] will have an opportunity of conversing with you. You will find him very intelligent and well-informed on all commercial matters and an out-of-hand free trader, but somewhat of a "doctrinaire" and indeed rather a visionary, I think, upon some other political matters. As regards the object of his mission to China, however, the appointment is a good one.
>
> You will see by my despatch No. 129 of today that there has been a Slave Insurrection alarm at New Orleans, and that an Englishman has been arrested as implicated therein,[45] and it would seem with sufficient evidence for a New Orleans Jury at least to deal harshly with him. It is difficult to know what to do in these cases. If we give assistance and counsel openly to prisoners in this predicament, it generally does them more harm than good, and it is very difficult to do it secretly. Mure,[46] however, is very discreet in these matters and well acquainted with the South and its feelings and prejudices. I am sorry for the occurrence of this business, particularly just now that a more favourable feeling has begun to show itself in South Carolina in respect to an alteration of their Coloured Seaman Law. This is very much owing to the abandonment of the case of "Ruben Roberts", which I directed the Vice-Consul to drop.[47]

In July the fisheries dispute flared up again, and Crampton decided to visit Canada to observe things at first hand. He reached Halifax, Nova Scotia, on 7 July and was back in Washington on the nineteenth. A week later he described a conversation that he had had with Secretary Marcy. Here we have the first rumblings of what developed into the Crimean War: a conflict initially between Russia and Turkey that eventually dragged Britain and France into an alliance with the Ottoman Empire in order to curb Russian expansion.[48]

> He, Marcy, then referred to the Turko-Russian question and asked me if I could give him any recent information as to the views of Her Majesty's Government in regard to it; he added that he did so because the Russian Minister here had been reading a good many despatches and documents to him on the subject, and was evidently anxious to propitiate the favourable opinion of the United States Government to the Russian view of the question. Mr. Marcy then said that altho'

the introduction of the subject by him might appear a little irregular, he had done so frankly because he felt anxious to take an opportunity of expressing his hope that Her Majesty's Government would feel confident that no difficulty which might arise out of any European Question would have the slightest unfavourable effect upon the fair and friendly spirit in which the United States Government were desirous to treat every question between themselves and Great Britain.

The President held the same language with even more frankness and emphasis. He said he considered the maintenance of friendly relations between the United States and Great Britain to be the most vital question in the whole range of Politics and that which affected the general interest of the civilisation of the World the most essentially; adding that he could not conceive a deeper responsibility devolving upon a human being than would be incurred by him who should risk their disturbance.

All this (and a great deal more was said in the same spirit) is extremely satisfactory, and it is difficult to doubt his sincerity. On the other hand we must regret, if such sentiments are sincerely entertained, not only the want of courage to announce to the American People that which is so emphatically declared to a Foreign Minister, but the fact which stares us in the face, that almost on the very same day, other members of the same Cabinet are pouring forth to delighted auditors floods of bombastical but mischievous trash of exactly the opposite tendency.

Early in August Crampton spent a few days in Berkeley Springs, Virginia, conversing with Marcy between games of whist. Fishing rights and commercial reciprocity dominated their discussions. In his letter of 8 August, Crampton recapitulated much of the argument.[49]

We think that all these points [British Demands] ought to be conceded, and are desirable in themselves independently of any Treaty. We also think that they will inevitably be conceded by Legislation within a very short time. It is, however, our intention to proceed boldly in the line of Free Trade Policy in which these Concessions will be necessarily involved, and our strength in Congress is sufficient to enable us to do so. But though we have a decided and increasing majority in both Houses there still exists a pretty compact Protectionist Party which becomes formidable whenever it can contrive to throw the votes of some local interest into the scale, and it is to be observed that almost every State, however strong in favour of Free Trade generally, makes its exception as to some particular article in regard to which it is always pledged and ready to rally to the Protectionists: as for example, Pennsylvania—coal and iron; Maine—lumber; Maine and New Hampshire (Mr. Pierce's State)—Ship-building; Maine and Massachusetts—the bounty on fishing; and so on. Now, the advocates of Free Trade proceed to say "altho" we shall, in all human probability be able to carry the three articles in question by Legislation, if we introduce them into a Treaty with Great Britain, we shall be defeated". In order to understand how this can be, it is necessary to refer to the mechanism of the Constitution of the United States. The passing of a Law requires the consent of both Houses of Congress. . . . For the passing of a Treaty a simple majority of two-thirds is required. Now the smaller States, whose voice is weak in the House of Representatives, are thus on an equality with the great ones in the Senate; and it is in the smaller States, generally speaking, that protectionist principles are still held to. It is clear therefore how much the "two-thirds rule" increases their power of obstructing a Measure when it comes before them as a Treaty.

"This may all be very true", I have remarked in reply to these considerations, "but our Colonies would probably prefer to see the Legislation you speak of effected before they give up all, to taking their chance as to what is to be done in the United States Congress hereafter." . . .

Although our conversations were principally confined to the Commercial Questions, Marcy made me a sort of overture in regard to another subject to which I have not yet adverted, but which, in the way that the United States Government seem inclined to treat it, seems to me to be big with important consequences, as regards the politics and balance of power, if there is such a thing, in this Hemisphere: I mean the Opening of the Amazon River.

This subject has been the theme of a good many essays in newspapers and periodicals, the most significant of which, however, are those which I enclose, written by Lieut. Maury, the clever Superintendent of the Observatory here—pretty evidently with the authority of the Government as a sort of feeler. Mr. Marcy introduced the subject by talking of our joint efforts to get the Paraná and other great rivers of South America opened to the Commerce of the World, saying he supposed we should equally like to see the Amazon so opened, and that he would be glad to have our aid and cooperation to that end. He added, however, that the United States have determined to go a little further than we might perhaps be inclined to do; in other words, he said "*we mean to have it opened*: we intend of course to do, and indeed *are doing* all we can to persuade Brazil to do this quietly by Treaty, but" he added (pulling up his Pants very much after the fashion of King Francis in Tristram Shandy), "if she won't we mean to have a fight with her". He said he thought it right to be thus frank with me on the matter as the United States had made up their minds that Brazil had no sort of right to shut up such a large portion of the world from the uses of Mankind, and that the United States having already obtained from Peru the privilege of navigating the upper branches of the Amazon in their Territory, did not conceive that Brazil should be allowed to block up the lower portion of the River. He alluded to some of the negotiations in regard to the Rhine and Danube in illustration of his argument, but did not seem to know much about them. I told him, of course, that I had no instructions about the Amazon, but that for obvious reasons I could not suppose we would ever agree that Brazil had not a right to retain the exclusive navigation of that River if she thought it proper. Such a principle would indeed at once deprive us of the right of reserving the navigation of the St. Lawrence and St. Johns etc. this however I said nothing about, and the conversation ended. Altho' all this was urged in a somewhat jocose vein. I have no doubt that Mr. Marcy is perfectly in earnest. The existence of this scheme throws some light upon the alacrity now shown to settle or "fix off", as Mr. Marcy calls it, all outstanding questions with us, and it looks very much as if the game which was played in regard to the Oregon Question by Mr. Polk's Administration (in which it is to be observed Mr. Marcy was Secretary of War, and Mr. Buchanan Secretary of State) is to be played over again now. In the Oregon Question when they found nothing was to be made out of us, and swaggering was answered by the equipment of heavy frigates, Mr. Buchanan suddenly closed with Pakenham's proposals which he had been scouting with great impertinence for more than a year, and before the ink was dry on the Treaty of June 1846, General Taylor was ordered by Mr. Marcy to fall upon the Mexicans, the result being what is now complacently alluded to by the present Government as "the glorious achievement of James K. Polk's brilliant administration". I shall not therefore be surprised to see the arrangement of the Fishery and Central American Questions with us immediately followed by an onslaught on Brazil upon the subject of the Amazon in order to confer equal illustration on the Administration of Franklin Pierce. There will be one feature in regard to the Amazon which will ensure the popularity of any move in that direction in a great part of the Union, —I mean the South—there will be no objection to the Southerners proceeding to that part of the world "with their property" (that is their negroes) as there was in regard to California from which that "property" was excluded by Congress altho' the country was conquered, as they (the Southerners) said with their blood and treasure as much as with that of the North. They are still indignant at this prohibition. The Mexican War is unpopular with them, and they would never consent to another war in which it was not stipulated beforehand that they might settle with their negroes in the territory which might be conquered.

During 1853 Anglo-American relations were chronically plagued by crises in Greytown and along the Mosquito coast, despite the joint efforts to provide Greytown with a degree of autonomy and self-government at the expense of the Mosquito King. In 1852 the inhabitants of this village elected their own governing council with an American settler, T. J. Martin, as mayor. Americans controlled the municipal council, in fact, which should have facilitated good relations with the Accessory Transit Company. The company, however, clung to the premise that its privileges stemmed from the king of the Mosquitos, who had granted it the right to erect a warehouse on Punta d'Arenas, a promontory on the north bank of the San Juan River. However, by 1853 this modest structure had been enlarged to include storerooms, living quarters for employees, shops for travelers, and even hotels of sorts. As it was situated outside the jurisdictional boundaries of Greytown, no revenue accrued to the town. To remedy this, the council addressed an ultimatum to the company on 8 February 1853, insisting that part of the buildings be dismantled within five days and that the whole area be evacuated within a month. When there was no compliance, the council organized a raid on Punta d'Arenas (21 February), and after it became apparent that nothing was going to be done by the company, the city fathers scheduled a second and final assault for 11 March. However, Captain George N. Hollins of the United States Navy arrived just in time to interpose his ship, the *Cyane*, between the warring factions, thus restoring an uncertain peace.

Initially the British took this affair quite calmly and even smugly, for it did not concern them directly and seemed to be just another example of two sets of thieves falling out among themselves. Nevertheless, Britain still felt obliged to protect the Mosquito Kingdom from one group of Americans or another.

On 22 August, Crampton brought Lord Clarendon up to date on the most recent state of affairs.[50]

I enclose you a copy of an unofficial letter which I have received from Mr. Marcy regarding the Greytown affair, being the result of the enquiries which I mentioned to you in my last letter [Aug. 14] he was about to make of the Transit Company as to the fact of their having made a voluntary agreement with the Government of Greytown in regard to Punta d'Arenas. Mr. Joseph L. White still denies the existence of any such voluntary agreement between the Company and the *Government of*

Greytown, but acknowledges its existence between the Company and the *Government of Mosquito*. Mr. White is the very incarnation of American *Attorneyism*, and his conscience therefore did not oblige him in the least to tell the whole truth when the enquiry was made of him in the first instance. The Mr. Martin of whom he speaks, is an American of the very worst character, an escaped convict from the Penitentiary at New York, who consequently found it convenient to go to Greytown where his "antecedents" seem to have secured to him the office of Mayor. Mr. White finds it convenient now to deny Mr. Martin's Agency in the affairs of the Company, but I strongly suspect that Mr. Martin and he understood each other perfectly well. I presume that the point Mr. Marcy will now make will be that as the United States Government have recognized the *de facto* Government of Greytown, but not the Government of Mosquito, no agreement made with the latter could be recognized by them.

All this chicanery, and the sort of transactions and people with which the two Governments have to mix themselves up so long as this Mosquito Question remains open, ought, if the Government of the U.S. is sincere in its pacific assurances, to show them the paramount importance of bringing the matter at once to a conclusion. I suppose, however, that by this time you will have had an opportunity of judging whether Mr. Buchanan's instructions are really meant to effect this object. Nothing of any importance has occurred here since last I wrote. Calderon de la Barca has left for Madrid to be placed at the head of the Administration of Foreign Affairs. He does not himself seem very sanguine of success, and he seems to be broken in health as not to be likely to have a very long reign. On the other hand the Spanish Government will find it difficult to replace him here, for he was personally liked, spoke the language and understood the ways of the Country as well as it was possible for a Spaniard to do so tho' this perhaps is not saying much. You are probably acquainted with his successor, Gonzalez Bravo, who is not yet arrived here.[51] He will have a difficult game to play.

I enclose an article from the "New York Herald" on the Eastern Question, not for its intrinsic weight, but because I feel pretty sure that its authorship is due to my Russian Colleague, Mons. de Bodisco. This old gentleman, whose age is lost in the might of ages and veiled by wigs, dyes, and other contrivances, is a perfect specimen of a "diplomate de la vieille roche". He came here some five and twenty years ago, *en retraite*, but has managed to keep himself alive, I suppose, by the excitement of speculating in American stocks. I don't believe he ever receives a despatch, and therefore having nothing else to do, he piques himself on traversing and counteracting "les intrigues de l'Angleterre". His "profondes combinaisons" however are pretty generally reported to me, and in general don't amount to much, altho' I believe in 1837 Fox "suspected him very grievously" of some little "intelligences" with the Canadian Rebels.[52] He is quite mistaken however in supposing that anything he gets put into the Newspaper will have the least political influence here. I am sorry to see that Mr. Pierce has been weak enough to appoint as Consul to London a Mr. George Sanders, Editor of the "Democratic Review", the most violent and outrageous of the Young American and Filibusters Publications. The man himself is too stupid to do any mischief, but you will see from the subjoined article that if he does not, it is not for want of the good wishes of the "New York Herald".

A month later Crampton returned to the theme of international waterways in both continents of the Western Hemisphere.[53]

I have had some more conversation with Mr. Marcy about the Amazon, and I was happy to find him much more correct and moderate in his views of the subject than when he first broached it to me at Berkeley Springs. He expressed himself much gratified at hearing that England would join the United States in an appeal to the common sense of Brazil to open the Amazon to the commerce of all Nations. He said, "That is exactly the way in which we would propose to proceed. I wish it to be distinctly understood that we do not, as certain parties here would wish us to do, assert that *we have a right* to navigate the River. We assert no such right, no more than we do to the *Navigation of the St. Lawrence*, which is now a subject of negotiation between your Government and ours:—but, what we do maintain is that we are justified in asking for and in strongly insisting upon a Treaty arrangement with Brazil conferring upon us as on all nations the "innocent use" of that river on the same principle as is recognized and fixed by Treaty among the "riverain states" on the great rivers of Europe: the political use of the River would of course rest with Brazil and would be guarded by stipulations in the same Treaty which should allow us to participate in its commercial use. You are probably aware that there is a Company here, at the head of which is Lieut. Porter[54] of the United States' Navy, who wish to take a Steam Boat up the Amazon on an exploring expedition: they have moved our Navy Department to give instructions to our vessels of War to support them in going up the Amazon as a matter of Right,—but this we have positively refused to do.

This brings me to your question regarding the St. Lawrence. The feeling in Canada on the subject is, I believe, universal in favour of the navigation being thrown open to the Americans. The Canadians have constructed magnificent canals and other works for getting round the Rapids and otherwise completing the line of navigation from the Great Lakes to the Sea: these Canals can only be productive in proportion to the traffic which passes thro' them, and in general the prosperity of Canada must very much depend upon the St. Lawrence becoming one at least of the great channels for the commerce of the great Western States growing up with such unexampled rapidity round the Lakes. This of course can only take place to a very limited extent while the Americans are excluded from the navigation of the River. The Americans, on the other hand, have constructed Canals, (and are constructing more, to say nothing of railroads) which now bring the Western Produce, *including a great portion of the corn grown in Canada*, to New York. The consequence of this state of things is that the Americans, not feeling the immediate want of the St. Lawrence, are, in general as compared with the Canadians, indifferent on the subject of the proposed stipulation for its free navigation,—while those interested in the New York Canals and railroads are even opposed to it. There are however inherent advantages in the navigation of the St. Lawrence, the want of which must be more and more felt by Western States as they increase in population and wealth, and, in general, the Government and Nation consider the right to navigate it a valuable and important one, tho' they are apt to affect to undervalue it. The Canadians would be glad, I have no doubt, to throw the river open at once, except insofar that the free Navigation of it having been made "a moyen de negotiation" for the Reciprocity Treaty, they would object to do so unless that question was, at the same time, settled to their satisfaction. As things at present stand therefore, the decision of the question of the St. Lawrence will depend upon that of the other commercial questions, and I fear it would be difficult now to separate it from them—the more especially as the Canadians rely on the adoption of certain discriminating votes on the Welland Canal in connection with holding the navigation of the St. Lawrence, as a means of coercing the Americans into a Reciprocity Treaty. This would be a mistaken policy, in my opinion, but Mr. Francis Hincks and the Canadian Parliament seemed last year very much inclined to adopt it.[55] In relation to this subject, I enclose a report on the Trade of the Lakes showing the immense development of it and its importance. You will see that the traffic on the lakes in 1851 amounted to 326 millions of dollars and employed 215,000 tons of shipping.

With regard to the fisheries and commercial questions, I need not at present enter into them, as you are now in possession of Marcy's counter proposition and note. I will however take due note of your directions as to the manner in which any negotiation on the subject is to be carried on. I entirely agree with you as to the inexpediency of giving anything up on the chance or promise of receiving an equivalent by American Legislation. It is a promise which no American Government can honestly make, or fulfill if they make it. They have little or no control over Congress on such subjects, and they confess it. We however can promise, and are sure of being able to fulfill our promise, to meet with reciprocity any liberal measures that Congress may adopt. I, therefore, always say to them "Do you legislate in such and such a manner, and we will engage ourselves to reciprocate either by treaty or by counter-legislation."

As is so often the case, one American presidential campaign is scarcely over when politicians begin to plan for the next one. Crampton was always on the lookout for such aspirants, and in his letter of 25 September,[56] he mentioned that he thought he detected two: James Buchanan, the current American minister to London, and Edward Everett, the former secretary of state. Following the death of Daniel Webster, Everett roundly rejected the so-called Tri-Partite agreement whereby Britain, France, and the United States undertook to defend the independence of Cuba. This greatly displeased Lord John Russell, the foreign secretary, who reproved Everett for jettisoning what Webster had already negotiated. Six months later, Everett took revenge by publishing Russell's reproof followed by his own refutations.[57]

On receipt of your letter of the 9th instant, I immediately proceeded to stir up Mr. Marcy on the subject of Central America, and endeavoured to find out the reason for Mr. Buchanan's inaction. Mr. Marcy, as he has always done, explained himself very frankly, but of course confidentially in regard to Mr. Buchanan's position. Mr. Buchanan, you will recollect, was displeased at not being allowed to take all the questions, commercial as well as political, between the two countries to England, with "carte blanche", there to make them the subject of one negotiation with you. He was restricted to the questions regarding Greytown and Central America including Ruatan Island:—but with regard to these he was, in consideration of his standing and position, and (I think wisely) with a view to getting the question out of the entanglement produced by former discussion, given "carte blanche". This however did not satisfy him, for he seems to have run sulky like a horse that pulls when you hold him and backs when you give him his head, and he has written to say that he will not enter upon the discussion with you of the matters entrusted to him, until the President instructs him point by point as to the ground he is to take:—what he may yield etc., etc. To this they have replied by a letter which was only sent by last post, saying that the Administration must decline doing this at the present stage of the affair. He, Mr. Buchanan, is they say in full possession of their general views:—

they have full confidence in his ability and skill; and his knowledge of the interests of the United States in regard to their foreign relations is equal, if not superior, to their's. He is fully qualified for a full and free discussion of the matters in question with you, and it would only be after such a discussion after hearing everything the British Government had to say or propose, that they could with fairness or with prudence lay down points or assume positions which were not to be given up under any circumstances. Were this done in the first instance, ground might be taken from which it might be difficult to recede, however expedient it might be to do so.

These and similar considerations, Mr. Marcy says he hopes will have their due influence on Mr. Buchanan; but you may plainly perceive that there does not reign an 'entente cordiale" between the Administration and their Representative in London. It is equally true, however, that he holds too many strong political cards for them to quarrel with him as a partner, altho' they are not inclined to allow him, as he evidently wishes, to play the whole game from his own hand.

The struggle for political capital among public men in this Country, particularly when they have once been Candidates or look to be Candidates for the Presidency, is indeed, one of the most remarkable features of the System. The notion that a man may be put up for President, once taken up, seems to produce in him a peculiar mental disease:—like a person bit by a Tarantula, he cannot remain quiet, but by a curious retributive dispensation he almost invariably does some foolish thing or other which utterly disqualifies him for success in the very object he has in view. Webster, a man of undoubted ability and intellect, and Scott, a very inferior, but I think honest man, were on a perfect equality in acts of folly and insincerity at the last Presidential election. Clay and Calhoun distinguished themselves in the same way on other occasions. This disquisition I give you not for its own sake, but in some measure as an introduction to the next sake, but in some measure as an introduction to the next topic of my present letter, I mean the eccentric movements of apparently the most staid politician of them all—Mr. Everett.

Mr. Everett, the very incarnation of New England steadiness and Boston respectability, and who seemed for years to have given up politics for literature, on Mr. Webster's death seemed to have got it into his head that he was a fit and proper person to be President of the United States. Whiggism Yankeeism, and Bostonianism, tho' great in New England, are an abomination to the "general" and won't do for President. So of course a Candidate's first move must be to clear himself of these imputations. Accordingly, the first step in that direction was taken and a good bold stride it was, in the Note in answer to our proposition for a Tripartite Convention about Cuba—going further in reality than Cass or anybody else in Filibustero-ism, and in direct contradiction to the principles and opinions of the Party with whom Mr. Everett had hitherto been acting. However, he was Secretary of State and he was to be the organ of the whole Country, and not of New England. So far he was within bounds: but now Lord John Russell's despatch in answer to his appears— and altho' he is no longer Secretary of State, and admits, as he must well know, having been a diplomatist himself, a flagrant breach of diplomatic usage and propriety, as well in regard to Mr. Marcy as to Lord John Russell and yourself, he writes a long rejoinder to Lord John's despatch, addresses it to him, and publishes it in the newspapers before it could have reached its destination, as you will perceive by the enclosed copy of it, puffed and commented upon in the style of which I append a specimen. This desire of keeping his name afloat before the Public has, in this instance, carried Mr. Everett even further than one could imagine so cautious and discreet a man would venture to go—for there can be no doubt, as you will see by referring to the Act of Congress of which I enclose a copy, that in writing the letter in question he has actually infringed the Statute Law of his own Country. It is not likely that this act will be brought up against him on the present occasion, but if Parties ran high and Congress was in Session, I should not be at all surprised to see it done. The Act was passed in Mr. Adams' Presidency in consequence of a letter written with Mr. Adams' consent by Jefferson, who was himself Vice President, to the French Government, and therefore meant to reach the very offence Mr. Everett has committed.[58]

On 9 October, Crampton returned to the question of commercial reciprocity and was able to detect a glimmer of hope amidst the otherwise discouraging tactics employed by the Americans.[59]

I have received your letter of the 23 Ultimo, and I am not surprised at the effect produced upon you by Mr. Marcy's draft for a Commercial Treaty. The principle in Treaty making ascribed by Mr. Canning,[60] to the Dutch, of "granting too little and asking too much" has certainly been religiously deserved by Mr. Marcy on this occasion. The way of meeting this cool pertinacity is, as you would remark, not to break off the negotiation, for this would be made an excuse for throwing the blame of any future trouble upon us—but by making counterpropositions strictly fair in themselves, and which we are really willing and able to carry into effect the moment we are met in a fair spirit. These, if now made, must go before the American Public, and they ought to be accompanied, I think, by a Statement on our part of our whole case;—for as yet this Country has been mystified by partial and imperfect accounts, and discussions on isolated points regarding the commercial relations between the United States and the British Colonies. When the whole matter is considered, it will be seen that the United States have been treated with the greatest liberality both by British and Provincial Legislation on all matters affecting commercial intercourse, with little or no response from the American Congress. In fact they have uniformly refused to apply to us the principle of Reciprocity which they so often have put forward as the guiding maxim of their commercial policy. The immense advantages accorded to the United States by 1st The Admission of their Corn to British Markets; 2nd The Admission of American manufacturers on the same terms as those of the Mother Country by the British Colonies; 3rd The East India & Intercolonial Trade: 4th The Grant of British Registers to American vessels which throws the whole of our shipbuilding trade open to American competition:—without mentioning other concessions,—have never been responded to at all, and are studiously kept out of sight whenever they want to get any of the few remaining things we have as yet to concede. I am however glad that Mr. Marcy has at length been induced to make us officially the proposals he had embodied in his draft and note, such as they are, because it will give us an opportunity of making a counterstatement and counter propositions which must go before Congress, and Jonathan [i.e., America] will see that if we have still got anything he wants, it must be fairly paid for. There is no want of acuteness of perception on his part in regard to these matters, but unfortunately he has adopted it as maxim, that no American Government or Minister is to be forgiven for settling a question or making a bargain on simply fair and equitable terms, until it has been shown that gnashing and extortion have been pertinaciously tried and failed.

On 17 October Crampton sought again to help Lord Clarendon in the arduous task of unraveling the complexities of American political factionalism.[61]

On the other hand internal matters have not been so quiet. These party squabbles cannot of course have much interest for you, just now more particularly, and I should despair of being able to put you up even to the "terminology" of the science here, or to give you any clear notion of what is really meant by hard shells, soft shells, adamantines, old hunkers, Barnburners etc. However as these matters have collaterally considerable influence upon our relations with the United States, and some notion of them is necessary to account for symptoms which otherwise are apt to appear more alarming than they really are, I will state to you "a few" what I believe to be the general bearing and tendency of the agitation now existing, complicated as it is by local and personal feeling and disguised by incomprehensible party slang. The plain English of the matter then seems to be this. Mr. Pierce having been brought in by a triumphant majority made up out of all the sections of the Democratic Party got together with great skill and manoeuvring for the purpose of finally annihilating the Whigs, set to, as in duty bound, to exercise his unquestioned prerogative of "dividing the spoils". It was pretty evident that to do this in such a manner as to satisfy all his supporters, or even in a way to leave them no fair cause for complaint, was a task beyond human political wisdom, and certainly beyond that of poor Mr. Pierce. I mentioned to you that the distribution of the spoils was a long operation, and that even during its continuance, I already saw symptoms of division in the Democratic Party Camp: it was not however till the whole business of dividing the booty was got through, as it has only now just been, that the storm burst: but now it has come, and whether the Cabinet will survive it, I don't know, but that does not so much signify. Mr. Pierce is at all events bound to the stake to be baited for the next three years and a half. Already the "adamantines" (hardshells) of New York have resolved that he is a "villain". . . .

The key by which almost all political complications in the United States may be interpreted will not fail us on the present occasion. It is the Slavery question which, in one shape or another, is at the bottom of them all. The Democratic Party being, as you are aware, divided (as is also the Whig Party) into Freesoilers and Unionists, the present accusation against Mr. Pierce and his cabinet is that in spite of hard swearing to the contrary, he had favoured the freesoilers in his appointments, or at least that he has not, as the Unionists pretend he ought to have done, excluded them altogether from office. Those who have got the places, being of course the Minority, all those who have been disappointed, have, as you may suppose, become violent in their Unionism, and under the names of hardshells, adamantines etc. have united in an onslaught on the Administration. It is in vain that the office holders protest and endeavour to purge themselves from the suspicion of being freesoilers or abolitionists: it puts the disappointed office seekers to insist that they are so at heart, or else that some other corrupt motive has influenced their appointment.

The way in which this affects us is this: it puts the present purpose of the Unionists to ring the alarm on the subject of supposed Machiavelian schemes of England to ruin the United States by fomenting disunion between the North and South by agitating Slavery, and a thousand other imaginary devices. The consequence is we are regaled with articles on "Conspiracies between the British aristocracy and Louis-Napoleon to ruin the United States by Abolition Agitation and Emissaries"; "Treaties between Great Britain and Spain for abolishing Slavery in Cuba for the purpose of disorganizing the South" etc: in short every exploded story about the deep designs of England and her hatred of American liberty is brought out like an old play with all the scenery, decorations, and properties which are, I believe, kept in type in the Printers' offices ready for production when the piece is to be reproduced. Though almost everybody knows the meaning of all this, it nevertheless does a great deal of mischief among the masses and makes hatred and suspicion of England a sort of habitual feeling with them.

I enclose you, as part of the same business, a letter to Marcy from a Mr. Lester[62] employed by "The Times" as their correspondent at New York. Mr. Pierce told me that this Mr. Lester asked him for a Consulship, and, on his refusing, thrust a packet of manuscript into his (Mr. Pierce's) face, saying, "I shall feel it my duty then to publish this in "The Times"." Mr. Pierce found it to contain the most gross personal abuse of himself which, he says, he supposes "The Times" thought too low to allow to appear in its columns.

One of the periodic bugbears of American journalism surfaced late in October 1853. The "Africanization of Cuba" was alleged to be a plot on the part of Britain and Spain to eliminate slavery from Cuba by flooding the island with apprentices brought from Africa who would ultimately establish a black republic just off the shores of the United States.[63]

You will admire the characteristic pertinacity with which it is assured here that a treaty has been made between Great Britain and Spain for the abolition of slavery in Cuba by means of the introduction of apprentices from Africa—an operation which letters written from Havana to newspapers here state to have actually begun. This in itself would not surprise me, but after my unqualified contradiction to Mr. Marcy of the rumour and the expression by him of his own disbelief of it, I was rather astonished to see the enclosed article in the "Washington Union", the administerial organ, containing a stiff reassertion of the report as one of the truth of which there is no doubt, and a swaggering appeal to the government to act upon the information they are presumed to have received. Though my general rule is never in my communications with this government to take the slightest notice of newspaper articles, I determined to take an opportunity of calling Mr. Marcy's attention to this one in the "Union" which has, as might be expected, been taken up by the press in general as proceeding from authority and has produced a chorus of nonsense of the most mischievous character as well as it affects or relations with the United States as the safety of Cuba itself from the piratical attacks of the "Filibusters", the encouragement of which I fully believe to be the sole object of the false report in question and of the newspaper comment thereupon.[64] Mr. Marcy saved me the trouble of broaching the subject by entering upon it himself in the course of a conversation upon other matters. He said that he still disbelieved the report in question, and had expressed that disbelief to the Editor of the "Union" who had come to him to consult him upon the subject of the article in question, which it seems is founded upon a letter from the American Consul or Vice Consul at Havana. Mr. Marcy added that he had strictly prohibited the Editor from stating that anything he had to say upon the matter was founded upon information derived from the Department of State. The Editor, it is true, says that his intelligence is derived from private sources, but this has not in the slightest degree weakened the public impression that the whole statement emanated from the Government. You will see in this only fresh instance of the truth of your own remark—that they are always ready here to make political capital at our expense in public—giving us at the same time the most satisfactory explanations in private. As soon as the falsehood of the present report is demonstrated by fact, it will be proclaimed and believed here, that we intended to make the Treaty in question, but were deterred by the firm attitude of the American Democratic Administration and press. The trade of "making giants" for the purpose of killing them, is carried on here to the greatest extent, and altho' the trick would seem to be stale, it produces the same delight every time it is executed. The only alarming part of the present pertinacious lying is that it looks like a premonitory symptom of a filibustering expedition from the South, and I have already heard some vague reports of enlistment or engagement in Georgia for one to take place in December or January next. The warlike appearance of things in Europe, I need not say renders the existence of such a plan more probable.

At about the same time that the British were stoutly denying that there was any substance to the Africanization of Cuba rumors, they were troubled by vague reports that certain Americans were fomenting revolution in Australia. Lord Clarendon asked Crampton to look into the matter, and on 31 October the minister in Washington sought to allay any fear on the subject.[65]

> I will not fail to keep an eye upon any proceedings which may be undertaken here in regard to Australia. I thought it almost superfluous to say that a Revolution there would be hailed with delight here, and that every assistance would be given to it by the People of the United States, because that is a feeling which exists here in regard to all revolutions and all colonies. I have never, however, had any reason to think that any design had ever been matured here for effecting such a revolution. If any number of Americans, however, establish themselves in Australia, I would strongly recommend the Governor to keep an eye upon them, as they would undoubtedly be participators in and encouragers of any rebellion proceedings which might be afoot.

By mid-November a new issue intruded on Crampton's attention: the Irish revolutionary John Mitchel escaped from Australia and made his way to California, where Irish-Americans were hailing him as a hero.[66]

> You will see if you look at the enclosed article from the "Washington Union" that my prediction that the respectable organ, on the demolition of the Africanization of Cuba Grievance, would retire under smoke of a general discharge of abuse of England has been quickly fulfilled. The thing is now pretty generally looked upon as a political hoax, as you will see by the enclosed tract from the "Intelligencer" even by the Democratic Press, tho' the "Union" still continues to harp upon it in articles which I enclose some of, tho' scarcely worth the trouble of reading.[67]
> The immediate object of their promulgation indeed no longer exists, for the election of the legislature and other offices in the State of New York which they were meant to influence are closed. They have ended disastrously for the administration, and indeed for the whole Democratic Party—the Whigs having, to everybody's surprise, what they call "carried the State" by an overwhelming majority. The dissensions of the Democrats rendered their defeat probable but not to the extent in which it has taken place, and what is most remarkable is that the Section of the Democrats which supported Mr. Pierce and his administration have come off the worst of all, altho at the Presidential Election they seemed to carry all before them. So much for the difference of feeling before and after the distribution of the Spoils.
> This defeat may have some good effect on the Foreign Relations of the Country, if it does not drive the Administration to some desperate act of outrage or aggression in order to regain its lost popularity. Unfortunately an opportunity for something

of the sort seems to be offered by the State of things in the Sandwich Islands to which I allude in my despatch No. 176 of today,[68] and it has accordingly begun to be "intimated" and to be understood that the annexation of those Islands to the United States is to be a "point" in Mr. Pierce's message to Congress at its opening on the 5th of next month. However that may be, it is clear that the scheme of getting possession of that important point in the Pacific has not been lost sight of here.

John Mitchel has arrived at San Francisco, and has of course been received by the Governor of the State at a banquet at which what they call the "exercises" of the evening were exclusively devoted to the abuse of Her Majesty's government. I see it argued in some of the papers that it was quite excusable in Mitchel to break his parole, as it was given to a government which could not be looked upon in any other light than that of "Pirates" etc.

This resuscitation of abuse and insult against England which I observe has lately taken place, is evidently caused by the expectation that we shall shortly be engaged in a war in Europe, and would probably die away again if the Eastern question was settled. If that cannot unfortunately be done, it will, I fear, require all our vigilance and firmness to meet the spirit that will be called for here.

Mr. Bunch is here on his way to Charleston. I have put him into full possession of our views in regard to the Law affecting our coloured seamen, and given him letters to persons of influence in South Carolina with whom I have already been in communication on the subject. If the South Carolinians have not got the Africanization of Cuba into their heads, I have hopes that we may be able to effect some good in that quarter.

It was a continual frustration to Crampton that the Pierce administration was either incapable or unwilling to curb the anti-British sentiments printed in Democratic newspapers. He could understand why Anglophobic sentiments appeared in papers of doubtful repute, but why should the administration's organs be allowed such license?[69]

I took care to express to the President and to Mr. Marcy, as well as to some private friends of Mr. Buchanan, your favourable impression in regard to him, in such a way that I have no doubt it will come round to him. The President and Mr. Marcy were extremely pleased, and Mr. Marcy read to me the concluding part of a despatch which he had just received from Mr. Buchanan, reciprocating in regard to yourself the obliging expressions you made use of in regard to him. . . .

The "Union" still goes on, as you will see by the enclosed article, but in the midst of its impertinence I think I see it is taking ground for backing out. I need not say that the notion of my having directly or indirectly employed other newspapers, or the telegraph, to contradict its statements, is utterly untrue. . . .

I took an opportunity of telling him [Marcy] what you had done in regard to "The Times" [of London]. He expressed himself as very grateful to you, and I think he must have felt so, and perhaps a little as if "coals of fire" had been heaped upon his head, in as much as his own organ the "Union" has lately by no means been reciprocating with us in such friendly attentions. However he utterly repudiated its language, and declared that it was a mistake to suppose that the Executive could control the language of any newspaper. I am very glad to hear that Mr. Delane has so just a view of the effect of articles in "The Times" produced here:[70] it would be difficult to exaggerate it, more particularly when men or things here are *laughed* at, or held cheap—jokes are not understood. It is perfectly true that the name of Great Britain scarcely ever appears in *any* American Paper without being coupled with an insult: so habitual indeed has this become that they scarcely perceive it when you point it out to them. They therefore richly *deserve* to be paid off in kind. It is nevertheless the case of all others in which Hamlet's advice ought to be followed— "Use them after your own honour and dignity—the less they deserve the more merit is in your bounty." An attempt to reciprocate would only produce an endless Billingsgate,[71] and be just what the instigators of mischief would like. It has always been the greatest satisfaction to me to be able to point out that no Member of the British Parliament has ever dreamt of making offensive replies to the indecent outbreaks of Messrs. Cass, Douglas, and others in the American Congress, and altho' the Public Press and travelling scribblers cannot be utterly silenced, that there is nothing on our side to compare, either in quantity or quality to what appears habitually in all public proceedings and writings on this side of the Atlantic. . . .

You will perceive from my despatch No. 181 of today,[72] that the question of the Sandwich Islands comes up in a pretty tangible shape, and it seems to me that the time is come for the English and French Government to take some steps in the matter if they think it important that those Islands should not fall into the hands of the United States. If King Kamahenha was to ask to be put under the joint protection of the Three Powers—viz., England, France and the United States, instead of being annexed to the latter, there would be no valid objection on their part to them doing so; and if the United States thought proper to decline its part in such a Protectorate they could not complain of its being assumed by England and France, who, although they stand pledged to each other by the Declaration of 1843 not to assume the Protectorate, are not bound by any third Party. Whatever Plan however may be adopted it is clear that if something decided is not done, the annexation Scheme will be proceeded with here, and will probably form the subject of the earliest discussions of the approaching Congress, if indeed it is not presented to their consideration in the President's Message. . . .

I will endeavour to ascertain what has really taken place in regard to a supposed understanding between the United States and Russia in the case of our being engaged in war with the latter. I imagine that the idea of the Americo-Russian Alliance has arisen between M. Soulé and the Russian minister here. I do not think however that the notion would be at all popular with the American People. On the other hand in case of war with Russia we must expect to find renewed vitality given to all American "doctrines", pretentions and aggressive schemes.

On 4 December Crampton introduced the topic of Mexican-American relations. Since the war with Mexico, United States policy had been ambiguous. Certain Americans continued to covet Mexican territory, while others felt that it was their duty to protect Mexico from further encroachment either by treaty or conquest. Some Americans organized filibustering expeditions south of the border, hoping to force the United States into sanctioning official military action.[73]

He [Marcy] spoke of the Expedition from San Francisco against Sonora and expressed great regret that it had not been stopped. The United States, he remarked, were in a very awkward position in regard to their Mexican frontier. They had engaged by the Treaty of Guadaloupe Hidalgo to protect Mexico on that frontier from incursions, but the force they could dispose of was totally inadequate. He had himself, when Secretary of War, impressed upon President Polk the necessity of applying to Congress for a force for that purpose: this would, independent of other considerations, have been a matter of economy, for the claims of Mexico against this Country on account of Indian depredations on that frontier were already much heavier than the expense of such a force would have been. Mr. Polk however felt so anxious to be able to announce to Congress, after the Mexican War that the army had at once been reduced to its Peace establishment (not more than 9,000 men) that he would not listen to the proposal.

Perhaps because he had been in the United States an unusually long time for a diplomat, Crampton could not help being cynical concerning the "holier than thou" attitude that permeated American politics.[74]

I have received your letter of the 2nd Instant. All you say in regard to Mitchel is unfortunately too true. The effect of the tyranny of the "Demos" here is that like other tyrants, while it has become morbidly sensitive to any attack or imaginable indignity against itself, it has become proportionately obtuse in sense of justice or fair play when applied to its own proceedings in regards to others. Upon the principle adopted by certain religions of "pluribus omnia pura", they imagine because they are a Democratic Republic, and it has been inculcated upon them that every other form of Government constituted not only a political but a moral wrong, all things are to be permitted them and nothing to others. Accordingly, conduct which would be in their opinon highly offensive or indecent on the part of foreign Governments towards the United States is excusable and even laudable on the part of the United States to foreign Governments, because they, the United States, are the only chosen vessels of true liberty. I do not mean to say that there are not numbers of people in this Country who have too much good sense to adopt this reasoning, but that this is the popular feeling—the doctrine which is continually preached and that which is at the bottom of every movement in regard to Foreign Powers is incontestible. "To enlarge the area of freedom" is looked upon as a perfectly good excuse of any aggression whatever. They therefore think that the reception of Mrs. Beecher Stowe in London is shocking and indelicate in the extreme, altho' she did nothing there that is not done and legally done everyday here in many of the States of the Union:[75] but they are quite surprised that any objection should be made to the public reception of Mitchel and such is the obtuseness to which I have alluded, they really don't perceive that independent of political considerations, he has by the flagrant breach of his word of honour rendered himself unworthy of reception even as a private individual. . . . Mitchel is coming to Washington I understand, and I have no sort of doubt that he will be asked about, and that efforts will be made to bring me into company with him. I will take care however to propose a passive resistence to any such plan. Last year at a sort of public ball that was given to take leave of ex-President Fillmore, I found myself without knowing it invited to meet Mr. Meagher,[76] and it was of course "noticed" with great glee and exultation by the papers the next day. I will not however be so taken in again. Meagher has behaved comparatively quietly, but Mitchel's violence of character is such that he would be capable of getting up some disagreeable scene or if he did not, one would be invented for the occasion. . . .

With respect to the Sandwich Islands, I think the tone of aggression is somewhat lowered. The joint action of Sartiges and myself had, I believe, some effect. At least I feel convinced from what I have heard that some mention of Plan of annexing them *was* in the [Annual] Message but was left out after we spoke. The pear, I suppose, was not thought to be yet ripe enough. The presence of a sufficient French and English Force is the only thing I can think of which can keep things in status quo there: the King and the Islanders will be sure to follow the advice of the "big guns" if they are kept before their eyes. I hope therefore that Admiral Moresby will ere this have made his appearance in their neighbourhood.[77] I don't think that the United States have a single Vessel of War disposable to send there just now.

4

British Preoccupation with the Crimean War, 1854

On 4 October 1853 the Ottoman Empire declared war against Russia. Britain and France felt no great sympathy for either side, but fearing the consequence of Russian expansion and Turkish disintegration, they finally became involved at the end of March 1854. In his letters to Lord Clarendon, Crampton became preoccupied with concerns emanating from the war: signs of American favoritism toward Russia or Russian attempts to hire American privateering vessels, or any ways in which American neutrality might be compromised.

For its part, the United States anticipated controversy and even conflict with Great Britain concerning the definition of neutrality. America wanted to trade with any of the combatants: "free ships make free goods." The British agreed to yield on this point if it was understood that should American ships and crews hire themselves to the Russians as privateers, they could be seized on the high seas as pirates, according to international law. This was stipulated principally because Britain suspected that Russia would jump at any chance to augment its fleet, whereas Britain had no need of privateers from abroad because her navy was formidable. In his letter of 27 February 1854, Crampton assumed the stance he maintained throughout the year: vigilance against the machinations of the czar, tempered with assurances that there was little the Russians could do in America that would have any significant impact on the course of the war.[1]

I have had two pretty stiff conversations with Mr. Marcy about the neutrality law and privateering. He was all wrong at our last interview both as to the provisions of the law and their applications. I have however brought him up by making him look at Clayton's correspondence with Baron Roenne about the frigate built here for the Central Germanic powers to be used against Denmark.[2] I don't think they will be able to get over that precedent, particularly as popular feeling is strong on our side. Clayton is in the Senate ready to vindicate General Taylor's and his own course.[3] I know however that a law is generally valid here just in proportion as it jumps with the feeling of the people at the time and I have therefore endeavoured to set agoing some expressions of it in the press. I am however obliged to be very cautious in these matters. On the present occasion the "New York Herald" has responded to my hint in its own style of course, and others have come out in the same tune unasked, as you will see by the specimens I enclose. In fact public sentiment is all right here in that respect. I met old Cass a day or two ago at the State Department where, I suppose in order to balance his intended attack on your speech, he accosted me before Mr. Marcy and several other Sentors and shaking me by the hand said very emphatically "Well Mr. Crampton there is not at this moment one true American heart that is not with your country in this quarrel. Public sentiment is unanimous. The conduct of the Emperor of Russia is infamous. Nothing but insanity can explain it. I believe he is insane."

Not liking to trust this letter to the post and the risk of delay and loss in the terrible state of the roads, I have sent it by a special messenger to Boston.

On the eve of Britain's entry into the Crimean War, Crampton was able to report that American feeling was not unfriendly. To be sure there would always be those among the Democratic party, such as Cass, Douglas, and Mason, who would seek an opportunity to disparage British motives, but other American politicians would continue to favor English constitutional monarchy over czarist autocracy. Furthermore, by 2 March 1854 there were some hopeful signs that a commercial and fishing treaty might yet be concluded to the mutual advantage of Britain, Canada, and the United States.[4]

After my despatches of the 27th were made up, telegraphic news arrived from the North that the railroads had been so damaged by the recent snowstorm that it would be quite impossible for mail from here to reach Boston in time for the Cunard packet of Wednesday the 1st of March. I am accordingly determined to send them by the American packet which leaves New York on Saturday next, the 4th instant. They will go by messenger to New York and I have directed the Consul to select some trustworthy British subject among the passengers to take charge of the despatches to Liverpool. Consequently they will reach you without having passed through the American Post Office.

Those Senators whom I have met since Cass' attack on your speech[5] tell me that it made but little effect upon them and that there was a general feeling on both sides of the House not to follow his cry on the subject. The old gentleman seems to have out-talked himself lately and to have become a considerable bore to the Senate. This continued cry of wolf in regard to the aggression and deep-laid conspiracies of England against the United States although a popular theme is beginning to be disregarded. Echoes of his speech are I see in the newspapers, in the "Union" and the "New York Herald". I presume he put them in himself. I enclose copies of them.

In talking with Marcy he reiterated the assurances of the sincere desire of the United States to preserve strict neutrality in the coming war and said "We intend to behave so well in that respect as to soften considerably the objections of England and France to our getting hold of Cuba". This was propounded after the fashion of a joke and I so received it, but I think it was at least half in earnest and was most likely foreshadowing of some proposal to go the whole extent on our side in this war if we only wink very hard at a little filibustering and other operations in regard to Cuba.

I have had today a conversation with Mr. Marcy on the fishery and reciprocity question. I communicated to him the substance of your despatch (No. 19 of the 2nd Ultimo) and also some parts of the letters which I had received from Sir Edmund Head and Gaspard Le Marchant on the same subject.[6] I enclose copies of them. They are answers to what, at your suggestion, I wrote to them confidentially. Mr.

Marcy expressed himself very loath to break off the negotiation and very fearful of the consequences of another fishing season under the present state of the question. He said that he thought (speaking for himself) that all the objections made by Her Majesty's Government might be got over by a concession on the part of the United States except the registry of vessels.[7] On that point he could give me no encouragement at least for the present. There would be too strong an interest arrayed against it to render it possible to carry it. I remarked to him that unfortunately that was the very point upon which the colonies most insisted. He concluded by saying that he would nevertheless do all he could to bring the matter to a negotiation and he is about to send to his Mr. Andrews the United States Consul in New Brunswick who has been confidentially consulted by him in all this business and who is in full possession of the views and feelings of all parties in the United States in regard to it. Mr. Andrews is the author of the able and full report upon the commerce of the United States with the British colonies, of which, I think I have already sent a copy home, but of which I sent another in my despatch number 48 of today.[8] He thinks he can exercise some influence upon the colonial legislatures of New Brunswick and Nova Scotia favourable to the negotiation.

With regard to the plan suggested by Sir Edmund Head and Sir Gaspard Le Marchant of sending gentlemen from the colonies to confer with me—if it is thought expedient to adopt it, I would much prefer that they did not come to Washington but I would willingly meet them at New York or elsewhere. Here, while Congress is sitting, they would, as on former occasions, go about the members, talk and do more harm than good.

The tone of the Press with regard to Privateers continues to be all that we could desire, and denounces any attempt of that sort by American citizens in the strongest terms. . . . The great difficulty the Russians would have in the Atlantic would be the want of ports to take their prizes to, but their nominal ports in Russian America and Asia would render it more easy for them in the Pacific. The Russian Consul General in the Sandwich Islands, Monsr. Stoeckl, who is at present virtually in charge of the Russian Legation here, since the death of Monsr. Bodisco, told me that he could give me "his word of honour as a gentleman, that no Russian agent was employed here to organize or suggest privateering by Americans".[9] I have known Monsr. Stoeckl long and intimately, and I don't believe he would have volunteered this declaration if it were untrue. He admitted however that his Government would not *refuse* assistance of this sort if it were offered to them, but insisted that they had not sought it, and that the reports that letters of marque had been sent here by the Russian Government were false.

By 6 March that hardy perennial, Central America, returned to plague Anglo-American relations. Not that the crisis was very acute; rather, it was an irritant which was difficult to ignore. Crampton also mentions the congressional agony concerning how to admit the Kansas and Nebraska territories to statehood without upsetting the balance in the Senate between slave and free states.[10]

The buccaneering projects in regard to Central America on the part of the Transit Route Company seem to me to be a piece of swagger got up by Mr. Joseph L. White to frighten the Government of Nicaragua into terms he wants them to accept. The Transit Route has, from the great numbers of passengers to California, become very profitable, and the Company and Nicaragua are squabbling about the division of the spoils under the terms of the charter. The Nicaraguans claim ten percent on the net receipts. The Company refuses to pay them more than ten percent on the net profits. This seems to be the principal point and by the last advices it would seem that it has been compromised by a new agreement on the part of the Company to pay Nicaragua so much per passenger without relation to receipts or profits, thus avoiding mutual accusations of cheating in the examination of accounts. With regard to taking forceable possession of the Sheppard Grant in Mosquito, I cannot think that the notion is seriously entertained![11] It seems to me, though I may be wrong, to be a part of the same bullying system, because such a project could not possibly pay, if I am to believe those few people who know anything about the country. It would take millions of capital to colonize with the least prospect of success, and the climate is the most deadly on the whole continent of America. If Mr. White or his friends were to go there on such a speculation we should be deprived of the advantage of ever seeing them again. The Schemes of Mr. Squier in regard to Honduras I regard as more dangerous because they may give food to Messrs. Cass and Company and breed trouble for us in Congress about Ruatan[12] and Mosquito.

I am sorry to say that the Nebraska Bill has passed the Senate.[13] Not that it signifies to us in itself, but because it leaves the Senate idle and consequently ready for mischief.

Mr. Marcy has spoken to me again very earnestly about the fisheries. He fears collision there next season if we break off the negotiation. Upon every point except the registry he seems inclined to give in. With regard to this point however and the coasting trade there is feeling beginning to grow up in the country favourable to our views. The agriculturalists and the Southerners say that refusal to admit foreigners to the coasting trade and shipbuilding constitutes a monopoly in favour of the North and East and keeps up freights on their produce, and that now that Free Trade has been adopted in other things they won't stand an exception of this sort in favour of New England: this feeling will I think ripen, but I fear it will be a long time before it bears fruit. However, an influential Southern Senator is getting up an onslaught on the subject, and it will at least be fairly brought before the country. You can easily understand that Mr. Marcy, a New York man, does not dare to show a symptom of yielding on it;—neither does Mr. Cushing of Boston—and they are the two strongest in the Cabinet. Mr. Pierce is also a "down Easterner" and would have Yankee land upon him if he gave in on the shipbuilding interest. Mr. Hincks of canada is going to England and will probably converse with you on this question.

Two weeks later a new episode, the *Black Warrior* affair, provided an awkwrd diversion. The *Black Warrior* was a merchant ship that sailed from Mobile, Alabama, carrying a hundred bales of cotton to New York. En route it stopped at Havana, where it tried unsuccessfully to conceal its cargo from the Spanish customs officials. In theory, therefore, it was liable to seizure of the goods and a fine amounting to twice their value, or confiscation of the vessel itself. However, the Spanish were always reluctant to provide the United States with any pretext for a punitive expedition against Cuba.[14]

In spite of the bellicose message and the swaggering newspaper articles in its support, the thing [*Black Warrior* affair] has fallen very flat. Nobody believes that a good quarrel can be made out of it, and everybody sees why the attempt to get one up is made. The truth is that the Nebraska Question, although it was got thro' the Senate, is going all wrong in the House and in the Country. Mr. Pierce, by suddenly throwing himself into the arms of the South on that matter, has *not* propitiated them and has injured himself irreparably in the North, on which, being his own section, it is of course more essential for him not to lose his hold. A state election in New Hampshire, his own state, where his party was paramount, has just taken place, with so awful a falling off of their majority that they nearly lost the Governorship, and are left in a minority in one of the branches of the Legislature.

The other subject of tribulation is the Gadsden Treaty with Mexico.[15] This is now before the Senate in secret session. I understand, however, that it is in a bad way and, what is worse, that its opponents have got the evidence of a monstrous pecuniary job in connection with the Garay Grant in which Mr. Whipple, the President's partner in legal business at Concord, in New Hampshire, and other intimate friends of his are deeply concerned.[16] All this will probably soon come out, and the Treaty very likely be rejected in consequence. You see therefore that they have good cause for wishing to give a sop to the "Demos" to divert his attention. I am only afraid that they are desperate enough to rush into a war with Spain, or do some other outrageous thing to save themselves.

A week later Crampton was able to report that, as improbable as it seemed, certain American politicans were willing to contemplate a rapprochement with Russia in order to facilitate America's acquisition of Cuba.[17]

Although the "Black Warrior" affair may, I think, if the Spanish Government acts with prudence, be settled without producing an international quarrel, there is, I fear, mischief brewing about Cuba. This European war will not pass over without a question . . . of whether we are to see Cuba become part of the United States, or to determine to prevent it by force. . . . As they say here, "we shall have to face the music" on that point before long.

I have reason to think—but as this letter goes by post I must defer entering into particulars—that something wrong in regard to this subject is going on in the Executive or secret sessions of the Senate which have lately been long and frequent. Certain political leaders of influence who expressed other opinions before are, it appears, now leading off in favour of an alliance or friendly understanding with Russia against us, giving as a pretext what they call your hostile declaration in the House of Lords, and as a political reason the excellent opportunity such position would afford for the acquisition of Cuba. . . .

The Nebraska bill has been referred to a committee of the whole House on the state of the Union by a vote of 110 to 95. This, I am told, virtually *kills* the bill for this session as it gives its opponents the power of prolonging its discussion ad infinitum. This vote is looked upon as a severe blow to the Administration.

The Gadsden Treaty with Mexico is not yet confirmed by the Senate, and is, I am told, strongly opposed.

Any diplomat worth his salt had to have private sources of information in Congress, and in 1852–53 John M. Clayton, the senator from Delaware, was perhaps the favorite governmental liaison. By 1854, however, Clayton was frequently under fire from his senatorial colleagues for having deceived them with respect to the 1850 treaty on Central America, whereupon Crampton increasingly came to depend upon Charles Sumner, senator from Massachusetts and a staunch advocate of emancipation, for inside information.[18] Sumner remained a strong advocate of good Anglo-American relations, a regular correspondent of British politicians like John Bright, and a vital force for understanding and moderation during the American Civil War.

Although this Government [United States] will of course be very glad to take any concession they can get in regard to neutral rights, I do not perceive any disposition on their part to respond to our desire to go hand in hand with the United States in making privateering piracy. Mr. Marcy indeed said that he could hold out but little encouragement to me that any more severe penalties would be attached to privateering than those provided by the existing laws of neutrality of 1818, and he recurred to the fact that this law does not prohibit a citizen of the United States from equipping privateer vessels *without* the territory of the United States. I could not help expressing some surprise that any difficulty should be felt on the part of the United States to make the same agreement with us on the subject of privateers as they had made with other nations:—for instance, Spain. Mr. Marcy could give me no better reason for this than his opinion that Congress would not agree to the same arrangement being made with us. I am not however disposed to agree in this with Mr. Marcy. I believe on the contrary that the general feeling of the country is pretty strong against privateering, and I cannot think that there would be any objection in Congress to make privateering by neutrals piracy, more particularly if the measure was coupled with some relaxation on our part in favour of neutral commerce.

What I hinted to you in my last letter as having occurred in the Senate in secret session very much confirms this view. It was that Mr. Douglas and several other Democratic Senators and great pillars of the Administration had "led off" strongly in favour of an alliance between the United States and Russia—founding their arguments upon the proof afforded by your Speech in the House of Lords on the 31st. of January, that an alliance already existed between France and England hostile to the United States. My informant was Mr. Sumner of Massachusetts, a strong free-soil Northern man and anti-annexationist. Now, altho' his fears of the machinations of the South may lead him to take an exaggerated view of things, I cannot help thinking that there is something in what he says. It will, at all events, explain the un-natural partiality affected by certain ultra Democrats here to the Czar, and the evident backwardness of the Government to enter into our views in regard to maritime affairs. . . .

With regard to the reports of the proceedings of Russian Agents here for building vessels of war and securing the services of privateers, I think that on the whole (tho' I may be wrong in this) that they have been greatly exaggerated, and that these ideas, although they have no doubt presented themselves to the minds of many, are gradually being abandoned on the true American principle that on the whole such operations are not likely to pay. In fact, the nearly complete blockade which we shall be enabled to keep up of every Russian port seems to place an almost insuperable difficulty to the profitable execution of either of these objects.

Crampton may have taken malicious pleasure describing the pathetically crude ways recommended by American politicians to acquire Canada, but underlying his sarcasm was the genuine fear that such a fantastic undertaking could in fact be tried. Should rebellion occur again in the North American provinces as it had in the 1830s, Americans might well seize the opportunity to invade; alternatively, if John Mitchel's scheme to get at England through an attack on Canada succeeded, it could precipitate a larger conflict.

Once the Crimean War had broken out, Britain felt especially uneasy about her overseas colonies. Periodically she would make gestures of armed power, particularly by dispatching naval reinforcements, in order to remind the world that she was still a force to be reckoned with. Similarly, during the American Civil War, England looked on as if it were being held hostage by the United States, and should Britain provide the South with too much support, the North might attack Canada and become embroiled in a two-front war. This threat underlay the British government's generous grant of a large measure of self-government to Canadians in 1867.[19]

A Mr. Campbell of Ohio has offered a Resolution in the House of Representatives that the President be requested to negotiate with Great Britain for the cession of Canada to the United States: the thing was laughed at, but still 29 members voted for it.[20] It was done of course for Irish popularity and with reference to a sort of Proclamation that I send you today in my despatch No. 89 issued by John Mitchel to the Irish, ordering an invasion of Canada by the Irish here, to be aided by a rising of the Irish there.[21] Canada seems, however, to be now very prosperous and therefore very loyal, and even the worst Canadian radical papers scotch Mitchel's amiable proposal.

I had written so far when the mail arrived bringing me your letter of the 24th Ultimo containing the confidential draft of the Declaration respecting Neutrals & Letters of Marque.[22] Altho' it is Sunday, I immediately called upon Mr. Marcy at his house and have just had a long and satisfactory conversation with him on this subject and in general upon the relations of the two countries, including an explanation of the passage in your speech to which exception was taken or pretended to be taken. Mr. Marcy was evidently delighted with this declaration and said emphatically, "you may say to Lord Clarendon that the position taken by the British Government in regard to this matter is *entirely satisfactory* to us. It relieves us from a load of apprehension as to the effect which might be produced upon the friendly relations of countries by a harsh or even stringent exercise of belligerent rights against our commerce by England and France, even admitting that those rights are in accordance with the acknowledged Law of Nations. You have been long enough here," he said, "to know as well as I do that there is a nerve in this country in regard to maritime questions with Great Britain which will be touched, and we have unfortunately a sufficient number of madmen among us who would not fail to avail themselves of any opportunity which might be afforded to them to press upon it with a view to forwarding other wild plans and schemes which they favour in regard to Cuba. With regard to privateering by our citizens, the British Government have now adopted the very measure best calculated to prevent it. By leaving our commerce undisturbed, they have removed the temptation to individuals to engage in such hazardous enterprises. My apprehensions in this respect were founded upon the consideration that if any great amount of our merchant shipping was thrown out of its natural and usual work by a strict enforcement of belligerent rights, then it would naturally seek for employment in less legitimate and more hazardous pursuits. This will not be the case if they find they can carry on their usual occupation. Our people, as you know, are not very apt to embark in speculations which are not likely to yield a good return. Now, altho' by privateering a great deal of mischief might be done by the destruction of property, little gain would attend it when we consider the difficulty that a privateer would have getting his prize regularly condemned and sold, and this under the circumstances of the present war would be attended with great difficulty. It is true however that a smart steamer or two on the Pacific might do you injury by destroying your whaling vessels, but they could not make prizes of them, and no Yankee would engage in such an operation. Although I think your Government may be relieved of any serious apprehension on this score, and at all events we will rigidly enforce our neutrality law which is sufficiently stringent for the purpose."

I shall, nevertheless, keep this subject steadily in view.

On 1 May, Crampton had more to say about the Gadsden Treaty with Mexico.[23]

I am afraid the sort of suspension of hostilities against us by our friends in the Senate has been only owing to their being engrossed continually in secret session upon the Gadsden Treaty with Mexico. The discussion of that matter is however now over. The Treaty was, it appears, in the first instance rejected; and then taken up again by a vote "to reconsider": when it, or rather a very much modified version of it, was adopted. I presume, however, this will not be rejected by Santa Anna, as it still gives him ten millions of dollars cash in hand; and the money was of course his main object in treating at all, as he wants it to enable him to hold his ground as dictator. The remarkable part of the thing is that a party has formed itself in the Senate sufficiently strong to be able to reject the clause for taking another slice of Mexico on the avowed ground of being opposed to any further extension of the territory of the United States. Mr. Clayton some time ago told me that he and some others here determined to form a party and take their stand on this principle, but I confess I did not feel sanguine as to their success.

It continued to be a source of some comfort to Great Britain that the United States had such a small navy. On the other hand, this also played into the hands of those who advocated the use of privateers.[24]

I am sorry to say that I am not able to contradict what was told you as to the view taken of privateering here. So far from countenancing any change in the law of nations by which the practice should be abolished, it is now the fashion to cry it up as a truly national and pre-eminently American mode of carrying on warfare: privateers are spoken of as the "noble militia of our seas" and mild and virtuous men like Mr. Everett actually become sentimental and indulge in "ornate oratory" in favour of pensions being granted to the widows and orphans of such of them as were knocked on the head during the last war with us. You will have already seen from what I said in my letter of the 1st Instant, the sort of argument which is used on the subject; and you will also have remarked that in his answer to the communication of the Queen's Declaration respecting neutrals and privateers, Mr. Marcy does not say a word about the latter subject. The fact is that, having a very small navy and that in no very available condition, they make no secret that they would let loose every private ship that could be armed, in case of a war. They avow that they can't afford to be magnanimous or civilized in this matter; and therefore take the line of crying up privateering as a popular, national and patriotic proceeding as compared with the manner in which war is carried on by the "hired assassins" of which the armies and navies of Europe are composed.

On 26 May 1854 a riot broke out in Boston over the incarceration of Anthony Burns, a slave who had escaped from Virginia and made his way to Massachusetts. In the ensuing fracas, one soldier was killed and about sixteen whites and blacks were arrested. Under the provisions of the Fugitive Slave Law, Burns was eventually returned to Norfolk, Virginia. This law of 1850 had been part of the so-called compromise and allowed slave owners to recover "property" anywhere in the country.[25]

The Nebraska Bill is passed at last. It will produce no immediate effects, if indeed it ever produces any in the part of the world to which it immediately relates: but it is a victory of the South over the North and will be, and indeed to a certain extent already is, attended by a reaction against the South in the North: the bitterness of feeling which its advocates pretended it was to eradicate does not appear to have been much appeased, if we are to judge from the very serious riot which occurred at Boston the day before yesterday about a fugitive Slave, in which the Deputy Marshall of the United States was killed, and troops had to be called out. The South however are triumphant and have advanced their standard further than they would have dared to do during the last thirty years. An article was pointed out to me in the "Southern Quarterly Review", a journal of high reputation[26] and the organ of the South, and occupying a position in regard to that party analogous to that which the "Quarterly" does to the Conservatives in England, in which it goes so far as to advocate the reopening of the African slave trade as the only means of fixing and perpetuating the power of the Southern States and guarding them from Northern encroachment.

The spring of 1854 seemed auspicious for the passage of a reciprocity treaty: Crampton had devoted several years to preparing the ground, using the services of the secret lobby called the Organization; and Lord Elgin, the governor-general of Canada, returned from London, where it had been decided to make him Britain's chief negotiator in the proceedings. The British thereby hoped to assure the tacit compliance of the Canadian provinces with any commercial treaty that Lord Elgin might conclude with the American secretary of state. Lord Elgin reached Washington in early May, and by 12 June Crampton was able to report success.[27]

You will no doubt have received from Lord Elgin the Treaty which he has signed with the United States Government. He is now gone North, and altho' he will probably have to face a good deal of grumbling in Nova Scotia and New Brunswick in consequence of the cession of the fisheries without the American registry for colonial vessels or the abolition of the bounty on fish being obtained, I feel no doubt that he will have sufficient influence in the colonies generally to get their legislatures to act without delay and pass the necessary acts for carrying the arrangement into effect. On this side we have to face Congress, and here I must confess that my experience of the unmanageable nature of that illustrious Assembly and of its extreme slowness in all matters of practical importance (for it is quick enough in blowing up mischief and agitation) does not leave me without the apprehension of some provoking defeat or postponement of the measure by the adoption of artful dodges either by some one of the local interests that may not be pleased with their part in it, or by the South, out of spite to the North in regard to the anti-Nebraska excitement now prevailing—the

Slave Riot at Boston—or some other cause.[28] I yesterday spoke to Marcy on the subject, asking him what the prospect was, and how the Government intended to proceed. He told me in substance, that the Treaty would shortly be submitted to the Senate, but that he preferred in the first instance to have some talk with the representatives of those Interests more immediately affected by it. He said he feared we should have a good deal of opposition with regard to coal—the delegations from Pennsylvania, Maryland & Virginia declaring themselves strongly opposed to it. Maine also is making opposition to the admission of colonial lumber. He did not seem to despair of overcoming or neutralizing this opposition and concluded by saying "if we can fix these points, I think with the rest of the Treaty we shall get along". Whatever Congress may do, I nevertheless sincerely rejoice that Lord Elgin signed the Treaty. If we are obliged to defend our rights at the fisheries this season, we shall at all events stand in a better position than we have hitherto done. The American fishing interests can have no pretext for complaint against any measure we may take for the purpose, as their exclusion from free participation in the colonial fisheries will henceforth rest upon the shoulders of their own Government and Congress.

As regards the Colonies, Lord Elgin entirely agreed with me in the opinion I have before expressed to you that the admission of their produce free to the immense and increasing market of the United States was a general advantage to them so important as to be well worth purchasing even at some sacrifice to local interests. We also concur in thinking the measure of the greatest political importance, as removing the only disadvantage under which the Colonies labour in consequence of not being members of the American Union, and thus taking away every motive for annexation. The old exclusive Colonial System by which a sort of wall of brass was to be built between a Colony and every other Country but the Mother Country having been necessarily long since abandoned, it was really most impolitic to leave just sufficient restriction to cause annoyance, without being enough to check the growth of large commercial relations and consequently community of interests between two Countries in the relative positions of the British Colonies and the United States. . . .

With regard to Central American affairs, it would seem from the last news from Greytown that the municipal government of that place is falling to pieces. In the meantime we, who have all the odium here of attempting to make ourselves masters of Central America thro' our Protectorate of the Mosquito Government at that point, have neither Consul, Vice-Consul, nor Agent of any sort there to represent or protect it or even to let us know what is passing. The Mosquito Government without a British Consul and Man of War to represent it, I need scarcely say, is one of those things which will utterly disappear in any scrimmage which takes place among the Yankee and other desperados and adventurers who frequent that country in the shape of Canal Companies, Land Companies, and Passengers to and from California. Mr. Borland has, I understand, been urging this Government to send an American Man of War to Greytown to protect American interests and to average the indignity done to his diplomatic character, but I don't think Mr. Marcy has espoused his cause very warmly.

Two weeks later Crampton was still preoccupied with the prospects of the Reciprocity Treaty and highly desirous to secure Senate confirmation before the congressional session ended.[29]

The Treaty signed by Lord Elgin is now before the Senate and Mr. Marcy says that on the whole it has a fair prospect of success. He has had a good deal of conversation with the members from Pennsylvania who object to the admission of colonial lumber, and he sums up by saying that in his opinion things at present "look auspicious" for the passing of the Treaty. I am however bound to tell you that some of the Senators who I am afraid are more likely to judge correctly how things are going, do not concur in this opinion. They tell me that they fear the admission or rejection of Reciprocity is going again to be made a *sectional*, that is to say a Northern and Southern question, and that consequently the Treaty will be defeated or at all events not passed this Session; thus leaving us with the "fishery difficulty" on our hands again this season.

Some of the Southern members, I am informed, are going to propose as an amendment to the Treaty that the Fugitive Slave Law should be extended to Canada as a *sine quá non* to the Southern States entering into any reciprocal commercial arrangement with her! I have expressed the hope to some of the better-disposed Southern men that if they really feel it their duty to oppose the Treaty they will do it on some grounds in regard to which a reasonable compromise may be found and not by a proposal which would seem as if they meant to laugh at us, and which would be sure to call forth both in England and in the Provinces those very remarks about slavery in regard to which so much soreness is felt, and which are by no means calculated to increase the good feeling which all reasonable Southern men admit it to be their interest to maintain with Great Britain. The South is however just now both elated by its late success in the Nebraska question and irritated by the anti-slavery reaction which has been produced thereby in the North, as evinced by the late fugitive Slave riot at Boston and the frequent hanging in effigy of Mr. Douglas and other Northern men who voted for the Nebraska Bill. I fear therefore that they are bent upon mischief, and this brings me to another Southern move of a very michievous character mentioned in my despatches of today: I mean the proposal to abrogate the 8th article of the Treaty of Washington and to transfer their Squadron from the coast of Africa to that of Cuba.[30] Some of the principal Northern men, particularly Mr. Seward, Senator from New York, who is a very clear-sighted politician, has expressed to me a good deal of alarm at this proposal which seems to him to look more like a real step in the direction of Cuba than anything which has yet occurred; and both on this account and on the account of its objectionable character as regards the slave trade, he is going to oppose it with all his forces, which are very considerable. I have furnished him with all the arguments against it which our slave trade papers contain, as well as with a complete refutation of the "Africanization" charge against us, which is made to be one of the excuses for the measure. I think he will succeed in defeating it, for the anti-slavery feeling of the North is now fairly aroused, and the more so that the South are beginning to take ground in regard to Slavery which they never dared to do before.

Notwithstanding Buchanan's opposition to the treaty, the chances of its passing were still good, as reported by Crampton in his letter of 24 July.[31]

Congress is to close on the 4th Proximo, and I have consequently been watching the progress of the Reciprocity Treaty with some anxiety. Although the proceedings are in secret session I get pretty good information of what passes, and on the whole the prospect of its ratification is good. I have just had a long conversation with Marcy on the subject when we took the list of the Senate and "counted noses": the result is that, although some important interests oppose it, we shall nevertheless have, unless something unforeseen occurs, a fair majority. You are aware that it requires a majority of two thirds in the Senate to confirm a treaty. The most formidable opposition which we have to encounter has, I have good reason to believe, arisen, as I hinted to you as probable in my last letter of the 17th Instant, from Mr. Buchanan's disapproval of the Treaty; for I find that Mr. Slidell and some others who are "affides" of Mr. Buchanan, and who some little time ago were favourable to the Treaty, have now declared themselves against it. I do not think however that they are sufficiently numerous now to upset it. It is only justice to Mr. Marcy and the President to say that they have been indefatigable in their efforts, and that I have reason to know that the "screw" has been very vigourously applied in several quarters.

During the course of 1854 the British government had hoped to settle their outstanding differences with the United States concerning the definition of neutral rights in time of war. However, there was such an accumulation of resentment on both sides dating back to the American Revolution and the War of 1812 that an accommodation of attitudes was highly unlikely. However, because *no* unpleasant legacy existed between the United States and Russia, it was not surprising that in late July 1854 these two countries concluded a treaty on this subject. In his letter of 31 July, Crampton discussed the ways in which this came about.[32]

A Treaty has been concluded here between the United States and Russia upon the subject of Neutral Rights, and has been approved by the Senate in Executive Session. It has not yet been made public, but I am informed confidentially by a Senator that it consists simply of two articles: the one stipulating that Free Ships are to make Free Goods; and the other that the property of a friend captured on board an enemy ship is to be restored. In short it is just such a treaty as Mr. Marcy last week . . . told me he was about to propose to the Maritime Powers. There is a rumour prevalent that a Russian agent has come or is coming to negotiate the sale of the Russian North American possessions, including Litha,[33] to the United States. I cannot make out that there is any truth in this report yet, and the Russian Legation deny it stoutly. Marcy however has been lately throwing out hints to me of the wish on the part of the United States to purchase Vancouver Island from us, which, if the story of the Russian treaty is true, would look as if a design was entertained by the United States of getting exclusive possession of the whole North West Coast of this Continent.

I cannot quite agree with Mr. James[34] as to the "alarming extent of the pro-Russian feeling here which is biding its time to burst forth". In fact there would be no reason for its holding back nor could it be held back in this country if it really existed. On the contrary, I think more of it is even now manifested than is really felt. You have the exact state of the feeling of a large party in this country when you say England's difficulty is America's opportunity. Those who wish to pursue aggressive schemes are glad to believe or at all events to make it appear that we have our hands full, and they are therefore fond of exaggerating the power and resources of Russia and deprecating ours when they speak of the War: but few attempts are made and none have certainly succeeded, to enlist the sympathies of the country in favour of the Emperor of Russia or his cause. He has been too long looked upon here as the great "Anti-Republican" for any party to venture upon such a course. Besides which the foreign refugee vote, consisting of Germans, Poles, Hungarians, Italians etc., now a very important electioneering element, could never be brought to countenance this idea. The Irish too have been told by their priests that the Emperor is a persecutor of the Roman Catholic Church, which I need not tell you at once settles their opinion of him. The attempt to get up a pro-Russian feeling was principally owing to Senator Douglas who is an arch-Filibustero and anti-Britisher, but his having dropped the subject of late is enough to convince me that it has not been found a productive electioneering speculation, —for it must be observed that catching votes is always at the bottom of any "pro" or "anti" movement undertaken in this country. The great monied and commercial classes in this Country who are very powerful tho' less noisy than the mere politicians, are not favourably disposed to the Emperor, nor do they view the war with satisfaction. They desire peace for the obvious reason that the war has already affected them unfavourably, and they know that peace would not be brought about by any partial successes of the Emperor.

You will see by my Despatch No. 206 of today that an attempt has been made in Congress to bring a bill into the House of Representatives to place ten million dollars at the disposal of the President during the Recess to meet the contingencies alluded to by him in his message respecting the "Black Warrior" affair: in other words, to put it into his power to make war on Spain and seize Cuba without having obtained the previous consent of Congress. This bill has utterly failed, but even if it had succeeded in the House it would have been rejected by the Senate. In fact the jealousy of the different branches of this Government in regard to their Constitutional prerogatives is a much stronger feeling than even the wish to acquire Cuba, which is saying a good deal.

Mr. Marcy still speaks as if he thought the Senate would pass the Reciprocity Treaty: but he admits that it hangs fire sadly, and that time is now very short. I believe from what I hear from other quarters besides Mr. Marcy that there is the requisite majority, but I begin to fear that although the Treaty will not be rejected, it will be staved off by some Parliamentary maneouvre, and that the Senate will separate without voting on it at all, thus leaving us in a very awkward position in regard to the fisheries. But even if the Senate does now pass the Treaty, it will be impossible to get the requisite legislation in the House of Representatives before next session, and it would be a delicate question to know how far we might practically relax our protective measures at the fisheries upon the faith of the House of Representatives performing its part as soon as it reassembles in December next.

Crampton was understandably delighted to report on 3 August that the Senate, in executive session, approved the Reciprocity Treaty, and he promised to keep Clarendon apprized of developments towards its eventual implementation by Congress.[36]

I profit by the departure of the American steamer from New York the day after tomorrow to announce to you that the Senate yesterday approved the Reciprocity Treaty in Executive Session. Every effort will be made to get the House of Representatives to pass the necessary legislative acts *today* or tomorrow morning. The Bill was drafted & printed last night and laid on members' tables this morning. If no factious opposition is made, or anything else untoward occurs, we may yet have the Treaty complete as far as the U.S. are concerned before Congress adjourns at midday tomorrow. I shall endeavour to let you know its fate thro' the telegraph[37] if I cannot otherwise get the news to New York in time for the Packet.

Four days later Crampton described how the treaty squeaked through the Senate at the last possible moment. He then advised Lord Clarendon concerning the extraordinary events that had led up to the most recent nasty occurrence at Greytown. There had been considerable tumult back in May 1854 because a man named T. T. Smith, the captain of an American steamer on the San Juan River, had allegedly killed a native Mosquito Indian. When Smith next returned to Greytown, the local authorities tried to arrest him and have him brought to trial, but the American consul to the Central American states, Solon Borland, gave Smith sanctuary, whereupon the Greytown Council ordered Borland's arrest. However, both managed to escape the town's jurisdiction. Captain George Hollins and the steamship *Cyane* next appeared on the scene and ordered the local council to make formal apologies to Borland and Smith. He also claimed twenty-four thousand dollars in damages supposedly done to the property of the Accessory Transit Company.

When no response was forthcoming to this ultimatum, Hollins bombarded the village for six hours; not entirely satisfied, he then organized a landing party and set fire to the remaining huts and buildings of the town. Although the inhabitants had previously withdrawn to safer ground, their abodes were destroyed. Therefore, the inhabitants—American, British, French, Indian, and Latin American—sought in vain to recover damages from the United States government.[38]

The Reciprocity Treaty passed by a good majority in the Senate, and no opposition was made to it in the House; but it was a close run thing in point of time. The Government certainly took pains to get the measure passed, which was only done by pacifying the South. We were however very near losing the Treaty, for this Session at least, by the difficulty of getting the Senate into Executive Session before the adjournment. There were matters of public discussion in which they were hotly engaged, and the motion for a secret session had several times failed by one or two votes. On this I appealed to my old friend Mr. Clayton, who I knew to be at the bottom of it, and I must say he acted fairly. He told me frankly that he must vote against the Treaty but he admitted that there was now a two-thirds majority for it, and he consented to withdraw his opposition to the motion for going into secret session. This accordingly carried the next day just in time to get the Treaty through. When once brought to a vote the direct opposition was small, being principally confined to Pennsylvania on account of coal, and to Maryland, Delaware and some others of what are called the Middle States on account of wheat, the price of which they think will be lowered. Mr. Clayton's opposition, besides this, was founded on the, I think, erroneous idea that the measure will accelerate the annexation of Canada to the United States. A great many votes, however, have no doubt been given *for* the Treaty on the same grounds. I hope the colonies will now make no unreasonable opposition or delay in passing the necessary legislation, & I think it lucky that Lord Elgin is still in office there, for he will be better able to keep their shoulders to the collar than a new Governor General.

Unlucky too as the Greytown catastrophe is in itself, it is still fortunate it did not occur earlier, for a stirring up of the Central American question in Congress would very likely have spoilt all: as it is they have separated without having the time to enter on the subject. Public feeling is certainly not in favour of the Act or the manner of the destruction of Greytown, but I am afraid that when we come to make our representations against it an attempt will be made to justify Capt. Hollins and to conceal his misdeeds in the smoke of abuse of the British Government for their interference in that part of the world. . . .

. . . I send you today (in despatch No. 214) the President's message with the accompanying documents respecting the destruction of Greytown.[39] I don't think Marcy's instructions quite bear out what he said to me in regard to the alleged insult to Mr. Borland, *not* being one of the chief grievances which Capt. Hollins was to redress. It seems to me to figure quite as conspicuously in the Demand as the alleged robbery of the Transit Compy's property. The monstrous part of Capt. Hollins' and Mr. Fabens'[40] proceeding seems to me to be that they took advantage of the state of anarchy of Greytown to make a demand which they must have known the place was not then in a condition to answer and without giving the more respectable people of the place time to meet and form some sort of Government; a demand too with which they must have known it was utterly out of the power of anybody at Greytown to comply; for I suppose Capt. Hollins might as well have thought of finding 20 millions Sterling as $24,000 dollars among the 500 wretched ragamuffins, most of them negroes, who compose the population of Greytown. Even supposing the story of the robbery of the boat with flour and cornmeal is true, the demand was exhorbitant; and a cannonade of six hours was not very likely to help the people of Greytown to form a government or to find the money. I am afraid our friend Mr. Joseph L. White of the Transit Company is at the bottom of all this. It is evidently in the interest of the Company, and it has accordingly always been their endeavour to monopolize all the collateral profits which accrued from the forwarding of passengers across the Isthmus, and almost all the squabbles which have taken place have arisen from the jealousy of the Greytownians participating in this business. By the destruction of Greytown the Company will have everything their own way, and their interests alone are subserved by this iniquitous proceeding. . . .

The plan for removing the United States' Squadron from the Coast of Africa to that of Cuba has been successfully staved off for this Session, tho' I suppose it will be tried again when Congress reassembles.

The subject of domestic interest which, from the excitement it created, was near swamping the Reciprocity Treaty, was the "River & Harbour Improvement Bill". It was passed after hot debates by both Houses—but it has been vetoed by the President. Under so unassuming a title it involves one of the great questions upon which the whig and Democratic Parties are divided. The latter contend that the Federal Government and Congress cannot constitutionally spend the federal revenues on public works, and that such works must be undertaken by the governments of the separate states within whose limits they are to be constructed: the whigs maintain the contrary and I believe more popular opinion.

Another question regarding internal matters, but which affects us indirectly, lies over in an incomplete state. It regards what is called the Homestead Bill, by which, if it is passed, as I believe it will be, every person declaring his intention of becoming a citizen of the United States will be entitled to 160 acres of land *gratis*, such a grant being now given for about 200 dollars. The policy of the measure is very justly impugned, but it is of course popular among the masses; it is evident however that it would add a fresh stimulus to emigration from Ireland, which scarcely seems to be required.

My French colleague, Monsr. de Sartiges, is in a state of great alarm at a report which I have already alluded to, that a negotiation is on foot for the sale to the United States of the Russian territories in America. He wants me to draw up with him a joint protest against this plan and send it to the United States' Government. This I object to because there is really nothing to go upon but newspaper gossip, and we should only expose ourselves to an impertinent answer. Besides which I have ascertained that no proposal of this sort has come to the Senate and consequently, even supposing that such a project was entertained, which I confess I do not believe, it could not be acted upon until Congress meets again in December, and this would afford ample time for our governments to determine upon what ought to be done, and instruct us accordingly. Both the Department of State and the Russian Legation deny the existence of anything of the sort, but the idea is kept up by the "New York Herald" in consequence of the arrival of a Dr. Cottman[41] from Russia who they say is charged with the mission in question.

By 13 August Crampton was hoping to escape the heat and inactivity of Washington in order to visit Canada and Nova Scotia to urge the prompt approval of the Reciprocity Treaty there.[42]

Congress has now adjourned, and Marcy, completely prostrated by fatigue and the heat which has been more insufferable this year than I ever remember it, is going to revive himself by going for a few weeks to one of the watering places. As under these circumstances no business of importance can be transacted, I have thought it a good opportunity to fulfil my promise to Admiral Fanshawe and to pay him a visit at Halifax.[43] He has pressed me lately to do so, as he wishes to be "insensed" about Greytown and our position in Central America—subjects which are quite new to him. I shall therefore start this evening and go by the Cunard packet which leaves Boston on Wednesday the 16th Instant. I may perhaps be also of some use in pressing on the colonial governments the expediency of speedy legislation in regard to the Reciprocity Treaty, and I shall be back in Washington in time to exchange the Ratifications of that Treaty as soon as they can be sent out.

By Crampton's next letter of 10–11 September, American public opinion was divided regarding the exploits of Captain Hollins at Greytown. Some regarded him as a hero who had avenged insults to American pride. Others justified his actions on the grounds that he had warned the inhabitants and had resorted to force only as his patriotic duty, not standing to gain anything personally from the action. An undercurrent of criticism also existed, deploring such high-handed measures and urging the government to make amends.[44]

The attempt to whip up public opinion has been made just in the way I anticipated in my last letter: a series of venomous articles against England, raking up every lie about us from the last war, bringing up Copenhangen,[45] Warren Hastings,[46] and all the hacknied topics of abuse, has appeared in the "Union"—together with letters from "Our Correspondents" who probably reside in Washington City, proving that we have been terribly beaten by the Russians—but without the desired effect. The cry has now been taken up: all the considerable Papers continue to reprobate the Greytown business, and the "Union", tho' after a fashion the Ministerial organ, is not a paper of sufficient influence or circulation to turn the tide of public feeling. All these difficulties and dilemmas, however, make Mr. Pierce's Administration, as you justly remark, about as dangerous a one as we have ever had to deal with: they would be too glad to avail themselves of any chance collision which might occur between our ships, or any other accident to change the ground of the questions which embarrass them, and as I before said, to trick the Country into a course of violent action, for the effects of which they would evade all responsibility.

A short conversation I had writh Mr. Marcy the day before yesterday gave me a pretty clear idea of what was going on about the Sandwich Islands, and my interview today, which I have not had time to report fully in my despatch No. 224 has, as you will see, entirely confirmed my suspicions.[47] In fact, they have thrown off the mask completely, and it would be useless to trouble you with any of the circumlocutions by which I was informed that the annexation of the Sandwich Islands is a "fixed fact" in the intention of Mr. Pierce's Government. There will be a considerable opposition to it in the Senate no doubt; but I do not trust to its ultimate efficiency when material ambition or vanity is to be gratified. My interview with Mr. Marcy took place so late as only to allow me time to give an account of it in this very hasty manner.

In a long letter written on 25 September Crampton reiterated his abiding distress concerning the American newspaper press, repeating his lament that in private the government would speak well of Britain but would do nothing positive to discourage the press from continuing its personal vendetta against almost all things English.[48]

The efforts of the "Union" and "Star" have not succeeded in whipping up public opinion in favour of Capt. Hollins, nor are they likely to do so. Other papers, such as the "New York Herald", which would only be too ready to adopt any feasible pretext for defying England, and which would be the first to bully their own Administration into doing so, have never attempted to take up the present Greytown affair and Mr. Borland for that purpose—a pretty good proof they don't think them available. You will perceive from the enclosed article that the "Herald" still condemns Hollins and Borland, and also deviates into truth about Soulé. The "Union" and "Star" are both very insignificant papers and little read or quoted out of the immediate neighbourhood of Washington. The "Union" in fact, I have reason to believe, would not, in the hands of its present Editor, pay its own expenses by its circulation and is only profitable by the money it receives for the official printing. This "bonus" I need scarcely tell you was part of the "Spoils", and was given as a reward for electioneering and other political services. Hence the *real* reason why the Government can't or won't, even if they disapprove of the outrageous language of the "Union", adopt the obvious remedy of selecting a paper of more moderate principles for the publication of official documents. The truth is that Public Printing, being a very lucrative concern, and one of the best things the Government has to give away, is in reality conferred upon some individual who represents a whole clique of political jobbers among whom the money is, I believe, divided. The Government is of course engaged and committed with these people, and this kind of underhanded political engagement has, in this country, all the cogency of "debts of honour" among low gamblers and lags, who are obliged to be punctual in paying them in order to be able to carry on their trade.

I had, a few days before I received your letter, a long discussion with Mr. Marcy on the very subject of the "Union". He went over the old ground and I made to him the very observations you make to me. I said it was no doubt satisfactory to me to be informed that the insults and reiterated misstatements of the "Union" did not proceed from the Government, but as this statement was not appended to the articles which contained those insults and misstatements, and as I could not publish his (Mr. Marcy's) disclaimer of them, they necessarily went forth to the world clothed with the apparent sanction of the Administration. If, I said, the Government cannot undertake to review each article before it is printed and thus become responsible for them, why not put the paper into the hands of an Editor whose decency and discretion they can confide, and in whose general opinions they concur? To this Mr. Marcy found no better answer than that it was extremely difficult in this Country to find a man of sufficient intelligence to carry on a paper at all, and that those who were thus gratified would not submit to be controlled from putting in things they thought "would take". I concluded this I fear very useless discussion by saying that the melancholy part of the matter appeared to be that such things do "take", and that I firmly believed that "those things" created the appetite which they fed. The true answer to my question is however, I suspect, to be found above.

I have been informed on very good authority that the actual penner of the abusive anti-English articles in the "Union" is a Mr. Forney, who is clerk of the House of Representatives and who is supposed to be "par Excellence" the leader or worker of the Kitchen Cabinet above alluded to. He is an intimate personal friend of Mr. Cushing and also a boon companion of the President in certain jolly conciliables, in which it is said that Mr. Pierce reverts to his former taste for too much brandy and water. There may be some gossip in this, but at the same time Mr. Forney certainly is one of the principal "faiseurs" of the Administration: what is more surprising, however, and what does not exactly harmonize with devotion to Mr. Pierce, he is Mr. Buchanan's "Âme d'aimée" and one of the principal workers for running Mr. Buchanan for the next Presidency, the campaign for which is already beginning to loom up.

One of the repercussions of the Democratic party victory that brought Franklin Pierce to the White House in 1852 was the shattering of the Whig party. For a time there was nothing to take its place. While some Whigs tried to revive their party's forces, others abandoned it in favor of the abolitionist or Free-Soil movements. Still others sought to rally support around the cause of native Americanism. The latter was in reaction to the flood of Catholic immigrants arriving on American shores each day from Ireland and the Continent. The Know-Nothings were accused of systematically intimidating foreigners, and the party derived its name from denying knowledge of any such activity. Greytown again presented difficulties that Crampton painstakingly tried to sort out, especially regarding colonization rights according to the Clayton-Bulwer Treaty.[49]

The "Union", wonderful to relate, has let us alone for nearly a whole fortnight and have even gone the length of inserting an article from another paper which talks of the "improved feeling of England" on American affairs. I scarcely flatter myself however that this truce, which may have been the result of my last conversation with Marcy, will be of long endurance; and I rather attribute it to the attention of the Government and its Party being now engaged in Home Politics. The "organs" are in consequence fully occupied in discussing the "Know-Nothings" and other political organizations whose operations in the elections have lately been very disastrous to the Democratic Party. "Know-Nothingism" is a revival of what was called the Native

American Party, and its chief object is to resist by counter-organization the pressure of the Irish vote which, from the effective discipline exercised by the Roman Catholic Priests, acted with a power disproportionate even to its numbers, and was felt to be a real tyranny. The Democratic Party having especially courted the Irish vote, the "Know-Nothings" have for the present thrown themselves into the arms of the Whigs who have consequently been carrying everything before them, especially in the State of New York where Mr. Seward, to the great grief of Mr. Marcy and his friends now reigns paramount.

I fear nevertheless that some more mischief is brewing in regard to Greytown. Mr. Barclay writes to me from New York that he hears from a source on which he relies that the *"Räzee"* "Independence", and the steam frigate "Princeton", the latter to be commanded by Capt. Hollins, are to be sent shortly to Greytown, for what purpose does not well appear, unless it be that they really wish to get into collision with us.[50] I also understand from Mr. Barclay that he is informed that what is called the "Central American Land and Mining Company", whose purpose is supposed to be to take possession of nearly the whole of the Mosquito Territory under the pretense of a Grant from a former King of Mosquito to a Mr. Sheppard, which they have bought, are about to commence their operations by sending down several hundred colonists to take possession of the territory including Greytown itself. It appears that Mr. Cooper, the Senator from Pennsylvania, and Mr. Shields, an Irishman and Senator from Illinois, are engaged in this scheme. It was set on foot as I formerly mentioned to you by Mr. Joseph L. White, Mr. Morgan, and other gentlemen connected with the Canal Company, a circumstance which, taken together with the stories which are circulated in regard to the immense riches of the Mosquito country in mines and land, and the large sums of money which are said to be invested in the speculation of Mr. Cooper and other "prominent citizens" lead me to guess that the whole thing is a stock jobbing humbug, very congenial to the soil where the great Poyais swindle was enacted some thirty years ago, and suitable to the genius of the projectors of the famous Interoceanic Nicaraguan Canal which has been the occasion of so much trouble to us but which I fairly believe neither Mr. White nor anybody else ever dreamt of executing.[51]

Admiral Fanshawe has however written to me to know what course of action I think he ought to adopt against the landing of "Colonists in the Mosquito" and whether "colonization" would not be contrary to the Clayton-Bulwer Treaty. To this I have replied that the Treaty binds both parties not to "colonize" Central America, but that I presume colonization by either of the Governments, or with their sanction is thereby meant. On the other hand I said that the forcible occupation of the country by armed parties under the pretense of colonization would be an act of piracy or filibustering. Of course the United States Government would deny having anything to say to an attempt to colonize by their citizens, particularly under a claim granted by the Mosquito Government which the United States Government does not acknowledge, and would say they could not prevent American citizens settling where they chose. It has always appeared to me that the bargain in the Clayton-Bulwer Treaty that neither party should colonize was an unequal one—for it gives the United States the right to object to the establishment of a colony in the only way we ever do or can found one, that is by the action of the Government, while it leaves them free to colonize in the only way they ever do colonize, that is by the independent squatting of individuals or bands of their citizens. Admiral Fanshawe tells me that he is going to send the "Vestal" down to Jamaica and place her at the disposal of Capt. Henderson to make use of her as circumstances may require. I hope however if the American vessels I have alluded to go to Greytown, that they will either meet with a British force fully equal to their own, in which case I have no doubt they will behave themselves properly, or else that they may meet with none—otherwise we shall have a repetition of Capt. Hollins's late swaggering & violence.

Whenever the Americans were preoccupied with domestic political concerns, Crampton never breathed easily, as he had diagnosed that there was always a tendency for politicians to divert public attention away from internal problems toward external affairs, often at the expense of Britain's reputation.[52]

I have received your letter of the 29th Ultimo. I entirely agree with you that the proceedings of the United States government look very much as if they intended to fall out with us; and altho' I am still of the opinion that they would not like to push matters to actual war, I am very apprehensive that the course they are pursuing may, even without their intending to go so far, really involve us in some serious quarrel. Under the loss of popularity which every election that takes place makes it daily more evident they have incurred in regards to their internal policy, the Administration are evidently trying to draw the attention of the people to Foreign Affairs: with this view they take measures for the annexation of the Sandwich Islands; they seek to acquire a footing at Samana to show they have Cuba steadily in view;[53] they dispute our right to Ruatan; throw doubts on our title to the Falkland Islands; endeavour to eliminate us from the Mosquito protectorate in a manner which may carry with it a humiliation to us and a triumph to them; and all this in order to bring themselves before the people as what they call "whole-hearted Americans" and stiff asserters of the Monroe Doctrine, as well as to show that Mr. Pierce has been endeavouring faithfully to carry out the declarations of his Inaugural Address in favour of the policy to territorial aggrandizement in general and the acquisition of Cuba in particular, altho' nearly half his term is now over without any of these objects having been attained, while the acquisition of Cuba, in spite of Monsr. Soulé's able diplomacy, looks further off than it did some time ago. For the old Anti-English feeling is revived—as the no Popery cry has sometimes been in England, & intense vexation is felt and even avowed by Mr. Marcy and Mr. Cushing that England and France are now formally disapproving and setting their faces against those precious plans, or as they say, interfering in and intriguing against the little acquisitions which the United States want to make while they have acted so differently towards those Powers in generously allowing them to acquire whole empires in India and in Africa without a word of objection. Hence, the Alliance of France & England is gall and wormwood here. It upsets the old established policy of the country of playing them against each other. A good understanding between England and France would never be acceptable to the United States upon general principle, but it is particularly distasteful now that it interferes with some of their favourite objects. It is in vain that they affect to feel and try to get up a sympathy with Russia in order to counteract it. It is not that they hate the Emperor of Russia less, but they hate the Anglo-French alliance more; and altho' they draw imposing pictures of Russian Power, and eagerly adopt and copy the most gloomy croakings they can find or invent as to the prospects of the allies, I can easily perceive that they don't believe them themselves, or at all events, feel a secret misgiving which even their own national vanity to a certain extent is calculated to raise, that Anglo-Saxon fleets & armies are not likely to be demolished as quickly as the "own correspondents" of the "Union" and the "New York Herald" are fond of predicting, or that England and France are about to retire baffled and defeated from the field. It is, however, necessary to show these people that even while the contest lasts, we are not quite reduced to the last gasp, and this is better done by *facts* than words: arrival of the "Colossus" & "Termagant"[54] is a fact exactly of the nature that will be appreciated. To say the truth however, I rely more than anything else on news of some decisive event in the Black Sea, which I trust is by this time taken place, for bringing them to their senses.

American politicians were continually fascinated with the possibility of acquiring Cuba, and President Franklin Pierce was no exception. During the summer of 1854 he encouraged his envoys to Spain, France, and Britain—Pierre Soulé, John Y. Mason, and James Buchanan—to gather somewhere in Europe and assess the prospects. Fearing publicity, the three met at Ostend, Belgium, in October, drew up a "manifesto," and went their separate ways, hoping their deliberations would remain secret. They urged the United States government to purchase Cuba from Spain, but if the mother country proved obdurate, the Americans would be fully justified in seizing the island.

By Crampton's letter of 6 November, news had leaked out, and Secretary of State Marcy, no friend of the Ostend Conference collaborators, had to deny such rumors of potential American aggression.[55]

Mr. Marcy then, dropping the subject of the Sandwich Islands in particular, went on to descant at some length, but without ill humour, upon the general view taken of the policy of the United States by England and France: "I really begin to think," he said, "that you have taken up the idea that we are a dangerous and aggressive sort of people, and yet look at the facts. Here we are with a population and a commerce very nearly equal to your own, and while you maintain strong positions all over the world and large fleets and armies, we have not yet a navy fit to defend one half of our own coasts, and as to an army, why Congress won't give us men enough to keep off the miserable remnants of the Indian tribes which still remain in our back country, much less to make aggressions on our neighbours. Even after the Mexican War when we had got a few more troops together and when I was in the War Department, I was not able to keep a single regiment from being discharged, tho' some of them were actually wanting to protect the frontier from the Indians, and, consequently, you may see in the papers today an account of a shocking massacre by the Indians—a thing perfectly shameful at this time of day, but which arises solely from the exaggerated jealousy of the people and of Congress in regard to giving troops to the Government.[56] Now, is this a state of things to excite, I won't say the fears and suspicions, but the extreme watchfulness which seems to be kept up with regard to the smallest of our movements by some of the European Powers: Sartiges comes here and says "Why you are all Russianized". Well, that's all nonsense: we have nothing to do with Russia and you know our people must always be talking and writing; but if there is any feeling of that sort about just now, it entirely arises from the notion that France & England are to be found thwarting us at every step and interfering with things at this side of the water. As for us, I can safely assure you that far from wishing to get mixed up in those questions of Balance of Power which have involved you all in war in Europe, it is our earnest desire to keep aloof from them altogether. . . ."

Our conversation then turned upon the "Conference" of American Diplomatists at Ostend: I asked him what it all meant: "Well," he said, "there's another thing that has been taken up by your papers as a grave matter, and yet there's nothing in it; at least I know nothing of it. I suppose Mason and Buchanan wanted to talk over matters and things: this, however, I will tell you quite between ourselves that I did not want Mason to go over there, and in fact I told him to come back and he is to come back: you know the sort of man he is, and it was with great unwillingness that I gave him leave to go to Europe strictly about his private affairs; but he spoke to the President and begged very hard to go: my last words to him however were, Mind, Mr. Mason, I have no orders or hints to give you of any sort. You are going to Europe on your own private business or amusement solely." Mr. Marcy then went on to say that Mr. Mason's position as Assistant Secretary of State was very much mistaken if it was supposed that he had any voice in determining the measures taken at the Department of State. In short, he took so much pains to shake off any connection with Mr. Mason that I shall not be at all surprised if it turns out that Mr. Mason has been doing something or other in Europe which Mr. Marcy does not desire to be responsible for.

He then for the first time for many months adverted to Soulé, saying, "there's Soulé too who is *quite* a peculiar man,"—upon which hint I spoke havig hitherto carefully abstained from introducing the subject, and put it to Mr. Marcy's own judgement whether the presence at Madrid of such a *"peculiar man"* as Mr. Soulé, taking into consideration both his former history and late proceedings, was calculated to convey to Europe the impression that the policy which Mr. Marcy had just announced to me of keeping strictly aloof from European complications, in the wisdom of which I entirely concurred, really was that of the United States. Mr. Marcy made very little defence of Soulé, but turned to the subject of Cuba, saying that he could not see what was our objection to its acquisition by the United States, or why we should *interfere* in that matter. To a very obvious remark of mine that our policy in the matter was one of noninterference & of leaving things as they are, he said, "Oh, but even now you are almost as good as possessors of Cuba, for the Spanish are ready to do exactly what you like to tell them." I said to this that in regard to the only thing we had ever desired the Spaniards to do in Cuba, namely to put down the Slave Trade, they were so far from doing what we told them, that it was with the greatest difficulty that we could get them to pay the slightest attention to the treaty engagements with us: but that if he meant that Spain now looked with a more friendly eye to England and France than to the United States as regarded Cuba, that this should excite no surprise when it was considered, as Mr. Marcy himself must admit, that the Spaniards, between threats of piratical invasion on the one hand and the Presidential Inaugural Address and Messages presaging open war with them and asking Congress of money to carry it on on the other, actually lived in a state of siege in Cuba, almost as onerous to them as if actually at war.

Ten days later the implications of the Ostend Conference were still very much in the public limelight, and Marcy continued to deny any sinister overtones.[57]

Mr. Marcy continued our conversations by entering on the subject of the conference of American Diplomatists at Ostend. . . . He said that this matter had been misapprehended; that he could assure me there was no intention on the part of the United States Government to "meddle or make" in the affairs of Europe; the conference had no such object in view. . . . "You know," he said, "that I have never concealed from you that we *want Cuba*. . . . We want it honourably by cession, and for a handsome consideration. Well! there were various facts and considerations connected with that business (which by the bye does not just now offer at all a favourable aspect) in regard to which Buchanan and Mason wished to compare notes and to hear what Soulé had to say." I asked him to what sort of facts and considerations he alluded; he said, "Why, for instance, there's your own people to whom Spain owes money which she will never be able to pay in this world unless she gets the money from us: then there are your merchants, whose business would be immensely increased, as you may judge by California. And Buchanan thinks that there is a feeling of this sort growing up among your business men in England (no doubt "the Buck" has been "incensing" the Spanish Bond-holders, and cultivating the "middle classes") that it would be better for all parties if we had got Cuba. Mason had been looking about him; and in short, we wished to know in what position the matter stood; but there was no notion of stirring up revolutionary sympathies or getting ourselves mixed up with European quarrels, out of which it is already our Policy to keep."

Mr. Marcy however did not inform me to what *conclusion* the Conference had come, or what line of action they recommended. . . . Whatever truth there may be in Mr. Marcy's account, it is nevertheless quite compatible with an intention on Soulé's and Buchanan's part to encourage the discontented spirits of Europe. The ostentatious meeting at Ostend was quite unnecessary for the purpose Mr. Marcy avowed, and signified to the republicans all over Europe, plainer than words could have expressed it, "Hark! we are *conspiring* in your favour!" and this was of course the real meaning of the *meeting* whatever may have been the subjects discussed at it.

I then entered upon the Mosquito question. I expressed your sincere desire to settle that matter once and for all—and my own opinion that the exchange of long historical and argumentative notes, however ably composed, would not do it: Mr. Marcy entirely agreed in this; and after some conversation said that he thought he and I could settle the matter in a short time *if it were left with us*; but I found exactly the sort of unwillingness, or rather fear, which I expected of taking the matter out of Buchanan's hands. Mr. Marcy however spoke out his opinions of "the Buck" so freely on this occasion (though of course as between ourselves) that I cannot help thinking that some rupture between them is at hand. "There's Buchanan," he said, "who's a singular man! Sometimes all easiness and confidence and friendliness; and then again, all of a sudden, God knows why, as captious and jealous as can be. He gets suspicious and gets discontented with himself I believe and everybody else—and what is more singular, and what you'd scarcely believe in a man of his ability, he goes now and puts himself completely into the hands of two fellows, who between ourselves be it said, are about two as arrant knaves as exist—I mean Sanders and Sickles—men of an inferior stamp too altogether.[58] Now in order to give you an idea of the sort of trickery which is resorted to in these matters people have come to me and told me that I ought to send that long concern that Buchanan lately wrote to Lord Clarendon about Mosquito down to Congress with the message; and because I would not do this while the affair is under negotiations, they impute to me political jealousy of Buchanan, and he and his friends are as cross as possible about it. Now I can assure you, upon my honour, that it is not nor ever was my intention to run a political race with Mr. Buchanan for the Presidency or anything else."

I then tried to ascertain, putting aside all controversy in regard to titles and claims and the interpretations of treaties, what it is that the United States Government really want in Central America, and what it really is in our position there that is obnoxious to them: To my enquiries on these points Mr. Marcy said; "My opinion is that (with the exception of Cuba) we want no more territory—our stomach is pretty full already in that respect—all that we require in Central America is the freedom of passage across the Isthmus, now necessary for our communications with California; for if we had a railroad across our own territory, as I trust we shall, I would not attach such importance even to that.[59]—So long however as we are dependent upon that passage for our communications with California, so long will you find our people looking with some jealousy upon any position of yours which seems to give you the power of obstructing it.''

"In that respect," he added, "I think that you will find the question of Ruatan Island most difficult to deal with." I assured Mr. Marcy that he might depend upon it that Great Britain had no design of forming new colonies or taking possession of menacing positions in Central America. I referred him to the negotiations which had already been on foot between Sir Henry Bulwer and Mr. Webster—between Mr. Webster and myself—and to all the communications I had since made to him from my Government, for proofs of this. He would see that Great Britain had been not only willing but anxious to get out of a position which, right or wrong, would give rise to jealousy or misunderstanding between the two countries; that if these negotiations had been without result it was from no indisposition on our part to consent to arrangements which might be satisfactory to the United States, but to the pretension which was set up by a party in this country and which the Government of Nicaragua had evidently been encouraged to take up and persist in, that we were to be triumphantly driven from our position as the acknowledged perpetrators of wrong—the humiliation to be thus inflicted upon us seeming in the eyes of that party to be in fact the great desideratum in the settlement of the affair. This of course could not be submitted to. In the same manner with regard to Ruatan Island, it was not, in my opinion, a possession of any great importance, and had not been settled as a military position, but certainly the way to come to an understanding with us on the subject, was not to summon us peremptorily to haul down our flag—and to threaten to drag it down if we demurred. . . .

Mr. Marcy said, "certainly not . . . and I really think there ought to be no difficulty in adjusting the interests of both countries in Central America.''

In many respects, the year 1854 was the high point of Crampton's diplomatic service in America. The Reciprocity Treaty had at long last been enacted, and American designs on Cuba and the Sandwich Islands failed. Greytown was in shambles due to American high-handedness, inducing the British to reassert their protectorate over the stricken town and its environs. To be sure, Britain was increasingly distressed about setbacks in the Crimea, but Crampton took satisfaction in knowing that the Russian machinations in North America had accomplished little. By the end of the year it was also apparent that American privateers would not flock to the aid of Russia, nor would American shipyards construct vessels for the czar's navy. Americans continued to insist on their right to trade with any nation whether that nation was at war or not, provided that the goods were not contraband, and the British reluctantly acquiesced. As in the First World War a half a century later, the British found that their relative proximity to American markets and shipping worked very much to their advantage, as compared with Britains more remote allies on the Continent. Besides, as Crampton was fond of noting, the Americans found it difficult to wax enthusiastically about czarist autocracy and only pretended to support the regime as a way of getting at England, and although this may have made eminently good sense to Irish Americans, it did not sustain the rest of the inhabitants. On the whole, the United States practiced neutrality with reasonable consistency.

5

Recruitment, 1855

Nothing so preoccupied John F. T. Crampton's attention and dominated his private correspondence with Lord Clarendon during 1855 than the issue of "foreign recruitment." It all began innocuously enough. The British consul in Philadelphia, George Mathew, addressed the following private query to Lord Clarendon at the end of October 1854:[1]

> I have had several applications from medical men (Americans chiefly) proposing to serve in the East or Baltic: many of whom, I doubt not, would be found fully competent. Men have also applied (British subjects) as sailors and as soldiers. If in either case it was thought proper to give any discretionary powers to Consuls, I apprehend that a free passage would be the primary requisite.

Upon receipt of this communication in mid-November, Lord Clarendon proceeded to sound out some of his cabinet colleagues as to their opinions.

> This letter from the Consul from Philadelphia is important. Should not a discretionary power be sent to him and to other Consuls in the U.S. to give a free passage to men willing to serve in the British Army and Navy? Should the power be restricted to *British subjects*? I think not.

From the Admiralty, James Graham rendered an affirmative response.[2]

> I see no objection to the trial of the experiment and our Consuls in the United States may be entrusted, until further orders, with a discretionary power to accept the service of all Volunteers speaking native English, whether American or British-born, and to give them a free passage to England, in consideration of their enlisting either in the Army or Navy of Great Britain.

On the basis of this response, Lord Clarendon lost no time writing to Crampton asking him for his reaction to Mathew's proposal. Crampton's reply was not very encouraging.[3]

> I have received your letter of the 17th Ultimo, and I have addressed to our Consuls in the chief ports of the United States the confidential Circular, of which I enclose a copy, desiring them to report to me what prospect there may be of getting men

to enlist in our Service. I do not, I confess anticipate that we shall be able to do much in that way, nor does Consul Mathew's opinion weigh much with me, for he is a terrible talker and discoverer of mare's nests, and not a very discreet person in his proceedings. However, if the thing is managed with prudence, there can be no harm in trying the ground. It will be necessary to take great care not to do anything which could be legally construed into enlisting people here, for there are but too many aspirants to political fame who would be ready to pounce upon a British Consul with a prosecution for violating those "Neutrality Laws" which we ourselves have so frequently invoked against filibusters, Irish rebels, etc., in this country, and however laxly those laws are usually enforced against such people,—judges, juries, and District Attorneys would all pull together in straining them to the utmost against *us*. The difficulty would be to get any efficient hold over the people we may send over, which would ensure their enlisting when they got to England; for I suppose that any written engagement made with them to that effect here would bring us within the meaning of the Provisions of the Act of Congress.

After Christmas Crampton returned to this topic in a private letter to Lord Clarendon, this time in bahalf of Consul Barclay of New York City.[4]

I enclose a copy of a Letter which I have received from Consul Barclay about the prospect of getting recruits at New York for our army. There would appear from this account to be the possibility of getting some men, but the difficulty is now how to do so without infringing the Neutrality Laws of the United States, any appearance of which on *our* part would raise a terrible outcry. I have answered Mr. Barclay that I must wait to hear from you before I can direct him to take any other steps than those he has already taken. The accounts I have received lately from Philadelphia, Boston, etc. do not seem to promise much in this way. From New Orleans I have not heard.

While this correspondence was being exchanged, the British cabinet framed legislation facilitating foreign enlistment, which Parliament duly passed. In the interim between its passage and the time when instructions to enact the legislation could be received by Crampton, he reported at length of a conversation he had with President Franklin Pierce.[5]

He [Pierce] began our present conference by saying that he wished to tell me confidentially of some steps he had taken in regard to the reputed organ of the Administration the "Union". He repeated that it was not the organ of the Government, but he admitted that it was supposed by many to be so, and that in consequence, though he seldom or never read the paper himself, he had learned with regret . . . that an article had lately appeared in the "Union" of a very hostile and illiberal character towards the allies— . . . "Well," said Mr. Pierce, . . . "I have however thought it right to send for Judge Nicholson (the editor) and to tell him, that although, as he well knows, I have no pretentions to control the editorship of his paper, or to interfere with the expression of his political views in any way—or above all to render myself responsible for them—that nevertheless I would most earnestly request of him that unless he wished to *disoblige me personally*, to abstain from all discussions whatever on the question in dispute between Russia and the Allies, and from all animadversions on the conduct of either party in the war—in short to let the subject drop; and I think," continued Mr. Pierce, "that I can now promise you that neutrality at least will be observed by the "Union". . . ."

We then conversed pretty freely upon almost all the questions which could affect the friendly relations of the two countries, and the subjects of Cuba, the Sandwich Islands, Capt. Lynch[6] at the Falkland Islands, and Capt. Hollins at Greytown were brought up—I also touched upon the subject of Central American affairs in general, and the final settlement of the Mosquito question.

With respect to Cuba the President said, "You know that I have never concealed from you my policy in regard to this matter and my opinion that it would be a benefit to yourselves as well as to other nations that Cuba should be in our possession—but on the other hand I have never swerved and never will swerve from the determination which I have also expressed to you that nothing shall be done while I am at the head of affairs, towards the acquisition of that island which is not strictly in accordance with the honour and integrity of this Government. Circumstances do not now seem to favour any advance toward the acquisition by those means, and no other shall be employed. I think therefore that this is a question in regard to which we need feel no present uneasiness."

I took this opportunity . . . to say that we had on our part been equally frank in regard to Cuba; that our policy in this respect was purely conservative and altogether removed from that of a "meddling interference in the affairs of another hemisphere," which had been attributed to us—we wished to see Cuba in the hands of its lawful possessors—we thought that this was the best position under all the circumstances of the case in which in the true interests of all parties it could remain; we saw no good reason for any change—and I then put it to Mr. Pierce's own impartial judgment whether Great Britain in feeling and expressing a deep interest in the fate of Cuba was justly liable to the charge of intermeddling in the affairs of a part of the world in which she has no concern—and of endeavouring to entangle the United States in the system of the "Balance of Power in Europe". "Those," I said, "who make such a charge seem totally to forget that exclusive of commercial interests, a great and important portion of the British Empire is actually situated in this hemisphere— that Great Britain is in fact an American Power—and even as such, second to none in importance with the exception of the United States themselves—how then could it be expected that the British Government with any regard to its responsibility to the nations whose interest it is entrusted with, should regard with indifference any important territorial change on the Continent—We wished to act on the best understanding and in the most friendly spirit with the United States in all such matters—but to abdicate all right to watch over the interests of Great Britain on this side of the Atlantic was what I thought could not reasonably be expected of us."

The President then spoke of the Sandwich Islands and what he said confirmed the impression I had received from my conversation with Marcy that the design of immediate annexation was not going forward. Mr. Pierce said that he could assure me that no treaty for that purpose had been signed—and that there were difficulties about it which appeared to him to be insurmountable—for instance that the admission of the Sandwich Islands as a *state* was out of the question, and that the acquisition of them as a Colony would be entering upon a course of policy which was so totally at variance with the Spirit of the Constitution that he doubted the possibility of its being adopted by Congress—. . .

I concluded by touching on the Central American affairs, and after expressing your sincere desire to have them amicably settled, and your wish to ascertain what would be an acceptable arrangement of them, I tried the ground in the way you suggested in your last letter, by proposing a provision by Nicaragua for the Mosquito

Indians and an arbitration respecting the parts of the Clayton-Bulwer Treaty upon which a difference of opinion exists. Mr. Pierce concurred heartily in the wish to arrange these questions and made no objections to the sort of basis which I put forward. There was however evidently a hesitation as regarded Buchanan—and in this I was confirmed by a conversation I had with Mr. Marcy the next day who avowed to me that "delicacy about Buchanan" was the real obstacle in that matter—He told me however that Buchanan was *really* coming home and going to give up the mission in the course of next summer in order, he (Mr. Marcy) supposes, to run for the next Presidency—I have no doubt therefore that you are right in "guessing" that the *Buck* has no notion of settling the question before he returns, but only makes it a peg on which to hang "wholehearted American Notes" to be produced hereafter for the purpose of raising political capital for himself. Marcy again told me that Buchanan was very angry that his Notes have not already been produced, but that Mr. Marcy is determined not to lay them before Congress while the question is under negotiation. . . . Strange revolutions take place in the public opinion of this country— and I only hope that the sort of lull which now exists here may last long enough to allow us to get into a position to be able to make head against the next storm of aggression which springs up. Among the remarkable and important changes which have lately taken place is that of the language of the "New York Herald", an extract of which I enclose.[7] I have sent you many of its former articles about Cuba—which you can compare with this one—you will see that they not only don't want Cuba, but they would not take it as a present—nor Canada either!

I send you more reports about the enlistment of recruits for our army. It seems that some might really be got, but I shall await your orders for further proceedings. Many applications are made to me by surgeons to be employed in our army, and I dare say some might be procured if they are wanted.

It was with much satisfaction that Crampton announced on 22 January the resignation of Pierre Soulé and his replacement by a much more moderate envoy.[8]

The news of the week is the Resignation of Soulé, and the appointment of Mr. Breckenridge to reign in his stead. The latter is well spoken of by those who know him. He has never indulged in violent or filibustering declarations and his manners are quiet and respectable.

Congress has done little, and that little has been directed to internal matters. The commercial crisis in the Eastern Cities still continues, and by a strange and sudden revolution—the streets of New York, where a few months ago the commonest Irish laborer could not be got to carry a hod of bricks for less than 2 or 2½ dollars a day, are now paraded by bands of artisans and workmen of all sorts without employment or food, while their wants are very inadequately supplied by soup kitchens and other charitable contrivances. This is a state of things by no means safe at such a place as New York where the police and other institutions are by no means well prepared for a successful resistence to a Rebellion of the Belly.

I have just received your letter of the 5th. For the reasons alluded to in my last letter I do not think we shall be able to do anything here in the Central American Matter until Mr. Buchanan returns to the U.S. in August or September next. . . .

The newspapers have been more moderate of late on the subject of the War, and the "Union" since I last wrote has not contained any unfriendly criticism on the cause or conduct of the Allies.

While Crampton and the consuls were aware of the possibility of Russia hiring privateers for the war on the Crimea, they were also zealous in furthering Britain's own interests by making discreet inquiries concerning the lawful purchase of American merchant ships. However, as noted in this letter of 28 January, the prospects were not too encouraging, since there was so little space below decks in which troops might be conveyed.[9]

> With regard to the purchase of Steamers here for the conveyance of troops and horses, I send you Mr. Barclay's opinion that nothing of the sort could be got at New York, which I think renders it unnecessary to inquire elsewhere. This entirely coincides with the result of my own observations as far as I have been able to make them on the Steam Navigation of the U.S. With the exception of the Collins and Southampton Line of Ocean Steamers which we could not of course get as they are reduced to the minimum necessary for the conveyance of the Mails, the steamers used here are entirely wanting in the requisites pointed out by the Admiralty.[10] They are almost inevitably paddle boats with light draft of water consequently low between decks *below*, though with high hurricane decks, and they have the machinery nearly entirely above board. In short they are very good boats for coasting and running up estuaries and rivers but bad for going to sea, as was shown in the case of the "San Francisco" last year, a vessel of that sort in which it was attempted to send U.S. troops to California.[11]
>
> On the other hand numerous proposals are made to me for the enlistment of recruits for our Army. They generally proceed from Germans who have served in Schleswig-Holstein, Hungary, and other lands, and who aver that were I to give the word and furnish the means of transport they could at once send thousands of their countrymen to England for enlistment. Of course allowance must be made for exaggeration in these statements, but nevertheless the extreme dearth of employment now existing in New York, Philadelphia, and other large towns would, I think, enable us to procure a considerable number of men, if means could be found for getting them safely to land without violating the Neutrality Laws of the U.S. Not having yet received any instruction in regard to this matter I have been extremely guarded in my replies to these proposals at the same time I keep the matter in view and leave the question open, taking care not to commit myself by writing or otherwise do anything which might afterwards be turned against us.

Later in the year, Crampton learned that certain American shipowners were prepared to modify their steam vessels in order to accommodate British requirements, which made purchases more viable.

Early in February, Crampton received his first official authorization to proceed with the recruitment experiment. It is significant to note that this came in a private letter from Lord Clarendon dated 19 January 1855, whereas the formal dispatch for the record was not penned until 16 February. As with Pakenham in 1844, this discrepancy opened the way for potential embarrassment and misunderstanding.[12]

Because Lord Clarendon's instructions of 19 January set the tone for subsequent events, it is important to quote directly from them.

If depots were established in Canada, and the other Colonies for British Subjects, it is possible that they might *draw* recruits from the U.S. They might go there voluntarily as Emigrants without any enrollment or being collected together in the U.S., and if it was made known in Canada that a free passage would be given and £6 or £7 be received on arriving here I should not be surprised if we got a considerable number of useful men. Sir G. Grey has already written to Sir E. Head and the other Governors about establishing depots, and I wish you would put yourself in communication with them and endeavour to forward the scheme by all the means you think safe.

Crampton's reaction was again one of concern. As he had said from the first, any such recruiting would fly in the face of the Neutrality Law passed by the United States Congress in 1818.[13]

I have received your letter of the 19th Ultimo, and have already written to Mr. Barclay upon the subject you allude to, and I shall immediately communicate with Sir Edmund Head. So soon as we shall be able to tell people where to go, I think something may be done in that matter. The difficulty is as to the means of helping those who are inclined to go but have not the means of defraying their travelling expenses. If we were to *advance* money we should have no security as to its being used for the proper purpose; and although we might promise that such expenses would be reimbursed on the arrival of the people at the Depot, this would only enable those who could pay their own way in the first instance to come. As the wish to join us arises out of want of work and distress, I fear the numbers of those who could do so would be small. Nevertheless by the invention of a trustworthy agent the thing might be managed, and I hope to be able to tell you more about it by the next packet.

I am still confined to the house and have consequently seen nothing of Mr. Marcy.[14] I am happy to say however that nothing has occurred in Congress or elsewhere which would have rendered it necessary.

There was never in Crampton's mind any serious thought given to sending recruits directly from the United States to Great Britain. The trick was to facilitate their travel to Canada without seeming to contract for their services while on American soil.[15]

I am in communication with two or three persons who appear to be sufficiently trustworthy and intelligent to enable us at all events to make the experiment on a moderate scale, and without any risk of being charged with a violation of the Neutrality Law of the U.S. If we succeed in the first instance we can extend our operations.

All my informants agree that the method proposed is the best that could be adopted, and profess themselves to act upon it the moment I say the word. If there is no great delay in the arrangements in Canada, I think we might obtain a considerable number of men from the U.S., but our chances of doing so will diminish as the spring advances and the demand for labour increases.

The moment therefore that I am informed that depots are formed in Canada for the reception of recruits and that I am enabled to let it be known upon what terms they will be enrolled and to what point they are to direct themselves, I propose to set one or two of my agents at work to convey them to the appointed places. Such advances of money as I shall have to make must necessarily be made on trust to the Agent who shall undertake to convey the men, for any written engagement would bring us under the provisions of the Neutrality Laws. But the outlays will not be considerable in any one instance; and if the Agent was to fail to fulfil his engagements as to the first batch of men, we should of course not employ him again and abandon the whole project as a failure. The thing must therefore be looked upon as an experiment, but it is one which I think likely to succeed, and of which the risk of trying is not great.

Until otherwise instructed I shall charge any money which I may advance for this purpose to the *Secret Service Account.*

The people we shall get, if we get any, will be principally Germans, and among them I am promised a good number of intelligent non-commissioned officers and others who have served in Schleswig-Holstein. The number of British subjects will I think be small. . . .

. . . Mr. Breckenridge whose appointment as Minister to Spain in Soulé's place I announced to you, has after some consideration declined to go and a gentleman has been named in his stead rejoicing in the name of General Augustus Caesar Dodge, now Senator for Iowa—an appointment with which "Punch" at least will be pleased. He is the type of a Western Gentleman, that is to say a very dirty savage, but in other respects bears a good character; at least I have never heard of his ever having settled any difficulty with his colleagues by a recourse to what are called the "appropriate western weapons"—viz: the bowie knife and rifle. He will at all events be a fish out of water at Madrid, but this perhaps is so much the better.

By 25 February news reached Crampton of the resignation of Lord Aberdeen and his cabinet due to the worsening of the war abroad, the ineptitude and inefficiency of the government, and the consequent clamor in and out of Parliament. The pugnacious Lord Palmerston became prime minister, but Lord Clarendon survived the upheaval at the Foreign Office.[16]

The last Packet brought us news of the re-formation of the Ministry, and it is with infinite satisfaction that I find that the changes which have taken place do not affect the Foreign Office. . . . A strong free soil feeling has in fact manifested itself in the disagreeable shape of Resolutions passed by the Michigan legislature disapproving of the votes of the Michigan delegation in the U.S. Congress upon the Nebraska bill, and consequently of the course of Cass himself, who is emphatically what is called a "Northern man with Southern principles;" in other words, one who tries to be popular both North and South in hopes of the Presidency or other *Federal* honours. It is easy enough to be a great man in the North by going the whole figure on the "free soil abolition" ticket; or in the South by a "chivalrous defence" of the "peculiar institution" of that part of the Union; but the material for political capital all over the Union is comparatively scarce and one of its chief elements has from the beginning been and still is to a great extent a malignant hatred and jealousy of England which I am sorry to say still lives and reigns in the bosom of the people of this Country. When things look ill for one political party as opposed to another, in this country, and particularly when *"Sectional Differences"* (i.e. Northern and Southern differences) spring up, this nerve of the body politic is the one which is always pressed by the losing party. Many of the politicians who do not scruple to avow to me their belief that the notion of danger or aggression from Great Britain is a delusion, do not on the other hand scruple to disseminate and foster it by public speeches and writings whenever it suits their purpose. They are not ashamed to use the argument—"resistence and hatred of England and its Government were what created and has maintained our Union—if we cannot keep up the notion among the people or substitute some other equally binding motive we shall infallibly drop to pieces before long."

Nothing demonstrates the precautions that Crampton felt it necessary to take to protect the contents of his private correspondence than the following letter of 6 March, which had to be conveyed across American territory without benefit of special messenger. Its very subject, foreign enlistment, is not mentioned at all, and only if this were known could the reader understand its meaning. The "competent officer" alluded to turned out to be a prominent Nova Scotian politician, Joseph Howe.[17]

> I have received your letter of the 16th Ultimo. You will have seen that I have been giving my attention to the principal subject of your letter and I shall not fail to use every exertion to forward the matter. Nothing however can be done until I hear that Sir Gaspard Le Marchant or General Rowan have made some arrangement in the Colonies. Halifax is in some respects better than Montreal for the required purpose, at least it is not subject to many of the difficulties set forth in General Rowan's Memorandum which was enclosed with my Note of the 19th Ultimo.
>
> I intend to send up a Messenger to Sir Gaspard, and to propose to him to send me down a competent officer who can at least form some idea of the efficiency or non-efficiency of the material before we allow them to be sent off. I shall also send a person to Cincinnati.

By the time Lord Clarendon's official instructions regarding recruitment reached Washington, Crampton had already begun a serious examination of the topic. In a private letter of 12 March and in the official dispatches of the same day, he assured the Foreign Office that the subject had been thoroughly examined by the legation's attorney, J. M. Carlisle, who reported that under the Neutrality Law of 1818, no active recruiting could go on within the jurisdiction of the United States. Crampton nevertheless indicated that he believed that there remained a legitimate loophole whereby prospective recruits could anticipate a cordial reception and cash bounties in Canada. However, for the record, Crampton repeated his stern warning to the chief recruiting officer: "Mr. Howe will avoid any act which would connect his proceedings with her Majesty's Legation, and he has received the strictest injunctions from me to abstain most carefully from the slightest infraction of the Neutrality Laws of the United States." And further, he took the precaution of supplying Howe and the British consuls in major American cities with copies of Carlisle's admonitory opinion. Unfortunately, Howe later ignored these warnings in the interest of securing immediate results.

One might question whether Crampton acted precipitately in his eagerness to lure potential recruits during a time of economic hardship. The following letter suggests this, but in fact Crampton was responding to Lord Clarendon's pressing appeals.[18]

> I am hard at work on the subject of the recruitment. What it may bring forth I don't know but at least the experiment shall be tried.
>
> Sir Gaspard Le Marchant has sent down Mr. Howe (formerly Provincial Secretary), a sharp and active man who seems well qualified for the work we have in hand. Sir Gaspard, you will see by his letter herewith enclosed, doubts that *he* has any authority to raise troops and wants to know whether I have.[19]
>
> I don't exactly know what he means as of course he cannot imagine that I could levy men in the United States; however as he says he will receive any men I send him, and as you wish me to act promptly, which indeed is a *sine qua non* to success, I have determined to go ahead at once and do what I can. As Her Majesty's Government wish the thing to be done we can of course run no risk in acting before technical and detailed instructions are sent out. Merely to report as to the practicability of the scheme and then to wait two months for authority to try it would be in fact equivalent to abandoning it altogether, for if anything is to be done it must be done *now*. So soon as the present state of the labour market changes, as it is sure to do as spring advances, there will be an end to the numerous offers which are now made to me. The Neutrality Law you will see by Mr. Carlisle's opinion which I send you in my No. 57[20] confines us to narrow limits in our measures here—but I think we shall be able to manage to show some people the way to Halifax without "hiring or retaining" them. The expense of a voyage from Boston or New York to Halifax is small and if we can get some Nova Scotian vessels whose masters will give credit, the passage money can be paid on arrival.
>
> Once there I have no fear of the recruits not enlisting, for in Nova Scotia at this season they would find nothing else to do. I hope if instructions to Sir Gaspard to raise and enroll troops are not already on the way that they may be sent out at once —for otherwise some technical difficulty or delay in providing for such people as may first go from here may deter others from following their example.

By 23 March Crampton was dismayed to see the issue of recruitment openly discussed in the columns of the *New York Herald*. Reprinted there was a handbill that a certain Angus McDonald had been circulating. Attention was drawn to a bounty of six pounds (thirty dollars), which would be received by anyone making his way to Canada, where he would thereafter be supplied with clothing, rations, and warm living quarters. Further, it was noted that "the subscriber (with the view of assisting those who have not the means of paying their Passage) hereby gives notice, that he has opened a Passage Office, No. 36 Pearl Street, (near Broad,) where he proposes to engage passages by good vessels to Halifax, leaving twice or three times a week, for the sum of $5."[21]

Although there was no public mention of it, McDonald was one of Joseph Howe's recently deputized agents who, as soon as he learned that the New York district attorney might prosecute him, fled abroad. Crampton promptly instructed Consul Barclay at New York to disavow such recruitment. He also sought an audience with Secretary of State Marcy to convince him that the British legation in Washington had nothing to do with the handbill. In one sense, this was true because Crampton never knew McDonald; in another, he was anxious to stay aloof from the undercover tactics of Howe.[22]

Thinking that the distribution of tickets alluded to in Mr. Howe's letter of the 17th Instant, herewith enclosed, as well as the circulation of handbills or advertisements was dangerous as well as unnecessary, I have done what I could to put a stop to them.[23] For although these facts do not, taken separately, constitute a violation of the Law, they might, taken with others which might be elicited on a prosecution of any of the individuals who had done them, make up a case which, going to an American Judge and Jury in the present temper of the country, would bring those persons sufficiently within the meaning of the words "hiring or retaining" persons to go beyond the same (the U.S.) with "*intent* to be enlisted", to result in a verdict against them. I accordingly summoned Mr. Howe (between whose proceedings and the Legation however every counection has been avoided) to come to Washington, which he did this morning, and I have had a full discussion of the whole matter with him along with my legal counsel, Mr. Carlisle, upon whose knowledge of the law and good advice as to the best mode of proceeding I entirely rely—I had already sent to Mr. Howe by a confidential Messenger, and the few tickets which were given out have been re-collected, and all proceedings by handbills or the opening of offices which were done "on their own hook" by the people who have been offering us their services under the idea that they were quite safe, have been stopped. The District Attorney of course talks loud as you will see by his letter herewith enclosed but Mr. Carlisle is not of opinion, even if a prosecution should be attempted and some of these people held to bail, that any case can be made out against them; and Mr. Howe is fully instructed as to the legal precautions he is to take in the event of any attempt being made to implicate him. In short I think that what has happend will do no more than practically to test the matter, and let people see what can and what cannot be done consistently with the Law.

I took good care to explain to Marcy with perfect frankness our position and intentions as regards this matter. I said, besides reading to him my letter to Mr. Barclay (enclosed in my No. 75 of today)[24] that we were certainly anxious to obtain efficient recruits from whatever quarter they should come and that depots for enlistment had been established in the colonies where those who should voluntarily present themselves would be received and enrolled, but to the enquiries which had been addressed to me upon that subject by persons in this country I had invariably replied by referring them to the provisions of the Act of Congress 1818, and stating that neither I nor any of the Agents of Her Majesty's Government could either "*enlist*" them in the U.S. or "*hire or retain*" them to go to any part of the British Dominions with the intent of there enlisting, that consequently all I could do was to give such persons the information of which I was in possession as to terms, and the time and place at which they might, if so disposed, be received into the British service; being aware of no law which prevented citizens of the U.S. or others from emigrating from this country for whatever purpose they might think proper. If, however, individuals either from the hope of making money or from ignorance should, notwithstanding what I had said to them or as in the case of McDonald without any communication with me, proceed in a way which might bring them within the Provisions of the Act, I could only regret their having done so without the power of preventing it; and would make no objection to the rigorous enforcement of the Law in their case. Mr. Marcy concurred in the correctness of my positions, and said that he had never doubted that this was the view I would take of the question, adding that the U.S. Government felt obliged to act with perfect impartiality and to cause the laws to be enforced in this as in the case of a like attempt from whatever quarter proceeding. He remarked, indeed, that he had rather suspected that the pretext of an enlistment for the British Service had been made use of to cover some intended filibustering expedition against Cuba.

Occasionally, in spite of his preoccupation with the Crimean War, Central America, and Cuba, Crampton had the opportunity to sound out Marcy concerning some of the most fundamental characteristics of American policy.[25]

Mr. Marcy then proceeded to speak at great length of the feeling of the U.S. generally, making very sensible observations which I only wish he could act up to; and making some candid avowals as to [the] way in which political matters are conducted here, which, though I know them to be true, perfectly astonished me as proceeding from a "wholehearted American" to an Englishman. He said, "this policy of [American] extension if it is persisted in will be our ruin;—if we are to have islands and outlying territories we must have large armies and fleets to protect them—that this would entail upon us large establishments of every sort—and in that case I can assure you we should not be troubled with a "surplus" in the Treasury, for there is one thing in which our people certainly *do* surpass yours, and that is in the art of cheating their Government. The expenses of the Federal Government are comparatively small now and therefore the field is restricted, but where we should be if we launched out into great operations, I don't know. Then again with regard to Congress—you have been here for some time, and you have eyes, and therefore it would be useless for me either to point out or to disguise from you the corruption which prevails there. There is a power which you are perfectly well aware of—the "Lobby" which before the second Session of Congress invariably gets the entire control of the Legislature. There has not been a single President of the U.S. within my recollection, and I can go as far back as Madison and Monroe, who ever commanded a majority in a second Session of Congress. In that respect your government is in reality a more popular one than ours—but if *we* had to go out whenever a measure was carried [against] us our administration would not average six weeks duration. Every one of their evils would be multiplied a hundred fold if we had to maintain great establishments, levy high taxes, and what not, which would be necessary if the ambitious projects of some of us were carried out." Mr. Marcy continued in this strain for a long time, uttered a great many wholesome truths, and in general spoke in a very friendly way—but how far this spirit will be fused into the public acts of the Government remains to be seen.

Mr. Howe is at work at the recruitment, but I am not aware how far he has succeeded as he has been lying by during the hubbub which was made in New York and Philadelphia and did not like to risk corresponding with me by the Post.[26] He has sent me today an appeal which he has published and which may perhaps do good. It does not seem that anything can be made of the prosecutions which were attempted against one or two Germans who stupidly established what they called recruiting offices, and an insane man at Philadelphia of the name of Perkins whom I never saw or heard of but who has been swearing that he had an interview with *me* and *Mr. Marcy* at the State Department, when we arranged together everything about the recruitment.[27] I enclose Mr. Howe's manifesto and a note which accompanied it—but which tells me nothing of what progress he has made. I see it announced that a cargo of about 90 recruits has already arrived at Halifax and I have given letters of introduction to Sir Gaspard Le Marchant to a few German officers who have been recommended to me by the Prussian Minister here. We may pick up a few people of this sort in the U.S. but I doubt that either their numbers or those of the recruits will be very considerable.

By 23 April Crampton still seemed oblivious to how badly Howe was managing recruitment, since he always seemed to be able to keep one step ahead of the authorities. Minor indiscretions, at least, appeared harmless.[28]

With regard to the recruitment I enclose the Reports I have received from Mr. Howe which do not look as if he was having much success. The ground left by the Neutrality Laws is so narrow that it is scarcely possible to expect the sort of people who must necessarily be employed to treat it with discretion.

It is also unfortunate but too certain that exorbitant zeal in thwarting or annoying the British Government is a certain means of attaining popularity in this country and hence the activity of all sorts of officials in throwing any possible obstacle in the way of our proceedings.

It is perfectly well known that there is no case against the people who have been held to bail by the district attorneys, but the alacrity of these gentlemen will redound as much to their glory among their people as their supineness has done on occasions when Filibustering attacks on Cuba were quietly organized, and when armed bands were publicly recruited and marched through the streets of New York, as I saw in 1848, with flags flying and drums beating for the conquest of Ireland—on which occasion Mr. Buchanan, then Secretary of State, told me with perfect truth I believe, that though no doubt the thing was illegal yet that as no jury could be found in New York who would not instantly acquit the delinquents it would only increase the excitement if the District Attorney was to attempt prosecution.

Mr. Howe has not yet written to me from the West where he is gone with a Polish Officer Colonel Korponay, whose promises I hope will be better fulfilled than those of our other purveyors of recruits.[29]

Ten days later, Crampton came to the awful realization that Howe had bungled everything, and worse—that he might have compromised the British minister in Washington as well. There seemed no alternative but to take matters into his own hands and go to Canada to discuss the matter personally with the Canadian officials.[30]

Not feeling altogether satisfied or easy about the proceedings of Mr. Howe with respect to the recruitment, and finding that I cannot possibly prevent the occurance of blunders and misunderstandings unless I take the matter into my own hands, I have decided to go up to Canada in the first instance and speak to Sir Edmund Head, and then to Halifax to confer with Sir Gaspard Le Marchant. By starting today for Quebec I can manage to do this perfectly and avail myself of the Cunard steamer to Halifax on Wednesday next. I can then return to Boston and New York and see what can be done in strict conformity with the Neutrality Laws the real bearing of which I have found is very difficult to impress upon anybody who has been involved in the business. My notion is that whatever is to be done can be effected without violating them in the least; but that any attempt to *evade* them by artful dodges will only defeat our object and give "beau jeu" to Cushing and the other malignant spirits

under his control who only want to make themselves of importance by annoying
us. My objection to Mr. Howe's proceedings, tho' I fully recognize his zeal and
cleverness, is that he has given an air of mystery and intrigue to what can only be
done with any effect publicly and legally. Besides I am most anxious not to have
the appearance of taking one position in regard to this matter in my communications
with Mr. Marcy and another thro' Mr. Howe or any other real or supposed agent.
I am therefore not sorry that he has gone back to Nova Scotia, for his movements
have lately been so erratice and obscure that I have had difficulty in following or
understanding them, much less controlling them.[31] I hope therefore that by putting
my own shoulder to the wheel I may be able to prevent any mischief, if I cannot
effect any good.

While Crampton was away, a decision by Judge Kane in Philadelphia greatly
cheered the British legation in Washington. Although Hertz and Perkins, the
two chief defendants charged with recruiting, were held over for trial by jury,
the judge declared that "the payment of the passage from this country of a
man who desires to enlist in a foreign port does not come within the Act of
1818."

By 3 June Crampton was back in Washington, and he too was more hopeful.
Despite the refusal of General William Rowan, the commander of Her
Majesty's forces in North America, to allocate barracks and other facilities
for newly arrived recruits, other arrangements were made for receiving those
who crossed the frontier. Crampton's new plan, which involved more or less
abandoning the sea route via New York or Boston to Halifax and henceforth
concentrating on attracting recruits overland, had the tacit support of Edmund
Head, although he could not condone the project openly because there was
at the time a bill pending before the New Brunswick legislature to encourage
enlistment by Canadians into their own provincial militia. However, Gaspard
Le Marchant, the lieutenant governor of Nova Scotia, had openly espoused
enlistment from the United States.[32]

At Niagara Barracks one of the German Officers remains . . . while the others go
across to Buffalo, Detroit and Cleveland, from which places it will be easy for those
who wish to enlist to pass over into Canada without any previous enrollment or
organization whatever, and without the necessity of distributing to them any money
or doing anything else which could be taken as an infringement of the Law. They
will merely have at Buffalo and Detroit to cross a ferry and at Cleveland to cross
the lake by a steamer which goes twice a day. They will be received on the Canadian
[bank] opposite Buffalo and Detroit by a German Officer, who will be stationed at
each of those points and transferred on by rail-road through British territory to
Niagara barracks. So soon as a small number shall be collected there, they will be
forwarded by either the regular plying steamers, or if a sufficient number of men
can be got within a reasonable time by steamers which can easily be taken up for
the purpose, down the St. Lawrence to La Prairie. There arrangements have already
been made for procuring schooners for sending them on to Halifax where when once
in Sir Gaspard Le Marchant's hands they will be pretty safe. Indeed they will have
little opportunity of deserting or misbehaving on the road, for they will never be

brought into contact with the populations of the larger towns in Canada where they might be tempted by the offer of high wages or otherwise to repent of their engagements to enlist.

In spite of otherwise strained relations, the United States and Britain were prepared to cooperate with respect to the international use of waterways in Latin America.[33]

You will see by my despatches of today that Mr. Marcy actually professes to go "hand in hand with us" in securing our right to the free navigation of the La Plata and the other great South American rivers. There has generally been on the part of this Administration so evident a fear of being even suspected of the slightest community of feeling with England or of appearing to accept our cooperation or assistance in any affair, in short, there has been so marked a disposition on Mr. Pierce's part to exhibit to the public, whatever he may really feel, that "wholesome mistrust" of us so strenuously recommended by the "Union" and by General Cass, that I apprehend there must be some very sufficient reason for invoking our aid on the present occasion; and that reason would seem to be the real want of the necessary disposable naval force to carry their point alone now that the Brazilians seem inclined to take the wrong side of the question. However this may be, I think the symptom is a favourable one to a certain extent and the American public may perhaps end by discovering that Great Britain may on some occasions prove a more useful ally to them than the Emperor of Russia himself.

The recruitment is going on, but it is up-hill work and beset with difficulties. The opposition of the United States authorities by fair means and foul is unceasing; and they are egged on and encouraged by Russian agents who I have good reason to believe spend enormous sums of money in espionage and bribes to the New York Police. We nevertheless succeed in getting small portions off by every vessel that goes to Nova Scotia, and Sir Gaspard's forces are gradually augmenting so that I don't despair of his being shortly able to turn out a respectable battalion on the glacis at Halifax well armed and equipped. That I think will *draw*, as it will soon become known in the United States, and the Germans are now so abominably persecuted in all the large towns by the "Know-nothings" that I am sure numbers of them would join us if they felt certain of a good reception. The men are not coming over by Niagara as fast as I could wish but still I received an intimation today that the recruits are on their way from thence to Halifax. There has been some mismanagement I fear among the German officers, and from the sad mistake committed by General Gore of giving me Lieutenant Preston who is a mere boy, instead of a much more experienced officer for whom at Sir Gaspard Le Marchant's suggestion I asked him, there has been a want of authority and caution which is much to be regretted.[34] But Gore, it appears, was foolishly piqued at Sir Gaspard's being entrusted with the raising of the Legion instead of himself and made all sorts of difficulties. As Sir Gaspard has now succeeded to military command of the Province I hope this defect will be remedied forthwith, for he is fully aware of its existence.

The month of June proved critical regarding foreign enlistment. On the ninth Marcy told Buchanan that recruiting was still taking place in America despite British assurances to the contrary, and therefore the American government was determined to act. On the twenty-second the British cabinet decided to discontinue the experiment, and Crampton was informed that he should bring recruiting to a halt.[35] However, he was given some leeway regarding precisely when to call a halt to it.[36]

It seems to me that the expense of the recruits we may obtain when reckoned by head including the outlay which under the circumstances must often be lost altogether from the roguery or the stupidity of our agents on the one hand and the interference and intimidation by the United States Government on the other, will be out of all decent proportion to what we can produce as a reinforcement to our armies; and will be such as would if expended at home in increased bounties or more active recruiting arrangements, produce a greater number of soldiers. . . .

. . . With regard to the recruitment I have put a stop to all fresh measures for carrying it on or enlarging it, merely allowing Korponay and Smolenski to whom promises were made on Sir Gaspard's part by Mr. Howe that they should have the command of bodies of men they undertook to bring.[37] I thought it but fair to hold our word to them and to give them a fair chance of holding theirs. They would of course have been very indignant if we had suddenly backed out, and would probably have shown us up by publishing in the papers the very imprudent letters which Mr. Howe wrote to them. I have thought it right however to fix with them by agreement a limit as to time and expense at the expiration of which their plans if not accomplished must be regarded as failures and definitely abandoned. From what I observe I think they themselves will very soon have to acknowledge that the thing cannot be done, at least not within a reasonable time or at a reasonable expense. The inherent difficulties of the enterprise are great. Besides the "acharnement" of the American Authorities and Press against it, the utter want of control over our agents and over the recruits they may collect in a foreign and in this case I may almost say an enemy's country, paralyzes the whole operation. Even the very partial success we have already had in connecting a few men at Halifax has excited a storm of pretended virtuous indignation supported by all the calumnies and lies that the peculiar malignant ingenuity of American Newspapers can devise. The law authorities of the U.S., stimulated by the desire to show their zeal, are overstretching the law in a way that the lowest village attorney would be ashamed to attempt. In their extreme admiration of Russia they have adopted her system of Police; every gentleman who comes from our Colonies is immediately surrounded by spies and followed about by waiters of hotels and hackney coach drivers. This is no exaggeration, for the district attorney at Boston had the "naiveté" to tell Mr. Perley, with whom he was acquainted, as a good joke, that he had attached a waiter and a cabman to his suite, and could name to him every person he had spoken to since he left New Brunswick.[38] The money for this extra service *cannot* come from the U.S. government for there is no fund out of which it could be taken, so I leave you to guess its source. Among other ingenious contrivances, fabricated letters have been sent to the President supposed to have been written by victims of British treachery and oppression who were inveigled by false promises into going to Halifax where they were immediately put in chains and shipped off to the Crimea to be offered up to the "Moloch of an unjust and wicked war"[39] Our friend the "Union" is very strong on this point, and papers all abound in general abuse of the Allies, so much so that I have great difficulty keeping my French colleague from some outbreak of feeling which would only render matters worse and delight the "talented Editors". I have just received a dispatch which I send you today from Mr. Rowcroft our Consul at Cincinnati informing me that he has been arrested and placed under Bond because people came and asked him whether they might go to Halifax and be enlisted.[40] This it seems is now considered sufficient cause for legal proceedings against any body and as evidence of it can at any time be obtained by giving a dollar to some half-stewed German there is no lack of arresting and bailing—but they have not got a single conviction; and finding that the first cases brought to trial were all discharged, they have adopted the dodge of postponing the trials indefinitely by one pretext or another, keeping members of the supposed recruits in prison all the time as *witnesses*, and thus effectually preventing them from getting to Halifax which is the real object in view. All this in any other country would look as if Peace could not be preserved between us, but I don't apprehend anything of the sort here as long as we are able to buy their cotton and lend them money to build their Western cities. The result however is I fear our recruitment will not prove a profitable transaction.

Considerable confusion ensued during the next few months. On 15 July Marcy reiterated to Buchanan his determination to put a stop to foreign enlistment. Buchanan conferred with Lord Clarendon and was assured that recruitment had indeed ceased. However, by 30 July Crampton was still procrastinating, feeling some obligation to Korponay and Smolenski as well as acting oblivious to the ever-hardening American position.[41]

With regard to the recruitment, although it is true that men are coming in somewhat quicker than they did, I think that it is on the whole advisable to put a stop to it. "Le jeu ne vaut pas la chandelle"—what with the opposition of the U.S. Attorneys aided and abetted by the congenial help of the "United Irishmen"—what with the great distances over which the men have to be conveyed, the consequent losses and desertions by the way, the treachery of many of them, the impossibility of controlling them or our own Agents in a country as hostile to us in feeling as Russia itself—all this makes it evident to me that, even supposing that a certain number of soldiers might ultimately be obtained by persevering and paying our way through every obstacle, we might lay the money out to better advantage in bribing recruits at home or even in our own less thickly peopled Colonies than in the United States.

Once Crampton learned about Lord Clarendon's explicit assurances to Buchanan, he put a prompt end to recruitment. As irony would have it, after six months of effort and risk, the British authorities in Nova Scotia could credit themselves with a mere five hundred foreign recruits.[42]

On the receipt of your letter of the 20th ultimo I immediately put a stop to *all* proceedings in the business which forms the subject of your correspondence with Mr. Buchanan. It is absolutely necessary that no case, legitimate or illegitimate, if an attempt to go on in that matter, should be brought up as having occurred *subsequent to your assurance to Mr. Buchanan*, and any loss that we may incur by suddenly breaking up our arrangements is of course not to be taken into consideration.

Shortly after Crampton terminated enlistment, President Pierce ordered the attorney general, Caleb Cushing, to gather and summarize incriminating evidence against the British agents and diplomatic personnel who had been involved. While Cushing prepared his report, a major new witness against the

British emerged: Max Strobel, whom Howe had hired as a recruiter in the spring, and who had been fairly successful until late June, when he began to feel undercompensated by the authorities in Halifax. Strobel's disgruntlement fit in nicely with Cushing's ingrained dislike of Great Britain, fostered for many years by his family's involvement in mercantile shipping. Thus, at the same time that he instructed his district attorneys to continue gathering evidence against the British agents, he made a formal recommendation to his cabinet that the charges against Her Majesty's government be broadened. Marcy seconded this argument six weeks later, suggesting to Buchanan that the point at issue was no longer a breach of American statute law but "an offence against our sovereign territorial rights" under international law as well.[43]

At this same time, the activities of various Irish organizations came to Crampton's attention. Although he did not take their efforts too seriously, he decided to alert Clarendon about a recent convention in Boston of the Massachusetts Irish Emigrant Aid Association, whose object was to unite all of the emigrant organizations throughout the country against the tyranny of British rule in Ireland.[44]

> With regard to the "Irish movement" of which I speak in my Despatch of today no. 183,[45] I do not think it will amount to much. I have no doubt that it is an "Anti-Know-Nothing" manoeuvre, in order to organize the Irish vote at the elections in November next. In 1849 there was an organization of the same sort for invading Ireland, under much greater excitement than what now exists, and yet the subscription all over America only amounted to 9,000 dollars. This money disappeared without being either appropriated to revolutionary purposes nor returned to the contributors. This has been a standing joke against Irish "Directories" ever since, and will scarcely encourage people to book up on the present occasion.

On 5 September the storm burst.[46] Marcy informed Crampton that the United States government would only be satisfied by his recall or some other appropriate acknowledgment of British violation of the United States Neutrality Law. Crampton was outraged because Marcy, with whom he felt on good terms, had intimated nothing of this throughout the whole of the summer.[47]

> The result of the "advisement" of the American Cabinet on the recruitment question has at length been communicated to me; and although from Mr. Marcy's manner and the hostile articles in the "Union" I expected something disagreeable, I was not, I confess, prepared for what has occurred. . . .
>
> You will at once perceive that the result of the "Cabinet advisement" has been a determination on the part of the Government to make the most of the recruitment question for the purpose of embarrassing and humiliating the British Government, and thereby making political capital for themselves.
>
> In order the better to succeed in this object it is evidently their intention to give their vindication of the dignity of the United States against the pretended insults of Great Britain the greatest "eclat" they can.
>
> Accordingly—instead of accepting the frank explanations contained in your note

to Mr. Buchanan and resting satisfied with the assurances that the whole plan of obtaining recruits from the United States was abandoned, they do not even allude to that assurance as causing them the slightest satisfaction but persist in pursuing the matter retrospectively and vindictively. In short, to use Mr. Cushing's metaphor on the subject, they have made it a "nut to crack" which having once got between their teeth they are determined not to relinquish. They have now moreover determined to make a more brilliant affair out of it by turning their fire on the British Minister at Washington as well as on the British Consul at Cincinnati.

The concluding part of Mr. Marcy's note, though mysteriously expressed and rather a bungled piece of composition, can have no other meaning than this: viz—that you have the alternative of disavowing my part in the matter and recalling me, or else of sustaining me and having me *dismissed by them* after the fashion of Mr. Jackson, Mr. Guillaume Tell Poussin and others; and the latter course is that which would suit their purpose best.[48]

Under these circumstances it seems quite evident to me that I cannot remain here in any case.—I have therefore today addressed you an official despatch requesting my recall and begging to be authorized to leave this country forthwith.[49]—I have made it a "Separate" despatch and enclosed it in this private letter:—You will thus have an opportunity of retaining it in your hands or of cancelling it altogether, in case upon mature consideration the adoption of any other course by me or the modification in any way of this should appear to you to be adviseable. In that event I need not say that I shall be governed by your directions. But I confess I can see no alternative.

Should the fact of my removal at my own request being already a "fait accompli" when this Government come to demand their "measure of satisfaction", disembarrass the question of one of its difficulties I shall rejoice in having taken this step. This will besides disappoint these people in their contemplated "coup de théatre" of packing me off in case your explanations are not "deemed satisfactory by the President", and you may rely upon it they will find means to pick a hole in them whatever they may be. I asked to be released at once because I do not even now feel sure that before your answer can arrive they will not trump up some pretended "disclosure" as an excuse for putting their design into instant execution. If it was to leak out that I had already resigned I feel confident they would do so; in short they would execute me "instanter" lest, like Pierre in Venice Preserved, I should "deceive the Senate" by suicide.[50]

But I fear that, assuming that the part of the question which regards me may thus be disposed of, great difficulties remain behind.—The United States Government, you will see, have taken new ground. It is now no longer of the infringement of their laws which they complain, but of a "want of respect to the policy which", they say, "those laws indicated as well as of a violation of international law" and of the sovereign territorial rights of the United States. In this offence our diplomatic and Consular Agents in this country together with nearly all the Civil and Military Authorities of our North American Colonies are, according to Mr. Marcy, now implicated; and their observance of the municipal law is now brought forward, not as an *extenuation* but as an *aggravation* of the supposed outrage. The disavowal and dismissal of all these functionaries would I presume be the "measure of satisfaction" which Mr. Pierce now modestly requires. I can only say that the view of the matter and the policy of this country now put forward in Mr. Marcy's note was never alluded to by him in any conversation on the subject with me. He indeed seldom alluded to the subject at all, and when he did I understood his view of it to be this—that every Citizen or Resident in the United States had a perfect right to emigrate therefrom without being accountable to anybody for his motives or intentions, but that *recruiting* and *enlisting* within the jurisdiction of the United States was *illegal* under the Act of 1818 and consequently that the United States Government would be compelled to punish any person or persons who violated that Act. I am particularly diffident in relying upon my own powers of seizing the precise meaning of a principle or opinion expressed in conversation or upon my own memory in retaining it completely, especially when thrown out in a disjointed manner and in an indistinct tone and clothed in the sometimes expressive but often to me obscure American Metaphors which my friend Mr. Marcy sometimes adopts, but in this case I am fortified as to the correctness of my impression by precisely the same impression having been made upon Lumley at a conversation on the same subject he had with Mr. Marcy during my absence in Canada in May last.[51] I can only infer from this that Marcy's present view has been adopted in the late "Cabinet advisement" to which I have alluded, and that it was *not* his opinion till then although I have no doubt that it was that of some of his Colleagues. Mr. Marcy's present Note in fact gives the sentiments and almost the very *words* of numerous articles in the "Union" paper, some of which I sent you, and which I am morally convinced were written by one of these Gentlemen. Should this not have been the case, Mr. Marcy's conduct to me must appear to have been extremely treacherous and unfriendly, as indeed the proceeding of the United States Government taken as a whole decidedly is:— For had Mr. Marcy at any time asked of me to tell him the exact nature of the part I took or proposed taking in obtaining Soldiers from this country, and on my explaining it to him frankly as I of course would have done said that the United States Government would feel compelled to take the line they *now have taken* if I persevered, I should have instantly held my hand and advised you to drop the whole plan.

Mr. Marcy would not then have been obliged to have recourse to spies and hired informers as he has now done for "disclosures" which he could have got much more easily and correctly from me. Of the exact nature of these disclosures I am of course ignorant, but from the threatening letters I have received from some of the Germans whom Sir Gaspard was obliged to dismiss from the Legion for crimes and misconduct, I can pretty well derive their tenor as well as the way in which they were obtained.

As regards my own part in this disagreeable business I can only say that I have always given you to the best of my ability a faithful account of every step I took in it. It was my sincere desire, no doubt, to test the possibility of our obtaining in this country some part of the force we so much need; but at the same time every precaution I could devise was taken to avoid the slightest infraction of the laws of the United States.

That I was violating international Law and insulting the Government to which I was accredited certainly never occurred to me. If nevertheless upon a retrospect of the transaction it is thought by Her Majesty's Government that I have proceeded further than they could have wished, I shall not complain of being disavowed and of terminating my connection with this country.

While the recruitment issue simmered and Crampton awaited London's response to his proffered resignation, he returned to discussing an incident involving the Irish. In Louisville, Kentucky, where there had been an election in August, there was a riot when the Irish and German supporters of the Democratic party resisted the determined efforts of the Know-Nothing party to win by tactics of intimidation and violence. Guns and even cannon were brought in, and afterward the local press placed the number of dead at twenty and the wounded at forty.[52]

Mr. Rowcroft has been here and tells me that he has got some important information as to the organization of the Irish population for the purpose of seizing a favourable opportunity of invading their native country.[53] It appears that they are collecting arms and money and that the association has very extensive ramifications. I have no doubt that since the Election battle at Louisville where the Irish it seems got much the worst of it,. . . there has been a great impetus given to all sorts of Irish combinations in view of similar fights in other parts in the Union; and I also think it slightly probable that they prefer to give as a reason for this increased activity and especially for the collection of arms, their intention to use them against the British Government rather than against the "Know-Nothings" which I, notwithstanding, take to be the real object in view.

Whether, as Crampton believed, Cushing was determined to pick a quarrel with the United States or not, the last quarter of 1855 saw repeated attempts to strain Anglo-American relations. Added to the dispute regarding recruitment were disagreements concerning Central America, the Crimean War, slavery in the South, and Irish pressure groups. The press seemed to thrive on exposing the differences between the two countries. Crampton tried to convey both his amusement and frustration about this state of affairs.[54]

Although I am not disposed to credit reports of an offensive and defensive alliance between Russia and the United States, because I know this Government will not and indeed could not venture upon such a step, their late conduct nevertheless taken with other symptoms convinces me that they are acting more or less on an understanding with Russia to annoy and thwart us and to create the impression which Russia naturally wishes to exist in Europe that we are in a most critical position as regards this country; that we are awfully terrified at the very thought of a rupture with it, and moreover that it is in the power of Russia to precipitate such a rupture whenever she pleases and throw the United States into the scale against us in case the war should last.

This I take to be the object steadily kept in view by the Russian agents in this country and there are a variety of circumstances which make it the interest (or supposed interest) of the present American Administration to become partners with Russia in playing this game to a *certain point*. But further than that point I do not apprehend that they could or that they wish to go.

The point in question would in my opinion be exactly that at which it could begin clearly to appear that England has made up her mind to put up with their various acts of insolence and aggression no longer, and bring the matter at once to an issue with them whether there was to be peace or war between the two countries. The very moment that the question of a real rupture with us came before the country here as an *imminent event*, the troubles of the Administration would begin, and they would have to change partners and begin a totally different sort of dance, or else be reduced to finish their present performance in solitude. To this point I believe it is in our power to bring them at any time. There would be a tremendous clatter to be sure of speeches, of articles, and of impertinent notes, but it would all end like the Oregon humbug of Mr. Polk: Congress and the country would leave the President in the lurch in any line of proceedings leading to a war with England about a few German recruits, or indeed about any other matter which did not involve some positive and vital interest of the country. Marcy I believe knows perfectly well that his onslaught on us will not lead to war, but he hopes to make us "eat a quantity of dirt" as the Persians say; to humiliate and bully us; and then to boast of it in the President's next message. Everything in regard to internal matters is gone wrong with this Administration, and lately more than ever; a perfect storm of Northern and Southern feeling is brewing, and will burst upon them next Congress; and they have managed to place themselves so ingeniously between the parties that they will be perfectly *flattened* when, the collision occurs.

Under these circumstances they have determined to play their ace of trumps, and put the match to the old Powder Barrel of Anti-British feeling which is in reality the great underlying "stratem" upon which, as they remind us every fourth of July, their "glorious institutions" are built.

By 2 October news reached Washington that the British and French had finally triumphed over the Russians at Sebastopol. Crampton was delighted, for he felt that this would help quiet those doomsayers in America who had been predicting Anglo-French defeat for months. He also informed Lord Clarendon of the latest legal maneuvers to discredit the British over the recruitment issue. The trial of two of Joseph Howe's alleged agents, Hertz and Perkins, had finally begun in Philadelphia, but Crampton did not think that the testimony would be too damaging. His expectations of James Buchanan, American minister to London, were less sanguine, however.[55]

With regard to the "Buck's" [Buchanan] note about Mosquito I feel sure that you are quite right as to his views in writing it. I am however, not so sure that the Administration would not back him up, although I know they generally dislike him. The American Government reproaching us for delaying to settle the Mosquito question is somewhat cool, considering first that we have for 6 years been vainly entreating *them* to settle it with us; and secondly that the present Administration has with equal coolness, and without other notice than by allowing us to find it out by their acts, withdrawn and repudiated the terms upon which their Predecessor's and we had *fully agreed* to settle it. The project of Treaty signed by Mr. Webster and myself, though rejected by Nicaragua seems to me to constitute in point of honour and good faith, between friendly nations at least, an *obligation* to settle the question on those terms, by which Mr. Webster's successors are bound, unless they could show very satisfactorily that he was wrong in Constitutional Law, which I defy even Mr. Cushing to do—or that circumstances had been changed by *our acts*. This they have not done and cannot do. With regard to the sense of the Clayton-Bulwer Treaty, Mr. Clayton has one doctrine—Bulwer another—Mr. Webster a third—Messrs. Cass and Douglas the party in the Senate a fourth and Mr. Buchanan it appears a modification thereof making a fifth! How is it then to be determined? It is at all events but a very one-sided bargain for us even by our own interpretation, for the United States are not in the least bound not to colonize or occupy in the only way they ever do colonize or occupy, that is to say by the United States citizens on their own hook, and as are now actually doing through Col. Kinney;[56] while we *are* prevented from colonizing or occupying in the only way we can do so, viz, by the action of our own Government. The "Buck" is a very cunning old gentleman and a great schemer in matters of private interest. I should not be surprised if he has been urging the renewal of the onslaught on the recruitment and the threat of dismissing me if not recalled. This would besides his political plans subserve a little private object which I have told you he had, and the nature of which you may understand by referring to my private note of the 9th September, 1854 in which I related what Mr. Marcy told me about my being replaced by Sir William Ouseley in view of pleasing his American wife, with whose family Buchanan is intimately connected. Ouseley I believe is a very good man and I daresay worthy of the place, but I must say that I don't think the American wife should make him better fitted for it, or make it more agreeable to himself, but quite the contrary.[57]

Crampton was understandably pleased when Lord Clarendon, on behalf of Her Majesty's government, reaffirmed confidence in his conduct.[58]

I have received your letter of the 28th ultimo respecting Mr. Marcy's note and the course which has been pursued by the United States Government in regard to the recruitment question; and I can truly say that I never perused a letter with more heartfelt satisfaction.

You have in the first place summed up the position in the most masterly manner, leaving not a shadow of doubt upon my mind that it is thoroughly comprehended by Her Majesty's Government; and in the second you have pointed out with equal clearness the course which is to be pursued to meet every event which may arise in regard to it. Perfect firmness in *essentials*, good temper and moderation as respects minor provocations are the only arms by which the malicious, mean, and tricky braggadocio of this Government can be successfully met.

Simplicity of purpose and a determination not to be turned off from the main issue of the case, but to oblige them to make the option *at once* is the only way to defeat the tortuous and insincere policy which guides their councils. The question simply is, do the United States want to pick a serious quarrel with us or not? If they do, we are ready to meet them, if not, we are ready to let by-gones be by-gones and be friends. The "measure of satisfaction" which we can give them consistently with the national honor should at once be stated to them; if they accept if frankly as it is offered—good—if not, they should at once be made to *see* that we have made up our minds that a rupture is inevitable and are acting accordingly.

The present plan of the United States Cabinet is evident: It is to keep the matter as much and as long before the public as they can by mock trials and other contrivances of that sort until a national feeling is got up that an insult has been put upon the country and not atoned for; and in the meantime to keep up an angry but indecisive discussion of the matter diplomatically, with the intention of enduring it hostilely . . . to be prolonged if possible until the meeting of Congress in December next. . . .

. . . But Mr. Marcy's conduct in this matter is of a piece with the rest and more specifically with that of Mr. Cushing, who is our *real enemy* and whose Old Bailey diplomacy will not have escaped your admiration.

You will see that he has profited by his position as a member of the American Cabinet and his consequent access to the diplomatic correspondence of the Government to produce in an open Court of Justice[59] his [Mr. Cushing's] reply to your note to Mr. Buchanan!—in terms hostile and disrespectful, and in which he actually presumes to talk of the Agents of the British Government as *malefactors screened* by your devices from justice.

But this Gentlemen's object is plain and it is fully confirmed to me by what I hear of the language he is now using.

He evidently is insane enough *really* to wish to bring on a rupture with England, and is therefore determined to seize every opportunity of widening the breach he has continued to make.

That he was desirous of getting the country into a War I was always told on the best authority from the very commencement of the Administration. His warlike propensities appear to have been on one or two occasions overruled by his Colleagues, but he now seems to have persuaded them, under the idea I suppose of our defeat in the Crimea, to go with him. I believe *they* would like to back out now that they know the value of Mr. Cushing's prophetic power, but *he* is evidently determined to force them on the course he has got them to adopt. I *know* that he goes about saying that my *dismissal* is inevitable and boasting of the immense fleet of armed merchant men which the United States could at once call into action, which would ravage our coasts and burn all our small towns. I could scarcely believe in such folly if I had it not from a source which for various reasons I know to be certain.[60] However, I believe that he will be grievously disappointed in his expectations and, partly by the better sense of the owners of those very merchant men and their cargos whose practical aid he counts upon.

His breaking through every rule of international propriety and courtesy in commenting in such a tone upon a diplomatic note publicly, which is still in the hands of the Secretary of State as part of a correspondence upon a question under discussion . . . seems to me to be an outrage which I at first thought of at once pointing out to the United States Government in an official Note. On reflection, however, I thought it better to leave it to you to deal with.

A sore spot between the two countries was the issue of who should control Nicaragua. Although William Walker held sway there, it was quite natural for the British to speculate as to the best means of restoring stability to the region. In Washington, the former Nicaraguan chargé d'affairs, Marcoleta, was advising Crampton to settle the Mosquito Indian question by granting Nicaragua sovereignty over the Mosquito territory.[61]

With regard to the establishment of the Mosquito as an independent nation in some allotted portion of the Mosquito coast Marcoleta urged objections which I confess I have always felt have some weight as well for our own sake as that of Nicaragua.

The evil of such an arrangement seems to me to be that we should have to continue our Protectorate of the Mosquitos and get into fresh questions with whoever interfered with their political independence, a state which it is obvious they are totally incapable of maintaining for themselves against *anybody*.

If they are not to be politically independent it seems to me the sort of arrangement now proposed in Marcoleta's 6th and 7th Articles is better than the one by which they would be given an allotted territory as the Indians are in this country, under the sort of quasi-treaties which are made with them by the United States Government; for in that case they would be confined to a territory so allotted and it would probably be filched from them in a few years for a few casks of rum or other "notions" after the manner and fashion of that respected class of persons called the Indian Agents in this country, the rascality of whose proceedings cannot be parallelled.

The only question therefore is whether the securities now offered for the future existence of our Protegés sufficiently conform with our honour; for practically I really imagine it will make no difference whatever.

The whole Mosquito Nation does not amount to more than a few hundred persons and there are deserts and swamps where they may hunt and fish ad infinitum, and where no Nicaraguan authority ever has or probably will in our time set their foot.

If the Indians are allowed to come to any little villages or ports which exist on the coast where they can dispose of such things as they have got to sell, they will have all the advantages of which they are capable of availing themselves, or which they now really enjoy under the supposition of their being the possessors of the "Eminent Domain" of the country.

During the course of November, news arrived in the United States that the British were reinforcing their naval squadron in the West Indies. To Crampton this was a great tonic for his otherwise flagging spirits, as he was growing weary of the continued personal abuse against him in the press. Although the recruitment issue quieted down, he still could not take much pleasure in his work.[62]

The idea of a war with England on this subject of recruitment or indeed on any other pending matter has now, in spite of every effort of the Administration to stir up hostility, been so universally scouted by all the great interests of the country that I feel pretty certain that Mr. Marcy is now looking out for means for backing out of the business altogether. He will of course endeavour to throw as much of the blame as he can upon us as the provokers of the quarrel, the idea of which has proved so unacceptable to the American people, but the Cotton Gentlemen of Manchester and Glasgow may be perfectly easy as to the existence here of just the same base feeling which animates them in regard to their Mills and Markets.

The only difference that I know of is that here there is somewhat more baseness in the feeling because it is half-concealed in a cloud of swagger, and because it in no degree results from an absence of malignant hostility; they are "willing to wound and yet afraid to strike," and I shall much regret to see the Manchester and Glasgow men do all the peacemaking; for if they were only to preserve a firm attitude and their own dignity, these people would come more than half way in conciliation; if however they find that we are to keep peace with them "à tout prix" they will bully us now and hereafter to the very last inch they can; for a more unrelenting set of devils when they think they have got anybody "on the hip" never existed. A soft answer does *not* turn away wrath *here*; they make a cool calculation of the injury they can inflict without hurting themselves and at the same time inflict it without reference to any general considerations of the better policy of keeping up a feeling of kindness by a little giving and taking and a little of that blindness to the faults of their friends which I am sure we have on many occasions shown toward them to the very limits of what was proper or possible in justice to ourselves.

Violence in the Kansas-Nebraska Territory, Irish agitation in New York, and the chaotic situation in Central America preoccupied Crampton in early December.[63]

One of the principal and most exciting questions to be dealt with this Session is that relating to the Kansas-Nebraska Territory. It is one of those questions that bring Northern and Southern principles face to face in a new form and with somewhat more than their ancient animosity.

The conditions of as "pretty a quarrel" on *the subject as Sir Lucius O'Trigger*[64] could have desired already existed in a disputed election of a delegate from that Territory, both parties having elected their man and each having repaired to Washington with the intention of taking his Seat in Congress as the legitimate Representative of the Territory. The feeling on the subject was already very bitter but the news which has just been received from the Territory has raised the excitement to red-hot pitch. It appears that the Northern and Southern parties in the Territory have actually come to blows; skirmishes have taken place, people have been killed, houses burned and the Governor of the Territory has made official application to the President for Federal troops to put down the "Civil War" which he finds himself unable to suppress by the ordinary legal means at his disposal. This is the result of Mr. Pierce's great Peace and Conciliation measure of last year! You may therefore imagine the state of favor in which the Administration now is—and you will the better understand why, having the prospect of this ugly affair in their hands, they were seeking for a desperate issue out of their difficulty by a quarrel with England. That resource has however failed them and I find that even the most anti-Anglican papers now openly say, "we have little time to waste on recruitment difficulties and other minor affairs of that sort, with Civil War and bloodshed and Dis-Union at our doors".

I send you today an account of the Irish Convention at New York[65] (enclosure no. 1). . . . The thing could not have been better done in Dublin itself or Cork.

One of the chief organizers, Mr. Doheny (late from Australia) denounces another chief organizer, Mr. McClenahan, the talented Editor of the "Citizen" as a "mean spy" who in "five minutes after the meeting will be closeted with the British Consul"; a general scrimmage in the usual style ensues; "You lie!" "You ruffian" etc., etc., in the midst of which Mr. O'Mahony jumps to his feet impelled by an excuseable misgiving to ascertain whether the "epithet ruffian" could be meant for *him*, for if so, etc., etc. All this, and other considerations, do not make me very apprehensive of the invasive designs of these heroes, and I am still of the opinion that the whole organization is meant to be used for voting purposes in *this country*. . . . One of their plans is to form affiliations with the Irish population in *Canada* and this I confess appears to me to be the most dangerous because the most practicable part of the scheme.—For some reason or other, however, the Catholic Priests are unfavourable to this organization. Perhaps those holy men having hitherto had the sole drilling and selling of the Irish vote in their own hands don't like it to be interfered with. Neither do the newspapers give the plan much support. . . .

Nicaraguan affairs are in a bad condition. The total want of energy of the Central Americans allows Walker to hold his own; and the Representatives of the Central American States here are amusing themselves by addressing protestatory and supplicatory Notes to Marcy not to recognize Walker's Government; to which he returns no reply, or answers verbally by jokes and chuckles. Of course it does not signify a farthing to Walker whether he is recognized or not by the United States. He knows he will be recognized if he holds his ground; and he knows that the United States Government will do nothing to prevent his doing so. It appears that there were quite a sufficient number of Nicaraguan troops under arms to have crushed him but that they have marched off in two divisions—one to Costa Rica and the other to Guatemala. Even now it is evident that Walker feels the precariousness of his position, for he is having every man of the least consequence on whom he can lay his hands instantly shot, shows that he is aware that he has nothing but terror to trust to for maintaining himself.

Although Congress assembled on 3 December for a new session, a deadlock developed in the House of Representatives about who should be Speaker. By 17 December, when Crampton wrote his next letter, there had been sixty ballots, and no decision was in sight. With little news to report, he offered instead a few descriptive comments about his diplomatic colleagues.[66]

We have nothing new about the Nicaraguan tragi-comedy except the arrival here under the title of Envoy Extraordinary and Minister Plenipotentiary from Mr. Walker's republic of a friend of his, Mr. Parker H. French,[67] a gentleman who having stood within danger of the Law in the United States on account of extensive forgery which he committed in Texas where there is little Law, fled to California where there is none at all, and from thence joined Walker.

He now imagines that his diplomatic character will shield him; and although it appears that the President has concluded that it would be *too bad* to recognize him at once, I have no doubt he will not be molested. If the United States Government were consistent with their professions they ought at once to arrest him as a violator of the Neutrality Laws, and have a detainer filed against him as a forgerer besides; but this would be considered "ungenerous and ungentlemanly-like" in this country as Mr. French has, in his Pocket, a most advantageous "Treaty" between the new Republic which he represents and his former country. . . .

. . . and I have since understood that both he [The Austrian minister to the United States] and the Prussian [minister] are very decided in advocating Mr. Cushing's course in blaming me [concerning recruitment]. This I attribute to some degree to a habit I have remarked on the part of a certain small fry of diplomatists to curry favor "à tout prix" with the Government to which they are accredited. . . . They have been followed in this course by the Dutch and Belgian representatives who have really nothing to do with the matter. The Belgian (a gentleman rejoicing in the appropriately sounding name of M. Bosch) had rendered himself particularly offensive—so much so that I think I must give him a hint to devote more of his talents to purely Belgian questions.

All these diplomatists are personrally of the very smallest calibre, underpaid and generally under-bred. The Swedish Minister, M. de Sibbern, on the other hand, is a Gentleman in every respect, and has as well as my French Colleague, M. Boilleau, behaved in the kindest and handsomest way. The Dane, M. Bille, has also behaved well.[68]

As of 24 December there was still no Speaker. Not only did Congress seem to lack leadership, but there was a vacuum of power in the White House as well.[69]

Mr. Pierce you may have already perceived is given to continual vacillations; a week ago he told somebody he had never dreamt of my recall or dismissal; and if you doubted he was an indiscreet talker, what I have now told you would convince you of it. I cannot help thinking too, as others do, that although he has taken "the pledge" [against drinking] there are moments at which the "*veteris vestigia flamma*" appear, and this would partly account for silly speeches which he has made on various subjects.

I don't believe him by any means the most malignant member of his Administration but he certainly seems to be the weakest and least to be relied upon—such indeed is his character pretty generally. . . .

Mr. Parker French, the piratical Nicaraguan envoy, has not been received; and yet I think it is only a delay. Mr. Jefferson Davis, the Secretary of War, whose Department it was which was cheated by Mr. Parker French's forgeries, being asked why he did not immediately have him arrested said—although it is true that we have not recognized him, yet such is our respect for international obligations that we allow "the gloss of his diplomatic character to protect him!". . .

P.S. As I should not like to trust the above to the Post I have sent it by a Special Messenger to New York and thence by an English Gentleman to England. . . . I enclose an article giving an account of a little incident which has just taken place here. I think I mentioned to you that Mr. Douglas Wallach the Editor of the "Star", is the confidential friend of Mr. Cushing and particularly of Mr. Pierce who calls him "Dug" and treats him with great familiarity. I could always see some traces of official confidences in the "Star", sometimes partially obliterated by brandy and water perhaps, but of course with no want of low impudence towards us. Well-merited retribution has however you will perceive overtaken this gentleman through the "Providential" instrumentality of the Honorable Mr. Smith, a Member of Congress for Virginia, and he has had his hand nearly bitten off in a difficulty with that gentleman. These being the sort of gentlemen by whose means the politics of this country are really *worked* you will understand the absolute necessity of a Foreign Minister "declining" to go down into the arena of their discussions even for the simplest purpose of self-defence or for mere statement of a matter of fact.

Unbeknownst to Crampton, on 28 December Marcy addressed a monumental dispatch to Buchanan in which the American position on recruitment was further buttressed and justified. Buchanan was instructed not only to relay this elaborate condemnation of British policy and British agents in America to Lord Clarendon but also to insist on Crampton's recall from Washington.[70] What had begun in February as a modest inquiry into the feasibility of recruiting a few unemployed foreigners for military service in the Crimea thus mushroomed into a major diplomatic crisis, perhaps the worst since the Oregon Affair ten years earlier.

At the end of the year the strain was beginning to tell on Crampton. Although he took comfort in the fact that Lord Clarendon and the cabinet continued to support him, he became increasingly bitter concerning the way he was treated by the American press and the Pierce cabinet. The possibility that he would soon leave Washington therefore did not dismay him.

6

Expulsion, Transition, and Restoration: Crampton, Lumley, and Napier, 1856–1857

As the year 1856 began, Crampton was faced with the same problems that had plagued him during the previous year. Rumors of an impending Anglo-American conflict were rife. The Americans continued to insist that their neutrality laws had been willfully violated by numerous British agents. In addition, they charged Great Britain with having dealt falsely with the United States in 1850, promising under the provisions of the Clayton-Bulwer Treaty to withdraw from Central American affairs and then refusing to do so. Britain maintained that the treaty was merely prospective; therefore she was under no obligation to cease protecting the inhabitants of Greytown and the Mosquito Coast or to abandon her Crown colony of the Bay Islands off the coast of Honduras. Moreover, she was exceedingly upset by William Walker's invasion of Nicaragua and his establishment of the puppet Rivas regime, actions that threatened to convert another filibustering gamble into a future American possession.

Crampton was convinced that the Pierce administration, goaded on by its attorney general, Caleb Cushing, would exploit these diplomatic tensions.[1]

Your letters of the 14th and 21st ultimo only reached me yesterday. The Packet has had a bad passage and we are also now so blocked up with snow that I have serious doubts that I shall be able to get this mail down to Boston in time for the Wednesday's "Cunarder".

I am sorry to say that I have not a good account to give you of things here.

The Government and Mr. Cushing in particular seem bent upon mischief of some sort. Their political position at home is desperate and having nothing to lose they are, it appears, determined on doing something striking to arouse public attention and fix it on foreign relations. They have seen that the country will not support them in *War* with Great Britain, but they think nevertheless that something may be done.

My dismissal, and a menacing position with regard to the Central American questions, are the subjects selected for offensive proceedings. Out of them they think a sort of *pot* stick can be made by which the whole country may be stirred up. Mr. Cushing I unerstand makes no secret of this plan and I believe he makes no secret either that *he* would if he could push things somewhat further and get the United States into a foreign War; this being the great cure for the black disease which is now tearing the vitals of the Union.

His real motive is however that he, Caleb Cushing, should for once stand at the head of the nation—whatever ruin or confusion might afterwards ensue.

He knows however, I believe, that he has not got the country, Congress or even all his colleagues embarked in so extreme a plan: but he will shove them as far upon that road as he can.

The present state of Congress unfortunately rather favours the success of the scheme the Administration are now engaged upon. The House is still *not organized* and Congress is thereby paralyzed as to the measures which they would otherwise be enabled and I am convinced are anxious to adopt to put a stop in time to the contemplated violence of the Executive.[2] The dodge of withholding the correspondence on the recruitment difficulty, which I foresaw was intended, makes it difficult for the Senate even to take hold of the question, and several of the more conservative Senators who know the real state of things have told me that they are most anxious to put a stop to the dangerous course which the administration are taking, and that the Senate would undoubtedly do so if they could only get an opportunity.

Like many British observers, Crampton relished pointing out the uncouth and often violent behavior of Americans, especially those of Irish descent.[3]

I don't know whether Mr. Rowcroft's prosecutions of the Irish conspirators at Cincinnati will do much good.[4] I perceive that the usual Irish "stratagem" has been adopted in the case, viz. that of shooting the principal witness. The ball went through his hat however.

When Crampton next wrote, political campaigning had already begun for the election that would take place ten months hence. Opponents of the Democratic party were in great disarray: Northern and Southern Whigs divided over the issue of slavery; the Know-Nothings opposed Catholics and foreigners and were hopelessly split regarding positive goals; and the fledgling Republican party tried to cut across these factions and draw support from those in the Northern states.[5]

The most alarming part of the matter, apparently at least, is the line which has been taken by Mr. Seward and followed by Mr. Foot of Vermont, one of the parties of which Mr. Seward may now be considered the leader.[6] These gentlemen you will have seen have thought proper to make strong war by themselves. . . . This object is two-fold. First, to gain for the new party to which they belong (the "Black Republicans") the reputation of being "whole hearted Americans", ready to fight with England for a straw, a reputation which they are the more anxious to establish from the fact of their party being made up in a great degree of the remains of the old federalists and Whig elements—they would naturally labour under the disadvantage of being thought by the masses too peaceful and conservative, a reproach which was always made against the Federalists and Whigs and one which ever since 1812 has made them the most unpopular people in the country. In the second place they wish to deprive Mr. Pierce and his Administration of the credit of being the most forward in the war cry and by joining him and even going beyond him to bring the question of peace or war at once to a point at which they conceive that he and his party will flinch and have to back down instead of enabling him by their opposition to keep the question before the country until the time of the Presidential nominations in May and June next. . . .

Mr. Dallas is here taking his instructions, and I believe will start next week for England.[7] I have had some conversation with him of a very friendly and pacific character, although without entering into particulars of the "difficulties" the details of which he told me he had not yet mastered. You will find him a respectable-looking old gentleman of better manners and address than most of his countrymen. He is however a strong Democrat and "anti-Briton"—though less likely to adopt "artful dodges" than his Predecessor. . . .

Mr. Rowcroft's Irish prosecutions have, as I foresaw they would, failed; they have however rendered the fact apparent that there is an extensive organization of Irishmen here ready to do us any little good turn they can combined with political objects here[8] The Judge who has discharged the accused evidently thinks that any conspiracy or arrangement entered into in the United States for overthrowing the Government of another country is perfectly legitimate if not praiseworthy, as long as the execution of it is put off until a war breaks out between the United States and that country. As this "saving clause" will infallibly be appended to the Program of every future "Emmett and Wolfe Tone" Lodge which may be established, it will of course be quite useless for us to attempt to check the proceedings of such persons here.[9] All we can do will be to keep a strict watch on their proceedings and I shall instruct the Consuls accordingly. . . .

I never, to say the truth, thought the Clayton-Bulwer Treaty worth one farthing as restraining these people from pursuing their aggressive plans in the only shape they do or can pursue such plans—but it has turned out unfortunately to be worse than nothing by entangling us in engagements to which these ingenious gentlemen give any interpretation they please while they are carrying out their manifest destiny without the smallest check under cover of an outcry against British encroachments.

There would therefore be no great misfortune in the abrogation of the Treaty altogether, or even the loss of the Belize and the Bay Islands, but still it would be fatal to do anything which would countenance the idea of our having violated a treaty. I know for certain that Mr. Clayton has prepared an historical statement for the use of a Senator who is about to make a speech on the question by which he pretends to prove that we have violated every treaty we ever made, and ergo, the Clayton-Bulwer Treaty!

When statesmen of Mr. Clayton's standing resort to such stratagems it is not surprising that the masses, who of course believe them, should be inveterately hostile to and distrustful of everything we do.

By 3 March Crampton realized the implications of Marcy's lengthy dispatch to Buchanan of 28 December 1855, including its firm request for his recall.[10]

With regard to my resignation of the Mission, which I think Marcy's note justifies and renders natural . . . personally I should care very little for this [voluntary resignation] and I should heartily be glad to get out of this country in which I have now spent upwards of ten of the best years of my life, broken by one very short leave of absence. Washington, never a pleasant post, is under the present circumstances detestable, and I really think that just now the Legation would be better in the hands of a Chargé d'Affaires and a new hand who would keep quiet and who would at all events afford a smaller mark than a Minister for the poison arrows of these savages.

Lumley is perfectly well qualified to carry on the business and is entirely imbued, as well he may be, by what he has lately witnessed, with the necessity of caution in this dangerous and hostile region.[11] However I shall be entirely guided by your opinion in this matter; and if it is judged useful or expedient on any account that I should hold on until my respected friends have made up their minds either to turn me out or to shake hands with me, I shall willingly do so.

Whenever the subject of Central America was raised, there was heated debate in the Senate on the subject. John M. Clayton, who still served in the upper chamber as a Republican, would defend his treaty and accuse Britain of violating it in spirit if not in fact. Democrats countered that Clayton's treaty betrayed America's real interests, and the Senate Foreign Relations Committee was blamed for having ratified it in 1850.[12]

It would give me sincere pleasure to see Bulwer explain his own meaning in the Treaty, as it would be a much more expeditious process to be able to refer people to it directly, as expressed by himself, than to deduce it from the terms of the document itself and from such correspondence as he has left here about it. Indeed, nothing would please me more than to meet him out here on a special mission to fix and repair his own hand work; for it was the misfortune of it to give endless bother and to be a source of blunders and misconceptions without end to everybody else who has had anything to do with it since. The truth is, if I may say so confidentially, it is a pity it ever was made. At all events it should not have been made till *after* all questions regarding our Protectorate Rights and territories had been fixed and defined.

I always expressed this opinion and was astonished on my return here in 1851, to find that the Treaty had been signed without any of these matters being settled. But Clayton was in a great hurry to get the Treaty done before he was turned out of office and Bulwer was (very naturally) anxious to get it done and to get out of this blessed country. So that they both of them agreed to constructions which would get round the obstacles instead of reading them out. I have no doubt that Clayton persuaded Bulwer that the construction adopted saved all Bulwer wanted to save and at the same time told his own colleagues and the Senate that he had got a construction which gained all they wanted to gain and eliminated us out of Central America under pretense of protecting a canal which never was to be made. In order to enhance his supposed services in this respect he has now the effrontery to talk to the Senate of the "*troops* and *bands* of *colonists we had in readiness to pour upon the Isthmus* in order to keep its use from the United States!"

As the Treaty stands however and with the talent possessed by these people for interpreting *everything* to suit their own purposes, it is a peg upon which eternal discussions can be hung and moreover, every dispatch written or communicated about it has become the subject of fresh misinterpretation.

Nothing therefore it seems to me but arbitration on the construction or abrogation of the whole thing can possibly settle it.

The war scare continued unabated, prompting Crampton to explain to Lord Clarendon why the Pierce administration insisted upon pursuing a policy of deliberate provocation.[13]

One of the chief ends of the Administration has been to raise a sort of war alarm under cover of which they have succeeded in passing some Bills and are endeavouring to pass others which could not have been got through Congress under ordinary circumstances.[14] The measures I allude to are the 10 Sloops Bill for which they have got ten millions of dollars, the small arms Bill for which they are to get three millions, and the fortifications Bill for which they hope to get three millions more. This you will observe shall give Mr. Pierce and his party some sixteen millions worth of patronage and small jobs which he will have to distribute between now and the Presidential nomination in June next. Of course I need not tell you that the doctrine "to the victors belong the spoils" will be rigidly adhered to and that every dollar will go to the political supporters of the Administration.

As the other side would do the same thing were they in the same place, they of course do not object, but they would be very glad to have a good excuse for passing no more money; and I have not a doubt that the three million bill would fall through if our difficulties were supposed to be ended. It is the direct interest of the Administration therefore to keep them open, and to do them justice they spare no pains to keep up the impression that they are in a most precarious position.

No sensible man or *politician* of *any party* believes a word of it; but of course it has its effect on the Masses and furnishes topics for such speeches as those of Mr. Iverson of Georgia and Mr. Brown of Mississippi, with creatures of the Administration.[15]

Three weeks later Crampton accepted the inevitability of his expulsion, but determined that when it occurred, the United States government would gain no satisfaction from it.[16]

With respect to my resignation, although I certainly should not be sorry that people here should clearly understand and feel that no English Gentleman would, from a love of office, wish to cultivate their society unless they treat him in a different spirit from what they have lately displayed toward me, I nevertheless entirely agree with you that it would be much better that they should be allowed to dismiss me than that I should resign.

For in the first place, explain it how we might, my resignation would always be held up here as a victory obtained over the British Government, and in the second it would be converted into a precedent which would render the tenure of office of any future British Minister in this country, to whom any political party or even clique of individuals might take a dislike or for political effect wish to get rid of, so insecure as to endanger the friendly relations of the two countries upon the most trifling pretexts. Precedents of the successful bullying of a foreign Power, and particularly England, would be more dangerous here than in any other country in the world. Each succeeding Administration is goaded and taunted into not following behind its predecessors in embodying the vulgar impudence and vanity of the already *spoiled* democracy in some scandalous act of national aggression.

The more personal and insulting such an act can be made, the better it pleases. Nothing rendered General Jackson so popular as his swaggering though puerile message to Louis Philippe that he would hold him *personally* responsible for some American claim upon the French Government and *force him* to pay whether the

Chambers chose to grant the money or not.[17] Personally I do not in the least mind the attacks which are or may not be made upon me here. After torturing their ingenuity to the utmost they have produced little else than vague abuse and moreover all the noise proceeds in reality from a very limited number of people who have a particular political object in view.

In mid-April American policy assumed a less bellicose tone. At the same time, reports from Central America suggested that several states had combined forces in order to topple Walker's precarious government in Nicaragua.[18]

All the Administration, even including the warlike Cushing, now wish to put "water in their wine".

In fact the evident state of opinion both in Congress and in the Country at large would not warrant the Government in taking violent measures, and no good electioneering purpose would now be served by such a course. The "Recruitment" and the Central American questions were taken up for no other purpose than as means for influencing the Presidential canvass; but as the whole attention of the public is now directed to that canvass, and it is at the same time evident that in spite of all efforts to draw public attention to Foreign Politics, the contest must take place on "other issues." To *these* all the politicians are addressing themselves, and the Clayton Treaty and the Recruitment are put like empty bottles under the table. . . .

Costa Rica has declared War on Walker and announced to the United States Government that She claims all the rights of a Belligerent. M. Molina tells me that Marcy received the intimation with evident *ill*-humour; and I see that the newspapers are asserting roundly that I made Molina take this step in order to make the British and French Governments take possession of Central America under the pretense of acting as *allies* of Costa Rica, in the same way that they were allies of the Turks.[19] I fear that the poor indolent Indians, who compose the forces of the Central American states, even though superior in numbers will form no match for the desperadoes who have gone and are, (the Neutrality Laws interpreted by Caleb Cushing notwithstanding), going by hundreds every week to join him.

One week later Crampton was pleased by the news from Nicaragua because Walker's forces had met heavy resistance.[20]

The news from Nicaragua has been an agreeable surprise, for there seems to be no doubt of the fact that a portion of Walker's forces have been completely defeated by a very slightly superior Force of Costa Ricans, and this I hope may encourage the other Central American States to make some exertion to put an end to the notion that fifty or sixty drunken ruffians from the United States can take possession of any part of this Continent they choose to select as a field for plunder. . . .

Of course the discomfiture of the gallant Filibusters is attributed here to secret aid to Costa Rica from Great Britain, and it is also discovered that Walker's force consisted after all only of Irishmen and Germans—and consequently American glory is intact.

News reached Washington that while Costa Rican troops were stalking Walker and his supporters in Virgin Bay on Lake Nicaragua, they had mistakenly killed several unarmed Americans working for the Accessory Transit Company. Similarly, reports from Chagres in Panama alleged that on the night of 15–16 April the local inhabitants attacked a group of Americans en route from the East Coast of the United States to California, killing an estimated thirty of them and wounding many others.

Although the British were in no sense responsible for these manifestations of anti-American feeling, they were blamed because most of the incidents happened in countries that were thought to be her client states. Accordingly, the United States augmented its naval squadron in Central American waters and punished those judged responsible. Crampton's letter of 5 May expressed his concern that America might grant diplomatic recognition to Walker's recently established dictatorship in Nicaragua.[21]

The Panama riot is unfortunately timed, and it is also unlucky *if true* that the Costa Ricans should have killed any unoffending Americans at Virgin Bay.

Walker, however, in spite of the victories he boasts of must be in a bad way.

On the other hand, there is little trust to be put in the valour of Central American natives and I shall not allow myself to exalt in their having disposed of Walker until I hear that they have shot or hanged him.

I apprehend however that whatever may be the result of the present contest in Central America, we must expect before long to see one or all of the passages across the Isthmus to be under the direct control of the Americans. Quarrels with the natives will be sure to succeed each other, and consequent outrages and inconveniences will be experienced by Passengers to California, so that the U.S. Government will be at last forced to take up the matter and lend its aid in establishing either in its own name or that of some piratical "Branch American Government" Yankee supremacy in those countries. You may judge that this notion may possibly be carried out ere long by referring to the Speech of Mr. Douglas in the Senate (see inclosure no. 4 in my despatch no. 113 of today)—and coupling it with the fact that Mr. Douglas is now "the favorite" for the Presidency. . . .[22] Marcy has written a very savage note to M. Molina upon the subject of the alleged massacre of non-combatant American Citizens by Costa Rican troops at Virgin Bay—I have no doubt the charge is very much exaggerated if not totally false; but I have advised M. Molina to answer at once that if any such thing has occurred the Costa Rican Government will make reparation; and that they as much as the U.S. Government utterly repudiate the practice of putting non-combatants to death. With regard to shooting fillibuster prisoners, even when taken with arms in their hands, I have strongly advised M. Molina to press upon his Government the bad effect which such a practice, even if justifiable, will produce on their cause, and the small influence it can have on the success of their army in the field. Marcy is already trying to make capital out of the indignation excited by these acts, and Mr. Douglas and others are using them as arguments for the necessity of the United States wresting the countries through which passages across the Isthmus have been made, from the "barbarous" race which now occupies them, as a measure necessary for the safety of American citizens going to and coming from California peaceably on their legitimate business. This language of course finds an echo from numerous classes here, and I have no doubt that Mr. Douglas as well as Mr. Pierce will make it a "plank of their platform" at the Convention at Cincinnati in the beginning of next month.

It appears that another Minister Plenipotentiary from Walker has arrived at New York and the newspapers are very confused that the President will receive him. The new Envoy is a priest, Padre Vigil, and is described as a "venerable and highly intelligent ecclesiastic."[23] M. Molina, who knows him, tells me on other hand that he is a villain of the deepest dye, and that he was un-priested as far as the Catholic Church could unpriest him, and banished from Nicaragua for being concerned in several murders. This is much the most probable account of the two.

I fear that the moment would not be opportune for me to carry out the instructions in your despatch nos. 85 and 89 to propose to Marcy a joint action against Walker.[24] Whatever Mr. Marcy's personal opinion may be, or whatever may be the real wishes of the Government to see that free-booter uprooted, they would never dare to countenance anything which would seem like letting us have a finger in the Central American pie.

If they *do* wish to see Walker disposed of, (and I very much doubt that all the Cabinet do), it is because they fear that a section of the Democratic Party *opposed* to them is making capital by supporting him. They are therefore now evidently, as you may judge by the late notes to Molina which will be laid before Congress in a week, trying to head off Mr. Douglas by being even more indignant than he is against the Central Americans. To take any effective measures to help them now and more particularly in *conjunction with us* would throw the whole game into Mr. Douglas' hands.

During the second week in May the United States learned that preliminary terms for peace had been accepted by both sides in the Crimean War. Meanwhile, Walker was far from suffering defeat and in fact appeared stronger than ever.[25]

You will not, perhaps, be surprised to find (by my despatch no. 118 by this packet) that the United States Government is taking ground for recognising Walker;[26] you may, however, have some astonishment left for the coolness of our friends here in alleging that it is our unauthorized interference in that gentleman's affairs which compels them to adopt this scandalous course.

The facts I believe to be simply this. A pressure from without has been brought to bear upon Mr. Pierce's Government in favour of the recognition of the gallant Filibuster, as a measure necessary to place Mr. Pierce in an advantageous position as an "Aggressive Patriot" at the Democratic Convention at Cincinnati on the 2nd of next month. In order to do this with good grace, and to have an excuse *for not having done it long ago*, it was necessary that a case *should be got up* to show the present necessity of it as a measure required in order to counteract British Influence in the matter. Accordingly this is done in the usual way. A *"disclosure"* of British designs is brought forward by means of a letter, stolen by Walker, handed over by him to the United States Minister in Nicaragua; and by him published in the American Newspapers. Add to this that it is suddenly discovered that the Right of Search has been exercised, and the American Flag insulted by Captain Tarleton of the "Eurydice," because he ventured to ascertain whether 500 armed ruffians in an American Steamer were going to seize upon Greytown; for such I infer must have been the object of his enquiry.[27] At all events no objection was made to his investigation, and the 500 filibusters or passengers were allowed to go their way without hinderance on his part and may, and probably have, joined Walker. . . .

I am told that Marcy still opposes immediate recognition of Walker and that he has threatened to resign if the President and his colleagues insist upon it. His language and manner at our last interview, I confess, gave me the impression that he is wavering. He said that he did not know "how the matter will now be handled," and added very pointedly that it was at all events a very painful and disagreeable one to *him*.

I presume however that the Government will wait for the next news; and if possible feel the pulse of the Cincinnati Convention before taking any decision. If the news is that Walker has been hanged, it will relieve them from a great embarrassment; and I daresay that they would not be sorry in their hearts to hear it.

By 19 May there was little doubt in Crampton's mind that his expulsion was imminent. As a last effort toward reconciliation, he accepted the good offices of the French minister to the United States, the comte de Sartiges, in order to avoid the inevitable.[28]

If I am not misinformed, the Government has determined to adopt the hostile course and send me my Passports at once.

Sartiges happened to be with me when I received your letters, so that I was able at once to put him in train to try the chances of a friendly offer of French "bons offices" in the matter. As from being absent during the whole course of the affair he is not naturally "au fait" to it in all its bearings, I impressed upon him the necessity of not plunging into the details or entering into arguments on the merits of the case on either side, or for the present, the offering of specific conditions of accommodation.

He perfectly well understood the position he was to take and I believe correctly performed his part at an interview he had with Marcy the next morning (the 17th). His reply is "Marcy est hostile—il est furieux contre *vous* personellement. . . ." He also saw Cushing by chance and had a long conversation with him: "Cushing montrait moins de mauvaise humeur," said Sartiges. . . .

[I am] most grateful to you for what you say in regard to my own affairs and future prospects. We have exactly the same feeling as to the necessity of not giving these people triumph and they shall not have it from me. I shall therefore pass over with perfect equanimity all their attacks in Congress or the papers, *and never reply to them* except through the official channel of a despatch to my own Government.

A week later, Crampton's fate was still in doubt. Meanwhile a shocking episode occurred in the chamber of the United States Senate: an outraged Southern congressman, Preston S. Brooks, mercilessly beat Charles Sumner, the renowned abolitionist senator from Massachusetts.[29]

The hesitation which I told you in the postscript of my last letter Sartiges thought he perceived in the councils of this Government seems in reality to have existed for I have not yet received my passports. . . .

I shall keep this letter open till the last moment in order to tell you what more I may learn on the subject; but up to the present time all is uncertain. . .

On Wednesday last Mr. Brooks, a Southern Member of the House of Representatives, entered the Senate Chamber, and approaching Sumner, the Senator from Massachusetts, who was sitting in his place in the Body of the House, felled him to the earth by a blow on the back of the head with what (by courtesy) the papers call a *cane* but which it seems was a rod of iron covered with *gutta percha*. This was done without a word of notice, so much so that Mr. Sumner had not time to rise from his seat. He was knocked senseless by the first blow, upon which Mr. Brooks proceeded to belabour him while on the ground without it appears any sort of opposition by the Spectators, Mr. Sumner's colleagues. Mr. Brooks indeed it seems had brought a "friend", Mr. Keitt of South Carolina, to prevent impertinent interference in the "difficulty".[30] Sumner was carried off bleeding and senseless and has been in a precarious state for two days.—He is now however recovering. Mr. Sumner is really one of the best-educated and most gentleman-like men of the Senate, but he had made an anti-Nebraska speech in which the peculiar institution of the South was rather roughly handled. Mr. Brooks' exploit, though of course it excites the indignation of the North, is highly and openly approved of by the Southern members who applaud the justice of punishment being inflicted on the spot where the offence was committed.

Two days later the talisman of diplomatic dismissal, a returned passport, arrived in Crampton's mail. At the same time, similar expulsions were delivered to the British consuls in Philadelphia, New York, and Cincinnati.[31]

On the other side of the Atlantic, the American minister George M. Dallas, anticipating retaliation by the British, made preparations to leave London. Talk of war, which had lessened in the late spring, was revived briefly but proved erroneous. Weeks passed without Dallas being dismissed by Her Majesty's government, and there was delay in appointing a new minister to Washington. Eventually John S. Lumley, a former secretary of the legation, was designated as chargé d'affaires; and later in the year, as if to underline their continued confidence in Crampton, the British government conferred a knighthood upon him.

For a time following Crampton's departure, there were few private and confidential letters to Lord Clarendon from Washington. Lumley wrote occasionally, as did several of the British consuls, but regular diplomatic correspondence was sluggish. However, one incoming letter to the foreign secretary during this time was of particular interest. It came from a British traveler, Charles D. Archibald, who had obtained a lengthy interview with the newly designated Democratic candidate for the presidency, James Buchanan, lately United States minister to Great Britain.[32]

During a visit which I lately made to Mr. Buchanan at his residence in Pennsylvania I had an opportunity of learning his views and opinions, expressed without reserve, upon a variety of questions foreign and domestic. Altho' he does not speak with absolute certainty of his election he thinks he has the best chance, and his friends are everywhere sanguine of success. The Hon. Mr. Ingersoll,[33] late U.S. Minister in London, and other zealous supporters of Mr. Fillmore, have expressed to me their (unwilling) belief that Mr. Buchanan will carry the day. . . .[34] I believe than no man will be more tenacious than Mr. Buchanan of what he considers the rights and interests of his country, and he will defend and maintain them by every art of diplomatic strategy; but there will be no appeal to the God of Battle in his time, at least so far as Great Britain is concerned.

Speaking of the British ministry he said, Lord Palmerston has greatly strengthened his position and his Government seems likely to last. He then referred to the last interview with His Lordship on the occasion of his taking leave of the Queen, when, after some "playful" conversation, His Lordship assured him that he would rather see him President of the United States than any other man. He remarked that altho' his official career in England had not been without annoyances, he could look back with the kindest feelings towards all with whom he came in contact.

He had not, he said, heard who was likely to be sent as Minister to this Country but hoped a judicious selection could be made. He had, when Your Lordship did him the honor to consult with him at Paris, recommended that it should be someone of high rank and title if possible; and from my own knowledge and observation of the American people I venture to express my humble concurrence in the opinion that *ceteris paribus* a nobleman would be more acceptable than a commoner. . . .[35]

Referring to the future of the British North American Colonies, he said that so long as they continued a part of the British Empire the United States would not attempt to interfere with their institutions and form of government; "but as an independent state it must necessarily be a *republic*—We should oppose the establishment of a Monarchy in Canada as we shall certainly do in Mexico should it be attempted. Our Southern States have an intense hatred of kings and lords." I remarked that this was contrary to the received opinion in England where we regarded the people of the Southern States as essentially aristocratic in their feelings—They are, he said, ultra Conservative and ultra democratic at the same time.

He said he believed in his heart that "if it were put to the test there was more real love for old England in the United States than in any other country under the sun. The French do not like you, altho' it is the policy of the Emperor to make it appear so. The Germans are not to be relied on; and the Russians as a matter of course are burning with vindictive feelings. It is from Europe therefore, and not from America that England has anything to apprehend. Every right minded American citizen next after the well being of his own country, must wish for the prosperity of England even upon selfish considerations, but we do so from higher motives, and as in times past so for the future, "my thoughts are turned on peace."

The next noteworthy private and confidential letter came from Edmund A. Grattan, the British consul at Boston, a man whose experience in America dated back to 1848. He and other seasoned foreign observers were greatly troubled by the condition of near civil war existing in the Kansas-Nebraska Territory. It may be recalled that in 1854 Congress sought to resolve the status of this area by using Stephen A. Douglas's doctrine of "popular sovereignty," which allowed the inhabitants of a territory to hold elections in order to determine whether they approved or disapproved of slavery. Once this determination was made, Congress entertained applications for statehood. In this case, proslavery elements in neighboring Missouri were afraid to risk the outcome of random migration into the new territory and therefore undertook to persuade about five thousand Missourians to move into Kansas to vote in favor of slavery. This tactic succeeded, and Kansas petitioned Congress to come into the Union on the side of the South. The Senate was willing to grant the petition, but enough members of the House of

Representatives balked to put its passage in doubt. Meanwhile, Free-Soil advocates in Kansas mobilized their forces and launched a series of violent raids into the newly settled territory. Local law enforcement agents could not maintain order, so federal troops had to be sent to the area. Grattan's letter of 7 September was written as this drama unfolded.[36]

The public papers, as well as other sources, will inform Your Lordship of the events now taking place in the Territory of Kansas. A large number of the settlers of that Territory being emigrants from the New England States, the condition of affairs in Kansas excites a deep interest here. The region of country in which Kansas is situated, having always been considered in the North as destined to become free territory, the movements now going on in Kansas are looked upon with extreme anxiety by all persons opposed to the further extension of slavery. It is very generally believed that the South is determined upon establishing slavery in the Territory if possible, with a view to its ultimate admission into the Union as a Slave State. From its geographic situation on the banks of the Missouri River exactly opposite to the State of Missouri, it is deemed by the Slave States generally, and by Missouri in particular, to be of greatest consequence to their interests that the institution of slavery be established in Kansas and there can be no doubt that the repeal of the Missouri Compromise was carried through Congress mainly with a view to the conversion of this Territory as well as that of Nebraska into Slave States. Otherwise the previously existing laws legalizing the Northern limits of slave territory would never have been disturbed at the risk of reopening the agitation of the Slavery Question with the long train of difficulties sure to follow its revival. I think that there can be little doubt as to the intentions of the South in this matter.

The latest news in regard to the Territory is to the effect that the President has declared the Free-State men in the Territory in a state of rebellion against the territorial Laws, and the Governor and the General commanding the United States Troops in the Territory are authorized to suppress the Rebellion by force of arms and are further empowered by the President to call upon the authorities of the States of Kentucky and Illinois for assistance in case the regular troops and militia of Kansas should prove insufficient to reestablish order.[37]

I should mention to your Lordship that it is asserted on behalf of the Free-State men that they have only taken up arms in self-defense having been driven thereto by the menaces and violence of the Missourians and the so-called "Border-Ruffians" who at different times illegally, as has been proved, invaded the Territory and succeeded in forcing upon the legitimate settlers by means of fraudulent votes, a set of Laws entirely repugnant to their views and at variance with their sense of right and justice. These Laws certainly as far as they have been published appear to be eminently unfair and tyrannical towards the Free-State settlers and seem to have been introduced with the object of intimidating and if possible driving the latter out of the Territory. The Federal Government is clearly accused of conniving at the design of the pro-slavery party in this matter, it being asserted that no efforts have been made by the government to suppress the illegal proceedings of those who in violation of every principle of right and justice entered the Territory for the purpose of imposing upon it a pro-slavery code of Laws, whereas as soon as an attempt is made by the Free-State men to rise up in opposition to these unjust aggressions, the whole power of the government is directed to put them down. When party spirit on both sides was so high and reports so materially contradict each other as they do on this one question, it is not easy to arrive at a very definite idea of the real state of affairs. Looking back however to the history of the Territory since the passage of the Kansas-Nebraska Bill and the repeal of the Missouri Compromise, it is difficult to avoid coming to the conclusion that the Democratic Party and consequently the actual Government of the United States are implicated in the design of converting Kansas into Slave Territory. A short time will doubtless show what the result of this policy is to be, but were immigration into the Territory allowed to proceed undisturbed there can be no doubt that Kansas would become a Free State, for according to the best authority it would seem that the settlers from the North and West greatly outnumber those from the Southern States. Late events have, however, as may be supposed, considerably checked emigration from the North, and I understand that the number of settlers now proceeding to the territory from New England has become very small.

I beg leave to transmit to Your Lordship herewith a report of the speech recently delivered in the Senate of the United States by Mr. Wilson of Massachusetts upon the army Appropriation Bill in which the Northern view of the present condition of affairs in Kansas is stated with great force.[38]

As the time of the Presidential Election approaches increased interest attaches to every political movement tending to throw light upon the relative strength of parties in the country, especially at the North and West. As far as the Southern States are concerned it seems to be generally understood that they will vote in a body for Mr. Buchanan. The recent State Elections in Iowa and Vermont have been favourable to the Republican party, but the Election to which the greatest importance is attached is that which took place in the State of Maine yesterday, the result of which has been completely favourable to the Republicans.

Two weeks later Grattan reported that the situation in Kansas was more tranquil, although the ingredients for further bloodshed were still present.[39]

Since the date of the observations which I had the honour recently to address to your Lordship on the subject of Kansas, a change seems to have taken place in the aspect of human affairs in the Territory.

The measures adopted by Governor Geary for the pacification of the Territory appear to have been atended so far with success, and though hostile movements are still reported to be going on in different parts of the Territory the general impression seems to be that matters are gradually becoming more settled, and that the crisis in the affairs of Kansas may now be considered to be passed.

At the same time some of those best acquainted with the state of things in Kansas look upon the present comparatively quiet condition of affairs as merely the result of an understanding entered into between the Administration and the pro-slavery party, with a view to conciliating by a show of moderation the good will of the Northern States previous to the Presidential Election, and are convinced that as soon as the election is over the South will make a new effort to recover lost ground in Kansas and that the real struggle for supremacy in the Territory will then take place. Meanwhile, however the people of the Free States are taking advantage of the favourable turn of affairs to push forward emigration as rapidly as possible, and are transmitting the utmost amount of aid that can be collected in the way of money and clothing to those already in the Territory. I understand that about four hundred Emigrants now assembled at Chicago, will move into Kansas in the course of the present week, and it is said that from one to two thousand free-state settlers may be expected to proceed to the Territory during the present Autumn. From all that I can gather after careful inquiry, I find that but little doubt is really entertained in this neck of the country, that Kansas must ultimately become a free State, whatever efforts the South may hold in reserve with a view to recovering its ascendancy in the Territory.

The chief causes which lead to this conviction are 1st, the climate of Kansas and the general feeling of the country which are favourable to white settlers and make the employment of Negroes unnecessary, and 2ndly, the great numerical preponderance of the free state settlers over those favourable to the establishment of slavery, many of the former being themselves emigrants from the Southern States who nevertheless from motives of personal interest are entirely opposed to the introduction of slave labour into the Territory.

The contest attempted to be maintained by the South under these circumstances can therefore only be carried on at a great disadvantage, and with a small prospect of final success.

Toward the end of September Americans became increasingly obsessed by the forthcoming presidential election. Chargé d'affaires Lumley tried to minimize the petty details of campaign rhetoric while at the same time providing Lord Clarendon with a flavor of the political scene.[40]

The results of the State Elections in Pennsylvania and Indiana having turned out favourable to the Democratic Party, Mr. Buchanan's election as next President of the United States is looked upon almost as a certainty. As at those elections members were likewise chosen for the next Congress, and the result was an increase in the number of Democrats chosen to represent those States, it is probable that Mr. Buchanan, if elected will have a good working majority in the House of Representatives which will give his administration a support in that branch of the Legislature which Mr. Pierce's Administration did not enjoy.

Unfortunately the persons most intimately connected with Mr. Buchanan in politics, and who are supposed to exercise a powerful influence over him are men who, even in this country, are considered to be of a reckless and unscrupulous character, amongst these are Messrs. Forney, Sanders, Sickles, Slidell and Soulé and General Quitman, all of whom expect important or lucrative appointments under his administration in return for the assistance they have rendered Mr. Buchanan during his Presidential canvass.[41]—That such appointments are contemplated by the individuals themselves and their friends admits of no doubt, and though it seems difficult to believe that Mr. Buchanan should so far yield to their importunity as to place the interests of his country in such unsafe hands, the general opinion is that these persons have claims on Mr. Buchanan and will enforce them. I find for instance that it is generally believed that Mr. Slidell, Senator from Louisiana, whose aid to Mr. Buchanan has been of such a valuable nature that he will receive any appointment he may ask for, will most probably choose the post Secretary of State.

General Robbles informed me a few days ago that in the course of a conversation with Mr. Ward, the President of the Democratic Convention in Philadelphia, he had asked that gentleman whether it was true that the choice of Secretary of State lay between Messrs. Forney, Cushing and Slidell, upon which that gentleman replied that as to the two former he knew that hey had no chance, and as to the latter it was hoped he would be satisfied with some other Department.[42]

The character given to me of Mr. Slidell, by one of his fellow Senators, (how truly I will not venture to state) is that of a fortunate gambler in private and public life, by no mean scrupulous in the means he adopts to attain his ends;—he is moreover, without doubt, a man of considerable ability, perseverance and determination, which in addition to his being one of the most ardent advocates of filibusterism and annexation, to the utmost extent, accounts for his being considered one of the most dangerous men that ever aspired to a position of such importance. When I add that one of the favourite candidates for the post of Secretary of War (though such an appointment is scarcely probable) is the present occupant, Mr. Jefferson Davis, whose filibustering propensities have only been held in check by Mr. Marcy; and that, although such a report appears to be truly ridiculous, the friends of the notorious General Quitman express great hopes of seeing him appointed to that Post; Your Lordship will not be surprised to learn that Mr. Buchanan's election is looked upon with much alarm and anxiety by the Spanish, Mexican, and Central American Representatives in this country. It is to be hoped however that these apprehensions will prove to be unfounded and that Mr. Buchanan will make a very different selection; for the choice of such men as I have mentioned would be the announcement of a policy of such an aggressive nature as might compel not only independent States of this Continent but even European nations to unite together in self-defense.

I have abstained from troubling Your Lordship with conjectures respecting the chance of success of the respective Candidates for the Presidency and it seems equally unnecessary to indulge in suppositions as to which Candidate would be the one under whom the peaceful relations of this country with the world would be the least likely to suffer interruption.

Judging from the different declarations of principles, the so-called "platforms" put forward by the three parties in the field, it has been generally believed in Europe that the Presidency of Mr. Fremont[43] would be the most favourable to the peace of the world, and that the success of Mr. Buchanan would give full scope to the development of American aggression under the name of manifest destiny.

But in this country one is continually warned against placing too much confidence in these "Platforms"; they are, to use their own figure, but the hustings employed at elections, made for the occasion, and liable to be used for very different purposes than those for which they were originally constructed.

On 14 October Lumley wrote again to Lord Clarendon, reporting on his long conversation with John S. Bartlett, a British subject living in America who had strongly opposed Canadian federation and home rule. For many years Bartlett edited a literary magazine called the *Albion* and, with Crampton's encouragement, had recently established a political weekly called the *Anglo-Saxon*.[44] On his own printing press he ran off copies of a memorandum he prepared for the private consideration of the British cabinet.[45]

THE FEDERAL UNION

We are opposed to the Federal Union of the British North American Provinces, because it will lead to early declaration of independence of the so confederated colonies, and their consequent loss to England. An Independence so obtained would not be permanent, because the new State, Confederacy, or whatever it may be called, will be subject to the intrigues of the politicians of the United States, who would leave nothing undone to bring it into the Union. This was the case in regard to Texas. Texas was an independent Republic for some time after its severance from Mexico, and was fast rising into power and importance, for being *free*, it had abjured both *Slavery* and the *Tariff* and was about to have an independent European trade and political connexion. This did not suit the people at Washington, the slave-holders of the South—nor the High Tariff men of the North; and forthwith every engine was put in motion in order to bring Texas into the general fold. In the grand assault on the new and infant republic the newspapers led the van, followed by speeches in Congress and elsewhere. The resident British minister in Texas, Capt. Elliott, was assailed with every speech of obloquy; his dress was described in the public journals, so that he might be known and insulted by the rabble, and he was designated "The man with the white hat."[46] Bribery, intrigue and corruption were employed to bring over the leading men, which ultimately succeeded, and Texas became an American State, putting on the black livery of slavery, and adopting the high tariff proscription against European goods. And so it will be with the federated provinces of England when they separate from her. They would not adopt slavery, of course, but they would acquiesce in its continuance in the South, and adopt in a greater or lesser degree the system of American protection. This, no doubt, will be the result, the new Republic will fall into the jaws of, and be swallowed up by the American Union.

And how will it be brought about? By intrigue, cajolery, and, if necessary, *force*, for be it remembered, the lost colonies will no longer have the protection of England, and they will fall an easy prey. The abundant supply of food now produced in the colonies, and the vast capabilities they possess for water power operations, will presently make them able to become a manufacturing country—whether for their advantage or disadvantage we pretend not to say, but the point will be urged with force and effect, and England may some day see a tariff barrier opposed to her from the Rio Grande, in lat. 26 to Hudson's Bay.

All this being accomplished—that is to say, the British Provinces confederated—subsequently independent, and lastly absorbed into the Union—the daring object of the Americans not only in their views southerly, but also northerly, each section of the country pursuing its object in its own direction by a process which the late Mr. Calhoun called the process of "accretion"—what becomes of England as a naval power? What will she be without her North American Colonies? How would she bear the loss of her coal, iron, ship-timber and sea ports?. . .

The North American colonies are well as they are—let them remain so. They are prosperous and happy, advancing with unexampled rapidity to greatness, wealth, and power. Each is independent. If grievances arise in either they are settled, and the mischief goes no farther, but when all are united or represented in one Congress, local grievances will become general ones, and mischievous in proportion to the magnitude of the field of their operations.

England *must* retain her North American colonies, and can do so with good management. She should distribute among the colonists of good character and ability some of the Imperial appointments, admit them freely into the army and the navy, and adopt the plan of transferring able colonists from one colony to another. True, England has given away nearly all of her patronage, but a clever man may be appointed Governor of another colony, as in the case of Mr. Daily and Mr. Hincks.[47] The titles, too, given to Sir Allan McNab, Sir John Robinson, and others were well bestowed, and the practice should be continued.[48] These things give the colonists an interest in the affairs of the whole empire, and make them part and parcel of us. Nor should a few thousands of pounds be grudged now and then, to be laid out in public improvements, especially in the matters of Light-Houses, Coast Surveys, Mail Steamer Contracts, &c, particularly to the line just established so successfully between Liverpool and Quebec. This enterprise is a most favorite one with the Canadians, and should receive a mail contract as soon as possible. Mr. Cunard must not oppose this, but be content to divide the Imperial patronage in a case where it is so desirable he should do so, where the mail and steamer business will be increased thereby, and where the colony as well as the mother country will be so much benefitted. Ten or twelve well disciplined regiments should always be retained in these colonies, as the expenditure of the army is advantageous to the community near which it is placed and the intercourse of the officers (who should be enjoined to conduct themselves with signal propriety) with the inhabitants gives a British tone and feeling to society.

Undoubtedly there is much loyalty in British America, but it must not be conceded that there is an Annexation party, or a set of men desirous of joining or annexing the country to this United States. The French *Rouge* party is of this kind, and their journal boldly advocates separation from England, and "emancipation from the British yoke." This fact being known, it should be the business of the Imperial Government to foster the loyal portion of the people by such means as have just been pointed out. All internal improvements which are really beneficial should receive the countenance of the Home Government, and the inhabitants should be made to see that England is sensible of their value, is proud of them, and feels a deep solicitude for their welfare.

One month later Lumley was still very much preoccupied with Canadian affairs, especially the question of whether American residents in the provinces constituted a threat to stability and tranquility.[49]

Although there may be no immediate danger to be expected from the attempts of American citizens to excite feelings of hostility towards Great Britain in Newfoundland referred to in Mr. Bunch's letter to Your Lordship of the 25th September last; there can be no doubt that such designs do exist and extend not only to the Colony of Newfoundland but to all Her Majesty's North American Colonies.[50]

I consider these designs to be twofold, one of an insidious character which has been for some time in practice, the other boldly avowed but not yet attempted, neither of them to be underrated, though from neither of them is any danger to be expected at the present moment.

It is not to be supposed that the United States Government or its lawless citizens would openly attempt anything like an invasion of any portion of the British American Colonies, except under peculiar circumstances; but there can be no doubt that a settled purpose does exist in this country to expel the British Power from every part of this continent, a purpose in which the Government and people go hand in hand, for this is but a part of the policy of expansion which has become the fixed policy of the United States and remains unchanged no matter who might be the individual elected as the President of the Republic.

I have already attended to this idea though in a crude form in one of my letters to Your Lordship, of the 24th June last, when I stated that there was reason to believe that the proceedings of the United States Government in the Enlistment question were but part of a system the object of which was to extend the Monroe Doctrine to the British Colonies on this Continent.

I did not by that expression mean to say that the true character of the Monroe Doctrine (which was originally laid down for the purpose of protecting the Spanish American Republics who had declared their independence against the attempts of European powers to bring them again under subjection) could in any similar way be applied to Her Majesty's Colonies which could not be the case till those Colonies had declared their independence; but the fact is that in adopting the Monroe Doctrine as their Palladium American politicians have given it a totally different signification, for to them it means the eviction of Foreign Powers from this Continent and the annexation of the Territory they have hitherto held.

There can be no doubt that it is in this sense that Americans of all classes understand the Monroe Doctrine, and that they expect that in this sense it will be applied to Her Majesty's Colonies whenever a favorable opportunity occurs. That such an opportunity had presented itself during the late war was very generally believed, and accordingly indications are not wanting that preparations were being made to put the idea into practice.—The American Government did not even at that time entertain the idea of annexing the Colonies or any portion of them by force, but they do hope and believe that they be induced sooner or later to dissolve their connection with the Mother country and join the Union.—They know full well however that there is little chance of the Colonies falling away as long as they feel that England is the most powerful nation, for they are proud to belong to her, and fully aware of the immense advantages which they derive from the connection; but if it could be shown that England had fallen from Her high estate, no matter whether that decadence had been produced by pressure exercised or the action of Her Government by the cotton interests, or by force of arms, the effect would be equally liable to diminish the prestige she now enjoys and the bond which unites Her with the Colonies would be loosened.—I cannot but think that considerations of this nature must have guided the conduct of the U.S. Government in the Enlistment Question which appears to have had for its object, either the humiliation of Great Britain in the eyes of her Colonies, or to drive Her into a War by making demands to which the U.S. Government knew she could never accede:—The alternative depending on the posture and duration of the war in the Crimea. . . .

The second, and bolder plan of annexation to which I have referred is connected with questions of internal policy, and may be said to depend upon the balance of power between the Northern and Southern Sates of the Union.

Your Lordship would be surprised at the frequent allusions that are made whenever that question is broached, not in a spirit of boasting or hostility to the period when it may be necessary to annex the Canadas to the Federal Union. This question is discussed as a system of policy and considered to be one merely of time and expediency. Nothing is more frequent than to hear it said "as long as the South leaves Cuba alone so long will the North put off the annexation of Canada." One of the principal checks indeed on the filibustering designs of the Southern States is the fear that the immediate annexation of Canada which would follow, would give the North a number of additional States of more populous character than the South would obtain, thereby neutralizing the effect which the annexation of Cuba, Mexico, it is tended to produce; viz the perpetuation of the power which the South has hitherto held in Congress.

What is extraordinary with reference to this plan is that it never seems to enter into the minds of any one that the Canadas either could or would offer any opposition to such an arrangement.

On one occasion Count Sartiges mentioned to me the question of annexing Canada had been discussed in his presence by several staid and sober Senators and Members of Congress. I asked him how it was expected to succeed in such an extraordinary attempt to which he replied, they reckon on the anti-British feeling in the Provinces and the sudden inroad of 200,000 volunteers. . . .

One of the most common means employed to excite a hostile feeling towards H.M. Government is to seize upon some imaginary or accidental circumstance for which a want of interest in the Colonies on the part of the Mother country can be inferred.

The two idle reports which have afforded the most fertile ground for these insinuatons of late are 1st: the slight notice taken of the offer of the Canadians to raise a Regiment for the Crimea and the other, that Her Majesty on visiting the Paris Exhibition passed by the Canadian Department without noticing it.[51] I mention these circumstances only to show the avidity with which any subject is seized upon which is likely to excite a feeling of discontent in the British Provinces.

Sharpwitted as American citizens usually are they seem to have been altogether blinded by self-confidence in their estimation of the character of the Canadians, the strengths and resources of that magnificent Colony and above all to the imminent dangers to which their own country would be subjected by such a rash undertaking as an attempt to annex the Canadas by force. In an incredibly short time their ports on the East could be blockaded and at the same moment their most flourishing cities in the very heart of the West would be at the mercy of a fleet of British Gunboats to which the Barque "Richmond" has served as Pilot. It is certain that no greater safeguard could be devised against the ambitious designs of the United States than the encouragement of the establishment of rapid communication with the Mother country and no assistance that can be rendered to the lines of Steamers now plying to Quebec would be thrown away.

There is doubtless a feeling of anxiety with regard to the policy which Mr. Buchanan may pursue but it may be four years, or it may be four months before any evidence of danger to the Colonies appears. I cannot but think however that a most effectual remedy is at hand if any such exists; though its very simplicity may make it appear ridiculous, its only recommendation is that it requires no demonstrations likely to offend American susceptibilities nor alarm the cotton interests in England, it requires no greater fleet than a few private yachts and no greater force than a few thousand tourists. Let it only become fashionable to shoot and fish in Newfoundland instead of Norway and to visit the Falls of Niagara instead of those of Schaffhausen[52] and the British Colonies will have nothing to fear from the designs of the U.S. Govt. or her independent citizens.

One of the most salient features of Anglo-American journalism was the practice of reprinting lengthy extracts from each other's papers, which was fostered by the trade custom of exchanging free copies. For many editors this represented a great saving of time and investigatory labor. It was commonplace, for example, for the *Washington Union*, the *National Intelligencer*, the *New York Herald*, and the *Baltimore Sun* to borrow freely from *The Times* of London. However, when American newspapers began to reprint articles from British antiestablishment papers like the *Manchester Guardian*, Lumley took offense.[53]

It may perhaps be somewhat galling to the feeling of independence of Englishmen and to our national pride to admit the possibility of anything like foreign influence being exercised in the internal policy of England; and yet My Lord, it may be as well to state at once that the pretensions of the United States to have the power of directing the action of Her Majesty's Government is a conviction very generally entertained and by no one I have reason to believe more positively than by Mr. Buchanan, whose long residence in England it is said has given him a thorough insight into our weak points.

One of the means by which it is imagined that this influence may be exercised with effect is through the medium of the Press, not by the agency of the principal expositors of public feeling in England but by the aid of the paltry cheap papers which have sprung up within the last two or three years chiefly in London on the American principle and some of which are as thoroughly American as if they wre published in Mr. Buchanan's own state of Pennsylvania.

In the course of last year I made some inquiries, at Mr. Crampton's request respecting the character of one of these papers called the "London Telegraph" from which the United States Government organ continually quoted articles, and which paper General Cass declared in the Senate had as large a circulation as all the London morning papers together; and I was informed that the "Telegraph" was one of the most inferior of its class, that very few people knew of its existence, that it was conducted by a notorious swindler of the name of Sleigh and that it was altogether such a miserable production that it was beneath notice.[54]

In consequence of the very complete exposé given in the Boston Paper the "Anglo-Saxon" of the character of the "Telegraph" and its Editor, the American papers and U.S. Senators ceased to quote from it; but papers of the same class and others of a better standing took its place; and, thanks to the "Union" I am able to designate the following papers besides the "Telegraph" which are peculiarly favourable to American or, I may say more correctly, peculiarly hostile to British interests and which not infrequently contain articles that can be traced even to Washington, these papers are the "Morning Star", and the "Morning Advertiser" published in London; the "European Times" of Liverpool and the "Guardian" of Manchester.

That these papers though published in England are to all intents and purposes American, the extracts which I have the honor to enclose will I think prove conclusively to Your Lordship; those articles can only have been written by Americans—Worthless and insignificant as some of these papers may be for any good purpose they may nevertheless be the means of doing infinite mischief and it is to be feared that this is the purpose for which they are intended. . . .

Although I cannot at this moment send Your Lordship an extract from this paper, [*Manchester Guardian*], I may state that it is believed to be more especially in the interests of Mr. Buchanan, indeed I have the authority of H.M. Consul at Richmond for stating that the exact period when that paper first espoused Mr. Buchanan's interests dates from the visit paid by the U.S. Minister to Manchester in 1854; nor is it a coincidence to be overlooked that this period tallies with the return of Mr. Buchanan from the Ostend Conference.[55]

It is very easy to conceive that although many people in London, and even "The Times", may be in ignorance of articles published in the papers I have mentioned, it may be possible, without giving them the notoriety which the Government organ procures for them in this country, that the occasional publication of some of these malicious articles in France, may with a little management be calculated to create a very natural feeling of irritation, especially if there is an object to be gained by exciting that feeling. Contemptible therefore as these wretched publications may be considered in England, they are not beneath notice, especially when, as I think I have indicated, there is reason to suppose that their malign influence is directed by a power whose interests it is to dissolve that bond of Union which so happily unites the French and English nations.

I considered the circumstances to which I above alluded, although they might not have the importance I attach to them, to be of sufficient interest to warrant my calling the attention of the French Minister to them; who, far from treating them lightly thanked me for my observations and said that the principles of *working* the press, which may be said to be reduced to a system in this country, was so often practised by public men in this country that he should not be at all surprised if an attempt had been made to introduce it in England and France.

Following a lengthy conversation with Sartiges, Lumley summarized for Lord Clarendon the French minister's shrewd conclusions as to what would happen if the United States continued to placate Walker in Nicaragua or sought in some other way to acquire Cuba or part of Central America. [56]

> I said that I did not think it too late at all events to point out what had not occurred to me before, and possibly might not have occurred to Her Majesty's Government, that the true character of Walker was that of a Slave Agent and the object of his employers was the extension of Slavery and probably the restoration of the Slave Trade.
>
> Count Sartiges said that that really appeared to be the case, and was becoming more evident every day. Indeed, he said, is it not possible that Mr. Soulé or his friends may have sent vessels already to the Coast of Africa for Slaves, which might without difficulty be landed at a convenient and safe distance from Greytown.—However, Count Sartiges said, he did not think the time was yet come for throwing off the mask.
>
> I was much struck at hearing the same observation from the Mexican Minister who called on me yesterday and who likewise believes that the scheme now being carried on by means of Walker will [be] used for the extension of slavery in any part of Central America that may be conquered or acquired—it is true he said that the plans entertained by men of the Southern States of this union were so extravagant and wild that they would be riduculous, if it were not a fact that those who indulged in them were the very men who attained to power in the United States.

Based on press cuttings, Lumley was convinced that Walker's intentions in Central America were worse than ominous. It was small comfort that some of the sentiments were ludicrous, since they accurately portrayed one virulent strain of American patriotism. [57]

> On the whole notwithstanding a gentle flush of indignation from Mr. Marcy in his organ the "Star" and the harsh words used by Mr. Thomas[58] there is no reason to expect any great opposition to Walker's scheme on the part of the present government and still less on the part of Mr. Buchanan's government. As to Walker's pretended hostility against the U.S. government no one believes in it, it is considered to be a blind put forward to induce H.M.'s government to give up Greytown to Walker (that is to the United States) as a convenient harbour for the naval force which will be required in the Caribbean Sea when Central America shall have been conquered by lawless citizens of the U.S. who, at the risk of losing their American citizenship, *will* persist in occupying and colonizing that country in spite of all the efforts of the United States Government, and thereby rendering the Clayton Bulwer Treaty a dead letter.
>
> It is certainly an extraordinary circumstance that the United States should be the only country in the world that is not to be held responsible for the misdeeds of her citizens; it appears that because Her people are daring and lawless, they are to be permitted to invade with impunity neighboring lands, wage a war with the inhabitants, and confiscate their property; and because the U.S. govt is too weak or affects to

be too weak to prevent it, while those countries suffer, she is to reap the advantages of her want of power to restrain her filibustering citizens. The Federal Govt is in short an ingeniously contrived device which while it offers to European Powers the semblance of a Government responsible for the acts of her citizens is in reality an excuse for not interfering with acts of aggression which though fatal to others, may result in her own infinite emolument and advantage. I do not think a more striking illustration can be given of this successful assumption by the U.S. Government of a right to place themselves above the Law of Nations, than by referring to an equally successful attempt which appears to have been made by an American citizen to infringe the Laws of England with impunity; I see by the papers that a man who had fired a revolver loaded with ball in the streets of London and threatened the life of a policeman was let off by the Lord Mayor *because he was an American* of decent exterior, and declared that it was the custom in New York to discharge loaded pistols in the streets: in saying this he spoke the truth, for it is done not only in New York but at Baltimore and in Washington continually, for the authority of the Law is absolutely in abeyance in this country; but if the man had been punished with the utmost vigour of the law, the whole of the respectable community of this great nation who are now living under a reign of terror and ruffianism would have applauded the due assertion of the majesty of the law and it would have strengthened the hand of every magistrate in this country.

We may have cause enough to rue the introduction of one American Institution, the establishment of the American Press in England without having to submit to the disgraceful and cowardly institution of American revolvers which has already made such a fearful progress here, and bids fair to become the distinctive badge of American democracy all over the world.

Six months after Crampton had left Washington, there was still no replacement for him at the ministerial level. According to Charles Archibald, this was causing considerable anxiety in the nation's capital.[59]

No one who has lately visited Washington can have failed to observe the unusual gloom which hangs over that dullest of Capitals or the appearance of isolation which pervades the departments of State. Unlike the great countries of Europe, America has, or at least professes to have, no political sympathies or alliances; and the interruption of diplomatic relations with Great Britain has given the authorities a "long vacation" which has evidently become tedious and irksome. They say that the only alliance they desire, or ought to have, is with England; and moreover, that the only true and natural alliance which England can ever have must be with the United States. We may trust alliance or ententes with the Emperor of the French, the King of Prussia or the Government of Spain; but between England and America it is the alliance of people with people based on the sure and lasting foundations of their common origin, kindred sympathies, cognate conditions and mutual interests. Above all they dwell upon the obligations of a common faith; and the necessity of union and good will between the two great protestant communities of the world who have alone solved the problem of self government; and whose co-operation is essential to the advancement of true christianity and enlightened civilization.

The toleration of violence in mid-nineteenth-century America never ceased to amaze British envoys. At the same time, they readily acknowledged that many decent citizens shared their dismay with such lawlessness. In his letter of 7 December Lumley repeats this common complaint.[60]

> I fear that some of the expressions made use of by me in my Private letter to Your Lordship of the 30th Ult. in alluding to the state of society, the practice of carrying concealed weapons and the efficient manner in which the laws of this country are carried out may have appeared to Your Lordship to be exaggerated.
>
> Being aware of the unfavourable impression which an ill chosen word or an exaggerated expression may produce by throwing doubt upon statements that are in themselves correct, it is with the view of removing from Your Lordship's mind any such impression that I venture to lay before you the accompanying extracts taken with two exceptions from the daily papers published within the last month. . . .
>
> It would not be such a matter of surprise if these accounts related to occurrences at San Francisco, where the inhabitants were compelled for several months together to take upon themselves the execution of the Law upon criminals whose misdeeds the authorities either connived at or were afraid to punish,[61] nor would one be so astonished to hear similar accounts of the border life in the far West, or of the social conditions of the Territory of Kansas of which descriptions of the utmost fidelity have been given to the British public by Mr. Gladstone in his letters to "The Times":[62] but it is to the state of society in the Great Eastern Cities, in the very heart of civilization to which I refer.
>
> I do not pretend to say that crime is more prevalent in them than in the great cities of the continent of Europe; but there it is less daring, and of a different character, the value of human life is more regarded and the crimes committed against it do not escape with impunity as is too often the case in this country.
>
> I will not trust myself to write on this subject, but to give Your Lordship some idea of it, I will quote from the first article in the enclosure A the following passages taken from the "Baltimore Sun" of Nov. 18: showing that the daily outrages committed against life did not subside with the election riots in that city but are the result of a deeply seated disorder.[63] "As incident to the diabolical spirits which possess some of the very worst most vicious and depraved we find them parading the city armed to the teeth flourishing their weapons when and where they list and utterly indifferent to if not defiant of the nominal municipal authorities etc., and this is but the index to a purpose the consumation of which has over and over again startled the public ear, the deliberate act of homicide, the killing of men upon the slightest provocation, upon no provocation at all, and in one instance at least as a sort of *pastime*, consistent it is true with the character and tastes which recent events have brought into view. *We know all of us* that *the very diabolism of murder is abroad in the community*. Men's hearts are full of it. It would be the merest affectation to deny that it is so, or to modify the expression of fact. A very considerable number of men and youths in this community are at this day *utterly bereft of an adequate sense of the crime* of *murder*. Blood guiltiness is with them reduced to its very minimum as an offense against society, and it is fit that we should ask ourselves the question whether there are not *very many who are ambitious of distinction* among their fellows *for having killed their man*. Concede that it is so—We do not doubt it, and what a hideous emulation must be secretly agitating the minds and hearts of too many of the profligate youth banded in various associations amongst us."
>
> The article marked No. 2 will give Your Lordship some idea of the extent to which the practice of winning and using concealed weapons is carried in *Washington*, since it has become necessary to denounce it from the pulpit.[64]

As another instance I may state that a member of Congress mentioned at the table of the French Minister that having had occasion to select his overcoat from a number of others of the same colour and appearance which were hanging in the Lobby of the House, out of seven that he took down, five had revolvers in the pockets.

The extract No. 3 is a leader which is from the *New York Herald* written at the time of the well known case of Mr. Herbert, a member of Congress, who shot a waiter in the breakfast room of a Hotel at Washington, and refers to the general apparent approval with which that act was received—from which the editor comes to the conclusion that society at Washington is so utterly debased and degraded that people think nothing of a murder if the murderer is a "man of condition" and his victim is a "nobody."[65] Since that time however the evil has fearfully progressed, for it is scarcely to be doubted that the practice referred to in the "Baltimore Sun" of taking life for "pastime" has reached Washington.[66]

Such is generally supposed to have been the incentive of the murder of a poor and inoffensive negro, referred to in the extract No. 4.

This murder took place at 8 P.M. in the best part of the most frequented Street in Washington, the fatal blow was struck with remarkable dexterity by someone passing the negro; the weapon used was supposed to have been a Stiletto, the wound being very small and without effusion of blood, the negro was stabbed to the heart and died instantly; his murderer has not been discovered.

It is not surprising to find after this in extract No. 5 that even the coloured population have armed themselves;[67] but what will strike Your Lordship with astonishment is to find from the same extract that even young children go about armed with revolvers, knives, sling shots and brass knuckles: more mischief is indeed caused by the boys than by men, and as from their youth, and their being often of respectable families the authorities are loath to punish them, impunity only encourages them in the imitation of the vices of those older than themselves.

As an illustration that even the most respectable citizens consider it necessary to carry arms in self defence, I may mention that as I was walking home last night, a gentleman who was with two ladies on arriving at his house discharged his pistol in the air before closing the door.

The extract No. 4 contains a short account of a common practice at Washington, that of setting fire to a stable or empty house, which used formerly to be done to give the volunteer fire companies an opportunity of exercising their engines but which is now practice to give the rival companies an opportunity of fighting: in the case referred to no attempt whatever was made to throw a drop of water on the burning building, but the fireman actually ran past the fire to meet and drive back a fire company that was coming from another part of the town. *It was known beforehand* that a fire was to break out that night in the first ward, the firemen were prepared to start at the first signal, and being well armed a fight immediately ensued in the principal street in Washington in which revolvers were freely used; the Russian Secretary of Legation who happened to be in the street at the time very narrowly escaped being shot.[68] The person whose property was thus willfully destroyed is an honest industrious Irishman whom I employed to carry my despatches of the 20th Ult. to New York.

This lamentable state of things arises no doubt from the manner in which party politics affect every class of office; with the exception of the Judges of the Supreme Court every civil officer is liable to be changed from the President whose term of office is of 4 years to the Policeman who is changed every 1 or 2 years: this short duration of office makes the latter unwilling to take active measures in the performance of his duties which may make him enemies after the expiration of his office; there are however other reasons why these crimes go unpunished as Your Lordship will see from extract No. 10 that the injured persons are often afraid to prosecute even where the guilty parties are known "lest the forfeiture of life should be the penalty of such a proceeding" and "any one who interferes is made to suffer by being knocked down."[69] Some attempts have lately been made to remedy this evil by taking away their arms from all persons arrested and as Your Lordship will see by extract No. 14 that in 24 hours no less than 60 revolvers were handed to the Mayor of Baltimore but it appears from the last extract in this enclosure that this measure is of little use as the persons thus deprived of arms purchase others. . . .[70]

I have however another reason for drawing Your Lordship's attention to this state of society since I conceive that it explains to a certain extent why it is that the Federal Government is powerless or unwilling to prevent the Lawless acts of their citizens against States with which this Government is at peace; the indisposition to take measures which may militate with self-interest, and the fear of becoming unpopular which renders the municipal system so ineffective may affect the action of the Federal Government; thus it is to be explained that while the Neutrality Laws could be carried out with the utmost vigour against British subjects, they are in abeyance as regards the unlawful acts of U.S. Citizens: for though we know those Laws can be enforced even to an arbitrary and unjust degree, such a proceeding as against U.S. Citizens would be improper and inexpedient and would probably raise a violent opposition to the Government.

In the consideration of the wild schemes of conquest entertained by citizens of this Republic it is therefore essential that European Powers should bear in mind that the character of the persons with whom their agents are placed in contact in this country renders it necessary that these mad plans should not be treated as impossible absurdities; they are not the dreams of wild enthusiasts, *but the calculations of the most practical people in the world*, who unite with the astuteness of the Russian a reckless daring and disregard of consequences utterly unknown to any other country or age.

It may be taken as a rule that there is nothing too desperate which offers a fair chance of gain, if successful that will not be attempted; should the attempt fail they will merely laugh at the gullibility of those who could imagine them capable of entertaining seriously such a wild scheme, should it succeed they will say there is nothing a handful of Yankees cannot accomplish.

It is impossible to call to mind too often that since the most respectable portion of the community appear to have abandoned interference with politics, conducted as they now are in this country, as inconsistent with self respect; the power and conduct of the nation has fallen into the hands of a most cunning, daring and unscrupulous race of men; and that although there are some bright exceptions amongst the politicians of the present day, there are others who have reached and will attain to the highest positions under Government whose aspirations are identical with those entertained by the most desperate characters in Walker's lawless band.

On 7 January 1857 Lumley sought to clarify a point which Lord Clarendon had raised in his dispatch number 36 of 18 December 1856. It had to do with an episode taking place in Hong Kong, where the British authorities had arrested an American officer from the *Annie Buckman* on a charge of assaulting a member of that ship's crew. The man, aided by the American consul in the area, presented a learned defense based upon the opinions of several leading authorities in international law. Lord Clarendon had indicated puzzlement regarding this case, and Lumley was quick to enlighten him.[71]

> I am not aware whether it has struck Your Lordship as somewhat remarkable that United States Consuls and Commanders of United States Vessels of War should appear to be equally conversant with the works of the Publicists on International Law as appears for instance in the correspondence communicated to me in Your Lordship's despatch N. 36 of the 18th December. This country it is true may be said to be governed by Lawyers; the President is a Lawyer, each and every member of his Cabinet is a Lawyer, the 62 Senators are all with one or two exceptions Lawyers, and of the 251 Members of Congress there is scarcely one that has not practiced or studied Law. The study and practice of the Law may in truth be considered as the chief branch of education, it is indeed the stepping stone to preferment of every kind; there are few young men in this country with any ambition who do not practice it; success at the County Courts may secure their election to Congress, and finally to the Senate, while the practice of pleading gives them a facility in elocution which is very remarkable; there is scarcely a member in either House that speaks with difficulty or hesitation.
>
> That United States Consuls should be chosen from this class is not surprising, but it does appear rather remarkable that naval officers should be equally well-read in Wheaton & Kent, as appears in the correspondence above referred to; the secret of it is this: five hundred copies of the 7th edition of Wheaton's Elements of International Law edited by Mr. Lawrence have been purchased by the State Department from Mr. Wheaton's Widow and every United States Consulate and Vessel of War is provided with a copy of this work.[72]

Since Admiral Perry's expedition to Japan in 1853, the United States had been interested in the Far East, and while refraining from the acquiring of territory there, it had nonetheless sought trading and revictualing privileges in China and Japan. Like the British and the French, America assumed its right of acccess to overseas harbors and markets based on international tradition and the law of nations, and any resistance on the part of Asians to its friendly overtures was bound to be met by prompt and firm retaliation.[73]

> The news of the destruction of a Chinese fort at Canton by the American Frigate "Portsmouth"[74] has been received with great and unconcealed joy, and there can be no doubt that this act is considered as the first step toward a system of acquisition of Chinese territory which has long been contemplated and may before long be put into execution; the object in view, being, as far as one may judge from the American papers, the acquisition of Shanghai; which it is generally believed in the United States is destined to become the great entrepôt of Chinese Trade. In some of the maps lately published in New York a proposed route for Steamers is laid down from the mouth of the Columbia to Canton as the nearest route between the American Continent and the Chinese Coast. This may be true as regards the United States Possessions but there can be no doubt that the distance between Vancouver Island and the Island of Chusan[75] is considerably shorter. I merely mention this circumstance as one of the many indications of the policy of the United States towards China, of which although no positive manifestation has yet been given, there is good reason to believe

will be one of aggression and acquisition and though it may lie dormant for a time is not less steadily pursued.

Meanwhile, plans were underfoot in London to appoint a new envoy extraordinary and minister plenipotentiary to the United States. Francis Napier was approached privately by Lord Clarendon in late 1856 to take the post, but due to ill health, he was unable to arrive in Washington until March 1857.[76] Although he was only in his midthirties, Napier had acquired considerable diplomatic experience in Vienna, Constantinople, Naples, and St. Petersburg. Because the Crimean War broke out when he was in Russia, he returned to Constantinople due to the withdrawal of British diplomatic representation and there undertook special missions throughout the Middle East.

His appointment to the United States marked his first ministerial position, and in an early private letter to Lord Clarendon showed interest in America's preoccupation with Chinese affairs. He had a long-standing personal involvement with China, as his father had led the first British diplomatic mission there and had died prematurely from the stresses he had experienced in the post. It was thus not surprising that his son adopted a similarly critical view of the Manchu dynasty and urged Clarendon to deal sternly with Chinese officialdom.[77]

I have to thank your Lordship for your private letter of the 6th Instant. I beg you to believe that I have the strongest personal as well as official interest in the Chinese affair. You may remember that my father, acting under Lord Palmerston, was the first victim of the obstinacy and perfidy of the Canton authorities in the year 1834. They have been pursuing the same course ever since, and I trust Her Majesty's Govt. will not lay down their arms without obtaining the right of access not only to Canton but to the whole Empire, as freely as in Turkey, and that you will insist on having an occidental Minister at Peking, which is not only necessary for the control of the Provincial Mandarins, but for watching the Russians, who, under the exterior of a seminary, keep a legation there, and are as aggressive on the Amur as they used to be on the Danube.

I will do all I can here, but the impulse must come from the commercial Towns, and I hope that Boston and New York are beginning to bestir themselves. You cannot hope at present for *armed* cooperation, that is against their constitution, which they only violate on greater occasions, and for purely selfish purposes, but they may send out a Plenipotentiary in a 1st class steamer with good Instructions, he may pass through London on his way to Aden where his vessel will meet him. They may strengthen their squadron and place it at the orders of the Plenipotentiary; the latter may have orders to follow the course of operations and remain at the allied headquarters; the rest may be left to the chapter of accidents. The Chinese will fire into American ships by mistake, reprisals will occur, and our peaceful counselor will soon be launched into active hostilities. I will promise the Govt. here that their representative shall be admitted into the confidence of the English and French Agents, and have the same voice in the negotiation as if he came with 20,000 men; and I will also take the liberty of disclaiming all views of territorial acquisition on your part, which alarms them, and I will hold out the prospect of a subsequent movement to Japan which interests them since Commodore Perry made his barren Treaty.

The Russian Minister here, Mr. Stoeckl, has a good deal of influence, not directly on the Cabinet, but by his social relations and intimacy with the Senators. He is a coarse jovial fellow, and a good companion. He has certainly been holding opinions and expressing them to our prejudice in this matter. I opened the subject with him frankly a day or two ago, told him I knew the language he held, explained in general terms the objects of Her Majesty's Govt., asked him whether there was anything in them which his govt. was opposed to, and required an engagement from him that until he received Instructions from St. Petersburgh he would observe a perfect neutrality in the present affair. Mr. Stoeckl would not give me his engagement for some mysterious reason which I am to know hereafter, but he said he thought his government would have nothing to object to in your Lordship's policy in China, and he regretted that a fuller participation of your views had not been made to St. Petersburgh at an earlier period, for Russia being a coterminous Power with China, and having a direct land Trade with that Country, and great material Interests at Stake, had at least as good a right to be made acquainted with our designs as France which had no commerce at all in that quarter. . . . Mr. Stoeckl obtained his present rank, as Envoy Ext., and the favour of his Govt., by his activity in opposing Mr. Crampton and Count de Sartiges during the late war, and I find that he is rather disposed to carry on the same course at present. We parted on the most cordial terms, and are the best friends in the world, but he will do us a mischief if he can.

During the many months when there was no British minister in Washington, negotiations to resolve outstanding differences regarding Central America continued in London between the American minister in London, George M. Dallas, and Lord Clarendon. From these discussions emerged the Dallas-Clarendon Treaty, whereby Britain agreed to transfer the Bay Islands to Honduras and to reassign jurisdiction of the Mosquito Indians to Nicaragua. The latter were required to guarantee respect for the rights of the tribe; and in return, the United States agreed to recognize Britain's colony of Belize in British Honduras.

At long last, it looked as if the vexed bundle of problems unresolved by the Clayton-Bulwer Treaty had been laid to rest. However, when the United States Senate approved the treaty on 12 March 1857, it appended a number of amendments unpalatable to the British government. When Napier wrote to Clarendon on 14 April, he did not yet know his government's decision concerning the Dallas-Clarendon Treaty, but he reiterated America's displeasure with Britain's recalcitrant attitude concerning New Granada, especially her unwillingness to compensate for the lives lost and the property damaged at Panama the year before.[78]

I beg to thank you for your private letter of the 27th of March. The view you take of the apprehended rejection of the Central American Treaty strengthens me in my persuasion that it will be accepted by Her Majesty's Government in its modified form. I have therefore read a passage from your letter to Mr. Cass[79] to confirm him in a favourable view of the subject, for I observe that both he and the President are not devoid of anxiety on this point, and that the suspense affects their disposition towards us in the Chinese affair and in other matters.

General Cass continues to offer me every assurance of good dispositions towards England, but if he does not retain any personal rancour, he certainly inherits a large share of the maxims of the old race of politicians in America in reference to cooperation with foreign States and "entangling alliances." I find that there are here just as many traditional commonplaces as with us. They are drawn from the "Testament" of Washington, and the Messages of Jefferson and Monroe, instead of from Magna Carta and Lord Coke.[80] Sydney Smith could have composed a "Noodle Oration" for an American Senator as well as for an English Squire.[81] The younger men have thrown off these venerable notions, but unfortunately they have emancipated themselves beyond measure, and despise all the principles of faith and justice as much as the "Wisdom of our Ancestors."

The advanced age and feeble health of the President and Secretary certainly operate towards the neglect of business.[82] I have never found General Cass informed upon a single subject or in earnest about it. He seems delighted with his position and content to do nothing. This has its good side as well as its bad. He may do no mischief. . . . But surely the emancipation of the Amazon is a very reasonable project, would be as beneficial to us as to the Americans and might be promoted by Your Lordship with less alarm and suspicion than by General Cass. . . .[83]

Mr. Reed the new Commissioner for China is a man of fair capacity and gentlemanlike manners. He is an old Whig who joined the Democrats on the *preservation of the Union motive*. I fear he will be too prudent and not let his navy loose. Lord Elgin must corrupt him. I will do all I can to get him sent to London. He is a grandson of a favorite hero in the mythology of the American Revolution.[84]

Although written in distinct tones of irony, Napier's letter of 20 May displayed his growing understanding that there would apparently be no stopping American Manifest Destiny and that it was merely a matter of time until the United States acquired additional territory either in Cuba or Mexico or Central America.[85]

You are making such rapid advances in the affections of General Cass that I do not know where he will stop. You will see in his last note how full of amenity and repentance is this devouring orator who used to swallow the British Empire before the Rustics of Michigan and the Senators of Washington. . . .

I have wearied you in a very long Despatch about Cuba.[86] The more I reflect on the subject the less cause of apprehension do I feel of its transfer doing us any harm, but I am open to conversion and correction. It would be an excellent thing if the United States would annex all the Spanish Colonies, (and then appropriate the Mother Country), saving always the Central American Transit Routes which as Your Lordship observes must be secured as neutral ground by general treaties.

On 8 June Napier wrote the first of several private letters to Clarendon defending himself against allegations made by the French Minister, the comte de Sartiges, accusing him of bias in favor of America. The charge was originally mentioned in a letter to Paris, but it evidently became known in Whitehall in due course.[87]

I knew that M. de Sartiges had made an attack upon me. He has got a leaky vessel in his chancery. It is merely the result of personal jealousy and malice. The French Minister fell out with the Americans when he first came over, on some ceremonial question of precedences and visits, in which he is a high and punctilious authority. Then he has a pleasant and sarcastic humour which he exercises at the expense of this people. The result is that he is extemely unpopular and he feels it. He is disappointed too in his professional ambition, and considers himself banished and slighted in a barbarous country. He is married to a Bourgeoise of the austere city of Boston notwithstanding his amours, which were notorious from Persia to Peru, but the propitiatory sacrifice to the Casta-Diva of American society is not accepted. Madame de Sartiges is blamed for her condescension to a depraved Count, and the frailties of the Count are commemorated with cruel satisfaction by the ladies to whom he did not pay his addresses. I am on excellent terms with M. de Sartiges and I beg Your Lordship will never countenance his removal. I willingly accept his bad offices at Paris, when I observe the good he does me here. He has endeavoured to fasten a reputation on me of a Filibuster and a democrat, but it does not make the Americans dislike me, and our Colleagues recognize the motives of malevolence and vexation. He is now gone down to Cincinnati to attend a great Railroad festival where he may make a speech which no one will understand, for he speaks English like the French Correspondents of Punch, and where he may serve up the old dishes of Lafayette and Rochambeau if the Representative of a Bonaparte may allude to the Republic or the Bourbons.[88] You may depend upon my never quarrelling with M. de Sartiges, I have no unfriendly feelings towards him, and I have long ago determined never to add an angry word to the incalculable incriminations of my Napier kinsmen. I will talk it over gently with M. de Sartiges when he returns about a fortnight hence. In the meantime I have had occasion to expostulate with my Russian Colleague who appeared disposed to endorse the ironical observations of the Frenchman. He took it very well, and is really a good natured underbred man.

I beg to offer to your Lordship my best thanks for your support at Paris. M. de Sartiges has, I apprehend, continued the secret war. Your Lordship will receive by this mail the answer to your proposal for a new Treaty. It is rather rude, but it was much longer and ruder in the first draft. Cass, Appleton, and the President all cooperated in this production.[89] I have also volunteered more advice and suggestions than is perhaps becoming, but I suppose I must frankly say what I think if I am to be of any use, and then submit to your Lordship's better judgment. The best settlement then, in my opinion, is to adopt the American version of the Clayton-Bulwer Treaty and get rid of the Bay Islands and Mosquitia, on decent terms, as fast as possible, but if Your Lordship wishes a new treaty, it could perhaps be made. I have transmitted some hints. I have not sounded the President. It is no use, he is too sly. He commits himself to nothing. He would ask for something in writing, and that would get abroad, and my suggestions would be riddled by the shot of newspaper commentary for two months, before they could obtain official consideration. General Cass is more hearty and open than the President, but he is weak and faithless, and has no real influence on the solution of affairs. Both are trimmers and cowards, who flinch before the least symptom of public discontent. The other Ministers are very good fellows and have no prejudice against England whatever, neither have most of the Senators and politicians I meet with. Some jealousy there is blended with a great deal of respect and affection, but, all, with one accord have that sort of contempt for *Foreigners*, Frenchmen and Spaniards, which seems to have prevailed in England in the days of Hogarth and Smollett.[90]

One week later Sartiges was still very much on Napier's mind.[91]

I know that Sartiges will never forgive me, and yet I treat him very well. I conform myself to all his fancies and punctilios as if he were a pretty woman. There never was a Colleague more *aux petits soins*. But all will be of no use, it is an unpardonable offence to have more of the public attention than himself. I beg your Lordship not to be persuaded that I am a propagandist of the Expansion Doctrine in the filibustering sense. I contemplate no other expansion than that of immigration, settlement, and the ballot box, with an occasional rational *purchase*, and by these means the Americans will be down to the Isthmus in another generation. My creed may be very shortly stated, or rather my *impression*, for I am not vain enough, or so like Sartiges, as to suppose that I must be right on a view of six weeks. I believe that it would be advantageous to England that the U.S. should possess Mexico and those parts of Central America which do not intercept the Transit. I believe that it would be advantageous to England that the U.S. should possess Cuba; that it would stop the Slave Trade, mitigate the severity of Slave Labour, and diminish the area of Slavery. But if H.M. Govt. think I go too far and if they deem it right to lay down a barrier against the boundless encroachments of the U.S. I may be converted by their arguments, or, at least, I can obey their orders. I have a letter from Lord Palmerston which is full of his Lordship's characteristic spirit. If he will take a stand, tell me where, and I will stand as fast as anyone. In the meantime you may depend upon it not a word shall pass my lips which is not perfectly in harmony with your views, either in public or in private. As for my correspondence with this Govt. Your Lordship may judge whether I have left any means unused to fix their attention to *our* rights and *their* obligations and engagements. . . .

I have taken the liberty of offering you my opinion on the great questions under discussion. I have now tied up the Central American Question, and turned my attention to the Copyright Treaty, which might be brought foreward next winter with some chance of success.[92] I hope to be able to go down to New York in about ten days to confer with a Convention of Booksellers favourable to that project, and I have explained my purpose to the President and the Secretary of State. The Secretary is in our favour, the President, cold and doubtful, but not positively hostile. I am very happy to hear from Your Lordship that the Russians go so far with us in China. I will take care to let it be known through the newspapers. Mr. de Stoeckl is very pleasant and we get on perfectly well, yet I presume that he makes a little opposition over his cards. His strength lies among the gambling Senators and generally with the Rowdy Interest. He was also formerly very mighty in the houses of ill fame, but he has been driven off that field of propagandism by his late marriage with an angular angel from Boston, Massachusetts.

The Kansas difficulty is clearing off very rapidly, and, in my opinion, slavery is in a declining state all over the west and centre of the Union. It will be pushed out by the expansion of free labour, and the demand for negroes in Texas. The accounts of the Slave Trade in Cuba are really horrible, but I think the account of the *profits realized* in the Traffic, as estimated by the British Authorities in Cuba must be overrated.

On 19 June Napier felt called upon once again to justify the remarks he had made in a speech in April, since Sartiges continued to harrass him.[93]

I am ashamed to occupy your Lordship's attention for a moment with my personal concerns but I must once more allude to my unhappy Speech which has carried so much consternation into the bosom of my French Colleague: I called on Count de Sartiges yesterday at his house in the Country and opened myself to him on the subject. I told him he was at liberty to form any opinion on my words and actions he pleased and report accordingly to Paris but that I had two points of complaint against him: 1. that he had written so seriously on the subject without ever mentioning a word to me on the matter; and 2ndly that in the course of his jocose conversation here had to my colleagues and others qualified me as "le Lord Filibustier", and suggested the propriety of my asking General Walker to dinner, a mere pleasantry to the same purpose, all of which tended to place me in a false position with my Central American Colleagues. Count de Sartiges said a good deal in denial or extenuation which I need not relate. He was quite civil and good humoured, and we parted better friends than we met. Moreover I intend to show him every degree of confidence possible and communicate to him whatever papers about Central American affairs he ought to see and which the Department of State does not send him because he restricts himself to verbal communications.

Count Sartiges is a clever man and witty, and not an unpleasant colleague except where his temper or jealousy are aroused. His susceptibilities are the result of bad health and bad fortune. I am determined to be on exccellent terms with him. He has been rather spiteful however behind my back, and once or twice rude to my wife, but as this was with quarrelsome, and not with amorous intent I forgive him freely. And now I hope that I have buried my speech forever or at least till next St. George's day.

On 23 June the Central American question resurfaced. The British government rejected the alterations made by the Senate to the Dallas-Clarendon Treaty, leaving no choice for the two contending parties but to return to debating the Clayton-Bulwer Treaty. Partly in order to force a settlement and partly as a bluff, the American government let it be known that it was seriously considering abandoning the 1850 treaty altogether.[94]

When I had the honour of seeing the President on the 18th Instant after I had spoken to him about China and the recognition of Nicaragua, he spontaneously brought the conversation to bear upon our broken negotiations respecting Central American affairs in general. He said that he desired nothing more than to be able to say in his first message that all difficulties with Great Britain on this subject were laid at rest. He implied by his subsequent expressions that in his opinion the best way of terminating them would be by abrogating the Clayton-Bulwer Treaty and leaving the question open. This gave me an opportunity of declaring your Lordship's views in the frankest manner. I said that I gathered two things from your official communications and private letters, 1st that Her Majesty's Govt. were most sincerely desirous to effect the cession of the Bay Islands.[95] 2nd that Her Majesty's govt. were determined never to give them up without stipulating for the security of British subjects and vested interests, and I believed, for the exclusion of Negro slavery. I then pointed out to the President in your Lordship's sense, the disadvantages to the United States contingent on the abrogation of the Treaty, in reference to our possession of the Bay Islands, our territorial pretensions in Belize, and our undefined Protectorate in Mosquitia, alleging that under the open system we should begin with great advantages, while the Americans would set out on the race for superiority with nothing, and no claim to anything. I hinted at the negotiation of new engagements being preferable to the abolition of the Treaty. I made no impression on the President. He, like all other Americans, believes that under an open system the Americans would carry everything eventually before them, and acquire an ascendancy over all the Transit Routes though he stated his opinion that no portion of Central American Territory ought to be actually annexed to the United States. The President evidently dislikes the Clayton-Bulwer Treaty with all his heart, and if he could shake it off he would endeavour to evade the formation of any new agreement in the same sense. I then put it to him plainly if Her Majesty's govt. should before the meeting of Congress, by direct and independent negotiation with the Central American States bring our position into conformity with the American recorded Constitution of the construction of the Clayton-Bulwer Treaty, would he then abet and encourage an attempt to break that Treaty down in Congress. He said he would not as distinctly as he ever says anything. I asked him whether he would give your Lordship his good offices in Nicaragua in reference to the formation of an Indian Reserve for the Mosquitos. He replied that he would, and, barring the anti-slavery clause, he would do the same in Honduras regarding the Bay Islands. So at least, I understood him.

By the end of June Napier realized that Lord Clarendon's views on American expansionism differed markedly from his own. The foreign secretary rejected even the remote possibility of ceding Cuba to the Yankees. He was convinced that Spain would never agree to this and directed Napier to act upon this determination when dealing with the Americans.[96]

I have received your Lordship's private letter respecting Cuba, and my language shall be conformable to your sentiments on this subject. You must understand the disposition of the Spaniards in this matter better than any one, and if the Gov't of Madrid be definitely resolved against the cession of the Islands, whether from motives of pride or patriotism, it is obviously desirable not only to resist any illicit attempts at invasion from hence, but also to discourage a pertinacious and menacing system of overtures towards purchase. I think the Spaniards ought to sell, but if they will not sell, they ought not to be vexed either by violence or importunity. An attempt will certainly be made by the President for this acquisition. He is pledged to it in the eyes of the people and I imagine that it will not be concealed from the govts of England and France.

One of the perennial problems involved in pursuing a diplomatic career was securing adequate housing. In Washington, Napier was confronted with the dilemma of either choosing to be in the center of the city and paying a higher rent, or taking cheaper accommodations in the suburbs and possibly missing the social ambiance associated with his duties. Being a man of moderate means compared with others in the profession, he sought advice from London.[97]

When I took leave of Your Lordship you told me to take a house in an *ostensible* position in Washington, and open it to company, and that you would consider the means of giving me some assistance in addition to my salary, for entertainment.
I have accordingly taken two houses, the aggregate rent of which would be £530 per annum, if I kept both for the whole year. I have made, however, stipulations

for an addition to the larger one, during the present summer, paying 10 per cent for the outlay, and next winter I hope to have one commodious house for £500 a year, or rather less being the amount allowed to me for house rent, giving up the small one in which the archives, chancery, and one attaché are now placed. This house for £500 a year is unfurnished, and I have become indebted in furnishing it, and it is far from being furnished. Mr. Crampton had a beautiful house in Georgetown about two miles from the centre of Washington for £250 per annum. The French Minister has that house now. I could have got one equally or more spacious, in a fine garden, on a healthy elevation, with an Italian view, for less than £300 a year, and with it the pleasure of comparative seclusion and repose. On consulting a variety of persons, however, I determined on public ground, to come into the city, live with the people, and keep my doors open to everyone who wishes to call. I think this is good policy, but it costs me, first, £200 a year, by the higher rent of a house in town, secondly £120 or £150 a year for a house or cottage somewhere in the Country, during the months of July, August, and September, when the Town is uninhabitable or at least unwholesome on account of fevers and agues. If I lived at Georgetown, I could stay there the whole summer, or leave it for a very short while. M. de Sartiges is going to live there all the summer. But if Washington were ever so habitable in summer I am obliged to depart from it, for my house is being built. In short my aggregate rent for an unfurnished house in Town and for a cottage in the country is now £620 per annum, and I believe it will never be less. I receive about £480. Under these circumstances I leave it to your Lordship to decide whether it might not be reasonable to make me some allowance for a country residence in summer, or raise the general allowance so as to admit of one.

In regard to the general expenditure of the Mission I may say that the salary is higher than that of any other here, but I need not tell Your Lordship that the position and obligations are altogether different. Although the English Minister may occasionally be the object of jealousy or animosity, he has always a great share of public attention and generally of respect and everybody expects to be asked to his house. The French Minister has alone any pretensions to the same position. The present occupant, as I said before, lives at Georgetown, is rather penurious, and has married a woman with a considerable fortune. The habits of life here were once very quiet, and they are still below the standard of a great European Capital, or of New York, but they are becoming more luxurious, and the prices of commodities are as high as in England, and wages are one third higher.

Your Lordship spoke of giving me some allowance for entertainment. If I am to receive company during the approaching session of Congress this will certainly not be superfluous. I think it is right to advise Your Lordship that, if the thing is to be done well, I ought to have not less than the command of £1000 besides my salary, between the beginning of December and the beginning of the following August for it is the long session. I do not insist on this, for I can live without it, and I will do so if necessary, but I cannot live freely, and make entertainment a means of influence. My salary and house allowance are now, with deductions, £4800. If you should make me an allowance of £120 for a country house, and sanction, on the presentation of accounts, about £1000 for entertainment, the gross expenditure for the Mission would be £5920 which is, I believe, less than that of Berlin, a much cheaper place.

I enclose an account for the three most formal and official dinners I have given here respectively to the Cabinet, the Navy, and the Diplomatic Body, as well as a statement of the Ball on the Queen's birthday. This is by no means done in the proper way, or at the proper cost, but I could not do better until my house is enlarged. The sum total is £223–14–0. If you consider yourself justified in obtaining the reimbursement of this sum to my agent it will be of some use to me, for I am in debt for furniture and have more to do in that way yet; and if you are inclined to sanction a current outlay for entertainment I should like to know how the accounts are to be made out, whether vouchers be required, or whether a round statement under my own hand be sufficient. I repeat that it forms no part of my purpose to put anything bye. If you give me more I will spend what I get and if you do not, I will spend what I have, but I cannot contribute anything from my private resources, which are smaller than I venture to state, and which are necessary for objects of a strictly private nature.

I am aware that any proposal to raise my salary might be met, in Parliament, by the remark that the English Minister gets as much as the President. This is far from being the case. The nominal salary of the President is £5000 a year but he is lodged, served, heated, and partly fed, for nothing, and the later Presidents have lived so meanly that they have not saved less than £2000 a year. In reference to Mr. Buchanan I can only say, that I have been here 5 months, and neither I, nor any member of the diplomatic body have been asked within his house. I waited on his niece with my wife, and some others, one evening, and did not get a glass of water.[98] In fact no entertainment is expected from the President. He is exonerated on this ground; if he received anybody he would have to receive the whole population. The last ball at the White House was given by Mr. Van Buren, but he was nearly suffocated, and it has never been tried since.

I may add that I have been obliged to take my house on a lease of four years; though it is usual for Foreign Ministers to insert a clause vacating the lease in case of professional removal, death, or suspension of international relations, I could not get such a stipulation inserted in my lease, and if I had hesitated I would have lost the only tolerable house to be had.

At a later period it is my intention to bring under the consideration of Her Majesty's Government the propriety of purchasing a house. The house for which I am to pay £500 a year, might with the additions now in course of construction and a small garden, be bought for less than £6000. An adjoining plot might be bought, for safety against fire, for £1000 and £1000 laid out in a further addition, alteration, and improvement, would make the whole outlay below £8000. The situation is a good one, and the value of land and houses rapidly rising.

British ministers to Washington were in great demand as speakers on public occasions, and Napier was no exception. On 18 July he wrote bemusedly about his recent participation in festivities at Harvard College.[99]

I believe I forewarned your Lordship of my intention to attend a Festival at Cambridge or Harvard University near Boston. This commemoration is held biennially, it is accompanied by some public exercises on the part of the graduates of the year, by an oration from some popular man of letters connected with the College, and by a dinner, which assembled all the Academic Men of every age and condition who can come. On the 15th we heard the essays of the young men in public speaking. They were more remarkable for confidence and aplomb that for originality. Mr. Everett delivered on the following day the great discourse on the utility of classical and Mathematical studies.[100] It was a miracle of memory and ornament but without much strength of argument. He is an accomplished rhetorician and a very amiable person, but not a deep thinker. We sat down to dinner in the College Hall about 500. Mr. Robert Winthrop was chairman, a perfect gentleman, formerly speaker of the Federal House of Representatives, a fast friend of England, a teller of plain truths, with a good share of eloquence, humour and sense. He was placed opposite the portrait of his lineal ancestor John Winthrop first governor of Massachusetts who died in 1649. His son the second governor was a friend of Chancellor Clarendon from whom there is an autographed letter preserved in the family. The name of Her Majesty was received with remarkable favour. The whole company rose and remained standing while the music played God Save the Queen. The Chairman alluded very happily to Prince Albert's recent assertion on behalf of education. I made a speech of moderate length in which I said what I thought would be agreeable without being false, and admonitory without being offensive. I think it gave some satisfaction to my audience who were very much inclined to be pleased and there has been more commendation of it in the newspapers since than in deserves. It is reported correctly in the accompanying paper. I beg you will not impute egotism to me when I send you such a matter. A speech from the English Minister is regarded here as a half national and official declaration. It is treated as such. An error of taste or judgment would be very severely handled, and what is tolerably good is greatly magnified, after the fashion of this violent, impulsive, magniloquent people. It would certainly never do to come forward too often and make oneself common and unclean, but this was a rare occasion. The company were collected from the whole Union. They could not have been more pleasant and refined if they had met at Trinity or Christ Church. It is true that Harvard is tainted with the Unitarian heresy, but the absence of Athanasius was not apparent. I have since been down to Nahant by the seaside to dine with Mr. Prescott and Mr. Longfellow.[101] It is the watering place of Boston, and full of pretty women. There are sirens on those shores. It is good for me to go back to the unflattering realities of life and office, to Cass and Costa Rica.

Perhaps nothing shook British self-confidence during the middle decades of the nineteenth century as much as the Sepoy Mutiny in India. Like the Crimean War, it seemed to invite nations like the United States to exploit Britain's momentary weakness and preoccupation. By 26 July news of this uprising reached Napier in Washington, and he strongly urged Lord Clarendon to follow a policy of expeditious firmness.[102]

I have not observed any malignant feeling of satisfaction or triumph in this Country in respect to our embarrassments in India. In fact I believe that if you act with vigour you will have the sympathies of the people here on your side. If you halt, or invite the French to assist you in China and thus share the burden as it were, there might be a sneer at the declining power of the old Country, but if you were to raise 30,000 men, subdue India with one hand and conquer China with the other, then the Americans would cry well done, for they respect nothing but energy and violence, and side with the resolute and the strong. They believe it is *our* "Manifest Destiny", to possess Asia, and are apt to excuse their preposterous proceeding here by alleging our masterful actions in the Eastern World. It is good that the mutiny should be a formidable one for nothing short of a sharp crisis would impel Parliament to probe the question of Indian govt to the bottom and initiate the dissolution of the iniquitous Company.[103] I beg you will excuse this excursion. I belong to the party of Lord Ellenborough and the late Sir Charles Napier, if they have a party. Perhaps it is confined to *Sir William* and myself.[104]

Most of Lord Napier's private letters for June and July dealt with his personal concerns such as his relations with Sartiges, his search for adequate housing, or diplomatic crises *outside* of the United States. This was symptomatic of the relative calm in Anglo-American relations. For most Americans, violence in Kansas and the issue of slavery dominated concern over Central America or designs against Cuba and Canada. The summer of 1857 was therefore sufficiently quiet to allow Napier to escape the heat of Washington and take refuge in the countryside, where, it appeared, most American politicans had also fled.

7

Napier and Ouseley: A Conflict of Personalities, 1857–1859

Because of the inability of Britain and the United States to agree on the terms of a treaty that would resolve their outstanding differences concerning Central America, Palmerston decided to dispatch a specal envoy to Washington who could assess the situation en route to his post as Her Majesty's minister in Nicaragua. Just as in 1854 when Lord Elgin went to Washington specifically to negotiate a reciprocity treaty, so William Gore Ouseley was commissioned in 1857 to facilitate the settlement of the difficult problems involving Greytown, the Mosquito Coast, and the Bay Islands.

Ouseley had already served in Washington as an attaché between 1825 and 1832. He had also published a book entitled *Remarks on the Statistics and Political Institutions of the United States* (London and Philadelphia, 1832). His experience in the Western Hemisphere was not limited to North America, however. In 1832 he went to Rio de Janeiro as consul, becoming chargé d'affaires in 1838 and minister eight years later. Shortly thereafter he was assigned to Buenos Aires, where he remained until 1850.

Ouseley was also well connected. His wife, Maria, was the daughter of the former governor of the state of Vermont, Cornelius P. Van Ness, and his sister-in-law was the wife of Judge James J. Roosevelt of New York. But this was not all. President James Buchanan, a seemingly inveterate bachelor, had once proposed to another of Mrs. Ouseley's sisters. These connections help to explain why Ouseley was mooted as a replacement for Crampton during 1854–56. On the other hand, he suffered one distinct disadvantage in securing diplomatic preferment from Lord Palmerston. When that redoubtable peer was foreign secretary, he had recalled Ouseley from Argentina in circumstances that suggested a reprimand. Lord Aberdeen explained the situation to Lord Clarendon.[1]

He was employed by me in the River Plate, and although censured by me, and recalled by Palmerston, his views turned out to be correct, and he may have some reason to complain of both of us.

In October 1857 Palmerston allowed Clarendon to appoint Ouseley as a special envoy to Central America. The Ouseleys arrived in New York on 13 November and made their way without delay to Washington, where they had many old friends. Their presence was somewhat awkward to Lord Napier, since both men were equal as far as diplomatic rank was concerned but differed greatly in temperament. Each reported directly to Lord Clarendon by official dispatch as well as by private letter, and one of the first things that Ouseley did was to indicate his friendly relationship with President Buchanan to Lord Clarendon.[2]

On first arriving at Washington I did not, as I had intended, proceed at once to call on Mr. Buchanan as a private friend. I had been told at New York, that a certain degree of jealousy existed on the part of Lord Napier of my appointment. Several of the papers had given erroneous accounts of my mission—saying that I came here as Minister etc., a proper notice in the Gazette would have prevented this—& had, intentionally or otherwise inserted articles calculated to produce ill-feeling & distrust between Lord Napier and myself. Some of these articles and letters I have seen, & others still stronger were mentioned to me. Further the late treaty with Nicaragua, which had apparently been both precipitately & secretly signed, without the participation of H.M. Gov't., contrary to the spirit of the Bulwer-Clayton Treaty, also led me to think it better to suspend any resumption of my former more or less intimate intercourse with Mr. Buchanan & wait until we could see an authentic copy of the Treaty.[3]

I am not sorry that I acted thus. Lord Napier & I have had time to become better acquainted, and I think that if a shadow of anything akin to professional jealousy ever existed on his part, it no longer does in the slightest degree—while the first *demarches* came from Mr. Buchanan in the form of friendly reproaches for not having come to see him as I used to do. Ultimately, I received a note from him asking me to call, and fixing an hour.

I called on the President who—after having got rid of the Russian Minister who was, perhaps accidentally, in the ante room, and one or two others—shut the door (he received me upstairs in his private apartment), drew his chair to the fire, and taking (as he possibly had sometimes seen done at the Foreign Office) a cigar, at once dropped the President and began a familiar and apparently unreserved conversation, in the most friendly manner.

On my part I commenced by saying in a half serious manner, that I supposed I had nothing to do but to go back again—or to proceed to Central America and make such Treaties as I thought proper—that such had at least been the opinion expressed by others—as the Bulwer-Clayton Treaty was virtually set aside by this new Treaty with Nicaragua.

Mr. Buchanan instantly and with some warmth exclaimed against this idea. I have thought it best to state to Lord Napier what the President said on this & other matters, in order that he might report if officially to Your Lordship, & shall not therefore further refer to it.

By 30 November word reached Lord Napier of the impending resignation of Robert J. Walker as governor of the Kansas Territory. This was totally unexpected because Walker was not only one of Buchanan's strongest supporters for the presidency but for a time appeared the likely choice as secretary of state. This prospect having failed, Walker had accepted the challenge of directing affairs in Kansas, hoping that a successful resolution of dissension there would enhance his already considerable political reputation. However, he was doubly dismayed when he learned that Buchanan supported the proslavery elements advocating the Lecompton Constitution. Feeling betrayed, he submitted his resignation to the president in December.[4]

Governor Walker of Kansas has thrown up the cards there and has arrived in the capital like a thunderbolt. The Democratic party is not unlikely to be rent asunder. The Kansas Convention has framed a Constitution which contains a provision submitting the slavery clauses to the ratification of the people. That Constitution is not operative as an Instrument of State Government until it is approved by Congress. Walker maintains that the President should recommend its rejection unless it comes to Congress with the ratification of the People of Kansas *in all respects*, that is the true broad democratic doctrine; the President inclines to recommend it in its present form, that is with the ratification of the people only on the slavery question. Douglas stands by Walker with all the northern Democrats. The Southern men headed by Jefferson Davis and [Robert] Hunter adhere to the President or rather advocate his present inclination. The President who has no real vigour of character trims and hesitates. The excitement is very great and very favorable to us, as it weakens the action of the Federal Govt, and brings out those elements of disruption which are gradually dissolving the structure of the Union.

Following an interview with President Buchanan, Senator Stephen A. Douglas was convinced that there was no possibility of compromise concerning the Lecompton Constitution. Douglas had been the chief architect and advocate of the doctrine of popular sovereignty, whereas this so-called constitution flouted all notions of responsible self-government. Therefore, on 9 December the "Little Giant" from Illinois broke with the chief executive, fragmenting the Northern Democrats and at the same time irrevocably alienating the Southern wing of the party. Five days later Lord Napier bore witness to this rupture.[5]

The Kansas battle has opened with a vigorous speech from Douglas incriminating the govt. for adopting the resolutions of the Territorial Convention and countenancing the submission of the Slavery clauses of the new Constitution to the people without the remainder of its provisions. The subject is entangled and I do not like to write about it. I think, on the whole, Douglas will fail, that the President is right and will succeed, that the people of Kansas will vote on the Constitution and annul the Slavery clauses, that Kansas will be admitted as a free state and the good cause will triumph. Now I may easily prove mistaken as to the means and the exact time, but no man here doubts that, by one way or another, Kansas will be a free state of the Union within two years, and I find that there is no sincerity or patriotism on either side but that all the embarrassments are raised for personal and factious objects. Looking to the result, which is inevitable, we need not trouble ourselves about the embarrassments, intrigues, and agitation which may intervene. Kansas, Nebraska, and Oregon will all be free states. Oregon has just been decided. The people have cast a vote against slavery and even free negroes. The whole Pacific Seaboard is thus Free Soil, for Washington Territory will follow the example. Slavery will first be surrounded by free states then it will be expelled from somewhere it has now a feeble hold, it will be hemmed in more and more, and confined by the progress of free labour and white immigration to the shores of the Gulf of Mexico where the white man cannot compete with the black. The people, the democracy will vote slavery down, where it is unnatural and unprofitable, but this result will not be effected by the maxims of humanity and religion. It is no use preaching abolitionism here. Sumner is the voice of one crying in the wilderness. No one listens to him. Few would assert his sincerity, but I believe in that.

I was present when Douglas spoke. He reminded me of O'Connell both in face and in manner though he is a much smaller man.[7] In method he is more like Lord Derby.[8] His style is a rapid, impetuous, transparent argument, without much superfluous ornament or fancy. I observed a few vulgarisms but less than might have been expected from a man of 45 who was bred a mechanic. I have no doubt that he would be extremely admired either in the House of Lords or Commons. I was told that he was less extravagant than usual, and that the speech was one of his best efforts. He was certainly far, far superior to Mr. Whiteside whom I heard last year on his great motion against government.[9] The government Party were very feeble in reply, but they are to put forward their best men on Wednesday, Jefferson Davis, and Toombs, the chief of the Southern wing of the Democracy, the "Fireeaters".[10]

It is surprising to observe how little the House of Representatives is thought of here. All the public attention is bent on the Senate. The Deputies of the People are regarded as little better than a set of jobbers and adventurers.

On the same day, Ouseley focused his attention not on domestic affairs but on Buchanan's foreign policy goals.[11]

The key to Mr. Buchanan's moderation of tone with England, to his positive disclaimer of all wish to annex any part of Central America, his desire to "reciprocate cordially" Your Lordship's friendly overtures etc., etc.,—the key in short to his whole system of gov't. negotiations, & foreign policy is to be found in the one absorbing long-cherished plan of the later years of his life—viz., *the acquisition of Cuba during the term of his own Presidency*. With this in view he has disappointed his more fire-eating friends, for this he is on his good behaviour with us (and with France), for this he has virtually disavowed the Ostend Manifesto & for this he would be very sorry to quarrel just now, with any power, but Spain.

The employment of private and confidential letters to Lord Clarendon suited Ouseley well, although he sensed the possibility that it risked undercutting Napier's own reports. Cuba was again uppermost in his thoughts.[12]

I referred in a private letter of a late date, to the designs of the U.S. upon Cuba. Since then circumstances have come to my knowledge which induce me earnestly to recommend that H.M. Gov't. should be prepared for a more serious—though *not immediate*—attempt to get possession of that island, than any that has hitherto been made. Whatever may be the measures which H.M. Gov't. may adopt—either in conjunction with France, or separately—they must be prepared to act, and possibly sooner than I at present expect.

I shall however before long get at more exact information (to which I have a clue) that I shall immediately forward either through Lord Napier, or in the form of a private letter.

In the peculiar position that I occupy here, I have adopted this private form of communication for many reasons, in all matters not directly belonging to my Central American affairs; and even on these, perhaps Lord Napier would prefer being the medium of official correspondence from hence?

I shall, with your permission, continue to write thus from this place.

The ubiquitous William Walker now imposed his shadow again upon Anglo-American relations. For a time it seemed as though he had been finally thwarted by being arrested on 10 November in New Orleans for violating the American neutrality laws. However, true to form, after he was released on bail he took ship to Mobile, Alabama, enlisted additional recruits beyond the several hundred already accompanying him, and departed for an unknown destination suspected to be Greytown. In Ouseley's letter of 28 December 1857 he began by expressing his misgivings about the recent appointment of General Mirabeau Buonaparte Lamar (1798–1859) as American minister to Nicaragua. In spite of a distinguished military record—during the 1820s he had earned a reputation for frontier fighting, and when Texas became independent in the 1830s, he was rewarded by being elected its vice-president and later its president—Ouseley mistrusted his motives in accepting the assignment. Lamar's personal finances were known to be in disarray, and it was thought therefore that his acceptance of the mission was due in large part to the prospect of a large salary and travel allowance. Nevertheless, Ouseley considered it prudent to transmit Lamar's views concerning Walker to Clarendon.[13]

> I more than once brought on a conversation with the General [Lamar] on the subject of Walker & Co. This is the substance of what he said: that he augured no success for the present expedition of Walker who is not the proper man for such a great enterprise as that which he has undertaken. That he has neither prudence, knowledge nor tact, & is very indiscreet; that he is no soldier, i.e. he has only brute courage both in politics and fighting—is not wholly uneducated—is rather a repulsive than a popular man—that he has none of those qualifications so important for a military leader except that of rushing blindly at his opponents and the possession of great perseverance, or obstinacy of purpose, but without strategical resources, plans or technical knowledge. Worse than this, he is destitute of humanity, sacrifices his men, if not wantonly, uselessly, and is utterly regardless of his sick and wounded, & is not therefore likely to gain that good will and confidence so essential in adventures such as his.

William Walker's threat to the stability of Central America was cut short by the energetic action of the American naval commander in the Greytown vicinity, Commodore Hiram Paulding. In mid-December 1857 he surprised

Walker and his men while they were still in the mouth of the San Juan River, forcing them to retreat before they had reached Nicaragua. As Napier reported on 5 January, this ambush created a storm of controversy.[14]

I perceive by Your Lordship's private letter of the 18th of December that we have been going too fast with reference to the intention of our Navy in Central America. It is fortunate therefore that the difficulty has for the present been extinguished by the single action of the United States Squadron. I thought that circumstances had so materially changed that Her Majesty's Government might have been disposed to sanction a more active course of proceeding, and I was even under the impression that the Government of the United States would not have been sorry to see the expedition frustrated by our interference, which would have perhaps given them less embarrassment than the "untoward" energy of Commodore Paulding. The President has been placed in a very difficult position. I believe he desired to prevent the departure of Walker, and he hoped the Filibusters after getting away would have been captured at sea, but he hardly counted on such a vigorous and unpopular step as the arrest of the whole band on the Nicaraguan soil, which being an irregular proceeding has given the Southern men some colour for their complaints and menaces. The whole of the Southern Democrats were loud in their protestations and they believed at first that the President would disavow the Commodore. Even the Senators held this language. Slidell of Louisiana, a zealous supporter of Mr. Buchanan, avowed his dissatisfaction to me, and predicted that the Government would bend to the Democratic storm. I affirmed the contrary, and I believe I shall be justified by the result. The Government have very properly reserved their decision. The subject is already beginning to lose its zest, and the Commodore will probably be quietly supported. The President is now thoroughly committed and I am confident that he will continue to act against the Filibusters with all the vigour which the Laws allow. Walker has been liberated from arrest because there was no warrant for his detention, but I hear privately, that the Government have it under contemplation to arrest him again on the charge of violating the Neutrality Laws if sufficient evidence can be collected. Your Lordship may, however, imagine that there are many difficulties attending this course and I am not sure that it would be desirable to give him the prestige of a public trial with the prospect of his acquittal.

The removal of Walker from the Central American scene tends to facilitate the mission of Sir William Ouseley, and Her Majesty's Government may now be justified in sanctioning concessions which they might otherwise have denied. I therefore take the liberty of reminding Your Lordship of my recent Despatch in which I recommended earnestly the propriety of deciding in favour of one or two alternatives—either to propose the abrogation of the Clayton-Bulwer Treaty, or to execute it according to the American interpretation. I am constantly afraid of the intervention of Congress on this ground. Happily they are occupied with Kansas which is a worse imbroglio than Central America, but the question may be stirred by the vexation of many of the Southern Members in the failure of Walker's enterprise. They may vent their dissatisfaction on our heads.

A few days later Ouseley confirmed the fact that Paulding's intervention had aroused widespread consternation among politicians in Washington.[15]

Lord Napier doubtless informs you by this mail of the feeling in favour of the late piratical attempts on Central America existing in some quarters here. Several Southern members warmly and openly defend Walker and actually insist that he and his confederates should be sent back to Greydown at the public expense and that Commodore Paulding should be condignly punished.

During a dinner party lately at the President's, conversation turned on this all-engrossing subject. Mr. Toombs, Senator from Georgia, was very warm in his denunciation of Commodore Paulding and in defense of the filibusters. He said that he never would rest until he had procured the disgrace and dismissal from the service of Commodore Paulding. Mr. Buchanan to or at whom these observations were directed replied: "leave the matter to me—do not interfere injudiciously—wait a little, and you shall find that I get possession of Central America or all these countries much more effectually and in a much shorter time than would be done by the filibusters." I did not myself hear this remark but can entirely rely on the accuracy of my informant.

Following the failure to secure ratification of the Dallas-Clarendon Treaty by both Britain and America in 1857, Lord Napier strongly urged Her Majesty's government to adopt one of two alternative courses. Britain could either abrogate the Clayton-Bulwer Treaty and thus have a free hand in Central America or she could accept the American interpretation of the Clayton-Bulwer Treaty, thus avoiding future clashes over Greytown and Nicaragua. Lord Clarendon like neither of these alternatives, however, and so informed Napier.

In his private letter of 11 January Napier broached the subject of policy differences between himself and Ouseley, some of which were as much temperamental as they were philosophical.[16]

I understand Her Majesty's Government to have determined irrevocably in favour of maintaining the [Clayton-Bulwer] Treaty. In that case clear and prompt action is necessary or we shall drift into trouble. I would advise that Sir William Ouseley should have orders to go at once to Honduras without waiting at Guatemala and that Mr. Wyke should have orders to give him.[17]

The cession of the Bay Islands is the first thing to effect if anything is to be done at all. It is highly desirable that Mr. Wyke should be with Sir William, who has not much alacrity of mind. He is an amiable, kind-hearted, and in some respects, accomplished man, but he has not much energy in the transaction of business, and he is privately averse to the Clayton-Bulwer Treaty and would gladly see our possessions saved and the Treaty sacrificed, but once armed with distinct instructions he will, of course, honestly carry out the policy of government.

The next day Ouseley sent his own interpretation of events to Lord Clarendon, reminding him of the special relationship he enjoyed with President Buchanan.[18]

There are many matters of importance, but of too delicate a nature for me to touch on directly—or uninvited—in conversing with the President; but I have no doubt that opportunities for "ventilating them" as Lord Brougham says, will be afforded by biding my time.[19] I have abstained from calling or asking to see Mr. Buchanan as often as I did before the meeting of Congress for several reasons. He is now very much occupied as he personally transacts too much business, perhaps unavoidably, until he is firm in the saddle. Moreover there are persons both in and out of Congress, members of the Cabinet as well as others, even some of the *Corps Diplomatique* who are not overpleased at my frequent private interviews with the President for which they are inclined to feel jealousy and distrust. This I am anxious to avoid without losing the benefit of what I conceive to have been Your Lordship's chief motive in sending me hither; I mean, turning to useful account any personal intimacies of me and mine, with those who direct the Government of this country. I therefore avoid calling often for the present. Meanwhile opportunities are not wanting for indirectly ascertaining the opinions and intentions of the Executive.

After his first year in office, Buchanan maintained an aura of evenhandedness despite his inclination toward partisanship. Napier acknowledged this on 19 January.[20]

The Filibusters are extinguished as far as Central America is concerned for this Presidency. The President's special Message on this subject to the Senate has been referred to the Committee on Foreign Relations and I know confidentially that a report will be made in a conservative Spirit. The President has behaved in a polite manner, making, after his fashion, some verbal concessions to his Southern supporters, but virtually backing up the naval officers. I am assured that he has received an immense number of assurances from all parts of the Country that he will be sustained by the decent people of every party. He knows his strength, but does not boast of it, deeming it better to allow his antagonists to expend their passion in orations and resolutions which will lead to nothing. In fact the more the President is now abused the better; it hardens him in doing right.

Ouseley's initiatives to improve the social relations between Buchanan's niece and the Napier family were undoubtedly well-intentioned, but they highlighted Ouseley's personal rapport with the White House at the expense of the formal relationship enjoyed by his order colleague.[21]

With respect to the feeling existing between our Legation and the White House, I have endeavoured and am doing what I can to bring Lord Napier *et les siens* more in contact with the President and Miss Lane. As I think it cannot but do good. Admitting that Lord Napier and many others may be quite right in their feelings of distrust and distaste for Mr. Buchanan's policy and acts, more frequent personal interviews may do good and soften those feelings, I may say mutually, between the White House and our Legation. It is with this view that my wife and I have managed to bring about some informal quasi-accidental meetings between Miss Lane and the Napiers, and the Legation. I think the President will allow her to go to the ball which is to be given [by the Napiers] on the 25th to celebrate the marriage of the Princess Royal, albeit he strongly objects on the grounds (not imaginary) of the jealousy and latent ill feeling it would produce on the part of families of members of the Cabinet, Senators and other Americans.[22] Miss Lane, adopting of course, by Mr. Buchanan's desire, the role established for Presidents' wives, *viz.* not making or returning visits. The President is not wrong in this. It is incredible what a degree of jealousy and invidious enmity is excited in this country by the slightest show of preference or intimacy however natural or well-founded on the part of the White House.

Miss Lane is fond of riding and often rides with my little girl, and we proposed to the young Napiers, and some of the attachés to join in whenever a proposal is made to us to visit the Navy Yard, the Arsenal and with Miss Lane; we try to make it general to the legation and with some success. I do not mean to imply that there is any ill will *d'un part ou d'autre* but I think we have contributed to dispel a sort of shyness of each other—and that before long a more easy intercourse and more points of contact will be established than when we first came.

It may seem trifling to take up your time with this *politique de boudoire* but it is surprising among these hard practical dollar-making people how much more is done *dans les coulisses* than on the stage.[23]

By 20 January Ouseley, together with the majority of diplomats and politicians in Washington, regarded William Walker's active career at an end, which at last freed them to turn their attention to other pressing matters.[24]

There are doubtless many troublesome unsettled questions arising out of our position and that of the U.S. with reference to Central America, but Her Majesty's Government may look upon the affair of Walker as being no longer one of them. That source of embarrassment is during the Presidency of Buchanan at rest. I do not intend to take to myself an undue share in bringing about this result; but I do not think that my presence here has been quite useless in the matter. I enclose an extract from one of the speeches lately made by a supporter of the President. Others have also spoken in the same sense. At the risk of being considered a *mouche de cache* I will say that parts of these speeches, have in some measure, been suggested by myself.

Ouseley eventually supported one of the alternatives that Napier had suggested regarding the Clayton-Bulwer Treaty, namely its abandonment.[25]

The Bulwer-Clayton Treaty is no real hindrance to U.S. projects. If preserved it will be at our expense. The protectorate of Mosquito and the Bay Islands, as long as we keep them, are outposts to defend our West Indian possessions and powerfully tend to prevent the immediate absorption of Central America. The President's message gives a fair opening for us to take him at his word and propose the abrogation of the Treaty, thus forestalling him and, under the semblance of conceding a favour, we escape all disputes about the needless and damaging sacrifices which the U.S. gives nothing. Pray my dear Lord, understand that I do not, of course, act or speak otherwise than you signify the wishes of H.M. Government, but I think it nevertheless my duty to state what my observation here and previous experience enable me to ascertain. It is not by throwing away our trump that any game is to be won with these people. Concessions yielded in a generous gentlemanly spirit are never "reciprocated" but are only converted into a foothold, a standpoint as Carlyle would say, for further demands and an encouragement to continue to yield nothing.[26]

As time passed, Ouseley began to write almost daily to Lord Clarendon and showed little inclination to leave Washington for Central America. He continued to thrive on his special relationship with the President.[27]

I dined the other day with the President. This was not a private party but a large dinner. I was the only Englishman, I believe the only foreigner present. When the party was about to break up Miss Lane had, or affected to have something to say to my wife, and asked her to remain. When the other guests were gone the President took me up to his room "to smoke a cigar" and a long interview and some apparently confidential conversation of a desultory but not an uninteresting character ensued.

Among the subjects he spoke of [was] the Mormons and the troubles in Utah. He said that he had upwards of two thousand of the "best troops" ready to act against them in the spring; that they would probably migrate into British possessions and he wished me joy of them. He added that any number of volunteers were ready to march against the Mormons from California but that the Governor had decided upon not calling for their services. I asked why, he replied that "all the Mormons would be massacred if the Californians marched against them". He did not wish this and it was better to let them leave the country. (Yet General Scott is about to proceed to California ostensibly to conduct operations against the Mormons).[28] Possibly there is an intention of directing or forcing the movement of the Mormons so as to serve the purpose of the U.S. Government in Mexico to which I refer in my no. 14 of this year.[29] He said that the Pacific Railroad was an object worthy of the peculiar attention and support of this Government. When I remarked that it would be many years before such a gigantic undertaking could be completed, he replied that in less than ten years it would be opened. . . .[30]

He spoke of his personal liking for Lord Clarendon rather as though confessing a weakness against which he ought to be on his guard, than as having been of any use to him. In short he seemed to imply that he had got but little out of the Secretary of State for Foreign Affairs in return for his tender feelings.

He spoke (as on former occasions) unreservedly in praise of Lord Aberdeen and said that he was the safest, most upright and worthy Minister England possessed and a most estimable Statesman.

He spoke of Lord Palmerston as disliking him.

I was sorry to perceive, although I trust that I may exaggerate its extent, that a somewhat bitter feeling still rankles in Mr. B's mind at his not having been popular among the megaloi [31] in England as not having received as much attention from them as he expected. He regretted that the Queen however "amicable and gracious to him in manner" did not like him. (I think he attributed this to Lord Palmerston). He said he should have much liked to have seen the interior of Windsor—i.e. to have been invited thither. To this he referred more than once, and implied that he perfectly well understood that the higher powers in England disliked him. In short I suspect that he knows that he was regarded much as the ancient Dutchman described by Washington Irving as having looked upon the Yankee settlers "with great respect and abhorrence".

Since the Buchanan administration and its naval commanders were willing to enforce the neutrality laws against Walker and other filibusters, Lord Clarendon instructed Napier not to interpose Her Majesty's naval forces as well. Napier reluctantly acquiesced while at the same time reminding Clarendon of the chaotic situation in Mexico, where civil war continued. Such conditions usually provided Americans with an excuse to intervene.[32]

The condition of Mexico is most alarming. It looks as if the agony of that unruly and uncemented body has come at last. It is confidently asserted here that the Northern

Provinces will probably fall away and form a separate Republic which would soon be assimilated and incorporated with the Union. For Mexico itself, I mean the whole Republic, it cannot be doubted that the wisest course would be to make overtures for annexation to the Federal Union which would give them peace, freedom, and security for property, and might give us some degree of pecuniary recognition and indemnity.[33] For such a step however the politicians of Mexico who prey on the carcass of their country are not prepared. So the fabric will fall to pieces, and the contumacious portions will gradually be united to the Union, while the rest will remain a sacrifice to anarchy and Indians. The Americans would find it difficult to take in the whole of Mexico at once for it would involve the reception of some fourteen Senators and sixty Representatives all at first Roman Catholics and Spaniards. The crisis is an interesting one, and the attention of the Southern votaries of expansion is being drawn southwards rather than to Central America and Cuba. It is, however, certain that the President will make some effort towards a pecuniary negotiation for Cuba. My impression is that he will not conceal his movements from France and England but endeavour to propitiate them. Something he must do. In one form or another he must redeem the pledges of the Ostend Conference and as he has repudiated the method of marauding and conquering, he must operate by persuasion and purchase.

Although the United States was bound by treaty not to countenance the slave trade between Africa and the Western Hemisphere, there were always individuals who flaunted the law and engaged in clandestine slave trading. Lord Napier did not think it likely that the practice would be substantially revived, however.[34]

I am happy to learn by Your Lordship's private letter of 15 January that my Slave Trade note has given you satisfaction. Mr. Seward has moved in the Senate for the production of all correspondence relative to the present abuse of the American Flag and the diminution of the Squadron. It will be out in a few days and will produce a good impression. The Slaveholders are by no means universally in favour of a revival of the Trade, and many who have no conscientious compunctions respecting the principle of the Trade, are yet in favour of the enforcement of the Laws and the observation of the Treaty while Laws and Treaty exist. Any legislative movement for the restoration of the trade in Congress would be put down at once. The North has a decided majority in the Lower House and will shortly have one in the Senate— on this question it has won already in the latter, for many of the Southern Senators would not suffer the subject even to be debated.

It may be recalled that the admission of a territory such as Kansas to statehood required the consent of both houses of Congress. As Napier indicated in his letter of 9 February, violence often accompanied the debates preceding the vote.[35]

The Lecompton Constitution has come up, that is the Constitution framed and voted in the *form* of Law by the pro-slavery minority of the People of Kansas, with all the odious clauses establishing slavery in the Territory. The Free State party, I think by a most mistaken policy, having abstained from voting.

The President has recommended the adoption of the Lecompton Constitution by Congress by message to the Houses. . . .

In the House of Representatives the opposition, composed of Republicans and Free State Douglas Democrats, finding themselves in a majority moved on Friday last to refer the President's Message to a *special Committee* charged to investigate the whole subject. The Government Party, feeling their danger, moved the adjournment, and though repeatedly defeated, went on making the same motion all Friday night till at length wearied out the majority and adjourned at 1/2 past six on Saturday morning.

These nocturnal struggles in the American House are generally signalized by some scandalous disorder. On the present occasion Mr. Keitt of South Carolina, the son of a German Tavern keeper, and himself a cracked-brained intemperate pro-slavery enthusiast, had a verbal altercation with Mr. Galusha Grow, who though a Representative from Pennsylvania, does not disdain the arm of the flesh.[36] Mr. Keitt struck the first blow but Mr. Grow returned it with interest; several members on either side fell to; besides the active combatants, others rushed to the place and endeavouring to restore order made confusion worse. The action was fought in a convenient arena in front of the Speaker's chair, about 1/2 past two o'clock. No one was seriously hurt, and both parties are endeavouring to turn the incident to their advantage outside.

The division is to be taken today and will be a test of party strength, but the practical result involving the acceptance or rejection of the Kansas Lecompton Constitution will not be attained for six weeks or two months.

After hearing all that is to be said on both sides I am under the impression that the Lecompton Constitution will pass the Senate, and will be rejected in the House by a very small majority. There is no doubt that the opposition have a positive majority, but [the] Government count on buying off several of the Douglas Democrats with federal offices. On the other hand the Northern Constituencies will keep a sharp lookout on their delegates and whoever votes for Lecompton will be lost in political life forever. We shall see whether interest or apprehension will carry the day.

In the decade prior to the American Civil War there was a marked reluctance in Congress to increase the military budget. According to Ouseley, the Buchanan administration's response to this attitude was to hoodwink the members into approving larger military expenditures.[37]

The designs of the President respecting Cuba have met with an unexpected check in the refusal of Congress to allow the increase of the army or to appropriate funds for the expedition of General Scott to the Pacific Coast *une die.*

It may seem that there is little direct connection between an expedition ostensibly against the Mormons or involving relations with Mexico and plans for the acquisition of Cuba. The latter however is the real object; the other is subsidiary to it and serves to mask the real movement. The intention as to the Mormons was to bring about their emigration to Sonora and thus to turn their rebellion to account by making them pioneers for future annexation under a quasi-military colonial system, that General Scott was partly to inaugurate without however being aware of the full scope of the project for the execution of which he was to be one of the instruments. His personal experience and former relations with Santa Anna and other leading men in Mexico was also to be used to the furtherance of the object of the U.S. in profiting by the difference with Spain. In all these matters, the increase of the army and a large appropriation for expenditure by the Executive, would have enabled the President when this Session is over to begin to carry into effect his grand object. I look upon it as only deferred and should not be surprised if before Congress disperses the President should obtain the means he covets for a purpose on which he deems absolute silence to be as yet necessary. He will find other ostensible motives to cover his real object. The building and equipment of several war steamers now actively in progress, ostensibly for service on the African station and to reinforce the Gulf of Mexico squadrons have, I more than suspect, reference to the same purpose. The real intention as to the Mormons is to buy them out which will it is said cost two or three millions of dollars, and the surplus of the appropriation would have given the Executive means for commencing the execution of its real plans.

Occasionally Lord Napier mentioned a personal matter in his private correspondence with Lord Clarendon, such as the item related in the postscript to his letter of 15 February: "My house caught fire the other night and we had a narrow escape. My wife lost all her clothes which makes Lent convenient."[38]

In February 1858 Napier found himself increasingly denied access to President Buchanan and was therefore forced to rely on William Ouseley as his intermediary.[39]

Acting in the sense of Your Lordship's private letter of the 22nd of January I made overtures to the President for a private conversation on Central American affairs on the 18th. The President intimated to me that he would prefer the communications to pass in the regular official channel. I am thus cut off from all private access with the President and referred to General Cass, who takes no responsibility and remembers nothing. This is disadvantageous. I do not know what the President's motives are for this and I am sure, on a late occasion, I took every precaution against misunderstanding and doing him an injustice. I believe that General Cass was averse to that method of treating foreign questions, feared that it might be extended and thought it necessary to stand upon his dignity. I have consequently been reduced to deal with General Cass and Mr. Appleton. With the latter I could get on better for he is an accurate thinker, tolerably sincere and entirely in the confidence of the President; but the old Secretary of State is embarrassing. I saw General Cass on Thursday; explained to him that Her Majesty's Government had no further communication to make until they had received an official reply to our offer of arbitration and reiterated the opinion of Her Majesty's Government that this expedient was the most just and honourable one for the regulation of our disputes. General Cass told me he could not hold out any hope that the determination of the President on that point would be changed. I then told him that if on further reflection the method of arbitration were definitively declined, I had reason to believe that Your Lordship might listen to overtures for the dissolution of the Clayton-Bulwer Treaty by mutual consent and with some substitute providing for equal rights in the transit passages. I recommended the subject to the mature consideration of the President and suggested that if the project were adopted, some proposal to that effect might be insinuated in his official answer to our last overtures. I begged him however to decide on nothing without seeing me again and giving me an opportunity of considering the views of the President to which he may in the meantime ascertain. I subsequently spoke in the same sense to Mr. Appleton. I observed enough to be assured that this notion of abrogating the Treaty and returning to the *status quo ante* is not as agreeable to them as they have pretended. They would like to make us give away the [Bay] Islands and then dissolve the engagements of 1850. We here, of course, must be entirely firm. By next mail I hope to let you know the result of the President's reflection. I have begged Sir William Ouseley to try and get at him.

Napier's letter of 2 March 1858 reiterates the predicament created by the presence of two ministers in Washington, neither feeling responsible to the other and each undermining the other's credibility.[40]

The President and General Cass have for the last ten days been pondering on the reply to our overtures for a settlement of the Central American difficulties.

I learn from the Secretary of State that it is definitely decided not to accept arbitration. General Cass, would, I think, prefer making an overture for the dissolution of the Clayton-Bulwer Treaty. The President I believe is not disinclined to recognize Sir William Ouseley's mission as a method of adjustment. I am prepared, however, for a complaint that our communication of the nature of his instruction is not sufficiently explicit to warrant the President in accepting and supporting the mission and directing the United States Minister to cooperate with it. I do not apprehend any difficulty on the Mosquito question and not much on the boundary of Belize but they desire to have a more definite knowledge of the terms on which we are prepared to transfer the [Bay] Islands to Honduras. Such a definite knowledge I cannot impart to them for I am not authorized, indeed I do not possess it myself. I have always been under the impression that if Sir William Ouseley's mission was to be the means of solving these difficulties the surrender of the Islands ought to have been the first object, but the conditions should have been made simple and easy and that they should have been frankly communicated to the American Cabinet. We have over and over again declared that we are ready to give up the Islands for the sake of the neutrality of the projected transit route. . . .

In the meantime the United States Government will continue to make their separate Treaties and save the privileges they desire and thus obtain a practical ascendancy in the transit routes. . . .

The Kansas question was at last opened yesterday in the Senate in a practical form by a proposal to receive the territory as a state under the Lecompton Constitution. It will certainly pass the Senate; the House is doubtful.

By 8 March Lord Napier admitted that he needed to reassess his belief that the slave trade was declining, since rumors concerning its revival were rife.[41]

Your Lordship will see from my public correspondence and from the reports which I doubt not the Consuls are sending in, that the revival of the slave trade is being advocated in various quarters and forms by certain parties in the United States. This unhappy movement has been stimulated by the French project. It originates further back and deeper in the security of black labour and the immense remunerative field for its employment. Our coolie trade, especially the Chinese branch, has been a noxious example. General Cass has an answer to my slave trade note in preparation. We must expect some complaints about the arrest of American vessels and the ill-regulated importation of Asiatic apprentices. I believe that if the apprenticeship measure before the Louisiana legislature should pass that body it will be quashed by an act of Congress.

Mr. Benjamin,[42] Senator for that state, holds this opinion and it was confirmed by
one of the Senators from Maryland who came in while we were talking the matter
over. The whole North will rise against the revival of the Trade under any disguise,
and the middle and Western slave states would take the same side to preserve the
value of their breeding negroes and maintain the Union. Such is my impression of
the present state of public feeling on the subject. It may not be of long duration.
The influence of the middle slave states a moderating and conservative one is rather
on the wane. South Carolina, Alabama, Louisiana and Texas are coming to the front.
They are ardent fanatical advocates of the extension of slavery. They are roused
by the impending corruption of free labour with which the North menaces them.
They feel that the sceptre of the Union is passing away from them; that the majority
in the Senate will soon be decidedly adverse; that the House of Representatives is
lost already. They see their vast extent of unoccupied unprofitable territory, capable
of giving sustenance and employment to millions of negroes, without avail in the
political struggle. This fills them with resentment and despair. If they cannot get
negroes in the Union they will break the Union and get negroes as an independent
federation. I do not believe that the existing political structure can last long. It is
a question on which I have reflected and consulted a good deal. The most conflicting
opinions are held by the most competent judges, but I lean to those who think that
we see the last age of the great confederacy. . . .

P.S. My despatches are cut short by the secession of Hope who is gone off suddenly
to attend his wife.[43] She was taken ill unexpectedly this morning and had a son born
at ten o'clock, as I just learned. Mother and child doing well—the first instance as
far as I know of an unpaid attaché having a legitimate child.

By mid-March news reached the United States that the Palmerston
government had fallen. This meant that Lord Clarendon would be leaving the
Foreign Office after five years, to be replaced by Lord Malmesbury[44] in a
cabinet led by the new prime minister, Lord Derby.[45] This change in
leadership came about somewhat indirectly as the result of an episode in France
known as the Orsini Affair. Felice Orsini,[46] an Italian nationalist who had
taken refuge in England, was relying on Napoleon III to promote the unification
of Italy, but because the emperor didn't seem to be doing enough to bring
this about, Orsini crossed the Channel, made his way to Paris, and attempted
to assassinate the French ruler. Several people in the vicinity of the bomb
explosion were killed, but the emperor and his wife escaped. Nonetheless, the
episode ended the short-lived era of Anglo-French amity created during the
Crimean War.

Both British envoys in Washington hastened to establish private
communication with the new foreign secretary.[47] Napier followed his initial
letter with another six days later.[48]

I have to thank your Lordship for your private letter of the 5th inst. I am happy
to learn that you do not view the expansion of the United States southwards with
any jealousy. That expansion is inevitable and in its legitimate forms most beneficial.
It will reach Central America and renovate that region hereafter, but it is not desirable
that the ambition of the United States should take the form of Filibusterism, or that

it should be indulged by the infraction of Treaties. I have always been in favour of the principle of the Clayton-Bulwer treaty, so much so that I have advocated the preservation of that Treaty even by the surrender of the people of the United States. It only prevented the annexation of Territory to the present Union. Such annexation is most unreasonable and unnecessary while the vast extent of Mexico is unappropriated. The people of the United States might freely transport themselves to Central America, plant, mine, and devote themselves to every kind of industry, multiply and possess the land and govern it as independent states; there is no reason, no necessity for their present arrogation to the Federal Union. If, however, Her Majesty's Government decide that it is not desirable to maintain this bar to territorial aggrandisement by the sacrifice of our own possessions which though small are still of some significance and have been declared colonial dependencies of the Crown, let that resolution be distinctly taken and acted upon, and if the U.S. government will not dissolve the Clayton-Bulwer treaty with the provisions we desire, it may be simply abrogated and both parties may return to their positions before the year 1850.

On 22 March Ouseley furnished the new foreign secretary with verification of his personal relationship with President Buchanan.[49]

> I had a private interview with the president an evening or two since—His Excellency inquired with interest respecting the late ministerial changes in England. He observed (and in so doing merely repeated in fact what he more than once said to me in England) that curiously enough he had found that a "Tory Ministry"—as he styled it—was always more inclined to act in a friendly spirit than "the Whigs" or so-called Liberals and that the party to which Your Lordship belongs was in his opinion "better and safer for England than its opponents". (He said that were he an Englishman he should belong to the Conservative party). . . .
> I should premise that Louis Napoleon is no favourite of the President, and that it is very possible that His Excellency should not be sorry to see the late initiating incidents result in a serious difference or actual war between England and France.[50]
> A favourite political theory in the U.S. is that such a war would ensure the success of their designs on Cuba and possibly enable them to get possession of our West Indian Islands.

Although Lord Clarendon was no longer a member of the cabinet, he still exerted much influence in Parliament, and in this capacity he continued to receive occasional letters from Ouseley.[51]

> We were quite taken by surprise, in which I believe that we were not singular, at the late changes in the Administration. . . . It causes inconvenience (to say the least) inasmuch as it suddenly takes the direction of negotiations, now much advanced toward solution, into new hands and necessarily will occasion a pause, which our friends here will, as usual, turn to account. General Cass has lately attempted to act in imitation of Mr. Buchanan's part (about reference to arbitration) early in the negotiation with yourself, which I think I contributed to defeat by putting Lord Napier on his guard. . . .
> I mention this only confidentially to yourself, and should probably not have referred to it at all were you still at the F.O. Yet I cannot but think that it might be advantageous if Lord Napier could be advised to be a little less confidential and communicative

to General Cass and others here. They really do not deserve or return it and it does no good—and possibly a little more so (although this is comparatively unimportant and temporary) with me. It is only from a friend like yourself that such a hint might be useful. My mentioning it to Your Lordship can at least do no harm.

The President continues to see me in private on confidential terms and said more than once the other day after the change of Ministers had been announced that he regretted much your leaving the F.O. . . .

It continually frustrated Lord Napier to have to deal primarily with Secretary of State Lewis Cass, as he found it impossible to have a relaxed conversation with him.[52]

I understand Your Lordship's wishes respecting the affairs of Central America. No further overtures shall be made in any form until an official answer has been returned to our proposals. (In my late conversations with General Cass [which included] suggestions of an offer on his part for the dissolution of the Clayton-Bulwer treaty, I obeyed the wishes of Lord Clarendon conveyed to me in his private correspondence.) His object was that I should exert some private influence in shaping the decision of the American Cabinet, and procuring a proposal for the dissolution of the Treaty in a manner, and with a substitute comfortable to our interests and wishes. That kind of negotiation may do very well with many European Ministers but I fear it is impracticable with the American Cabinet. The President will not commit himself by personal intercourse and discussion, and General Cass is so old, so forgetful, and so false, so irresolute and so enslaved to his own popularity that he will decide nothing, and would adhere to nothing if he did, in conversation. The result of my short experience is that all communications with the American Ministers should be official and written. I expect an answer about Central America in the course of next week, and I am afraid it will be accompanied by a vexatious communication about the Slave Trade. Our cruisers have been occasionally making too free with the American vessels. It is possible, also, that some restrictions may be passed on the traffic between China and Cuba carried on principally in British bottoms and attended with such a loss of life among the labourers or apprentices transported that it almost rivals the atrocities of the Slave Trade. I venture to recommend this matter to the attention of Her Majesty's Government though I doubt not it is brought under your consideration from their other quarters.

There is a cloud gathering on the Northern frontier of Mexico. I have desired the consuls at New Orleans and Galveston to keep Your Lordship and this Legation well informed of the projects and movements of the filibusters who will find an opening by the dissentions of the Mexicans. The leading Southern Senators here are informed of the designs of the adventurers and favour them. Mr. Toombs,[53] Senator from Georgia, told me the other day that the independence of the *Sierra Madre* republic would be declared in three months.

As the year wore on, the Buchanan administration became increasingly unpopular, according to Napier in his letter of 5 April.[54]

The temper of this government, never very courteous to Foreign Powers, may at present be soured by their contemptible position in domestic affairs. The policy of the President in reference to the increase of the army has been defeated in both Houses of Congress, the Lecompton Constitution, so warmly pressed by Mr. Buchanan, has been stopped if not definitely rejected in the House of Representatives, and, moreover, there are two treaties out, one with Nicaragua, the other with Granada, neither of which has been ratified. The President is in a bad position, and it is always popular to be impertinent to England.

One reason why William Gore Ouseley remained in Washington instead of embarking for Central America was his realization that the United States government was reluctant to acknowledge him as an official bargaining agent regarding matters in that part of the world. He kept being asked for clarification of his powers, but he refused to be specific, believing that he would gain maximum flexibility if his assignment remained cloaked in mystery. By 12 April he considered this strategy vindicated.[55]

Since the rejection of the proposal for arbitration has been received, couched in language that completely confirms my anticipations of the unfriendly and captious spirit by which this government is actuated toward Lord Napier, and the unfair use they make of his confidential and personally unreserved remarks to them, I cannot remodel my dispatch nor indeed forward any numbered official report throwing blame on Lord Napier, for in the first place it was not unnatural for Lord Napier, with little experience of this government and people, to expect in return for the friendly, conciliatory and I may say concessionary feeling that he has constantly shown in his dealings with them, and his popular personal efforts and hospitalities to all classes here. . . .

In the next place Lord Napier, after receiving General Cass's note, called on me, and in the fullest and most candid manner admitted "his regret at not having attended to my cautions as to his extreme confidence in the utility of unofficial and private manner of transacting business here"—saying "that he never should again commit himself to these people—that the report of his confidential conversations and communications [are] not honest and are most uncandid, and the suppression of what fell from theirs were negatively quite as unfair as their positive inferences;" for all which I was fully prepared. . . .

I cannot but think that I perceive a great dread of an expulsion à la Crampton actuating Lord Napier's conduct. This is neither unnatural or unfounded—but I do not think that extreme concession, forgetful of the respect due to H.M. Government or his own dignity as the Queen's Minister, is the way to avoid it.

It will, for a time at least, be best to hold the reins in London—to negotiate there officially only—or send out the forms of notes to this government from the Legation. Her Majesty's present government is not committed to any line on this policy with this government as yet—even by Lord Napier's late acts—and things may take a better channel by removing them to the Foreign Office.

Because he had no alternative, Lord Napier graciously accepted Ouseley's help, although he rarely agreed with him on matters of style and policy.[56]

I do not think that Mr. Buchanan's government can make very much political capital out of this question as we have at present placed it.

Sir William Ouseley differs with me, I believe, more or less on this question. We

are on the most cordial terms, and I have begged him to give you the full benefit
of his opinions at the risk of invalidating my own. Public feeling is, on the whole, good.

Replaying a familiar scene that occurred prior to Crampton's dismissal,
Napier reported rumors regarding his own tenure in a letter that dealt primarily
with recent events in Kansas.[57]

The inducements to come into the Union at this stage are great and the ordinance
respecting the public lands is liberally drawn. Many people think that the constitution
will be accepted along with the ordinance and that it will be altered in reference to
slavery afterwards.

In all this prolonged and envenomed contest the question of slavery or no slavery
has never really been at stake. No legislation can permanently force slavery into a
portion of the United States unfitted by nature for slave labour. The people will sooner
or later make their will felt and sweep off the hateful institution. All parties know
in their hearts that Kansas must be a free state in a couple of years, at the farthest,
in name and law as it is already in fact. The question has been contended for party
purposes and for no other.

A report has reached me through Mr. Everett to the effect that the President has
intimated in one form or another to Her Majesty's Government that it would be
agreeable to him that I should be removed. This rumour would not have been noticed
by me if it had not come from such a respectable quarter. He stated that he had
it from good authority in the Department of State. If there be any foundation for
this assertion, I need not say that you would confer a great obligation on me by
informing me on what grounds the President has based his application, in order that
I may have an opportunity of removing any misapprehension that it might create.

At the end of May 1858 all other issues were eclipsed by an incident in the
Gulf of Mexico. British ships, zealous in their efforts to curb the slave trade,
periodically stopped and searched vessels approaching Western Hemispheric
shores, and mistakes were sometimes made because of inadequate identification. According to the United States, Her Majesty's vessel *Styx* had
undertaken searches of no fewer than six American ships in the Gulf of Mexico
and fifteen harbored in Cuban ports.[58]

You will be a good deal surprised at the tenor of my despatches today. The agitation
here about the detention of American vessels in the Gulf of Mexico has risen with
a rapidity and a violence which I never anticipated. Since the debate on the 29th
in the Senate I cannot do otherwise than treat this affair as a serious international
emergency. I have therefore sent an express to the Admiral advising him to suspend
the action of our ships, and to go down to the coast of Cuba at once, to keep the
Peace if possible but also to be prepared for war. I believe that it will all pass away,
but if the other issue occurred, and if I had not warned the Admiral as soon as possible,
my responsibility would be great and my condemnation deserved. . . .

I think it right to state that in my opinion you cannot practice any kind of
supervision, visitation, or inquiry over American shipping in the Cuban waters without
incurring the most serious hazards of war with the United States. The whole nation,

you may say, are of one mind on this question. They are determined, and will attempt to fight it out, though God knows they are ill-prepared. We are ill-prepared too. Our Indian and French embarrassments and the Naked state of our North American Provinces make the present occasion peculiarly unfavorable to us, while these circumstances offer a great temptation to adventurous spirits in America.[59] I should not be the least surprised by some attempt upon the Canadian frontier for the purpose of aggravating the difficulty and producing collision.

Napier also saw sobering implications for American democracy in the reports of recent riots in New Orleans.[60]

An extraordinary commotion has taken place at New Orleans. That place has been under the domination of a faction called "Know-Nothings" for the last two years, who are of the "American" party, one whose leading doctrine is the exclusion of foreigners from office and the adoption of severe laws of naturalization. This party was not without good grounds and if it had conducted its affairs with discretion might have risen to power. It betook itself, however, to bad courses forming sworn association, operating secretly, and using violence in the elections. The result is that it has become wholly discredited and has little ascendancy except at New Orleans and Baltimore where the most bloody barbarities are practiced and where the citizens come, especially if they be Democrats, to have no security for life or estate. The late revolution at New Orleans is unprecedentedly a manifestation, on the part of respectable men, to cast off the yoke of this tyranny and to give freedom to the ballot box and security to all in the exercise of their political privileges. The vigilance committee has obtained the upper hand and has begun to expel the ruffians from the town. We know of this affair, as yet only by telegraphic accounts and it may not prove to be so much a movement of the respectable classes as a mere effort of the Democratic Party to recover the municipal power. One thing is certain and it is privately avowed by all reflecting politicians here: viz., that government by universal suffrage in great cities is irreconcilable with peace and good order and freedom of opinion. The cities of America must either be placed upon another and an exceptional system with reference to suffrage or they must be governed by the intervention of the state governments, which have a more wholesome source of election instead of by municipal councils.

I have not met in America more than two persons of thought and political experience who in their hearts believe in the permanent working of the popular sovereignty and universal suffrage machine—but no one dares declare himself, at least in the North, and no one knows how the prerogatives abandoned to the mob are to be resumed by the better order of people.

For many people in England the decade of the 1850s was a time of soul-searching about imperialism. Some thought that it had served its purpose and should be replaced by informal commercial and diplomatic ties. The ideals of free trade with their corresponding attack upon mercantilist practices very much fostered a mood of imperial contraction, a view taken by Napier. On the other hand, there were others like Ouseley who urged Her Majesty's government to retain Britain's hard-won possessions in the face of any attempts to be rid of them.[61]

The secret of Lord Napier's readiness, nay, apparent anxiety to yield anything and everything that this government may exact—is not, as some think, merely on the "anything for a quiet life" system (which perhaps has been too much adopted by preceding governments in their dealings with the United States)—nor is it solely in order to gain personal popularity or to avoid differences with this government—but he is a disciple of the exploded and fallacious school whose theory was advocated by Roebuck,[62] and others some twenty-five years ago (but long since abandoned by them)—viz., that England has no need of colonies, and would be stronger and richer, perhaps even more powerful—without them. While this is merely treated as a sort of theme for a debating society, or even as one of the subjects on which certain M.P.'s—fond of defending paradoxes—exercise their talents in incidental and desultory debate, it does little harm. But it becomes positively dangerous when sincerely adopted by an English Minister. Lord Napier is firmly persuaded that England would gain by giving up not merely our more distant minor dependencies but even the Canadas, Nova Scotia, the West Indies, etc. Because a generation ago our colonies were injudiciously governed and the system of their management was not rightly understood, it by no means follows that when well-governed and prosperous, they should be a burden yet. Our magnificent American empire every day increasing its own strength, and adding to that of England, he thinks an encumbrance, and makes no secret of his opinion. This, and the irresistable desire by which he is animated for unreserved communication, and often misplaced confidence, made me anxious that the seat of all negotiations of a delicate or difficult nature should be transferred to *England*. . . .

Should we give up Canada, the West Indies, etc., which is the secret object the United States have constantly *in petto*—we should next be asked to yield Ireland. It is useless to blind ourselves to the impolicy of a system of concession without a return. They do not like us the better for it—and are only the more exigent. Their appetite grows by what it feeds on.

After eight months of preparatory discussions, Ouseley finally decided to leave Washington for Central America. He asked Lord Malmesbury to arrange for a British warship to stop in New York and collect him en route to the Caribbean. He thought it best to keep the purpose of his mission secret so that the American press would not undermine his efforts. He also reasoned that if only Lord Napier could be kept in check, his mission would have a better chance of success.[63]

Lord Napier now begins to see that the object here is to get us to give up everything without any equivalent and then give up the Bulwer-Clayton Treaty. But he is so honourable, so devoid of guile and trickery himself, that he can hardly believe in it in others, even of these people. He never had *sciemment* [knowingly] tried to deceive them—but he has done so nevertheless, once or twice completely—by telling them the exact truth—but this cannot last as I may explain by and by. On the other hand they suspect our good faith, and our expectant attitude not a little puzzles and annoys them. They suspect a price in everything and the contrast between the petulant cross-fire constantly kept up for some time between London and Washington—and the more dignified actual proceedings, takes them aback.

It is impossible to get Lord Napier to think that diplomacy consists in anything but a continual battery of notes, conferences and despatches, and he worries himself (and people here) by his unremitting and active mode of ventilating every question on every occasion.

Ouseley's criticism of Lord Napier had its effect on Lord Malmesbury, as may clearly be seen in the latter's private communications with the prime minister, Lord Derby, who commented to the foreign secretary, "Napier's own policy seems to be that of giving up everything the U.S. can wish for, even before they ask it."[64]

Not realizing the full extent of his impaired situation in Washington, Napier confessed to Lord Malmesbury a sense of relief following Ouseley's departure for Central America.[65]

I intend to investigate the schemes of the filibusters while I am about New York. This is the centre of all their machinations, and those of the rival commodores or steamboat proprietors whose mutual malice is such that they would sacrifice life and peace and every principle to do each other a mischief. The chief of these rogues are George Law,[66] Vanderbilt,[67] and this Joseph White,[68] who is however a clever fellow and well informed on Central American affairs.

Ouseley spent many weeks in New York awaiting the arrival of his ship, and during that time continued his reports to Lord Malmesbury.[69]

George Law (a steamboat speculator here, a wealthy man) who furnished Henningsen with a considerable sum (all expended or lost in Walker's expedition) refuses any aid to Walker—but peculiarly enough lately offered Henningsen $50,000 to take the command of an expedition against Nicaragua, the chief object of which appears to have been the hope of securing a monopoly of the transit route.[70] Henningsen refused, as he has separated himself from the Walker filibusters; with whom he is now ashamed to "march through Coventry". Besides, I am informed that he is anxious to be more or less legitimately employed by the U.S. against *Mexico*. The assertion of money having been furnished by General Cass, directly to the filibusters, and the suspicion of the Central Americans to that affect are not, I think, well founded. It is certain however that they now have friends. Vanderbilt, the present monopolist of the transit—has positively refused, alleging that he will have nothing to do with any but regular commercial (and profitable) speculations. I fear it is true that the President and Government will—now that they know of the treaty intended with *Costa Rica*—connive at all the present preparations and future acts of the filibusters, in order to throw impediments in my way there.

Improbable as it seemed, Ouseley reported that word was being spread that Secretary of State Lewis Cass helped William Walker undertake another unlawful expedition to Nicaragua.[71]

The first result here [New York] is that an immediate movement of the filibusters is expected. Private information from a reliable source has reached me, that in the low ale and wine houses where the adventurers meet, they say that now General Cass actually encourages their undertaking and supplies, through certain political adherents, money to fit them out—that it is true that the President still ostensibly disapproves—but will not, they say, act against them.

Like British observers before him, Ouseley was impressed by the legal knowledge of American politicans, including the president.[72]

Buchanan is a subtle man and lawyer, and like all American diplomats and public men (with very rare exceptions) considers it his duty to act for the U.S. as a paid advocate for his client, and more in conformity with Old Bailey practice that we are apt to like or think allowable.

They are all in fact, as regards public affairs, unscrupulous attorneys—at the same time Buchanan in private life and personal feelings is, I think, an estimable and right-minded man—and has been very friendly to me.

By mid-October Lord Derby regretted his and Malmesbury's decision to have sent Ouseley to Washington.[73] It had created jealousy between the younger minister and the older envoy, and furthermore, Ouseley had a tendency to panic when there were sudden shifts in policy, such as the unexpected rapprochement between Nicaragua and Costa Rica. Unaware of this growing unease in London, Lord Napier raised the question of his salary and housing for the next year.[74]

When I saw Lord Clarendon at the Foreign Office before starting for America, he gave me some instructions of a social nature. He told me to take a good house in an acceptable situation, to keep it open, to throw myself among the people, and to endeavour to obtain some influence by a hospitable and generous manner of life.

I replied that I foresaw much difficulty in a financial point of view. The salary was scarcely commensurate to the expenditure of a settled establishment on such a footing, that I had no ready money and no available private income, for the very little I possessed would be necessarily applied to some purposes of a purely private character at home. I consequently anticipated incurring some debt in my outfit and in furnishing my house, and that would impose on me a course of economy during the first two years of my mission.

Recognizing the justice of these reflections, Lord Clarendon told me nevertheless to follow his wishes, and that he would find me the means to a reasonable extent; and he added that if he went out of office he had little doubt that his successors would act up to his intentions.

Accordingly, I have kept an open house and made merry, in rather a rough way, to the satisfaction and entertainment of the Americans and perhaps in some degree to the promotion of a good feeling in influential quarters, though I admit it was not very apparent in the "visitation".

I have had power to draw upon the secret service fund for £1,000 and my allowance for house rent has been raised from £500 to £600.

The money is now all spent. I have dispersed all my outfit salary, and allowances, and something of my own and I find myself still considerably in debt, at the commencement of a new session, for furniture, etc., and but ill-provided in that respect.

Before beginning again it is desirable that I should understand my position. I can, of course, pull up and endeavour to live on my salary, though that might necessitate rather a sudden and indecent alteration. I can, on the other hand, continue my previous indulgent habits with rather less assistance than I had before.

Your Lordship has to decide.

Do you intend to sanction any further application of the secret service money? If you do I think, in consideration of the comparative shortness of the approaching session, and the fact that we need not anticipate another marriage in the Royal family, £700 in two payments—one, on the first of December and the other on the first of March—would answer my purpose and be a sensible enlargement of my ordinary means.

In regard to the expenditure of £1,000 last winter it is difficult to disentangle that sum from the general expenses of my household. I have, however, extracted from a good deal of miscellaneous hospitality some salient instances which will, in round numbers, account for the sum referred to.

Your Lordship will find them on a separate sheet.

Your Lordship will remark that the account contains both a ball on the Princess's marriage day, and that on the Queen's birthday, entertainments which have probably been paid for at several missions at extraordinary allowances on a much greater scale.

I need only add that I live in the midst of a shifting miscellaneous society altogether given to dining, drinking, and dancing and all pressing towards the house of the "British Minister". I therefore think that I have some claim on the public purse. Certainly, Washington is dearer than Berlin and the Americans are more extravagant than the Prussians, but my salary is I think £1,000-or £1,500 below that of Lord Bloomfield.[75]

EXPENDITURES

Professional Concert:[76] Frezzolini, Strakosch, Vieuxtemps, Thalberg; 20 Nov. 1857 100

Ball on the occasion of the marriage of the Princess Royal, 25 Jan. 1858 200

Enlarging a room permanently on that occasion 130

Ball on the Queen's Birthday, 28 May 1858 150

During the months of December, January, February, and March: 16 dinners to 18 persons at £25 each 400

Amateau concert, rehearsals, suppers, professional orchestra, etc., June 1858 90

Total: 1,070

* * *

On 9 November Napier sought to interpret the significance of the state and local elections that had just taken place.[77]

The elections continue to run strongly against Mr. Buchanan's government. This may be in some respects useful as it weakens the Administration and prevents their adopting a threatening or energetic attitude in Foreign Matters, but it may result in subverting the Democratic Party and bringing the Northern Republicans into power, whose commercial principles are less consistent with the practice and interests of England. We cannot forget that the Democrats, with all their faults, are for a low Tariff, and the Republicans with all their pretensions, are protectionists.

Since Ouseley was now well out of the country, Napier resolved to defend himself against the recriminations that Ouseley leveled against him. One wonders whether this unburdening would have enhanced Napier's position in the eyes of Malmesbury and Derby had it come earlier in the year.[78]

I forward to Your Lordship by this messenger the long note on Central American affairs promised by the last mail. In my accompanying Despatch I have added a good deal of explanation and something which has the air of controversy.[79] I have done so with great reluctance, first because I feel the impropriety of inflicting on you a recitation of details so complicated and repulsive, and secondly because I have a peculiar motive for keeping out of all disputes.

I differ with Sir William Ouseley in his views and I think he has misconceived and, in some degree, misrepresented my proceedings. I have felt tempted to dispute his reports to H.M. Government on more than one occasion, but I have refrained because I will not be a combative and polemical Napier. If I get involved in a contention with my colleague I am condemned at once.

Sir William Ouseley has however, so confidently and frequently assumed, in conversation and apparently in writing, that I have on my personal responsibility promised concessions to the U.S. Government without authority or approval from the Foreign Office, that I have been constrained to place my course in a more correct light.

I have indeed held out to the President and to General Cass that H.M. Government would evacuate the Bay Islands and Mosquitia. Mosquitia is to be evacuated and the surrender of the Bay Islands was officially, though conditionally, proposed in an official note of 30 November 1857 drawn by me, on Sir William Ouseley's first instructions—shown to Sir William, altered by him, and sent in with his full sanction. It was afterwards approved of by H.M. Government. This official offer to surrender the Bay Islands has never been formally revoked by H.M. Government. It still stands as the record of their intentions. It may have been an impolitic offer on the part of the late government, I think not, but if it be so it is not my doing. It is a public act. If Her Majesty's Government have definitely resolved to alter the policy of their predecessors in that respect, they have a good opportunity of doing so, in answer to General Cass's present note.

I have never held out the expectation of any other concessions than the transfer of Mosquitia and the Bay Islands. The remaining point, the Belize frontier, has always remained in the dark.

On the subject of the Bay Islands I think Sir William Ouseley had a morbid feeling. Before he went away he was extremely unwell, he had a dangerous fever and was reduced and debilitated. He conceived that I was opposing him, he thought my course calculated to frustrate the objects of his mission, persons in this country endeavoured to sow jealousy between us and did not stick at telling us the most malicious things of each other. Whether the Bay Islands are valuable or not, they might become as

Mr. Ouseley thinks another Gibraltar, and whether they be as I believe an unprofitable and embarrassing appendage, since Her Majesty's Government has informed me of their resolution to act separately, to stand apart and independent, and deal with the Central American powers alone, I have never held out to the President or General Cass any prospect of concessions at all, other than those respecting Mosquitia which are comprised in Sir William Ouseley's present instructions.

All I respectfully contend for is that the cession of the Bay Islands should not be laid at my door as my private sin.

On the very day that the above letter was written, Lord Lyons accepted Lord Malmesbury's offer to become envoy extraordinary and minister plenipotentiary to the United States, requesting time to set his affairs in order and visit his father, who was gravely ill.[80] Lord Malmesbury informed Napier of this decision in terms which avoided injuring his pride by suggesting that he was not being recalled but rather being offered the opportunity to return to Europe, where he would be assigned to The Hague, always considered a desirable posting. Napier accepted the inevitable with grace.[81]

The steamer, having been behind time, I have only this morning received your letter of the 26th of November, announcing my nomination to the Hague.

As you have employed such kind expressions it would ill-become me to use any expostulations on the subject. It is not good striving against Fate and the Foreign Office. I certainly do not desire to leave America at this moment. I have long cherished the hope that after the settlement of our Central American difficulties it might be reserved to me to make an expanded reciprocity treaty, and a limited copyright convention. With a view to those great objects, I have endeavoured to lay the basis of the cordial feeling in this country toward England, and to gain a hold upon the leading politicians in both Houses of Congress. I believe that I have in part succeeded, and though Her Majesty's Government may possibly think that I have been too much disposed to concession on certain points and that I am the advocate of a policy too favourable to American pretensions, I trust that I have not committed Her Majesty's Government, and I think that the good effects of my general action would have been practically felt hereafter. I confess I could have wished to remain, and even now I could not receive a more welcome piece of intelligence than that Lord Lyons had preferred Holland and that Her Majesty's Government had decided to retain my services here.

On private grounds, irrespective of ambition, I have not only no reason to complain but many reasons to rejoice. There is not much here to make life agreeable. My wife would prefer Europe. My children must go to school. If I had been offered the choice of the missions in Europe I would have chosen The Hague. In short, if the question be definitely decided I am content to repair to the land of tedium and Teniers.[82] I am fond of pictures and resigned to do nothing. But if there be any election I avow that I would rather remain at this post, which seems to be the Castle Dangerous of English diplomatists.

Will Your Lordship permit me to ask, a favour. It is to appoint Mr. William Hope unpaid attaché at The Hague. He is my relative and a young man of unusual character and abilities. I brought him here and I conceive that he would be glad to follow my fortunes. I had great attachment to his father who was many years Lord Justice Clerk in Scotland, and his grandfather the Lord President Hope, my great uncle, was the friend of Pitt and Dundas (which I am not). You see that Hope is my cousin, and a Scotchman must have a cousin about him.[83]

On looking over my letter I see there is a little bitter mirth mingled with my submission. I hope Your Lordship will excuse it under the circumstances. Seriously speaking I am very sensible of Your Lordship's goodness. If there be a motive for changing my destination, and of that Her Majesty's Government are the only judges, the intimation could not have been conveyed to me more delicately, nor could I have been provided with a more convenient and pleasant post.

Napier's first letter in the New Year made use of the cloak of the private and confidential convention, reminding us of the importance of this method of communication with the Foreign Office as a supplement to the ordinary public dispatches.[84]

I send you today a full explanation of the grounds on which I made overtures for the dissolution of the Clayton-Bulwer Treaty last year, and I have forwarded an Extract from Lord Clarendon's private letter instructing me on that subject.[85] I hope I have not gone wrong in putting a private communication into a confidential Despatch. A letter of the kind has almost the force of an official instruction. It could not be suppressed because I necessarily intimated to the Secretary of State the nature and extent of my authority when I made the overtures to him. It could not be left without some allusion or record in the correspondence of the Legation, for reference may be made hereafter to my proceedings in the matter by the Government of the U.S. when it suits their own purpose, as reference has already been made. . . . I am also under the apprehension that a very incomplete and incorrect version of my opinions or conduct may have been conveyed to the Foreign Office, though not intentionally, by Sir William Ouseley on some points. Your Lordship will observe that as I am about to retreat I am protecting my rear.

I fear that nothing is to be expected from the United States in regard to a combined intervention in Mexico. Mr. Otway urges a Foreign Protectorate and M. de Sartiges has spoken to me in the same sense.[86] I have told my French Colleague that in my mind Parliament would never consent to Her Majesty's Forces being employed for the maintenance of any form of Government in Mexico, monarchial or republican, and that the settlement of a country by force of arms is chimerical as far as we are concerned. If a Foreign Protectorate involving the military occupation of Mexico be requisite, the only country which could afford such a protectorate and the only one which England would wish to see do it is the United States. Such a protectorate, however, the United States at present cannot exercise or accept, and I thought it possible that the Confederacy of Mexico might be once more tranquilized and united by a benevolent mediation on the part of the European Powers and the United States. If the United States would not come in, the European Powers might attempt it alone. I do think it worthy of Your Lordship's consideration whether such an effort might not be made now. If the English and French Ministers were instructed to withdraw to some neutral position in connection with their ships, and to make a strong appeal to the rival Government and Presidents, would it not be possible to induce both parties to resign a sterile and disputed authority.[87] A provisional President such as General Robbles might be brought forward and an administration formed from persons not deeply engaged on either side, until a Convention should be assembled from all parts of the Country in Mexico. I throw out these suggestions as they occur to me without any local knowledge, which I fear must deprive my opinion of all value.

Although manifestly illegal under American law, a slave trade with Africa continued under a variety of subterfuges and clandestine arrangements. In December 1858 a pleasure yacht called the *Wanderer* stationed itself off the coast of Georgia in order to meet a larger ship carrying slaves. It then ferried about three hundred Africans to an island in the Savannah River, where they were sold and dispersed. Those responsible were apprehended and brought to trial, but Lord Napier foresaw future ramifications arising from the episode.[88]

Your Slave Trade despatch with Commodore Wise's Report has, in conjunction with the late arrival of the "Wanderer" with a Cargo of Slaves in Georgia, had the effect of waking up the American Cabinet to a sense of their disgraceful position in regard to the abuse of the American flag on the Coast of Africa.[89] General Cass told me the day before yesterday, that the subject had been under discussion in the Cabinet, that the Secretary of the Navy would send on a Steamer directly, and that every effort would be made to substitute Steam Power for the present old-fashioned sailing vessels. General Cass also adverted to some change which he thought might be desirable in the terms of the Ashburton Treaty.[90] That Treaty now prescribes the maintenance by either party of a proper squadron bearing 80 guns, and on the part of the United States there have been usually three or four old-fashioned Brigs or Corvettes with about that number of guns on board. Now, as General Cass observed, the *number of guns* is certainly quite indifferent. Ten light steam vessels with two guns apiece would be infinitely preferable to four sailing vessels with 80. He thought some modification of the Treaty might be introduced stipulating the employment of Steam Power and reducing the number of guns. I told him that I thought H.M. Government would entertain any proposal having for its object to render the blockading squadrons more efficient.

The "New York Herald" reports the overthrow of Zuloaga and the elevation of General Robbles.[91] This change, if it prove to be well-founded, will no doubt draw on a negotiation between the two factions, for Robbles is an honest, well-intentioned man, and before leaving Washington had already conceived the project of mediating and restoring peace by reciprocal concessions.

Congress has reassembled in a very quiet mood. There is no excitement or expectation of great political results. . . .

Mr. Toombs, the Senator for Georgia, who may be regarded as a violent advocate for an aggressive foreign policy, told me recently that there was nothing to be apprehended in regard to Mexico. Congress would not even endorse the timid proposal of the President to establish posts in the border provinces of Chihuahua and Sonora for the protection of Arizona.

As to Cuba, all parties agreed that there is no prospect whatever of any step being taken toward its acquisition. It is understood that Spain is resolutely bent upon rejecting any overture for negotiation and no one here, of any recognized party, dreams of the annexation of the island either by filibustering or by public war. If Spain will show a reasonable disposition to adjust the pecuniary claims of Citizens of the United States I see no reason why the relations of the two Countries may not become perfectly easy and friendly. All that Mr. Buchanan said on this subject in his message was forced upon him by his unprincipled participation in the Ostend Manifesto, which was in fact, as far as he was concerned, an election manifesto and not the programme of a practical foreign policy.

The only subject which obtains much attention is the scheme for a Railroad to the Pacific, which is presented under various forms but which will not, I think, obtain the sanction of Law during the present session.

Not yet knowing that Napier was due to be replaced at Washington, Ouseley continued to caution Lord Malmesbury about entrusting the minister with any information relating to Ouseley's mission. From his vantage point at León, the capital of Nicaragua, Ouseley felt that Napier had already done enough damage.[92]

In your note of the 5th of November (of which only the duplicate has reached me) you say that I am "too suspicious of the U.S. Government," etc. May I take the liberty of saying that I am not properly speaking *suspicious* in as much as suspicion implies *uncertainty*. Now *I knew* before I left New York that the moment Lord Napier volunteered his incontinent communication on my affairs to General Cass—especially as regards Costa Rica—instructions were sent off instantly to Lamar here to obstruct, and if possible prevent, all satisfactory negotiation on my part. This is only what anyone who really knows the people and *cosas do los Estados Unidos*, would be prepared for. As to Lord Napier the extreme candor with which he accepts everything and anything from Americans, amounts almost to infatuation, arising doubtless from his unaccountable admiration and predilection for everything republican: so that when he wrote to me that General Cass had promised his good word, etc., to Lamar and the government for me (see also His Lordship's no. 39 of October 16) he was indignantly surprised at my utter disbelief on and deprecation of all such aid. Cass is in this case a *dona pasens* who knowingly wants to deceive us; Lord Napier in the innocence of his heart is likely to deceive because he is himself deceived. With the best and most upright intentions I admit, and with a large share of good, even brilliant, qualities he is the very last coadjutor—at least in all relating to the U.S. or to practical affairs of any sort, that I should ever select. Indeed, my dear Lord, if I may venture to speak with entire frankness to you, less a secretary of state than as Lord Malmesbury, all I wish from Lord Napier—much as I like him personally—is that he would entirely abstain from all interference with Central American affairs, and that nothing whatever should be mentioned respecting my measures, opinions or the negotiations going on here, to that *enfant terrible* of diplomacy, at least while I have anything to do with it. I know how unreasonable this may appear; I beg you to excuse me *outre guidance* on this point. Had I not had, before I left the U.S., sufficient grounds for what I say, I have them now amply on becoming acquainted on the spot with Lamar—*faits et gestes*, since my instructions even prematurely explained (not in general terms as directed by you) so copiously, that without sending a copy they could not have been more entirely laid before the U.S. Government, which act has been represented here, as I expected, as asking permission or at least approval of the Government at Washington.

On 21 February Napier reported that President Buchanan's legislative program was in jeopardy. It looked as though Congress was going to refuse to appropriate a request for $30 million to purchase Cuba as well as to deny any extraordinary powers regarding Central and South America and Mexico.[93]

In fact the President is reduced to a nonentity. He is even pitied by his enemies.

I learn from General Cass this morning that, in a few days, instructions will be forwarded to Mr. Dallas in reference to the suppression of the Slave Trade.

Some allusion will, I think, be made to the severity of Your Lordship's language in qualifying the proceedings of the Americans and the abuse of their flag. You will then be informed that the U.S. Government proposed to send two steamers to Africa and three to the coast of Cuba; a desire will be expressed for the revision of the Ashburton Treaty with a view to the reduction of the stipulated number of guns, to the substitution of a stipulated number of appropriate vessels armed with Steam Power; and a hope will be expressed that you will be able, under existing treaties, to enforce the cooperation of the Spanish Government in suppressing the trade in Cuba.

On the eve of his departure, Lord Napier wrote his last private letter to Lord Malmesbury, informing him that Lord Lyons had arrived safely and all seemed in order for a smooth transition.[94]

Lord Lyons arrived at Annapolis on the 8th. I could not dispose of my house and effects until he had seen them. That domestic business, the presentation of our respective letters, the explanation of affairs and other matters have occupied ten days. I trust that this delay of the ship will not be thought exorbitant. We sail tonight and I hope to be able to pay my respects to Your Lordship in about a month.

Lord Lyons is pleased with the country, and has already made a very agreeable impression.

Even after Napier had left Washington, Ouseley continued his vituperations against him. From Costa Rica came further rantings.[95]

I can only repeat that one must distrust all the United States Representatives, Agents or representations on all that relates to their policy and intentions. Lord Napier sincerely thought that by giving up everything in the Bulwer-Clayton Treaty, he was insuring the realization of what the subtle Buchanan always put forward—viz., that there would be no further difficulty between England and the U.S., if we gave up in this matter. Lord Napier anticipated after that a sort of millennium of good feeling and friendship between Great Britain and the United States. I fear this will prove a great mistake.

With the United States, it is from system not accident that there is always a grievance got up against England—already they are preparing one on the Oregon and the Vancouver's boundary—and probably also on Belize.

On May 24 Ouseley offered his latest assessment of Anglo-American relations. His letter began, however, with a reference to his wife's sister, whose family connections reinforced his links with New York's inner social circle.[96]

Her husband is Judge Roosevelt of the Supreme Court of New York, who has been spoken of as the intended successor of Dallas in London.

It is not at present the intention of Buchanan to recall Dallas—not only have his friends been strenuously supporting him, but his plausible respectability of appearance is thought useful in England, as it is reported that what he says is actually believed at the Foreign Office and that his representations have weight. . . .

Mr. Cobden has been on a visit to Mr. Buchanan—Mr. Bright is in frequent correspondence with him. By working on the vanity of these people (and that of old Edward Ellice and others also), Mr. Buchanan and his friends completely cajole and make use of these people;[97] really very ignorant as they are of the true intentions and feelings of the U.S. people towards England. No one who speaks so much of the U.S. knows less of them than Mr. Bright (except perhaps Lord Napier, but his ideas are more dangerous because he is convinced that he is *well*-informed, whereas he is purposely and cunningly misled). It is a great misfortune for England that in the House of Commons there should be a *clique* if not a party—absolutely in the service of the U.S. In fact they are, more or less *scienment* traitors to their own country.

I used to meet Bright, Cobden, Milner-Gibson,[98] etc. at Buchanan's in London and saw the beginning of the net-work which he has thrown around all that set— chiefly of the Manchester school. We have no similar, or counteracting footing in the Congress of the U.S. To do them justice, their nationality would be proof against any attempt to magnetize it.

A short while after writing this, Ouseley himself was recalled to England, his original mission having partially succeeded and at the same time been somewhat foiled.

8
Lord Lyons and the Buchanan Administration, 1859–1860

Richard Bickerton Pemell Lyons began his worldwide travels at the age of twelve, serving as a midshipman on his father's sailing vessel. Thereafter, his professional development followed more conventional lines, and included attendance at Winchester College for his secondary education and then Christ Church, Oxford, for a bachelor of arts degree. In 1838 he took up the post of attaché in Athens, where his father was British minister, and remained there until 1852, when he was assigned to Dresden. The following year he was transferred to Florence, becoming secretary of the legation in 1856 and minister plenipotentiary in 1858. In December 1858 he accepted Lord Malmesbury's offer to become minister to the United States. When he assumed this post in April 1859 he had already succeeded to his father's title as Second Baron Lyons. Thus the British were again sending a member of the peerage to Washington in order to flatter the American ego.

Lord Lyons's first private letter to his foreign secretary was written from Washington on 12 April.[1]

> I am just about ready to set out for the White House to present my letters of Credence, and shall probably not get back in time to write you by this Messenger a report of the Audience. The President will probably attack me about Sir William Ouseley's treaty—your *private* letter of the 25th (which reached me last night) will enable me to say just what is desirable about the "anti-filibuster" clause.[2] I shall be careful to say no more than you authorize, and to confine myself to observing that this clause is *perhaps* one of those with which you are not satisfied. The point, however, upon which I am told public feeling is most excited here, is the conclusion of the Transit Treaty, without the simultaneous abandonment of the Mosquito Protectorate.
>
> Lord Napier has exerted himself very much to assist me in every way, and has done all that was possible to start me well both socially and politically.
>
> I hope Mr. Warre is on his way out. It is indispensible to have a thoroughly efficient, paid attaché at this mission.[3]

One week later, Ouseley's treaty with Nicaragua still monopolized Lord Lyons's attention.[4]

213

On the 13th I spoke to General Cass, as you desired me to do in your private letter of the 25th of last month, respecting the anti-filibustering article inserted by Sir William Ouseley in his Treaty with Nicaragua. I said exactly what you told me—that is that I had no instructions on the subject, but that you had mentioned to me in a private letter that Sir William Ouseley had signed a treaty and inserted of his own accord some articles of which you did not approve. General Cass replied that of course the Article respecting filibusters was one which you disapproved—I answered that I was not able to tell him whether it was or not—all I could say was that there were articles which did not satisfy you. In the conversation which I had with him today upon the same subject, and which is reported in my despatch no. 13 of this date, he said, as you will see, that perhaps the President would wait to see what you did about Sir William Ouseley's filibustering Article before deciding upon what course to pursue respecting the similar Article in the American Treaty with Nicaragua which has just arrived.[5] I did not say anything whatever as to what you might be likely to do or not to do, but left the matter just as I had placed it on the 13th in the conversation of which I give an account at the beginning of this letter.

General Cass spoke much more hopefully and cordially about the whole Central American question than he has hitherto done to me. The great object with a view to our relations with this Government of course is to get all our Treaties and Arrangements with the Central American States completed as soon as possible.

Six weeks passed without the appearance of his long-promised paid attaché, prompting Lord Lyons to register a complaint, since his handwriting was nearly illegible and he badly needed an amanuensis.[6]

I am very much obliged by your sending out Mr. Warre and am impatiently expecting him. It is absolutely necessary to have a good man here to direct the Chancery; I think too this Mission would be a very good school for a young man who really wished to learn his business, and I should welcome anyone who was industrious and wrote a thoroughly good legible hand.[7]

It is particularly desirable that the Staff should be complete, because if the Minister is to have any knowledge of the Country and People, it is indispensable that he should visit from time to time the principal cities. This is not like a European State in which politics and business are centred in the Capital and can be studied more advantageously there than elsewhere. No political men make Washington their principal residence, in fact they cannot do so, as it sends no members to Congress, either to the Senate or the House of Representatives. Commerce it has none. In fact it is little more than a large village, and when Congress is not sitting it is a deserted village.

By 21 June Mr. Warre had not yet made his appearance, and the Ouseley treaty with Nicaragua was still under debate. Lord Lyons endeavored to reassure Secretary of State Cass that its provisions would bring mutual benefit to both their governments.[8]

I think it may be convenient for you to have in a despatch a summary of what General Cass said respecting the Nicaraguan fears of filibusters, and I will accordingly write one on the subject. He spoke in a friendly, good-humoured tone—but he seemed to think that Sir William Ouseley might easily have brought the Nicaraguans to reason, if he had been more firm with them. How this may be I know not, but I quite agree with General Cass, that it is a thousand pities that we cannot get rid of these Central American questions. They give a handle to the Press to stir up ill will against England, and to irritate the President by asserting that he had been over-reached by us. I trust that whoever may take up the negotiation, upon Sir William Ouseley's departure, will remember that after all, the relations between England and the United States are the important element involved in the Central American affair.

You will see by my despatches that I apprehend some trouble here, unless I am able to announce, simultaneously with Sir William Ouseley's recall, that measures are already adopted for proceeding with the negotiations. I am also afraid that the continuance of our Protectorate for a year after the Treaty will not be relished here. It is quite true that the Americans have only to blame the inefficiency of their own measures to check filibusters, but the more they are in the wrong, the more noise and bluster they make. I suppose General Cass meant to imply that the President had done all he could against filibusters, and consequently it was for the British Government to find the means of bringing the Nicaraguans into a more reasonable state of mind. I hope to hear tomorrow that Mr. Warre has arrived at New York by the "Persia". The Staff of this Mission has hitherto been composed of a Secretary of Legation, a paid attaché, and two unpaid attachés. Of all these it may be said that only one unpaid attaché is at his post. For when you were so kind as to transfer Mr. Monson to this Mission, you did so with the intention of giving the comfort and advantage of a Private Secretary; considering the number of private and semi-official communications upon all sorts of Subjects and from all sorts of people which come to me, the very great importance of not giving offence and the extreme readiness of people here to take it, I think that few ministers abroad have so much need of a private secretary's help as I have.[9] As it is, Mr. Monson is necessarily employed all day long about Chancery work and has very few spare moments in which he can assist me in other matters. Mr. Irvine's unfortunate illness has deprived me of a Secretary of Legation—but secretaries of legation in general are of little use when the Minister is at his Post.[10] What is required in order that the business should be properly done, and that I should have time to give to matters which are at least as important as the routine business, is a couple of efficient Chancery attachés.

In July Lord Palmerston succeeded Lord Derby as prime minister, and Lord Malmesbury was replaced by Lord John Russell. Lord Lyons took this opportunity to acquaint the new incumbent with the outstanding issues between England and the United States.[11]

I thank you very much for the permission to communicate with you confidentially, which you have given me by your private letter of the 24th of last month.

You will have seen by my despatches by the last two packets that I am uneasy about the effect likely to be produced here by the suspension of our negotiations in Central America; and that I am anxious to give the Govt of the United States an explanation in some written form. I may add to the reasons thus stated in my despatch, No. 100 of the 5th a consideration rather characteristic of this Country.[12] It is not only desirable really to satisfy this government of our good intentions, but it is important to put it out of their power to assert that we gave them no explanation if it should happen to suit them to make "political capital" (as they call it) by complaints against England.

At present the President and his Cabinet appear to desire both to be and to be thought by the Public to be on the best terms with us. They are however so weak in Congress that I doubt whether they would continue to do anything for us which would be the least unpopular. It is not therefore to be hoped that they will make any effort to open to us the Coasting Trade, to extend the provision of the Reciprocity Treaty with Canada to make a Copyright Convention, or, in short, take any liberal course in commercial matters. Nor indeed is it likely to be in their power to carry any measure tending to put us on equal terms with themselves in these respects. The democratic spirit appears in this country to be all in favour of Protection and Exclusion Privileges. Happily, the interest of the South is against a high Customs Tariff; and this checks the Protectionist Tendencies of the manufacturing North.

One of the peculiarities of Anglo-American relations during the summer of 1859 was the extent to which they were dependent on third-party negotiations in Central America. While the United States was relying on Britain to surrender the protectorate of the Mosquitos to Nicaragua and the Bay Islands to Honduras, there were partisans on the scene still maneuvering to secure particular advantages.[13]

The long confidential despatch which I write today will show you that I have delivered to the President the message contained in your private letter to me of the 1st; and that it produced a good effect.[14] The anxiety of the President and of General Cass that the whole Central American Question should be at an end before the meeting of Congress in December is extreme. I entirely concur in their views with regard to the importance of this to the Relations between the two Countries. No doubt they are still more influenced by considerations affecting their own position before Congress—but I think this is an additional reason for us to desire to settle the questions in time. The Cession of the Bay Islands is the point to which they attach most importance.

I only hope that whoever conducts the Central American Negotiations will steadily keep in view the real object of his mission. We have sacrificed everything in this matter to the sole desire to keep upon good terms with the United States. I take it for granted that we acted wisely in doing so, but I have never thought it worth while to examine that question, for the thing was inevitably done long before I had anything to do with the subject. What seems annoying is that we are likely to lose the fruits of our sacrifice by the difficulty of bringing the Central American Petty Republics to behave reasonably. Perhaps I am influenced too much in my opinion by the point of view from which I regard the question, still I cannot help thinking that the local objections raised by those small governments should be put aside at once—at all events that they should weigh now but as the dust in the balance compared with the consideration of the Relations between England and the United States. We have (in effect if not absolutely in form) positively promised to give up the Mosquito Protectorate and the Bay Islands and to carry out in practice the American Interpretation of the Clayton-Bulwer Treaty. The time is gone by for considering whether this was wise or dignified,—the Negotiator in Central America has now only to fulfill the promises in such a way that we may at least reap the advantages of the sacrifices we have made.

You desire me to give you any candid opinion respecting the mode in which the negotiation has been managed by Sir William Ouseley. I have very little means of forming an accurate opinion. The despatches of his, of which copies have been sent to the Mission from the Foreign Office and from Sir William Ouseley himself, show that the local difficulties and embarrassments have really been very great. That little or nothing has been done, unless the Mosquito Treaty is by this time concluded, is self evident; for so far as the Relations between England and the United States are concerned, the Transit Treaty concluded by Sir William has been an additional difficulty. I have an impression, which I certainly should not mention, if you had not expressly desired me to give you my opinion. It is an impression not deeply fired because it has been made not by a careful examination of facts and arguments but merely by a sort of tone which pervades the correspondence. It amounts to this, that Sir William Ouseley (probably quite unconsciously) has in feeling become a sort of Partisan of the Central Americans against the United States, and has been very naturally and very amicably more inclined to protect these two weak countries from the overbearing proceedings of their great Neighbour—than to press upon them a settlement of the question in such a manner as to content that Neighbour. I should have defended Sir William Ouseley more stoutly against General Cass's insinuation that he not sufficiently considered the bearing of his proceedings upon our Relations with the United States if I had not remembered that unfortunate Anti-Filibustering Article which he and the Nicaraguans introduced into the Transit Treaty for the sole purpose of embarrassing the United States, and forcing them to agree to a similar article in their Treaty.

I feel moreover that I am hardly right in making these observations—for they are founded on little more than conjecture. I mention them indeed rather with a view to the future negotiation than to Sir William Ouseley, who is now I suppose on his way to England.

By 22 August both Cass and Buchanan impressed upon Lord Lyons the necessity to clarify the Central American situation before Congress convened in December, threatening that if Britain dragged her heels over a settlement there would be a "devil of a row."[15]

I have to thank you for your private letter of the 5th which reached me on the 19th. The President and General Cass are very much pleased by the prompt and satisfactory answer which you have enabled me to make to their representations on the Central American Negotiations. They would indeed have been very unreasonable had they not been satisfied. It will be an immense point gained with regard to our Relations with this Country if we can get the negotiation actually finished before the Message to Congress—but the time is very short. I hope the new Negotiator will be sufficiently impressed with the importance of taking advantage of every means of giving me the earliest possible information of his proceedings.

I do not know whether you will attach any importance to the Treaty which is in the course of negotiation between the United States and Mexico. I have said a good deal in my despatch upon the necessity of not using the information contained in it in any manner which might compromise General Cass. The fact is that I am not sure that he did not tell me, on the spur of the moment, more than he intended; and our communication would become very awkward and reserved if he should get into a scrape with the President or his Colleagues in consequence.

On 11 October 1859 Lord Lyons reported that disruptions in Mexico might invite American intervention, since a protracted civil war would undoubtedly encourage filibusters.[16]

With regard to Mexico, it seems probable that the President may apply to Congress for leave to occupy the frontier Provinces; or even that he may take occasion from the affair at Brownsville or similar occurrence to send Troops, upon his own responsibility, to maintain order in those Provinces. I am glad that you do not think it necessary that we should interfere with the proceedings of the United States towards their Southern Neighbour. For I see no means which we possess of interfering with effect, even if our interest lay that way; and there is nothing which has so bad an effect upon our relations with this Country as making remonstrances which we do not enforce and showing what the Papers civilly call "impotent discontent and ill will." I do not think that the term "Central America" in the Clayton-Bulwer Treaty is held to include Mexico—but I believe all the wise heads have considered that the immediate annexation of Mexico would be fraught with imminent danger to the Union. We must only be on the lookout to prevent the Mexicans granting the United States *exclusive* Commercial or Transit advantages. General Cass positively denies that the present Cabinet desire, or would accept, any such advantage.

Two weeks later Lyons mentioned in passing a raid on Harper's Ferry in the state of Virginia led by John Brown, a fanatic abolitionist who had gained notoriety in 1856 by massacring five proslavery colonists at Pottasatomie Creek in Kansas. On the evening of 16 October 1859 he and about twenty others, both whites and blacks, seized the federal arsenal and held local citizens hostage. In the assault on the building by a force of United States Marines, Brown survived but was later hanged after a well-publicized trial.[17]

The American Public are absorbed by a foolish affair at a Place called Harper's Ferry, where eighteen Abolitionists contrived to obtain possession of the United States Armoury and to frighten the Town and the Governments here and in Virginia out of their property. It is to be regretted as it will add to the excitement in the South against Abolitionist doctrines and indeed against all fair treatment of coloured people—whether Slaves or Free.

In his letter of 8 November Lyons continued to lament the delays regarding the situation in Central America, but also introduced another area of dispute between Britain and the United States. It involved the island of San Juan, located off America's northwest coast but considered by the British as part of Vancouver Island and therefore under their jurisdiction in accordance with the Oregon Treaty of 1846. The United States, on the other hand, claimed that because that treaty omitted mention of the island, it belonged by implication to them. Toward the end of the summer of 1859 federal troops from the territory of Washington occupied the island, forcing the issue and compelling Lord Lyons to seek a compromise.[18]

The President and General Cass appear, as the Session of Congress draws near, to become nervous about our Central American Negotiations and perplexed about the terms in which to mention them to Congress. I hope to have some good news for them from Mr. Wyke before the end of the month. If not, it would I think be very desirable that I should be enabled to give effect as fully as possible to the alternative stated in your dispatch of the 4th August (No. 26), and "make it clear that that it has been from no fault of Her Majesty's Government" that the negotiations have not been already brought to a close.[19] I think the President and General Cass themselves are quite convinced that Her Majesty's Government have used their utmost efforts to accomplish this object, but I can see that they would be very glad to have some definite and detailed communications in order to produce an effect upon Congress.

I do not think that this unlucky San Juan has diminished the desire of the President to announce the settlement of the Central American Questions—though it will interfere very materially with his intended statement of there being for the first time no serious question between the two Countries. I confess I can hardly hope that there will ever come a time when this statement can be made; for with such subordinates as the United States Government employs and so great an amount of laxity of official discipline, any petty American officer on our immense frontier may get up a serious dispute. You will see by my despatches of to-day, that a Deputy Collector of Customs has set up a claim to a part of Canada and threatened to assert it by violent measures.[20] He had indeed been immediately disavowed by the Govt. here—but the affair is remarkable as an illustration of the extraordinary way in which the small official people conduct themselves.

Some of the newspapers wrote violently about San Juan. That the President will venture to acknowledge our right to it I have no hope. If the Senate were convinced that we should really go to war rather than give it up they might take upon themselves to advise the President to accept our terms, as they did in the case of the Oregon Treaty in 1846. But the idea that happen what may England will never really declare war with this Country has become so deeply rooted that I am afraid nothing short of actual hostilities would eradicate it.

A few weeks later Lyons took up the financial plight of Edward Mortimer Archibald, the British consul in New York who had come from Newfoundland two years before to reestablished a permanent consulship following the expulsion of Crampton and others in May 1856.[21]

The inadequacy of the Salary and Emoluments of the New York Consulate to enable the Consul to procure sufficient assistance in order to discharge the duties properly causes so much injury to the Public Service that I have not hesitated to write to you a strong official recommendation of Mr. Archibald's request for an increased allowance. The scruples I feel in adding to Mr. Archibald's labours deprive me of much useful and important information and are a serious inconvenience in carrying on the business of the Mission.

I have never seen Mr. Archibald and have no interest concerning him except that which arises from our official connexion. But I believe him to be a most able and labourious Public servant, and I have been informed by many people not particularly connected with him that he is ruining his health by overwork.

On the same day, Lyons wrote another private letter describing the American government's increasing frustration with the Juarez regime in Mexico, especially in view of several alleged provocations along the Mexican-Texas border.[22]

The President and his Cabinet seem to be at their wit's end about Mexico. Their immediate perplexity of course is to know what to say about it in the President's Message. They are so weak in Congress that they are afraid they shall not be supported if they propose vigourous measures, while they are sure to be attacked if they do not. Strange to say, they do not appear to have received any official account on the accuracy of which they can rely of the attack from the Mexican Frontier upon Brownsville. The day before yesterday they ordered Eight Companies of Regular Troops (between five and six hundred men) to be in readiness to embark at Old Point Comfort near the mouth of the Chesapeake, for Texas. To-day news appears to have been received that Brownsville is safe—the inhabitants finding themselves strong enough to hang without trial one of the Marauders whom they had made Prisoner. It is announced that in consequence of this intelligence the departure of the troops from Old Point Comfort has been countermanded. The President will be glad to avoid taking any decisive measure till Congress assembles at the beginning of next month. I had a conversation with General Cass yesterday about Mexican affairs in general; but it was clear that he did not know what to tell me about the President's intentions.

The extraordinary excitement and alarm which exist in Virginia since the Harper's Ferry affair are not very confirmatory of the confidence which the Planters profess to feel in the "happy and attached Peasantry" by which euphonious appellation they love to designate their Slaves. There have been alarms and movements of Militia and volunteers almost daily; but all that has really occurred to justify apprehension is the burning of the Ricks of some of the Jurors who found Brown guilty.

On 28 November Lord Lyons returned to the topic of Mexico.[23]

I spoke to General Cass the day before yesterday about Mexico in the sense of your Private Letter of the 11th (that of which the copy is enclosed). I did not speak very definitely about your recognizing Juarez, but said rather that you would be disposed to do so if he succeeded in establishing himself. I used this as an argument that the United States should strengthen Juarez' hands by being moderate with him and not weaken the party they wish to support by asking for concessions humiliating to the Pride which the Mexicans inherit from their Spanish Ancestors. General Cass seemed delighted with the idea of your recognizing Juarez. He said there was nothing in the Treaty which Mr. McLane proposed that could be offensive to Mexican Pride except the clause respecting the Protection of the Transit Routes, but that this clause was absolutely necessary.[24] It provided only (as the Nicaraguan Treaties do) that the United States should have a right to use their own Forces to keep the routes open upon an emergency. The Transit Routes were all the United States were to get in return for their Four Millions of Dollars—and the Routes would be useless unless there were the means of protecting them. The Purchase of Lower California (General Cass added) had not been insisted upon; and as for the rest of Mexico, the present Administration would certainly not accept it if it were offered.

John Brown's raid on Harper's Ferry continued to exercise the imagination and stimulate the emotions of Northerners and Southerners alike. In his letter of 6 December, Lyons discussed the mounting concern that the government would not deter the slave trade or be willing to protect free blacks.[25]

You will see by despatches of this date that there is very little prospect of any satisfactory result from our remonstrances concerning the Slave Trade.[26] Lamentable as it is, I am afraid that the President goes beyond Public Opinion already in the measures he takes against it. In the South the rendering it legal has many avowed advocates: and it is to be feared that some of the professed abolitionists of the North derive too much profit from dabbling themselves in the trade to desire any efficient measures for its suppression. The greater part of the Vessels engaged in it seems to be fitted out at New York. The state of feeling at this moment in the South upon the whole question of Slavery is shocking. The Harper's Ferry Affair seems to have excited Southern Passions to an indescribable degree. The dissolution of the Confederation is but one of the measures which are loudly advocated. There are plans for the reenslavement of all the emancipated Negroes, for the purging the South of all Whites suspected of abolition tendencies, and what not. The difficulty which we shall have in obtaining decent treatment for Coloured British Subjects will be almost insufferable. I grieve to see that Bills have already been proposed to the Legislature of South Carolina for the reenactment of the law which consigned all free coloured Seamen to gaol during the time their Ship is in a South Carolina Port. Even if we should find a case, either in South Carolina or in Louisiana, which will do to bring before the Supreme Court of the United States, and should obtain in any reasonable time (which is most important) a decision that this Coloured Seaman law is unconstitutional, we shall have gained little but a good *casus belli* against the United States. South Carolina and Louisiana will certainly set the Supreme Court at defiance; the Federal Government will as certainly have neither the will nor the power to compel those states to submit to the Court—and we shall be left to enforce respect to our rights and our Treaties by our own Arms. I trust Mr. Bunch, the Consul in South Carolina, may succeed in preventing the infamous coloured Seaman law from passing. He has had great experience of such matters, and has shown on previous occasions great tact and judgment in the management of them.

Another source of trouble between us and the Southern States may arise from the measures which they are taking to drive out all persons suspected of unorthodox notions on Slavery; and the orthodox notion seems to be that Slavery is a divine institution. In many parts of the South Vigilance Committees are formed who turn people out at a moment's notice without any pretext even of law. If any attempt is made to treat British Subjects in this manner, I trust you will approve of my encouraging the Consuls to insist upon the law being observed in their case and to resist any endeavour to inflict banishment or any other penalty upon an Englishman except in due form of law. But it will require a great deal of prudence and discretion to act in each case; for a fair trial is a thing impossible in this Country of elective judges and partisan juries when public feeling is excited and any redress we may expect for the wrong to England will be too late for the individual in the hands of the Lynch Law Assassins.

The great hope is that the excitement may be too violent to last, but before it subsides it may do incalculable harm to these States and raise very painful and awkward questions for us.

Ordinarily the president postponed delivery of his annual message to Congress until the House of Representatives elected its Speaker, but because such extreme animosity existed between Northerners and Southerners on the subject of slavery, no Speaker could obtain a majority and the House was deadlocked. Nevertheless, Buchanan was tempted to give his address.[27]

I suppose it [the message] will not be delayed much longer—The President is understood to be impatient to issue it and to be determined to send it to the Senate without waiting for the House of Representatives if the Speaker be not elected this week.

It seems to be universally considered that matters are nearer a crisis with regard to the disruption of the Union than they have ever been before. After making the allowance for the tendency to consider the "present" crisis as always the most serious that has ever occurred, I am inclined to think that North and South have never before been so near a breach. I suppose North and South would lose equally in the end, but the South is willing to run the risk and the North is not; and thus very probably the North will as usual avoid proceeding to extremities and not venture to elect an Anti-Slavery President next year. The Southern members even talk of making the Election of Speaker a Repeal of the Union question and of seceding in a Body from Congress if the "Black Republican" Candidate is elected, as he probably will be. The great importance of the Office in this Country consists in the fact that the Speaker nominates the Committees of the House and is expected to pack them for the purpose of the Party which elects him.

The matter likely to give us immediate trouble is the violence with which, in many parts of the South, abolitionists and free coloured people are being persecuted and expelled. Mr. Mure, the Consul at New Orleans, arrived here yesterday on his way to his post. I am glad to find that he does not anticipate quite such outrageous proceedings in New Orleans as those which Mr. Bunch states to be going on in South Carolina. But Mr. Mure looks forward to great difficulties with respect to the Coloured Seaman Law; and to consider the abrogation of the law as hopeless now. Unhappily the Supreme Court of the United States is *Pro-Slavery* as its notorious decision on the Dred Scott case shows; and even if we could get a good case of an imprisonment of a British Subject of Colour before it, it would be very much inclined, if it could not decently decide against us, either to get rid of the question upon some technical ground or to postpone indefinitely giving its decision.

The election of a Speaker continued to elude the House, and by 20 December Buchanan still had not presented his annual message. Not least among those wishing to know its contents was Lord Lyons, who had to repeat his request of Lord Russell to have patience.[28]

I wish the Message were out—until it is actually delivered changes will constantly be made, and I have no hope of its being changed for the better as far as England is concerned. The way in which England is mentioned is important, because it will have great influence on Public Opinion and in some measure bind the President to the sentiments he expresses in it.

I do not think this Government are particularly pleased by the prospect of soon receiving their Treaty with Juarez, signed and ratified at Vera Cruz. They have great doubts whether they shall get the United States Senate to ratify it; and they are not without fears that Juarez and his Government will have ceased to exist before the Treaty can be submitted to the Senate here. I believe the President still means to ask for Authority to use force in Mexico if necessary, but he is so very weak in Congress that he has great doubts whether he shall obtain it. I fancy that it is the extreme uncertainty as to what he will be enabled to do by Congress which prevents his responding to our overtures for acting in concert with the United States in that Country.

By late 1859, Miguel Miramón (1832–67) commanded the Mexican forces controlling Mexico City, opposing Juarez's troops in Vera Cruz. Lord Lyons's private letter of 26 December accurately forecast not only that Europeans would intervene in Mexico but also that a European monarch would be asked to quell republican factionalism in the interest of national unity. Lyons further anticipated the virulent American reaction to such a flagrant violation of the Monroe Doctrine.[29]

Time will not admit of my answering officially by this Mail your instruction to give my opinion upon the suggestions for adjustment of Mexican affairs. . . . In fact, so far as the question depends upon the course likely to be pursued by this Country, I could say very little until the President's Message has been sent down and some indication of the feeling of Congress been given. Unless the moral effect in favour of Juarez be much greater in the case of the Treaty than it was in that of the Recognition of his Govt. by the United States, he will not have gained much by it. Some considerable time must elapse before he can receive the United States dollars or even be able to show such a prospect of obtaining them as may induce speculators to advance him money at a discount upon them. In fact he will very probably not receive them at all. The Treaty itself will, I suppose, arrive to-day. I do not think that the Government, as at present informed, expect that the Senate will ratify it; and after that comes the question whether the House of Representatives will vote the four millions of dollars. General Cass observed the day before yesterday in speaking to me about the Treaty, that the supplementary Convention authorising the intervention of the United States in Mexico whenever and wherever it may be necessary, appeared to be precisely what the President had positively refused to agree to some time ago. He had however no knowledge of the existence even of the supplementary Convention, except that derived from a Newspaper Telegram. It seems to be thought here that Juarez only accepted the Treaty when he found himself at the last gasp—and that his main inducement to do so was a promise from Mr. McLane to defend Vera Cruz against Miramón with the guns of the American Ships. People observe that it was very easy to promise this, but that it remains to be seen whether Congress will give the sanction necessary to carry the promise into effect. So far therefore as the principal question which I am desired to answer is concerned, I may say that I cannot consider Juarez' prospect of maintaining himself to be so good as to render it advisable that Her Majesty's Government should select the present moment for recognizing him.

It appears to be the deliberate opinion of almost all Foreigners in Mexico that a Foreign Intervention is the only chance left of restoring order in that Country. But it seems to me, who have no local knowledge on the subject, extremely difficult to understand in what form this intervention is to be exercised. If the Mexicans have sufficient regard for the moral right of the United States or of one or more of the Great Powers of Europe to lay down their arms, adopt a form of Government recommended by their Foreign friends, and submit quietly to it when adopted, then certainly the Foreign Powers have only to agree among themselves *what to recommend*, and the question is settled. There would probably be some difficulty in getting Countries with such very different notions of Government as England, France, and the United States, to agree upon *what to recommend*, but this obstacle might perhaps be got over.

I suppose however that it is contemplated by people of all opinions that some Foreign Military Force must be employed at all events just to set the new Government going.

I imagine that the United States would be extremely unwilling either to send a Force of their own—or to see the Troops of any other Nation occupy Mexico. I conclude there is no probability of England's having any Troops to spare for such a purpose. France would have the Troops, if the Emperor thought fit to use them;—but I do not know how far either England or the United States would acquiesce in an exclusively French occupation of Mexico.

Then comes the question of the relation in which the occupying Force, whether belonging to one or more Powers, is to stand with regard to the Govt. it is sent to support. It can hardly be supposed that it can play only the part which the French Garrison played at Rome during the five years I resided there.[30] During that time the French Garrison was little more than a visible Sign that the Emperor would not allow an insurrection against the Pope. Neither the Troops nor indeed their Imperial Master interfered with, or exercised any considerable influence over the Government. This seems a state of things possible only at Rome with the Head of the Roman Catholic Church at the head of the temporal government also. In a Country like Mexico, whoever commanded the occupying Force must no doubt command the Government also; and it would be very difficult to determine when the Government would be able to go alone. My experience of Greek affairs does not make me desire for the Mexicans a triple protection. The result of this in Greece seemed to be interminable questions between the three powers themselves, and interminable intrigues on the part of the Government, which was always seeking the support of one or other of the Foreign Powers, and very often sacrificed the welfare of the Country to the real or supposed views of the Power it wished to conciliate at the moment. A Foreign King would probably be the best Governor to combine with a foreign occupation. The prestige of Royalty, the security which it affords for the cotinuance of power in the same hands, the visible sign which it is of National Unity and Independence—the respect which it inspires abroad—the consideration with which a regard for their own Title and Dignity leads all Sovereigns to treat it—these and the other advantages inherent in the institution might render it an instrument for establishing a Government in Mexico which might outlast the necessity of being maintained by Foreign Troops. Even in such incompetent hands as that of King Otto, the Institution has achieved for Greece not indeed prosperity or good government but a considerable amount of stability, union, and independence. To establish Monarchy however in Mexico, the opinion of the United States must be set aside and their hopes of overthrowing it checked with a firm hand.

The actual annexation of Mexico to this confederation raises immediately one of those questions between the Northern and Southern States which have already gone a great way to dissolve the Union altogether. The Southern States desire the addition of Territory South, with a view to extending Slavery, and adding to the Pro-Slavery Votes in the United States Senate. To this the North is conscientiously opposed on religious grounds—to say nothing of the indignation it feels at the notion of its own vast superiority in wealth and population being swamped in the Senate. Even now, since every State sends equally two Senators whatever may be its population, the North has not the influence it ought to have in the Senate, which is the more important branch of the Legislature. As the religious sentiment on Slavery in the North approaches very nearly to fanaticism, and as the Southern feeling on the point has become furious passion, there is little chance of their coming to an agreement upon a matter which calls these feelings into play. In this particular question the South have on their side the National vanity, which seems always childishly gratified by any addition to the already enormous extent of the Territory. In the meantime the course of events seems to be bringing about the gradual annexation of Mexico. The

Mexicans in the Northern part of their Country have fallen to that point that they can neither maintain order on the Frontier nor even hold their own against the Savage Indians within it. They will (to use an American expression) be "squatted out" of the country by their Anglo-Saxon neighbours whenever and wherever any considerable number of the more energetic of all choose to settle. But this is a very different thing from the sudden incorporation of a vast territory and of a large population totally different in Race, Language, Religion and Feelings, and (so far as the enforcement has been tried) utterly incapable of maintaining order among themselves under the United States system of Government. All the wiser and more conservative Politicians in this Country deprecate as an unmitigated evil the sudden annexation of Mexico; nor are such men willing to undertake a Protectorate of Mexico. This they say would be an enormous innovation upon their whole political system which has never admitted of any other connexion than that of perfectly equal Sovereign States bound by a Federal tie on terms the same for all.

Judging from this distance, I should say there was not much to choose between the two Parties in Mexico. An Englishman's sympathies are certainly more with the Name of "Constitutional" than that of "Clerical"—and Juarez has behaved much better to us than Miramón, but then Juarez is at Vera Cruz within reach of the guns of our Ships. If the mere fact of our recognition would terminate the struggle in favour of either Party and then give a chance of a stable Government, I should myself be quite willing that either Party should have it—but knowing so little as I do of Mexico, I do not understand why our recognition should do more for Juarez than that of the United States did.

I have written at this great length from want of time to arrange and abridge my ideas. I have not enough knowledge of Mexico nor sufficiently recent intelligence of the events on the spot to make my opinion valuable. But as you desired me to give it, I thought it right to say what occurred to me without losing a post. My impression certainly is that this would not be a good moment to recognize Juarez because his prospects at home seem far from good and his chance of receiving any material support from this Government is so uncertain that it is impossible to calculate upon it. I shall perhaps be able to speak more definitely upon this latter point when the much expected Message at last comes forth.

When Robert McLane concluded the treaty with Juarez late in 1859, its provisions seemed relatively innocuous. The United States agreed to pay Mexico four million dollars for the opportunity to submit bids on the construction of alternative transit routes across Mexico from the Atlantic to the Pacific oceans. Mexico reserved the right to oversee the drafting of such contracts as well as the right to police the routes and maintain law and order. There was one clause in the treaty that rather alarmed the British, however. If Mexico proved incapable of providing protection to travelers and companies using these routes, then the United States government reserved the right to send its troops to the affected area until the Mexicans could reestablish stability. This provision equally troubled the Buchanan administration, and realistically, the treaty as a whole had little chance of passage in the Senate.[31]

The President has made his policy respecting Mexico known at last by his Message.[32] In accordance with the Monroe Doctrine, he repudiates the intervention in that Country of any European Power—while in disregard of a much older maxim of American Statesmen, he advocates intervention on the part of the United States. The supplementary Convention made by Mr. McLane with Juarez is no doubt intended to give some regularity in point of form to the armed interference of this Government. Divested of the involved roundabout arguments by which it is introduced and recommended, the President's plan is to send a Force from this Country to carry Juarez to the City of Mexico and establish his Government over the whole Mexican Republic. The President has dated his Message the day before he received the telegraphic news of the conclusion of Mr. McLane's Treaty, but the Treaty itself was in his hands when he actually sent the Message forth.

In order to be able to carry out his views the President must get the Senate to ratify the Treaty, the House of Representatives to vote the four millions of dollars, and both Houses to sanction his warlike intentions. The late Congress refused him all he asked of this nature, and it is by no means certain that he will find the present Congress more tractable.

If Congress refuse to sanction the President's proposals, Juarez will be in a much worse situation than if they had never been made: for this would make it public and certain that the United States would *not* use force to support him. Judging from present appearances, it may be a considerable time before Congress comes to any decision upon the question, and it seems to be doubtful whether Juarez will be able to hold his own without prompt assistance. I do not know enough of Mexico to say whether he will gain or lose in popularity by the Treaty. He himself seems to have had very strong objections to it, and to have accepted it only as a last resort, after the defeat of Queretaro.

Judging from this distance, I certainly do not think that the position of Juarez is sufficiently secure to render it desirable for us to recognize him at this moment. Such information as I have does not lead me to suppose that now our recognition would have much moral effect; and our prestige would not be increased by recognizing a Government which did not succeed in establishing itself. Our recognizing Juarez would certainly give pleasure to the Cabinet of Washington, but I am not sure that this would not in part be caused by the desire of having us in the same scrape with themselves. If however Congress allow the President to establish Juarez at Mexico by force, then no doubt it would be convenient for us to have recognized him in due time; but I hardly think the due time is come yet.

When the President speaks of the "intervention of European Powers" I suppose he alludes to the assertions that France and Spain will interfere in favour of Miramón. The moderation of his language on this point is no doubt to be attributed to his consciousness that the United States have no Naval or Military means of resisting such an interference.

I postpone writing officially about Mexico until next week, in the hope that I may be able to learn something in the interval of the probable conduct of Congress. A great number of Senators and Representatives are now absent, having gone to their homes for Christmas.

The President took an opportunity to see me alone on the 31st and said in allusion to the Message that he had hoped at the end of his administration to leave a clear score with England. I told him that the Cession of the Bay Islands to Honduras had already removed the principal difficulty in Central America. The President expressed his satisfaction with the terms of Mr. Wyke's arrangement as I had stated them to General Cass;[33] and he went on to say that he concluded that Her Majesty's Govt. were satisfied with the course he had pursued with respect to General Harney's occupation of San Juan.[34] I answered that Her Majesty's Govt. would not fail to be satisfied with General Scott's proposal for a joint occupation on equal terms; for they had themselves suggested such an arrangement before they knew that General Scott had been instructed to affect it. The President proceeded to express his great anxiety that the question of the Sovereignty of the Island should not lead to a serious dispute between the two countries. It seemed, he said, a little matter, but little matters had before now led to great wars. . . . His sending General Scott was, in American eyes, very much the same thing as sending the late Duke of Wellington upon a similar mission would have been regarded in England. The necessity of having recourse to such a measure shows how difficult it was to reconcile public opinion to backing out of Harney's aggression, and to enforce obedience on the spot to orders to that effect. The President has reaped the reward of having behaved fairly, for his conduct seems to have been more generally approved in this matter than in any other which had come under my notice. I am afraid however that he will deem it necessary to be extremely tenacious about the title to the Island.

I see with great regret that an opinion seems to be gaining ground that a foreign war would be the most probable mode of promoting Union between North and South. I find men who ought to be wise and prudent, not averse to trying this desperate remedy for the distracted state of the Country. I am afraid there is little doubt that England would be the Country selected for the experiment if it were to be made. But it will not be made if England have her hands free from European difficulties and if the Americans believe that she would put forth her whole strength at the outset and give them a sharp lesson, before they have time to get up an Army or Navy. What is however to be apprehended is that the feeling in favour of war may add to the numbers of those who would join in the provocations to England which are favourite weapons in the struggles for the Presidency. The next presidential election already occupies all minds and influences all political moves.

On 23 January 1860 Lord Lyons reported the latest rumors about Mexican internal dissension and the possibility of war.[35]

I thank you most heartily for the kind wishes for the New Year, which have been brought to me by your private letter of the 30th. I do indeed trust we shall have no more American difficulties, but the Confederation seems to be in so extraordinary a condition, that very desperate measures may be resorted to in the hope of getting out of the "fiasco".

I suppose it is partly with this view that the President is carrying on a war with Mexico, for it seems to become more and more evident that the Ratification of the McLane Treaty would lead to that. General Cass, however, told me confidentially this morning that the Senate had done nothing yet about the Treaty, and that he did not regret it, for he was sure that at this moment they would not ratify it.

Baron Gerolt, the Prussian Minister here, has just read to me confidentially extracts from despatches addressed by M. de Wagner, the Prussian Minister who has just reached the Mexican Republic, to the Government at Berlin. The most striking fact mentioned by M. de Wagner is that McLane talks openly at Vera Cruz of annexing the Northern Mexican States to this Confederation, and in that case of depriving the Indian and mixed races of political rights. This is rather strong considering that Juarez himself is of pure Indian blood. I do not feel very competent to judge Mexican matters, but I confess I should be sorry to see England committed by a recognition of Juarez. The object of the Southern Members who support the Treaty is of course to introduce Slavery. It is to be hoped that would be rendered impossible by the nature of the Country, which is said to be unsuited to Negro labour. But however desirable the triumph of the Constitutional Party may be, I should be glad to be a little more certain, first of its taking place, and secondly of the nature of the means by which it will be accomplished, before England is in any way pledged.

General Cass and (I think) the President are becoming very touchy about our remonstrances against the laxity of the American officers in suppressing the Slave Trade. There is no doubt that the President is sincerely opposed to the Trade, but unhappily he is very little supported by Public Opinion, especially in his own Party; and he is no doubt made unstable by thinking that he gets no credit from anybody on this subject.

America's appropriate role regarding Mexico was delicate, since her sympathies rested with the Juarez faction, but it was uncertain whether Juarez could successfully withstand the assaults of the Miramón forces.[36]

I have been with General Cass this morning, and have been kept so long and heard so much from him on so many subjects that I have barely time to give you partially an outline of what he said upon the most important of them. . . .

The General said that Mr. McLane himself had arrived at New Orleans and been summoned to Washington by telegraph, and that he would probably be here to-day or tomorrow. He represented (the General said) that the great majority of the Mexican People were in favour of Juarez, but stated that the Juarez party were at the end of their resources and were only too likely to succumb to the Miramón if they were not promptly succoured.

Mr. McLane had landed a hundred United States Marines (General Cass told me) at Tampico in order to protect American Citizens if Miramón should attack that place; they were ordered to resist Miramón's Troops unless he have satisfactory assurances that the life and property of the United States Citizens would be respected. Mr. McLane had asked for instructions as to whether at Tampico and elsewhere the U.S. Ships should interfere by force to protect American Citizens—or whether they should join the Liberal Forces in restricting Miramón under any circumstances.

I observed to General Cass that the measures of Mr. McLane might save the Senate the trouble of considering whether it should sanction hostilities with Mexico, for if they caused a collision with Miramón's Troops the United States could not avoid supporting their own men.

The General said that the duty of the United States officers to defend the lives of their Countrymen in Foreign Countries could hardly be questioned. With such a Constitution as that of the United States, the Executive would not give the officers instances beforehand. It had no power to give orders for resorting to hostilities without the sanction of Congress. It was obliged therefore to leave the responsibilities very much with the Commander on the spot, and could do no more than support them afterwards if their conduct appeared to deserve it. The most convenient thing would be for Miramón to solve the question by declaring (as it was said he threatened to do) war against the United States. General Cass said that his hopes of getting Mr. McLane's Treaty through the Senate were hardly stronger than they had been when he saw me last; and if the Senate did ratify the Treaty, the embarrassment of the Government would not be at an end. No doubt the United States Troops could easily march to Mexico—but what was to be done when they got there? The Executive was strongly opposed to any annexation or permanent protectorate; and the Senate would never consent to anything of the kind—It was only to be hoped that the information given the Gov. by Mr. McLane and others was correct, and that the Constitutional Party, if once established in the Capital, would maintain itself by its own means and govern firmly and wisely.

By March the Mexican situation insinuated itself into the political arena, with both parties supporting tactics calculated to benefit their own electoral position.[37]

If one were to judge by present appearances, one might feel certain that the Mexican Treaty would not pass the Senate. But as the question has become one of Party Tactics with a view to popularity at the Presidential Election, there is no knowing what a day or an hour may bring about. The Republicans wish to withhold from the Administration Party the means of obtaining popularity by a military expedition; above all they dread the influence the two millions to be kept back for American Claimants may be made to have upon the Elections. On the other hand the Administration seem to be doing their best or get up some fighting in Mexico, which may enable them to pander to the popular love of blood and conquest. I only hope that they may be content with this and not consider a hostile demonstration against England essential to their Electioneering. One Party or the other is pretty sure to bid for the Irish vote by some violent anti-English proceeding—but the Administration might be led to acts which it would be difficult to get over—while the opposition could not go much beyond words.

Mr. Mure has sent me a copy of his despatch (Slave Trade No. 5 of Feb. 16) reporting his proceedings with regard to the Law in Louisiana for the imprisonment of Free Coloured Seamen.[38] I think he has managed extremely well. He appears to have succeeded in preventing the law being practically enforced against British Subjects for the present. In this way we may give time for the present fierce excitement to subside, and then either get the Law repealed or test its Constitutionality by an Appeal to the Supreme Court. In the present state of Public Feeling, and with the present Constitution of that Court, we should have no chance of getting a favourable decision from them.

I am afraid that the President will not dare to let Mr. Dallas take any part in the proposed Conference in London on the Slave Trade. Both he and General Cass are unmoveable on the subject. The fact is, that the country is becoming more and more divided into an absolute Anti-Slavery and an absolute Pro-Slavery Party. The President's is the Pro-Slavery party—and that Party does not like to have even the Slave Trade with Africa denounced. On the contrary the success of their struggle in supremacy in the Senate depends upon their getting new states admitted into the Union as Slave States, and they are beginning to think that they must import Slaves in order to have enough to send into these new States.

In early April the San Juan affair was still unresolved, partly due to the appointment by the American government of men whom Lyons considered "unfit" for their posts. The first section of his next letter begins with a series of almost whimsical proposals concerning suitable arbiters of a settlement.[39]

I am very glad that General Cass' mind is at last relieved about the declaration concerning San Juan, and that he will at all events continue the discussion on the same terms as if the declaration had not been made. I do not know whether he will go so far as to propose arbitration in his next communication. The plan of appointing an arbiter on each side, to draw lots for the choice of Umpire, is a very roundabout way of leaving the matter to chance. It would be more simple, and quite as just, that General Cass and I should toss up for San Juan at once. I suppose however it would be possible to find some Sovereign to whose decision both Parties would agree to refer the matter, and whom the Americans could not, if he decided against them, accuse of "gross and revolting partiality". It might perhaps be desirable that I should know beforehand whether there are any particular Sovereigns whom Her Majesty's Government think unsuited for the office, and particularly the idea of selecting the Emperor Napoleon, if the Americans should put it forward. I mention this at once, although I think the chances are against General Cass' making a proposal in his next communication to have recourse to arbitration rather than argument.

The Capture of Miramón's Steamers is curious as an illustration of the manner in which the Americans carry out, where they are strongest, their principles of freedom of the seas and territorial rights.[40] I have not felt called upon to express an opinion of the proceeding here. It does not seem to concern Great Britain, except as a general question of Maritime Law. I conclude the Government has completely guarded itself against being proved to have given any instructions beforehand. It has of course approved the conduct of the officers. In this case the affair has been useful in defence of the policy of the Administration towards Mexico; but had it been otherwise, acts of violence whether justifiable or not are too popular to be disavowed. . . .

The President has sent a Message to the House of Representatives complaining of their having appointed a Committee to inquire into certain very vague undefined charges against him and the administration of using corruption to influence Elections. I imagine Mr. Buchanan is at least as pure in such matters as any of his predecessors since Washington.

A Protectionist Tariff has been proposed to the House of Representatives. As it is brought in by a Private Member and not by the Committee of Ways and Means, I hope there is great doubt about its passing the House—at all events there cannot be much reason to fear that it will be agreed to by the Senate. For obstructive purposes this Constitution works admirably at the present moment. The Party is a decided Majority in the House of Representatives—its opponents a decided Majority in the Senate—the Government is in a decided minority in the House, and has not a working majority in the Senate.

In response to continuing pressure by the British, the Buchanan administration tried to enforce legislation against the slave trade, but its efforts were frustrated either by the navy, which found excuses not to comply, or by politicians who feared repercussions if offenders were arrested openly.[41]

General Cass told me that he had himself recommended the Navy department to send one or more of their Cruisers to the East Coast of Africa, but that the Naval Officers had made so much objection that he saw that the thing would not be done. This being the case, he thought it better not to mention the objections in detail in his note to me (Enclosure in my Slave Trade No 8), lest doing so should lead to a controversy on the validity of them, which could produce no result.[42] He did not, however, mind telling me privately what they were. In the first place the Naval Officers doubted whether there were any American Slavers on the East Coast; secondly they thought that it would be impossible to intercept vessels from Mozambique because such vessels would bear too much to the South (I don't think General Cass understood this professional point, and I am sure I did not). Thirdly, they think the present Squadron is fully employed on the West Coast and is so well posted there that it would be a pity to disturb it. Fourthly, the Government is unwilling to agitate the question of the Slave Trade in this Country by applying to Congress for the means of adding to the Squadron.

General Cass said he told me all this very confidentially in order that I might see that the representation of Her Majesty's Government had been taken into respectful consideration. He begged me not to enter into any discussion about the reasons which he gave; for it was expressly to avoid discussion that he had not stated them in his Note. The Administration were doing their best, and any attempt to go farther might diminish their means of acting against the Slave Trade instead of increasing them.

By mid-April 1860 Buchanan himself was beginning to think about the way that history would assess his presidency. In a conversation with Lord Lyons, he indicated his overarching vision for Anglo-American relations.[43]

I met the President out walking last Thursday (the 5th). He stopped me and said a few words about San Juan. He began by repeating an observation he often makes to me, that it has been his great ambition to be able to say at the end of his Administration that he had left no question with Great Britain unsettled; that for the first time since the Revolution *"the docket was clear."* He went on the say that the only obstacle which now remained was San Juan—that he hoped and trusted that a matter of such small real importance would not be allowed to cause a war between two great nations; but that the People of the West Coast were becoming very excited, and he really did not know what to do. He concluded by begging me to set my wits to work to devise some plan of coming to an amicable settlement.

Questions of foreign policy receded into the background toward the end of April, when the badly split Democratic party assembled in Charleston, South Carolina, for their presidential convention.[44]

The only two subjects which the Americans appear able to talk about at this moment are the Fight of the Benicia Boy with Sayers,[45] and the Charleston Convention for nominating the "Democratic" Party's Candidate for the Presidency. The total uncertainty as to who will be nominated is very extraordinary. The most significant circumstance which has yet occurred at Charleston is the marked line of division between the Northern and Southern Branches of this Democratic Party on the question of forming the *Platform*, or declaration of the Principles to be held by the Candidate; *all* the Southern States voted one way—and the Northern *all* the other. The South threatens to secede from the Convention if the Platform it advocates be not adopted. This would break up the Democratic Party which forms the only remaining bond between North and South.

The Democratic convention did indeed widen the division between North and South, with the proslavery delegates seceding and reassembling in Richmond, Virginia, and the antislavery delegates adjourning to Baltimore, Maryland. This turn of events promoted speculation that a Republican candidate might win the election as a result of this split. Lyons also recognized the possibility that Britain's supply of raw cotton could be in jeopardy.[46]

You will receive by this Post a despatch from Mr. Bunch, the Consul at Charleston, giving an account of the "Democratic" Convention held at that place to fix upon the Candidate to be supported by the Party at the Presidential Election.[47] The ultra-Slavery States seceded and adjourned to Richmond in Virginia. The other States adjourned to Baltimore. The Ultra Slavery States require not only that Congress shall not interfere to prevent the importation of Slaves into any of the "Territories" (the parts of the Country not yet formed into States) but that it shall interfere to force the inhabitants of a Territory to admit Slaves if they shall endeavour to exclude them. The dispute turns upon what is at present a mere abstraction; for there is not at this moment any Territory to which the principle can be practically applied. But it is one of the indications of the great struggle for political power which is going on between the North and South; and the division of the Democratic Party which has taken place at Charleston has gone very far to divide the Nation into two by a distinct geographical line. The complications in the modes in which the President may be elected render it very difficult to conjecture the results of the split. I see that Mr. Bunch thinks that the success of the Republican Candidate will be the consequence.

Whether this would be a good or bad thing for us, it is not easy to determine. I do not think the Republican President would really effect or attempt to effect much on the Slavery question. In order to get on at all with the Senate (and without the consent of the Senate he cannot make a single appointment to any office) he must allay the fears of the South upon this head. He would probably find it necessary to be very punctilious with England, because his Party is reproached with being led by its anti-slavery sympathies to be too friendly to us—a reproach which its conduct has certainly done nothing whatever to justify. "*Protection to Native Industry*" is part of the Republican Programme and so far as their advent to power would enable them to carry out their illiberal commercial views, it would be injurious to us in the extreme. As I have already said I do not think that the Republicans will for the present effect anything against Slavery, whether in or out of office. But as Slavery cannot be abolished without at all events a temporary suspension of cultivation in the South, it is all important to us to have the means of getting cotton from some other quarter, before abolition makes any great progress.

Whichever Party is in Power in this Country, we must, I am afraid, be always prepared for a Declaration of War from the United States if we are involved in serious difficulties in Europe—with the lowest class, which is the governing class, a war with England would always be popular; and this class have been flattered into the belief that the United States are a great naval and Military Power. Even with many Conservatives a Foreign War finds favour as a remedy for intestine divisions. I do not think any [American] government would intentionally bring on a war with us at a moment when we could bring all our forces to bear upon America. The danger is that almost everyone in this Country believes that we should endure anything rather than go to war with the United States; and with this feeling the temptation to curry favour with the populace by a display of arrogance towards us is too great to be resisted. At the last Presidential Election Mr. Crampton was offered up as a propitiatory sacrifice to the Irish Vote. I hope and trust a quarrel with England may not be looked upon as a good Party move upon this occasion.

The Japanese Embassy is expected here daily. As the American Government has ordered a Steamer to go round Cape Horn to Panama to be ready to take the Ambassadors back, I suppose they do not at present intend to go to Europe. I am a little puzzled to know how to treat them. Their Government appears to be behaving extremely ill to us, so that any great demonstrations of friendliness on my part would probably be misplaced. I am disposed to think that I had better do what the rest of my Colleagues do, and not make myself conspicuous one way or the other.

Toward the end of May, it was the turn of the Republican party to capture the limelight, but Lord Lyons registered little enthusiasm for their unknown candidate, Abraham Lincoln.[48]

The Mexican Question seems as far from a solution as ever. General Cass does not appear to me to wish Mr. McLane's Treaty to be ratified. The opposition are willing to ratify it, since they have become sanguine of electing their man for the new President. I suppose they trust to its being impossible to get the agreement of Juarez to the amendments in time for Congress to vote the four millions dollars this Session—and they are willing enough to have the dollars and the Powers given by the Treaty in the hands of their own President.

It would be idle to trouble you with a weekly account of the ins and outs of the Electioneering Proceedings. The Republicans have thrown over the head of their Party, Seward, and chosen for their Candidate a Mr. Lincoln, a man unknown, a rough Westerner, of the lowest origin and little education. They are very confident of electing him. But as there will be at least three candidates in the field, it is very commonly thought that no one of them will have the absolute majority of all the votes given.—In this case the House of Representatives elect from the three highest on the Poll—and if they do not give to either an absolute majority, the election falls virtually into the hands of the Senate so that amidst all these complications it is impossible to foresee what may happen. The most curious thing is the total ignorance of the leaders of the Parties as to the turn things may take. Seward went away from Washington a few days ago feeling perfectly certain of being named as the Candidate of the Republicans; and I never heard Lincoln even mentioned by the heads of the Party here.

In his private letter of 19 June, Lord Lyons continued to worry about the widening split between the two factions of the Democratic party.[49]

The House of Representatives has passed by large majorities a series of Resolutions censuring the President and the Secretary of the Navy for employing the Patronage of the Navy and granting Navy Contracts for party purposes. However, as the late Congress upon the same evidence passed resolutions exactly contrary, the President may set one against the other. The fact I suppose is that the present Administration has acted in these matters in the same way as all Administrations have done since General Jackson introduced the system of distributing the "spoils" among the Party after each election of a President. I imagine there can be no doubt at any rate that Mr. Buchanan personally is at least as free from reproach in such matters as any of his recent Predecessors.

The Newspapers which will go to Europe from New York by this Packet will perhaps have got from Baltimore by Telegraph intelligence of the results of the Democratic Convention which reassembled there yesterday after the adjournment from Charleston caused by the split of the Party there. If the Northern and Southern sections of the Party cannot now come to an agreement the Union may really be considered to be in some danger. For if all the Southern Members in Congress are on one side, and all the Northern on the other, the Southern will be in a minority, which, with the increase of the population and the admission of New States, will be daily diminishing—and the South would rather break away from the Union than endure this. If on the other hand the Northern and Southern sections of the Democratic party can agree upon a Candidate for the Presidency and a Declaration of Principles, that Party will have a fair chance of bringing in its man for President and of holding its own in Congress for some time longer.

The summer of 1860 saw the Democratic party divided irreconcilably over the selection of a presidential candidate, and so the Northern delegates nominated Senator Stephen A. Douglas of Illinois, while the Southerners chose Buchanan's vice-president, John C. Breckenric'ge of Kentucky. Lord Lyons evaluated the candidates and tried valiantly to explain the issues to Lord Russell in a private letter dated 23 July.[50]

I had intended before leaving Washington to have laid before you in a Despatch some prognostications respecting the issue of the coming presidential Election. But upon reflection, and talking to the most sagacious political people within my reach, I have become convinced that I could say nothing which would not be likely to mislead.

There are four sets of Candidates for President and Vice-President in the field.

Lincoln—the Republican will undoubtedly have a much larger number of votes than any of his Competitors, but he is by no means certain of having the absolute majority of votes necessary to ensure his "election by the People," as it is called.

Personally he is, I understand, a rough farmer who began life as a farm labourer and got on by a talent for stump speaking. Little more is known of him. Our danger from his triumph lies in the probability of his trying to bring in a Protectionist Tariff and to upset the Reciprocity Treaty. His party are often loud against England in order to counteract the suspicions to which they are exposed by their sympathy with English feeling on the Slavery question.

If *Breckenridge* be elected President, we shall have a continuation of the present system of Administration, perhaps with some more vigour (as he is a young man) and fiercer *verbal* attacks upon Cuba. He is now Vice President, a well educated and well mannered man. He is a native of Kentucky and is the Candidate of the ultra pro-Slavery Party which includes all the Southern States.

Douglas is the Representative of the Northern Democratic or milder Pro-Slavery Party. His distinctive tenet is *"Squatter Sovereignty"*—which means that the People of a Territory have a right to exclude Slavery before they are admitted into the Union as a Regular Sovereign State. The ultra Pro Slavery partisans hold that it is the duty of Congress under the Constitution to enforce the Right of Slave Holders to carry their "Property" into a Territory whether the inhabitants already there like it or not. Douglas' chance is thought at present to be but small. He began life as a Carpenter—then became a small lawyer—and like Lincoln got on by his talent for stump oratory. He is a thorough Political Adventurer, and has been pursuing the Presidency for years by all the usual political maneuvres. He is supposed to be over head and ears in pledges to give places, contracts etc. in case of being elected. He is suspected of Filibustering tendencies. His Foreign Policy, especially that towards England, would no doubt be directed entirely by Party considerations at each moment and by the popular cry.

Bell, the Candidate of the Neutral or respectable Party, is considered just now to have no chance at all.[51] He would probably establish an honest and well meaning but perhaps timid and weak administration.

The office of Vice President derives almost all its real importance from the chance of its holder's becoming President by the death, incapacity, or *non election* of a President.

The difficulty of forming a probable conjecture on the result of the present contest arises in some measure from the complicated plans introduced into the Constitution, mainly I suppose with a view to prevent the chance of the Union's being left without a President.

Originally each State chooses a number of Electors equal to the number of its Senators and Representatives in Congress. In this way New York sends I think 35 electors to the College, while some of the smaller States send only three. If any Candidate gets the absolute majority of votes in this Electoral College, he is said to be "elected by the People" and the Election is over. Practically, the Candidate who runs with him for the Vice-Presidency is sure to be elected also.

But if no Candidate gets the absolute majority in the Electoral College, the House of Representatives elects the President from the three candidates having the highest number of votes for President from the two candidates having the highest number of votes for Vice President.

In the elections, however, in the House of Representatives the smallest State gives one vote and the largest gives no more than one. The Practical effect of this on the present occasion is remarkable. For although the majority of the population are "*Republican*", the majority of the States are "democratic"—and consequently (as the 35 members of New York are of no more weight in the vote for President than the one Member for Oregon)—the House would probably elect a Democratic President if it elected anybody.

But as the House has three candidates to select from, and as the Democratic party is split into two Sections, it is possible that no Candidate may get the absolute majority of votes which is required in order to be elected. The House may thus go on taking vote after vote for an indefinite time without coming to any result, as happened at the beginning of this Session with respect to the Election of Speaker. The Constitution has provided however against this chance of the Country's being left without a President. If the House cannot agree upon a new president on the day before the old one goes out of office (the third of March) then the new *Vice* President becomes *ipso facto* President for the whole ensuing term of four years.

This arrangement would also in the present case probably lead to the Election of a Democratic President. There is no danger of the Senate's not making an Election of Vice President, as it has only two Candidates to choose from, one or the other must have an absolute majority of the votes given, unless in the very improbable case of a tie. The majority of the Senate is undoubtedly democratic, and there is little doubt that it would elect for Vice President General Lane who runs on the same "ticket", as it is called, with Breckenridge, and would form a similar administration.[52]

In this way Lane is thought to have by no means the worst chance of getting into the White House.

The tactics of the Republican Party are to get their Candidates elected by the People. The *Democrats* having no chance of doing this since their split, aim at throwing the election into the House, and if they cannot elect their man there, at preventing any election at all by the House so as to leave the office of the Vice President elected by the Senate.

I can hardly hope to have made anything more intelligible by this long story than that there are a mass of contingencies and complications which render it impossible to predict with any approach to accuracy the result of the Election. Perhaps I should add that it is equally difficult to form an opinion as to the success of which Candidate is to be desired for England.

During the summer of 1860, Edward, the Prince of Wales, came to the United States and Canada. His visit revived the question of whether the Hudson's Bay Company was still entitled to its "possessory rights" south of the forty-ninth degree of latitude. These had been granted in the Oregon Treaty of 1846, and the United States government was anxious to terminate them, but at a compensatory price that the company claimed was inadequate. On the eve of the presidential election, however, every issue, whether domestic or foreign, was ignored, especially in view of the threat by the South to declare sovereign independence if Lincoln was elected. In his letter of 22 October Lord Lyons intimated that momentous events were about to unfold.[53]

In fact, the minds of the President and his Cabinet as well as those of most men here are almost exclusively occupied by the alarm created by the proceedings in the South with regard to the Presidential election. The Southern States now declare that if Lincoln be elected they will not wait until he is installed in the Presidential Chair in March but will take measures for their own security at once. This plan is that the Legislatures of the several States shall at once call together Conventions to consider the propriety of seceding from the Union. These *Conventions* are provided for by the Constitutions of most of the States as forms of enabling the People to exercise their Sovereignty when changes in the Constitutions or other matters beyond the powers of the Constituted Authorities are in question. Some of the States even declare that if Lincoln be elected they will at once refuse to allow Customs Duties for the Federal Government to be collected within their limits. Anything of this kind would be a terrible blow to Mr. Buchanan, as it would devolve upon him to enforce if he could the Federal Authority in the refractory States; and that too against his own Party. I am astonished to find so much serious alarm existing among calm and reflecting men. I would myself be disposed to think that the cry was mainly to be attributed to the desire to influence the elections which are close at hand—especially that of New York. For if the State of New York can be frightened out of giving its votes to Lincoln the election may be thrown into the House of Representatives.

Following Lincoln's successful election, Lyons pondered its implications for British trade and diplomacy, pointing out the potential mischief of which Seward was capable.[54]

Things look as if we are going to have troublous times here, though it seems impossible that the South can be mad enough to dissolve the Union. If they could do it quietly, we might in some respects gain, as they would in all probability establish a low Tariff and throw themselves fraternally into our arms if we would let them. But one cannot but tremble at the idea of serious troubles in the Southern States while we are so entirely dependent upon them for cotton.

One plan not unlikely to be resorted to by Mr. Lincoln's Party to divert men's minds from disunion is to get up a question with Great Britain. I don't think they would have really the least idea of going to war with us, but they would think it a safe game to bully Mr. Lincoln's Counsels. Mr. Seward has more than once played this game before, professing to do so from friendship to England—a course which he explains by a mode of reasoning which I confess it passes my diplomacy to understand.

This is one consideration which makes me extremely desirous to get the San Juan and Possessory Rights questions out of the way before the new Administration comes into Power. Another is that small as is Mr. Buchanan's power of getting a Convention through the Senate, Mr. Lincoln's will be much smaller unless indeed the Southern Senators throw up their seats. I am myself far from sanguine. I doubt very much whether Mr. Buchanan will agree to any convention which we can accept, and I doubt still more whether the Senate would ratify one. Still I think the good feeling occasioned by the Prince of Wales' visit, and the desire of Mr. Buchanan to announce that he leaves no question with England unsettled are favourable circumstances, and I am very nervous about the Administration which will come into office in little more than three months.

By 25 November secession by one or more Southern states seemed likely, prompting Lord Lyons to speculate on the potential difficulties which would be faced by Her Majesty's ships that customarily docked at Southern ports.[55]

I do not think any conjectures as to the fate of the Union between these States can be made now which are sufficiently probable to be worth recording. It seems however to be considered nearly certain that South Carolina will secede from the Confederation at latest on the 4th of March when Mr. Lincoln takes office. It is thought to be by no means improbable that this troublesome little State may secede in a month or six weeks time. The practical question which her secession would be likely to raise for us would relate to the payment of Customs Duties by British Vessels at Charleston. Upon seceding, the State will refuse to allow the Federal Customs dues to be collected in its Ports. The Federal Government may send United States Ships to collect the duties on Vessels and their Cargoes bound to Charleston before they can enter the Port. On the other hand, the State of South Carolina may determine upon levying Customs Duties of its own inside the Port. If other States secede, the same thing may happen at other Ports. This would place the Consuls in an embarrassing situation: for if they advise the Masters and Consignees to pay both duties under Protest, they must give the advice without any confidence that either duty will ever be repaid.

Another mode by which it is suggested that the Federal Government may attempt to bring the seceding States to submission is a regular blockade of the Ports by the United States Navy. I suppose however that if such a Blockade be regularly established, Foreign Vessels have no other course than to submit to it, at all events until their governments formally announce that they will not recognize it.

The first thing which always occurs to the Consular mind when in trouble is to ask for a British Man of War. There are however many considerations which should, I think, be well weighed before one of Her Majesty's Ships is sent to a Port at which a contest is going on between the Federal Government and a seceding State. In the first place the appearance of a British Man of War at Charleston or any such place is so unusual an event that it would, even in ordinary times, give rise to all sorts of conjectures and interpretations throughout the Confederation. If one appeared in the midst of a dispute between the Federal Government and the South, a violent situation would be very probably produced against Great Britain in the minds of both the contending Parties.

I presume that you would wish the British Agents in this Country to be particularly careful to avoid any step which would embarrass Her Majesty's Government in determining eventually the policy to be pursued. A Consul would I think, in this point of view, be safer without a Man of War than with one. As to the moral weight which the presence of a Man of War would give to a Consul's representations, this with a people like the Americans would depend upon her power to use actual force against them and upon their belief in her readiness to do so. They are more likely to be irritated than awed by a demonstration which they believe to be no more than a demonstration.

There is also to be taken into account the risk of actual Collision with the United States Navy—which not a few American officers would be willing enough to provoke under such circumstances.

The case will be somewhat different if the British Residents at Charleston or elsewhere should be in actual danger, whether from a servile insurrection—for the Lynch law—of from a Bombardment. Under such circumstances a Man of War to escape in would be most desirable. Of the probability of a servile Insurrection I have little or no means of forming a judgment. The application of lynch law to the class of Englishmen likely in the present states of affairs to be resident in a Southern City does not seem probable. That the United States Forces should actually bombard a town in the Southern States, I should have thought inconceivable if I had not heard it seriously suggested. It may be supposed at all events that Foreigners would at least receive due notice to quit.

Indeed the more general opinion appears to be that no attempt will be made by the Federal Government to bring back a seceding State by force. But however this may be, it seems particularly desirable to avoid as far as we can, without neglecting to provide for the safety of our fellow Subjects here, anything likely to give the Americans a pretext for quarreling with us. For a Foreign War, and a war with England as being the most exciting, is the remedy very generally prescribed for the intestine divisions here.

With the Country in this State, it is hardly to be expected that we shall be able to get the President or the Senate to attend either to a Convention for settling the San Juan question or to one embodying Mr. Lindsay's suggestions on Shipping Matters.[56] I should nevertheless be myself disposed to try both, not from any great expectation that I should make any near approach to concluding either now, but because I do not like to throw any chance away, and do not think that to fail now would increase the difficulty of succeeding hereafter.

Lord Lyons was correct in assuming that American foreign policy would soon be eclipsed by domestic upheaval, but he little imagined just how profoundly it would affect Anglo-American relations.

9

Prelude to Civil War, 1861

In December 1860 the Southern states began to break away from the federal Union one by one. First to act was South Carolina, followed in January 1861 by Mississippi, Florida, Georgia, Alabama, and Louisiana. In state conventions, each formally seceded from the United States; recalled their senators and representatives from Washington; and defied Buchanan to intervene. Early in February Texas joined the other secessionists, and these seven states chose delegates to a forthcoming assembly at Montgomery, Alabama, at which they lost little time proclaiming a new Confederacy with Jefferson Davis as its provisional president. The Buchanan administration stood meekly by and did nothing.

What excitement there was in Washington grew from speculation about the composition of Lincoln's new cabinet, but one thing seemed abundantly clear: William H. Seward would be its dominant personality. In his letter of 7 January Lord Lyons reiterated his fear of Seward's bellicose tendencies.[1]

It is considered almost certain that Mr. Seward is to be Mr. Lincoln's Secretary of State. This will be regarded as a defiance of the South, unless (as is expected) Mr. Seward comes out with a conciliatory speech in the Senate. With regard to Great Britain, I cannot help fearing that he will be a dangerous foreign minister. His view of the relations between the United States and Great Britain has always been that they are a good material to make political capital of. He thinks at all events that they may be safely played with—without any risk of bringing on a war. He has even to me allowed his belief that England will *never* go to war with the United States. He has generally taken up any cry against us—but this, he says, he has done from friendship to prevent the other Party's appropriating it and doing more harm with it than he has done. The temptation will be great for Lincoln's Party, if they be not actually engaged in Civil War, to endeavour to divert the Public excitement to a foreign quarrel. I do not think Mr. Seward would contemplate actually going to war with us, but he would be well disposed to play the old game of seeking popularity here by displaying insolence towards us. I don't think it will be so good a game for him as it used to be, even supposing we give him an apparent trump; but I think he is likely to try to play it.

This makes me more than ever impatient to settle the San Juan and Hudson's Bay question. I confess however I am almost in despair about them. If General Cass had started in office, I really believe the thing might have been done in time. The choice of the Attorney General, Mr. Black, for a successor to him is most unfortunate.[2]

He is a lawyer who can only attend to one thing at a time, and neglects all other business now in order I suppose to give the President legal advice on the Crisis. There are not eight weeks left of Mr. Buchanan's Administration. It was impossible to get the simplest bit of business through Mr. Black's office in that time when he was Attorney General.

Whenever crises arose in Europe or America, friendly as well as unfriendly powers offered their services as arbitrators. However, Lord Lyons doubted that any outside mediation would be tolerated in this situation.[3]

Mr. Everett, who is here with a monster Union Petition from Boston, came to me a few days [ago] in a state of great despondency about the Country. He said that it had occurred to him that perhaps the mediation of the great powers of Europe between the North and South might be beneficial. It would not do, he said, for England alone to offer her mediation, but she might do so in conjunction with France and Russia. Such a mediation he thought would probably take place in Europe, if any of the States on that Continent should be in the same condition as was this Confederation. I reminded Mr. Everett that the States of Europe regarded themselves as belonging to the same political family, while hitherto the United States of America had haughtily repudiated the notion that the powers of Europe had any title to interfere, (and this not only as to the affairs of the United States themselves but as to those of any other part of America) would it not cause a great deal of irritation in this country if Europe now came forward to settle the domestic quarrel now raging here? Mr. Everett said, perhaps it would, but still he thought a declaration of the great powers of Europe would have great effect on the Southern States, which looked a great deal to Foreign support. He said that he had hinted something of the kind to the Russian Minister M. de Stoeckl—but that he had not mentioned the idea to any one else here—and he begged me not to allow it to transpire here that he had spoken to me about it.

I have never heard anything of the kind suggested by any one but Mr. Everett. I should very much hesitate to proffer mediation unasked. Among other difficulties, I doubt whether public opinion in England could be brought to the point of toleration of Slavery, at which even Northern Americans (except the most ardent abolitionists) have arrived. It would, I should think, be difficult for England to be a party to an arrangement for securing and perpetuating Slavery anywhere—and the Northern States are quite ready to yield on everything except the *extension* of Slavery.

I have given you an account in a Despatch today (No. 40) of a long conversation I had yesterday with Mr. Seward.[4] He is extremely friendly to me personally—but I confess my fears of him as Foreign Secretary are increasing. He was especially unsatisfactory on the Tariff question. He repeated (no doubt for my instruction) a conversation he had with M. Schleeder, the Bremen Minister, who appears to have suggested the imprudence of giving European Commerce and consequently European Governments strong reason for supporting the South. Mr. Seward said that he had told M. Schleeder that nothing would give so much pleasure as to see a European Power interfere in favour of South Carolina—for that then he should "pitch into" the European Power, and South Carolina and the seceding States would soon join him in doing so. I am afraid he takes no other view of Foreign Relations than as safe levers to work with upon public opinion here.

He says that the reason he will not commit himself to any definite plan for a settlement of differences at present is that he is sure that at this moment no plan would be accepted by both parties—and that he does not choose to weaken his position by making himself responsible for a rejected plan. In this I think he is wise. Whether he will bring about a better state of things as soon as he expects, remains to be seen.

Lyons's next letter of 12 February 1861 was filled with foreboding. Three weeks remained before Lincoln would be taking office, and already Seward's influence was creating difficulties for France and England.[5]

I am very glad indeed to get the draft of a Convention about San Juan, etc., and I shall attack the President himself about it immediately. I am afraid he will tell me that it is impossible for him to attend to it, that it is too late, or (what I fear is true) that it would be impossible for him to carry it in the Senate now that the Seceding Senators have withdrawn. Nevertheless it is our last chance, and I am more than ever anxious to get these questions out of the way before Mr. Seward comes in. For he shows more than ever a disposition to play his old game of raising excitement by a dispute with Foreign Powers, and of course England is the power most useful for his purpose. He has asked one of our Colleagues to invite the French Minister, M. Mercier and me to dinner, in order that he may talk politics with us. I should not be the least surprised if he were to tell us both not to be annoyed if he used a high tone with us, and appeared hostile to France and England, for that he would be merely conforming to a necessity of his position, and would be actuated by the kindest motives towards the two countries. I had hoped that he had been convinced of the dangers of this game by a conversation which he had with the Duke of Newcastle at Albany; but he has such unbounded confidence in his own sagacity and dexterity that nothing which can be said to him makes much impression.[6]

Such being, as I believe, the disposition of the man who will be at the head of the Foreign department and Prime Minister of this government in three weeks time, it may perhaps be worth considering whether it will not be more than usually important to act, if possible, in concert with France, should it become necessary to resist attempts to exclude our vessels from Southern Ports.[7] As I mentioned in my last letter, Mr. Seward himself told me that he *wished* some Foreign Power to resist any measures taken against South Carolina. He would hardly I suppose adopt an intolerable tone of bullying towards England and France united; although, in language at least, nothing would probably exceed his fierceness towards England if he thought he had her alone to deal with.

He is playing a difficult game in home politics. On the one hand, he tries to rally moderate opponents by vague conciliatory speeches; on the other hand, he keeps his own Party together by pointing out that he has never *voted* for any concession whatever, and declaring that he never will. Moreover he has little or no personal acquaintance with the President Elect, and very little knowledge of his views or intentions, or means of judging of the amount of influence he himself will have with the new chief magistrate.

As the North and the South drifted toward open hostilities, Secretary of State Seward sought to discover the implications of such a struggle as seen by diplomatic representatives in Washington. At a private dinner party, several ministers discussed this, but Lord Lyons was chiefly concerned with the impact it would have upon British commerce and trade relations.

As time went on, it became increasingly clear that the North wanted to contain the conflict in order to maintain the legal fiction that America was undergoing a rebellion, not a civil war. Such a distinction was important because of the legal difference as defined by international law. If the North admitted that a condition of civil war existed, the Confederacy would be accorded a sovereignty of its own and therefore have the right not only to exchange diplomatic representatives with foreign powers but also to receive direct aid of a non contraband nature from them. On the other hand, if the North could succeed in persuading other nations that the American struggle involved merely the putting down of insurgents by the federal government, then no outside power could communicate directly with the South and it would be easier to blockade Southern ports with minimal naval capacity, since they were part of the normal extension of federal jurisdiction.

Lord Lyons felt compelled to point out, however, that the North was obliged not to proclaim a blockade if it could not enforce it, since "paper blockades" by nonexistent warships were not binding upon foreign states under the law of nations. In addition, if the North proved powerless in sealing off Southern harbors, the South's successful defiance would soon lead to the diplomatic recognition of the Confederacy by those European nations trading with them.[8]

Mr. Seward came to me on the evening of the 20th instant and asked me to let him speak to me very confidentially. He went on to express great apprehension lest *any* Power should recognize the Southern Confederacy. He seemed even to feel alarm lest Brazil or Peru should do so. In fact the immediate object of his visit appeared to be to endeavour to ascertain through me whether there could be any truth in private information which had reached him that Brazil had determined already to recognize the new Confederacy. Brazil, he said, might perhaps be led to do so by community of feeling on Slavery. . . .

I said that with regard to Brazil I thought it very unlikely that that Power would recognize the Southern Confederacy unless some of the European Governments set it the example. I added that I did not suppose any European Power was likely to quit "an attitude of expectation" provided that in practice its commerce was not interfered with.

Mr. Seward observed that he considered it all important to ward off a crisis during the next three months—that he had good hopes that if this could be affected, a counter-revolution would take place in the South—that he hoped and believed that it would begin in the most distant State, Texas; where indeed he saw symptoms of it already. It might be necessary towards producing this effect to make the Southern States feel uncomfortable in their present condition by interrupting their commerce. It was however most important that the new Confederacy should not in the meantime be recognised by any Foreign Power.

I said that certainly the feelings as well as the interests of Great Britain would render Her Majesty's Government most desirous to avoid any step which could prolong the quarrel between North and South or be an obstacle to a cordial and speedy reunion between them, if that were possible. Still, I said, if the United States determined to stop by force so important a commerce as that of Great Britain with the cotton growing States, I could not answer for what might happen.

Mr. Seward asked whether England would not be content to get cotton through the Northern Ports, to which it could be sent by land.

I answered that cotton, although by far the most important article of the trade, was not the only point to be considered. It was however a matter of the greatest consequence to England to procure cheap cotton. If a considerable rise were to take place in the price of cotton, and British Ships were to be at the same time excluded from the Southern Ports, an immense pressure would be put upon Her Majesty's Government to use all the means in their power to open those ports. If Her Majesty's Government felt it their duty to do so, they would naturally endeavour to effect their object in a manner as consistent as possible, first with their friendly feelings towards both sections of this Country, and secondly with the recognised principles of International law. As regarded the latter point in particular, it certainly appeared that the most simple, if not the only way, would be to recognise the Southern Confederacy. I said a good deal about my hopes that Mr. Seward would never let things come to this, with which it is not necessary to trouble you.

I thought Mr. Seward, although he did not give up the point, listened with complacency to my arguments against interference with Foreign Commerce. He said more than once that he should like to take me to the President to discuss the subject with him. The conclusion I came to was that the question of a forcible collection of the duties in the Southern Ports and of a blockade of those Ports were under discussion in the Cabinet, but that Mr. Seward was himself opposed to these measures and had good hopes that his opinion would prevail.

It would appear however that a change took place in the interval between this conversation and yesterday. Mr. Seward, the principal Members of the Cabinet, the Russian Minister M. de Stoeckl, and the French Minister M. Mercier, with some other people dined with me. After dinner Mr. Seward entered into an animated conversation with my French and Russian colleagues and signed to me to join them. When I came up I found him asking M. Mercier to give him a copy of his instructions to the French Consuls in the Southern States. M. Mercier made some excuse for refusing, but said that what the instructions amounted to was that the Consuls were to do their best to protect French Commerce "sans sortant de la plus stricte neutralite".—Mr. Seward then asked me to give him a copy of my instructions to Her Majesty's Consuls. I of course declined to do so, but I told him that the purport of them was, that the Consuls were to regard questions from a Commercial not from a political point of view: that they were to do all they could to favour the continuance of peaceful commerce, short of performing an Act of recognition, without the orders of Her Majesty's Government.

Mr. Seward then alluded to the Peruvian Papers, and speaking as he had done all along very loud, said to my French and Russian Colleagues and me, "I have formed my opinion on that matter; and I may as well tell it to you now as at any other time. I differ with my Predecessor as to *de facto* Authorities. If one of your ships comes out of a Southern Port without the Papers required by the laws of the United States, and is seized by one of our Cruisers and carried into New York and confiscated, we shall not make any compensation." My Russian Colleague, M. de Stoeckl, argued the question with Mr. Seward very good humouredly and very ably. Upon his saying that a Blockade to be respected must be effective, Mr. Seward replied that it was not a Blockade that would be established, that the U.S. Cruisers would be stationed off the Southern Coast to collect duties, and enforce penalties for the infraction of the United States Customs Laws. Mr. Seward then appealed to me. I said that it was really a matter so very serious that I was unwilling to discuss it; that his plan seemed to me to amount in fact to a paper blockade of the enormous extent of coast comprised in the seceding States; that the calling it an enforcement of the Revenue Laws appeared to me to increase the gravity of the measure, for it placed Foreign Powers in the dilemma of recognising the Southern Confederaton or of submitting to the interruption of their Commerce.

Mr. Seward then went off into a defiance of Foreign relations, in a style of braggadocio which was formerly not uncommon with him, but which I have not heard before from him since he has been in office. Finding that he was getting more and more violent and noisy, and saying things which it would be more convenient for me not to have heard, I took a natural opportunity of turning, as host, to speak to some of the ladies in the room.

M. de Stoeckl and M. de Mercier inferred, as I do, that within the last two days the opinions of the more violent Party in the Cabinet had prevailed, at all events for the moment—and that there is a danger that an interference with Foreign Trade may take place at any moment. I hope it may still be prevented by the fear of its producing a recognition of the Southern Confederacy. But I am afraid we must be prepared for it.

It may perhaps be well, with a view to the effect on this Government, that the Commissioners who are on their way to Europe from the Southern States should not meet with too strong a rebuff in England or in France. Such a rebuff would be a great encouragement to violent measures here. In fact, notwithstanding my contradictions, the Senate and indeed, I fear, the President is not uninfluenced by the bold assertions made by some members of the violent party, that they have positive assurances from Your Lordship and other Members of Her Majesty's Government that *under no circumstances whatever* will Great Britain recognize the independence of the South.

M. Mercier thinks it advisable that he and I should have a discretionary power to recognise the South. This seems to me to be going too fast. I should feel a good deal embarrassed by having such a power in my pocket, unless the contingency in which it was to be used should be most clearly stated. What does appear to be of extreme importance is that England and France should act in concert.

Three days later Lyons reported that Seward continued to try to manipulate the responses of diplomats to the American political dilemma, although he noted that "Prudent counsels appear to be again in the ascendancy," making it unlikely that "any interference with foreign commerce is *at present* contemplated."[9] Meanwhile, the Spanish sent troops into Santa Domingo in defiance of the Monroe Doctrine.[10]

I think Mr. Seward hopes that he has got by the Spanish invasion of Dominica the question with a Foreign Power, for which he has been on the lookout. He was not clear about the mode in which he hoped to turn the Cuban Question to the profit and glory of the North and the confusion of the South. He can hardly I suppose think that he has the means of annexing Cuba and emancipating the Slaves there. His notion of sending a Ship of War to Dominica was that it would ensure a rising of the population of the Republic against the Spanish Intruders. I have given a long report of what he said to me in a Confidential Despatch today (No. 129).[11] It may be well to avoid alluding to it in communications to this or any Foreign Government;

lest the freedom with which he talks to me should be checked. He has a foolish habit of asking to see Despatches either by me or other Ministers here. I think it better and more straightforward to refuse civilly, than to compose Despatches expressly for his eye.

I have nothing to add to my Despatches about the intentions of the Government towards the South. Where nothing is decided, nothing can be known. There had been a stormy sitting of the Cabinet on the question of Fort Sumter, on the morning of the day on which Mr. Seward made his strange tirade *after dinner* at my house, which I mentioned in my private letter of the 26th. But the Cabinet has not (or had not up to Saturday night) had a single sitting to deliberate on the general line of policy towards the Southern Confederacy.

It was perhaps fitting that South Carolina, the first state to secede, became the first to provoke a military showdown with the Lincoln administration. It occurred at Fort Sumter, a federal stronghold in the harbor of Charleston that stood as a symbol of United States jurisdiction in the midst of the newly proclaimed Confederacy. In an attempt to maintain a presence there, the government in Washington decided to resupply the garrison by sea. However, unexpected bombardment from shore batteries forced the surrender of federal troops, sending shock waves along the entire Eastern seaboard.[12]

The American Packet by which this letter is to go will take news from New York at least twenty-four hours later in date than any we have now here.

There appears to be no doubt that the first object of the expedition from New York is to re-victual Fort Sumter; and that if the Charleston people do not allow that to be done peaceably, the attempt is to be made to introduce provisions and, in that case, troops also, by force.

Immense activity is shown in fitting out ships of war in several of the dockyards. In fact the coercion party having at least got their own way in the Cabinet, are doing their best to make up for lost time.

If solemn declarations are adhered to, the immediate consequence will be civil war and the secession of the Border States.[13] There is still perhaps *some* hope that the evident disinclination on both sides to shed blood may render the coercion mild and the resistance nominal. I am afraid the probabilities are the other way.

I do hope that they will not be so ill-advised as to interfere with Foreign Commerce. But all these naval preparations look painfully like a blockade.

Considerable preparations are being made to collect Militia from this District, and, if necessary, from the neighbouring Northern States to protect this town from an attack from the Southern Confederacy.[14]

Once the South fired on Fort Sumter, the likelihood of a Northern blockade of the Confederacy's ports loomed larger, greatly increasing Lord Lyons's anxiety regarding British shipping. In his letter of 15 April he sought Lord John Russell's opinion concerning a proper course of action, at the same time reiterating his lack of confidence in those formulating American policy.[15]

I am getting very uneasy about the intentions of this government with regard to stopping intercourse with Southern Ports. Now that war has begun, it seems difficult to suppose that they will abstain from taking advantage of the one great superiority they have, which is their Navy. I suppose a regular Blockade would be less objectionable than any such measures as closing the Southern Ports as Ports of Entry, or attmepting to collect duties for the United States by ships stationed off them. The rules of a Blockade are to a great extent determined and known; and our ships could at all events resort to any Ports before which the United States did not establish a regular effective Blockade. But if the United States are to be permitted to seize any ship of ours, wherever they can find her within their jurisdiction, on the plea that by going to a Southern Port she has violated the United States Customs Laws, our commerce will be exposed to vexations beyond bearing, and all kinds of new and doubtful questions will be raised. In fact this, it seems to me, would be a paper Blockade of the worst kind. It would certainly justify Great Britain and France in recognising the Southern Confederacy and sending their Fleets to force the United States to treat British and French vessels as neutrals in conformity with the law of Nations.

Just as Mr. Seward was confident that he had prevailed in the Cabinet, the President and the violent party suddenly threw over all his policy. Having determined not to resign, he pretends to be pleased, and one of his Colleagues says of him, that in order to make up for previous lukewarmness, he is now "the fiercest of the lot." It is a great inconvenience to have him as the organ of communication from the United States Government. Repeated failures have not convinced him that he is not sure to carry his point with the President and Cabinet. He is therefore apt to announce as the fixed intention of the Government, what is in reality no more than a measure which he himself supports.

I am in constant apprehension of some foolish violent proceeding of the Government with regard to Foreign Powers. Neither the President nor any man in the Cabinet has a knowledge of Foreign Affairs. They have consequently all the overweaning confidence in their own strength which popular oratory has made common in this Country. I believe the best chance of keeping them within bounds will be to be very firm with them, particularly at first, and to act in strict concert with France if that be possible.

As I have mentioned in some of my Despatches information coming from the Southern Commissioners sent to negotiate with the Government here, it may be as well to mention that they did not seek any intercourse with me, and that I never had any communication with them direct or indirect, nor to my knowledge ever set eyes on any one of them. I do not know that I should have thought it necessary to refuse to communicate with them, if it had been proposed to me, but the fact is as I have just said.

Although a blockade had not yet been announced officially, Lord Lyons became increasingly convinced that one was imminent, and Britain would have to respect it.[16]

As I hardly know when the Bag in which I shall send this letter will reach Your Lordship, nor indeed into what hands it may fall, I cannot write quite without restraint.

The Blockade has not yet been officially announced to me. If it be carried on with reasonable consideration for Foreign Flags and in strict conformity with the law of Nations, I suppose it must be recognised. At all events it could hardly be disputed without express order from Her Majesty's Government. Before such orders could arrive, the season during which British vessels ordinarily frequent the Southern Ports would be over.

I understand that the Northern Ports insisted upon a Blockade as a *sine qua non* condition of their giving their support to the Government. Of course they could not endure to see Foreign trade diverted to the South.

As regards the Southern Privateers, I suppose the principle of Neutrality would prevent our interfering with them either—unless they threatened danger to our Merchant vessels, or filibustering expeditions against places not in the United States. The United States Navy ought to be quite sufficient to keep them down; and there can be no doubt of its desire to do so. As a matter of technical law, I suppose we have the right to seize Privateers, if we please, which sail under a flag which we do not recognise.

I have just seen the Consul and Vice-Consul from Baltimore who have come over to report to me the state of affairs there. They describe the anti-Union and anti-North excitement as tremendous. The town seems to be entirely in the hands of the Mob. The Vice-Consul who has managed to get through from New York, says that the excitement there against the South, and especially against the Baltimore people is equally fierce.

At Washington great alarm is felt first lest the town should be immediately attacked from the South; and secondly lest it should be starved, as both Virginia and Maryland refuse to allow provisions to come to it. These alarms seem not to have much foundation.

The resignation of the Virginia officers has within the last two days deprived the U.S. Army and Navy of a great number of the best officers.[17]

Following Jefferson Davis's announcement that the South intended to outfit privateers by means of letters of marque and reprisal, President Lincoln formally ordered the establishment of a blockade on 19 April. A week later, Lyons described the repercussions arising from these two new contingencies.[18]

In common with the most influential of my Colleagues, I exhausted every possible means of opposition to the Blockade. The great North Eastern Cities insisted upon it, not only as a measure of vengeance, but as one essential to the preservation of their own prosperity. They could hardly be expected to make sacrifices for the contest, unless they were secured from seeing their Trade diverted to Southern Ports. I think the Blockade is less likely to be injurious or to raise awkward questions than any of the irregular modes of closing the Southern Ports which were proposed. Until September it will interfere very little with any Trade which we carry on with the South in the ordinary course of things. But it will of course effectually prevent the new trade which might perhaps have sprung up under the influence of the opposing Tariffs of North and South. The official announcement of it, which I have only just received, seems extraordinarily vague. I conclude the exact date of the commencement of the effective Blockade [at] each particular Port will be announced in proper form hereafter. I hope that we shall succeed in obtaining a tolerably liberal application of its rules as far as Foreign Vessels are concerned.

Mr. Seward has talked (not to me) of the United States' being now willing to adhere to the Declaration of the Congress of Paris abolishing Privateering.[19] I am always rather afraid of touching upon the principles laid down in the Declaration. It may perhaps be a good thing to secure the adherence of the United States to them— though how long after the present crisis the adherence may be maintained, is, I think, not a little doubtful. The time at which the offer would be made renders the thing rather amusing. It would no doubt be very convenient if the navies of Europe would put down the Privateers, and thus leave the whole Navy of the United States free to blockade the Ports against European Merchant Vessels.

The Consuls at New York and Boston having been withdrawn by the interruption of Post and telegraphs from the influence of the calming potions which I administer to them when I have the means of doing so, seem to have taken the Northern War Fever. As the Governors have refused to send the Arms from the British Public Stores without my sanction, I hope no great harm is done. Mr. Archibald is so valuable a public servant that I have been sorry to send him even the very mild reproof of which I send you a copy officially today.[20]

I have been rather puzzled what to say to the Admiral.[21] Every Consul and every British Subject wishes to have a Man of War or a Fleet if possible at his door. I don't see that the Man of War could be of any practical use, except as places of refuge, in case of bombardment or actual fighting in a town. There are naval as well as political objections to having our ships here without strong necessity. The temptation to desert is very strong and very generally yielded to by our Man of Wars men in American Ports. With the practice which has grown up here of putting out lights and removing Beacons and Buoys it might be easier to get a ship into one of these harbours or rivers than to get her out again. I should like to have ships as near at hand as possible without being actually in American Waters.

During the hectic and uncertain weeks in late April and early May, Lincoln was without his own appointed diplomatic representative in London because Charles Francis Adams, grandson of the president John Adams and son of John Quincy Adams, was unable to reach London until 13 May. Upon his arrival he was greeted by disconcerting news: Great Britain had in the interim recognized a condition of "belligerency" in the Southern part of the United States and Her Majesty's government proclaimed neutrality with respect to both belligerents. Temporarily stunned, Adams was nevertheless quick to realize that this stance was far from a disaster for the North. To be sure, the Lincoln administration would have preferred no pronouncement, but a declaration of neutrality meant that the South in its turn could take no comfort from across the Atlantic. Furthermore, belligerency was not civil war, and the Confederacy would not be viewed as an independent government.

As far as Britain was concerned, she would be bound to observe any effective blockading of Southern ports, as would France. Lyons's letter of 14 June again portrayed Seward as the puppeteer pulling the strings.[22]

I consider that we may take it for granted that this government will admit without hesitation that the principles of the second and third articles of the Declaration of Paris are to be observed by them in the present context. I do not apprehend that the Southern Government will make any difficulty in doing the same thing.

Both governments will no doubt also be quite ready to declare a principle that a blockade to be recognised must be effective. But this government is not willing to admit that it has not as much right to close the port of New Orleans by an act of Congress as it has to close the port of New York, or that it may not confiscate foreign vessels for a breach of the revenue laws if they attempt to go to New Orleans after it has been closed by law as a port of entry, whether it be in fact blockaded or not.

This is likely to be the *practical* difficulty with regard to the question of the belligerent rights of the South. But after all, the *sentimental* difficulty is the great one. The present apparent triumph of the South in founding an independent government is so galling to the North that anything which implies the admission of this self-evident fact irritates them beyond measure. As you will have seen from the tone of Mr. Seward's despatches, the recourse is to deny the existence of the fact, not to explain it; to threaten anyone who shall dare to assert it, or even to perceive it.

I hope to be able to take advantage of the present lull in the storm to set things with Mr. Seward on a better footing. The prohibition to carry prizes into our ports, and your reply in the House of Commons to Sir John Ramsden have thrown oil upon the troubled waters.[23] Mr. Seward sent Baron Gerolt, the Prussian Minister, to me last night with a sort of friendly overture. Baron Gerolt told me that Mr. Seward was ready to yield all, and more than all, that England and France asked for the security of their commerce, but that he would not and could not endure recognition by those two powers of belligerent rights in the South, that this was to imply that the Union was dissolved, that there were two nations and two governments; that England and France were treating the United States like Japan or China. Mr. Seward appears to have said further to Baron Gerolt that he had received satisfactory despatches from Mr. Adams; that he had himself the best disposition now towards England; that he had not had a political conversation with me for some time, that he hoped I should be ready to enter upon friendly explanations with him.

I told Baron Gerolt that I had kept under cover like a prudent man while the storm was raging, but that I had been carefully watching the signs of the weather. I had purposefully postponed discussing the question of belligerent rights with Mr. Seward until I could completely reassure him on the point which had caused most irritation and which possessed the most practical importance. I was anxious to be able to tell Mr. Seward positively that the Southern privateers would not be allowed to dispose of their prizes in British ports. I had received the intelligence only that evening. With the disposition in which Baron Gerolt said Mr. Seward now was, I had every hope that our discussions would be quite satisfactory to both.

I do not think Baron Gerolt himself had detected the real object of Mr. Seward in sending him to me, nor did I give him any hint of it, although it was quite plain to me. Mr. Seward evidently wished to divide Messrs. Mercier and me upon the question of belligerent rights. He no doubt desires to avoid having the fact established that he has official cognizance that the belligerent rights of the South have been recognised either by England or France. But what he desires much more is to have it believed that France has not really taken the same course with England. He may even have some hope that France may retract, if she be not committed by some official act. England has bound herself by the Royal proclamation—but no similar document has emanated from France. Mr. Seward is therefore still at liberty, if he thinks it may suit his political object at home, to be violent against England, without being obliged to adopt the same course with France. These are no doubt Mr. Seward's real motives for urging Mssr. Mercier to put off communicating to him the instructions relative to the Declaration of Paris and the belligerent rights. To counteract these schemes appears to me to be at this moment the most essential step towards maintaining peace and friendship between the United States and ourselves. I have not perceived any sign of desire upon Mons. Mercier's part to give in to Mr. Seward's plan, but he has become extremely cautious of giving offence, which he did not seem to be some time ago. I have not seen him since he received his despatches by the mail last night. I hope however that either this afternoon or tomorrow he will go with me to Mr. Seward. I propose to be extremely yielding as to the form of the communication. All I aim at is to establish beyond contradiction that France occupies precisely the same position as England with regard to the question of belligerent rights.

I think I have been lucky to get through the beginning of the blockade with so few awkward questions. The blockade is by no means regularly carried on—but as yet I hardly think any British vessel has practically suffered an injury or experienced treatment inconsistent with the laws of nations. Had there been a case which I should have been obliged to take up energetically during the height of the excitement, we should probably have brought our relations with the United States to a critical point.

British recogniton of a state of belligerency in the South created a great stir in the Union States. Public opinion and the press in the North exploded with unmasked fury.[24]

Mons. Mercier and I have by a course, perhaps a little pusillanimous, prevented an immediate explosion here on the subject of the belligerent rights of the South. But I cannot say that I am much reassured about the future. The only thing which prevented the explosion now was the unmistakable identity of the line taken by France and England. This manifest concert between the two great maritime powers is no doubt inconvenient to Mr. Seward. For it counteracts his plans of making "political capital" by violent language towards either. Except the maddest of the violent party, no one can help seeing that to quarrel with England and France both at this moment is not a proof of consummate statesmanship.

I do not know whether Mr. Seward will get off his instructions ot Mr. Adams and Mr. Dayton by this packet.[25] The tone of them will depend so much upon what the writer may suppose will be the feeling of Congress when it meets on the 4th that it is difficult to say what it will be.[26] They no doubt will make some sort of complaint of the concert between England and France. Indeed if Mr. Seward carried his doctrines as far in writing as he does in speaking, he will asset that not only are joint or identical communication from foreign powers disagreeable to the United States but that it is an offence for foreign powers even to communicate with each other on American questions. England and France must sooner or later, if this Civil War last, take a stand upon this point, and also upon the unreasonable objections made to their communicating however informally with the *de facto* government of the South. But I felt sure that you would not wish me to bring on a crisis here at this moment by insisting on Mr. Seward's receiving my communication officially. At all events I should have been very sorry to have done more than the French Minister.

One of Mr. Seward's objects in transferring the discussion to London and Paris is to gain time. He is divided between the fear that Congress may after all blame him for putting the country upon bad terms with Europe; and the apprehension that any lowering of the tone he so unfortunately assumed may lose him his mob popularity. His refusing to receive the communication from M. Mercier and me is just one of those safe half measures, which may be represented in one light or the other, according to circumstances.

Mr. Seward also no doubt calculates upon the effect which may be produced upon the governments of Europe by the events of the month which has elapsed since the instructions were sent to M. Mercier and me. No doubt that prospects of the North are brighter than they were a month ago. But nothing has yet happened to give any clear notion of the probable extent and duration of the struggle. The perseverance of neither side has yet been put to the test. No military engagement has taken place—and consequently the effect of defeat or victory on the spirit of the two divisions of the country can only be conjectured. Hitherto the North has advanced gradually into Virginia without opposition, but if the advance is to go at the same rate, it will take about half a century to get on to Florida. On the other hand we have been again threatened with an attack upon Washington; and no doubt if President Davis could move his troops with rapidity such an attack would have a fair chance of success. But the same causes which oblige General Scott to be so nearly immovable, no doubt operate as forcefully with his antagonist: lack of means of transport, lack of commissariat, lack of trained soliders.[27] Unless one side make up their minds to a dash at Richmond or the other at Washington, we may go on in the present state of uncertainty all the summer, and even much longer.

If this be so, we shall probably also remain in the same uncertainty about the conduct of the Cabinet of Washington towards Great Britain, and prudence must, I am afraid, lead us to consider ourselves at any moment, open to a declaration of war. Any symptom of disunion between England and France, any necessity on the part of the Cabinet or of some of its members to arouse popular passion or pander to it, might bring on a war.

Toward the end of June 1861 there was a lull in the bellicose atmosphere, yet Lord Lyons sensed that many serious problems lay just under the calm surface.[28]

Nothing of importance has occurred either in the military or political world since I wrote you on the 21st. We are promised as usual a great battle for the end of the week—but we have been promised this so often that we shall hardly believe it when it actually comes off, if come off it should.

Things at this moment are certainly more favourable to our being able to keep the peace than they were a month ago. I wish I could feel confident that the danger was passing away. But the same personal ambition in individuals, and the same irritability and ignorance in the multitude may bring it on again at any moment. I find that we were a month or three weeks ago even nearer to a declaration of war than I apprehended. The note which I had mentioned in my despatch no. 209 of the 23d of last month as having been prepared by Mr. Seward to send to Mr. Adams was, I understand, all but a direct announcement of war.[29] And it would certainly have been sent, if means had not been found of alarming the President and the more reasonable members of the Cabinet. I understand that sentences and even pages are scored out in the draft, and strong expressions altered in the President's own hand, and that a special injunction added by the President appears that Mr. Adams was to consider the despatch as intended for his own eyes only, and was on no account to communicate it to anyone. Among the phrases struck out by the President was, I am told, one which stated that the United States would stand to England in the same relation which they had already stood in two previous periods of their history.

Mr. Seward's motives for provoking a war with England can be traced only to his view of his political position as candidate to succeed Mr. Lincoln. He is supposed to think that the anti-slavery cry is worn out, or at all events that he cannot hope to continue to be the undoubted head of the anti-slavery Party. He is thought to wish to set himself at the head of a new party—which should be the Union party par excellence, which should rally to itself the old Democratic Party of the North by advocating the maintenance of the Union at any price, and which should rally to itself the important Irish vote, by hostility to England. I imagine that the precipitation with which Mr. Seward was disposed to act arose from the hope of beginning the war with éclat, by an invasion of Canada before any preparation could be made for the defence of that province. All this sounds like madness—but although the danger, I hope, escaped for the moment, we have the same man and the same motives and the same recklessness—and have therefore the same necessity for being prepared for the worst. . . .

There is another possible danger peculiar to England to be apprehended when Congress meets. In the endeavour to rearrange the tariff with a view to producing revenue, the Reciprocity Treaty is very likely to be attacked.[30] The objections already made to it have turned very much upon the amount of revenue of which it deprives the Treasury. Of course the argument will tell with double force now. I have not heard the question mooted yet—and shall certainly not put people up to it by premature remonstrances. Still it is a subject of uneasiness to me.

I believe it is the present intention of the President to say very little of relations with foreign powers in his message to Congress. The idea seems to be to state that with the greater number of powers the relations are perfectly cordial, that with some others questions are pending, but that there is no ground for apprehension.

It has indeed become apparent that hardly a dollar of the great loans which are in contemplation will be raised if there is any apprehension in the money market of a war between the United States and England. This consideration, the concert between England and France, and the apparent ill-success of the blustering policy, have produced the present return to comparatively moderate language and conduct. If the effect of these causes be increased by manifest readiness on our side to render the *immediate* result of a declaration of war disastrous, or at all events not favourable to American boasters—we may go on safely, I trust, for some time. . . .

Mr. Seward wishes me to explain to you that his determination is to take no notice of any recognition of belligerent rights which is not formally announced to this government—or brought home to them by some act affecting themselves; that he is willing to close his eyes to Royal proclamations, speeches in Parliament, in everything not addressed directly to the United States. I mentioned in my despatch N. 282 of the 27th that Mr. Seward had held this language to M. Mercier and me when we saw him together.[31] He repeated it to me the day before yesterday. I do not however think it safe to act upon such verbal assurances.

Until Congress met to authorize military expenditures for the coming fight with the South, Lincoln felt constrained merely to prepare for war, but once the existence of a rebellion was acknowledged and funds had been appropriated, the executive branch of the government moved with maximum speed, with little recourse to legislative approval—a pattern that has persisted in American history.

The precise mode by which the United States has embarked upon military action defies clear definition. In theory, a declaration of war requires a vote of Congress, but in 1950 President Truman committed American troops to defend South Korea, as part of a larger United Nations response to the aggression of North Korea, without seeking the approval of Congress. In Vietnam, Congress chose to view the conflict as a rebellion by the communist Viet Cong against the legitimate government of the south, so it never sanctioned American involvement per se. Congress's reluctance to declare that in fact a state of war existed led many Americans to challenge the legality of America's participation.

In 1861 Lincoln was determined, at one and the same time, to procure congressional support for waging a war while avoiding any suggestion that the government in Washington was itself engaged in a civil war. On 2 July Lord Lyons waited anxiously to hear the actions taken by Congress in an emergency session.[32]

Congress meets day after tomorrow. The Members have not yet arrived in sufficient numbers to enable any opinion to be formed of the mood in which they will set to work. The general impression seems to be that the "compromise" party has just shown itself enough to stimulate the passions of the majority, and that violent war measures will be the result. The wish of the war party is to make the session as short as possible, in fact to hold a council of war rather than a legislative sitting. It is thought that popular applause will be sought by the Administration rather in asking for an exaggerated than a moderate amount of men and money. The Administration will probably be attacked for the dilatoriness of its military movements and notwithstanding the great weight which still attaches to General Scott's opinion, will perhaps be forced into undertaking an invasion of Virginia immediately.

The best hope for moderation towards foreign powers lies in the absolute necessity of raising a very large loan: the difficulty of getting it taken in this country: and the importance of bringing it forward both at home and abroad under favourable circumstances. The announcement of the departure of [British] troops and gunboats for Canada appears also to have a sedative effect so far at least as the Government and its organs in the press are concerned. But there are men in the Cabinet itself who are not unlikely to resort to extreme violence of language if not of conduct towards England the moment they fancy that to do so would improve their own political position.

Awkward questions are I am afraid accumulating.

The question of the recognition of belligerent rights will at once come up in a practical form, if an attempt is made to close the Southern ports by act of Congress— and to enforce the exclusion of foreign vessels from them by penalties under the municipal law of the States, instead of by a blockade regulated by the law of nations. I have some hope that the Government have been made aware of the extreme danger of attempting to subject British or French vessels to such a system—and that they will hardly attempt to put it in force, provided Congress so settles the law as to leave them the option of a regular blockade. As the law stands, it seems more than doubtful whether any ship can be condemned for breach of blockade. This unhappily makes it necessary that some legislation should take place on the subject; and the debate will be on very dangerous ground. . . .

The military inactivity on both sides is becoming ridiculous. The impatience of the people must, one would think, force leaders to attempt something soon. Until some real collision takes place, opinions on the comparative strengths, efficiencies, and spirit of the two armies can be little more than conjectural. Most of the officers of high reputation in the little regular Army of the U.S., being Southern men, have gone over with their states to the Southern side.

The U.S. military authorities have taken violent measures to keep down disunion at Baltimore. I do not doubt that the Consul will send ample details of the affair, which has happily not led to bloodshed.

The special session of Congress was short, lasting only two weeks, and the members apparently showed no signs of wanting to go beyond Lincoln's earlier blockade of the Southern ports. Their dilemma was to be able to close the majority of ports in the South while avoiding a formal proclamation that all harbors were closed—something the North could not manage in any case.[33]

> The determination in both Houses to put down debate has saved us from some violent attacks which were mediated. I only hope Congress will adhere to its present intention of adjourning at the end of the week. It is anything but a check on the government and certainly the government requires no spur to violence against foreign powers.
>
> I am very impatient to know what is the real extent of the successes which the United States troops have achieved in Western Virginia, and if it turn out to be really a considerable affair, to see what effect it will have upon the spirit of the South. But it is very possible that as further intelligence comes in, the whole importance of it will melt away, as has happened with a dozen or more great victories, which have been announced.

By 19 July both the North and the South were poised for a major military engagement, further complicating British calculations concerning their response to a blockade.[34]

> You will have been informed by my telegraphic despatches that the law enabling the President to close the Southern Ports has passed. I am afraid the chances are in favour of its being put into execution without delay. . . .
>
> I do not understand from the opinion of the law officers, or from the case of New Granada, whether or not the seizure of a British merchant vessel within the territorial waters of the United States and her confiscation under the new Act of Congress for having entered or attempted to enter a Southern Port, would be an act hostile to Great Britain. In the case of New Granada only seizures on the high seas are (I think) mentioned as inadmissable. The common cases here are likely to be seizures either within the undisputed territorial waters of the United States, or within the territorial waters claimed by both the United States and the (so-called) Confederate States.
>
> The great battle is now considered to be imminent every hour, hitherto it was always to be at the end of the week.[35] It seems hardly possible that they can avoid fighting now, unless the Southern men continue to retire. Even supposing these to be abstractedly the best tactics for the Southern Army, it seems difficult to carry them on much longer without completely discouraging an Army composed of half trained volunteers and commanded by almost untried generals.

On 20 July Lyons related a private conversation he had with Seward in which the secretary of state was anxious to assure him that the legislation pending in Congress was not intended to disrupt European commerce. The bill enabled the executive to designate a blockade where necessary, but its timing was discretionary. Seward portrayed himself as the moderate in the cabinet, trying to withstand pressure by the war hawks.[36]

> Mr. Seward proceeded to enlarge upon the havoc which a war between the United States and a European Power would make among merchant vessels.[37] He said that

all the energy and all the commerical activity of the American people will be converted into a frightful spirit of cupidity—and that commerce would be swept from the face of the ocean.

I let Mr. Seward see that it was not the success either of the United States Navy or of American privateers which I thought alarming, but I observed that it needed no argument to make me feel that a conflict between Great Britain and the United States would be a fearful calamity.

Mr. Seward proceeded, with some hesitation, and with an injunction to me to be secret, to speak of his own position. The impression he seemed to wish to convey to me was that he himself was at least always inclined to peaceful and moderate counsels; but that he could not afford to "lesson his means of usefulness" by going against the current of public feeling. He wished Foreign Ministers to take this into account in judging of his conduct. If, for instance, he had used strong language in his earlier communications to Foreign Powers, it was from the necessity of making them clearly understand the state of Public Feeling here and the results it might produce.

He concluded by asking me to tell frankly and confidentially what I thought about the bill closing the Ports.

I told him that I had not been ordered to make any communication to him, but that since he had asked me, I had no hesitation in saying that Her Majesty's Government did not consider that the United States had any right, according to the law of nations, to close by decrees any Ports which were not in their own possession.

I observed that this ought to be a most important consideration in determining the course of the Government—and I pointed out to Mr. Seward that a measure of this kind would at once raise the questions he wished to avoid with Foreign Powers, and raise them in the manner least favourable to their views. . . . I was not altogether unprepared for the change in Mr. Seward's tone. I had reason to believe that since the meeting of Congress, he had become aware that the violent party would not take him as a leader; that the party opposed to him in the Cabinet and in Congress were urging the immediate closing of the Ports, with the intention of making him the scapegoat if it involved them in trouble with European Powers.

I am far from thinking it desirable that any language likely to irritate this susceptible people should be used in Parliament or elsewhere. But what has lowered the tone of Mr. Seward and of the public has been seeing that their bluster has produced no effect—that it has not changed the determination of Her Majesty's Government, nor created dissension between England and France. Firmness appears to have a much more quieting effect than any amount of conciliation or concession.

Finally, the long-awaited Battle of Bull Run took place on 21 July. As attackers, the Northern troops assumed that their superior numbers and spirit would overwhelm the Southern defenders. Instead, after an initial success, they were routed by Confederate reinforcements and retreated to the relative safety of the Potomac River. Lincolin, realizing that under these circumstances, the capital lacked adequate defense, called his cabinet together and they anxiously debated whether to remain in Washington.[38]

It is too soon to form any speculations on the results of the defeat of yesterday. Neither General Scott nor the government had calculated on the possibility of anything like it, and as for the people of the North, they talked, at all events, as if the victory was already theirs. If the North have anything like the spirit to which they lay claim, they will rise with more resolution than ever to avenge the defeat. The test will be the conduct of the militia regiments. The three months term of service of most of them has just expired; some had gone home and the rest were on the point of following, leaving the war to be carried on by the remaining volunteers and the regular army. If the militia regiments remain, and others come up, we may conclude that the war-like spirit of the North is unbroken. If they do not, there may be a chance for peace. For this battle will not facilitate recruiting for the army and the volunteers, and unless the capitalists are urged by patriotism or squeezed by mob pressure, the loans will fail and the money to pay the volunteers will not be forthcoming.

I am myself inclined to hope that Congress may show some dignity and good sense. The general opinion is that it will be violent and childish—vote men and money on paper by millions—slay its Southern enemies by treason bills, and ruin them by confiscation acts—decree the immediate and unconditional abolition of slavery in the Southern states, the closing of the ports and what not.

The mood of the North had been boundlessly optimistic on the eve of Bull Run; almost a carnival atmosphere accompanied the advancing troops. But now that the battle was disastrously lost, the North realized for the first time the enormity of the task confronting it.

10

The *Trent* Affair

A period of relative diplomatic calm followed the fiasco at Bull Run, due partly
to the dismay felt by the Northern troops and partly to Seward's sober
reassessment of their state of readiness.[1]

> The proclamation closing the ports has not been issued, and may perhaps not be
> issued at all. On Tuesday last, two days after the defeat of Bull Run the majority
> of the Cabinet were for issuing it forthwith, but they were successfully resisted, and
> chiefly, I believe by Seward himself. Mr. Seward is, I hope and believe, in the same
> prudent and pacific mood which I discussed in my private letter of the 20th. His
> declining to produce his correspondence is a proof of this. It is not very common
> here to refuse any application of Congress for papers.
>
> I am rather surprised by the spirit, or rather want of spirit, shown by the North
> regarding their defeat. It would seem to argue that the enthusiasm and the unanimity
> were still more fictitious than I thought, or else that incessant boasting and adulation
> have really had an enervating effect on the American character.

At the beginning of August Seward took some pains to explain to Lord Lyons
how the government proposed to invoke a blockade.[2]

> Mr. Seward spoke to me again yesterday very confidentially respecting his own
> position with regard to the question of closing the ports. He began by saying that
> he was very sorry that he had not been yet able to send off the exposition of the views
> of this government which he had mentioned to me in the conversation of which I
> gave you an account in my private and confidential letter of the 20th of last month.
> He said that it had been ready a week ago, but that he would tell me confidentially
> that it was only the day before we were speaking that he had obtained leave from
> the President and the Cabinet to send it. It would now however go to Mr. Adams
> by the first mail. He said it was very difficult to make a Minister of Finance and a
> Minister of Police understand the bearing of measures upon the foreign relations
> of the country; that in fact each member of the Cabinet was overwhelmed by the
> business of is own department; and he really believed not more than one despatch
> from abroad had been read by any of his colleagues.
>
> Mr. Seward then sent for the draft of the despatch for Mr. Adams and proceeded
> to read me a bit here and there, and to talk about it. The beginning, he said, was
> an assertion of the *right* of the United States to close the ports if they pleased. This,
> he hinted, he had been obliged to put strongly, lest the despatch should have to be
> produced in Congress.

Next came a long demonstration that the Act was enabling, not imperative; and the passing it by the legislature did not imply that in their opinion the President ought to close them, but only that he ought to have the power to do so. After this was an assurance, rather vague and involved so far as I could judge from the bits he read to me that the interest of foreign powers and the bearing of the question on the foreign relations of the country should be duly weighed in considering whether the proclamation giving effect to the act should be issued. At the end came some *rodomontade* (or buncombe as we say here) about the policy of foreign governments in this question being founded upon the consideration of interest and of commerce, while that of the United States was based on high and eternal consideration of principle and the good of the human race; that the policy of foreign nations was regulated by the governments which ruled them, while that of the United States was directed by the unanimous and unchangeable will of the people and so on—with a wind-up on the horrors of war.

The despatch appeared to me to be really written as a defence to be produced to the American public, if the Administration should be attacked for not issuing the proclamation immediately. Its adoption by the Cabinet may be considered in some sort satisfactory as a proof that for the moment, the intention is not to execute the act closing the ports. It is also satisfactory that Mr. Seward should have taken this line. I had learned from another quarter that he had had the greatest difficulty in carrying his point in the Cabinet.

I begin to hope that he may be opening his eyes to the real dangers of a quarrel with England; although no doubt party politics at home immediately affecting himself are the immediate cause of the great change in him.

He seemed very apprehensive lest the pacific views he now professes transpire here, or on account of them come back to him from Europe. I think his object in speaking to me was that I should endeavor to prevent any strong language being used in Parliament; or any strong despatch being sent out here which would embarrass him in carrying out his peace policy.

I am, however, convinced myself that neither Mr. Seward nor anyone else here will maintain a policy which they think will make them unpopular. I am convinced also that quiet firmness is what succeeds both with the government and the people. I am inclined to think that in the manner of asserting our rights, Mr. Seward's position at this moment may well be taken into consideration. But I think it should be made apparent that neither cajoling nor bluster can in the least degree change our determination. If the United States readjust their finances and reorganise their army, or (which amounts to the same thing), if the people fancy that these things have been done, we shall very likely have a return to the old tone and the old conduct. I hope, however, that the impression we have now made will be strengthened by evident readiness on our part to make an attack upon any portion of our dominions disastrous at the outset to the assailants, and by a manifest firmness in exacting due respect to us. The one thing necessary is to disabuse both government and people of the delusion that they can carry their point with us by bluster and violence, and that we are more afraid of a war than they are.

On 2 August Lyons reported the first of many instances when American authorities ignored proper legal procedures in their summary arrest of foreigners in the name of military necessity.[3]

The Congress and people of the United States seem bent upon placing their own lives and liberties and with them of course those of foreigners in their country, without any reserve into the hands of the officers of the army. I report two cases of British subjects confined without lawful warrant today. The proceedings in the Court at New York seem to be monstrous. I am very anxious to know what I am to do about these and similar cases. Theoretically, I suppose the Americans have a right to put the whole country under martial law: if so, what practical means are left of saving foreigners from arbitrary ill treatment?

Three days later Lyons was pleased to report that the two British subjects mentioned in his last letter were released from unlawful imprisonment.[4]

I persuaded Mr. Seward last night to set Quillan and Fitzpatrick free without any discussion on the merits of the question. There were certainly reasonable grounds of suspicion in both cases. I suppose even if the suspension of the *habeas corpus* at Baltimore be admitted to be legal—the refusal of military authorities to obey the writ at New York, where I believe there has been no pretence of suspending it, was a mere stretch of power. But, as it is a stretch of power supported by the judge who granted the writ, by Congress, by the government, and more than all by the mob, the men might have remained in prison until they died or were released by us *vi et armis*, if I had gone on with legal proceedings or had made a formal diplomatic demand for their liberation. . . .
   There seems to be no great change in public feeling—though the effect of the defeat at Bull Run diminishes as time passes and as the Confederates remain quiet. Some amusement has been caused by a Joint Resolution of both Houses of Congress commending the army [for] "the imperishable honour of the example" of the troops who ran away from Bull Run. It is so characteristic a document that I will attach it to the end of this letter.

Financing the war meant imposing new taxes as well as persuading bankers to issue revenue bonds, both unwelcome necessities following the Union's resounding defeat at Bull Run. Lyons hoped that reestablishing peace would be more appealing than either of these alternatives.
   Meanwhile, French interest in the Southern cause annoyed the government in Washington while at the same time reminding it that Europe was more than casually interested in the outcome of the burgeoning conflict.[5]

The government is concentrating as large a force as it can of troops here, but it will be some time before these levies will be even as good as those which were at Bull Run. Congress has raised the pay of privates from eleven to thirteen dollars a month . . . still recruits do not come in as fast as they are wanted. The Secretary of the Treasury is at New York trying to get his loans taken.[6] Much will depend upon his success. Much also upon the spirit in which the introduction of direct taxation and excise duties is taken by the people, when the pressure of the taxes is actually felt. A peace party is showing itself, but, as yet, timidly.
   The present discouragement has been favourable to peace with European powers; but we must be prepared for the old cry and the old provocations if the North gain a victory and succeed in raising money.
   I believe the people here are far from pleased with Prince Napoleon having gone

to the Southern headquarters, although they wisely manifested no reluctance to aid him in doing so.[7] He told me the Southern troops were still worse clothed than those on this side, and that their material "de guerre" was inferior. The officers with him, however, seemed to think that they would rather command the Southern soldiers. The Prince's visit has been useful in one respect, as from his dining with me and a variety of other circumstances, it has increased the persuasion of the union between England and France, on the American question.

Mr. Faulkner, the United States Minister in Paris, came here on his return from Europe to settle his accounts with the State Department.[8] He was arrested yesterday and is in prison on a charge, I suppose, of treason. General McClellan is, or pretends to be, in fear of an attack upon Washington;[9] and demands in consequence a larger concentration of forces, increased powers, and greater independence of General Scott. It seems however to be probable that we shall not have any serious military engagement until October, and that then the advance will be made by the United States.

By 16 August Lyons was made aware of a crisis for which he would ultimately be considered responsible. It involved in the first instance Robert Bunch, the British consul at Charleston, South Carolina, and secondly Robert Mure, a British subject by birth but who had long since acquired American citizenship by virtue of living for many years in Charleston, where he was an established merchant.

Mure was in the habit of making an annual business trip to London, but because he was a Southerner and subject to conditions arising from the declared state of belligerency, he asked Consul Bunch for a document validating his purely mercantile mission in order to protect himself against arrest by any Northern naval commander.

Bunch agreed to provide this but also seized the opportunity to entrust his diplomatic pouch to Mure's care, since mail service had been discontinued by the unofficial blockade against Southern ports. This commission was dubious enough without Mure also putting into the pouch a number of private letters from South Carolinians wishing to communicate directly with people in England.

Mure got as far as New York before he was arrested and deprived of the sealed diplomatic bag. On orders from Seward, it remained unopened but was sent by a special messenger to London. Once it had reached the Foreign Office and the official dispatches had been removed, Seward stipulated that the remaining private letters be turned over to the United States. However, the British refused to comply with this request on the grounds that their consul was justified in using Mure's services as a messenger since the United States was no longer providing mail service between the Southern states and England.

This episode occupied much of Lyons's time during the next several weeks, while other wartime pressures subsided temporarily.[10]

A brilliant victory by United States troops in Missouri near Springfield is announced, in which their General Lyon was killed.[11] But things do not seem to be going on well in that quarter, for the victorious army appears to have been in full retreat immediately after the battle, and considerable apprehensions to have been entertained for its safety. General Fremont too has found it necessary to put St. Louis, the principal town in Missouri, under martial law.[12] Not a word is to be believed of the accounts, official or otherwise, given by either party of the encounters which take place in Missouri, or indeed elsewhere. One can only judge of what really occurred by the relative positions of the two armies after the battles.

The New York bankers appear disposed to drive a hard bargain with the Secretary of the Treasury about the loan. The money question is becoming serious; the import duties produce next to nothing; the new taxes will not bring anything until February if so soon; and we are threatened with a paper money in the form of Treasury notes worth five dollars.

Mr. Seward told me confidentially this morning that there was no question now of issuing the proclamation closing the ports. He had no doubt heard of the increase of Admiral Milne's squadron.[13] A little success in raising money and a small turn of fortune in the field, may render a further sedative of the same kind desirable. . . .

You will see that Mr. Seward has had a messenger with despatches from Mr. Bunch to you arrested. In speaking to me on the subject this morning, he did not complain of Mr. Bunch; a month ago he would have taken away his exequatur. Mr. Seward said, that it would be very easy, if a Consul chose to put it in the bag addressed to you, and let the messenger open the bag when he arrives in England, and separate what was really for you from the treasonable correspondence. He should therefore wish the bag to be placed in your hands exactly as it had been sent off. I resented the idea that Mr. Bunch or any of our consuls would play such foolish and improper tricks, but said no more as he told me he should explain the whole matter to you through Mr. Adams. I made no endeavour to get him to give me the bag. I did not wish to afford the smallest motive towards these people including me in their small exposés.

I do not think the seal of the bag will be tampered with.

I doubt very much whether any grounds exist for the charge against the messenger, Mr. Robert Mure.

Among the topics dealt with in his letter of 23 August, his inability to stifle the publicity surrounding the Mure episode seemed to trouble Lyons most. On a more theoretical plane, he worried about the dangers inherent in the government's wanton suspension of personal liberties.[14]

The success about the loan at New York, small as it was, and smaller and smaller as it appears to be on examination, has raised the spirits of the war party. I am very sorry to observe that one of the first manifestations of this has been a return to violent language against England in the press, and to exhortations to the government to put in force the act for closing the ports. Mr. Seward is, I believe, at present, resolved not to close the ports. But we know the effect of a public cry in this country, and I cannot feel at ease. At present, however, great efforts appear to be made to render the blockade more effective. Gun boats and small steamers are being rapidly fitted out for this purpose; and it is announced that preparations are being made to sink hulks full of stones at the entrance of the small inlets on the coast. Activity in this respect is stimulated by the outcry in the papers against the ease with which the Southern privateers come out of Southern ports and carry their prizes back into them.

A strong blockading squadron is in fact equally necessary whether the ports are closed by blockades under the law of nations, or by a customs regulation under an act of Congress.

No military events of importance have occurred, to our knowledge, during the last few days. Small skirmishes are reported in all directions, both sides claim the victory, and no influence on the result of the war is produced. General Banks has retired from Harper's Ferry and come nearer to Washington.[15] Alarm is again expressed for the safety of the place, intentionally exaggerated no doubt to assist recruiting. A very inconvenient amount of discontent, which has led in some cases to open mutiny, exists among the volunteers. General McClellan has put down the mutineers with a strong hand, by the help of the regulars. One cannot yet judge whether these are merely the ordinary difficulties in reducing volunteers to discipline, or a spirit of disgust which will diminish the numbers and efficiency of the army. The present plan seems to be to concentrate as large a force as possible at Washington. It is generally thought that no advance is likely to be made, (at all events by the United States army) until the end of next month.

The people appear to me to be very recklessly applauding the suspension, without law, of all their liberties. It was found impossible to pass the resolution sanctioning the suspension of the *habeas corpus* act by the President through Congress, nevertheless the government sends anyone it pleases to a fortress, and orders the commandant to decline to make any return to a writ of *habeas corpus*. A passport system has been established by an unsigned notice from the State Department merely inserted in the ordinary newspapers. Last night the New York papers were stopped at the post offices, and the more obnoxious to the government kept back altogether.

This practical abrogation of legal securities may lead to serious difficulties concerning British subjects. The two (Quillan and Fitzpatrick) who were in prison were released on a private application from me to Mr. Seward. But anyone who has an enemy to inform against him is in danger.

This affair of Mr. Bunch's messenger, Robert Mure, is a disagreeable one. The letters found on him, which have been published in the newspapers so improperly, are not more objectionable than are, I suppose, all letters written in the South now.

But they contain plenty of "treason" on the hypothesis that the whole population of the South are simply ordinary rebels. It was from a fear of something of this kind happening that I gave the Consuls such stringent instructions not to forward letters. There is clearly some foundation for the account given in the published correspondence (which I send officially) of a conversation with "Mr. B." or "*Mr. Bunch*"—though the principal assertion, that of our having taken the first step to recognise the South by proposing a Commercial Treaty, is so completely false. It is true that I, like everybody else, made the remark that after the Battle of Bull Run it would be impossible to deny that the Southern States were *de facto* belligerents, but I am pretty sure that I did not write it to Mr. Bunch. It may be a long time before I receive any explanation from Mr. Bunch, for the communication with the South is rendered more difficult by the President's proclamation enjoining non-intercourse.

As it is quite certain that no application from me in favour of Robert Mure would be attended to, and as he is a naturalized American Citizen, I have thought it better for him, and more prudent altogether, to let the matter rest, until I have orders from you about it.

At the end of August Lyons repeated his concern about the widespread repression of civil rights and the implications of press censorship.[16]

The arrests continue and indeed increase very much in number. The Mayor of this town, and two ladies well known in society here are among the latest victims.

To advocate peace is now interpreted to be "giving aid and comfort" to the enemy—and the principal opposition newspapers have been accordingly stopped at the Post Offices, or suppressed by the government or the mob. I don't think however that the men in power here have the nerves, the talent, or the standing in the country, to set up a real reign of terror. What is more to be apprehended is that it may become necessary to their personal safety to keep up an excitement which will prevent their being called to account for their transgressions of the law and the constitution. This may lead them to the desperate measure of a foreign war. It will be a critical moment, when the intelligence arrives that there is no hope of raising money in Europe, or when the money is got in, if the loan be taken there. This hope of getting money from us has had a great deal to do with the comparatively moderate tone of the government and the press. As the hope diminishes, the press gets violent again.

Skirmishes of varying magnitude occurred regularly along the border between North and South, but reports of them could not be trusted. Furthermore, the blockade was far from total, since only key ports were selected in an effort to cripple the Confederate economy.[17]

I have to thank you for your Private Letters of the 16th and 17th which I have just received. The arrival this morning of the Messenger from the Foreign Office, and of the French Consul from South Carolina, with the accumulated correspondence of more than a month from the South, has given me so much to read, that no time remains to write to you officially on the state of Affairs. Not indeed that I should have much to write beyond what I have already made known to you by my private letters of the 23rd and 27th. I send you with this a newspaper account of the engagement in western Virginia. As usual the United States seem to have had the worst of it, and as usual the defeated party declares that it killed many more men than it lost. There have been some insignificant skirmishes on the Virginia side of the river near this place.

I am afraid there is a tendency on the part of the officers of Customs and others at the Ports to interfere vexatiously with our shipping, and the State Department, if it have the will, does not seem to have the firmness necessary to check it. I send reports of some of the cases officially. In two, in which the Secretary of State informed me officially that he had ordered the vessels to be released, he refused to enforce this order when it was disputed by the Law officers on the spot.

I have heard nothing from any good source to make me believe that there is any intention to allow our ships to go to New Orleans in ballast for cotton, or any intention whatever to relax the Blockade, except upon compulsion. On the contrary everything is being done to make the Blockade effective. It will never be really effective. Mr. Bunch's Despatches give a striking picture of its deficiency at present in his District. I suppose the best information will be that given to Sir Alexander Milne by the Captains of his Cruisers. Some of the Papers are crying out vehemently for the Proclamation closing the Ports.

In early September the North was still building defenses around Washington, fortifying the capital against attack, real or imagined. A Peace party also emerged and threatened to undermine Northern steadfastness, especially among the volunteers who tended to defect when no excitement was brewing.[18]

The enemy have brought up so large a force close to the United States entrenchments on the banks of the Potomac opposite this town, that General McClellan is afraid they mean to attack him immediately. He has in consequence sent all the troops he can dispose of over the river, and an engagement is considered to be imminent. Hitherto however I cannot say that either side has shown much wish to fight again since "Bull Run." . . . A victory on the Union side is very much wanted in order to put down the Peace Party which is showing itself in some force particularly in the State of New York, to induce the Bankers to take the second fifty millions of the loan next month, and to give General McClellan and the higher officers sufficient authority and popularity to check the want of Discipline and the Mutinous spirit which prevail among the raw volunteers which compose their Army. I don't think McClellan has under his orders more than two thousand of the old Regular Troops; the men who have enlisted for the Regular Army since the War differ very little from the Volunteers. At the breaking out of the war the United States had about seventeen thousand Regulars. A considerable number of these surrendered in Texas, others are still on the remote frontiers, it is surprising that greater efforts have not been made to concentrate them.

A victory would do much to set things straight; but some of the illusions with which the war was begun are gone forever. The appearance of unanimity in the North has completely vanished. It is deemed necessary to resort to actual violence to keep the Peace Party in check. Arbitrary Arrests—suppression of Newspapers—dispersion of Public Meetings—are things of everyday occurrence. It is now plain that the volunteers will serve only for high pay, and that even with the immense pay offered, it is difficult to get them, difficult to keep them when got, and most difficult to train them and maintain discipline among them.

When British merchant ships and crews were caught running the blockade of Southern ports, arrests were made and cargos confiscated, but Lyons was loathe to intervene in these cases when they came before Northern Prize Courts.[19]

I hope you will not think I am too tame about the arrests of British Subjects and such matters. The natural temptation to a man placed as I am is to write what the public regard as spirited Notes. My own view however at the present moment is that so long as I can get redress in the individual cases, it is better for me to be as quiet as I can here—and not to embarrass you by getting into a dispute. I therefore avoid raising questions of principle, and keep clear of strong language so as to leave all the cases for your consideration, unhampered by declarations made by me to this Government.

I am disinclined to ask for the release of Vessels captured by the Blockading Squadrons. Some of the captures appear quite unjustifiable; but my applications are unsuccessful, and I suppose the release of a Vessel without her being sent before a Prize Court can be asked only as a favour, not a right.

In the spring of 1861, at the outbreak of the Civil War, many Southerners were certain that the European powers, especially England, would support the Confederacy so as to keep their textile mills supplied with raw cotton. In order to put further pressure on the European countries to make this decision, the South imposed its own embargo on the export of cotton, reinforcing the blockade by the North. The British, however, refused to play this game because there was currently a surplus of raw cotton in Europe, and shortages were not forecast for at least a year. Lord Lyons consequently dismissed this threat of a cotton famine in his letter of 4 October.[20]

> Mr. Mercier observed that he supposed that the need of cotton in England was still more pressing than it was in France; and that Her Majesty's Government must be very seriously occupied with devising means to obtain a supply from this Country.
>
> I told him that I had no other information concerning the deficiency of Cotton in England than that which I derived from the Newspapers and from the other Public Sources;—that I had been unable to come to any definite conclusion as to the quantity in hand, or the exact time at which a lack of it would be seriously felt. I did not however perceive that any great alarm was yet felt in England. On the contrary men's thoughts appeared to be turned hopefully towards new sources of supply; and there seemed to be a very general opinion that if the momentary inconvenience was not very great indeed, it might be wise to endure it now, in order to be free in future from the danger of depending so very much upon one country for an article of the greatest importance to us. At all events I did not think that either the Government or the People in England were prepared for such extreme measures as recognizing the Confederates and breaking up the Blockade.
>
> On several points I agree with M. Mercier. I think disputes on small questions quite as likely to lead to a quarrel as the adoption of a determined policy with regard to recognizing the South. I do not think that either through a port in the hands of Northern Troops, or through a port from which the Blockade was temporarily withdrawn, the Southern Government would allow cotton to be exported. I have been so long without good information from the South that I do not speak as confidently as M. Mercier did. Still I doubt very much whether the Southern Government is really falling to pieces—or the people sick of the contest. I do not believe that there is anything like a Union Party left in the Southern States. I take perhaps a more hopeful view than Mr. Mercier does of the Military Prospects of the North, but I do not expect any considerable success this winter.
>
> On the other hand I think the time is far distant when the intervention of England and France in the quarrel would be welcomed, or, unless under compulsion, tolerated by the American people. If it becomes a necessity for those Powers to recognize the South and break the Blockade, they might perhaps avoid a conflict by such a display of Naval Force as would be irresistable, and if the necessity should arise, the measures would of course be taken promptly and energetically, and above all with no symptom of hesitation. But in my opinion the South has not gone far enough in establishing its independence to render a recognition of it either proper or desirable for the European Powers. Nor do I think that such a recognition would by any means put an end to the war, unless of course it were converted into a defensive (if not also an offensive) Alliance with the South.

Ten days later the prevailing military stalemate continued, causing Lord Lyons to speculate when and where the next confrontation would take place. He noted objectively that neither side had yet been severely tested.[21]

> I am inclined to think that Mr. Seward is really again led away by his sanguine disposition, and has again fixed a definite period (it seems to be two months this

time) for the restoration of the Union, or at least for the subjugation of the South.

It is true that the next two months will try Southern Resolution hard. The Blockade by land and sea has not only deprived the Planters of common luxuries (tea and coffee for instance) for themselves—but puts them to great straights about providing necessaries such as pork, winter clothing and above all shoes for the Negroes. The expeditions against various points of the Coast, if they have no more serious results, will keep the people in constant alarm. There is no doubt that the North will make great efforts to seize a cotton Port. It is thought that they might collect troops on Ship Island, and set out thence to capture New Orleans itself, with a very fair chance of success. If the spirit of the South be anything like what it is represented, it will take a great deal more than this to bring it to submission. But that Spirit has hardly yet been tried.

The two great Armies near this place seem equally unwilling to fight. The Northern Army continues to advance very slowly over the ground, which the Southern Army abandons. The movements are just like those which preceded Bull Run. Accident or pressure from the North, where people are again getting impatient, may however bring on a battle.

On 28 October Lyons wrote particularly eloquently about the possibility that if England and France acted in concert, they might convince the North and South to reunite. Conversely, if they were forced to take sides, their intervention would deepen the division between the two combatants.[22]

To speak coolly on a very serious subject. If we were convinced that our recognition of the South would be met by a Declaration of War on the part of the United States— the breaking up of the Blockade by our Fleets, would follow more properly and legitimately, as an operation in War; than as an act of violence performed in peace, to obtain cotton. I discuss the eventuality (as the Americans say) because France seems to be disposed to bring it under consideration; otherwise I should have shrunk from alluding to it.

To return to my own proper Province. I very nearly despair of getting on at all with this Government unless Great Britain and France come to some distinct understanding with it, on the nature and extent of the communication which they mean to hold with the *de facto* Government of the Confederate States. In vindication of this position, he [Seward] has already determined to revoke Mr. Bunch's Exequatur; if he is in his present mood, he will be glad to find a pretext for performing other half violent acts of the same kind.[23] If he finds these acts popular, and not too dangerous as far as England is concerned, he will probably play out the play, and send me my passports, on the plea of some Consul having communicated with the Southern Government under instructions from me. I have hitherto by taking the greatest pains to avoid annoying this Government on the matter—by extreme caution—and minute attention to small details, contrived to keep myself personally out of the scrape. But this cannot go on forever. And it has besides one great disadvantage. Anything conciliatory which I do, any concession which I make, serves as an encouragement to the people here to advance new pretensions. It is practically out of the question that we should hold some sort of intercourse with the *de facto* powers in the South. For instance there are cases of compulsory enlistment of British Subjects; of British goods on board vessels captured by Southern Privateers—and other similar matters occurring every day. Am I to refuse to transmit applications from British Subjects on such matters to the Consuls in the South? Are the Consuls to refrain from acting upon them?

It is now more than ten months since South Carolina left the Union. State after State has followed the example. The United States have made no apparent progress whatever in restoring their Authority over any State after it has seceded. This Government has ceased to exercise the smallest power of influence in any part of the New Confederation—on the other hand there is a *de facto* Government in that Confederation which is obeyed without question and exercises all the functions of Government with the most perfect regularity. On what pretext can the Government which is without the means of protecting our Subjects debar us from even the most necessary—and most informal unofficial communication with the only power to which our numerous Countrymen can look for protection and redress of grievances? Surely the United States ought to be content with our abstaining from official political recognition of the Confederate Government—and not be captious and punctillious about our carrying on unofficial communication in cases of necessity.

I mention this because it is a matter which will keep us perpetually in hot water with the Government here unless it can be settled once for all—and which is as likely as any other to lead the men in power to insolent if not hostile treatment of us.

I think the best mode of settling it would be that England and France should come to a regular agreement about it, and should announce their intentions to the Government of the United States simultaneously. I think it would be much better that this should be done by an identical or even by a collective statement. This form would no doubt add to the annoyance which the step would occasion here. But I have little or no hope of keeping the peace except by unmistakable demonstrations of the Union and the determination of England and France.

Soon after writing the above, the most serious crisis yet to plague Anglo-American relations since the beginning of the Civil War took place at sea on 8 November 1861. Charles Wilkes, captain of the United States warship *San Jacinto*, intercepted and then boarded the British mail carrier *Trent* as it steamed away from Cuba toward England. Among its passengers were James M. Mason and John Slidell, both former southern United States senators but now Confederate envoys to London and Paris respectively. Wilkes arrested the two men and took them to Boston but allowed the *Trent* to proceed. News of this incident reached Lord Lyons by 17 November, but he took no action pending instructions from London.

Quite naturally, the British assumed that Wilkes had acted under instructions from the United States Navy, but Secretary of State Seward revealed that Wilkes had acted "without instructions, and even without the knowledge of the Government," a fact which in no way deterred Americans from regarding Wilkes as a great hero, however.[24] Seward meanwhile prepared the ground for an American retreat, and Lincoln omitted any allusion to the affair in his annual message to Congress. On 22 November Lord Lyons outlined his own reaction to the episode before hearing from Lord John Russell.[25]

I have been all along expecting some such blow as the capture on board the "Trent." . . . Turn out how it may, it must I fear produce an effect on public opinion in both countries which will go far to disconcert all my peaceful plans and hopes. I aim to win out with the never ending labour of keeping things smooth, under the discouragement of the doubt whether by so doing I am not after all only leading these people to believe that they may go all lengths with us with impunity, that I am sometimes half tempted to wish that the worst may have come already. However, I do not allow this feeling to influence my conduct—and I have done nothing which can in the least interfere with any course which you may take concerning the affair of the "Trent".

If the effect on the people and Government of this Country were the only thing to be considered it would be a case for an extreme measure one way or the other. If the capture be unjustifiable, we should ask for the immediate release of the prisoners, promptly, imperatively, with a determination to act at once if the demand were refused. If on the other hand the capture be justified, we should at once say so, and declare that we have no complaint to make on the subject. Even so, we should not escape the evil of encouraging the Americans in their belief that we shall bear anything from them. For they have made up their minds that they have insulted us, although the fear of the consequences prevents their giving vent to their exultation. They would not consider it so manifest a proof of yielding on our part if we at once declared that we had nothing to complain of, as if we did complain without obtaining full reparation. Of course, however, I am well aware that public opinion in this country is not the only thing to be thought of on this question. While maintaining entire reserve on the question itself, I have avoided any demonstration of ill humour. My object has been on the one hand not to prevent the government's being led by its present apprehensions to take some conciliatory step; and on the other hand not to put Her Majesty's Government or myself in an awkward position if it should after all appear that we should not be right to make the affair a serious ground of complaint.

I have received this morning the instructions and full power to conclude the Mexican Convention.[26] I suppose that the proposal of the United States would hardly seem serious if it were any longer delayed. I think therefore that I had better not allow the affairs of the "Trent" to stand in the way of my joining my colleagues in making the proposal. But if they are willing, I shall make the proposal "collectively" with them—and at all events give it as little the air of a separate negotiation on my part as circumstances will allow.

Congress will meet on the 2nd next Monday week, which will not diminish the difficulty of managing matters here. It is supposed that General McClellan will be obliged to attempt some forward movement in order that he and the Government may be able to meet the fiery legislators. They hoped the Beaufort affair would have been sufficient, but like they all do, the effect is so much weakened, first by the preposterous boastings beforehand, and secondly by the fabulous accounts of the success first given, that something new must if possible be provided.[27] The troops appear not to be stationed at Beaufort itself, but to be entrenching themselves on an Island in the Harbour. The successes in Kentucky and Eastern Tennessee seem to have melted away completely, as further intelligence has come in.

The finances are kept in an apparently prosperous condition by postponing all but the most pressing payments. In this matter the New York Banks are not pressed to pay up the sum they have taken on the loan. The people are so enamoured of their last brilliant discovery in political economy that it was seriously intended to raise the Morrill Tariff in order that no money might go out of the Country, and nothing be imported but "gold and silver to carry on the war with."[28] The Cabinet has now however, I understand, determined to recommend that the Morrill Tariff be not touched. One cannot help hoping that some may be reasonable enough to suggest the idea of a Revenue Tariff.

General McClellan's own plan is said to be to gain a great victory, and then, with or without the sanction of Congress and the President, to propose the most favourable terms to the South if it will only come back. It is a curious sign of the confusion into which things are falling that such a plan is coolly discussed; I mean that part of it which consists in the General's acting without the consent of the President and Congress.

The general rejoicing following the capture of Mason and Slidell subsided once it was recognized that the British might retaliate in some way.[29]

I hope that this evening or tomorrow morning my French and Spanish Colleagues and I shall settle the form in which to invite the United States Government to adhere to the Mexican Treaty. Mr. Mercier spoke on the subject to Mr. Seward yesterday. Mr. Seward said that he was indifferent as to the form in which the proposal was made, but he did not give any hint of what the answer would be. I have not been able to see M. Tassara, the Spanish Minister, yet. I still incline myself to a collective note.

The people here are certainly frightened about the capture onboard the "Trent". The New York Money Market gives signs of this. Another indication is the moderation of the newspapers, which is (for them) wonderful. They have put in more correct accounts of my language (or rather silence); I rather suspect that this must have been done on a hint from Mr. Seward. As a general rule I abstain from noticing anything the newspapers say about me—on this occasion in particular contradiction from me would have been almost as dangerous as affirmation; so I left the assertions to take their chance.

The Consuls in the South do not behave well about forwarding private letters. There is a fresh case which I report today. Mr. Seward has, I think, behaved properly about it. I am afraid I shall be obliged to ask you to support me by some severe act, if my last instruction is not obeyed. I have not had a ship to send South before. I shall now however be able to send the "Racer" to Charleston as soon as I can get my despatches ready. The "Nimble" which has just arrived at New York, will remain there to enable me to communicate with the Admiral if necessary.

I write, as indeed I act, as if our relations with this Government were to be unchanged. Let the affair of the capture onboard the "Trent" turn out how it may, I am not confident that I shall long be able to do so.

A mood of expectancy always ushered in the opening of Congress in November, and 1861 was no exception. There still had been no official response by Britain to the *Trent* Affair, and the emancipation question loomed menacingly before the Cabinet.[30]

It is only three days to the meeting of Congress. I suppose the Presidential Message will be sent in on the first day, and that I shall be able to send you a copy by my Messenger of the 3rd of next month. I am very anxious to see what he will say of the capture onboard the "Trent". The wisest course would no doubt be not to mention it at all—so as to leave himself free to act when the views of her Majesty's Government are known.[31] I shall very probably see Mr. Seward tomorrow, but I shall not allude to the capture unless he does, and I shall at all events express no opinion about it. The Public here have with their usual silliness been making heroes of Captain Wilkes, and even of Lieutenant Fairfax[32] the officer who was sent to board the "Trent", giving them dinners, serenades, and so forth. But on the whole both press and public have been (for them) moderate in tone—and the principle result hitherto has been a tremendous outpouring of learning on international law. Nevertheless, turn out how it may for the moment, it is a serious and unfortunate affair.

I am a good deal puzzled as to how I ought to answer your question whether I consider the Blockade effective. It is certainly by no means strict or vigorous along the immense extent of coast to which it is supposed to apply. I suppose the ships which run it successfully both in and out are more numerous than those which are intercepted. On the other hand it is very far from being a mere Paper Blockade. A great many vessels are captured; it is a most serious interruption to trade; and if it were as ineffective as Mr. Jefferson Davis says in his Message, he would not be so very anxious to get rid of it.

The Consuls in the South are crying out for ships again. This is the solution for every difficulty in the Consular minds, as my experience in the Mediterranean taught me long ago,—though what the ships were to do, except fire a salute in honour of the Consul, I could never discover. I had some trouble, as you may perhaps recollect, in checking the Consular ardour to send ships up the Potomac to my own relief last Spring. Sir Alexander Milne objects strongly to sending ships to the Southern ports, unless with a specific object and definite instructions, and I think he is quite right. It is quite true that a town may be bombarded someday by the United States Forces—that British subjects may have their throats cut by the Negroes in a servile insurrection; or be tarred and feathered by a vigilance Committee. But we cannot keep a squadron at every point to protect them—and I do not know what points are particularly threatened.

I shall do all in my power to keep things smooth, until I receive your orders about the "Trent" affair. This can in any event do no harm. There is a story here that in a recent hypothetical case, the Law officers of the Crown decided in favour of the right of the United States to take Mason and Slidell out of a British Ship or Postal Packet. I do not know whether Mr. Adams has written this to Mr. Seward; but I am inclined to think that the Government believes it to be true.

The signs of the times are that the party question in Congress will be "immediate emancipation at all risks." Mr. Sumner has sounded the abolition trumpet loudly already. It will be a difficult point for Seward. He and the President are supposed to be against any measure rendering reconciliation with the South impossible, and bringing on the immediate issue of subjugation or independence. On the other hand the violent Party are beginning to fear that it will be independence, unless a servile insurrection or the fear of one is brought to bear upon the Southern Masters.

On 6 December Lord Lyons repeated his concern that Seward's violent language and his habit of publishing official dispatches no doubt had the effect of currying public favor, but his bombast also exacerbated already tense situations like that of the *Trent* Affair.[33]

I suppose it has been considered by this Government necessary to cover the poor and beggarly account it has had to present to Congress of its progress towards subjugating the South by a return to braggadocio about the European Powers. I believe the vanity of authorship has something to do with Mr. Seward's publishing his own interminable despatches. But the fact, taken in connexion with the tone of the Foreign Paragraphs of the Message (which are believed to have been written by him) certainly suggest that for the moment, he is going on his first and worst manner. To any one who has time to read through the series of despatches to France and

England, the remarkable feature is the curious manner in which, under cover of a cloud of words, he retreats from all the strong pretensions he has put forward whenever they are seriously resisted or paid no attention to. He begins by ordering Mr. Adams to suspend diplomatic relations, if you see the Southern Commissioners unofficially. He declares that the United States will never tolerate for a moment a recognition by any power of the Belligerent Rights of the South. Then he says that he does not care for the fact of recognition of the Belligerent's Rights, provided it be not officially announced to the United States themselves; then he accepts an official announcement and so on. The worst of it is, that he always tries violence in language first; and then runs the risk of pledging himself and the Nation to violent courses if he be taken at once at his word. I have not seen him since the news of the capture of Mason and Slidell. I have not taken any pains to keep out of his way but there has been nothing to render it necessary for me to go to see him on business. I am thoroughly convinced that I could only make the matter worse by talking to him about it. . . .

Mr. Galt, the Canadian Finance Minister, had rather an interesting conversation with President Lincoln the night before last.[34] The President abjured for himself and the Cabinet all thoughts of aggression upon Canada. He said that he had himself been opposed to Mr. Seward's Circular for putting the Coasts into a state of defense, but had been overruled. On being asked about what the recommendation to make fortifications and depots of arms on the Great Lakes meant, he only said, "We must say something to satisfy the People." About the Slidell and Mason affair he said, "Oh, that'll be got along with". He volunteered to observe that if he could not in a reasonable time get possession of Virginia, Kentucky, and Missouri and keep Maryland, he should tell the American People to give up the contest for it would be "too big" for them.

The impression made upon Mr. Galt was that Mr. Lincoln himself was honest and sincere in what he said, but that he was very far from being Master of his Cabinet.

Lord John Russell's long-awaited instructions finally arrived in two private letters to Lord Lyons dated 30 November and 1 December. They stated unequivocally that he was to demand the release of Mason and Slidell; that they were to be placed under British jurisdiction; and that an official apology was expected. If these terms were not met, Lyons was directed to break off diplomatic relations and leave the United States. On 19 December Lyons reported the effecct that these instructions had upon Seward and the Cabinet.[35]

Before I left Mr. Seward he said that there was one question which he would put to me "informally", but which it was most important that I should answer. Was any time fixed by my instructions within which the U.S. Government must reply. I told him that I did not like to answer the question; that what of all things I wished to avoid was the slightest appearance of a menace. He said I need not fear that—he only asked me to tell him privately and confidentially. I said that on that understanding I would say that the term was seven days. He then said that much time would be lost if I did not let him have a copy of your despatch "unofficially and informally"— that so much depended upon the wording of it—that it was impossible to come to a decision without reading it. I told him that the only difficulty I had about giving it to him at once officially, was that the seven days would immediately begin to run. He said that was very true, but I might let him have it on the understanding that no one but himself and the President should know that I had done so. I was very glad to let him have it on these terms. It will give time for the packet (which is indeed already due) to arrive in time with M. Thouvenel's[36] despatch to M. Mercier and in the meantime give Mr. Seward (who is now on the peace side of the Cabinet) time to work with the President before the affair comes before the Cabinet itself. I sent the despatch to him in an envelope marked Private and Confidential. Almost immediately afterwards, he came here. He told me that he was pleased to find that the despatch was courteous and friendly, not dictatorial nor menacing. There was, however, one question more which he must ask me—without an answer to which he could not act—but at the same time he must have the answer only in strict confidence between himself and me. Suppose I had told him in confidence that I was to wait seven days for an answer on the subject of the redress we required. Supposing he was within the seven days to send me a refusal or a proposal to discuss the question. I told him that my instructions were positive and left me no discretion. If the answer was not satisfactory and particularly if it did not include the immediate surrender of the Prisoners I could not accept it.

I was not sorry to tell him this in the way I did. I avoided all menace which could be an obstacle to the U.S. yielding, while I did the only thing which will make them yield if they ever do: let them know that we were really in earnest.

I don't think it likely they will give in—but I do not think it impossible they may do so—particularly if the next news from England brings note of warlike preparation and determination on the part of the Government and the People.

Mr. Seward has taken up all my time, which is my excuse for this scrawl. I shall be able to write again tomorrow.

As tensions mounted concerning Seward's reply to the British ultimatum, Lyons prepared for a possible rupture between the two countries. On 23 December he wrote:[37]

I have followed, I think to the letter in my communications with Mr. Seward on the "Trent" affair, the plan laid down in your private letter of the 1st. The Packet unluckily so late, that M. Mercier will not receive the promised instruction from M. Thouvenel until tomorrow: but I could not have again put off communicating your despatch to Mr. Seward without an appearance of vacillation, which would have been fatal. No time was practically lost by my consenting to the delay from Saturday to Monday: for whether the 7 days expired on Saturday next or Monday next, I should have been equally unable to announce the result to you sooner than by the Packet which will sail from New York Wednesday the 1st of January.

I feel little or no doubt that I shall have an answer of some kind before the seven days are over. What it will be depends very much upon the news which will be brought by the Packet tomorrow. If it convinces the people here that it is surrender, or war without any hope of a division in their favour by France, our terms will perhaps be complied with. If there is any hope left that there will be only a rupture of Diplomatic Relations, or that we shall accept no mediation of France, no concession will be made. There is no doubt that both Government and People are very much frightened, but still I do not think anything but the first shot will convince the bulk of the population that England will ever really go to war.

Mr. Mercier went, of his own accord, to Mr. Seward the day before yesterday, and expressed strongly his own conviction that the choice lay only between a compliance with the demands of England, and War. He begged Mr. Seward to dismiss all ideas of resistance from France; and not to be led away by the vulgar notion that the Emperor would gladly see England embroiled with the United States in order to pursue his own plans in Europe without opposition. He said that if he could be of use, by making these sentiments known to Senators and other influential people, he was quite ready to do so. Mr. Seward asked him whether he had received special instructions from his Government on the Subject. M. Mercier said no; but that he expected some immediately, and that he had no doubt whatever what they would be. Mr. Seward did not accept his offer to prepare influential men here for giving way, but merely said, "Let us wait and see what your instructions really turn out to be."

It is announced by telegraph that General Scott is more than halfway across the Atlantic on his way here; I suppose in the hope of appearing again on the stage as the fond pacificator. If he gives the sanction of his name to a compliance with our terms, he will certainly render the compliance easier to the Government, and less unpalatable to the people. But I cannot foresee any circumstance under which I should be justified in departing from your instructions. Unless I receive an announcement that the prisoners will be surrendered to *us*, and at least not a refusal to make an apology, Monday before noon on this day week, no other course will be open to me than to demand my passports and those of all the members of the Legation, and go away at once. In case of a non compliance or of the time elapsing without any answer, it will probably be desirable for me to take myself, the Secretary of Legation, and the greater part of the Attachés, off at once, leaving if necessary, one or two of the Junior Attachés to pack up the Archives and follow as quickly as possible. It is a case in which, above all others, delay will be dangerous. I am so convinced that unless we give our friends here a good lesson this time, we shall have the same trouble with them again very soon, under less advantageous circumstances, that even my regard for them leads me to think it all important that they should receive the lesson. Surrender or war will have a very good effect on them—but anything less will make them more self-confident than ever, and lead them on to their ruin.

I do not think there is any danger of this Government's deliberately taking any step to precipitate hostilities upon my departure. On the contrary if they let me go, it will be in the hope that the interruption of Diplomatic Relations will be all they have to fear from us. But they have so little control over their affairs that I think we must be prepared for acts of violence from subordinates—if they have the chance of performing them, in cases where no immediate danger is incurred. I shall suggest to the Governor and Naval officers to take reasonable forecautions against such acts. A filibustering expedition of the Irish on the frontier of Canada to damage the Canals, or something of that sort may also be in the cards.

New Orleans seems to be seriously threatened by the United States Troops—but I cannot propose to the Admiral, under present circumstances, to expose a detached ship to capture, by sending her to look after our Countrymen there.

It is generally believed that the Government will insist on an immediate advance of the Grand Army of the Potomac in the hope of covering a surrender to England with (to use President Lincoln's phraseology) a "sugar coating" of glory in another quarter if possible.

You will perhaps be surprised to find Mr. Seward on the side of peace. He does not like the look of the Spirit he has called up. Ten months of office have dispelled many of his illusions. I presume that he no longer believes in the existence of a Union party in the South; in his power to frighten the nations of Europe by great words; in the ease with which the United States could crush rebellion with one hand, and chastise Europe with the other; in the notion that the relations with England in particular are safe playthings to be used for the amusement of the American People.

He sees himself in a very painful dilemma, but he knows his Countrymen well enough to believe that if he can convince them that there was a real danger of war, they may forgive him for the humiliation of yielding to England, while it would be fatal to him to be the Author of a disastrous Foreign War. How he will act eventually, I cannot say—It will be hard for him to face present unpopularity; and if the President and Cabinet throw the whole burden on his shoulders, he many refuse to bear it. I hope that without embarrassing him with official threats, I have made him aware himself of the extreme danger of refusing our terms.

Lincoln's cabinet pondered the British ultimatum in discussions that continued for two days and finally concluded that they had no alternative but to restore Mason and Slidell to British custody. However, Seward still justified their seizure in a time of national emergency and claimed that their release was further proof of Northern confidence in the face of desperate attempts by the South to establish diplomatic relations abroad.[38]

The Americans are putting the best face they can upon the surrender of Mason and Slidell, and so far as has depended upon me I have done everything to make the pill as easy to swallow as possible. But I cannot disguise from myself that the real cause of their yielding was nothing more or less than the military preparations made in England. They are horribly out of humour—and looking out for some mode of annoying us without danger to themselves. There is a talk of discriminate duties on British goods, of a non intercourse act, and other absurdities. What is more serious is a proposal which it is said will be introduced into Congress next week, to repeal the act for carrying into effect the Reciprocity Treaty. This would be a direct breach of the Treaty—and would of course be an indisputable *casus belli*. It has often been suggested before, in the old belief that we should bear anything rather than go to war with the United States. I hope they have had a lesson which will make them wiser.

I cannot help fearing that it is as necessary as ever, maybe more than ever necessary, to be prepared to give a warm reception whether to regular invaders, or to filibusters from the United States, who may make an attempt upon Canada. In fact, I am not reassured respecting the maintenance of peace.

For the present we have some sincerity in Mr. Seward. For he must do his best to maintain peace, or he will have made the sacrifice in the case of Mason and Slidell in vain. As in that case, so in others. He sees now that besides the utter ruin of the country, a war with us would give the ascendancy to the ultra Party who are opposed to him in the Cabinet and in Congress. He fears too, and with great reason, that it would throw the country into a state of anarchy in which chiefs of a totally different frame of mind from him would have the upper hand. But he may be swept away, or, if he finds it impossible to hold his position on his own principles, turn round, and play a desperate game with the ultras. I have given him the opportunity of offering amends spontaneously in these rather awkward matters, and as you will see by my despatches, he has been prompt in seizing it.

On reading his enormous note at leisure, I find that it is much more of an apology than I thought from the hurried perusal which was all I had time to give to it before I sent it off to you. But with your letter before me, I should have taken much less *ad referendum*; for the surrender of the prisoners is in fact the whole question. On the other hand I should not have gone out of my way to declare, on my own responsibility, that the note was perfectly satisfactory, unless it had contained a formal apology in plain words.

I have a better opinion of the Boston Mob than Mr. Seward has, and should have had very little fear of the Prisoners being insulted, if I had taken them from Fort Warren directly on board a British Man of War.[39] I am not sorry however to spare the Bostonians (who are among the most friendly to us of the Americans) what they might consider a mortifying and humiliating spectacle. I have at Mr. Seward's request not made the name of the place at which the Prisoners are to be transferred generally known. Indeed I found that many people were going to Boston to be present on the occasion; and there is no advantage in having a crowd or sensation about it.

Thus the year 1861 ended with Anglo-American relations in a distinctly precarious state, an irreparable breach having been narrowly averted.

11

Decisive Victory Eludes the North,
January–June 1862

At the beginning of 1862, England had every reason to hope that her declaration of neutrality would provoke no further antagonisms such as the *Trent* Affair. At the same time, she was determined to protect her shipping and commerce while reluctantly observing the Northern blockade of Southern ports. As the American cabinet considered its next move, Lord Lyons feared the possibility of other forms of harassment.[1]

We are told that General Burnside's expedition is directed against Norfolk in Virginia, and indeed that his troops landed in three divisions at points not very distant from that place yesterday.[2] The attempt to take Norfolk in this way is regarded as a hazardous one, but the prize is considerable, and the necessity for something like a Federal success most urgent.

The country is in a state of great depression. The bankruptcy has come sooner than even the most despondent anticipated. The prospect of raising from twenty to thirty millions sterling in taxes from a people unaccustomed to pay any apparent taxes at all for Federal purposes, is almost hopeless unless the government can show the people something for their money.

The reduction of the South seems not so near now as it appeared to be six months ago. The result of all this is a more marked division of parties. The one may be called the Revolutionary Party, it is for prosecuting the war at all hazards and by all means— for proclaiming the immediate abolition of slavery in the South, promoting a servile insurrection there, turning out the Cabinet and even deposing the President if he be an obstacle to their schemes, keeping Congress permanently in Session to spur on the government and the generals, maintaining a paper currency by inflicting heavy penalties for depreciating it, and so on.[3] The Foreign policy of this party would be a return to reckless conduct and language towards Europe in general, and the attempt to obtain the support of France and England. . . . It will be rather provoking if just as we have cured Mr. Seward of this disease, we have to encounter it in a more virulent form in a successor to him.[4]

Happily, however, opposition to the tactics of the violent party may be expected to keep him in the hall of peace. A war, after the concessions he has made, would be most injurious to his personal reputation. I imagine his present game is to put himself at the head of a moderate reasonable party, not absolutely averse to listening to proposals for ending the war without a reconstruction of the Union, when the time for doing so shall come; that is to say, when the people shall be tired of taxes and suffering, and shall be unwilling to sacrifice liberty, the Constitution and material prosperity to the rage for reconquering the whole of the old territory, now lost. In the meantime there is the hope of so great a military success as may reduce the South, or of one at all events sufficient to induce it to treat on moderate terms. If the unhealthy season which comes on in the South in the early summer arrive without any great advantage having been obtained by the Northern arms, the violent and the moderate parties must break out into open hostility with each other. A great defeat of the North might bring on the question of peace, or revolutionary government, still sooner.

In either case there will be danger for us. The violent party will be reckless and risk anything. The moderate party may provoke a foreign war either as an *excuse* for giving up the contest with the South, or to divert popular irritation after having given up the contest.

At present the people are depressed, not to say cowed. I doubt whether they would resist any measures taken by France and England conjointly, even to the extent of breaking off diplomatic relations with both powers. But however friendly we may be, however hostile France, they will not give up their idea of getting France to unite with them against us.

The financial plight of the North became steadily more acute, because although each state was responsible for recruiting and sustaining its own volunteers, the mechanics of the blockade involved a drain on the federal treasury. Bank loans and a general tax levy seemed the only solutions, but there were serious objections to asking for funds from the public.[5]

The friends of the Union here are still very gloomy. The bankers, from fear of an immediate issue of paper money by the government, have come to a sort of hocus-pocus arrangement, in consequence of which it is hoped that the Treasury may hold on for three weeks or a month longer. It is wished, rather than expected, that by that time it my have become possible to raise another loan, which at this moment is out of the question. To bring this about Congress has already pledged itself to raise fifty millions Sterling by taxation. It is supposed that it will proceed immediately to vote all sorts of taxes, more with an idea of influencing the money market than with any great expectation of raising really any very large sum by them. As there are no Federal taxes at all now, except import duties, the whole machinery has to be created. The Western states can hardly pay taxes, and it is not certain they will if they can. In fact the difficulties are innumerable. The advantages of belonging to a Union saddled with an immense debt, enormous taxes, and rapidly losing prestige, both home and abroad, may appear very problematical to the outlying states.

A part of the programme of the bankers for getting off a new loan is an advance of the army, and a victory. But here too, according to present appearances, the prospect is not encouraging. The attack upon Norfolk (if it were ever intended) is now believed to be abandoned. It is now believed that General Burnside's expedition is gone to Albemarle Sound, [North Carolina,] and that the object is to intercept the communication between Virginia and the South and thus isolate the army at Manassas. But in order to do this effectually it must land on the mainland and march to the railroad which must be, I should think, fifty miles or more from the Coast. As a part of the same plan, an army is to advance from Kentucky to Eastern Tennessee and obtain the control of the other railroad which connects Virginia with the South. All this being accomplished, it is supposed that the Confederate Army must fall back from Manasses to the South of Richmond, and then, there being nothing to oppose it, the Grand Army of the Potomac is at last to advance to Richmond.[6] Besides all this, there is a great expedition which is someday to descend the Mississippi, and the Port Royal Expedition which is to take Savannah or Charleston or both.[7] It seems very doubtful whether any part of the plan will be executed in time to raise the Federal credit in the money market at home or abroad. Certainly the most remarkable feature in the present war has been the utter absence on both sides of anything like dash or enterprise.

The question is rapidly tending towards the issue either of peace and recogniton of the separation, or a Proclamation of Emancipation and the raising of a servile insurrection.[8]

It turns out that Mr. Seward has made much ado about nothing by ostentatiously granting permission to land British Troops, horses, munitions of war, and what not, in answer to a superfluous application from a private firm at Montreal for permission to land some officer's baggage at Portland. He is apt to create embarrassment for himself and those who have to do with him by offhand proceeding of this kind. He resorts to them more I think for the sake of making a sensation than anything else. I sincerely hope our military officers will not be led away by the apparent convenience and economy of the arrangement to take advantage of it. I hope and trust war is far off, but I should be very sorry indeed that we should accept favours which would in the least embarrass us in following our own policy in the subject. . . .

The French Admiral Reynaud is at Fortress Monroe, with a couple of ships.[9] He will probably visit Norfolk. There does not seem now to be much prospect of an attack upon that place, nor do I suppose that any British or French subjects who may be there would have any difficulty in getting away in case of danger. I would rather not, in the present state of feeling, have an English ship there if military operations were going on in the neighbourhood. In the very improbable case of our subjects' needing protection, the French Admiral would afford it.

Although the North's victory at Mill Spring, Kentucky, was not a major battle, it was a salutary boost to flagging morale. There had been many skirmishes since the Battle of Bull Run, but this was the first decisive and well-organized defeat of Southern troops. By 28 January Lyons had heard the welcome news.[10]

On the 19th the United States troops under General Thomas obtained what seems to have really been a success of some importance at a place called Mill Spring, near Somerset in Kentucky.[11] We are still without official details, and I do not know that when we have them we shall obtain much notion of what really took place. There can be no doubt however that the United States side was victorious. . . . If followed up (of which there are no signs at present) it will come in aid of the plan of obtaining the command of the communication between Virginia and the South through Eastern Tennessee.[12]

Of the naval and military expedition under Burnside we have little or no news, although it is more than a fortnight since it sailed. This looks as if it was to do no more than seize some point of the Coast and establish troops there in the same way that Sherman has done at Port Royal.[13]

The bill to introduce paper money is to be discussed in the House of Representatives to-day. No progress has yet been made in devising the ways and means of raising the hundred and fifty million dollars which Congress has declared its determination to raise by taxation.

The Reciprocity treaty is under discussion in a Committee of the House of Representatives. So far as I have been able to ascertain, it has been treated in a less unfriendly spirit than formerly. I don't' think there can now be any danger of their giving us a regular *casus belli* by abrogating it (as they used to threaten to do) before the term fixed.[14] They are not likely to venture upon anything which they think we are really determined to resist.

Still sanguine that the South could be subdued if its seat of government could be captured, Lincoln developed plans to lay siege to Richmond. Lyons's letter of 7 February was written with this knowledge, but he admitted that he had no idea when or how the Union would move against the state of Virginia.[15]

The present notion appears to be to overwhelm England and France with demonstrations of friendship and confidence. The effect which it is hoped an appearance of good understanding may have on the money market is no doubt the primary cause of this change of tactics. Very great dread of the two powers recognising the South and breaking up the blockade has a great deal to do with it. It is thought prudent to avoid giving them any pretext to do so, and it is not impossible that the same confidence is now placed in the powers of cajolery as was formerly placed in the effect of bluster and braggadocio. At all events materials are provided for a furious invective against the wanton treachery of either power if it does anything disagreeable. As much apparent strength as possible *in re* combined with a due but not more than a due suavity *in modo* is what is requisite to carrry any point here. If by any means we can avoid all interference until the affair settles itself, it will be I think a great point gained, both for the Americans, North and South, and for ourselves.

The paper money bill passed the House of Representatives yesterday under the pressure of a letter from the Secretary of the Treasury saying that he was at the last gasp, or something to that effect. I suppose that under the same pressure it must be rapidly passed by the Senate. An advance of the army is considered to have become a financial necessity. It is doubted whether it will be possible to levy the new taxes unless the people see something for the money. One cannot help having apprehensions for the result of an attack forced upon unwilling generals and troops by public opinion and political necessity.

In his letter of 11 February, Lyons was able to give Lord John Russell a surprisingly accurate account of several military encounters, due principally to the good fortune of his having heard the details firsthand. Meanwhile, Seward tried to make the North appear to dominate these fights in order to discourage diplomats resident in the capital from being tempted to recognize the independence of the South.[16]

The gloom which hung over the North has been for the moment dissipated. The Battle of Mill Spring or Somerset in Kentucky, the taking of Fort Henry on the Tennessee River, the excursion of the gunboats as far as Florence in Alabama up that river, and the occupation of Roanoke Island by General Burnside's expedition have followed each other in quick succession.[17] No one of these if of any great importance in a military point of view, but taken all together they have had a great effect upon the spirits of the union men. They seem to show that the tide is turning, and that victory is coming over to the Northern side. At Roanoke Island they have taken about two thousand prisoners; indeed compelled the whole Southern Force on the Island to lay down its arms. Both Northern and Southern accounts will I suppose recount prodigies of valour. I hear from an English eyewitness that there was in fact very little fighting.

The really important thing is to ascertain what effect will be produced in the South. Hitherto the Southern men have borne discomfort and privation well. But they have not yet been tried by any reverses to their arms. On the contrary they have had a marked superiority in almost all encounters. The Chancellor of the French Consulate who has just come from Richmond tells M. Mercier that the news of Roanoke had been received there with great grief and great surprise, but that the effect had been a still stronger desire to serve in the Army. The reenlistment of all the troops whose term was about to expire was ordered by the government and consented to by the men, not only without a murmur but with acclamation. This Chancellor, who went with the last despatches through the South from Richmond to New Orleans says that it is the same thing everywhere, that from boys to old men every one is ready to serve, but that arms cannot be provided for all. If this be the spirit, the North has not made much advance towards ending the contest.

It is announced too that the inhabitants of Elizabethtown, to which the Burnside men were to advance from Roanoke, had abandoned the town and themselves burnt it down. However we have yet to see how the South will bear a great reverse, such as a defeat of the Army at Manassas or the loss of Savannah or New Orleans.

The slowness of the North to mobilize for war and the initial disappointment felt as a result of failure to crush immediately the forces of the South led inevitably to changes in Lincoln's cabinet. At the War Department, Simon Cameron was replaced as secretary by the energetic Edwin M. Stanton, whose style had an immediate effect on Anglo-American relations, according to Lord Lyons.[18]

As you will have seen by my despatch by the last mail (No. 118) I am willing to give Mr. Seward and the government all credit for relaxing the extraordinary powers they have assumed concerning arbitrary arrest and matters of that kind.[19] The English victims have not been let out of the military prisons as quickly as I expected. I shall see in a day or two whether this is anything more than accidental. In fact the whole affair arose from a conflict between Mr. Seward and the new Secretary of War.[20] Mr. Seward has a habit of taking the command of all the departments, and this the Secretary of War could not stand. I think it is well that the arrests should be withdrawn from Mr. Seward. He certainly took delight in making them, and I may say playing with the whole matter. He is not at all a cruel or vindictive man, but he likes all things which make him feel that he has power.

I hope we may effect something practical as regards the Slave *Trade* while he is in the mood. He has sent a Bill to the Senate to give admiralty jurisdiction to the United States Consuls on the Coast of Africa. I hope too it may be possible to get a proposal which I made in vain to the late government taken up. It was to amend the American law so as to render the fact of a vessel's being evidently equipped for the Slave Trade sufficient evidence to condemn her. The enumeration of the *indicia* might be taken from some of our Slave Trade treaties with other powers. Mr. Seward spoke to me about this yesterday.

In order to be able to blockade Southern ports, the North withdrew its naval squadron from the West Coast of Africa, virtually ending efforts to intercept slave-trading ships. As a result, the British government proposed a treaty calling for mutual "visit and search" of suspected slavers. America had previously refused to permit any interference with her ships on the high seas, which induced many vessels carrying slaves to fly the American flag. Lincoln welcomed such a treaty but wanted the credit for initiating it. Another advantageous by-product of agreeing to mutual search was its subtle identification with antislavery, a linkage applauded by foreign supporters of the Union. On 31 March Lyons reported that the prospects of speedy passage were favorable.[21]

Mr. Seward seems very confident that he can carry the Treaty for the suppression of the Slave Trade through the Senate now, but doubtful whether he shall again have so good a chance. I am not so sanguine as he is about his success now, though it is a matter on which he ought to be pretty certain. But I am entirely of the opinion that we are not likely to have so good a chance again. I think therefore that I shall be doing what you wish if I sign it at once, with or without the clause limiting the duration. . . .

The continued resistance of Island No. 10 on the Mississipppi has much diminished the confidence of the military men in the feasibility of making the descent upon New Orleans by the River. We do not hear that the attack by Sea has been attempted.[22] General McClellan will have from 60 to 80 thousand men disembarked on the Virginia shore of Chesapeake Bay by the end of the week. There has been some hardish fighting at Winchester in Northern Virginia, but no important result.

Since you wrote the enquiries about the expectations as to the result of the war, you will have received several despatches from me containing information on the subject. In my No. 132 in particular I spoke of the effect on these expectations produced by the recent federal successes, and in my No. 177 of the 10th of this month, I mentioned the sentiments of the several parties on the questions of slavery and of governing the South when conquered.[23] I should not be able to add much to these and other despatches on the subject had I time to write at length.

The one point on which all parties are, or appear to be, agreed in the North, is not to lose an inch of the old territory. Since the recent successes, they will not admit the notion of doing so as a possible contingency. The one party is for a restoration of the Union by combining with a large military occupation, liberal and alluring offers to the South to work the old Constitution again. The other party is for pursuing the war to the complete subjugation of the South, then for abolishing slavery, and gradually raising the conquered territory to the condition of states again, as it becomes peopled by "loyal" white men. If things go badly, the North may become tired of the war, the financial difficulties will be great, there is not that enthusiasm in the Army which will keep it together without larger pay and a considerable amount of comfort, the government will not be able to take any very violent measures to enforce the circulation of its paper money; whether the new taxes will produce a revenue, whether it will be possible to collect them, are as yet matters of doubt. They are not voted yet by Congress. The great question still is, what is the real amount of the determination of the South. The Southern men in all the recent encounters have fought badly. Will they hold to their determination to bear suffering and privation to the last extremity? If they do they may wear out the North at last, and then the separation may be affected, which would have saved all the evils to both sides, if it had been consented to at once.

General McClellan and President Lincoln argued over the number of troops that should be committed to the main attack against the Confederacy and the size of the contingent to be held back for the defense of Washington. As a result, McClellan was relieved of supreme command and given responsibility only for the Army of the Potomac. In early April he embarked on the Peninsula campaign, the immediate object being to occupy Yorktown, but the ultimate goal was to capture the Confederate capital of Richmond.[24]

Yesterday was the anniversary of my arrival three years ago at Washington. I celebrated it by signing the Treaty for the suppression of the Slave Trade. Weary years they have been in many respects. But if I am as fortunate in obtaining your approbation of this last proceeding as I have on former occasions, I should be very ungracious and ungrateful to grumble about the annoyances and disagreeableness of the post. I have at any rate thought it better to run the risk of going a little faster than you intended about the treaty, than to throw away a chance which we have never had before, and are not very likely to have again, of attaining a great object.

This Treaty, like the president's anti-slavery message, and other measures of the same kind are no doubt intended to save the credit of the President with the party which elected him, if he should make concessions to the South, with a view to reconstructing the Union. Congress is undoubtedly more decidedly anti-slavery at this moment than either the President, Mr. Seward, or the country in general. The one thing the country desires and for which it is fighting is the greatness of the nation, and the people have learnt, even more than ordinary minds in general do, to attach the idea of national greatness to extensive territory. They do not care much for what in Europe is called the honour of their aims in the present quarrel. They neither felt nor professed any great shame after Bull Run, they do not regard it as a matter of any great importance to recover the military credit lost on that day. In fact they are so bewildered by their newspapers that they hardly know when they are victorious and when they are beaten, they have only a general impression that prodigies of skill and valour are performed daily. What they want is to get back the lost territory. The violent abolitionists would prefer separation to a reconstruction of the old Union, some because the result of readmitting the South with slavery would probably be to banish the abolition party from power for another half century. But the great majority of the country would, I think, make very great sacrifices of principle on the question of slavery in order to bring the South back and finish the war. In fact, however, the North has hardly yet felt the pressure of the war at all. It has paid no extra taxes, and there has been no great slaughter in the armies nor great distress among the people, and the recent successes make most Northern men confident that they shall be able to end the struggle on their own terms.

The government are expecting great military news almost every hour.[25] General McClellan has landed something like a hundred thousand men on the peninsula between the York River and James River and has attacked Yorktown. In the northwest General Pope is moving a force across the Mississippi to aid in the attack on Island No. 10, which has so long arrested the progress of the expedition down that river.[26] The Consuls at Charleston and Savannah appear to have recovered their apprehensions of an immediate attack on those places. We do not hear that the attack on New Orleans, which was undoubtedly intended, has yet taken place.

The Senate has passed the bill emancipating forthwith the Slaves in this capital and the little surrounding District, and given compensation to the owners. The number of slaves who would be freed would not be large, under two thousand, but it will be a great measure as a beginning if it pass the House of Representatives also.

Eyewitness accounts from the South were hard to come by, yet Lord Lyons was again lucky to receive a firsthand report by the French Minister, Henri Mercier, of his recent visit to Richmond.[27]

M. Mercier came back from Richmond yesterday. He went soon after his arrival to see Mr. Seward and came afterwards to me. He is fully persuaded that the confidence and the resolution of the Confederates are increased rather than diminished by the recent events. They consider (he says) the battles of Pittsburg Landing as a great military success on their side.[28] They admit that their troops have behaved ill when shut up in forts, but they declare that they are as firmly convinced as ever of their superiority in the field. They expect to inflict a disastrous defeat upon McClellan before Yorktown. They have good hopes of being victorious in Tennessee. If they are worsted everywhere, they will still not surrender. They will destroy their stores of cotton and tobacco, and all other property which they cannot remove. They will retire into the interior of their country, and defy the North to follow them. They will endure any privations and sufferings rather than be again united to the North. Their unanimity and devotion to the cause are wonderful. They are not carrying on a war in the usual manner for dominion as the North is, they consider themselves to be fighting for their homes and their liberty; and are making and are ready to make any sacrifices.

Such is the impression which M. Mercier says was made upon him by what he saw and heard.

I asked him whether he had obtained any specific information as to the extent of the naval and military reserves of the Confederates. He said that they offered him every facility for seeing whatever he chose, but that he had hardly thought it fair to avail himself of these offers. They admitted that they were in want of arms and ammunition, and said that but for this, they could keep a very much larger army in the field. They had no difficulty about men. It was a mistake to suppose that the act placing at the disposal of the government the whole able-bodied male population was a sign that recruiting had become difficult. On the contrary they had more men than they could arm. The object of the act had been to put an end to a system which had risen of certain regiments enlisting for limited terms, or on certain conditions, such as serving in a particular district, electing their own officers and so on. They had another "Merrimac" nearly ready at Norfolk; they had an iron-plated vessel on the James River; they had iron-plated vessels nearly ready at New Orleans.[29] It was true that the Federal vessels had been bombarding Fort Jackson on the Mississippi below that city for some days, but that Fort would probably detain them until the iron-plated vessels were ready, and then the Confederates would be relieved of all apprehension for the city itself.[30] If they lost New Orleans and all the seaboard, they would be as far from being subdued as ever. There could be no doubt that they would burn the cotton and tobacco in any place they were obliged to abandon. Why should they leave them to enrich their enemies?

I enquired of M. Mercier whether he had entered upon any particular matters of business with the members of the Confederate government; for instance, had he made any arrangement with regard to the large quantity of tobacco which belonged to the French government and which was at Richmond. He said he had avoided the appearance of having come to transact business, that the French tobacco would be spared if the rest were burnt, provided it could be distinguished and separated from that belonging to private persons.

I asked M. Mercier if anything had passed on the subject of the position of the Consuls. He said that if the idea of calling upon them to take out Exequaturs from the Confederate government or to withdraw had ever been really entertained, it was now abandoned. There appeared to be a very good disposition towards foreigners in general, less good perhaps towards the English as a nation than others, perhaps because more had been hoped from that country than from any other, and the disappointment had consequently been greater. On the other hand the Confederate leaders professed to have abandoned all expectation of succour from Europe, indeed they declared that all they desired was such an interruption of the blockade as would enable them to get arms.

I enquired whether any proposals had been made to him by the Confederates, whether they had offered commercial advantages to France in particular, or to Europe in general, as an inducement to recognize their independence. He said that no proposal of any kind had been made to him, nothing like a proposal had been sent through him to the government of Washington. He had spoken always as a friend of the Union, as a friend of all parties, but the particular language he had intended to hold was virtually inapplicable to the state of mind in which he found the Confederates one and all. It was idle to tell them that they were worsted on all sides, that the time was come for making terms with their enemies. What he had said to them about the recognition of their independence was, that the inducement to France to do it would be the hope that it would have a great moral effect towards hastening peace, at this moment it would certainly not have any such effect, it would embroil France with the United States and that would be all.

M. Mercier said that he was more than ever convinced that the restoration of the old Union was impossible, that he believed that the war would, if the powers of Europe exercised no influence on it, last perhaps for years, that he thought that in the end the independence of the South must be recognized, and that the governments of Europe should be on the watch for a favourable opportunity of doing this, in such a manner as to end the war. The present opportunity would however he thought be peculiarly unfavourable. It was evident that the armies in Tennessee and at Yorktown must first fight, that he supposed however that in a month something decisive must take place in both those quarters. Then the powers of Europe would see their way.

I did not express any opinion as to the policy to be eventually pursued by France or England, but I entirely agreed with M. Mercier that there was nothing to do at the present moment but watch events.

This morning Mr. Seward spoke to me about M. Mercier's journey. He said that M. Mercier had, probably without being altogether aware of it himself, obtained very valuable information for the United States government. He himself was quite convinced from M. Mercier's account of what had passed, that the Confederates were about to make a last effort, that they had their last armies in the field, and that their last resources were brought into action. Their talking of retiring into the interior was idle. If the United States were undisputed masters of the border States including Tennessee, and of the sea coast, there would be no occasion for any further fighting. Anybody who liked to retire into the interior was welcome to do so and stay there till he was tired. Mr. Seward went on to say that he had had some difficulty in preventing M. Mercier's journey making an unfavourable impression on the public. With this view he had caused it to be mentioned in the papers that M. Mercier had had a long interview with him on his return from Richmond, he had in the evening taken M. Mercier to the President, which also he should put in the newspapers, tonight he was to dine with M. Mercier to meet the captain of the French Ship of war the "Sassendi" which had brought M. Mercier back, tomorrow the President would pay a visit to that ship.

I suppose the truth lies somewhere between M. Mercier's views of the prospects of the South, and Mr. Seward's. Mr. Seward was of course anxious to weaken any impression Mercier's language may have made upon me.

The slave trade treaty has met with much more general approval than I expected. It has excited quite an enthusiasm among the Anti-slavery party. I have never seen Mr. Seward apparently so much pleased. Mr. Sumner, who had had the management of it in the Senate, was moved to tears when he came to tell me that it had passed unanimously.

The capture of New Orleans was heartily cheered by the North. In spite of significant land and river defenses, a flotilla under the command of Admiral Farragut had forced its way up the mouth of the Mississippi and occupied a key city. As Lyons pointed out in his letter of 2 May, the North could now contemplate operating and controlling a major Southern seaport for the first time.[31]

I have no doubt that the government seriously wishes to open the port of New Orleans. It would seem however from Mr. Seward's caution to me not to write anything to excite speculation in Europe, that he apprehends some obstacles. Perhaps he may wish to give American traders a start. The newspapers announce this morning that two large cargoes of Ice have already "by permission from Washington" been shipped at Boston for New Orleans. This however is an article in which no competition from Europe can be feared.

We have nothing important from the Army before Yorktown. In the mean time the approach of summer is making itself felt, and reminds me that I cannot hope to spend another summer in this unhealthy town with impunity. I will not however now trouble you with my lamentations on this subject.

Like his predecessors, Lord Lyons hated the semitropical climate of Washington, D.C., and therefore concocted reasons why he should not be asked to remain there during July and August.[32]

Under ordinary circumstances I should send by this packet an application for leave of absence. But I do not like to do so as things stand, without being sure that you will not be annoyed or displeased by it. I have myself strong and, I think, good reasons for very earnestly wishing to get away. The principal one is that I have little or no hope that, if I try another summer at Washington, I shall retain health and strength enough to do the business properly. There are no doubt cooler and more healthy places in the United States, but none from which Washington can be reached except by a long journey. To anyone who knows what travelling in this country is, it must be evident that any disadvantage to health from removing to a healthier air, would be more than neutralized by frequent journeys backwards and forwards. The expense of this post has so much increased, that I do not know whether I could afford to go to a watering place and live there in a manner befitting my official position. But this is a minor difficulty, which might be got over. My great objection to the arrangement is that I do not conscientiously believe that I could manage the affairs of the Legation satisfactorily or efficiently at a distance from Washington. I believe the work would be much better done by a competent Chargé d'Affaires on the spot, having the entire control and the entire responsibility. In short I feel very strongly that both for the public service and my own credit, I should do ill to attempt to do on, when I am sensible that my strength will not hold out. I have now been more than three years in this country, and so strongly have I been impressed with the necessity of being at the seat of government, that with the exception of the two months during which I was officially in attendance upon the Prince of Wales, I have been only four nights absent from Washington.[33] I will not importune you with the reasons affecting me privately and personally, which make me extremely anxious to get home. I will only add that I am much too grateful for the support and approval which you have given me to have the smallest desire to urge a request which you would rather not comply with. It is only the very strong feeling I have, that my being away during the summer is in all respects desirable, which has led me to beg you in this private manner, to take my wishes into consideration.

The fear that either the French or the British would give diplomatic recognition to the South, or worse yet, become involved in the war, plagued the North and tantalized the South. On 16 May, Lyons was disinclined to speculate about the future, preferring to await developments.[34]

The government here is very much disquieted by the rumored intentions of England and France with regard to intervention. This is not altogether without advantage, as they are more disposed to be considerate, or at all events, civil, when they have doubts about us, than when they feel sure of us. They are more civil to France than to England partly because they are more doubtful about her, and partly because they never will have, do what she will, the same bitterness against her, as they have against England. Mr. Seward is encouraged by some of his English correspondents (not, that I know of, by Mr. Adams) to believe that the Mexican affair will produce a serious disagreement between England and France.[35]

M. Mercier thinks it quite within the range of possibility, that the South may be victorious both in the battle in Virginia and in that in Tennessee. He is at all events quite confident that whether victorious or defeated they will not give in, and he is certainly disposed to advise his government to endeavour to put an end to the war by intervening, on the first opportunity. He is however very much puzzled to devise any mode of intervention which would have the effect of reviving French trade and obtaining cotton. I should suppose he would think it desirable to go to great lengths to stop the war, because he believed that the South will not give in until the whole country is made desolate, and that the North will very soon be led to proclaim immediate emancipation, which would stop the cultivation of cotton for an indefinite time.

I listen and say little when he talks of intervention. It appears to me to be a dangerous subject of conversation. There is a good deal of truth in M. Mercier's anticipation of evil, but I do not see my way to doing any good.

If one is to conjecture what the state of things will be a month or six weeks hence, one may "guess" that McClellan will be at Richmond, having very probably got there without much real fighting. I doubt his getting farther this summer, if so far. The armies in Tennessee will perhaps do very little. Savannah and Charleston may share the fate of New Orleans. Most of the cotton will have been destroyed in the places abandoned by the Confederates, very little will be planted. The campaign will not be pushed with any vigour during the summer. It may be begun again in the Autumn.

Thus, so far as trade and cotton are concerned, we may be next autumn, just in the situation we are now. If the South really defeated either or both the armies opposed to them, I think it would disgust the North with the war, rather than excite them to fresh efforts. If the armies suffer much from disease, recruiting will become difficult. The credit of the government has hitherto been wonderfully kept up, but it would not stand a considerable reverse in the field. It is possible under such circumstances that a peace party might arise, and perhaps just *possible* that England and France might give weight to such a party. However all this is a mere speculation. We are (as usual) supposed to be on the eve of a crisis which is to clear up everything.[36] Certainly it will be more easy to form an opinion as to the probable results of the war, a month hence than it is now.

At this point, the French kept reviving their desire to intervene in the war, but only in concert with Britain. Commercial interests doubtless underlay this steadily applied pressure, since Napoleon III's adventurism in Mexico was proving costly and futile.[37]

Some of the Foreign Ministers here have made reports from their Consuls at New Orleans as late as the 6th of this month. They represent the quantity of cotton destroyed at New Orleans and on the banks of the Mississippi as enormous. They state that the inhabitants of New Orleans are submissive but sullen, and that few, if any, can be induced to take the oath of allegiance. I do not know how it happens that I have nothing of more recent date than the 29th April from Mr. Coppell. It is very unlikely that it is by any fault of his.[38]

M. Mercier talks sensibly enough about intervention now. It would perhaps be still more sensible not to talk about it at all. He says that there is manifestly nothing to be done now, short of an alliance offensive and defensive with the South, and the employment of such a force as should keep the army and navy of the United States at such a distance from the plantations as to enable the planters to set quietly to work to cultivate cotton, and the ships to carry it unmolested from the ports. He of course sees that the attempt to make war, and war upon such a scale, with the United States would probably cause much greater evils than those which it would be intended to remove. In short, he says that intervention can hardly be useful or effectual except at a moment when one or other of the parties was willing to make peace *at any price*. At such a moment one might hope that intervention would be unnecessary. However M. Mercier thinks that intervention (which I am inclined to believe always means with him recognition of the South) might have a great effect at a moment when the North was weary and in difficulties. He says that the test of the North being shaken will be a great fall in government securities; that the test of the South's beginning to waver will be their bringing goods to market to the ports occupied by the Federal troops.

The generals both in Tennessee and in Virginia are slow and prudent, apparently to excess. The delay is against the North, as the sickly season is approaching, and the climate will then in great measure relieve the Confederates from the need of a defensive army. It seems that all the Federal generals are crying out for reinforcements, and that the government is about to call for one hundred thousand, if not two hundred thousand recruits immediately. . . .

I see with great satisfaction that you have put it clearly to Mr. Adams that he is not to expect us to help the United States to exclude our commerce from the Southern ports. No doubt the number of British ships which run the blockade is very irritating to the United States cruisers, and I am in constant apprehension of their committing some high-handed act of violence. Some of the cases of interference with our merchant vessels in the Gulf of Mexico are awkward. And then, English merchant captains do not seem to be aware that they are liable to be searched at sea. I don't think Mr. Crawford at Havana gives them the best advice.[39] He admits in theory the belligerent right of search, but seems to think it ought not to be exercised in the usual way in the present war. But as we have distinctly given both parties belligerent rights in general, and the right of search in particular, we are precluded from considering such points. I have always a dread of a disposition rather to get up a good case against a Foreign government than to prevent cause of complaint being given by one.

By 6 June it was clear that McClellan's forces were in for a long and difficult campaign in Virginia. The South, far from yielding easily, appeared to gain spirit and strength, and it was said that there were more volunteers than could be equipped.[40]

I have received this morning your despatch of the 20th of last month, giving me leave of absence. I am very grateful for the kind manner in which you have taken my wishes into consideration. I have not time to form any definite plans in the hurry of sending off the messenger. But I have become more than ever convinced that I cannot spend another summer at Washington with impunity, and that if I am not at Washington, I am better out of the way altogether. I shall therefore in all probability embark for England in about a fortnight or three weeks time, unless some turn in affairs here should make me feel it my duty to postpone my departure.

The sanguine Union men hope that the late attack of the Confederates may be a precursor to their evacuating Richmond. But, it seems more probable that they will fight a greater battle before they do so. The impression on both sides appears to be that they had the advantage in this last affair, but the positions of the two armies are the same as they were before.

The spirit of hatred manifested by the population at New Orleans and all other places retaken by the North exceeds in intensity and in tenacity anything which was expected even by those who knew the South best. At Norfolk the people must soon take the oath of allegiance or starve, as the federal generals keep up a blockade by sea and land or very nearly so, but beyond the satisfaction of making their enemies perjure themselves, they will not gain much by their success in their operation. General Halleck's telegrams from the West are so notoriously untrustworthy that it is not worthwhile to mention their contents.[41]

Preparing to take his leave of absence, Lord Lyons commented briefly on Seward's curious reaction to his departure.[42]

I was so unwell yesterday that I was unable to do anything, which has prevented my sending you by this mail some general information on the prospects of the war, and some other matters. It is however of the less importance, as I hope to pay my respects to you in person a week after this letter reaches you.

I did not think that Mr. Seward would object to my going. He has, in fact, taken up the idea with so much enthusiasm that I have been obliged to endeavour to check his anticipation of the wonders I am to effect, or rather to make him understand that my own opinions, not his, are those which I must express to you.

I take his willingness that I should go as a sign that he does not expect serious troubles, for I think he would rather be in my hands than those of a man new to him, if he did.

I am afraid there are three things to which we must not blind ourselves—

1st that we have a very small chance of getting cotton from this country for a long time to come.

2nd. That there is no Union feeling whatever in the South.

3rd. That the war has become one of separation or subjugation.

In his last private letter before leaving for London, Lyons described President Lincoln's homespun farewell.[43]

I had quite an affectionate parting with the President this morning. He told, as is his wont, a number of stories more or less decorous, but all he said having any bearing on political matters was, "I suppose my position makes people in England think a great deal more of me than I deserve, pray tell 'em that I mean 'em no harm." He does not pay much attention to foreign affairs, and I suppose did not like to talk about them without Mr. Seward. I am to hear Mr. Seward's last words at New York on Tuesday evening (the 17th). I embark the following morning, and hope to pay my respects to you in person a few days after this letter reaches you. It is quite time for me to get away from this place, the heat today is overpowering.

At the midpoint of 1862 it was becoming apparent that in spite of everyone's fond hopes for an early end to the war, both sides were prepared for a slow and grinding war of attrition. Differing loyalties and beliefs divided the country geographically as well as philosophically, and already thousands had committed their lives to upholding them, come what may.

12

William Stuart and the Interventionist Crisis, June–November 1862

When Lord Lyons left Washington on his leave of absence to England, he placed William Stuart in charge of the legation, even though Stuart had only taken up his post as acting secretary the previous November. His former assignments had been in Paris (1845–57), Rio de Janeiro (1858–59), Naples (1859–60), and Athens (1861). It is interesting to speculate whether someone with greater experience in American affairs would have interpreted the events differently during the last six months of 1862.

His first private letter to Lord John Russell was written on 23 June 1862 and carried no hint of the crisis looming on the horizon. Instead, it touched briefly on various issues that were pending and reinforced Lyons's impression that nothing major was likely to emerge during the summer to seriously jeopardize Anglo-American relations.[1]

There is no military news of any importance, nor up to yesterday any material change in the position before Richmond, except that both armies are said to be receiving reinforcements.

The British Vice Consul at Fredericksburg, Virginia, has been arrested—his flag has been seized and replaced by the United States' Flag—and he has been brought to Washington and allowed to go about on parole until the War Department finds time to examine his papers. Fortunately for us, he is an American citizen, but I suppose I ought to try and get some reparation for the seizure of the Flag, and also to procure the poor man's release, unless he can be proved to have taken an active part on the Confederate side in this war. So far, I have only seen Mr. Frederick Seward on the matter and asked him to suggest to his father to take the initiative in doing what is right.

I hope you won't think that I have commented on too much in my private note to Mr. Seward about cotton. It can hardly do harm, although it may not have any beneficial result, and it was as well to let him know in an inoffensive way that you had anticipated his propensity to throw the whole blame upon the Confederates for destroying their cotton.

Mons. Mercier tells me that the French Consul at New Orleans continues to give a deplorable account of the state of affairs there, and that he estimates the amount of cotton destroyed at 250,000 Bales. In spite of what Mr. Seward says, most accounts from the South represent that cotton will not be brought out in any quantity.

˶Absence of news concerning McClellan's Peninsular campaign frustrated observers who grew impatient for details of decisive victories or defeats. Communications from the front were sporadic, giving rise to loose talk and rumormongering. In these circumstances, Stuart was unsure of the accuracy of differing reports and turned to Henri Mercier, the French minister at Washington, for an experienced view of current events.[2]

There has been considerable alarm during the last two days, as it is known that McClellan's right wing was attacked on both Friday and Saturday last, and that he has quite changed his position, some say intentionally, to get another base of operations on the James River,—others supposing that he has met with a serious disaster. What seems to confirm the latter view of the case is that the War Office after announcing that all news, whether good or bad, should be communicated to the pubic, has since forbidden any to transpire. We are, therefore, too much in the dark as to what has really happened for me to attempt an official despatch about it.

It had been reported for some days past that Jackson was intending to attack McClellan's right wing in their rear.[3] This attack is said to have failed, but that same wing has abandoned its former locations, after a great deal of severe fighting; but whether it is a move for good or for bad remains to be proved.

The telegraph has constantly been cut, and the government may not possess the news which it is supposed to have. On all former occasions, it has hastened to announce even doubtful victories with great pomp. Hence all the present anxiety, which has been rather increased by Mr. Seward having suddenly started for New York on Sunday by a special train.

Mercier talked to me at great length yesterday about an eventual joint mediation as the only way of bringing this Civil War, and the calamities it is entailing upon us, to a close. He thinks it ought to be offered, as soon as it can be done without serious danger of bringing on wars with us, and that even now if offered energetically and with war as the alternative, it might be accepted. This would, however, be playing too great a stake at present, if I may be permitted to give my opinion, such as it is. By waiting for a disaster, we may find our opportunity. The credit of the North must be nearly exhausted, and when once confidence is shaken, the pace downhill will probably be very rapid. So far the people are buoyed up with arrogance and vindictiveness, believing that their fleets and legions could successfully oppose the whole of Europe, and whilst in this temper it would perhaps be the better for us to wait for some signs of exhaustion.

On 4 July Stuart began his letter by announcing the "great disaster which had befallen the Grand Army." According to information gathered by eyewitnesses, McClellan was in retreat and the Union army in serious disarray.[4]

They estimate the force with him, or which ought to be with him, at somewhere about ninety thousand men.

They describe the Army as completely disorganized—the generals as having with few exceptions lost their heads, and the men who did fight as showing no enthusiasm whatever for their cause, and as fighting more for life than as caring for the result.

Several superior officers were heard openly saying that the Confederacy must now be recognised, and they attribute the whole blame of their defeat to the Washington politicians.

The Confederates fought with great courage and desperation.[5] The truth is only partially known to the public, and as many still believe that it was a "splendid strategic movement" on McClellan's part to change his base to the James River.

It is impossible to conjecture what the effect will be upon the masses when the full extent of the disaster is exposed. The great call for 300,000 men was made when the govt received the intelligence of the first attack upon McClellan's right wing;[6] but even if these men do come forward in the numbers required, it will be some weeks or months before they can be prepared to enter upon a campaign, and confidence may be so shaken that it may be no longer possible to evade the financial difficulties by fresh issues of paper.

It would be very desirable that this should be so, before the folly of those in power becomes still more ruinous and incurable.

One of the most important sources of information about the South was the handful of war correspondents who could move freely about the country. Frank Vizetelly was one of these,[7] and Stuart spoke to him shortly before writing on 7 July.[8]

Mr. Seward was not at home to me when I went to the State Department this forenoon, so that I have scarcely anything worth telling you today. He is said to pretend to look upon McClellan's retreat as a piece of most masterly strategy, and to fish for congratulations rather than to accept condolences.

It seems inconceivable how these Americans are able to humbug themselves and each other. The Army itself is now, on its recovery from despondency, being persuaded that it has performed some wonderful feat, and McClellan's Proclamation shows at any rate his own wonderful revival. When our Officers left him the other day, he was in very different spirits. I hear 20,000 mentioned as the amount of the reinforcements sent to him; but his estimate is very uncertain.

Many people doubt the possibility of raising the 300,000 men called for.

Vizetelly, of the Illustrated London News has been with the Squadron on the Mississippi. He went from here some weeks ago a strong Unionist and has returned a complete Southerner. He saw no Union feeling anywhere in the South, and this is the story brought by other unprejudiced travellers from the South East as well as from the South West. There were some planters from Memphis who would be glad to sell their Cotton, if the price could be secured to them, but not from any Union sympathies. And he talked of some 5,000 Bales in that quarter which might be forthcoming. The 3,000 bales mentioned some time ago by Mr. Seward may have formed a portion of these.

The Confederate soldiers who were represented as coming in large numbers to take the oath of Allegiance were Conscripts coming for protection from military service, and not really converts to the Union cause. The hatred against the North must now be undoubtedly great and general throughout the South, whatever may have been the intrigues in which it originated.

During the summer of 1862, Stuart and Mercier pondered the feasibility and desirability of forcing an end to the Civil War by offering mediation that, if declined, would be followed by French and English recognition of Southern independence. They were aware that European intervention would be risky and would depend on the military strength and the civilian morale at a particular moment in time. Yet London and Paris both were interested in terminating the blockade and in restoring commercial relations with the South, so their representatives closely monitored a number of areas that might signal conditions favorable to diplomatic intervention.[9]

> We are certainly at present traversing a very important crisis in the history of the war, but it will take some weeks yet before we can exactly appreciate the full effect of recent events.
>
> There are several indications of a waning confidence in the future, such as the difficulty of procuring fresh recruits and the consequent prospect of having to resort to Conscription, the present attempt of the President to conciliate the Border states by securing to them full compensation if they will abolish slavery, the nervousness about the mismanagement of the war, which have chiefly been directed against Stanton, and have even ascended to the President, rather than against McClellan, and the rise in the price of gold which rose as high as 18% and is now at about 15 percent premium. . . . Mr. Sumner, who with Mercier came to dine with me on Sunday, talked of the confiscation bill as the death blow of slavery, but it will be necessary for the Federal Armies to conquer, before it can have much practical effect.[10] Mr. Seward yesterday told me that he looked upon the President's plan of compensation as much more fatal to slavery, which does not indicate his confidence in subjugation.
>
> Congress intended to adjourn tomorrow. I don't know whether they will stop to consider this message. It was the result of a meeting between the President and the members from Border States, and it will scarcely please the extreme abolitionists, who have been having pretty much their own way during the Session, and who have rendered the legislation of Congress as vindictive, and that, whatever else happens, I do not see that the Union, as it was, can by any possibility be restored. They have done all they can do to alienate instead of to conciliate the South, and General Butler at New Orleans is a fitting representative of their policy.[11]
>
> I have had no opportunity yet of questioning Mr. Seward about the present state of opinion in the South and the intentions of this government towards it. They are however almost sufficiently indicated by the Confiscation Bill, and Mr. Seward's statements have usually been speedily falsified by events.
>
> He now postpones the subjugation or surrender of the South until the winter.
>
> With regard to McClellan's army, there is great talk of reinforcing it and of recommencing hostilities, but many believe that he will either be shortly obliged to retire to summer quarters, or to come to Washington and advance thence in cooperation with General Pope's Army. I don't expect him to be able to do much at present from where he is.
>
> The fresh recruiting is called the "third uprising of the North". It does not however appear to be anything but a fictitious enthusiasm coming from above, and without much foundation. There must necessarily be some limits to the power of an extended agricultural country to produce soldiers for purposes of invasion, and the limits seem now to be nearly reached.

By 21 July pressure was building rapidly for intervention. The South went so far as to present demands for recognition directly to Paris and London, but these were dismissed by both Foreign Offices. In Washington there were accusations that motives of self-interest lay behind British and French offers of mediation.[12]

> M. Mercier came to see me as soon as the last mail arrived to say that he had a private letter, as I understood, from Mons. Thouvenel, which led him to believe that his government was getting very impatient at the prolongation of the war here, and that he might before long be instructed to intimate to Mr. Seward that the recognition of the Southern Confederacy must be taken into consideration, unless there was some prospect of an end of the struggle.
> Although M. Mercier has latterly observed great changes in public opinion here, yet he now thinks that the time has not quite arrived for mediation or recognition, that perhaps by October the change may be sufficiently great for a joint mediation to have some chance of being listened to. He never contemplates any action on the part of France except in conjunction with England.

As early as 29 July it was becoming apparent to Lincoln and his cabinet that they would have to take responsibility for governing conquered territories while at the same time conducting a full-scale war. The recognition that these commitments could be long-term was sobering.[13]

> I have been working Mr. Seward about cotton, and it is to be hoped that some good effect will ensue from the spirit in which General Shepley is returning to New Orleans.[14] The latter is represented to be a moderate and practical man. The great cry now is for a more energetic war policy, thereby meaning Confiscation, Emancipation, and the arming of slaves. There is no measure, however revolting, which would be found too strong, "Tous les moyens sont bons", according to present ideas, and it is argued that if the Slaves in the Southern States are encouraged to rise, the Southern Armies would dissolve owing to the necessity there would be for the Soldiers to rush to their homes for the protection of their wives and families. The Confederates have probably taken sufficient precautions to thwart such a result.
> So far the President has resisted the extreme pressures, although he has been obliged to yield to a certain extent in consequence of the Confiscation Bill. He is threatened with a lack of recruits, unless he gives way farther. On the other hand, if emancipation is once proclaimed, the effect upon most of the old army officers, who still, with a great portion of their men, suppose they are fighting to restore the union as it was, might be such as to endanger discipline.
> I am sorry to say that the general hatred of England appears more intense than ever, and any remonstrances from Your Lordship against vindictive measures which may be adopted toward the South would only render both the measure and their authors more popular, as has been the case in regard to General Butler.[15]
> It is reported to be under consideration to withdraw McClellan's army from the James River at all risks for the protection of Washington. If this is decided upon, it will be an acknowledgment of failure which will make a painful impression upon the public.

Although Congress did not pass a law drafting men into the Union army until 3 March 1863, vigorous efforts were made throughout 1861–62 to induce men to enlist. One such method was to threaten conscription if not enough volunteers were forthcoming. State recruitment had proved inefficient, unfair, and inadequate, and so the burden of filling quotas fell to the central government. Furthermore, British citizens were being intimidated by threats of being drafted even though the Foreign Office in London advised that domiciled aliens were not required to serve in a civil war. This formed the background to Stuart's letter of 12 August.[16]

It would be difficult to describe to you what a panic there is amongst British subjects all over the States with regard to this Drafting. The Legation is daily besieged by numbers asking for advice, and I receive numbers of Letters from the Western States, in none of which, except in Missouri, is there any Consul to apply to. So far, it is only panic, but I greatly fear from the present irritation against us that many may be forcibly impressed in some States, in spite of their British Nationality.

The subject is naturally giving me great anxiety, and as I cannot appoint Consular Agents for the emergency, I have determined to send Anderson round to the States from which the most of my Correspondents write.[17] He is a man of good judgment and conciliatory manners, and I propose that he should visit the different Governors, and ascertain in each case what proofs of Nationality will be sufficient for exemption. It will show the Governors that we take interest in the proper protection of our Subjects, and it may dispose them more favourably towards us. He would also put himself into communication with the principal British Residents in the large Towns, in order to advise and re-assure them.

He will possibly at the same time be able to pick up some useful information respecting arbitrary Acts. He will start tomorrow, and I shall ask Mr. Seward to give him Letters of introduction to the different Governors.

I can think of no other plan for assisting our countrymen in the present crisis. They cry out for Consuls, but it would be impossible to appoint such officials in all the Towns where they are now wanted. It will be a great thing if the Governors can be persuaded to be satisfied with Affidavits taken before a Notary Public, without the addition of Consular Certificates.

The threatened drafting has certainly given a great stimulus to volunteering. It is difficult to believe that the former will be everywhere submitted to without resistance, but this is a general reign of terror, and every encouragement is given to denunciations. The Victims meet with ridicule instead of pity.

By the end of July McClellan's Peninsular campaign appeared doomed. He could not resume an attack against Richmond without considerable reinforcements, and Lincoln lacked confidence in his ability to seize the initiative even if additional troops were supplied. Consequently, he was ordered to withdraw from the James River and support the beleaguered Army of Virginia under the command of General Pope, who had spent much of the month of August thwarting Robert E. Lee's efforts to cross the Rappahannock River on his march toward Washington. On 22 August Stuart sensed tension in and around the capital.[18]

The arrival of Despatches today from the Southern Consuls has left me very little time for writing.

General Pope has been retreating, the Confederates being in great force on his front, and it being their object to bring on a battle, and his to avoid one until General McClellan's army joins him. Mr. Seward hopes that McClellan will arrive in time to be the Bluecher of the impending battle.[19] It is reported that fighting is going on now, but we are kept very much more in the dark at Washington than they are at New York.

If Mr. Sumner is to be believed, it had actually been decided by the majority of the Cabinet, including the President, to proclaim Emancipation some three weeks ago, when Mr. Seward succeeded in getting the decision suspended for a day, and in the meantime telegraphed to his friend Mr. Thurlow Weed to come from New York to his assistance and it appears that the latter's influence over the President obtained a further suspension.[20] An offer has now been made to Mr. Cassius Clay, just arrived from Russia, of the command of the Southern States west of the Mississippi with power to proclaim Emancipation in those states at his discretion. I have not heard whether he has accepted the offer.[21]

Although McClellan had been ordered to withdraw his forces from the James River and link up with Pope's army as soon as possible, the operation did not get underway until 14 August, two weeks after the instructions had been issued. In the meantime, the Confederacy embarked on a bold strategy that involved dividing its forces and sending part of them, under Stonewall Jackson, on a flanking movement around Pope's army. This was successful, and Pope had to abandon his stores of food and munitions at Manassas Junction and retreat to a better defensive position closer to Washington. This Second Battle of Bull Run was in many respects the lowest point in Northern military fortune and morale during the entire Civil War. On 1 September, with admittedly incomplete information, Stuart did his best to acquaint Lord John Russell with the desperate situation confronting the Union.[22]

The latest trustworthy intelligence which I can give you is that General Pope has telegraphed to ask whether, if he is attacked to-day, this government can defend Washington. This I have from authority, but I do not know whether he has been attacked today or not. It was a great relief to him not to have been attacked yesterday, and his army is said to be completely demoralized. His present escape is ominous, after his pretended victories.

It is impossible to find out either what has actually occurred or what is to be done. All is confusion, and his generals are throwing the blame upon each other.

If the Confederates are in a position to renew the attack, this army may dissolve, in spite of the guns which are placed on the bridges to stop them.

General McClellan is at Alexandria and is much blamed for not having reinforced Pope, whom he hates. Pope is found fault with for not telling the truth in time. Burnside is reported to be cut off at Fredericksburg, the greater part of his artillery is said to have been lost.

With regard to the numbers on both sides, the three corps of his army can hardly have amounted to less than 200,000 and I have reason to believe that the Confederate army which was to start from Richmond amounted to 100,000, and that 40,000 were left for the defence of Richmond.

Of course I can form no estimate of how many were actually brought into action on each side.

In spite of McClellan's failure to come to Pope's support promptly enough, Lincoln appointed him commander of the Army of the Potomac, whose task was to defend the nation's capital in its hour of greatest peril. Already Lee had started moving his troops toward Washington, but he hesitated to attack directly, preferring to divert his forces in Maryland, where they cut railroad lines and tried to isolate the city. As of 9 September, Stuart was unable to report whether the Union had sustained a mortal blow or only a superficial wound.[23]

I am informed by Mons. Mercier, who has returned, that he wrote last week from New York, informing his Govt. of the grave aspect of Affairs and that he believed the time for offering Mediation to be approaching. He urged Mr. Thouvenel to come at once to an understanding with you and particularly to request that Lord Lyons would return as soon as possible. He acknowledges that the time for Mediation has not arrived yet, but he thinks it very desirable that he and Lord Lyons should have Instructions ready for it when it does arrive, as it might be only a fleeting moment which would be lost by a reference to London and Paris.

His idea seemed to be that the fact of Lord Lyons's return before the time contemplated might exercise a certain effect upon the public mind and prepare people for mediation; that it would be useless to merely make the proposal to Seward, who would only let such an interpretation of it go forth as would suit his private ends, and that some means should be taken to make it at once known to the Nation, in the hope that a Party would arise in its' favour.

As to the form of the proposal, he said it should be made with the greatest courtesy, and that it should be at the same time announced to the Federal Govt that we could no longer withhold our recognition from the South, and that we should wish to consult their wishes as far as possible in doing so, by waiting to see whether they would not first accept our good offices with a view to prevent the further effusion of blood.

Were Russia to join in this Offer, it would probably be accepted, and it possibly might be accepted from England and France alone, if a favourable moment occurs. . . .

I shall be anxious to learn what effect these events have produced in Europe, and whether the pressure for recognition may not have become irresistable.

We shall perhaps be hereafter reproached by our Northern friends for not having interfered sooner. Indeed the Belgium Minister heard it remarked in New York the other day that we must have some ulterior object in continuing to look quiety on. His opinion is that the War will never end, except under Foreign intervention.

I have scarcely given in this letter any opinions except those of my colleagues, and Lord Lyons will know what value to attach to each.

I can only add that a crisis is approaching, and that some risk will have to be incurred sooner or later. The result will depend upon the fitness of the moment chosen, unless we wait for complete exhaustion.

The diplomatic community buzzed with fresh rumors almost daily. One was that Stanton could not long remain as secretary of war in view of his lack of confidence in McClellan. The word being circulated had it that General Halleck would take Stanton's place, but he steadfastly refused to resign.[24]

We have never been more distracted by conflicting rumours than we are at the moment. Mr. Seward told me on Saturday that it had been discovered that the Confederates in Maryland did not amount to more than 35,000, and yesterday Mr. Mercier heard from good Authority connected with their side that they were 150,000, and that General Beauregard was on his way to join them with 35,000 more.[25] I don't see how they can possibly have mustered such large forces, as they are at the same time carrying on operations on a large scale in the Border States. All accounts represent them as being thoroughly confident, and that they are in no hurry, wanting to take Harper's Ferry and to defeat McClellan before going further. Their principal wants in Maryland were Shoes and Salt, and of these they have got large quantities.

If they succeed, the War may possibly come to a more speedy conclusion than we suppose, as the Federal Govt is fast losing its prestige, and were it once turned out of Washington, great confusion and panic would probably spread through the Country. There is an idea abroad now that the Confederates are coming to restore the Union and to throw over the Abolitionists. That it should have been published, however improbably, shows that great changes of feeling may shortly be expected, and that there is a growing weariness of the War, except amongst the many who are interested in sustaining it.

One obstacle to peace will be the unwillingness to look the final settlement in the face. It is somewhat the case of the gambler making desperate attempts to recover his lost money, and getting meanwhile deeper and deeper into difficulties. But the pace is getting too rapid on both sides, and unless they soon come to a check, the whole feature of the struggle may assume a very different shape.

Anderson writes from St. Louis, on his arrival there from Memphis, that it is impossible to imagine anything more deplorable than the State of things in Eastern Tennessee and Arkansas, the Country being given over to Brigandage, and the Federal Commanders not attempting to exercise any control over their troops. He heard from high authority that the course of General Curtis' Army through Arkansas was marked by inconceivable brutalities, and that the Officers would not or could not restrain their men.[26] Some of the most wealthy Citizens told him that they had decided to abandon their property which had become valueless and to take the first opportunity of removing to England.

Anderson's visit there appears to have been of great use to British Subjects. Under present circumstances, I have however thought it better to telegraph to him to come back, without going to the North Western States, as at first intended. His report of what he has seen and done will no doubt be very interesting.

On 17 September McClellan was finally able to attack Lee's army. Had he done so a day or two earlier, he might have trapped many of the Confederate troops between Antietam Creek and the Potomac River and inflicted a major defeat. As it was, Lee had time to withdraw his forces in an orderly fashion from Maryland into Virginia. Observers like Stuart were slow to grasp the significance of Antietam, since the Union failed to achieve a resounding victory. On the other hand, the South had been unable to inflict a crippling blow upon the North, and the city of Washington was secure. Soon it would become clear that these confrontations were degenerating into battles of attrition that ultimately favored the North. Writing on 19 September, Stuart based his observations on pure hearsay.[27]

The fighting this week must have been very desperate on both sides, and McClellan claims to have had the best of it on his Right and Centre, whilst it is acknowledged that his left has lost ground.

Yesterday, it is said, was devoted to burying the dead, and McClellan telegraphed that the result was in the hands of Providence. He had got all his available troops up, and expected to renew the Battle to-day. Two hours ago I heard that there was news from him up to 7 A.M. to-day, up to which time it had not commenced.

The Secessionists say that Jackson is working round to get in McClellan's rear, and also that Beauregard got to the Potomac yesterday with 40,000 fresh Troops. If this is so, or half of it, McClellan's fame is probably played out.

The moment is certainly one of intense interest, and a few hours may decide the result. What is very provoking is to know so little of what is passing so near. That Victory of Sunday appears to have been a comparatively small Affair, and it was very ingeniously announced to produce an effect in Europe. Nobody believes that McClellan can really have written those absurd Despatches.

Claiming victory at Antietam, Lincoln did what he had contemplated doing for several months. On 23 September he issued his Preliminary Emancipation Proclamation, declaring that as of January 1863, all slaves within rebellious states would be free. The emancipation did not apply to either the border or Northern states, and of course Lincoln knew that he could not enforce the decree in the Confederacy. Yet he judged that it was time to take this stand for both political and moral reasons.[28]

The Emancipation Decree has gone forth for the 1st of January next, but as it is only to apply to States which may then be in Insurrection, and in which consequently this govt. will have no *de facto* jurisdiction, it is not likely to be attended with much practical result. On the other hand, it is calculated to alienate the Democratic Party and to strengthen the Confederate cause. As it only came out this morning, I am unable to say what impression it is making upon the public mind.

The decisive Battle which was expected when I last wrote did not take place at all, the Confederates having retired to the Virginia side of the Potomac during the night, apparently without any further loss. It is supposed that their ammunition was exhausted, and that Beauregard did not arrive in time. Their retreat must have been perfectly orderly and not that of a demoralized Army. What they are now doing, or where they are even, is a mystery. It is perhaps as well that each Party should find out the difficulty of a war of invasion. There is considerable surprise at there having been no subsequent Despatches published from General McClellan.

As Stuart pointed out, one of the intentions of the president in issuing the Emancipation Proclamation was to appease those in England and France who found the Northern cause lacking in loftier goals beyond simply restoring the Union. Stuart's own assessment of its rationale and effect indeed contained serious doubts tinged with undisguised cynicism.[29]

The whole aspect of Affairs here is confused and uncomprehensible. To have to forward in the same week one Proclamation of Emancipation, and another suspending the Writ of Habeas Corpus throughout the Land, would make the situation, without any other complications, most difficult to realize. But there are, in addition, intrigues of all sorts, large and small, of parties and of persons, which make it impossible to see one's way for a day in advance, nor even to know what opinions are assuming shape, so extensive is the scene and so quickly does it shift.

There is a meeting of some sixteen or more Governors of "Loyal States" holding sittings at Altoona in Pennsylvania, who are said to be discussing the questions of the day with a view to decide upon different measures which, if they can agree, they will impose upon the unfortunate President. The Emancipation Edict is supposed to have removed the best part of their ground from under their feet, but they may require him to go further, to change his Cabinet,—to dismiss McClellan for Fremont,—to adopt all sorts of wild schemes for prosecuting the War. There is however a Conservative Element amongst them, which may exercise a moderating influence. We shall know in a few days whether they have been able to come to an understanding.

I heard that there had been a previous meeting of New England Governors, who had suspended the departure of reinforcements to Washington until Emancipation was proclaimed.

One of the President's motives must no doubt have been the expectation that it would change the course of public opinion in England and in Europe, and secure sufficient sympathy to render intervention impossible. But there is no pretext of humanity about the Proclamation. It is cold, vindictive, and entirely political. It does not abolish Slavery where it has the power; it protects "the Institution" for friends and only abolishes it on paper for its enemies. It is merely a Confiscation Act,—or perhaps worse, for it offers direct encouragement to servile Insurrections.

My surprise is that is should be found satisfactory by the Abolitionists, although it is probably only hailed as the first sign of the President's dependence upon them. If he has thereby gained their friendship, he has made more enemies, and he may find himself the Puppet of a Party, instead of the President of a Nation. There was certainly this excuse for him, that the incapacity of his Administration had lost him all support, whereas he will now obtain the support of one of the large Parties. All that is now done is with a view to the Elections, and it will be curious to see what they will produce.

The Convention of Governors bears rather the appearance of a Committee of Public Safety.

McClellan's position is a curious one. No other General could have fought the late Battles so successfully, as the Army would not have then fought under any other, and it is not likely that they would now submit to his removal. But the Campaign is still undecided, and he is not yet a great Conqueror. Had he more energy and decision of character, he might play a great part in the present confusion; but he may be victimised as before by his enemies in the Cabinet, now that he appears to be standing still. The next few weeks will be of great interest.

I dined yesterday with Mr. Seward, and he talked in his usual style about there having been difficulties which had, however, been surmounted;—all is to now go smoothly and prosperously! The great misfortune appears to me to have been that, from the beginning, not one of the men in power has shown any higher sense of responsibility than a Child who breaks his toys does.

I regret that I am unable to describe as completely as I should wish, for your information, what is passing around me.

When Stuart wrote on 29 September, politics dominated his thoughts. For the moment, both sides in the war were taking stock of their position, which appeared to be a stalemate.[30]

> I distrust Mr. Seward's proposal about Negro Immigration, in the present state of Affairs here.[31] It looks rather like a trap, and he seemed disappointed that I did not consider myself authorized to conclude a Convention with him off-hand. The President's own arguments to the Chicago Deputation against his subsequent Proclamation are curious and prove how entirely political and how little Philanthropical were the motives with which it was issued. One report is that it was so suddenly decided upon that Mr. Seward was not told of it, until he went to the Cabinet Council and was desired to sign it. He had been opposed to the same policy some weeks before, but he now makes out that it would then have been ill-timed, whereas the times have since changed!
>
> General McClellan's Army does not expect to move soon, and he wishes to give it rest. Neither Army is anxious to have the Potomac in the rear at this season when the rains may at any time render it impassable. The Confederates do not consider that they were defeated, and it was so near a drawn Battle as could be, only that the Federals have since held the ground.
>
> We appear to be drifting towards Revolution in the North, and things may take a bad turn any day, but it would be difficult to say in what exact form.
>
> Mr. Seward is really annoyed at the Treasury orders about Cotton being in contradiction to his previous assurances and he sent for me to ask for some proof in the shape of evidence of his having promised a liberal Policy, with a view to get up a case against his colleague Mr. Chase.[32] I accordingly made a memorandum for him, containing extracts from my reports of his language to me. It is unlikely, however, that Cotton will come out upon any terms.

The forthcoming state and federal elections were on Stuart's mind as he began his next letter of 7 October.[33]

> We have had a comparatively quiet week as far as Military or other "sensations" are concerned, and although there are battles brewing, the War is for a time becoming almost a secondary consideration, in view of the approaching Elections. It is expected that the Democrats will carry the day in Pennsylvania and perhaps also in New York; but in the latter State the struggle may be a close one, and it will certainly be a very violent one. Many are of the opinion that the Republican Party will carry Wadsworth for Governor of New York, unless there is a split amongst them.[34] Some intervening event may however quite change the aspect of Affairs. On account of the Emancipation Edict being intended to take effect on the 1st of January, the Abolitionists are in the meantime less anxious than formerly for the immediate advance of the Army.
>
> The Edict has, as might have been expected, raised a storm in the Congress at Richmond, and threats of raising the Black Flag and other measures of retaliation are under discussion.[35] There can be little doubt that if the War does continue, it will increase in hatred and barbarity. The Governor of Michigan or Minnesota (I forget which) in a speech here the other day called for the importation of the guillotine from France, and if the Republicans can maintain themselves in power, we may see reenacted some of the worst excesses of the French Revolution. Then, if they are defeated, will they after having tasted Power, submit to the decision o the Ballot Box? The tendency seems rather towards further disruption than towards reunion.
>
> Should an opportunity offer, I shall say more to Mr. Seward about the Cotton

Orders, but the matter seems no longer worth pressing, as the Confederates are less likely than ever to allow Cotton to come out.[36]

Both the French and Russian Ministers have been in the North for the last ten days. The President went last week to visit General McClellan's Army, and is said to have been much pleased. It is, however, currently reported that those troops who had been at Harrison's Landing on the James River will be incapable of standing the cold weather, that they have no stamina left. Intrigues of Politicians against McClellan are incessant, and General Hooker, a brave but swaggering Soldier, who was wounded in the last Battles, is being set up as a rival to him; at least an attempt is being made in that sense.[37]

The upcoming congressional elections began to have a perceptible effect on the calculations being made by politicians, diplomats, and military personnel in the capital. The majority seemed to favor a wait-and-see attitude while at the same time maneuvered into position for prompt action once the results were known.[38]

The Russian minister has just been with me, before returning to New York this evening. He is of the opinion that the time may come before long when intervention will be useful, that it should be reserved, if decided upon, until after the elections, when some of the leading Democrats might be sounded about it, if the war continues to languish. He says that M. Mercier (who is still in New York) is rather too anxious to precipitate matters.

He found Mr. Seward last night much depressed at the news about the elections. In the morning Mr. Seward had told me that the elections were not likely to be materially different in their result from those which brought in the present Congress, and had expatiated in his usual style about the crisis having passed, and all being over when the Armies advance, which they are ordered to do almost immediately. It was impossible at first to estimate the strength and duration of the Rebellion, but now its' days could be numbered. And this calculation appeared to be based upon an idea which he developed with great complacency, that materials are used up so quickly in this country that, taking the two sides together, no less than 100,000 men—50,000 in each—had been killed, wounded or invalided in a single month, and that at the same rate, the Southern Population would be exhausted in a given time and the Northern superiority be reestablished.

Mr. Seward further said to me that since General Grant's victory at Corinth, Negroes had been flocking into the camp in great numbers and that the same would be the case at New Orleans and wherever the Federal Armies advance, but he counts upon continual advances, whereas we have seen the tide turn more than once in this war, and it is as likely as not to turn again.[39]

The order to General McClellan to advance at once was very positive when taken to the President for signature but the latter added a postcript saying that it was not to be considered as absolutely positive if the general had serious grounds for opposition.

Seizure of two French consular agents and the commandeering of a Spanish ship outraged the representatives of both these countries, but because details surrounding the incidents were scant, they had little hope of redress. Stuart sympathized with their frustration but continued to feel that inaction by foreigners remained the wisest policy for the foreseeable future.[40]

The French Minister came back last night from New York and paid me a long visit today. He is much pleased at the Democratic tendency of his election, and does not doubt that the Democratic Party will soon have its desire for Peace. He appears to have talked with several of the most influential persons on both sides, and to have latterly found even Republicans more moderate, and going so far as to inquire whether in the event of Foreign mediation some modification, or arrangement for the gradual exhaustion, of slavery might not be stipulated for from the South.

Still, I fear that the President and his Cabinet have not as yet, as your Lordship seems to suppose, any idea that they are merely fighting to cover a retreat, and that they will not be ready to accept mediation unless forced to do so by this unexpected resurrection of the Democratic Party. It is, therefore, to the public, and not to the government that we must look, if we intend to proffer our services in the interest of Peace. If Seymour is elected Governor of New York, as now seems probable, the favorable moment will, perhaps, soon arrive.[41] He and his party are speaking out boldly for government according to the Constitution, and when in power they will oppose any unconstitutional acts within that state. Supposing then, as is generally admitted, that it is impossible to carry on the war vigourously whilst governing within the limits of the Constitution, the success of the Democrats will actually amount to a relaxation in the conduct of the war. It is here that it may then be too late to stop further separations, this may be a doubtful question which it may take some time to solve; but to secure the first separation of the South would be a great step gained, and if independence has ever been ably fought for and deserved, it has been so in the case of the Confederacy.

Mons. Mercier says that, in words at least, the general hatred of England has never been greater than now. He believes that the Russian Minister is trying to bring about a French-Russian mediation with an aim to separate France from England, but he is much opposed to this and has warned Mons. Thouvenel of the design, although he acknowledges that the best mediation of all would be that of the three powers combined. He had not received much of importance latterly from M. Thouvenel, who stated that the Emperor and other ministers being absent, nothing yet had been decided upon.

As the elections drew nearer, hopes for a settlement of the war increased. Stuart finally determined that the time had arrived to use recognition of the Confederacy as a threat in order to achieve this end, and he therefore hastened to inform Lord John Russell. Before launching into his reasoning, however, he began his letter with an unsubstantiated rumor from the front.[42]

A truly horrible incident appears to have occurred in Missouri, as described in the enclosed Extract from the "National Intelligencer" of this morning. I do not like as yet to send it to you officially, in the hope that it may be contradicted, but the details are given with such thrilling minuteness that the story can hardly be an invention. It is the actual execution by order of the Federal General McNeil of no less than ten of his Prisoners, in consequence of the capture and *suspected* death of one of the Unionist inhabitants of Palmyra by Confederate Guerrillas.[43] If it turns out to be true, we shall probably see terrible reprisals and perhaps the Black Flag hoisted, and then the War may become worse than any that we have yet heard of in barbarism and atrocity. It is the first instance of retaliatory threats in their worst exaggeration having been carried out to the Letter, and once begun, where will the system end?

On the other hand, the general aspect of Affairs has been latterly ripening very fast for mediation and Peace. People are speaking out more openly and are becoming prepared for mediation. In short, there are more hopeful indications of returning sense, and I feel almost convinced that any proposals which we might make in concert with France would, after a certain amount of threats and howlings by the violent portion of the press, be favorably received by the majority of the Public, if they are moderately and courteously worded.

I hope, therefore, that Lord Lyons is bringing out important Instructions, as the time for acting upon them is fast approaching, and the War may otherwise enter into a new phase.

The difficulty of getting information about British Subjects who have been arrested is very annoying, and after their release I have avoided pressing for explanation, lest by so doing the release of others should be retarded or refused. We can always bring forward the cases hereafter, if it is considered desirable to do so.

There are also considerable difficulties thrown in the way of obtaining the discharge of British Subjects who have been drafted, but in most of these cases the evil has arisen from their having neglected to take the proper steps in time to secure their exemption.

During the course of October and November 1862, Stuart was pressing vigorously for mediation just as Lord John Russell was reluctantly concluding that the Lincoln administration would never accept it. Furthermore, members of Parliament in London could not agree about a course to pursue, there being strong advocates for and against British intervention. This meant that Lord Lyons would return to America without clear instructions.[44]

The mail of the 18th has only just arrived, and Lord Lyons who started a week later may reach New York tonight or to-morrow if he has a good passage.

I rather regret to find that he does not seem likely to bring out decisive instructions, as both Mon. Mercier and I are of opinion that if Seymour carries his election today in New York, the opportunity for proposing mediation or an Armistice will have arrived. It is true that the Russian Minister thinks that we should wait a little longer, but he acknowledges the time to be very near. He would wish the Democratic Party to pronounce more strongly for Peace before we interfere. In the meantime, however, public opinion may start off in quite a fresh direction, and what he told me of a conversation which he had had with Seward, who is an old friend of his, certainly shows that we might now recognize the South without much risk to ourselves. Mr. Seward naturally declined to answer the direct question as to what he would do in the event of Foreign Mediation being proffered, to be followed by Recognition, if declined; but upon being pressed as to whether he would go to war, he said that he hoped it would not come to that. He asked Mr. Stoeckl whether Mr. Mercier or I had any knowledge of an intended mediation, to which Mr. Stoeckl replied that he could not tell for certain, but that he did not believe that we had received any instructions upon the subject. Mr. Seward then went on to say that he had information of his own which led him to believe that something of the sort had been on the topic, but that the British and French govts. could not agree about it, and that the idea would probably be abandoned in consequence of the failure of the Confederate invasion of England.[45]

This looks as if Mr. Seward considers mediation as sooner or later inevitable, unless the war is won or brought to a conclusion by some other means. He has not talked to me lately upon political matters, and has avoided any political conversations with Mr. Mercier.

Stuart wrote his next letter after the elections had taken place. Democrats nearly doubled their strength in Congress and obtained control of half a dozen state capitals previously held by the Republicans, both setbacks undermining seriously Lincoln's ability to prosecute the war. Stuart was left in limbo as to the precise inclinations of the Palmerston government and whether it was interested in acting together with France and Russia.[46]

> I did not intend in my last letter to be understood as supposing that the present moment would be decidedly better than any other for mediation or Recognition, but I believe that it is a favorable moment, and that it may be a pity to lose it. Although there are signs of approaching exhaustion which may produce still better opportunities later, yet there is always a certain amount of risk that the Democratic party, which is now getting the upper hand, may find its advantage in rousing some other cry than that of Peace, unless it sees at once some means of realizing that object. M. Mercier had certainly been preparing the way for mediation, and all that was asked of him was not to propose it until the elections were over. He did not hear anything from Mr. Drouyn de Lhuys by last mail, but he does not suppose that the change of ministers will make any change in French Policy here.[47]
>
> The success of the conservative party has exceeded all expectations. The unkindest cut of all is that the President's own village of Springfield, Illinois has gone against him, which is said to have annoyed him much. The country is in reality quite tired of the war, and of the jobbery of the Republican Party since it came into power. Not that it has become more impure than the other party was formerly, but that the war has given more opportunites for jobbing with contractors and Army appointments. The Radicals [Republicans] appear for the moment to be rather cowed than rabid, and so far their defeat has done them good.

Lord Lyons reached New York City on 8 November, and soon thereafter Stuart gratefully relinquished his authority as chargé d'affaires. With Stuart no longer in a position to urge a policy of intervention upon Her Majesty's government and with a change of foreign minister in Paris, drastic measures were unlikely to be adopted by either the British or the French. Lord John Russell also backed off, inclined to agree with Lord Palmerston that the time for mediation had not yet arrived.

13

Mediation and Domestic Emancipation, November 1862–June 1863

Newly arrived back in the United States after a five-month leave of absence, Lord Lyons remained a few days in New York City to assess political opinions before moving on to Washington. The recent state and congressional elections still dominated talk and fostered speculation about things to come.[1]

> I did not get here until the 8th. We did not meet with any accident, but were delayed by stormy weather.
>
> I found the people in this place in a state of great excitement and great delight at the Democratic triumph in the election—as much or more with the success in the Western states, and especially in the President's own state, Illinois, as with the more complete victory here.
>
> The political leaders here, and indeed the people at large appeared to be above all relieved and delighted with the idea that personal liberty and freedom of speech were secured to this State at least—they considered it impossible that the government would attempt to resist a Writ of Habeas Corpus in the State of New York—and certain that the state authorities would enforce execution of the Writ by the aid of the Militia, if necessary. Hopes were entertained that the result of the elections would be accepted by the President as the will of the people—that he would strengthen the moderate and conservative elements in the Cabinet and seek a termination of the war, by conciliatory measures, instead of by multiplying provocations to the South.
>
> A cloud was however thrown over all these brilliant prospects by the announcement the day before yesterday that General McClellan, the favourite of the Democratic or rather the moderate party, had been dismissed from the command of the Army of the Potomac, and ordered home—in fact removed altogether from active service. This was taken as a sign that the President intended to throw himself into the arms of the violent abolitionist Party, and it was thought probable that Seward and the other moderate members of the Cabinet would retire. Yesterday nothing new had come from Washington—and the excitement was kept up by a speech in a Democratic meeting by Mr. John Van Buren,[2] proposing McClellan as the Candidate of the Party for the next Presidency. People here seem however to be still convinced that the conservative Party must obtain the control of the Executive government within a few months. That Party does not conceal its desire for an armistice to be followed by a Convention, in which it thinks the South would be induced to take part, and in which such modification of the Constitution might, it believes, be made, a would induce the Southern States to return to the union. Suppose however that the more sagacious leaders of the party are in their hearts convinced that the union cannot

be restored—they probably regard the armistice as a preliminary to peace—and for the sake of peace would be willing to let the Cotton States at least depart—Such sentiments however cannot at this moment be avowed. The party calls, even more loudly than the Republicans, for a vigorous prosecution of the war. This it does partly with a view to embarrass the government, partly from a desire to place the North in as favourable a position as possible for proposing an armistice in the first place— and for obtaining a good frontier—if the armistice end in separation.

I have not encouraged people to speak to me on the subject of foreign intervention. I perceive however that the Democrats are very nervous on the subject. They are terribly afraid lest it should be proposed at a time at which the executive government is in the hands of the violent party. They think that that party would make use of the offer as a means of rousing the passion of the people, and that they might succeed in upsetting all the conservative plans and in producing a strong war reaction. If however the executive government should pass over to the moderates many of the Democrats would be willing, as a "pis aller" to receive an offer of mediation from *all* the powers of Europe. By *all* is meant principally *Russia* in addition to England and France and perhaps Prussia might be added with advantage. But the Democrats appear to be afraid of the effect on the public mind of foreign intervention under any circumstances, and to be willing to resort to it, only if it appears impossible to obtain a cessation of hostilities by any other means. Of course they would regard a simple recognition of the South by any European Power as disastrous to their moderate plans.

I have found however among Englishmen and Canadians here a stronger desire for the immediate recognition by Europe of the South than I was at all prepared for. This desire proceeds from a fear that the plans for reestablishing the Union might be successful, and that the reunited Confederacy would forthwith turn its arms against England and in particular Canada. I have, as you know, hitherto considered fears of this kind as simply chimerical. I have not yet changed my opinion, but I think it right to mention to you the fact that they are more strongly and more generally entertained than I had any idea of.

With regard to the hopes of the Democratic Party of morally coercing the President so far as to get the Executive Government into their own hands—it is to be observed that although Democratic Members of Congress have been already elected in this and other states in the room of Republicans, the Congress for which they have been elected will not meet until December 1863. The present Congress, which will begin its session next month, is strongly Republican—and the fact of its being already known that most of the Republican members will not be in the next Congress, will tend to make those members entirely regardless of the present wishes of the constituents. This system of electing members of future Congress, before the close of the existing Congress is one of the many curious peculiarities in the political system of this Country.

The government has hitherto shown signs of weakness. It does not seem willing to try the experiment of enforcing the compulsory draft of men for the army, and it has been very tardy in collecting the new taxes. But this may have proceeded from a fear of decreasing popularity before the elections. If the violent party in the cabinet now triumph, I suppose they will make a show of vigour, and I am not without apprehension that they may try the effect of vigour, that is to say of violence, in their Foreign Policy.

I have stated in this letter impressions made upon me on my arrival. I should say that they are derived almost exclusively from Democrats, indeed at New York almost all the upper classes are Democrats. This is now the centre of interest in American politics, and I should, on that account, have been glad to stay here a few days longer, but I am afraid my doing so might be misinterpreted at Washington.

It seems plain that at this moment Foreign intervention, short of the use of force, could only make matters worse here. Beyond this, I have not arrived at any conclusion from what I have heard here. If the army of the Potomac be pushed forward under Burnside, a great victory or a great defeat may entirely change the face of things. At all events the North are likely to obtain successes on the coast and on the rivers during the autumn, they will have a large number of small iron-clad steam vessels ready, and the autumn rains will render the rivers navigable. Successes may render the administration and the war less popular, and defeat the conservative plans. I confess too that I see no signs of the South's being willing to listen to any terms short of independence. There is believed to be a great divergence of feeling between the Border states and the cotton states, but they are kept together by the pressure of the war, by hatred of the North, and, I am afraid it cannot be denied, by the provocations of the government at Washington. Whatever quarrels there may be among the members of the Southern Confederacy, there does not appear to be a shadow of a desire to return to the union with the North.

I do not myself expect any great results from the financial difficulties on either side. I am told that such of the new taxes as have already been enforced in the North have proved to be more productive than was anticipated.

Once in Washington, Lyons lost no time conferring with the French minister, Mercier, and with Secretary of State Seward. Oddly enough, he felt things had not much changed since going on leave back in June. As before, Britain would need to wait upon events.[3]

I arrived here the evening before last. I saw both Mr. Seward and the President yesterday, but had no conversation of any great importance with either. No allusion whatever was made to the question of foreign intervention. Mr. Seward did not appear to expect me to make any special communication to him from you, and I was glad to avoid the subject. I do not think it desirable to put this government too much at their ease about the intentions of England and France, and I am very anxious to avoid saying or doing anything which might embarrass me in executing any instruction you may send hereafter.

Before going to Mr. Seward's I had a long conversation with Mons. Mercier. Intervention is always uppermost in his thoughts, and he is ever on the watch for an opportunity of effecting it. I did not however understand that he thought the present moment favourable. With the violent party predominant in the cabinet and a violent Congress to support them, there could in fact be little or no hope of a proposal for mediation being accepted. The alternative of recognizing the South, on the rejection of mediation, would simply produce a quarrel with the United States with little benefit to the South or to Europe, unless it were followed by strong measures with regard to the Blockade. . . . You may remember that I mentioned to you at Woburn that the Duke of Newcastle[4] thought that there was an objection, with reference to the lower Canadians, in allowing France to appear to take the lead of England in American affairs.

With regard to these and other questions, it is to be remembered that the position of the President will be very materially changed after the 4th of March next. On that day the House of Representatives is dissolved by the Constitution, and several Senators go out of the office. At present the President is sure of the support of Congress in violent and extra-legal measures. But it is already certain that in the new House of Representatives, the Democrats or conservatives will have a majority, and that the Democratic party in the Senate will gain strength. Consequently the action of the Executive government after the 4th of next March will come under the review of a hostile instead of a friendly Congress, and prudent counsels will have a better chance of being listened to.

You will hardly care to hear Mr. Seward's prognostications as to the immediate military successes to be expected, or the approach of the end of the war. Expeditions are prepared against Texas, Mobile, Charleston, and it is believed, Savannah. The success of some, if not all of these, is far from improbable. Less confidence must be felt in the prediction, which Mr. Seward makes of a great victory to be gained within the next few days in Virginia by the Army of the Potomac under its new General Burnside.

I find a new difficulty to contend with in managing matters here. Mr. Seward has apparently lost very much of his influence with the President and the cabinet. He seems to be very conciliatory, but not to be able to carry his points with other Departments. He has fallen very much in public estimation by signing the abolition proclamation, which was imposed upon him by opposition to all his own views, by the Radical party in the Cabinet. . . .

Mr. Seward took occasion to tell me that he was particularly pleased with the manner in which affairs had been conducted by Mr. Stuart during my absence.

I am very glad to find that Mr. Stuart has no wish to have leave for the next few months if his services are likely to be wanted here.

In assuming command of the Army of Tennessee, Major General Ulysses S. Grant (1822–85) emerged as the chief military figure in the West. His task was a formidable one: to force his way from Vicksburg to Port Hudson, a distance of some 210 miles down the Mississippi River. Vicksburg was high above the river, was well defended by artillery, and managed to hold out for many months to come.[5]

I cannot help looking with great apprehension on this campaign on the Mississippi. The United States armies are to bring with them wholesale confiscation of property and servile insurrection—the South may retaliate, and an awful series of horrors follow.

We have little means here of forming an opinion as to the amount of military resistance which the South can make on the Mississippi. Mr. Seward says they can make none—and that the result of the campaign is as good as accomplished. If it succeeds, it will be a much greater advantage to the United States than the capture of Richmond. General Burnside's advance to that place lags. He has determined to transfer his base of operations to Aquia Creek; this is the most convenient point of the Potomac for communicating with Richmond. It is about 60 miles from that place and there are the remains of a Railroad between the two. The rains have set in—so that after all Burnside may not get on better than McClellan did.

Mr. Chase, the Secretary of the Treasury, told me the other day that the new taxes were bringing in so much, that they would produce not only enough to pay the interest of the whole debt, but that they would enable him, if he pleased, to pay off five per cent of the capital in July next. We shall see how he makes this out in his report to Congress next month.

By 24 November, Count Mercier let Lord Lyons know that the French government was still determined to impose mediation upon the combatants or let them suffer the consequences. For his part, the British envoy was singularly unenthusiastic about the scheme.[6]

> M. Mercier has read me the Note to England and Russia proposing to them to join France in recommending the Belligerents try to agree to an armistice.
>
> As I have already said, I do not see that any great inconvenience can arise from the steps being taken, provided Russia is a party to it. If the proposal were made at a moment like the present, and if the answer were left to Mr. Seward, the answer would be evasive or temporizing. If the proposal arrived at a moment of military success, the violent party might induce the President to repudiate haughtily all notion of European intervention under any circumstances. I don't think that even if it arrived after a great reverse in the field, this government would accept it, unless they were absolutely in dread of losing this place, or of some other disaster, unless the Confederate Armies could be stopped. But if made at such a time, and consequently when the public was depressed and weary of the war, it might be taken up by the opposition.
>
> M. Mercier is much more confident than I am of rallying public opinion to Foreign mediation. I hardly think the idea of it will ever be so popular, that the opposition will be able to force the adoption of it upon an unwilling government.
>
> M. Mercier holds to his opinion that it is essential to the success that there should be an element of "intimidation"—felt, if not seen. That the government should have reason to apprehend that the rejection would lead to the recognition of the South and something more. He is no doubt right—but I draw a different conclusion from his premises. He thinks that the proposal should be made at once, in the hope that the "intimidation" will work of itself. I doubt whether the necessity of this element to success, is not a reason for putting off the proposal—unless we are determined to press upon the attention of the government (if necessary) the serious consequences of rejecting our offer—and to make the consequences serious if it be rejected. Otherwise we shall only weaken the effect of our future offer, by crying our wolf now, when there is no wolf.
>
> The *Blockade* is the critical point. The North will feel that to give up that is to give up the war for ever; and the South must be hard pressed before it accepts an armistice allowing the Blockade to subsist.

By 2 December it was apparent that the French would probably not seek to impose mediation upon North and South. With that issue more or less out of the way, Lord Lyons could turn his attention to Lincoln's annual message to Congress, with its plan for the gradual emancipation of slaves. It will be recalled that the Emancipation Proclamation of September 1862 applied only to states in rebellion and not to the rest of the country.[7]

> You ask me in your private letter of the 15th, what are the views of the Democrats as to quiet and gradual emancipation.
>
> It would be very difficult for them to announce at the present moment an opinion in favour of emancipation in any shape, because they repudiate the notion of the Federal Government having any right to deal with the question at all, and because they desire above all things to conciliate the South, which shrinks from all mention of interference with the subject. The President's Message will however elicit some

expression of opinion from the Democrats, for the greater part of it is taken up with an exposition of his own plan for gradual emancipation with compensation. I have not had time to make out exactly what the President's plan is. It appears to provide for the compensation of proprietors in such States as choose voluntarily to abolish Slavery before the year 1900; and for the preservation of the freedom of such slaves as shall have become free by the chances of war before the end of the "Rebellion". It appears to be intended to place the South between this proposal and the Proclamation of Emancipation, the execution of which will not, it is said, "be stayed because of the recommendation of this plan". The President seems seriously to suppose that if the plan be adopted, the Southern States will be induced by it to return to the Union. But in fact for it to be adopted legally some of them must virtually return beforehand, for it requires the assent of the legislatures or of Conventions in three fourths of the States, involving as it does a change of the Constitution. . . . The reports from the Army confirm the idea that they intend to make a serious attempt to get to Richmond at once. Indeed this is a political necessity for the party in power. Many of them feel that both the war and their tenure of power will be virtually at an end on the 4th of March if they have not made some real progress towards subjugating the South before that time.

A few days later, Lyons was able to consider more fully Lincoln's plan for gradual emancipation.[8]

The Democrats are affecting to praise the President's plan for what he calls "compensated emancipation". In fact it would be difficult for them to find fault with the principles of it. The abolitionists may object to its being left entirely to the choice of the separate States whether they will emancipate or not—but this is a democratic article of faith. No one can reasonably object in principle to offering compensation to the Slave owners if they choose to accept it, or to making the emancipation gradual. The purpose however of the Democrats in praising the plan is to convict the President of inconsistency, or to oblige him to withdraw his "Emancipation" or rather "Servile War" Proclamation. By that Proclamation all slaves in states which do not send to the United States Congress before the 1st of January Representatives elected at elections in which the majority of the persons entitled to vote have taken part, are declared to be at once free forever. Now the Democrats say it is impossible the President can believe he shall either conquer the Southern States or bring them back to the Union by persuasion in time for them to send members to Washington before the first to next month. Either, therefore, he intends to withdraw or modify his Proclamation, or his new plan is simply a "delusion and a snare". The President himself however declares that the execution of this Proclamation will not be "Stayed" on account of the proposal of the new plan.

It is needless to point out the practical difficulties in executing the plan. In fact there is nothing practical about it. It requires the assent (as the President himself says) of seven slave states. Does he expect to have seven slave states represented in his Congress in three weeks time?

Elected in November 1862, the Thirty-eighth Congress was not due to begin its first session until 7 December 1863, and in the meantime, the executive branch would exercise maximum power over governmental affairs. That left the "lame duck" second session of the Thirty-seventh Congress a few months in which to promote pet measures and generate a multitude of rumors.[9]

If Mr. Seward's resignation be accepted, which you will perhaps have information about by telegraph by this mail, it will show that Mr. Lincoln has thrown himself completely into the hands of the ultra Radical party. That Party will do anything to make its overthrow impossible—even possibly to risking a Foreign War—so that we may have to be ready for squalls. Unless they (Radicals) can do something *grand*, their doom will be certain—this may make them desperate.

They will endeavour to provide so lavishly for everything during this Congress—as to prevent any necessity for assembling the new one before its regular time (the first Monday in December)—but the separate States and their Governors have ample means of thwarting them in the mean time.

For many months there had been a crisis brewing in the cabinet, which came to a boil toward the end of December.[10]

Our "Ministerial Crisis" was supposed to be over, and Mr. Seward believed yesterday that the Cabinet would be unchanged. But Mr. Chase has not yet withdrawn his resignation, and if he will not withdraw it, there will very likely be a complete change in the radical sense. I believe Mr. Seward at bottom wishes to stay, and Mr. Chase at bottom wishes to go. This puts Mr. Chase in a better condition to make terms, and one of them may be that he is to have a united Cabinet of his own way of thinking. This would exclude Mr. Seward. The President however is afraid that Mr. Seward's departure would lose him the State of New York altogether, and will keep him if he can. But a quarrel with the Republican Members of the Senate is a very serious thing for him, for after the 4th of March, he will have nobody to look to but them. The House of Representatives will probably go entirely against him. There are now in the Senate 48 members, 30 Republican and 18 opposition. 28 of the Republicans were present at the Caucus at which the following resolution was adopted unanimously: "Resolved that a Committee of six be appointed to wait upon the President, and urge upon him the duty of changing his conduct and his Cabinet", so as to ensure to your etc etc etc. The point in the President's conduct objected to is, I believe, his irregular mode of doing business, and his not consulting his whole cabinet about important measures. The Committee had two interviews with him, the first alone, the second with all the Cabinet (except Mr. Seward who had sent in his resignation) present.

The whole affair seems very foolish as a party move, for it must weaken and discredit both the Cabinet and the President himself, and the possession of the Executive power is becoming more than ever important to the Republicans. But the fact is the reverses have made the Administration so unpopular, that the Senators thought it necessary for their own popularity to urge a change.

The result of the Crisis will no doubt be known at Boston by telegraph before the Packet sails. I shall be sorry if it ends in the removal of Mr. Seward. We are much more likely to have a man less disposed to keep the peace than a man more disposed to do so. I should hardly have said this two years ago.

The cabinet crisis soon subsided, and Lincoln persisted in his contention that what the North most needed was military success.[11]

It is believed that President Lincoln has his Emancipation Proclamation ready for the 1st of January. President Davis has already brought out his, threatening (or rather ordaining) retaliation. I suppose the friends of humanity must only hope that neither will be carried into execution.

The military prospects are gloomy at this moment. General Grant is said to be retreating instead of advancing in the West. It seems at all events certain that some bad news has arrived from that quarter. The Confederate Cavalry has made a raid, and carried off some booty between Washington and General Burnside's Army at Falmouth. That Army ought, it is supposed, if only military reasons were considered, to go into winter quarters, but party politics decide otherwise. It is said that it is to make another attempt to get to Richmond by the Peninsula, an expedition not very inspiring to the Soldiers, after McClellan's failure. Preparations for a move up the James River are said to be apparent at Fortress Monroe. It is supposed that the Iron-clads intended for the attack on Charleston will be diverted to this object.

The Bahama Islands are a constant source of anxiety to me. Considering that the Bahamians push to the extreme limit the advantages their position gives them for running the Blockade, they are hardly reasonable in expecting to find U.S. Captains always in good humour with them, or in pretending to anything more than a strict observation of international law, but to a strict observance of the law they have of course a right. I should have put the case of the "Elias Reid" more positively in my Note to Mr. Seward—had I not so often seen Bahama cases break down.

The 1st of January will see Governor Seymour installed as Governor of New York— and if it sees also the Emancipation Proclamation—the Democrats will have a magnificent opening for opposition to the Government, and for bringing about peace, if they really wish for peace. Their aims are too uncertain at present to make vigourous action likely.

The New Year 1863 began with little hope of an end to hostilities and with every prospect of growing discontent among the states of the Union.[12]

The Emancipation Proclamation appeared yesterday. It frees the slaves in all the states or parts of states in which the United States Government has at the present moment no *de facto* power. If it does not succeed in raising a servile insurrection, it will be a very unsuccessful political move for its authors. For it will not only render the South united and desperate, but increase the divisions in the North. The point immediately interesting is to see the use the [Democratic] opposition will make of it. The leaders of that party talked very loudly of their intentions beforehand, but they have not yet any definite policy to take a stand upon, and have hitherto been weak and vascillating notwithstanding their success in the Elections. They would declare openly for peace, but the Country is not yet ready for that. Nevertheless peace is now advocated more frequently and with less disguise in the newspapers, and endeavours are made to induce some of the State legislatures to pass resolutions in favour of an armistice and a convention. The most probable cause of peace will be the impossibility of raising or keeping together a great army, or even bringing what men there may be into action, unless the war spirit is revived by some military successes. It is said that it will soon be impossible to get more recruits even from Massachusetts, and one of the arguments of the favourers of the Proclamation was the necessity of getting black recruits to fill up the vacancies left by the Whites. The prospect is very gloomy, and if things go on in their present course we shall see retaliatory executions of prisoners on both sides, and every sort of atrocity.

The French Consul at New Orleans writes to M. Mercier that General Banks is doing wonders in conciliating the people and that there is even a probability that considerable quantities of cotton will be brought to market from the neighbouring plantations. I should fear the new regulations, by virtue of which cotton would be allowed to be exported only by the military authorities, will, if they are published and put in force, very greatly interfere with this hopeful prospect.

In late December 1862 and early Janaury 1863 one of the major battles of the war was fought in central Tennessee near the town of Murfreesboro. For a time, the Confederate forces under General Braxton Bragg (1817–76) inflicted devastating losses upon the Northern troops. These latter managed to hold out and eventually launched a decisive counterattack that drove the Confederates from the field. As the Union commander, major General William S. Rosecrans (1819–98), summed it up: "We have fought the greatest battle of the war and are victorious."[13]

I am not so much reassured as Mr. Seward appears to be by the latest news from Murfreesboro. All that seems certain is that there has been a frightful carnage. You will have three days later news by the telegraph to Halifax, than I can send today. The fall of Vicksburg is probable, for it can hardly hold out after the Gunboats get within range of it. If the Murfreesboro Battle is a decided victory on one side or the other, it will determine the fate of Tennessee and be a most important event, but drawn battles are the usual events of this war, the Federals having larger numbers and better material, and the Confederates, better Generals and more desperation.

I am rather alarmed by Mr. [Consul] Magee's announcement of his intention to send specie from Mobile in a British Man of War.[14] I should be very much alarmed, if I thought it likely that he would find a Captain of a Man of War as foolish as himself. I really could not answer for peace, if in addition to the irritation about the "Alabama"[15] should come the fury which would be excited if it were shown that our Man of War had carried Confederate gold through the Blockade. No proof that the money was intended for, or even that it had been actually paid to British Bond holders, would ever convince people here that it had not been used to purchase munitions of War.

On 9 January Lord Lyons returned to the familiar theme of a peace settlement and what it would take to convince the North. The prospects were exceedingly gloomy.[16]

In answer to the question in your letter of the 20th, I have no hesitation in saying that all men of all parties have lost heart about the war. They are not confident of success, but they have not lost confidence to such an extent as to reconcile them to the loss of territory. Governor Seymour's message shows how far the Democratic Party think it prudent to go in speaking of peace, and that, you will see, is a very little way indeed. It looks now as if the impossibility of recruiting would be the real cause of the end of the war. Mr. Sumner himself is reported to have told the President that he must not expect any more recruits even from Massachusetts, but then this was an argument for raising Black Regiments.

Mr. Stuart, who is at New York, has seen some of the Democratic leaders there. He says the Democrats give up the idea of the restoration of the Union by war, but that they still profess to hope to restore it peacefully, either by acting on the New

Jersey proposition for a Convention, or on Governor Seymour's vague notion of a combined action, on the part of the Central and Western States. They tell him that they are very despondent about the next two yars, but are anxious that the Cabinet here should play its game out and go to pieces as fast as possible. This means I suppose that they have lost the hope of getting Mr. Lincoln to take them into his counsels.

With the promulgation of the emancipation decree in January 1863, the Lincoln administration was faced with the problem of what to do with former slaves who might escape from the Confederacy. The proclamation had freed them without giving them the full rights of citizenship, and, as Lyons pointed out in his letter of 23 January, there was now some thought being given to encouraging their emigration.[17]

I must begin by begging you to accept my very hearty thanks for your kind wishes for the New Year.

General Burnside issued a Proclamation to the Army of the Potomac announcing his intention to lead them against the enemy, but his plans have been disconcerted by bad weather. Mr. Seward tells me that he cannot fail to do great things. If this effort does not succeed I do not know what is to become of the Republican Party.

Mr. Seward also tells me that the attack on Charleston will be made as soon as the iron-clads now on their way can get there. The "Cadmus" will however be in plenty of time to take off Mr. Bunch. Although I shall be sorry to lose his Reports, it will be a great relief to me to have him safely away when Charleston is attacked. I trust that you will be able to provide him soon with a good appointment. He has had a very hard time, and is the only one of the Southern Consuls who has remained uninterruptedly at his post. He is a very poor man, and by staying at Charleston in the summer has forfeited a life insurance, which was the principal provision he had made for his family.

The President told me the other day that he wanted to have an informal talk with me. He has not yet sent for me. The subject of the talk will no doubt be his hobby, the exportation of the Contrabands. I think something may be done on the Duke of Newcastle's Plan,[18] provided that we can control the Colonial Agents, so as to keep clear of directly exporting from the South. It is from the Southern ports, that the President most wishes to send Negroes, and it is from those ports that the most useful class, the "field hands", would be most easily sent. One of the plans of Mr. Mitchell, the Emigration Agent of the United States here,[19] is that he himself or some other agent or agents should be sent over to England to treat the matter with the government and to influence public opinion. I shall throw cold water upon this scheme until I hear from you what you wish about it. You might find the agents a great nuisance, and I suppose public opinion in England, would, without pushing, support at least as much as you would think it prudent to do. Public opinion in this country is much less unanimous about the matter.

M. Mercier's hopes about mediation have been raised by a visit from Mr. Horace Greeley, the editor of the New York Tribune, the principle organ of the Abolitionist Party. Mr. Greeley's object was to ascertain whether the Emperor Napoleon could be relied upon as a real friend to the United States, in case of his being accepted as mediator. What the Americans mean by a real friend in this sense, is one who would insist on the restoration of the Union. M. Mercier however says that he leaves those who talk to him under no illusion as to this point, that he tells them plainly that the Union is gone for ever. He mentioned to me that he was seriously thinking of writing to propose to M. Drouyn de Lhuys to authorize him to offer mediation, without reference home for instructions, if an opportune moment should arise. I don't know what you think of France's mediating alone, and so give him no opinion about it. So far as our position with this people goes, I should say that the less *we* had to do with the final settlement of their differences the better. If Burnside be defeated now, or even if he do nothing, the Republicans may perhaps look out for the means of peace. But even then success at Charleston or in the West might raise their spirits again.

One of the distinguishing characteristics of Lord Lyons's letters was an emphasis on the factional nature of Northern politics. In retrospect, his letter of 2 February seems to distort the mood prevalent in the North, but one must remember that the Union's chronic military disappointments bred much discontent.[20]

Mr. Seward sent for me and kept me so long, that I have little time left to write.

I think it would be a good thing to remove Mr. Magee as soon as possible from Mobile, and not to wait for this government to demand it. He has all along known it was a mere temporary appointment which was given him, and he has been lucky to hold it so much longer than he expected when he got it. I don't suppose the Confederates would object to our sending a man to Mobile as Acting Consul, but if they do, I think we are better with no one there, than with so incapable a man as Mr. Magee. I thought this, before the affair of the specie. We ought, I think, unless the U.S. Government object, to send a ship of war to Mobile to take him away, if he wishes to come, as otherwise he would have great difficulty in getting out of the Confederate states.

I had intended to write some speculations on the prospect of peace but Mr. Seward has left me no time. The Emancipation Proclamation has effectually divided the North, and now the two parties are at least as much occupied in contending with each other, as in fighting the Confederates. Each party is casting about for a policy which is likely to be popular, the Democrats would take peace more openly, if they did not fear that in the end the makers of peace will be unpopular, and therefore, believing peace must come soon wish to throw the odium of having made it on the Republicans. The Republicans are endeavouring to rule again by military power, but the opposition in Pennsylvania, New York, and New Jersey seems too strong for them, unless at least they can gain some military prestige. They are endeavouring to pack a majority for themselves in the next Congress by having sham elections, such as that at New Orleans, at all the points in the South where they have troops. They are also trying to place strong Republicans at the head of all the armies—but unless they can get some Republican to be successful and to win the confidence of the men, they do themselves more harm than good by their discountenancing Democratic officers. They are still hard at work trying to oust Mr. Seward. I can hardly believe that they will really send General Butler back to New Orleans.

All this looks like such a break up as to render the *vigourous* prosecution of the war impossible, unless, indeed New England, with a hundred and fifty thousand black troops, fight and subdue both the Confederates and the Central and Western States. I believe the people if polled would be for discarding New England and taking up with the South again.

France's military involvement in Mexico, combined with her predilection to weaken the United States, always manifested itself in some fresh behind-the-scenes proposal for imposing an armistice upon both North and South.[21]

I am rather at a loss to understand the French Proposal for negotiation without a suspension of hostilities. I suppose it is made chiefly to keep French people at home quiet, and to show that the Emperor is doing his best for them. Here it is not unlikely to be taken as a preparation for recognition or some more serious measure, as intended to be a last effort made to justify the Emperor in taking his own measures for his own interest. I don't think such a notion would do harm, for it is certainly not for the advantage of the North to feel too secure about Europe. The dread of foreign interference has become one of the arguments used by the peace party.

The Radicals intend, I believe, to make the account of Mr. Seward's messages to Richmond by M. Mercier, which appears in the French Yellow Book, a ground of attack upon the former.

The Union of feeling in the North is quite at an end. At first the Patriots called for a Foreign war to reunite North and South, now some of them call for a Foreign war to heal division in the North itself.

As Lyons reiterated in his letter of 10 February, the prevailing attitude in the North was that of war-weariness. There were no striking victories to quicken men's hearts and encourage voluntary enlistments.[22]

Mr. Seward told M. Mercier yesterday, that he was still unable to give any answer to the French suggestion in favour of direct negotiation, and that he doubted whether he should be able to give an answer in time for the mail of today. M. Mercier has no idea that it will be accepted, but he thinks the government will be very much embarrassed about the answer; to declare as they would have done a year ago, that they will never negotiate with Rebels would be throwing down the gauntlet to the prevailing feeling in the Country, which appears to be all in favour of an armistice and a convention. I do not think so many people would be in favour of negotiation, if they were convinced that it would lead to a final separation, but they still indulge illusions on this point. Discontent with the war is undoubtedly increasing, and if we have no success before the Spring, it will arrive at that pitch that it will be impossible to keep up the numbers of the Army. This I am inclined to think will be the real solution of the question.

In the meantime the Radical Party in Congress are bent upon bestowing unlimited powers on the Executive government, in order, as *they* say, to enable it to carry on a Patriotic war in spite of a faint hearted majority; in order, as their *opponents* say, to keep the Republican Party in power, and throw over the war or not as that Party may find convenient. Bills to enable the President to raise troops without the instrumentality of the State authorities and to legalize and extend the power of arbitrary arrest are the principal measures advocated.

Authority to raise money in almost any conceivable manner will also, if possible be given. But all this must fail, if the military administration does not produce some better results. The removal of all the Democratic Generals has only produced discontent among the troops. There must be a great change before the President could march a military force to coerce the State of New York. The Democrats are timid and seem more timid than they are. Beyond some impractical motions in the legislatures of New Jersey and Illinois, they have hardly shown any signs of life. The fact is that no important elections being at hand, the leaders do not wish to commit themselves to any opinions. They wait to see what will be unpopular when the Elections are nearer. Behind the Politicians however are the mass of the people, who are getting more and more tired of the war, although they have not yet made up their minds to sacrificing the integrity of the territory.

The offer of French mediation was rejected by the Lincoln administration in no uncertain terms, and as Lyons observed on 24 February, there was a growing conviction among Americans that the France of Napoleon III was proving increasingly hostile.[23]

The Conscription Law, the National Currency Bill, and the Letters of Marque[24] are those of the measures adopted by the Republicans to give the President so much power as to make him and his party independent of the next Congress or master of it. The cry against France is stimulated with a view to help these measures but there must be at bottom a great deal of hostility to France. It is a curious change that, even for a moment, a cry against France should be found more effective than a cry against England.

I don't like Mr. Seward's answer to M. Drouyn de Lhuys' proposal, nor his language to me about Letters of Marque. It looks too like a return to the old bluster, and he may not find the Emperor Napoleon so patient and unsuffering as we are. Whether he does it to recover his position with the Radical party and with the people at large, in his old principle that the Foreign Relations are safe materials to make political capital out of, or whether (which is not so inconceivable as it may appear) he really thinks he can frighten England and France with his Privateers, I cannot say. He is more cordial than ever with me personally, and I do my best to prevent his getting into hot water either with France or with me.

By 2 March Lord Lyons was still rejoicing in the novelty of American resentment of France and a corresponding complacency toward Great Britain.[25]

I have every reason to be glad that we kept aloof from the French proposal of mediation. The overtures of France were made before the country was ripe for them, and the result has been an outcry against them, and the introduction of Resolutions into Congress, which, if passed will increase the difficulty which the administration would have in accepting mediation at a future time. All the talk which Mercier heard before the Election from the Democrats was based on the persuasion that the South could be brought back by concession, and that the intervention of France would amount to a pressure of the South to return. There is no doubt that the Democratic success at the Elections was due in a great measure to the belief that the South would accept concessions. The offers have since been secretly made and contemptuously rejected. This has so much irritated some of the Democratic leaders that they are now louder than the Republicans in crying out for war. But the country is growing more and more tired of the war, and unless there is something to raise the war spirit again soon, the Democrats may venture to come out as a peace party. Long habit makes them look to the Presidential Election as the great object, and they become more and more inclined to postpone all other objects to success in that, as the time to begin the electioneering campaign approaches.

There are rumours of bad news for the Federals from Vicksburg but nothing which can be depended upon.

The concluding weeks of the congressional session, with its flurry of last-minute legislation, provided Lord Lyons with much anxiety. Authorizing letters of marque and reprisal could have only one object: to allow privateers to prey upon British merchant vessels, many of which risked blockade running in the anticipation of high profits.[26]

The Dictatorship measures were passed through Congress partly by the help of a war cry against France. It is thought that an attempt will be made to facilitate the execution of them by raising a war cry against England. The exasperation caused by the proceedings of the Privateers is so great, that the government might really find it difficult to resist making some demonstrations against us. If Mr. Seward is really desirous of peace, he has made a great mistake by pushing on the Letters of Marque Bill. I frequently suggested to him how much safer it was for the government to be without power. It is the old story, neither he nor any of the party have the least idea of really going to war either with England or France, but they would go to the verge of it for the sake of making political capital at home, and they may be carried beyond the verge before they see where they are.

Mr. Seward and the whole party calculate immensely on the effects of the anti-slavery meetings in England, and seem to fancy that public feeling in England is coming so completely round to the North that the government will be obliged to favour the North in all ways, even if it be disinclined to do so. This notion is unlucky as it makes those who hold it, unreasonable and presumptuous in dealing with us.

There is a new prize act which seems to contain some objectionable clauses, but it is impossible as yet to get a correct copy of it, as it passed. The same may be said of a modification of the Customs Act. So many acts are hurried through during the last night of the Session that neither Legislature nor President know what laws they have made, until they see them days afterwards in print.

During 1862–63 the United States was outraged by the Confederacy's ability to build and outfit commerce raiders in British shipyards. The most notorious of these ships was the *Alabama*, but the British government excused its procrastination by arguing that there was no way of determining the potential use of such vessels, since they were outfitted for combat only once they had left British waters. In London, Charles Francis Adams deluged Lord John Russell with reports from observers, private investigators, and consular officials to the effect that the purchasers of such ships were bogus intermediaries who would promptly turn the new hulls over to the Confederate navy. The Americans thought they had a *prima facie* case once the *Alabama* and others began to harrass Northern shipping.[27]

The prevailing feeling in the United States at this moment is exasperation against England on account of the proceedings of the "Alabama" and still more on account of the fleet of new vessels which are commonly believed to be building in England for the Confederates. Prudent men have tried to persuade the President of the folly of issuing Letters of Marque, and think they have convinced him. Unluckily both Mr. Seward and Mr. Chase are in favour of issuing them. Mr. Chase, I think, from genuine anger with England, Mr. Seward from a notion that they will serve him as a means of negotiation with Europe, or rather of terrifying Europe. Mr. Mercier says (I know not how seriously) that he has suggested to his government to open the Ports of France to the Privateers of both parties and their prizes, if the United States issue Letters of Marque. This would certainly be more in favour of the Confederates than the Federals, but it would be a singular mode of manifesting disapproval of privateering.

Nothing certain is known here of what has taken place either at Port Hudson or on the Yazoo River. The New York papers may perhaps have some definite news before the Packet sails tomorrow. The attack on Charleston is continually postponed. The Monitors are a disappointment, they did not do all that was expected of them during the experimental bombardment of Fort McAlister. It is said that they cannot fire quickly enough to be effective. Mr. Chase has been waiting for victories in order to raise loans, and Mr. Stanton in order to put in force the Conscription Act. Both will perhaps have to act without the long hoped for successes. I am beset with terrified British subjects who expect to be made soldiers of. The terrors are not altogether without reason in the case of those who have declared their intentions to become citizens.

As we noted at the beginning of this volume, British diplomats always dreaded the publication of a Parliamentary Blue Book, since it would contain the text of many dispatches that, although not private and confidential, were not always written with publication in mind. In his letter of 7 April, Lord Lyons felt a combination of annoyance and regret that one of his official dispatches should have created an outburst in the United States.[28]

The exasperation against England does not diminish. Mr. Seward certainly fans the flame, partly to make political capital for himself and partly in hopes of really frightening you. *He* does not actually mean to go to war, but he has no power to resist men more violent than himself, and may brew a storm which he may be unable to calm. General Butler's speech, which I send you officially, represents the popular feeling of the day. The Democrats have lost everything by not having courage to avow and stand by their real opinions. They now say that it is my despatch in the Blue Book which has lost them the Connecticut Election and ruined them, and even accuse you of having published it, from some Machiavellian motive, in order to destroy them. One hardly knows whether to wish the North success or failure in the field. Success will make them insolent, failure may render a quarrel with a Foreign power a necessity to the Republicans, as a screen for their shortcomings. I can only work quietly to keep things smooth. Unluckily since the arrival of the Blue Book I have a great deal of irritation against myself personally to contend with.

M. Mercier's cue appears to be to keep quiet and let the anger with England produce its usual effect of reviving the popularity of France. It has been a satisfaction to me to find that there is nothing in the Blue Book to produce embarrassment between him and me.

A week later the North's apprehension over Confederate raiders was considerably augmented.[29]

I have written as much as I have time and strength for officially. I have been unwell all the last week, but not seriously so. I think the state of things here, so far as peace with us is concerned, more alarming than it has been since the Trent affair. They are not a people who can be soothed by concessions, and they are a people who after any amount of bluster will give in if they think that their opponents are in earnest and are stronger than they. I would rather the quarrel came, if come it must, upon some better ground for us, than this question of the ships fitted out for the Confederates. The great point to be gained in my opinion would be to prevent the ships sailing, without leading the people here to think that they had gained their point by threats. I am in trouble altogether, for the goodwill to me personally, which miraculously survived so long, seems at last to have sunk altogether under the stroke of the last Blue Book.

Lord Lyons in Washington and Charles Francis Adams in London were both acutely aware of how serious Anglo-American relations had become and how close to war the two nations had drifted in recent months.[30]

Mr. Seward assures me that there will be no surprise as to any measures which this government may take to defend itself, if vessels for the Confederates should escape from British Ports, either in the United Kingdom or the Colonies. He says reasonable notice will be given to us beforehand. What he himself means to do is no doubt to issue Letters of Marque. I don't think he contemplates going beyond this. He likes however to say that he is fully aware that the issuing of them is likely to lead to war: and he makes no scruple in telling people that he has written to England to say that such and such things will tend to produce truth no more than a statement of a matter of fact. The despatch to Mr. Adams which he read to me a few days ago was not intended for communication to you. This mode of producing a spirited blue book for the American Public by writing strong despatches which are not communicated to the government against which they launch forth, is ingenious.

The failure of the expedition against Charleston is taken apparently with apathy, but one can never judge of the real impression things make here immediately. No man likes to be the first to express a strong opinion.

In early April the British government reluctantly took steps to detain several newly constructed vessels that the North claimed were destined for the Confederacy. Although one ship, the *Japan*, managed to escape, the *Alexandra* was prevented from doing so. By June 1863 the British Government lost its case and could no longer stop the *Alexandra* from sailing, but in the meantime, Lyons welcomed the easing of tensions in Washington. It looked as if the Palmerston cabinet was finally prepared to enforce the British neutrality laws.[31]

So far as I can judge in this short time, the Americans have eagerly grasped at the intelligence of the endeavours to stop the Confederate vessels building in England, as a relief from their dread that they were really drifting into a war with us. I cannot yet say whether the exasperation is subsiding. I have not much fear that they will ever really put a casus belli to us, but I do fear that they may force us to make demand upon them to which, however plainly just, party considerations may render it difficult for the administration to yield. I seem to be getting on pretty well again with Mr. Seward, but not with others since the Blue Book, and Mr. Seward cannot control the feelings or the actions of the other members of the administration, either as regards England or her representative here personally. However for the moment things certainly look more peaceful than they did a week ago. I mean peaceful towards us, for there are no symptoms of an approaching end of the Civil War.

At the beginning of May, the vastly outnumbered Confederate forces under Robert E. Lee inflicted a series of defeats upon the Union army near Chancellorsville, Virginia. Casualties were heavy on both sides, and the South sustained a higher proportion of dead and wounded than did the North, including the loss of the dashing commander Stonewall Jackson.[32]

Perhaps the New York papers of tomorrow will take intelligence to Europe of the results of the battles which have followed the onward movement of the Army of the Potomac. We only know now that there has been a great slaughter. In fact the news made public only goes down to Sunday afternoon. Every hour which passes without the publication of further intelligence increases the fear of the friends of the North.

I am doing my best to induce this government to put a stop to the questionable proceeding of their cruisers at St. Thomas and elsewhere before the arrival of a strong remonstrance from England. But I am afraid that as in the Trent affair, they will put off doing right so long, as to please themselves in the position of having either to make a marked concession to England or to run the risk of refusing just demands. I have kept the door open for spontaneous action on their part to the last moment, and have abstained from making anything like a demand or even an embarrassing observation. The difficulties are much increased by the quarrel between Mr. Seward and Mr. Welles, the Secretary of the Navy, about the mails of the "Peterhoff".[33] The ultra-Republicans are representing the giving up of the mails as a humiliating concession to British arrogance, and making use of it as a means of attacking Mr. Seward. The friends of England and of peace in that party cannot resist the temptation of an opportunity of attacking Mr. Seward, although they are at the same time increasing the exasperation against England. Among other devices is that of representing me as having made the most violent and arrogant demands about the "Peterhoff". No party is sorry for a chance of having a hit at me personally since the Blue Book. It is not any new light which the Book is conceived to throw upon my sympathies in the contest which has made people angry. Unluckily the book contains just the passages in my despatches which are most irritating to each of the parties, and which it is most inconvenient to them to have published. The Democrats are furious at the publication of their esoteric doctrines. They told M. Mercier at New York that my despatch had lost them two thousand subscribers to their paper, the "World". The administration does not like the passages about its mistakes and failures. The ultra-Republicans to not like the observations on the injury done to the government party by their factious attacks on members of the Cabinet. And what perhaps has more to do with the matter than all the rest, everybody is furious with England and with everybody and everything English. Mr. Seward's particular grievance about the book arises from a pretension he had that the Foreign Ministers here are to write nothing to their government but what he tells them.

Mr. Seward himself, however, talks pacifically, and I believe, he is acting in the same sense, but he has most of the Cabinet against him, and the public feeling here is in a dangerous state. All my experience goes to prove that firmness does better than concession with the Americans. It is well to build a golden bridge for the retreat of their national vanity, but not to yield in essentials.

I do not get worse, but I do not get well in health. It is particularly inconvenient to me not to be in full force just now.

As a seasoned diplomat, Lyons could not help looking beyond the confused impressions of the moment to the long-range implications of war and neutral rights on the high seas. What he foresaw as to possible British liability for building and releasing the commerce raider the *Alabama* would take eight years of acrimonious negotiation to resolve.[34]

I am doing all I can to persuade the government here really to stop the vexatious proceedings against our merchant ships. I think I shall get tolerably satisfactory written assurances from Mr. Seward, but he has no influence with the Navy Department, and it is on that Dept. the practical matter depends. Time has not yet elapsed sufficient to know how the people will take Hooker's defeat.[35] If it strengthens the moderate party, Mr. Seward will gain strength from it, but it may drive the ultra party into increased violence.

I do not know that anything like a formal statement of claims on account of the depredations of the "Alabama" has ever been presented to the United States government. I doubt whether there has even been any notion that we should under any circumstances admit our liability for them, and I suppose therefore no one has thought it worth while to make claims for individual losses.

If we make a convention on claims, we should endeavour to define very distinctly what sort of claims are included and what not, otherwise we shall have demands of all kinds brought against us, which will go far to defeat any real justice to bona fide losses.

The British continued to protest American interference with shipping between Liverpool and Matamoros, despite the North's claim that some of the goods sent to Mexico were ultimately destined for the Confederacy. Her Majesty's government claimed that Admiral Wilkes and the American squadron were taking advantage of the neutral harbor of St. Thomas to ambush such British merchantmen as the *Peterhoff*, the *Dolphin*, and the *Pearl*.[36]

I have been doing all I can to convince the people here that something practical must be done to remove the impression which has been produced in England by the capture of the "Peterhoff", the "Dolphin" and such proceedings. The two things which I have been most anxious to obtain at once, are the removal of Admiral Wilkes from the West Indies and Gulf of Mexico, and the withdrawal of the U.S. Squadron from St. Thomas. I have been obliged to go very cautiously to work, lest the appearance of a demand from me should have made the government too much afraid of public opinion to do either the one or the other. I did however go farther with Mr. Seward about Admiral Wilkes this morning than I had before ventured to do, and he has just been to tell me that Admiral Wilkes is off to the Pacific. I am particularly anxious that it should not appear that I had anything to do with this. I hope it is a sign that other conciliatory acts, not words merely, will follow.

The country seems to be taking the defeat on the Rappahannock very quietly for the present, but the losses were very severe, and the effect on the spirit of the Army and on the recruiting must be disastrous. Hopes however are entertained of a counter-balancing success on the Mississippi. Mr. Seward thinks that there will be little question soon of trade with Matamoros, because the Federals will have complete command of the Mississippi, and prevent goods being brought across that river from the West.

During the course of 1863 the question of black troops loomed larger in the minds of both North and South. As early as September 1862, the first regiment of blacks was organized by General Butler in New Orleans and called the Louisiana Native Guards, or Chasseurs d'Afrique. In November 1862, Union troops advancing along the coast of Georgia into Florida also included a regiment of blacks, the First South Carolina Volunteers (African Descent), under Colonel Thomas Wentworth Higginson. On 10 March 1863 larger numbers of black soldiers were employed in the occupation of Jacksonville, Florida.

In retaliation, the Confederate Congress in early May authorized the court martial of white federal officers commanding such troops, on the grounds that they were inciting insurrection among all blacks. Several punishments, including death, were recommended.[37]

> If the Negro Regiments are organized and taken to the South, we may look for a series of horrors, the White officers if taken prisoner will very probably be executed and the black privates made slaves of, and then there will be the retaliation on this side.
>
> The Presidential Election is the matter really uppermost in men's minds. Mr. Lincoln has as good a chance of being reelected, as any party candidate has of coming in.

Following his defeat and wounding at Chancellorsville in early May, Major General Joseph Hooker (1814–79) assumed a defensive posture in order to protect Washington and Baltimore. In the North, there was utter confusion as to Lee's ultimate objectives, but few guessed that the Confederates would be so audacious as to invade southern Pennsylvania.[38]

> We are supposed to be in a state of excitement here, because General Lee is believed to have left Fredericksburg with a great part of his Army, and gone upon some expedition. If General Hooker or the government know where Lee is gone, or indeed whether he is really gone at all, the public does not share their information. We are also kept in the dark about Vicksburg, all we know is that it is not taken yet. One assault upon Fort Hudson has also been repelled with great slaughter of the Federals. One can hardly suppose however that that place can hold out long.
>
> The administration and its friends are still more disquieted by the Peace Meeting at New York, and by the successful resistance at Chicago to the attempt of the military to suppress the opposition newspapers. The violent Republicans are beginning to say openly that the Army must be used to ensure the success of the Republican party at the Presidential Election, and that the enforcement of military rule must be begun at once. Whether the movement against the arbitrary measures will become formidable depends I suppose like everything else on the events of the campaign. . . .

. . . Even in this Country a military despotism can hardly be established by a Government under which no military successes are achieved in a war, and by Generals who are always defeated.

I am, I hope, better, but I do not get well.

Precarious health always dominated Lyons's thoughts as the heat and illness of a Washington summer progressed. On 12 June he shared these concerns with Lord John Russell.[39]

I thank you very sincerely for the consideration for my health shown by your letter of the 30th May, which I have received this morning. I cannot at this moment act upon the suggestion which you so kindly make, because I have let Mr. Stuart go to the far West on a shooting excursion, and he will not be back till the end of the month. It would however be a great comfort to me, if you would authorize me to go *on public service* either to Canada to confer with Lord Monck[40] or to Halifax to confer with Sir Alexander Milne[41] if I think it advisable to do so. This would put me quite at ease, if I were obliged to leave Washington, because I could then determine, according to the state of affairs at the moment, whether to keep within the limits of the United States and retain the management of the Legation in my own hands, or to cross the Frontier and make over the routine business to Mr. Stuart.

The implementation of emancipation during 1863 created many so-called contraband slaves who came under the expanding jurisdiction of federal troops. As Confederate forces evacuated an area, they tended to leave old or infirm slaves behind, while other blacks escaped Southern control and took refuge in cities under Northern administration. Back in September 1862, Lincoln had invited England, France, Holland, and Denmark to open their colonial possessions to would-be American black colonizers, but few former slaves availed themselves of this dubious opportunity. In May 1863 the American secretary of the interior, J. P. Usher, told the British he did not think there were any funds available to aid blacks wishing to emigrate to British colonies, but the combination of cheap labor and philanthropy still kept the issue alive in late June.[42]

It looks as if Mr. Hodge[43] had brought his negotiations to such a point, that we might reasonably hope that a beginning would be made of sending Negro Emigrants from this Country to our Colonies. But I am not yet quite sure what difficulties may not be made by this Government. The President's plan of approving papers submitted by subordinates, without coming to an understanding with his Cabinet, is not always successful. You will see that I made Mr. Hodge get the sanction of the Secretary of the Interior to his subordinate's Paper, and that I have myself formally put the question to the Government, whether they are willing or not that the Lt. Governor of Honduras should proclaim the three Ports.

I should very much like to get as many "Contrabands" as possible safe out of this Country—for I do not think that, at best, their condition in the Northern States will ever be a happy one—and they would, in all probability, be sacrificed without scruple, if the North and South should ever come to an understanding. In this case, however, our carrying them away might involve us in disputes with both North and South. The question is too large a one for me to pretend to settle.

The Delegation from Louisiana seems to be assuming rather the character of a political manoeuvre to strengthen the Peace party in the North and to embarrass the administration than that of a serious endeavour to restore the State or any part of it to the Union.

The panic continues—but no events have yet come to justify it.

Within a few days of the start of the Battle of Gettysburg, the movement of troops and the strategy behind them were still obscure to onlookers in Washington.[44]

It seems to be nearly certain that General Lee has invaded Maryland and Pennsylvania with the bulk of his army; a perilous move I should have thought both politically and strategically, but everyone seems to have confidence in Lee and none in Hooker. One of the results of the invasion may be that the communication between Washington and the North may be interrupted. This may prevent my writing to you by one packet, but I should hope to be able to keep up the communication eventually by having one of Admiral Milne's Gunboats or other small vessels in the Potomac.

On 27 June Lincoln replaced Hooker with Major General George Gordon Meade (1815–72) as commander of the Army of the Potomac. Meade knew nothing of this decision until early the next morning, and protested his unfamiliarity with Hooker's plan of campaign and the difficulties of suddenly taking charge. It seemed to many an inauspicious way to meet the Confederate advances.[45]

Things are looking very gloomy for the North just now. Still General Lee's advance is only compatible with "prudence", if he is right in the very low estimate he forms of the Army of the Potomac. It must be admitted that many Northern Officers, who have opportunities of knowing, give very desponding reports of the present condition of this army. General Meade can hardly be as bad as Hooker, but if the President has at last found a good general it is by accident, for Meade is untried. The Army still yearns for McClellan and says if there was to be a change, he should have been appointed.

Thus, on the eve of Gettysburg, Lord Lyons saw no cause for optimism as far as the North's military position was concerned. It would take time until the full magnitude of the battle sunk in upon both British and Americans alike.

14

From Gettysburg to President Lincoln's Reelection, July 1863–December 1864

On 1 July 1863 the armies of North and South blundered into a full-scale battle at Gettysburg, Pennsylvania: a three-day onslaught that many since have reckoned to be the decisive turning point of the war. Like others at the time, Lord Lyons sensed the magnitude of the occasion but lacked any detailed information.[1]

> The battle on which our fate depends is supposed to be going on at this moment. So far as I have the means of judging the Country is wonderfully apathetic about the result—a sign of weariness of the war I suppose. If there is a strong feeling at this moment, it appears to be one of dissatisfaction with the present Administration— the natural consequence of its ill luck in war.

A few days later it was clear that the Confederates had sustained a grave defeat at Gettysburg, but the longer-term implications were far from certain.[2]

> So far as we can judge from first accounts, General Lee's repulse has been a very serious one, and he has brought his army into a position in which to be safe, it must be victorious. However we have been taught by experience to distrust first reports— at any rate we have learned not to expect victories to be followed up—otherwise Richmond might be supposed to be now in danger instead of Washington. It seems to be thought that the best that can be hoped for Lee now is to get his army back to Virginia without any additional loss. If he succeeds in doing this, the campaign will probably end as usual, in an immense slaughter, without any real advantage on either side. But the Confederates cannot supply losses as easily as the Federals. If, on the other hand, Lee has ammunition enough to fight another Battle, he may turn the tables on Meade—but his man must have lost the feeling of superiority to the enemy, which constituted a great part of their strength.
>
> I cannot of course think of leaving Washington under present circumstances. For my health I can say that if I do not get better, I do not get worse, which is quite as good a report as I can expect to be able to make, until I have changed the air of this place for something cooler and healthier.

Begun on 18 May, the siege of Vicksburg finally proved successful, and on 4 July some thirty thousand Confederate troops surrendered to General

Ulysses S. Grant. It was a fitting parallel to Lee's retreat from Gettysburg that same day.[3]

I have just received your letter of the 27th and your Despatch authorizing me to go to Canada or Halifax on Public service. I am very grateful for them—and as soon as the fate of General Lee's Army is decided, one way or the other, I shall present Mr. Stuart formally as Chargé d'Affaires, and get out of this air as quickly as possible. If I find, as I hope, that the change of air restores me almost immediately, I shall make my absence a short one—at all events, I do not mean it to be a long one.

The defeat of General Lee has been followed rapidly by the fall of Vicksburg—and the North is now triumphant. The Administration will probably turn the opportunity to account in order to enforce the Conscription Act—at any rate they have gained strength to prosecute their war policy. It is difficult to form an estimate of the real value of the recent successes. It is supposed that the fall of Port Hudson[4] cannot be long delayed, and that thus the Federals, having the entire command of the Mississippi, will make an easy prey of the Confederate troops on the West of that river, and obtain possession of Texas, Arkansas, and Louisiana. If General Lee does not succeed in carrying the greater part of his army safe back into Virginia, I suppose the Army of the Potomac will at last get to Richmond—and then the Confederacy will be confined to the Cotton States—and of those the Coast will be very much under the control of the Federals. But the fate of General Lee's army is not yet decided. Meade does not seem to be in a hurry to attack him—nor if he has ammunition, does it by any means seem certain that he would be defeated if he were attacked. Of course it is not impossible that he may still defeat Meade,[5] but this is hardly likely; if however he only succeeds in withdrawing his army into Virginia, Richmond will, I suppose, be safe for some months, and in this neighbourhood we shall relapse into the old state of things. We do not yet know how the South are taking their misfortunes. If they even now remain united among themselves, and do not lose heart, they are still a long way from subjugation. If, however, serious dissentions spring up, one State after another will probably fall off from the Confederacy, and the end of the first Act of the Revolution may be near. It is premature to speculate upon the consequences of placing the executive Government permanently in possession of the control of an immense Army raised by conscription, and of accustoming the Government and the Army Officers to govern vast portions of the Country by Military Law. . . .

Competition for popularity in this Country is idle. France will always be popular, when there is any hope of her helping to gratify the ill will to England—the ill will to England is a sentiment, or a passion, which depends very little upon her own conduct. If the time should come when it would be proper to withdraw the recognition of Belligerent Rights, or take any other steps to manifest our belief that the war was virtually at an end, it would doubtless be well to come to an understanding with France, so that both Powers might not simultaneously take identical steps. If General Lee's army be destroyed—and if the Confederates fall out with each other, the time may not be very distant—but both contingencies are doubtful at present.

Once more begging you to accept my thanks for your very kind consideration for my health.

In March 1863 Lincoln had signed into law the first federal conscription act, requiring men between the ages of twenty and forty-five to be subject to a draft lottery. Some resented the provision by which substitutes could be hired and obligatory military service avoided by the payment to the government of three hundred dollars. Aliens who had declared their intention of becoming American citizens soon found themselves eligible for the draft as well. From 13 to 16 July serious riots, protesting the draft quotas and lotteries, broke out in New York City and spread to other parts of the Northeast. In New York upward of a thousand people were killed or injured, and over a million dollars of property damage resulted. It took federal troops to quell the disturbances, which had overwhelmed the local law-enforcement officials.[6]

The Floods, or the sympathizers with the Confederates, have broken up a part of the Railroad between this place and Baltimore during the night, so that I find that the only chance of getting despatches to New York in time for the Packet is to send off my Messenger in an hour's time with as much as we can get ready! General Meade's Army is very near that of General Lee—but it seems now to be considered doubtful whether Meade wishes to attack, unless he can take Lee at an evident disadvantage attempting to cross the River. It is really beginning to look very much as if we should ultimately relapse into the old state of things—with the Army of the Potomac on the Virginia Shore of that River and the Confederate Army between them and Richmond. General Lee's plans for invading the Northern States seem to have been effectually checked not only by his defeat at Gettysburg, but by orders from Jefferson Davis. The intercepted Despatches from Davis to Lee seem to be undoubtedly genuine. The purport of them really was to tell Lee that the authorities at Richmond had not at all understood that the advance of Beauregard[7] into Virginia with a large force was an essential feature in the plan of the invasion, and that this advance could not take place. The Despatches contained also some remarkable details showing the small force which Davis had at his command for the defence of Richmond, and of North Carolina.

Mr. Archibald[8] will report to you the real facts as to the Riots against the Conscription at New York—owing to the interruption of the Road we have here only confused and probably very much exaggerated telegraphic accounts. A serious resistance to the Conscription would be the most likely thing to put an end to the war.

Few details of the New York draft riots were yet available, but as always, Secretary of State Seward was putting the best face on events.[9]

General Lee has saved his Army, and the Confederates have lost less by their ill-advised inroad into Pennsylvania than might have been expected. But the loss of Vicksburg and Port Hudson are terrible blows to them. There is a report that Charleston was taken by the Federals on the 14th, but this is extremely doubtful.

I leave Mr. Archibald to report to you on the New York Riots, as his news will be at least 48 hours later than any I could send. Mr. Seward thinks they will strengthen the Administration, in the first place because they show the dangerous and abominable sentiments of the Mob of Democratic Voters, and secondly because the suppression of this riot will settle the question as to resisting the conscription in any part of the Country. On this last point, I think there is room for doubt.

The Mississippi being now clear, the time is come for Mr. Seward to redeem his promises to us about cotton. I have authorized the Secretary of the French Mission[10] to write to Mr. Mercier to say that I am quite ready to join him in pressing this upon

Mr. Seward—not that I have much hope of really gaining anything—but I am unwilling to leave anything untried.

If, as I expect, things settle down in the neighbourhood of Washington, I shall set out for Canada after the arrival of the next Mail from England—for I am coming to the point of health, at which I shall be of little use here.

Although the official British position during 1862–63 was that Her Majesty's government would respect effective Northern blockades of Southern ports, in accordance with the provisions of the Paris treaty of 1856, there were always those private Englishmen who were prepared to run the blockades for profit. Other British merchants plied the sea-lanes of the West Indies and the Gulf of Mexico, and bitterly resented any Northern interference in what they regarded as legitimate trading by neutrals. Secretary of State Seward was for making examples of potential blockade violators, while Lincoln and others in the cabinet preached caution.[11]

The operations against Charleston do not seem to get on rapidly. The President and Mr. Seward told me last night that there was no military news, and I have not heard that any has arrived since.

The Riots at New York appear to have subsided. We cannot however yet say whether they are the end as well as the beginning of resistance to the conscription and of persecution of the negroes.[12] Mr. Mercier writes from New York to propose that we shall make a joint effort to obtain some concession about cotton. I hope to settle something with his Secretary of Legation tomorrow. I am all in favour of making an effort, though I doubt our really getting any cotton in consequence.

I did not much like the idea of going with Mr. Seward to the President about the Blockade cases—because I wished to keep out of the domestic quarrels of the Cabinet. I could not however have refused an Audience to which I was invited by the President and Secretary of State, but I disliked having one ever so much—and the proceedings of the Navy Department seemed to me to be really a source of danger to our peaceful relations. The President promises fairly enough, and we shall now see what he will effect, when he "puts in the strength of his hand". It is not good general ostensible orders which are wanted, but a determination to enforce the observance of them by actions against the officers who disregard them.

I hope to get away at the end of this week or at the beginning of the next.

Lord Lyons was keenly interested in the draft riots since they had been perpetuated by many foreigners resident in New York, who claimed they were not liable to the provisions of the law. Any British subject wishing to escape conscription might well apply to the legation at Washington or the consulate at New York for protection and proof of citizenship. In a day when foreigners did not carry passports, this was no easy task.[13]

Military events or at all events military news, have been scarce during the last few days. The really important question seems to be the enforcement of the Conscription Act. On the one hand we hear of wide-spread plans of resistance to it, organized among the German as well as the Irish Population in all parts of the Country. On the other hand it is represented that the Government is determined to enforce it at the point of the Bayonet, and to begin at New York, as soon as it can get things ready. We have as yet no proof that any serious resistance to the Government will be provided by any measures it may take. The Democrats at New York, are, as might be expected, frightened by the Mob—they dare not encourage resistance to the conscription lest they should let loose an uncontrollable gang of plunderers. On the other hand, if the Government succeeds in getting military command of New York, there is very little chance of any but the Government Candidate coming in as President when Mr. Lincoln's term expires.

British Subjects are not the least violent in language about the draft, and are far from being pleased either with Her Majesty's Government or with Her Majesty's Minister here. I have given myself a world of trouble to make the burthen of proving their claim to exemption as light as possible. If I have not succeeded as well as I ought, I have done more than most people, who knew anything about the difficulties, expected.

On 10 July, Northern troops were landed on Morris Island in Charleston harbor and began their protracted siege of Fort Wagner. The possibility of capturing one or more major Southern ports had significant consequences for the North's relations with foreign powers.[14]

General Lee seems to have succeeded in passing the Blue Ridge, and in placing his Army again between Washington and Richmond. This being done, he has lost more in fame and prestige than in a material point of view by his ill-advised invasion of the North. The operations against Charleston were going on by the latest accounts, but no great progress towards taking Fort Wagner appeared to have been made. Mr. Seward tells me that an expedition is certainly to be made against Mobile, and that the capture of that place is already looked upon as a certainty. In Ohio General John H. Morgan[15] would seem to have been taken Prisoner; he will be a loss to the Confederates, as a Partison Soldier. About the Conscription the Government seems to be temporizing, enforcing it where it can, delaying it where serious opposition is made. In New Jersey it is announced that it is to be postponed until it is seen whether the quota can be made up by volunteering. The Government seems confident that by hook or by crook it shall obtain men enough, but it does not seem confident that it can enforce a systematic Conscription. It is very doubtful whether the war can be carried on with any vigour for many months longer except by means of a Conscription regularly enforced. If however Charleston and Mobile fall, the Federals will have very nearly realized their plan of occupying all the Ports and all the great lines of communication, and the Confederacy will be in a sorry plight. The Confederates who behave so well in the field, do not appear to hold out, when besieged, even as long as decency, not to say honour, requires.

In consequence of a letter from M. Mercier to his Secretary of Legation M. Treilhard,[16] I went to the State Department on the 25th, and spoke to Mr. Seward about the cotton. I told him that we had waited with the greatest patience while the military operations were going on upon the Mississippi, but now the River was open, and the time was come at which we had been promised an ample supply. What was he prepared to do to redeem his promises? There were, I said, two points on which I thought he might give us satisfactory assurances without further delay. First, he might declare unequivocally that cotton the property of Neutrals should be respected in districts recovered by the United States without any arguing from whom it had been bought; secondly, he might say at once that whatever facilities for exporting cotton were given either to the Agents of the United States Government or to American Citizens should be also granted to Neutrals.

Mr. Seward said that he would recommend me to postpone the discussion of these questions until the result of the attack upon Charleston was known. If the United States obtained possession of that port and of Mobile, the position would be so materially changed that they should probably be able to make a modification in the whole system of restriction on the trade with the South. It would be premature to enter upon the question, while operations were actually in progress before Charleston.

I said that it seemed to me that this state of things increased instead of diminishing the urgency of obtaining assurances on the first point. One of the principal reasons for asking for a declaration that Neutral cotton would be respected was to remove from the Confederates the temptation to burn it. Now it was just at such moments as the surrender of places like Charleston and Mobile that this temptation was most strongly felt. Neutral cotton would already have been burned in vast quantities, if he postponed his declaration.

Mr. Seward spoke at considerable length, and in a very friendly tone, but I cannot say the conversation made a favourable impression upon me. He did not by any means deny that the same facilities ought to be given and would be given to Neutrals as to American citizens or Government Agents with regard to removing and exporting cotton; but he hardly did more than allow me to take this for granted. With regard to the other point he did say plainly that the mode in which Neutral property had been acquired in cotton would be made the subject of investigation. It would never be allowed that Neutrals should retain possession of cotton, which they had received in return for subscriptions to the Confederate Loan, or in payment for arms and ammunition. If, as I contended, the law of nations allowed Neutrals to trade equally with both Belligerents, it also gave Belligerents extensive rights and powers in conquered districts.

I told Mr. Seward that I very much regretted his taking this view of the matter—and I tried to show him how important it would be to prove to Europe that she benefitted by Federal successes. I said that England and France were entirely of the same opinion on the question—although there was no intention of embarrassing him at this moment by any formal collective step on the part of the Ministers here.

By mid-August, Lyons was grateful to get away from the oppressive heat of Washington and make his way to Canada for a respite of several months. However, he was dubious about William H. Seward's invitation to accompany him on a tour of the state of New York for a week.[17]

Mr. Seward has made such a point of my going with him, that it has been impossible to get off without telling him plainly that I did not choose to travel with him. This of course I could not do: and he deserves some consideration from us, for if we managed to keep the peace at all without him, we should not manage to avoid a succession of critical questions. He has been summoning the foreign ministers, who are scattered in various bathing places, by telegraph to join us at New York. He had not received an answer from M. Mercier when I last saw him. I hope M. Mercier will come on all accounts, I expect to be deposited by Mr. Seward at Niagara in about a week's time and shall thence drop down the lakes and the St. Lawrence to Quebec.

I have told Mr. Stuart that I wish him to interpret your order that he shall correspond with me and receive instructions from me, as an authority to him to apply to me in any important matters which he may feel doubtful about, but not as a reason for delaying to act upon your instructions to me or to carry on the business of the Legation, on his own responsibility as Chargé d'Affaires.

Writing from Quebec, Lord Lyons was of necessity somewhat removed from the day-to-day business in Washington, but had some leisure to dwell upon longer-range considerations that might effect future dealings with the United States.[18]

Meanwhile, in Lord Lyons's absence from Washington, Chargé d'Affaires William Stuart reported upon the latest public reaction to Lincoln's further suspension of the writ of habeas corpus on the grounds of civil and military necessity.[19]

> The suspension of the Habeas Corpus, in the supposed interest of liberty and Civilisation, is startling and sweeping, and the Proclamation appears to go far beyond the authority granted to the President by the Act of Congress.[20] It will be a terrible blow for the unfortunate Democrats, and more especially for Governor Seymour of New York, who is said to have declared that no drafted man should involuntarily leave the State until the legality of the Conscription Act had been tested. The most painful feature in the whole proceeding is the apparent delight of a great portion of the Public, whose Liberties have as it were been blotted out by Mr. Lincoln's pen. One Washington paper last night had actually as a sensation heading HABEAS CORPUS KNOCKED OUT OF TIME IN NEW YORK AND PHILADELPHIA! How much blood may hereafter have to be shed to recover what is now being lightly and ruthlessly abandoned as valueless!

On 18 September, Stuart wrote a second private letter to Russell, passing on the latest rumors from Baltimore of growing Confederate desperation.[21]

> I enclose an extract of a letter from Consul Bernal[22] at Baltimore, and I am sending it in the same private way by a special messenger to Lord Monck[23]—relative to a supposed Confederate Project of fitting out an expedition on the Canadian Frontier for the purpose of making a raid upon Chicago or some other Federal town of the Lakes. The principal object would of course be to involve us in war rather than merely to inflict damages on a Federal Town, but I presume Lord Monck will have no difficulty discovering whether any real apprehension need be entertained on the subject, and in frustrating the project, if it has assumed any consistent shape.

[Bernal's extract follows]:

> A gentleman of my acquaintance, in whose security I have every confidence informs me that some individuals—citizens of the Confederate States,—have lately passed through here from Canada on their way to Richmond to procure commissions to enable them to fit out an expedition to some point in British territory with a view to making a raid on some town, or towns, of the United States bordering on the Lakes. I believe Chicago would probably be the place attacked. The plan is to send cannon to some island from whence the vessels of the expedition could embark them. This information was volunteered to me. At the same time it was imparted in such a manner as to preclude me from reporting it officially.

While Lord Lyons remained absent from Washington, Stuart had occasion to describe a recent dinner conversation that took place with William H. Seward at his home.[24]

He told us, in the course of the Evening, in a very complacent manner, how the Proclamation suspending the Habeas Corpus had been drawn up, and a very curious story it is, considering the immense importance of the Act. The Secretary of War had pressed for the suspension at a morning Cabinet Council, and it was agreed to. Then came the question of drawing up the Proclamation, and as it would be necessary to attach the Great Seal to it, Mr. Seward expressed his readiness to draw it up, the President being glad to be relieved of the duty. The Secretaries of War and the Treasury then said separately to Mr. Seward, that they would like to have an opportunity of seeing it before it was promulgated. Mr. Seward accordingly proposed to bring the draft of it to the Cabinet Meeting the next morning. Mr. Stanton objected, saying it must be out that afternoon. It was therefore decided to hold another Cabinet Meeting at 3 P.M. when Mr. Seward said he would be ready. He went to the State Department, asked for Copies of the Constitution and of the Act of Congress, upon which he concentrated his mind for two or three hours; he then wrote off the Proclamation, — had Copies of it made for each of his Colleagues, and went off to the Cabinet at the time named. One of two suggestions were made by Messrs Chase[25] and Stanton,[26] which had previously occurred to him; and upon his explaining his reasons for rejecting them, they all expressed themselves satisfied with the way in which it was worded, and it was signed by the President and immediately acted upon.

Such appears to have been all the deliberation thought necessary before suspending the Privilege of Habeas Corpus throughout the United States of America!

Toward the end of September, it was still unclear to observers in Washington like William Stuart just how serious had been the federal defeat at Chickamauga Creek, southeast of the city of Chattanooga, Tennessee. Each side sustained heavy casualties, but the Confederate forces had subsequently hemmed in the Northern troops by laying siege to Chattanooga. Unknown to Stuart and others, however, Northern reinforcements were being rushed to the front through an extraordinary utilization and coordination of railway resources.[27]

We cannot yet calculate the extent of the disaster near Chattanooga. That it was a most serious one there can be no doubt, as the urgent necessity of hurrying up reinforcements from all quarters will interfere with most of the other military preparations which were in progress. And although Rosecrans[28] appears to have succeeded in getting into a strong defensive position, yet if Bragg[29] is in sufficient force to flank him and cut off his communication before the reinforcements can reach him, the disaster, involving as it will, besides the loss of a large Army, the possession of Tennessee, and perhaps also of Kentucky and even of points of the Mississippi, will far exceed any that has yet occurred on either side during the war. As it was, Rosecrans seems only to have escaped annihilation by the stand of General Thomas's[30] Division, when all the others were utterly routed. Perhaps Bragg, as has hitherto been the case in all the battles here, has not the means of following up his success, or he may in the mean time be trying to cut off Burnside's[31] Corps from effecting its junction with Rosecrans. But we know little or nothing of either the strength or the plans of Bragg's Army. He has achieved a great success, but not a complete one unless he can do a great deal more.

I forgot to mention in my last that Mr. Seward had privately expressed himself to me as much relieved and gratified at the orders given to detain the Ironclads in the Mersey.[32] The effect was in a great measure weakened by my having been obliged to make the communication to him through his son. In order to prevent any flourish of trumpets in the Evening papers, I had reminded the son, in taking leave of him, that it was confidential and not official. The consequence, however, was that the Father would not even tell it to his colleagues, but only to the President, until the confirmation of it arrived!

On his way back from Canada to Washington, Lord Lyons stopped at New York City for a few days. He looked forward to the arrival there of Admiral Milne, the British commander of the North American fleet who, contrary to Lyons's fears, turned out to be a very popular guest among American political circles.[33]

I arrived here last night, having gained more in health from my holiday than I had anticipated and having, I think, turned the time I have been away from my post to good account. I have not of course anything to report concerning Canada and New Brunswick which would be new to Her Majesty's Government; but I have learned a good deal which will be very useful to me in conducting business at Washington, and I have gained a personal acquaintance with the governors which will I hope be advantageous and satisfactory with regard to the public service, as well to them and to myself personally.

Sir Alexander Milne is, I suppose, at this moment coming up the Bay in his Flag ship the "Nile"—but I do not think he will arrive here before my messenger goes. I shall be very glad to have some conversation with him. The comfort and advantages which his being in command of the Fleet have been since the war, are not to be told. I shall spend a few days here with him, and perhaps take him with me to Washington. This is so much the best place for obtaining a knowledge of what is going on in the political world, that it is a pity I cannot come here oftener, and stay longer when I do come.

I was surprised to hear that a Russian Admiral with several Ships was here. He and his officers are receiving public hospitalities and what are called here "ovations". There is no danger of our Admiral being troubled with anything in this way, I should think.

During mid-October, gubernatorial elections in Ohio, Pennsylvania, Indiana, and Iowa returned candidates who supported the Lincoln administration.[34]

Politically the Republican party will gain strength by its success in the Elections in Pennsylvania and Ohio. But the Democrats showed themselves so incapable of turning their electoral victory of last year to account, that the chance of their gaining another was small. They have moreover never ventured to make any definite announcement of their principles or their policy.

It is supposed that Mr. Sumner and the Ultras will make another onslaught on

Mr. Seward when Congress opens at the beginning of December; and that the Mexican Affair will be used as the principle weapon to attack him with. The object will, I imagine, be to oblige Mr. Lincoln to present himself as a Candidate for reelection on ultra Radical principles—and to bring in an ultra Radical Cabinet with him in 1865. All this however is very problematical.

In October, the Confederates under Lee tried to take advantage of the Army of the Potomac, which had been reduced in strength when troops were hastily sent West to help in the defense of Chattanooga.[35]

The Government has lost no time in turning its recent success in the Elections in Pennsylvania and Ohio to account by issuing a Proclamation calling out three hundred thousand additional volunteers, under a threat that the deficiency will be made up by a draft on the 5th of January if the number be not completed before that day. It is not easy to ascertain the number of men which will be furnished by the draft now in progress; but there can be no doubt that it will fall very far short of the number wanted and expected; and this new Proclamation is taken as a confession of the failure, but as a very ineffectual means of remedying it. If anything will end the war, it will be the impossibility of raising men to carry it on in the North, for the South seems as determined as ever not a give in.

We don't know where General Lee and his Army are—and are consequently in some alarm. I suppose General Meade has brought the Army of the Potomac so near Washington that this place is safe enough. No recent intelligence as to the position of Rosecrans' Army has been published, and this adds to the apprehensions of the public.

On 6 November Lyons readily admitted, as he often did, that he was quite at a loss to say what was going on militarily of any great consequence throughout the country.[36]

We are still without any decisive news from Chattanooga;—The accounts of skirmishes and small movements which are published are not to be depended upon, and give no grounds for forming an opinion as to the great result. The Army of the Potomac cannot do much until it has repaired the Railroads, which General Lee so completely destroyed during the late raid.

In the mean time the appointment of General Butler[37] to the command in North Carolina will be taken by the South as an earnest of what they have to expect, if they yield. North Carolina has always been the least ardent among the Secession States, and there were even signs of a union feeling there, which might perhaps have been made something of by conciliation. I suppose General Butler will effectually "crush out" any goodwill to the Federals. The sending of him seems a sort of demonstration of the intention of the President to apply the Radical system of extermination and confiscation—for North Carolina is just the place where the conciliatory policy which Mr. Seward is believed to advocate, might have been most naturally tried. . . .

What with the elections managed in this way, with the change in public feeling, and the imbecility of the opposition, the Cabinet will probably have a sufficient majority in Congress—and the ultra section of it will make a great push to obtain the mastery over Mr. Seward and the moderates, and as violence is generally successful here, will not improbably succeed. There seems to be rather a better feeling towards England, and perhaps Mr. Sumner and his radical friends will find their virulent attack upon us to have been a mistake.

I am disappointed and disgusted with Mr. Sumner's own conduct—and the more so as he is necessary to us to carry the Hudson's Bay Treaty through the Senate, and generally to manage matters affecting us (such as indemnities to owners of wrongfully seized Ships) which may come before the Senate.

Since the current military situation was obscure, Lyons took the next opportunity of writing on 23 November to speculate about the impact the war would have upon the United States.[38]

With what political institutions the North will come out of the war is becoming more and more problematical. The system of packing Congress, as developed in the Maryland and Delaware Elections seems to me to be the most dangerous symptom. The Elections in the United States were not peculiarly free from corrupt motives, but hitherto the Elections were respected as the undoubted results of the votes of all electors who chose to give them. But when the Administration of the day conducts Elections by the aid of Military Force, the results can only be respected while they are maintained by physical force.

In the mean time, the different Parties in the Cabinet are speaking against each other. Mr. Blair,[39] the Postmaster General denounced the plans of the extreme Abolitionists in a Speech in Maryland some time ago. Mr. Chase spoke in Ohio in support of the Abolitionist Plan. Mr. Seward's speech at Auburn was something between the two, inclining to Mr. Blair rather than to Mr. Chase. The President's own plan is supposed to be to readmit the seceding States as fast as they can be recovered, but to require them to adopt new Constitutions, abolishing slavery, and, I suppose, establishing his scheme of "compensated emancipation".

A quarrel between the Commissioners, and it is said, irritation on the part of the United States Secretary of War,[40] has put for the present a total stop to the exchange of Prisoners. The Federals detained in the military prisons at Richmond appear to have really suffered severely from insufficient supplies of food and necessaries, though there is no reason to suppose that they were much worse off than the Confederate Soldiers. The Confederates have now allowed the Government here to send food and other supplies to the Prisoners at Richmond, but the questions about the Exchange are still unsolved. The Secretary of War is believed to be in no hurry to settle them, being of opinion that the scarcity of men is so much greater in the South than in the North, that the South would gain by giving two or three Federals in exchange for one of their own men. I suppose, however, public feeling on both sides will soon compel a return to exchanging on the usual system.

The long-awaited opening of the first session of the Thirty-eighth Congress in early December generated the usual quota of rumors and speculations.[41]

It seems to be generally thought that the military campaign is over for the winter. It is even said that the siege of Charleston will be suspended. The political campaign begins today. I shall not be able to hear what has been doing at the Capitol (which is a long way from this, the "Executive" end of the town) before the Messenger goes. There is some idea that the Clerk of the House, who presides till the Speaker is elected, will play into the hands of the Democrats, and retard the Election of Speaker.

I am very glad you are going to send out military and naval officers. My incompetency to give anything like useful information on the state of military and naval preparation in this Country, in case of a sudden rupture such as that which the Trent Affair might have produced, has been weighing on my mind. I hardly think I can venture even to mention to Mr. Seward the notion of sending officers to the Confederate States. He would probably be very angry and decline to receive any of these officers, except on an assurance that none should be sent to the Confederates.

On 8 December 1863 a Northern steamer, the *Chesapeake*, was boarded and seized off of Cape Cod by Confederate supporters, temporarily made its escape, but was recovered nine days later in Sambro Harbor, Nova Scotia.[42]

Mr. Seward appears very desirous to prevent the affair of the "Chesapeake" becoming a serious one—and to be ready to give reasonable satisfaction if the case requires it. He is, however, a good deal afraid of the excitement which this affair and the Confederate schemes in Canada appear to be producing in the public.

I have so very vague a notion of what has really happened in Nova Scotia, that I think it provident to wait for written communication from General Doyle[43] before doing anything more.

In June 1863, French troops occupied Mexico City, in the face of steady opposition by Republican forces under Bonito Juarez. The French then set about establishing a monarchy there, culminating in the invitation to Prince Maximilian of Austria, in the spring of 1864, to become emperor of Mexico.[44]

Mr. Seward showed me very confidentially the day before yesterday a Despatch which he had received from Mr. Corwin,[45] the United States Minister at Mexico. Mr. Corwin appears to consider the quarrel between the French and the Clergy so serious, that the Clerical Party will now swell the resistence to the Monarchy France seeks to establish. Mr. Corwin intended to stay himself at Mexico for the present. American agents abroad are I think still more prone than others to see things as they themselves and their Government wish them to be, and I think this is to be taken into account in estimating the value of Mr. Corwin's opinions.

Mons. Mercier embarks for England and France on the last day of the month. I shall be very sorry to lose him. He is very agreeable and has been, I really think, a very good Colleague to me. He has his Christmas dinner with me tomorrow, devoutly hoping that it will be the last he will eat in this Country.[46] At this season, I feel more than ever weary of my own exile to this place, but I will not indulge in grumbling. I will rather take advantage of the opportunity to offer to you and to Lady Russell my best wishes and very kind and grateful rememberances.

Once Lord Lyons had received further details of the *Chesapeake* affair from General Doyle in Nova Scotia, he came to appreciate its potentially grave consequences. What seemed clear enough, however, was that American naval officers had entered British waters off Nova Scotia in order to seize the *Chesapeake* and return her to federal jurisdiction.[47]

The conduct of the United States Officers in Nova Scotia in the affair of the "Chesapeake" is far more than I had any idea of, until I received the written accounts from General Doyle. I have put off saying anything about it, until Mr. Seward comes back. Nothing would be done without him, and he will manage the affair better if he have it in his own hands from the beginning. It will probably be better for me to make no written remonstrance until I hear from you, and so to be free to make as much or as little of the affair as you may think desirable. I don't think it would be prudent to pass it over lightly, because if we give the United States Junior Officers an inch in such matters, they will be apt to go to such lengths, as to force us into a quarrel at last. I should be very loath to make any specific demand without instructions. I shall be guided by what Mr. Seward says in determining whether a formal general remonstrance from me now would be likely to promote or impede a satisfactory settlement. He may very likely be glad to gain time in order to let public excitement here subside.

While Secretary of State Seward reluctantly offered an official apology for the *Chesapeake* incident, the British pondered their possible risks in overreacting to American encroachments in the Gulf of Mexico. The new year of 1864 had ushered in a number of fresh complaints that Britain and America leveled at each other.[48]

Mr. Seward has been showering long notes upon me all day, and the consequence has been that I have been obliged to send them on to you almost without reading them.

I hope that on the "Chesapeake" Affair will be considered to contain a sufficient apology for the violation of our territorial jurisdiction. Mr. Seward showed me some days ago an instruction which he had prepared to send to Mr. Adams[49] directing him to protest against the "Chesapeake's" having been sent before the Admiralty Court at Halifax. I tried to convince him that it would be an ungracious, and as far as I understand the question, an unwarrantable protest. I thought however that he seemed to be of opinion that it was essential to do something of the kind, as a set-off to the apology to be made to us.

The general impression made by the notes, and indeed by all the information I send you officially today is disagreeable. I am in hopes that the proceedings of the Cruisers in the Rio Grande[50] may not be as unjustifiable as they look at first sight, or as they appeared to Sir Alexander Milne,[51] but the matter has an ugly aspect. I do not know whether the Captors ever tell truth—judging from my experience of this Blockade the Captured *never* do. I think even the Law Officers hardly make sufficient allowance for the lying of owners of captured Vessels, and I tremble lest the new Admiral should believe their statements and act upon them.

By early 1864 the Northern blockade of the Southern coastline was more effective than ever. Still, it was estimated that two of every three attempts to evade the blockade were successful. Profits ranging upward to 700 percent lured many on, including numerous British subjects. Only when they were apprehended or suspected of dealing in contraband did these latter seek the protection of their foreign citizenship and their legation in Washington.[52]

This Government is making a violent attempt to break up the system of sending supplies to the South from New York, and to frighten Blockade Runners in general.

Hence the detention of British subjects taken on board captured vessels, and the arrests at New York, which are the subjects of so many of my Despatches of today. I have tried to make Mr. Seward see how dangerous all these legal proceedings are—but I think he and his Colleagues trust to have succeeded in producing a consternation among the Blockade Runners before they get themselves into any serious difficulty with Foreign Powers. I found it impossible to get Mr. Seward to think of the effect of these proceedings on Foreign Governments, until I brought him to book by asking him in writing for explicit and definite information. I have not gone beyond this, because the explanation when he comes to write it may perhaps be more satisfactory than his vague observations would lead one to suspect. I think too I have succeeded in persuading him to be as reasonable as his Colleagues at the Navy Dept. will allow. Their theory is, so far as I can make it out, that there is so strong a presumption that the Blockade Runners are owned by Confederates that this Gov. has a right to call upon the Masters and Crews to disprove this, before they are released, although these may be no proof at all against the individual vessel.

The Reciprocity Treaty of 1854 had sought to promote friendly commercial relations between Canada and the United States. It was to remain in force for ten years and then to be renewed or canceled by either party with a year's notice. By the late 1850s there were growing pressures within the United States to raise tariffs and thus abandon the treaty. During the Civil War demands to abrogate it multiplied, as Northerners sought ways to punish Britain and Canada for recognizing Southern belligerency and for harboring Confederate agents.[53]

I am very sorry to say that the agitation against the Reciprocity Treaty has gone on increasing, and that it now appears probable that a Resolution calling on the President to give as soon as possible the Notice for abrogating it, will be passed by Congress. The Canadian Ministers are very anxious to be doing something in the matter, in order to cover this responsibility as regards their Constituents hereafter. They had a desire to send an Agent here to advise with me, and to speak to the American Cabinet and to members of Congress. This I have told Lord Monck, privately and confidentially, I will not hear of. I could not undertake to keep the peace for a month, if I had a man here, by my side, over whom I could have no practical control, and who would be really guided only by Canadian Party Politics, but who would yet be supposed to be more or less in my confidence, and therefore to be entitled to speak for me and for Her Majesty's Government. My troubles are great enough without adding Canadian Electioneering views to the difficulties I have to contend with. Mr. Seward's opinion is that the quieter the Canadians kept the better, and so is mine, and so it would be still, if Mr. Seward had not changed his. He now thinks that discussion on the subject cannot be avoided, and that a good effect would be produced by visits to Washington of influential Canadians coming "on their own hook", and talking in a friendly manner to Senators and Deputies. He does not recommend that they should appear to have any special connection with me, nor any resemblance of an official or quasi-official character at any time, nor does he consider it to be desirable that any one individual should stay long.

I am corresponding privately with Lord Monck about this notion of Mr. Seward's, and defer writing about the Treaty officially until I come to some understanding with him about it. Mr. Seward's opinion is so much more likely to be correct than mine, that I do not like to discourage Canadians coming in the way he suggests. Besides which I have very little hope of staving off the Resolution for the abrogation of the Treaty in any way, and therefore do not feel justified in preventing efforts being made by the Canadians themselves, provided I am clear of all connection with them, and that they do not compromise me or the Imperial Government.

I think that Mr. Seward is inclined to use the abrogation of the Treaty as a means of working with you, in aid of the great attack he is making upon you, on the subject of the dangers arising from the use made by the Confederates of the neighbouring British Provinces. The object of course is to make the most of the inconveniences arising from the belligerent's rights of the South, with the hope of inducing you to withdraw the recognition of those rights. I nevertheless believe him to be sincerely desirous of saving the Treaty, or at least of avoiding the necessity of giving the Notice, or approving a Resolution of Congress in favour of giving it.

The attack on the Treaty is now caused much more by ill-will to England and her colonies, than by any commerical or financial considerations. The same spirit has caused the introduction of a Bill into Congress to repeal the Act allowing goods to pass through the United States without paying duty in transit to and from Canada. In fact the absence of any serious opposition in Congress, renders both houses very unmanageable.

There are rumours of increased activity on the part of the Confederates in several quarters, of the abandonment of the siege of Charleston, of an attack on Mobile, and of other naval and military movements, but there is nothing yet so important or so certain as to be worth recording.

During February and March of 1864, Lyons continued to be preoccupied with the plight of British merchants and sailors accused of running the North's blockades. This left him little time to speculate about military and political matters.[54]

We are very much interested here in surmises as to how General Sherman[55] is faring in Mississippi, what has become of General Kilpatrick[56] and the Cavalry of the Army of the Potomac, and what will be the results of the defeat of the Federals in Florida, but none of these matters are of sufficient moment to be interesting in Europe in the present state of affairs there. Nor are the signs of the coming Presidential contest sufficiently distinct yet to be worth recording. The general impression of the day is that the Military prospects of the Confederates are more promising than they were a month ago, and Mr. Lincoln's prospects of being reelected less promising.

With the military and naval situation so very unclear, Lord Lyons welcomed the insights of career military officers, sent out from Britain as observers.[57]

The two Military Officers, Col. Gallwey and Capt. Alderson, sent by the War office to report on military matters here, are about to set out for the Army of the Potomac. Some great attempt will probably be made by that Army within a very short time. The Peninsula between the James and York Rivers will most likely be the scene of the operations; and everything is supposed to depend upon their success—the Presidential Election, and the Finances in particular hang in the balance. Capt. Gore Browne,[58] the Officer sent here by the Admiralty, went home four days ago. He has sent me a very interesting and able report, of which I will forward a copy to you by the next Packet. It confirms my impression that the Americans are very seriously preparing for a Foreign War. I think we should never be for long without Naval and Military officers here to watch and report on these matters: and I should be very glad to hear that a Naval Officer is on his way out. I think the men employed should be made to understand that their principal duty is to keep Her Majesty's Government so well informed of the state of preparation, and of the position of the Naval and Military Forces of the United States, that if a War were to break out at a moment's notice, our Admiralty and War Office would know exactly what to do. It is quite impossible that a Diplomatic Mission can do this, without the assistance of professional men; and the more completely the responsibility is thrown on the professional men, the more effectively will the work be performed. With the present feelings of the U.S. people, I think the officers had better come with a decidedly official character, either as Naval and Military Attachés to this Legation, or under any other name; but I do not think the most effective mode of obtaining the requisite information, would be to let them subside into permanent attachés residing here, and making their routine reports by each mail. It would, of course, be well before publishing any appointment of a definite official character, to let me ascertain that it would be acceptable to this Government to have officers here in that particular character. There can unhappily be no doubt that three-fourths of the American people are eagerly longing for a safe opportunity of making war with England; and to that extent this feeling may be played upon, and with what results, during the Presidential Canvass, no one can say.

The ill will shows itself in many ways—principally in actions proceeding in regard to the neighbouring Colonies. The last attempt in Congress is to repeal an act of 1831 in virtue of which there are no higher duties levied on British Crafts, boats, and Colonial Vessels in the American Ports on the Lakes, than are levied on similar American Crafts in the British Ports. I have spoken to Mr. Seward about it, and I hope, if it is a matter of importance to Canada, that we shall be able to stop it.

As Grant's troops sought to advance upon Richmond, they were suddenly blocked by some of Lee's forces in the wooded area near Spotsylvania Court House.[59]

There has been hard fighting the last four days between the Army of the Potomac and General Lee's forces. All we know is that there has been great slaughter. It is idle for me to try to conjecture what has really happened in order to inform you, as the Telegraph to Halifax will take you three days later news than I can write.

I am dissatisfied with the Government here for maintaining their obnoxious order for imprisoning the Blockade Runners—and for their excessively arbitrary proceedings in some of the cases of the Prisoners under Military arrest. I have pressed Mr. Seward hard upon these matters in conversation, and he has been exerting himself to set matters on a somewhat better footing, but he is not as much listened to as he ought to be by his colleagues in the War and Navy Departments.

A more serious matter is the outrageous commercial and financial legislation in which Congress is indulging, but it does not torment me as much, because I know that I am utterly powerless to influence it, in one direction or the other.[60] The English at New York and elsewhere are getting restive at not obtaining as much protection as they think they ought, from Her Majesty's Government. Considering their notions of the amount of protection which is due to them, it is only wonderful that we have kept them in tolerably good humour so long. Some of the cases, in which the

Government has behaved most arbitrarily, are cases of such very doubtful merit in themselves, that even in the interest of the Prisoners, it would be inexpedient for us to press them too far.

We have had a sudden plunge into our worst summer weather, which has knocked me up.

Washington, D.C., was always reckoned to be an expensive post for British diplomats, but the war, with its inflation, made Lord Lyons's financial position even more precarious.[61]

You will perhaps recollect that when I was with you at Woburn just before I left England in 1862, you were so kind as to say that you understood that when Lord Napier was Minister here, he was authorised to draw on the Secret Service Funds, for £1,000 a year in addition to his Salary, and that if, on my return to Washington I found it necessary, I might draw in the same manner. The arrangement was subsequently put into form in a letter from Mr. Hammond,[62] by which I was authorized to draw on the Secret Service Fund for £500 on the 1st January and 1st July 1863 and 1st January 1864. If the circumstances which rendered the salary insufficient continued to exist after January 1864, some permanent arrangement would, Mr. Hammond wrote, be made.

This contingency has now arrived. The expense of living at Washington is beyond all comparison greater than it was in 1862, and the incidental expenses occasioned by the War, and the enormous increase of the business of the legation, get larger and larger. The rise of prices in this place is out of all proportion to the depreciation of the currency.

I should on all accounts very much prefer a regular avowed increase of the salary, which would place this Mission in the relative position to other English Missions abroad, to which the increase in its importance, its laboriousness, and its expensiveness seems to me to entitle it. Indeed if I can contemplate remaining here much longer myself, I should be disposed to urge this with great earnestness. But in truth I feel that during the past five years I have gone through as much or more than my mind or body is equal to. I am worn out, and utterly weary of the whole thing. The people here too are beginning to be very tired of me; and I feel that if I can by any means get through this summer without breaking down in health, and without getting into any very serious scrapes, it will be as much as I shall be able to do. For however short a time I may remain, I would still very much rather have a regular increase of salary than an allowance from the Secret Service Money. But under present circumstances, I shall be thankful for any arrangement which will enable me to get on from day to day; and if it will be more convenient simply to authorise me to draw some Secret Service Money on the 1st day of July, than to put the Legation publicly on a better footing, I shall be quite content to have the matter settled so, and be grateful for the consideration shown to me.

The Profession is too important to me, and too interesting to me, for me to be willing to retire from it, or to go back to it: but I hope I may without presumption ask you to consider me as a Candidate for an equal or superior post in Europe, if one should be vacant. I have been led to say more than I intended when I began this letter. I meant indeed only to write on the question of the additional allowance, which the approach of the 1st July made it difficult to postpone. I have however for some time felt that I am becoming more and more weary and less and less useful here, and I really have not the heart to talk of any permanent rearrangement of the Salary as of a matter in which I have any strong personal interest.

Toward the end of May, General Grant's army moved relentlessly farther South through Virginia, while Lee tried to balk them at every turn.[63]

I send you officially the summaries of the military events, because it may be convenient to have the dates recorded in the Foreign Office for future reference— but the events themselves have little interest. They give very little clue for guessing at the results of the campaign. General Grant appears to be getting up every man he can lay his hands upon, to carry out his plan of crushing Lee by force of numbers. He has left himself nothing to fall back upon, in case of defeat.

The opening of the Presidential Campaign cannot be deferred much beyond the end of this month—though all Parties are holding back, in hopes that the Military events may give them something to take advantage of. Mr. Lincoln is still the favourite—though there is a split in the Republican Party, and a Convention has been called at Cleveland to nominate a Candidate on the principles of immediate abolition of Negro Slavery, and preservation of the liberties of the Whites from the Military despotism now exercised by the Executive Government.

I am far from satisfied with the manner in which my representation respecting the Blockade Runners, and the Prisoners in Fort Lafayette[64] and other matters are treated. I should do better perhaps if the Foreign Secretary had more influence in the Government, but I think I have reason to complain of Mr. Seward, too, who partly perhaps to conceal his own want of power, has taken to making light of my grievances. I am out of heart altogether.

Early in June, President Lincoln was renominated by the Republican party's convention at Baltimore, but Lyons thought there was nothing very remarkable in this, since it had been rather a foregone conclusion. He did take pleasure in reporting to Earl Russell a change of policy on the part of the American secretary of the navy, Gideon Welles, which promised to discontinue the imprisonment of British subjects implicated in blockade running.[65]

Your very kind letter of the 4th which I received yesterday has done much to revive me. With a hope of promotion, and the prospect of getting quit of my troubles mental and bodily and in some definite time, I can endure a great deal. It will probably be impossible for me to remain here all this summer, at least to remain in health enough for work—but it will be very difficult for me to move until an addition of at least two more secretaries is made to the staff of the Legation. It seems to me impossible to force men out here—but it is not a question of my head but my hands. I don't see how the mere manual writing would be got through, if the mere writing which I do with my own hands were thrown upon the rest of the men without further help.

It was symptomatic of Lord Lyons's feeling, that he was badly overworked and understaffed, that he wrote fewer private letters to Earl Russell during 1864. It was nearly a month since he had penned his previous one when, on 12 July, he summarized the North's gloomy military situation.[66]

There is a good deal of alarm here. The prevailing impression appears to be that the Confederates are waiting for reinforcements which are coming up the Shenandoah

Valley, and that then, unless Grant sends up a considerable force in the meantime, they will really make an attack upon this place. If Grant sends up a large part of his Army, then the Confederates will, it is supposed, retire, having succeeded in one of their objects, that of interrupting Grant's operations.

I don't myself think we are likely to see that Confederates at Washington. The place is defended by a complete circuit of Forts. The line of Forts on the side on which the Confederates are is about five miles from the town. I really *know* nothing. The military men this morning say that there will be an attack today.

It is frightfully hot.

Worsening military affairs prompted Lord Lyons to write again the very next day.[67]

The Confederates have torn up the Railway between this and Baltimore (the only Railway which connects Washington with the North) and appear to be in possession of all the country round on the North of the town. There has been skirmishing in the neighbourhood of some of the principal Forts, but no attack upon any of them yet. The numbers of the Confederates are at present mere matters of conjecture to us, and we do not even know who is in command of them. I abstain from conjecture as to the probable result of all this, for I really know nothing of what the Government is doing for the defence of the place. I suppose they will not move Grant's army from Petersburg except at the last extremity.[68] Her Majesty's Ship "Phaeton" is at Fortress Monroe. I have asked the Captain to come up here, if the communication between this place and Fortress Monroe is interrupted so that I cannot write to him, but otherwise not to come without a request from me. The French Chargé d'Affaires has sent the same instructions to the Captain of a French Man of War, the "Plegethon" which is at the same place. I suppose the Federals will keep the communication with Fortress Monroe by the Potomac open. If the Confederates should contrive to establish Batteries commanding the River, as they did once before, they would still I suppose allow Neutral Men of War to pass.

I made every possible effort to get off a Messenger yesterday, so that the Packet from New York might not go today without any Despatch from me, but I found it impossible. I have just heard of a chance of sending one this morning who will I hope get off and be in time for the Packet of Saturday the 16th.

The heat is intense, which makes the present state of affairs extremely irksome.

By mid-July, Lord Lyons was equally concerned about Confederate troop movements and the arrival of diplomatic personnel to help lessen his burden at the British legation.[69]

The siege of Washington has come to an end, and people are as usual in such cases, beginning to wonder why they were so much frightened. I suppose the result will be that some respectable force will be kept here. This will rather disconcert General Grant, if it be true that he considers constant reinforcements to the army of the Potomac to be necessary to the success of the enterprise against Richmond. The Peace Party in the Country has constantly made great progress, though no one of any note has yet ventured to place himself at the head of it. That the taking of Richmond would overthrow that Party, there can be little doubt; but whether an unsuccessful campaign would strengthen it so much as to enable it openly to put forward a Candidate for the Presidency, is not so certain.

The heat is overpowering. I am anxiously looking out for the arrival of Mr. Burnley[70] and Mr. Adams,[71] and I hope they will be immediately followed, if they are not accompanied, by one or more Third Secretaries or Attachés—otherwise the whole Legation will be knocked up.

Insofar as the North could take comfort from the military news, it did so over unconfirmed reports of General Sherman's advances in Georgia.[72]

The President called for 500,000 more recruits. It will depend very much on the events of the present campaign whether he gets them. If it is unsuccessful, the difficulty of enforcing a new draft will be immense, particularly in the West. The new levy will not in any case furnish any appreciable addition of men for this year's campaign.

The papers are full of stories of confabulations on peace between Confederate Agents and half-authorized Agents of this Government. I don't know what real foundation there is for the rumours. The negotiation has as usual broken down at the outset. The Confederate sine qua non is independence, the Federal's return to the Union without Salvery.

The War and the Administration are exceedingly unpopular at New York. I wish public indignation would put a stop to the system of arbitrary arrest, but of this I have very little hope. The Anglo-American Opponents of the Administration want to get up a quarrel between England and the present Cabinet here—and try to worry me into making peremptory and extravagant demands. I, however, adhere to my own rule, and do not make peremptory demands without instructions, unless there is some chance of their being complied with. It is for Her Majesty's Government, not for me to determine whether a matter is to be made a casus belli.

During the summer of 1864 the so-called Peace party seemed to gain support as Northern troops bogged down in Georgia and near Petersburg, Virginia. The federal need to protect Pennsylvania, Maryland, and the District of Columbia from future attack also removed any threat of a Northern campaign against Richmond. Some impressive Northern victory would, by contrast, greatly facilitate the recruitment of fresh troops and the raising of funds.[73]

I heartily wish I could get away from Washington, and go at once to Canada—but with two Members of the Legation away on account of their health, and two more ailing, I am afraid the work cannot be done at all without me. I don't think my opinion on the Military and Naval questions concerning the defences of Canada worth anything. My general impression is that the province is altogether indefensible unless the Canadians are prepared to make such a stand and such sacrifices as the Southerners have done. I don't think it will be attacked under the present Administration—in fact as the Administration goes out of office at the beginning of March, the winter will, I suppose, be a sufficient protection for the rest of Mr. Lincoln's term. If he should after all be reelected, it may be on such terms as may compel him to alter his policy on this as on other matters. . . .

It is very desirable for me personally on account of my health to get away, and I think also that it is very desirable for the public service that I should confer with Lord Monck on many subjects, and among others, on the wholesale system of seducing, and trapping, and kidnapping recruits for the U.S. Army from Canada.

But of course I must provide first for the regular business of the Legation. I am a little nervous too as to my own position with reference to quite a new man,[74] nominally at the head of the Legation, while I am in the country, which I shall literally be during a great part of my absence, and virtually be during the whole time.

On 6 August the Confederate cruiser *Tallahassee* slipped out of the harbor of Wilmington, North Carolina, and began three weeks of raiding Northern commerce, which netted her some thirty prizes. Successfully eluding the federal blockade, she returned to Wilmington on 25 August, and a few months later resumed her attacks under the name *Olustee*.[75]

> We have still no military news of importance from any quarter. Grant seems to be sending a great number of men up to the Shenandoah Valley, and the impression now is that the siege of Petersburg is to be practically abandoned, and that the campaign is to wind up with a great battle in the Shenandoah Valley or thereabouts. This however is only conjecture.
>
> A new Confederate Cruiser, the "Tallahassee", appears to be taking and destroying Ships on the Coast near New York. This increases the outcry against the Navy Dept. here. The "Tallahassee" is said to have come out of Wilmington. She is called of course in the newspapers an "Anglo-Rebel pirate".
>
> In the meantime Mr. Lincoln's chance of the Presidency for a second term seems vanishing, and the Peace Party is increasing and getting more and more bold. An armistice is openly called for in the *New York Herald* and other newspapers. The fall of Atlanta or even that of Mobile might however change all this. The advocates however of an armistice still go on the supposition that there is a party in the South willing to return to the Union on advantageous terms—I can see no signs of such a party. It is also taken for granted that the Blockade is to be maintained during an armistice, but I cannot conceive that the South would ever consent to this. The time might come when England and France might say a word on this point with effect, but it is not come yet.

After days of suffering from intense Washington heat, with no relief at night, Lyons finally determined to flee to Quebec on 25 August. He would undertake his journey slowly and observe the mood of the country as he went along.[76]

> Peace in prospect, and an armistice at once, are now openly advocated by a great part of the press. It is true that it is a peace *with* the Union, and an armistice *with* the blockade—still it is a wonderful change, which has enabled the words to be pronounced at all. Much depends on the Chicago Convention, but the Democrats have no party principles at all. They are only looking for a man and a programme to turn out the Republicans—and this makes them vascillating and insincere. I should say the quieter England and France were just at this moment the better. If an armistice be made, they may consider whether they should not insist upon its being by sea as well as by land—but I think anything from them just now, would only weaken the peace party. There is still a *possibility* of some military successes before the winter, which might make a great change in public feeling. Now, Mr. Lincoln's star is very pale. The new loan lags—the pay of the Armies is in arrear—and the Conscription, if it is to be made at all on the 5th of September, will be made under most unfavourable circumstances, and not without some hazard of serious resistance.

On 30 August, Lyons wrote gratefully from New York City.[77]

> I find myself wonderfully revived already by rest and fresh air. I intend to stay here a few days, in order to pick up a little political intelligence. I am so entirely absorbed in Washington by the endless complaints of real and pretended British subjects, that I have really no time to give to general politics. This is of course not a proper state of things, and some means must be devised for relieving the Chief of the Legation at Washington of some of the ordinary business. I shall think this over now, and try to make some suggestions. Since my return to Washington last October, it has been as much or more than I have been able to do, to keep the daily business from getting into arrear and confusion. I have had to work so incessantly at the pumps to prevent the water rising above my head, that I have not been able to think of any measure for stopping the leak.
>
> The military news seems more favourable to the North. It is no doubt cooked a little for the Chicago Convention—but at any rate the surrender of Fort Morgan[78] must be a fact. The Democrats do not seem to be so harmonious at their Convention as was expected. McClellan[79] is decidedly the favourite Candidate, but he is not in favour with the thorough-going-peace Democrats—and they threaten a secession if he gets the nomination. This would ensure the election of Mr. Lincoln, or at all events that of a Republican President. The feeling in favour of an attempt to make peace seems to be growing so strong, that some attempt of the kind may very probably be made. The North is not yet convinced that the South will not come back to the Union on *any* terms, and would rather give any terms than go on with the war—but whether it is yet ready to sacrifice all hope of the Union for peace, is still very doubtful.

By mid-September, Lord Lyons had reached Montreal on his way to Quebec. While declining Lord John Russell's kind offer to spend the autumn in England, he still hoped that a new appointment to some European capital would be eventually forthcoming to him. For the sake of his career and personal finances, however, he hoped the transfer would be comparable or better than his current position, and in the meanwhile he would stick it out in North America.[80]

> The reaction produced by the fall of Atlanta[81] may be taken as an indication of the real feelings of the people in the Northern States. The vast majority of them ardently desire to reconquer the lost territories. It is only at moments when they despair of doing this, that they listen to plans for recovering the territory by negotiation. The time has not come yet, when any proposal to relinquish the territory can be publicly made. The Union and the Constitution are mere words—what the people really want is the territory—what they cannot bring their minds to submit to is a diminution of the territorial greatness of the Nation. The Republicans are no doubt right in thinking that the possession of the territory will never be secure, if Slavery is allowed to exist in it—and their endeavour to exterminate, politically at least, the present race of Slave Owners and recolonize the South from the North is supported by this argument. The success of it, however, can only be procured, if it can be procured at all, by a ruthless war, and after that, by a relentless persecution. I doubt whether the people of the North are ferocious enough or persevering enough to carry out such a policy thoroughly. At present however the presumption is that Mr. Lincoln will be reelected—that the war will go on—and that the Northern Government will be more and more committed to the views of the ultra-Republicans. It is likely that

as the Presidential Contest goes on, it will be felt more and more that Mr. Lincoln is really the War Candidate—and that McClellan will be regarded as too peaceful by the War Democrats and too warlike by the Peace Democrats. There is a geographical division between the two wings of the Democratic Party, which is ominous as a further disruption of the Union, if the War goes on much longer. The Western, and border States, are really anxious for peace at any price—for they suffer cruelly from the War. The Eastern States which have comparatively not suffered at all, are still nearly unanimous in preferring war to separation for the South. For the moment the fall of Atlanta has revived the hope that the war may be speedily terminated. The immediate results have been that Mr. Fessenden[82] has got off his new loan—and that a great impetus has been given to the volunteering for the Army. The bounties given in some of the States are enormous. In addition to the bounties given by the United States Government, in some of the towns of the State of New York through which I have passed, the Municipalities were giving a thousand dollars bounty a head to men volunteering for one year's service. However, by this means, and by enforcing a draft in places where it will be submitted to, the Government seems likely to have an Army ready for next year's campaign, and they will certainly get money by hook or by crook.

There remains however quite time before the Election in November for one or more changes in public feeling—and if the actual Election takes place at a moment of depression, such as that which existed a month ago, McClellan may be President.

On 24 October, Lord Lyons wrote from New York City, on his way back to Washington. There had occurred in his absence on 19 October an audacious Confederate raid on St. Albans, Vermont. With their base in Canada, twenty-five Confederates or sympathizers, under Lieutenant Bennett H. Young, stealthily traveled the fifteen miles separating the frontier from St. Albans, held up three banks there, and then withdrew across the border unscathed. However, the Canadian authorities soon placed Young and a dozen others under arrest.[83]

I intend to be at Washington tomorrow. It seems desirable that I should be there to confer with Mr. Seward respecting the seizure in Canada of the men who made the "raid" upon St. Albans in Vermont, and some other matters. I am very much dissatisfied with the state of my health, and I have very little hope that I shall be able to get through the mass of business, which awaits me at Washington. I will however do the best I can for the present, and trust to your indulgence if I am obliged to make some temporary arrangements for my own relief.

We must be prepared for demonstrations of a *spirited Foreign Policy* by Mr. Seward during the next fortnight, for electioneering purposes. On the 8th of next month the election will be virtually made, and the necessity for pandering to popular passions be in some measure passed. But there is no doubt that success in the field will lead to arrogance in foreign relations, and France and England should be prepared to act, if possible, together, with coolness but great firmness.

It seems to be taken for granted that Mr. Lincoln will be reelected, unless some extraordinary event, such as a great military reverse, makes a sudden change in popular feeling before the 8th. It does not seem at all certain that he will be able to keep Mr. Seward as Secretary of State, in spite of the ultra-Members of the Republican Party. I believe however that he would be glad to keep him, but when the ultra-

Republicans have reelected him, they will be as much in his power as he in theirs, and indeed more so.

During the autumn of 1864 and early 1865, the federal armies under Grant tightened their hold over the area surrounding Richmond and Petersburg. It was difficult to know who was getting the better or worse of it: the besiegers or the besieged.[84]

The military prospects are held to be rather gloomy at this moment. In particular, the repulse of Grant's last movement forward, is believed to be a much more serious affair, than the published accounts have represented it to be. Consequently gold has gone up, and the hopes of the supporters of McClellan have revived. There appears to be a great danger to the Country if Lincoln be reelected by so small a majority, that the votes obtained by the various devices, to which the possession of the Military power have enabled the Government to have recourse, alone turn the scale. For in that case the election undoubtedly will not have been a fair one, and will perhaps not be acquiesced in by the defeated Party.

Amidst all the horrors of war, and iniquities of politics, there appears to be one gleam of consolation. Slavery seems to be doomed. The South appear to be seriously disposed to arm and free and grant land to a large number of slaves: and if this be done, the emancipation of the whole body of Slaves must follow. Slavery is this day abolished in the State of Maryland. The new Constitution is of course not the real expression of the will of the people of the State—and the more the pity—but nevertheless Slavery is effectually put an end to. In fact Slaves have become nearly worthless in that State—and even before the war the institution was generally admitted to be injurious to the general prosperity of the State.

Within a week of his return to Washington from Canada, Lord Lyons had to confess that he was again broken in health and must request a leave of absence.[85]

I hoped that my visit to Canada would so far restore my health, as to enable me to get through the work here on my return, with tolerable comfort and regularity. In this I have been very grievously disappointed. I did not get as much better during my absence as I had hoped to do, and since I have come back, it has become plain to me that I ought not to attempt to stay in this place and manage the immense amount of business, with which I am beset. I am so thoroughly convinced of this, that I feel it to be my duty to the public service, and indeed to myself, to ask to be allowed to come away without delay.

It would have been for many reasons much more satisfactory to me to hold on here, until I could be actually appointed to some other Port, and it is only the feeling that I cannot do my duty properly here, which makes me anxious to come away immediately. I am naturally extremely desirous, after my long and laborious mission to come away as creditably as possible, and I have the strongest possible wish to continue in the profession and to get on with it. You have always been so very considerate and kind to me, that I feel a real satisfaction in leaving myself in these matters in your hands.

It took somewhat over a month for Lyons to hear whether or not his leave had been granted.[86]

I am truly obliged to you for so promptly sending me leave to come home. When I wrote to you on the 1st of last month to ask for it, I hardly expected to have such urgent need of it, as I have now, but a few days afterwards I became so ill, as to be utterly unable to do any work. I have not made any satisfactory progress toward recovery, and am scarcely in a state to travel. There seems however to be no prospect of my getting any better while I am here, and I shall therefore, if possible, set out for New York tomorrow, in the hope of being able to embark there for England on the 12th by the Packet "China".

I am told that the American papers have stated that I have been dangerously ill with typhoid fever. I have had no fever at all. My principal malady is a nervous headache.

On 27 December 1864 Lord Lyons reported in person to Earl Russell that he was feeling better, despite the rough transatlantic voyage. He was given an extended leave of absence from active duties, but later in 1865 took up the appointment of British ambassador to Constantinople. After two years there he was assigned to Paris and successfully stayed there until his death, some twenty years later.

15

Sir Frederick Bruce and the Opening Stages of American Reconstruction, April 1865– July 1866

Born in 1814, Frederick William Adolphus Bruce was the youngest son of Thomas, seventh earl of Elgin, and brother of the eighth earl, who had served from 1847 to 1854 as governor-general of Canada. Frederick's first exposure to the Western Hemisphere came in 1842, when he accompanied Lord Ashburton to Washington for the negotiation of boundary disputes with the United States. In 1844 the Foreign Office assigned him to Hong Kong, but two years later he returned to North America in the capacity of lieutenant governor of Newfoundland. The year 1848 found him in Bolivia and 1851 in Uruguay. In 1853 he was promoted to consul general in Egypt, and from 1857 to 1862 he assumed the precarious role of minister to China. Upon his return to England he was created a knight, remained there for several years, and was then offered the post of Washington at rather short notice, when it was clear the Lord Lyons would not be returning there. Thus, on 27 February 1865, Bruce tentatively accepted Lord Russell's proposal.[1]

> I have received your kind letter, and in thanking you for its very friendly expressions, I think it right not to delay my answer.
> Personally I should have preferred remaining in Europe—or at least passing one summer in a temperate climate before encountering the heat of a Washington summer. But if Her Majesty's Secretary thinks that I may be of use in procuring friendly relations with the United States, and avoiding the great calamity of a rupture, I put that the object is of such importance, as to overbear personal considerations altogether. I know that I may rely on Your Lordship's support and consideration both as to the period of my departure, and to the discharge of my duties.

At about the time Lord Lyons left the United States, General William T. Sherman was successfully carrying out his three-hundred-mile march through Georgia to the Atlantic Ocean. In mid-December 1864 the Confederate forces were also routed at Nashville, Tennessee. The Northern blockade was inexorably tightened with the capture of Fort Fisher in North Carolina on 15 January 1865 and nearby Wilmington on 22 February. At about the same time,

Charleston, where the war had broken out in 1861, fell to Sherman's army.

While Sherman sought to subdue North Carolina thereafter, Grant relentlessly besieged Petersburg and Richmond, which Lee finally evacuated on 2 April. Then on 9 April, two days after Sir Frederick Bruce reached New York harbor, Robert E. Lee surrendered to Grant at Appomattox Courthouse, southwest of Richmond.[2]

> I reached New York yesterday after a stormy and tedious passage.
>
> Petersburg and Richmond had fallen two days previously. Lee seems to have extended his lines in proportion as Grant extended his, till they stretched over a length of 35 miles. But Lee's army being numerically inferior could not occupy them throughout in strength, and Grant harried them in parts without resistance.
>
> Lee's troops were further dispirited by the disastrous results of the attack on Fort Stedman,[3] which is admitted to have been a mistake. There is no doubt that large numbers of his men prefer being made prisoners to escaping, the privates being out of all proportion to the officers taken.
>
> The Confederates are insufficient in cavalry, and their retreat is conducted with difficulty. It is doubtful whether Lee will be able to save the wreck of his army.
>
> Of General Johnston's[4] movements nothing is known. He seems before the Richmond catastrophe to have succeeded in checking Gen. Sherman's advance. He is said to have had between 40 and 50,000 men.
>
> I leave this evening for Washington. The sooner we get out of this hot-bed of the Democratic party the better.
>
> I am glad to find that Mr. Archibald[5] thinks that success will not tend to make this Government or people more unreasonable. The speeches made on the fall of Richmond were moderate in their allusions to foreign powers.

Once in Washington, Bruce lost no time dining with the one American politician of note who he knew from times past, Senator Charles Sumner of Massachusetts. In his letter of 14 April, he also explained to Earl Russell that he was scheduled to present his credentials as British minister extraordinary and plenipotentiary to President Lincoln on the following day. That evening the president was assassinated.[6]

> Of Americans of note, Mr. Sumner is the only acquaintance I have made. . . . He is constantly with the President, as representing the extreme Republicans—but he did not conceal his disapprobation of the conciliatory course pursued by the President, and recommended by him in a speech he made two nights ago to the people on the organization of Louisiana. The impression among my colleagues is that the Republicans, backed by a majority of the Senate with the principle of exclusion to be so carried out, as to annihilate the influence of the leading men in the South, will thus secure themselves against the return of the Democrats to power. The army, as represented by the successful generals, is not in favour of this policy. But they consider it doubtful, though the President may be inclined to moderate counsels, whether he has resolution enough to pursue this policy, and avoid calling Congress together which would support the advocates of extreme views.
>
> In the meantime persons of all opinions seem to think the Confederacy is at an end. I hope that the career of their cruisers may soon be stopped. They are now powerless except to destroy innocent property.

Lincoln's vice president and successor, Andrew Johnson, shared his predecessor's humble origins. Born in 1808, he did quite well for himself as a tailor in Greenville, Tennessee, before becoming mayor and a state legislator. During the 1840s and 1850s he successively served in the United States House of Representatives, then as governor of Tennessee and in the United States Senate. A contentious Democrat for much of his life, he was the one Southern senator who sided with the Union when war broke out in 1861. The following year, Lincoln appointed him military governor of Tennessee, and two years later he was nominated to run as Lincoln's vice president, as a gesture of Unionist solidarity. He was sworn in as president on 15 April, the day following Lincoln's murder. By 18 April, when Bruce next wrote to Russell, he had not yet been formally presented to the new president.[7]

> My audience is to take place the day after interment. The new President out of respect for the dead, did not wish to name an earlier day.
>
> There is good grounds for believing that the ultra-Republicans are making great efforts to induce Mr. Johnson to employ men of their Party, and to pursue a more violent course towards the South. The destruction of his property by the Confederates in Tennessee, and the illness, if not the death of his wife, consequent on the terror produced by their proceedings, will not incline Mr. Johnson to mercy. But on the other hand, he owes his nomination to the Vice-Presidency to Mr. Seward, and should the latter recover from his wounds,[8] it is not likely that he will be removed. How far Seward's own views may undergo a change, remains to be seen. Hitherto I fancy his counsels have led on the side of moderation both in domestic and foreign questions. Should he not recover, Mr. Sumner is named the likely candidate for the Secretaryship of State.
>
> I saw him on Sunday, and he talked at some length on the present posture of affairs. He dwelt much on Mr. Lincoln's conciliatory disposition, and on his determination (expressed shortly before his death) to maintain peaceful relations with Great Britain. He said, that Johnson had been urged to call Congress together, but that he had however opposed it, on the ground that the House of Representatives would certainly cast a unanimous resolution to demand payment by Great Britain for damage done by the "Alabama", and to request France to evacuate Mexico.[9] That he would rather these questions not be brought forward, than be obliged to oppose them in the Senate, and that he hoped these matters would be settled before the usual time of meeting arrived. I said nothing, but Col. Raasloff,[10] who was with me, kept up the conversation, which was evidently a war address. Sumner is reported to have declared that if the "Alabama" claims are not settled, he will not support in Congress any act of Appropriations for the payment of claims by British subjects.
>
> I fear that the President's death and Seward's state, will exercise an unfavourable effect on our negotiations with the Government. Mr. Lincoln had considerable weight in the country, and the course he was pursuing tended to weaken the influence of the New England fanatical and protectionist party. It is doubtful whether the new President's views are the same, and he certainly has not the same influence in the country, and will be less able to withstand pressure in domestic and foreign questions. Men of all political colours seem to agree in this, that the South is too much crushed to offer any armed resistance in the field. Supposing their hatred of the North to continue, they may, if reconstructed, seek to embarrass the Government, by institutional means in the State Legislatures. If hampered in the exercise of their

rights, they must either submit under the pressure of an armed force, or gratify their revenge by such acts as those which have been committed in Washington. The ultra-Republicans are not likely to consent to reconstruction on a liberal basis, because they fear that the power so constituted would coalesce with the Northern Democrats against them, and deprive them of the predominance, which as a Minority they are able to exercise while a Revolutionary order obtains, and arbitrary Power, exists. Such acts, therefore, as Lincoln's assassination favour their party interests.

An incident which occurred after Mr. Lincoln's visit to Richmond illustrates the above remarks. While he was there alone, he got a communication from a Mr. Campbell,[11] an influential Virginian, who had held office under Davis. In consequence of what passed between them, Mr. Campbell proceeded to call together the members of the Virginian Legislature, and other respectable persons, with a view to re-organizing the State, and on his application the General in command, Weitzel,[12] granted them a safe conduct to repair to Richmond. On Lincoln's return the Republicans remonstrated so strongly that the permission was revoked, and the persons who had obtained papers were compelled to leave Richmond in twelve hours. General Ord[13] was directed to proceed and take command of the place. The President's object, was to endeavour (in his own terms) "to replace Virginia *in her proper relations to the Union*" without enquiring into the past, and doubtless on the basis of loyalty to the Union, and non-slavery. Whether he was right in affirming that the time had come for making the experiment, or that he could have relied upon the Virginians to carry it out, I do not presume to decide, but the pressure at Washington was so strong that he was not able to give it a trial. No other person, as far as I am aware, has proposed a scheme of reconstruction which would embrace the proprietary classes in the South. Other members in the dominant party who have spoken confine themselves to describing how far proscription is to be carried. This position, not his sentiments, has led to his death at a moment, when he was the only friend of the South in his party.

During his first fortnight in the United States, Bruce was struck by the war hysteria that still gripped the nation.[14]

I ought to mention, that there is no relaxation of arbitrary Power in this country. The Government, acting through the military authority, arrests anyone it pleases, brings him to trial or not as suits it, and detains him as long as it pleases. Witnesses are kept in prison till required to give evidence, without being admitted to bail. And as the jurisdiction of the State Courts is overridden, there is no appeal except to the War Department at Washington. In fact personal liberty is at an end throughout the Northern states, and as long as the War party, which is in the ascendant, professes to consider this power necessary to the national safety, there is no reason to suppose that it will terminate. It would appear, that individual rights have no foundation here, except in the Will of the Majority. It would not surprise me to see a "loi des suspects" enacted. If, as is likely, the feelings of the North and the South became more and more embittered, the future condition of incidents foreign and native, will be far more than it has hitherto been.

The Americans are singularly naive. The North has beaten the South, has suffered little, and is in good humour. Its people are bona fide astonished, that the Southern men, who are vanquished, who have lost relatives in the struggle, and see poverty staring them in the face, hate them more bitterly than ever and are ready to resort to any means of vengeance open to them against those they look upon as unjust aggressors. I doubt whether Lincoln would have been able to carry out his conciliation policy under such circumstances, and I doubt still more whether the present man will make the attempt.

On 20 April Bruce wrote a second letter in which he described his formal meeting with the new president and Andrew Johnson's response on that occasion.[15]

> The President's manner at my reception yesterday, was simple, self-projected and befitting his position. After the formal speeches, (the acting Secretary of State read his reply) the President said, "what you have heard is the official answer intended for publication, and I wish to add personally, that I am desirous to cultivate friendship with Great Britain as involving the welfare of both countries—I have not been accustomed to etiquette, but I shall be at all times happy with you, and prepared to approach questions in a quiet and friendly spirit with more to this effect." In speaking of the ladies of the South, he stated, in accordance with his late speeches, that Treason of the laws of the United States was a crime, and opinion demanded that it should be punished in their persons. However he did not dissent from my opinion that perhaps it was better for all parties that they should escape.
> On the whole the impression he made upon my colleagues as well as myself was not favourable.
> Mr. Sumner paid me a visit in the course of the afternoon, and enlarged much on the ignorance of the President on all the foreign questions—alleging, that he had no ideas beyond the popular and prejudiced ideas, which on these subjects he may have derived from newspapers. It struck me that the drift of his conversation was to lead me to the conclusion that I should enter into confidential communication with himself. This I am reluctant to do, as long as there is a hope of Mr. Seward being able shortly to resume his duties as Secretary of State. Mr. Seward and he do not agree politically and if Mr. Johnson's ideas on Foreign questions are narrow, and prejudiced, I do not think that Mr. Sumner is the person likely to present them and him in a juster and more comprehensive point of view. It is yet doubtful whether he will have any influence with his President, and I am disposed to think, that the impression of an anxiety on my part to conciliate, which would be inferred from my departure from the usual official channel, would tend to defeat rather than promote, any attempt to smooth over difficulties. There is a want of frankness in him, which coupled with the language he has held on the "Alabama" and the "Reciprocity Treaty", makes me suspect, that his object in making these advances, is to increase his own political influence by becoming the opponent of my views, rather than to forward them. Such a result, would in itself be undesirable.

It did not take long for President Johnson to project an image of vindictiveness toward the South, in contrast with what had formerly been called Lincoln's vacillation and now was considered his moderation.[16]

> Mr. Lincoln was inclined to bury the past in oblivion, in the case of any one who would accept after defeat the new order of things. Johnson's speech since his nomination, enclosed in my despatch No. 251 of the 23rd Instant shows that he considers that the Confederate leaders have been guilty of treason, and ought to be dealt with accordingly.[17] That the Union and its supporters ought to be

indemnified out of Southern property, and that Southern men of influence should be impoverished, so as to deprive them of the means of being mischievous.

General Sherman's conduct has surprised every one, and grievously annoyed the Government—During his march through the Southern States he pushed to the utmost limits, the rights War gives in an enemy country—and of all the Northern Generals he has obtained the worst reputation in this respect. Including the reinforcements sent to him by Grant, he has at least 100,000 men well equipped and supplied, and a large body of Cavalry under Stoneman in possession of the Railway forming Johnston's line of retreat.[18] Before him lies Johnston with an indifferent force not exceeding 25,000 men and with apparently no choice but surrender or destruction.

Luck being the position of the opposing forces, Sherman has granted a suspension of arms to Johnston, hostilities not to be resumed until after 48 hours notice; he recalls Stoneman, so as to leave means of escape to fugitives, and proposes an arrangement which would reconstitute the Legislatures elected under the influence of the Confederacy, and leave it to them to deal with Slavery and all other internal questions. This scheme would restore the Union without any conditions, and is therefore not only antagonistic to the policy proposed by Johnson but is at variance with the more moderate policy acted upon by Lincoln up to the hour of his death.

I have heard no explanation of his conduct. He is said to be an ambitious man— Does he wish to become the candidate of the Democracy? Or is he one of the Generals, who looks simply to the restoration of the Union, and to a foreign War, as the best hope of obliterating the traces of this terrible civil contest?

General Grant has been despatched South, and Sherman is ordered to resume hostilities.[19] I can hardly suppose that the latter will be continued in his command, unless he is strong enough to set the Gov't at defiance.

This incident ought to alarm the political leaders of the country, as to the dangerous consequences of Wars which call for large armies, and may form a successful General. Perhaps the American Robespierres may, like their prototype, find in it a sufficient motive to incline them to peace with the outer World.

Mr. Seward is improving daily—and I hope will soon be sufficiently recovered to take a part in affairs. His son grows weaker, and though conscious at times, cannot be roused from a state of stupor. Two out of the six men directly concerned in the plot of assassination, have been arrested—but Booth, Lincoln's murderer has not yet been taken—nor is it known where he is.

As war came to an end, the British legation in Washington was still besieged by fellow subjects who had been interned in the North.[20]

All I can do at present is to try and affect the release of British subjects who on various pretexts have been seized by the Military Authorities. Rather I should say, I try to have their cases inquired into by the War Department, in the hopes that any favourable circumstances may be considered and lead to their release. But it depends entirely on the humour of the office referred to, what is done in their cases—for Martial Law as administered here, is really no Law at all. And the feeling against Blockade runners, and foreigners who have served in a civil or military character in the South, is so strong as to make a fair trial almost hopeless.

These cases require great delicacy in handling—for to insinuate unfairness on the part of the officers composing their Military Commissions, would render the execution of a sentence only the more certain. The certainty now felt of suppressing the insurrection inclines the people against leniency where a foreigner is concerned, and the Govt will not openly thwart the popular sentiments in that respect.

With the Civil War over, American attention could be turned to the precarious empire of Maximilian in Mexico. The sympathies of the United States had always been with Benito Juarez and the Mexican republicans, who by early May 1865 were actively recruiting mercenaries in New York and elsewhere. With many federal troops still under arms, it was now possible for the American government to apply much greater pressure on France to withdraw her troops from Mexico.[21]

I think there is less bitterness against the French, than against us. But there is a strong feeling against Napoleon as having played a shabby trick, and European interference creating an Empire in Mexico, as looked upon as an attack on the American continent. Mexico moreover offers greater temptations than Canada and the cupidity of American adventurers.

It is doubtful whether Jefferson Davis[22] will escape, or where he will go. If to Mexico, the Emperor will have a thorny question.

I think this Govt is quite alive to the necessity of economy, and wishes to avoid foreign complications. But the popular opinion, is, that their armies are irresistible, and their resources boundless, and there is danger as long as the armies are on foot at their present strength.

On 6 May, Bruce again relied on his cordial rapport with Senator Charles Sumner of Massachusetts to report upon the latest views of the administration. Significantly, however, Bruce well recognized that Sumner was far more radical on the emancipation issue than were many of his colleagues.[23]

The question of most interest at present, is that of the re-construction of the South, and Mr. Sumner ̤ esterday explained to me the course the President intends to pursue till the meeting of Congress next winter.

He is anxious that the State Government should be reformed upon the basis of universal suffrage without distinction of colour. The propriety of an educational test was discussed, but it was rejected on the ground that as no such test was imposed on Whites, the Blacks ought to be free from it.

The President wished this result to be brought about by a spontaneous movement on the part of the Southern States themselves, and he expects to evoke their action by refusing any assistance or protection by the Federal authorities until it is taken. He has sent Chief Justice Chase[24] on an informal tour to the South, who will make these views known privately to the most influential among the residents. In this way the re-construction of the States without Slavery, and on the basis of equal rights to all colours, would be effected without any intervention on the part of Congress.

As to the punishment to be inflicted on the Insurgents I could not ascertain on whom it is to fall, or to what extent. The Constitution forbids the confiscation of any thing more than the life-interest in Real property, and Mr. Sumner seemed to admit that if properties were to be seized and divided amongst the Negroes, the subject must be referred to Congress, as being *ultra vires* of the President—at the same time he said that the eatables of large rebel proprietors would be confiscated, and partitioned among the Negroes, so as to crush the political leaders of the South, and for the nucleus of a negro proprietary class.

Mr. Seward expressed considerable doubts, as to the realization of the President's scheme, if it were left to the Southern men to take the initiative in such, to them, revolutionary changes in the social condition of the South. The President relies, as a constraining motive, on the anarchy and disorganization which will follow the disarming of the Southern forces, and the sudden emancipation of the Negro—and he appeals to the experience he has had as Governor of Tennessee. But in that State, there are 800,000 Whites to 200,000 Blacks—a fertile soil and a temperate climate—and the problem of settlement offers far less difficulty than in the Atlantic Slave-States.

Opinions differ as to the manner in which the Salves will exercise the rights of citizenship. The masters, who have treated them well, think they will vote with their masters. Probably the Southern men overrate the attachment, and the Northerners, the animosity, of the Negro. And it remains to be seen whether the black man will be allowed to go to the polls, whatever the theory of the Constitution may be.

Mr. Sumner leaves in a few days for the North, which is, I trust, a proof that he has little influence with the President. The views set forth above, differ little from the Black Republican programme, and I doubt whether it is embraced by the President as firmly as Sumner himself. The latter is so engrossed in the idea of Negro equality, that every other question is subordinate to it. He and his school wish to crush and persecute the White Southerners, as a necessary means towards realizing Negro Equality. But the political leaders of the party in force, and probably the President himself, look upon Negro emancipation as the *means*, and the destruction of the political influence of the White Southerners, as *the end*. In this respect they represent the general feeling of the country, and they will be ready to postpone the realization of the Negro-White programme, if they find they can, by proscribing the Southern leaders, and ruining the large proprietors, secure the political adhesion of the South, while, by apprenticeship or some modified form of forced labour, its material prosperity can be preserved.

I paid the President a friendly visit last evening. From his language about the leaders of the South, I infer that their proscription is a measure of policy as much as of vengeance, for he justified it on the ground of the great influence they exercise over the poor Whites. I observed to him, that the failure of their predictions, and the ruin they had brought on their followers, seemed to me more certain than any thing else to destroy that influence, and that Davis would probably run a worse chance hereafter in the South than he would in the North. This administration will not have Davis, if he is caught.

He maintains that in Tennessee, Alabama etc., cotton can be cultivated by white labour, and that its production will be increased and the quality improved by the influx of small farmers from the Free States which will take place. He put very well the economic argument against Slavery—"In a Free State, the immigrant brings both lands, and capital. In the Slave State the population only increases by its natural growth, and if you want immigrants you must sacrifice capital to obtain them." He must be a man of considerable natural ability, and his manner is simple and befitting his position. He is evidently quite engrossed with the internal question.

The trials of the persons charged with participation in the murder of the President etc., will begin this week. Every means will be resorted to, to get up a prima facie case against Davis, and the refugees in Canada.

Bruce fell into conversation with an Englishman who had spent the past year in the South and whose observations threw valuable light on conditions there. He relayed these comments to Lord Russell in a private letter of 10 May.[25]

> He estimates the quantity of cotton in the Southern States at a million and a half Bales.—But a large part has been much damaged by rain and exposure—and his impression is that not one-half will be fit for use. Then there remains the great difficulty of bringing it to market. No means of transportation as yet—the railways are much injured and in many places destroyed, and the rolling stock burned and useless—Beasts of Burden, waggons, etc., have disappeared, having been all taken for the use of the army.
>
> He thinks therefore that no considerable amount of cotton can be brought to market for months.
>
> As to the prospects of tranquility he says that the burden of the war, has been only borne by what he calls the *blood*, that is the proprietary classes of the Southern States. That they as a class, and Virginia as a State, have shrunk at no sacrifice of blood or treasure. But that the example of Virginia, in putting all her resources at the service of the Confederacy, has by no means been followed by the majority of the Southern States—that the latter have acted, as if they hoped, if fortune was adverse, to make some arrangement which would save them.
>
> He further told me, that the poor Whites, never took any interest in the War, though being ignorant and thoughtless they at first, went with the leaders. But that they evaded by every means the conscription and that when forcibly taken, they behaved badly in the field, and deserted and surrendered in masses. According to this account, the failure of the Confederacy is due chiefly to the lukewarmness of this class, which when reverses began, would not be induced to fill up the ranks, and make up by patriotism for inferiority in numbers, as was the case with the first volunteer Confederate troops, which consisted of the best blood in the country.
>
> His impression is, that the country will be less difficult to pacify than is supposed—Some persons will be irreconcilable foes, and will probably leave sooner than to submit to Yankee rule. The women also are very hostile, and to their influence may be attributed the prolongation of the War.
>
> But the population at large have suffered so much from the want not only of luxuries, but of the necessaries of life, are so sick of war, and so convinced of its hopelessness, that he thinks if the Govt follows a liberal policy, and encourages trade, they will readily be reconciled to the restoration of the Union authority by the return to the enjoyment of civilized life which will accompany it. Even if harshly treated, their tone is, that they will leave the country, rather than resist.

On 10 May 1865, President Johnson declared a virtual end to the war, authorized the United States Navy to arrest any Confederate ships' crews, and warned foreign ships not to shelter these commerce raiders. A week later the problem was still very real to Sir Frederick Bruce.[26]

> The Confederacy is at an end. It has no Government, no leaders, no army.—A few bands for some time may pillage in Texas, cruisers harm American merchant-ships, if they can find coal and supplies in neutral Ports. The Confederate navy thus achieves one of their objects, embroiling us with the United States, where they can be of no assistance to us and can derive no benefit, but the gratification of revenge.

Three days later, Bruce was even more concerned about the implications of Her Majesty's government being in any way involved with the remnants of the Confederate navy. In April, for example, the *Shenandoah* captured a number of Northern whalers in the South Pacific, and as late as June, it was doing the same in the Bering Sea.[27]

> I hope you will not think me obtrusive on the "cruiser" question. I must urge it on the attention of Govt. It is vital to our relations—and as I see the Confederacy is dead, and gone, the sooner an end is put to the system the better of our interests. It is more desirable that the crews of these vessels should disband peaceably, for if they are taken they will be hanged, as you see guerilla bands are to be treated on shore. And it seems to me a sound principle, in case of insurrection, to hold, that as they are simply Govt de facto, and not de jure, their rights, around the outer World cease, when de facto the Govt ceases to exist. Surely every regular Govt is interested in maintaining this distinction between legitimate and insurrectionary organizations.
>
> I can assure you, my dear Lord, that if the "Shenandoah" for instance gets coals in an Australian Port . . . and burns vessels, it will be represented by the anti-British here, and believed, that we are lending ourselves to the destruction of their commerce. And I cannot help asking the question—cui bono are we to create this bad blood? Certainly not from a feeling of chivalry to the fallen. Because these acts only render more bitter the last drops of this contest, and as the captain and officers only are Southern, we expose to death the crews, most of whom are English, who if they understood their position now, and were free to act, would decline increasing the risk. And as far as the questions with the Govt here, this practically friendly act following on the friendly sympathy shown, would do much to facilitate a solution. Particularly as now it can be put upon strong grounds of principle, and not in the light of a concession to a demand.

Ever since Sir Frederick Bruce had reached Washington, he had composed long private letters to Earl Russell of a much greater frequency than was usual. On 22 May he explained why he was bombarding the foreign secretary with so many such missives.[28]

> The course events will take is so uncertain, and it is so desirable that my opinion should not be made public, that I prefer embodying my speculations in Private letters.
>
> It is remarkable that Mr. Seward, who is still prohibited from talking, attended a meeting of the Cabinet for the first time last Saturday (the 20th). It was there decided that the evidence hitherto produced does not sustain the charge against Mr. Davis[29] of complicity in the assassination of Mr. Lincoln etc.; and that he was to be charged with Treason, and tried by a Civil Court. Unless further evidence is found among the papers captured at the same time as Mr. Davis, I apprehend this decision will be adhered to, and it will be a blow to Stanton's[30] influence, as his assurances led to the precipitate issue by the President of the proclamation charging him and others with the crime.
>
> I mentioned to your Lordship that Chief Justice Chase left for the South for the purpose of sounding popular feeling on the plan to be adopted for the re-construction of the Seceded States—This first attempt was made at Charleston, where he appears to have satisfied the views neither of the Whites, nor of the Blacks. No reprint of his speech has been received, and I am unable to state the purpose of it.

The antagonism of the Negro breaks out constantly—At Philadelphia, though the Abolition element is strong, the pretension of the coloured people to ride in the railway cars are strenuously resisted, and threaten to end in serious riots. On the occasion of the funeral procession of Mr. Lincoln at New York, the Municipality first refused to allow a coloured delegation to take part in it, and when obliged by the Govt. to give way, the delegation was accompanied by a strong force of police, to protect them against the mob. Everywhere measures are being taken to force the Negroes to work, and to teach them that freedom means working for wages instead of masters. The question of suffrage presents great difficulty. The negroes in general are totally ignorant, and much debased, and are unfit to exercise it. On the other hand if the Southern States are reinstated in their rights, how are the Whites to be prevented from legislating toward them in a class spirit—if the negro element is entirely unrepresented? The negro/white party, of which Mr. Sumner is the exponent, are prepared to carry through their theories of Equality at all hazards, but I doubt whether the President and the people at large are prepared to sacrifice the material-prosperity of the South for the sake of an abstract principle. Mr. Johnson will not unnaturally look to re-election and he will reflect before opposing popular sentiments on behalf of a race for which he has little sympathy.

General Sherman has left to take command of the forces destined against Texas. Kirby-Smith[31] and his adherents will be disappointed in their hopes of European support, for the Emperor Maximilian has sent an agent to assure the public through the press that the rumours of a cession of the frontier provinces to France are unfounded and that he has opened no negotiations with Kirby-Smith, or the Insurgents in Texas.

I trust the "Stonewall"[32] will cause us no embarrassment. According to the latest accounts she was still at Havana closely watched by United States vessels. I hope she will not obtain supplies at our Ports—for after the Review to-morrow, the troops are to be sent to their States to be disbanded—and any fresh cause of excitement against England would facilitate the views of Irish and other adventurers, who would rather use their swords against Canada, than turn them into reaping hooks. The greatest caution is required at this moment—and by friendly action we must endeavour to strengthen the hands of the Govt. and those who do not wish for fresh complications.

The presence of French troops in Mexico continued to act as a powerful irritant to the Johnson administration.[33]

General Sheridan[34] takes two Army Corps to Texas—where the naval force will be largely strengthened. This will bring the war unpleasantly close to Mexico.

The Govt. discourages expeditions to that country and has stopped the sailing of a vessel with arms and men from San Francisco. But I don't know what course may be taken when Congress meets. That body, it is believed, will endorse the most violent resolutions—and Johnson's action will probably depend on the state of men's minds with reference to War. The Army of Georgia (Sherman's) which to my unprofessional eye, looked far better both in material and discipline than that of the Potomac, will have been disbanded—and as it consists chiefly of farmers' sons, they will probably not be anxious for another campaign. The Army of the Potomac is largely composed of young recruits, and of very indifferent material attracted in the Northern cities by high bounties. I don't suppose that money would be as recklessly spent for a foreign War, and without it, the Govt. would only get the worst part of the indifferent material of the Potomac Army.

On 29 May 1865, President Johnson proclaimed amnesty for most of the inhabitants of the Confederacy and promised to restore all private property, provided that such individuals took an oath to uphold the Constitution of the United States. Those not coming within the terms of this proclamation were most Confederate officeholders and military officers, as well as large landowners and others who had blatantly abandoned the cause of the Union. However, these people could seek special pardons from the president, who would weigh the merits of their applications. Within the next few years over thirteen thousand such special pardons were granted.[35]

The amnesty proclamation has been explained to me by a good, though an unofficial authority, in a manner which I trust will prove to be correct.

He says that the sweeping exceptions introduced into it, are intended to deprive of political rights the classes of persons affected by them. That this Government considers it essential to future tranquillity, that the pretensions of individual States to secede on Account of the constitutional action of the electoral majority, should be dealt with as treasonable, and that therefore examples will be made of some of the principal leaders. That moreover the task of re-construction can only be safely confided to persons who are bona fide loyal to the Federal views and that it is therefore necessary to exclude from any participation in this task, all men who have filled political or military offices of importance under the Confederacy, or who have used on its behalf the influence they exercised among their neighbours, arising from the possession of large landed properties. But that it does not all follow that these men are to be made criminally responsible, or that their properties are to be confiscated, for the course they have pursued.

According to this, President Johnson's views are in favour of States' Rights, but he seeks to confine their exercise to such persons in the Insurgent States, as will exercise them in uniformity with the policy of emancipation, and in subordination to the supremacy claimed by the Federal Government.

During May and June 1865, there were many who clamored for scapegoats in connection with the assassination of Lincoln. Foremost of these was Edwin M. Stanton, the secretary of war, who was in charge of the investigations.[36]

The author of this system is Mr. Stanton, and the upholder of Mr. Stanton, and his Reign of Terror, are the Black Republican party headed by Mr. Sumner etc. This party are conscious that their policy and ideas are repugnant to the great majority of the American people both in the North and in the South— partly from fanaticism, and partly from love of Power, these men are ready to stifle free enterprise of opinion, and to suppress the constitutional guarantees of liberty during at all events the period that must elapse before the meeting of Congress, in which body, as at present composed, they have a majority—This can only be effected by maintaining military authority throughout the country. In the North, they seek to justify the continuance of martial Law by bringing forward witnesses who swear to the continued existence of plots and conspiracies to burn Northern cities, and assassinate Northern statesmen. And by raising the question of Negro-suffrage in the Southern States, which no White residents loyal or the reverse, will concede, they hope to continue there a provisional order of things based on military authority, until Congress meets, in which body they would propose to admit no representatives from the South, unless elected by the votes of Whites and Negroes without distinction of colour. Of this policy the President, is, I believe fully aware, and in order to thwart it, he as an advocate of States' Rights, is pushing forward the re-construction of the Seceded States, through the agency of the loyal Whites alone. He has already proclaimed the restoration of peace in Tennessee, Missouri, North Carolina, Georgia, and Texas. In these States he has directed Conventions to be called consisting of such of the voters according to their old Constitutions, as are loyal. These Conventions are to elect State Legislatures etc., to determine who are the voters, and to propose such alterations in their Constitutions, as are required by the emancipation of the Slaves. He appoints the Governors in the first instance to call these Conventions, and he seems to choose Southern men who will be acceptable to the people of the State and who are adherents of the Union. His own opinions are against Negro-suffrage, and he knows that he will have to encounter the hostility of the ultra Republican party. I was told by the President of the Georgian delegation, that Mr. Johnson stated to him that the Southern insurrection having been put down, he should now have to fight the Northern party, and he counted upon the support of the South in the conflict. To obtain it, I should think he must abandon the policy of punishment and confiscation—or at least he must confine it to a few individuals.

This gentleman assured me moreover that the tenor of Mr. Johnson's conversation left no doubt in his mind, as to his desire to avoid complication with Gt. Britain and France, and to devote himself to the peaceful development of the resources of the country. He added that the South was heartily sick of War, that they are grateful for the sympathy of foreign nations, and that their bitterness towards the Yankees would indispose them to join them in a foreign War. With the exception of a few restless men, and of some who wish to leave the country, the mass of Southerners are anxious to get to work, and to endeavour out of the ruin that surrounds them to save something for the families. He himself is an Irishman by birth, and will be Chief Justice of Georgia under the new organization, but he is so impressed with the uncertainty of prospects in this country, that he discussed confidentially with me his chances of success if he returned to the Irish Bar.

If the President's plan of re-construction works satisfactorily, and if while withholding political rights, the legal rights of free men are canceled by the Southern States to the Negro, I think the President will be sustained by the country whatever the ultra party, or Congress may do—The danger to be apprehended is legislation in the South which would give ground for asserting that Slavery was to be virtually re-established. In that case Congress would interfere, in the internal affairs of the Southern States, and if it were to do so, it would claim the right founded on necessity of deciding the privilege of voting so as to give to the Negro the protection of a vote. With our ideas on race, it is hard for us to understand, how averse are the people of this country to admit that a Negro is capable of exercising, or is entitled to, those rights to which *we* think all men whatever be their colour, had a claim. The address of the coloured delegation from Richmond to the President, inclosed in my despatch No. 352 of the 19 Inst.[37] will show you the treatment the Negro experiences at the hands of the Union soldiers. And in Tennessee, Johnson's own State, the new Legislature has passed Laws, which, among other marks of inferiority allow coloured people to give evidence in Courts only, in cases where coloured people are alone concerned.

In fact Emancipation was a War-measure intended not to relieve the Negro, but to weaken a hostile White party—and the White population are perhaps less prepared to understand it and act in its spirit than the Blacks themselves. How the negroes would use the right of suffrage, and whether it might be confined to those who have property or education I do not know. But looking at the principles of Government held in the United States, namely, that States are Sovereign in legislation etc.; within their limits, and that Govts only exist by the consent of the governed, the Republican programme of treating the negro as a citizen, and of giving him the means of self-protection by vote, does seem to promise the only way of ensuring Emancipation on the one hand, and of preserving States-Rights on the other. Whereas the Presidential or more properly the Democratic scheme seems likely to continue the Negro question in a new shape as a sectional question between the South and the North and re-produce party combinations in which the support of a "peculiar institution" in the Southern States, will be the price paid by a Northern party for the co-operation of Southern members, and out of which will grow a fresh conflict on States-Rights, arising out of the desire of the Southern White to extend his power over the Negro, and the efforts of the Free Northern party to check this tendency by the action of Congress.

As a British traveler through Virginia told Bruce, land speculation was rampant due to President Johnson's amnesty proclamation of 29 May. Anyone who owned a plantation valued at more than twenty thousand dollars and who voluntarily took part in the recent great rebellion would not be pardoned automatically with the others, and therefore the title to such estates was uncertain.[38]

Of the capabilities of Virginia, he talked in the most favourable terms.
     Large properties are to be bought very cheap—the proprietors having lost slaves, stock, and working plant of every description, and being without capital or energy to carry on cultivation. They are ready to sell to a foreigner, but not to a Yankee. These estates however come within the $20,000 clause, and consequently no title is to be had. This clause is a great bar to the renovation of Virginia—for large properties are those chiefly sought by speculative capitalists. The President however declines to extend the amnesty to the owners, though urged to do so by a delegation from Richmond. His democratic instincts may perhaps prompt this severity, and the fears, that if he is too lenient to the Southern aristocrats he may find himself at issue with Congress. . . .
     The country is desolate—mills, steadings, fences destroyed. The spirit of the people broken, but bitter as ever, no capital in the country to set to work with—and no means of getting it. The Negroes are restless and unwilling to work. In his opinion neither the Master nor the former Slaves can accommodate themselves to paid labour.
     It appears that there is every probability of English and Scotch speculation and immigrants turning their attention to Virginia. I begged him to point out to his clients, that every thing connected with the South must remain in an uncertain and provisional state at all events until the meeting of Congress. The cheapness that attracts these people is due in a great measure to a sense of insecurity.

During the summer of 1865, the question of the Reciprocity Treaty between Canada and the United States frequently surfaced. Its duration of ten years had more or less run out, but many in the United States opposed its renewal, either because they were protectionists wishing to restore higher tariffs on imported Canadian produce or because they resented the passive role that British North America played during the Union's subjugation of the South. Anglo-American feelings also ran high over claims for compensation arising out of the Civil War and over pending cases involving the imprisonment of British subjects. By early September, Bruce felt he could get away from the legation in Washington for a much needed time of travel and rest.[39]

I took advantage of a lull of Washington to visit Boston, where thanks to Mr. Burlingame[40] I passed ten days pleasantly, and I think profitably. I made acquaintance with the Governor, the poets, and the leading statesmen of Massachusetts, and was cordially received by all. I think they were agreeably disappointed in finding an Englishman, who, assuming a connection between the progress of the country and its institutions, sought rather to understand and appreciate the latter, than to criticize them. And this friendly attitude is all the more valued in one supposed to belong to the aristocratic class in England.

These men influence opinion, and it will be something gained, if they approach questions under discussion in a less bitter spirit.

Massachusetts, which is the head and brain of New England, where unmixed British descent, and traditions prevail most strongly, has fought and won in the main the battle against Slavery. By virtue of her strong convictions, and in league with the West, which her surplus population has leavened, she over-powered the indifference of the hybrid inhabitants of the Central States deprived as the latter were of their Southern leaders. For it is remarkable that as the North found its most able representatives in New England, so, Southern ideas have found the ablest supporters in British Virginia—New York and Pennsylvania have only furnished money and indifferent soldiers during the War, and before that event almost always followed the guidance of Southern men.

New England however, though devoted to Emancipation, is hardly less so to money—to be manufacturers largely, and is I believe a large holder of Government stocks. The latter she wishes to exempt from taxation and the former she wishes to protect by a high tariff. On both these points she will encounter the opposition of the Western and Southern States, though she may count upon support from New York and, particularly from Pennsylvania.

There are symptoms both in New England and Pennsylvania, of a coalition between those concerned in monopolizing interests, and the men of extreme views such as Sumner, for the purpose of overthrowing the President's views of re-construction. Sumner and his adherents believe bona fide that negro suffrage, and certain guarantees should be insisted on before the Southern States are allowed to send members to Congress, and they are desirous of prolonging the military occupation until this new order of things is established. And the classes interested in high tariffs, and in exempting the public securities they hold from taxation, will support from personal motives this apparently negrophile policy. There are many men in this party who would not be displeased to see War with England, as a means of fostering their manufacturers, and because they think it would lead to the annexation of Canada, which would extend the area of their concerns, and would put an end to smuggling in the Northern frontier. These men have an interest in promoting the bitterness felt towards us.

General Butler,[41] who is a very able man and a powerful speaker, was the only speaker at the Republican Convention in Massachusetts, who did not declare against the President's policy. He does not wish to quarrel with the Govt, and he succeeded in maintaining a neutral position between them and his party, by treating Johnson's policy as an experiment which might be abandoned, and by pointing out very forcibly all the circumstances which make its success improbable.

The Democratic Convention in New York, have entirely thrown overboard the *copperheads*[42] element. Their manifesto endorses Johnson's policy, and they have put forward candidates against whom the Republican party have nothing to allege. Indeed many of the moderate Republicans seem disposed to join them, and thus form a powerful coalition in support of the President. And if the Southern States act wisely, there is every probability of this party being largely recruited.

In October 1865 Viscount Palmerston died, and Earl Russell succeeded him as prime minister. Lord Clarendon again headed the Foreign Office, and on 24 November, Sir Frederick Bruce addressed his first private letter to him.[43]

I have been in the habit of putting in this form such facts or such speculation on events as it is not desirable to make public, and my recollection of the system in force, when I previously had the pleasure of serving under you, encourages me to begin at once.

I dined on Saturday the 18th at Mr. Seward's. . . . During the course of the evening he entered at great length and with much apparent frankness into the questions which agitate this country. We made no allusions however to Mexico.

On reconstruction he declared himself favourable to the readmission of all states which passed the Constitutional Amendment against slavery and which repudiated the rebel debt. I did not gather that he thought any other condition should be exacted. He seemed confident that the spirit of resistance was entirely quelled and that in no case was any fear to be apprehended of disloyalty in the South. This opinion appears to be, that the support of the North is more than ever necessary to the South, as a means of keeping the negro population in order. There is much force in this argument.

He then discussed with much earnestness the necessity of a pacific policy. He said the United States should give the example to the world of the extinction of their debt and that nothing but foreign war would prevent its being affected in half a century—that the estimates for the army and ordinance had been prepared and would not exceed thirty-three million dollars as against 530 million dollars for the past year. He talked of the difficulties offered by the Constitution of the country to carrying on a protracted war except for purposes of self-defence. He said we are like a snake with thirty-six vertebrae;[44] the best-fitted of all animals for safe progress on the ground; that if trod upon can coil itself up and strike a blow with deadly force, but that it cannot easily repeat it as the connection between the vertebrae was very imperfect—that a war might be acceptable for instance to New York but would excite great opposition in New England or other states, and that the result would be very difficult to pursue, and that the development and true interests of the country [were] peace and immigration.

Although events were relatively quiet during the summer and autumn of 1865, the topic of possible Irish revolutionary activity along the Canadian frontier was always ready to crop up again at any time.[45]

Seward has urged strongly the expediency of not making a formal representation about the Fenians on the grounds that it would reanimate their cause and tend to secure for them the sympathy of those who hate England but have no friendly sentiments towards the Irish. I state unhesitatingly my conviction of Mr. Seward's language being bona fide and sincere. . . . I am strengthened in the opinion that our policy in this harassing business is to act in concert with Mr. Seward and I am quite prepared to accept the responsibility of adhering to that course. It is to be recollected that Fenianism represents the lowest part of the Irish Roman Catholic population—the element which is antagonistic to the Protestant and free Anglo-Saxon race—and their position is that the abolition of slavery will be followed by the downfall of the power which under the leadership of the Democrats they wielded while the North was divided on the subject of slavery. . . .

No reliable evidence has reached me to show what the resources and members of the Fenians are, as stated by the "New York Herald". . . . But I can understand the motive of these publications, if their object is to add to the existing sources of misunderstanding between Great Britain and the United States and to embarrass this government who are I believe anxious for peace.

For the next few years the respective demands by Britain and the United States for compensation arising out of wartime exigencies would bedevil their relations. The chief American grievance stemmed from the British construction of commerce raiders like the *Alabama*, but Britain was far from willing to admit that she was liable for the damage that such cruisers inflicted upon Northern shipping during the Civil War.[46]

A paragraph in the [annual] message[47] stating that the President did not recommend legislation for redress for the "Alabama" is much criticized as being a lame and impotent conclusion after so much bluster. . . . The danger is that when the papers are presented to Congress some violent resolution will be proposed which would lead to a distinct issue. I have reason however to believe that both Mr. Sumner,[48] Chairman of the Committee on Foreign Relations in the Senate, and General Banks,[49] who holds the same office in the House, are in favour of a pacific policy; and I am in hopes that the difficulty of arranging the Southern question will strengthen them in their course, for I am deeply impressed with the constant embarrassments in foreign relations consequent on democratic forms of government. Passion and prejudice decide arguments and authority has no weight for every man is taught that his own opinion is as good as anyone else; and men in Adams'[50] position seek to make capital at home by unhesitating advocacy of the most extreme pretention. Will and not law is adopted as the standard by this community. These are the facts we have to deal with and we must not ignore them. All I can hope to do is to soften asperities and to gain time. . . . Mr. Seward seems hopeful about reconstruction. He says the Southern states are now as anxious to be in the Union as they were before to be out of it—that they are so sick of war that it is difficult to get up a militia for self-defence and that they want to be protected by Union troops—that he does not anticipate any outbreak among the negroes on a large scale though there may be local disturbances. He discourages the idea of negro emancipation and I am inclined to think he is right for the negro here seems, like his brother in Jamaica, to object to labour for hire and to desire to become proprietor of his patch of land. He seems confident that Congress would not be guided by extreme men like Sumner and Stevens[51] in imposing upon the South unreasonable conditions while on the other hand they will not throw open the doors and admit them on their own terms. In this as in other questions he is a Confucian and in favour of the via media. It is this tendency which makes his presence in the Government invaluable and which leads me to attach faith to his pacific profession—a man of unpromising mind, no longer young, sobered by experience, and just emerging from a long and doubtful contest, offers in himself moral guarantees against embarking again on the desperate game of war at the present critical juncture. If I am right in believing that peace is his aim, I think it is judicious to allow a man of his political experience to choose the means of effecting it.

On 18 December, Bruce related his matured impressions of President Andrew Johnson, based on several conversations he had had with well-informed Americans.[52]

I have information which may be confidentially relied upon of the impression produced on his mind and his feelings toward England and France respectively.

He has two strong opinions on the foreign policy of this country. *The one* is the Monroe Doctrine as it is popularly called—that is to say hostility to monarchy on the Southern frontier of the United States and hostility to all attempts by the European powers to seizing territory in the American continents or to interfering by force in its internal administration. In these views he will be supported by all parties in this country. . . . *The second* is a profound distrust and aversion to the European Napoleon as the head of a great scheme or conspiracy for extending imperialism through the world. On this point he used the expression "we shall have to fight, in combination with England, in defence of the principles of Anglo-Saxon liberty." . . . The President stated distinctly that he was not in favour of war with anyone at present on account of the unsettled state of the country and the financial conditions, and that he would not be the aggressor; but that he would not recede one step on the Mexican question and that if France forced a quarrel upon him on that ground he would spend the last dollar and the last man in the contest.

I do not think the prospects of the present Cabinet good. Seward and Stanton both have "Presidency on the brain" and it is impossible that Johnson who is aiming at re-election can feel confidence in men who are likely to be his rivals. He belongs moreover to the Democratic Party, who have a strong dislike for Seward and Stanton and a wish to occupy their places. Mr. McCulloch[53] of the Treasury, who is not a professed politician, is I think the member of the Cabinet most in the President's confidence.

There is a growing desire on the President's part to take more into his hands the direction of foreign affairs and I fancy, is rather suspicious that men of any independent ideas and information are studiously kept away from him. All these politicians distrust each other and every man in office works it with a view to his personal interest. There seems little of party leadership as we understand it. Every man can aspire to the Presidency and every man's vanity magnifies his hopes of success.

By the beginning of 1866, the American demands upon France to withdraw her forces from Mexico had become more strident. On a private mission to Paris, General Ulysses S. Grant reminded the French that the United States still had fifty thousand troops under arms in Texas and that prolonged French interference in Mexican affairs could only worsen Franco-American relations.

Whether or not Maximilian's empire would survive without French support was problematic; the Americans simply wanted the French withdrawn from Mexico, or else American "volunteers" might begin to aid the republican forces of Benito Juarez.[54]

I feel convinced that this government are doing what they can to avoid a war with France about Mexico. Orders have been sent to reduce largely the force in Texas. Mr. Stanton told me that he considered the prospects of organizing the country under Maximilian hopeless, that France would get tired of the pecuniary sacrifice it entailed for no object and would give up the cause—and that it would be absurd to go to war for a matter which will terminate of itself. Even General Grant, though expressing himself as embarrassed about his journey to Europe, while the French remain in Mexico, and characterizing it "as a proceeding which was not peaceable" did not talk of war as a contingency likely to occur. I particularly remarked that he did not allude to Maximilian. His sole idea is, that the French shall leave Mexico. . . . The disbandment of the volunteers is no symptom of peace. Grant and other leading officers are anxious to get rid under any circumstances of those expensive and ill-officered levies and so to organize the army of 50,000 men as to admit of the cadres of being fitted up so as to institute a regular army of above 100,000 men.

In his conversations with Americans, Sir Federick Bruce took pleasure in undermining their stereotypes about Great Britain. He pointed out that she no longer pursued an aggressive imperialistic policy internationally and, if anything, was in the process of divesting herself of control over some of her possessions. Domestically, he contended, Britain was not the benighted and reactionary society caricatured by the American press.[55]

I had a long conversation with Mr. Raymond[56] who is the Editor of the "New York Times" and the exponent of the views of the moderate Republican party in the House of Representatives. I attacked him on the question of Canadian annexation and argued from the disastrous effect on our connection with the American Colonies produced by the expulsion of the French from Canada—that our presence on this Continent was of the greatest service to the Union in keeping it together and in overcoming sectional jealousies—that it acted for a millstone about our necks in our relations with the United States and that the effect of our losing our foothold in North America would be to give a more purely European character to our policies. These views seemed to strike him as sound from the American standpoint. . . . It is astounding how much ignorance there is among all dupes here as to the condition of foreign countries and governments. What I endeavour to impress upon leading men is the steady and uninterrupted improvement of the condition of the masses in England—the uniform tendency of our modern legislation in that direction and its necessarily gradual advance owing to the transition that has to be made from ancient and widely different social conditions. I claim, on the ground of this essential similarity with the United States, sympathy and appreciation in our career of peaceful progress and discouragement of the revolutionary agitators who, by resorting to acts of violence and barbarism, aggravate the difficulties of our position. This line of argument evokes a more hearty response than appeals to common origin do, for the Americans are jealously bent on claiming a nationality, and the war has done much to increase that feeling—but

THE OPENING STAGES OF AMERICAN RECONSTRUCTION   371

the idea is far from unpleasing to them, that we, whom of all nations they respect the most, are carrying out in practice the main principles of civilization for the benefit of the masses which they claim to be the most marked characteristics of their conception of the aim and duty of government.

As long as French troops propped up Maximilian in Mexico, their presence would have a disturbing impact on American foreign and domestic policies.[57]

The breach between the President and Congress seems to widen, and I do not see symptoms of any serious split in the Republican party. The bills they are passing all look to a continued military occupation of the South. Mr. Myers,[58] Vice-Consul at Norfolk, informs me that in Virginia the course pursued by leaders in Congress is acting most unfavourably on opinion. He said that at the close of the war the Virginians were ready to re-enter the Union as loyal citizens. They felt and acknowledged that secession was at an end. Now however disunion which was at first confined to a few politicians was becoming the popular creed—and he assured me that in the event of a war with France sympathies and even the aid of the South would be with the foreign invader. The close of the war threatens to be the commencement not the end of the real alienation of the South; and under these circumstances tranquility will only be obtained by the native white population being swamped by immigrants from the North and Europe.

Each British envoy to the United States coveted those opportunities when he could secure a private audience with the president. On 9 February, Bruce recounted such a conversation with Andrew Johnson.[59]

He himself was anxious to see friendly relations existing with England, and he did not wish to rely exclusively on the reports of what passed between me and the Secretary of State. After some general remarks I alluded to the proceedings of the Fenians in this country, and to the preparations, as if for a State of War, that they obliged us to keep up in the frontier of the Provinces. He said with some emphasis— that this movement met with no sympathy on the part of the Government, which on the contrary was anxious to discourage it—that he was much dissatisfied with the impression in Mexico the Irish wished to create in this country—that the attempt to combine particular nationalities on this continent was contrary to American interests and inconsistent with their duties as American citizens—that he did not think the Fenian affair so formidable as was supposed and that it would die out for want of fuel. . . .

On the internal policy of the country the President appears to be quite settled in his views and confident that they will be ultimately successful. He said there are a few extreme Radicals who are bent on pushing theories to extremes and that the way to deal with them is to allow them to lay their plans fully before the people who will decide against them. He remarked on the inconsistency of those who, while advocating in the Freedmen's Bureau bill[60] provision for the maintenance and tutelage of the Negro, which could only be justified on the ground of his helplessness and inability to take care of himself, wished at the same time to confer on him a right by means of suffrage of taking part in the government of the country. He gave it as his opinion that the right of voting in this country requires to be raised not lowered. He said that in the towns it had become a source of corruption and that voters were publicly bought and sold without any regard to the public interest. The only remedy he saw was to provide that, after a certain time, a qualification should be required—perhaps a moral and educational qualification—for the electors of the lower Houses and a small free-hold qualification for the election of the Senators, etc. He said you can depend on the morality of the rural voters, but not on that of the town voters of the poorer classes. That the rural voters however poor, felt that he had an interest in the country and identified himself with it but not so the poorer class of town folk. Such a change would be beneficial to us for you may recollect that . . . the country Irish took little part in the Fenian movement and that it was chiefly confined to the town Irish and was taken up by the politicians in order to gain votes.

Every reflecting person I have talked to concurs in thinking that the successful working of this Government depends on the preponderance of the land being maintained in the electoral body.

Our conversation lasted about half an hour. During the latter part of it Mr. Stanton came in, and I thought it better to turn it upon general topics.

On leaving the President's he expressed himself as much pleased with the interview and added, that though all business must go through the Department of State, he should be glad to see me at any time, and hear any suggestions which I might wish to offer. I shall be very cautious of availing myself of this permission, as Mr. Seward's jealousy might be easily aroused. . . . There is a singular charm in the President's manner. He is evidently a man of strong convictions and much thought, combined with tenderness of heart. He expresses himself with much clearness and with an absence of anything like Americanism in his language and accent.

Toward the end of 1865 and the beginning of 1866, the former states of the Confederacy passed so-called Black Codes. Coming at about the same time the Thirteenth Amendment outlawed slavery, the codes sought to reimpose many of the restrictions of the antebellum South, with respect to labor contracts, apprenticeships, and vagrancy. In February 1866, Congress responded by introducing legislation that would augment the powers of the Freedmen's Bureaus and protect the former slaves from exploitative employers and landowners.[61]

I do not think Seward's trip to the West Indies had any very definite object. He wanted repose—he was glad to be absent—and he was not sorry to see the state of the Negro in different places. He has come back with the theory that in process of time the West Indies will form a black confederacy in amity with the United States. I have no doubt that there are many people who would like to see the United States in possession of stations in distant lands, which would place them on more equal terms with England in case of a war; but such projects would not I think find favour in the West. And in speculating on the future march of events it must be borne in mind the next will increase very largely the representation of the West in Congress. During the War the population of Illinois has increased by 500,000.

I am very glad to say that the wages of artisans have decreased 25 per cent in the West and I fancy in other places. A respectable Irishman with whom I travelled from Philadelphia told me that the Fenian funds were due to the prosperity of the Irish labourers, and if they are a little pinched money will not flow in so readily. He came from Pittsburgh and described the Convention as a set of ragamuffins.

The President's speech has mortified the more judicious of his supporters. Cleon got the better of Pericles[62] on that occasion; and remarking his antecedents, it is not to be wondered at. But I doubt if it will do him much harm in the country at large. The people are not sorry to see the President descend from his pedestal and play the tailor demagogue. They pardon easily an indiscretion which is due to frankness and courage. Seward is now very civil to the Democrats. He thinks he may become the leader of a third party formed of the moderate elements of the Republicans and their opponents. BUT he is not trusted and there is something pitiful and degrading in an acrobat of 66. The Democrats are full of hope, but I do not think that victory is as near at had as they suppose. The President's course has delighted the South and will I trust make him more willing to comply with their advice. He has in his favour the reputation of being inflexible.

The Irish question and possible Fenian raids upon Canada were topics that continued to haunt Bruce month in and month out. So did the political infighting that characterized the Johnson administration. Bruce felt that Seward played a pivotal role in all this.[63]

I believe Johnson distrusts him, & would willingly get rid of him & of Stanton. But Seward has checkmated him by taking the lead in the attempt to break up the Republican Party, and Johnson could not carry any fresh nominations to the Cabinet through the Congress.

Altogether the condition of this Gov't. is most singular. An overwhelming majority in Congress against the Executive; a Cabinet in which Johnson has little reliance; neither party able to carry out their views now that two-thirds of the Senate are not to be had against the President, and both parties speculating on the result of the elections next Autumn. Even then the elections will not materially affect the Senate.

You will see here an instance of the radical difference of American institutions from ours. There is no power to dissolve, and rapid changes in the representative body are necessary to get out of a dead-lock like the present. Senators are elected for six years; & a certain number are changed every two years: the comparative permanence of that Body being considered necessary.

In some respects this state of things is not favourable to peaceful relations with Foreign Powers. But as a War would tend to strengthen the President, it is to be presumed this Congress would be opposed to it. Moreover Johnson is confident of success in his home policy, and is inclined to make that his sole object at present. The Southern States according to the evidence before Congess are not to be relied upon, & if called upon to take part in a Foreign War, they would doubtless make their conditions which would be fatal to the predominance of the Radical party, and it is to be recollected that among the Radicals power is at least as warmly hugged as the Negro, who is simply their footstool. . . .

I ought to mention that I have been warned of my assassination having been discussed among the Fenians, as a mode of embroiling affairs. The warning was sent me through an officer by a Free-Mason who believes that I belong to that honourable fraternity. I am in the habit of walking home at night from parties, & the plan is to attack me on the road. I have little doubt that the idea may have been started, & I shall be careful. It is a consolation to think that any such act would do such harm to their cause, but with Irishmen that is no reason why it should not be tried.

A week later, on 16 March, Bruce relayed the latest rumors of Fenian machinations but admitted that sources of information were still fragmentary.[64]

> I read to Mr. Seward yesterday one of the many letters I receive from persons in different parts of the country professing to give an account of the plan of Sweeny for attacking the Maritime Provinces. This led to a long conversation on the rise and present position of the Fenian conspiracy.
>
> Mr. Seward describes it as having originated at the time when the Public in the United States believed that the South was likely to obtain recognition from England and France. The Irish conspirators here foresaw that this event would lead to a desperate struggle from the deep-seated reluctance of the North to acquiesce in disruption of the country. They proceeded to organize themselves and to propagate their idea in Ireland, and among the Irish wherever they were to be found, in the hope that they might raise somewhere the standard of Irish Nationality, knowing well that they would be supported by the United States warmly in an enterprise which threatened to be the most serious blow to the power of England. "In such a case", Seward said, "I myself and every American would have become a Fenian".
>
> Now, he continued, the question presents itself under a different form. The unity of this country is established beyond dispute, and what it requires is repose and peace for its complete consolidation. The conduct of the Irish during the War in spite of their military services, has not rendered them popular. In point of sentiment they did not show themselves friendly to Northern ideas, and they went with the Democratic, and not with the Republican party. If they were strong enough to make the Independence of Ireland a probable result of their enterprise, the irritation against England would acquire for them considerable moral support, but there is no faith in their success, and no real sympathy with Celtic aspirations, and the humiliation of England is not of sufficient interest to the United States, to induce them to ally themselves with a desperate cause, in the struggle which such an enterprise would produce.
>
> He continued "the first idea was that of O'Mahony[65] and his party, in favour of a descent on Ireland. But the difficulties in the way of such an enterprise, unless a formidable civil War were to break out in Ireland are insurmountable. Hence the plans of Sweeny & Roberts which contemplate the attack and seizure of the Provinces, as a first step towards the end they have in view".[66] He argued that this scheme would break down also, and that the best way of putting an end to the influence of these agitators, would be to let their dupes see, that after all their panaches they would effect nothing. . . .
>
> It is not so clear however that these are the real reasons for the reticence of this Gov't. The President and Seward are at this moment asking for aid from every quarter in his conflict with Congress. The Democratic party support him, and the Irish vote has hitherto always been given in favour of the Democrats. He will therefore shelter himself as long as he can, under the pretext that there is no violation of the law, and that the affair is not so serious as it is represented to be. He may hope that the leaders may disagree, or that something will happen to defeat their plans. But it is evident that this course keeps the Provinces on the qui vive, that it paralyses trading relations on the frontier, and that it allows these agitators to do their wont. On the other hand, it excites much hostility in the provinces, towards the United States, and the internal state of the country and of parties, is such, as to render it more easy for us to deal vigorously with these brigands without a rupture between the two countries, than it would be if the country were united and tranquil.

The "Civil Rights Bill", which has passed both Houses by large majorities is, I understand, to be made the test. If the President allows it to become law, it will be taken as evidence of his adherence to the Republican Party, and a rapprochement between him and Congress will be the result. If he vetoes it (which he must do within 10 days) the leaders of Congress will consider that he has gone over to the Democrats and the South, and they will embarrass his administration in every way.

While Fenian leaders like William Roberts and Thomas Sweeny plotted an attack upon Canada, a handful of others, including the Fenian General Gleeson, slipped back into Ireland. When arrested, they claimed the right, as naturalized American citizens, to speak with an American diplomatic representative.[67]

Mr. Seward begged me to call upon him to-day, and after some remarks on the Fenian project for St. Patrick's day having come to nothing, and on the divisions among the leaders, as proofs of the wisdom of leaving them alone at present, he said he wished to talk with me on a question from which he apprehended the Fenians will derive material support unless it be kept in abeyance during the present excitement.

He then mentioned the arrest of Gleeson[68] and some others, with whom the American Consul had not been allowed to communicate as being native Irishmen, though naturalized subsequently as American citizens.

He said that the principle of protection to naturalized citizens was one too firmly rooted in the minds of the American people, to allow any public men here to abandon it. That he was aware of the opposition the doctrine met with in Europe and in England—But that he wished me to represent to Her Majesty's Gov't. how desirable and indeed how vitally important it was at present not to raise it particularly in the case of men who have served in the United States army. He said "I am not much afraid of any serious difficulty arising out of the Fenian affair, but I do apprehend very serious complications, if this question is to be raised in connection with the Fenian movement." He recommended strongly as a middle course, that without waiving the principle the Consul should be allowed to see these men, and lay their case before Her Majesty's Government, who would still retain in their hands the power of dealing with it as they thought fit.

In order to appreciate the importance given to this pretension of the Americans, it is necessary to bear in mind the enormous and increasing foreign emigration to these shores. They take a deep interest in this claim to protection, and the native Americans support it, as a sine qua non condition of their support in elections.

I cannot conceal from myself the gravity of this question at the present crisis, and the unfortunate influence that will be produced on public opinion here, if the Fenians are able to present themselves to the American people, as denied the privileges of American citizens in this respect. I feel convinced that no party in America will hesitate in supporting the Gov't. in asserting the principle, and I also am persuaded that in a few years, looking to the rapid growth of this country, we shall find it impracticable to maintain our old doctrines on the subject without involving us in serious difficulties. But apart from the general question, I believe that to allow Fenianism to be mixed up with this collateral issue, will give them that ground of sympathy with the American people, which at present they do not possess, but which will render them really formidable, and may even acquire for them material support.

I look upon Mr. Seward's suggestion as made in good faith, and with a sincere desire to arrive at a pacific solution of the Fenian difficulty. It strikes me that whether these men are treated as natives or allowed to communicate through the Consul they are still liable to the consequences of the suspension of the Habeas Corpus Act, and that if they are unable to enlist sympathy on this extraneous ground, there will be no disposition on the part of this Gov't. to relieve them from the consequences of their own unjustifiable acts. There are not wanting symptoms that the Fenians are approaching a crisis, which will force them to action, or discredit their leaders. And we have more hopes of the aid of this Gov't. in defeating their designs, if this question can be avoided or postponed for the present.

Of course I made no remarks in the above sense to Mr. Seward. I confined myself to simply hearing what he had to say on the subject, and to expressing my intention to repeat it to Your Lordship.

In the spring of 1866 Congress passed a Civil Rights Act, which sought to bestow on all people, white or black, who were born in the United States equal political and legal rights. President Johnson vetoed the bill on the grounds that it was an invasion of states' righs, while Congress overrode this on 9 April. The Supreme Court then declared it unconstitutional, thus paving the way for the Fourteenth Amendment, with its provision for equal protection before the law.[69]

The telegraph will probably inform you of the Veto by the President of the "Civil Rights Bill". He is determined on defending the Constitution against the attacks of the Legislature. It is significant of some hesitation in the Republican ranks, that they have passed a "Loan Bill" enabling Mr. McCulloch to deal with the debt and currency within certain limits, though they must have suspected at the time that the President would reject their favourite measure.

General Grant, with whom I had a long tête à tête ride the other day, volunteered the information that his attention had been directed for some time to the Fenian movement, and that he had altered his disposition of the troops on the frontier accordingly. He seems confident that the plans against the provinces will end in nothing, and laughs at the idea of anything serious with Sweeny at the head. He says that to interfere with them unless they commit an overt act, would be to give them the bridge they want to get out of their difficulty with a certain amount of credit, and to preserve their influence over their dupes. General Grant has the character of being a truthful and honourable man, and I hardly think that he would have initiated the Fenian subject if he had no other intention but to deceive me. His views coincide with those of Seward, and corroborate the assertions of the latter but their Gov't. are not unmindful of their duties to their neighbours.

Sir Frederick Bruce took evident pride in his grasp of American domestic politics and lost few opportunities to share these insights with his superior in London.[70]

Mr. Seward takes the breach between the President and Congress very coolly. He says "We elect a king for four years. It generally happens that he is in a minority in Congress during the first Session, on account of the members having been elected in a former reign. The new President during that time shapes his policy and it goes to the country backed by his influence and patronage and with the strength he derives from the fact that during the remainder of his term he must govern or the country remain at a deadlock. Then parties begin to organize themselves with a view to the future, and the struggle is conducted not to obtain power immediately but to carry the next Presidential election.'' This is the substance of his views, and it is evident that the position or role of Congress is essentially different from that of Parliament. They can thwart the President's policy and the Senate can embarrass him in making appointments, but if he is firm they can hardly impose upon him in the country a different policy while his term of office lasts. They can only prepare the way for the triumph of another party or the principles of the upcoming Presidential election. This delay and the time afforded for reflecting and for a mature development of the policy of the Executive are very favourable to the working of ultra-democratic institutions. It is a pity that this feature is not better understood by the democrats of Europe. I feel certain that no democracy can work without a strong Executive.

As part of his reconstruction policy of restoring power to the individual states of the former Confederacy, Johnson authorized the issuing of state bonds and the collection of local taxes rather than seeking to retain these functions, as the Radical Republicans wished, in the hands of the United States Congress.[71]

The President's Proclamation included in my despatch of this day's date seems to be a formal declaration of war against the majority in Congress,[72] and places in a distinct form before the country the issues between the Executive and the Legislature. He takes his stand as the champion of the restoration of the Union according to the principles of the Constitution. He says that peace is restored, that the Southern states have loyally accepted the new order of things, and may be trusted to carry it out by state legislation and state authorities without further constitutional changes and without the continued exercise of arbitrary power; and he gives it as his opinion that they are entitled to the full enjoyment of their political rights as a part of the United States. It is a very singular result so soon after the Civil War. The Executive is now heading the South and the Democrats of the North for the Union against the bulk of the Republican Party in the North who are practically upholding the doctrine that union is impossible without organic changes in the Constitutional Charter of the United States. The position of the North and the South may be said to be reversed, for if the South were formerly for secession, the North are now for Revolutionary change, and both agree in dissatisfaction with their institutions. They feel in turn the influence of the principle which has always ruled in the contest between the Federal and States' Rights: the dominant party has invariably sought to extend Federal authority and the weaker party has always sought shelter under States' Rights. Insofar as the feeling of loyalty may exist among the masses to their institution it may safely be predicted that it is felt more strongly to the state authority to which the people are accustomed to look for protection of their lives, liberties and properties and the presence of which is felt in the daily affairs of life, than to the Federal Government which previous to the Civil War was hardly known except in their foreign relations and in questions of foreign trade.

No such grave question has ever been raised in this country and it is impossible to calculate what may happen if the Radical Party succeed in the next Congressional election. They already talk of not adjourning Congress at all this year and of continuing to sit for the purpose of embarrassing the President and for preventing him from using his patronage to advance his views. The leaders are prepared to go to any length in favour of their scheme which is to keep out the Southern States until the next

Presidential election has taken place. If they succeed it remains to be seen whether the South will recognize their President. In such an event they would have a most powerful argument for secession in which they would be supported by the Constitutional Party in the North. It remains to be seen what effect this proclamation will have on the President's cabinet.

A year after he arrived in Washington, Bruce felt he was in a good position to command the respect of Secretary of State Seward and to evaluate his character and style.[73]

The key to Mr. Seward's line is to be found in a great dread of saying or writing anything that may be politically injurious to him here. In his official utterances he will therefore always be captious, extreme in his pretensions and often arrogant. He will be as offensive if not more so when he means to recede as when he means to advance. He will cover his retreat by a tremendous fire. In delicate questions where it is possible it is therefore desirable to avoid paper discussions and to be satisfied with his acting. For instance in the Fenian affair he has always maintained that arms could not be seized, and if I had called upon him for an official declaration he would have answered in that sense. But the Government have authorized the General to seize arms as soon as there was something like an expedition on foot, and I know General Meade's[74] action in this respect has been approved. If it is seen that this Government will not allow their neighbours to be molested by criminal enterprises from their territory, and that their course is to all appearance spontaneous, the very fact of their reticence on the merits of Fenianism will give greater moral weight to their action and will inflict greater discouragement on the agitators.

Up to the present time not a criticism has been made on the conduct of the Government. No one ventures to blame them for enforcing the law, and my official silence deprives English-haters of the opportunity of presenting to this country a false issue. . . .

My intercourse with Seward does not lead me to think that he is a dissimulator, rather I should say that his bark is worse than his bite, but he is at first suspicious of a new man. He does not know whether his discretion is to be relied on or his friendliness. He puts himself on the defensive till his mind is made up on the point, but if he confides in a man, I think him inclinded to be frank as far as a man can speak openly or positively in a country so changeable and where a politician must be largely guided by opinion.

I believe he is sincere in stating that it is his fixed determination to have no more war while he is in power, and I believe him as capable as any man of carrying through a pacific policy, but circumstances may be too strong for him. In the meantime the best course for me is to act in concert with him as long as I can, to urge my views in a friendly spirit, and to avoid the semblance of anything like intrigue with rival parties. He is vain, and to show deference to his judgment in internal matters is a species of subtle flattery which is not without weight. Les politiques du salon are of little use here, for the ripples on the surface of society only serve to confuse the sight. Even the violent language used in Congress rather indicates the existence of prejudice than a deliberate purpose of action. The acts of the Executive are the best criteria of the direction of the undercurrent of interest and stable opinion. . . . It is impossible to predict what the future has in store, but for the present the desire for peace is on the increase.

In his private letters, Bruce seemed to thrive on the exploration of abstract issues, in response to such queries from Lord Clarendon as to the fate of blacks in the postwar Southern states.[75]

The question put in your last letter as to the position of the negro in the Southern States, supposing the President's policy of re-establishing States' Rights to be carried out, is one of great interest and of great difficulty. I cannot speak on the subject with confidence amid the conflicting reports I hear of Southern sentiment. It does not however admit of doubt that the freedom of the negro is accepted in the South. The state legislatures have sought to give it effect and have generally recognized his civil rights in all cases where he is concerned. In some instances they have refused to admit his evidence where white men only are concerned, but the question between the President and the majority in Congress is not fairly stated if it is represented as being solely a question of the more or less protection to be afforded to the negro. There is a much wider issue involved: how is a minority consisting of an ignorant and despised race to exist and be protected in the midst of a dominant and a haughty race who yesterday knew them only as slaves and chattels.

The President, a Southern man, knowing the state of opinion in the southern states and the condition of the negro, says in substance that the existence and safety of the negro race depend on their position being harmonious with and not antagonistic to the whites. He maintains that they will be the victims of the hatred and suspicion engendered by any attempt to force them, by any constitutional legislation and Northern influence against the opinion of the South. He asserts that there is no feeling of hatred or revenge in the South against them, that their well-being is essential to the interests of Southern cultivators, that their interests are safer guides to dealing practically with the question than theories of ignorant Northern sentimentalists, that if left alone (under the menace of interference if acting unjustly) the Southern States will establish relations beneficial to both races, and that in all events the experiment ought to be tried before tampering with the Constitution of the country. Finally, he does not hesitate to say that the sympathy professed by the radical majority in Congress for the negro is insincere, and that their real object is to use him as a means to prolong their tenure of power. Moreover, he objects to the Radical plan of action: that it is impracticable. He denies the possibility of extending over the vast country known as the Slave States any effectual protection based on the assumption that the resident Whites are hostile to the Negro. He is in favour of accepting the Constitution as it is and of legislating if necessary for *proved* but not for presumed evils. He is as anxious that the negro should become a useful member of society, as that he should be secured in the enjoyment of the rights of man, and if he is unequal to the exigencies of his position in an industrial community, he is indifferent to his fate. In this view of the case he represents I believe truly American sentiment in its cooler moments, though the hostility to the South produced by the War shows itself at present an artificial sympathy for the negro.

The negro is not an ideal being except perhaps in New England, where he is as little known as he was in Old England at the period of emancipation. In the other Free States he is looked upon as *Punch* describes, not as a brother but as a bother, and there is no disposition to make sacrifices to save him from destruction if he is too idle and improvident to take care of himself. The Irish particularly hate him as a probable competition in the lowest description of labour which has hitherto been exclusively their field.

You will never get out of the heads of men like Johnson (himself originally a mean white) the idea that the negro is an inferior being totally inept for the higher development of civilization. The objections entertained by his class to slavery were political and proceeded largely from the feeling of envy to the rich proprietors which republican institutions tend to produce. His class were the severest taskmasters in the South, and they are now the negro's worst enemies. The badge of slavery was the only distinction between them and the black man, and their pride of race is severely mortified now that it has been done away.

It is remarkable how entirely the President has abandoned the agrarian ideas which he apparently entertained at first. I think he now perceives that, if his policy of reconstruction is to be carried through and the Southern States are to be restored to their aristocracy, the interest and safety of the negro will be best protected by the large proprietors. He has no faith in the plan of turning the negroes into small proprietors, and thus depriving them of the care and civilizing influence of dependence on the white man. He believes that, if they become squatters, they will become idle, thievish and dissipated. They will be exposed to the hostility of the whites and through bad usage and improvidence will soon disappear altogether. He wishes them to become a necessary link in the chain of Southern industry, and that can only be effected by a combination between their labour and the capital and intelligence of the whites. It is only in this way that the negro can hope to escape the fate that has overtaken the Red Indian. Indeed if, as many suppose, white labour can be substituted for black in the raising of cotton, he will soon be driven for subsistence to the rice swamps of South Carolina and the sugar plantations of Louisiana. If therefore I am right in this statement of the views of the President and his adherents, it is evident that he looks upon the fate of the negro as dependent on economic laws not on direct legislation. He will therefore oppose to the utmost all revolutionary changes in the Constitution of the United States, not only because of his reverence for it but because he does not think the object of the philanthropists will be thereby attained. He will not refuse to consider any specific measure intended to meet a specific necessity, once that necessity is proved to exist, but he will resist all *a priori* legislation which is based on the idea that the negro must be put under the tutelage of the Federal Government as unconstitutional and as prejudicial to the interests of the negro himself. The question between him and the Radicals is not one of humanity but of sagacity, dealing with this most difficult problem, and I think, though I speak with diffidence, that the President's plan will work more favourably for the slave than any scheme which his opponents have hitherto been able to elaborate. I do not enter upon the political objections to schemes which will render necessary a quasi-military occupation of the South and which will give to the South the support on constitutional grounds of a large party in the North itself, but it is impossible to consider that question fairly without taking into account the Constitution of this Government which is not a republic, one and indivisible, but is an agglomeration of separate republics with a federal head, the powers of which are jealously specified and circumscribed.

Ever since the French had invaded Mexico, ousted the republicans under Juarez, and paved the way for a monarchy under Maximilian of Austria, the United States had sought redress of this flagrant violation of the Monroe Doctrine. By the spring of 1866 Napoleon III promised a phased withdrawal of French troops, but there were those in the United States who welcomed this pretext to justify American intervention.[76]

Mr. Seward told me two days ago that there was a strong feeling growing up in the country in favour of a more decided line of policy in the Mexican question, and that the Government would have great difficulty in resisting it. The nomination of Mr. Campbell[77] as Minister to the Republic of Mexico is a proof of it, and it seems not unlikely that the Mexican loan will be brought forward in Congress. Mr. Sumner and Senator Thurman[78] opposed Campbell's confirmation by the Senate but were defeated. The extreme Radicals, who are averse to war as it would lead to the immediate admission of the Southern states, declare that this is the game of the President and his advisors. I have good reason to believe that the President, in conversation with Mr. Andrew[79] (late Governor of Massachusetts and a Republican friendly to the President) said that he would not take the initiative in the question because Congress would reject anything he proposed; but that he would go quite as far as Congress in that direction. His position is so uncertain and would be so much strengthened by finding a common ground on which he and Congress could agree in the adoption of which would turn to his advantage any internal questions, that I should not be surprised if this Government were to take advantage of any plausible ground for abandoning their neutrality in the Mexican question. No doubt Sonora[80] or Lower California were pledged as security for the loan, and without embarrassing Juarez and without embarking in war it might permit him, with the funds thus required, to organize on the frontier a force for the invasion of Mexico in support of Juarez. Many of the unquiet spirits in the South would enter, and the Government would be very glad to see them disposed of. In a party point of view, this course would have certain advantages. It would gratify the Army, as many of the officers would find employment, and it would disunite the Republican party, many of whom, such as General Schenck[81] of Ohio are strongly opposed to the Mexican Empire. It would be a popular move with reference to the forthcoming elections, and would enable the President's supporters to recommend his policy of reconstruction on the ground of the strength the immediate restoration of the Union would give in maintaining Republican institutions on this Continent. Altogether, the Mexican question is at this moment in a very critical condition. Mr. Seward cannot conceal his wish for war between Austria and Prussia,[82] and I see he is apprehensive of a change of ministry in England,[83] as he thinks it would lead to a closer union with France in dealing with questions on this Continent.

Early on the morning of 1 June 1866, several hundred Fenians crossed over the Niagara River near Buffalo into Canada, under the command of Colonel John O'Neill. As Canadian forces gathered to repel this modest invasion, the Fenians withdrew across the Niagara and many were duly arrested by the American authorities.[84]

I cannot say I am surprised at the attempt of the Sweeny faction, as it has always appeared to me that Killian's[85] failure did not relieve Sweeny from making an attempt. The Government were however unprepared. There are only fifty men in the fort at Buffalo, and the revenue cruiser was away on a trial trip when the crossing was effected. The whole force in the northern district from Maine to New York only amounts to 1,200 men, so that even allowing that this Government are doing what they can, it is evident that the Canadians had to look to themselves for protection, and could not rely on the United States to keep peace along the frontier. As for the militia, our previous experience does not encourage us in placing much reliance upon them. The revenue force seems to have acted well. It is impossible to conjecture whether any further serious attempts will be made or not. I have urged most strongly upon Mr. Seward the propriety of arresting Sweeny and the other leaders as a means of preventing it, but if they are with the Fenians, I do not think the arrests can be effected. By the time the steamer sails from Halifax, events will I trust have developed themselves.

By 10 June it was clear that little was to be feared for the time being in the way of further Fenian incursions into Canada, and Bruce could turn his attention to a multiplicity of other issues as well.[86]

I think Seward was mislead by his sanguine disposition, and trusted to something happening which would relieve him from the necessity of open opposition to these enterprises. For the result of his course is that the Fenians plead the toleration as their defence, and his opponents attack him for having, by his reticence, lured these people to their destruction. The consciousness of being open to this charge and the desire not to break with the Irish party will lead to the offenders being dealt with very leniently if they are tried for violation of the Neutrality Acts. They will leave it to us to show severity to the prisoners in our hands. In this as in all foreign questions, the Government will be mainly guided by party considerations, and it is both dignified and politick to allow them to enforce their laws in their own way and of their own accord. If they decide in making examples of the leaders they will do so at greater care if not officially urged. If they do not they will be stopped in their complaints against us for not having succeeded in bringing to justice the offenders against the Enlistment Act. . . . But looking to the power of the Irish in elections and to the unscrupulousness of politicians in this country, I do implore Her Majesty's Government not to underrate the great danger to our relations with the United States arising out of a state of chronic discontent in Ireland. If a serious insurrection were to break out there, I doubt whether the will or the power would exist to prevent the recognition of the insurgents as belligerents. Opinion here and a certain national pride, support the national pride in enforcing its laws, but it would as surely support it in recognizing Irish belligerency and allowing privateers to slip out of their harbours to attack our commerce. It must not be assumed that the action of the Government is a proof of friendly feeling towards us. The wiser and calmer men have no faith in the possibility of an Irish republic and little sympathy with its advocates, but the people at large are more ignorant and all would see with pleasure England crumble or in difficulties. This feeling may perhaps die out in time or the increasing power of the West and a large German immigration, who do not love the Irish, may modify the power of the Irish element in elections. But no argument is of any avail against this strong prejudice. If the Reform Bill[87] will give England a Parliament which will deal promptly and broadly with Ireland, it is most devoutly to be wished that it may pass. All other questions seem to be trivial as compared with this. In looking back upon the difficulties arising out of the Civil War here and those I had to encounter in China, I see clearly how much they were due to the balanced strength of parties in Parliament and to the consequent paralysis of the Executive. Putting aside all discussion as to the merits of the two great opposing parties in the state, one point is clear: that no country can avoid finding itself in a labyrinth of confusion if it cannot constitute for itself an Executive strong enough to carry out consistently its views. And, if the present Constitution of the electoral body renders this impossible, the sooner it is changed the better. Otherwise we shall make good the Duke of Wellington's maxim: "How is the King's Government to be carried on?" though not perhaps precisely in the sense in which he used it. In the eyes of every patriot and of every impartial foreigner, the condition of Ireland and the inability to apply a remedy to so glaring an abuse as the Irish Church, are a serious slur on our Parliamentary system; a pretext more than plausible for Irish aspirations to self-government. A study of Irish history might disabuse them of confidence in the proposed specific.

I think it more than probable that the proclamation of the President and the subsequent action of the Government will tell against the President at the approaching elections,[88] and he deserves all the more credit for having laid down so broadly the principles of public and municipal law applicable to such cases. In view of the little force at his command and the strong Irish element in it, the proceedings of the Government and of General Meade seem to have been judicious. The seizure of arms and the arrest of the principal leaders were probably as much as they could with safety attempt. Mr Seward is anxious that the few remaining Americanized Irishmen who are in custody in Ireland should be released, on condition of their leaving the country. I do not think that their presence here will do much harm, and this Government will feel grateful for a proceeding which will relieve them from being attacked for not protecting American citizens. I think it good policy to strengthen the position of the President at present in relation to the Fenian question, and I therefore recommend a compliance with the suggestion.

Throughout the Fenian agitation in North America, Bruce tried to remain in the background as much as possible, so as not to provoke needlessly anti-British feeling. However, he was anxious to assure Lord Clarendon that he had not been idle.[89]

I have little in the way of fact or speculation to add to any despatches on the subject of the Fenians. The attempt on Canada is entirely over for the present, and my efforts are directed to advocate such a course of action as may prevent any attempt hereafter to make Canada the battlefield of Irish politics.

The Irish, by their defiance of the law and their open interference with the course of justice, are dong what they can to turn public opinion against them and against the armed organizations generally. Our true policy is to let this feeling work and to be satisfied at present with the enforcement by this Government of the law against those who have violated it. No government here will put itself in opposition to popular Irish sentiment, and it is hopeless to attempt it, but I am convinced that the President and Seward would with pleasure see the conviction of the leaders in this criminal enterprise, and will be more likely to be able to effect it if we do not embarrass them with demands.

The difficulty arises from the balanced state of parties, the approaching elections and the perverted state of public opinion. Had the President been a man of less firm character, we might have had very serious complications. As he has committed himself and his government in an unpopular cause, it is wise to consult his wishes as far as possible. The government will try and convict the leaders. If they succeed, well; if they do not, owing to the state of opinion, their position in complaining of us will be materially weakened. . . .

This country has much of the feeling of the "parvenu". They think that their position among nations is not sufficiently recognized and that feeling makes them wince under criticism, especially from England. They resent dictation in matters which concern their internal administration, and they will act better and more honestly if it is not attempted. The Executive is far more powerful than is supposed, provided that it is left to work in its own way and is not forced into direct collision with public opinion; and I venture to say that the Government at present are inclined to a more reasonable and pacific policy than the excitable masses, and have a juster idea of the true interests of the country. We have to make common cause with them against the self-confidence and resentment of the arrogant Democracy—a very special and peculiar sort of diplomacy is required—one which makes allowance for a double-faced course on their part, and whatever despatches they may write to flatter popular opinion, we may consider them of little moment, as long as their action is in the right direction.

During the summer of 1866, President Johnson and his supporters made plans to convene in August at Philadelphia a convention of moderates from throughout the country. It was hoped that this new National Union party could supercede the older ones, but many in the North perceived the effort as one playing into the hands of former "rebels" and "copperheads."[90]

The Philadelphia Convention summoned on August 14 from all the states and the support given to the proposal by the President and Mr. Seward, have produced a difference of opinion among Johnson's Republican supporters. Some of the most influential, such as Dennison,[91] the postmaster; Speed,[92] the Attorney-General; and probably Harlan[93] of the Interior, prefer their allegiance to their party to their adhesion to the President. They consider that the Republican Party ought to be kept intact and that the Government ought to be carried on by effecting a reconciliation between it and the President. The National Convention, which is proposed to call, will be largely composed of Democrats and men of Southern sympathies, and is indeed designed to break up if possible the Republican Party, and to bring about an understanding between the North and the South on equal terms. This is in direct opposition to the policy and ideas of the great majority in Congress. It is consistent with the Presdient's principles, and I can hardly understand, after what has passed during this Session, that any man could have hoped for a reconciliation or could have flattered himself that a rupture between the President and the Republican Party could have been avoided.

I see Raymond of "The New York Times", who both in Congress and in his paper has supported the President's policy as against the Convention. He declares that the attempt to form a new Presidential party has entirely failed, and that Seward has lost all influence even in his own state. He says there is no change in opinion in the North—that the extreme Republican sections are paramount. He told me they thought the President would, when the new Congress meets, try and fence the admission of the Southern members with the aid of the Democrats—that they went so far as to believe him capable of a coup d'état, and had passed a resolution in the House two days ago for the distribution throughout the states of all spare arms. It is a fact of some gravity if true, but such an impression should prevail as to what the President is capable of doing, and is a proof of the character of bitterness and suspicion that the political contest is beginning to assume.

Mr. Seward appears to be more anxious and preoccupied than he was some time ago. He is less confident as to the issue of the struggle on the internal question and is evidently afraid of some violent resolutions on the foreign question, which would be adopted in Congress to gain popularity at his expense. Altogether it appears to me that the internal difficulties augment, and are likely to do so if foreign questions are so managed as to keep them in abeyance, and allow domestic ones to engross popular attention. There is always danger of a diversion in that direction.

By 22 July 1866, news had reached Bruce in Washington of the resignation of the Russell cabinet, including Lord Clarendon as foreign secretary. The Liberal party under Earl Russell had confidently expected to bring about an extension of the franchise, but it was this issue that forced the government to resign. Bruce had good reason to regret Lord Clarendon's leaving office, for he had won the latter's respect and confidence during the late 1850s. Now it was very likely there would be a new foreign secretary who had not occupied that position previously.[94]

> I have served too long under you, and have received too much indulgent consideration for my efforts at your hands, not to feel a very sincere regret at losing you as my chief. I feel the deep obligation I am under to you for the confidence you have reposed in me, which has given me the self-reliance without which the difficulties of such a post as mine could not have been successfully met, and though your kindness may over-rate my merits, I will not conceal how much I am gratified at the expression of your approbation. Indeed, I think by acting entirely in concert with Seward in Fenianism, Canadian provinces, etc., some difficulties, and those not inconsiderable, have been avoided, and the tone of this Govt in its communications has sensibly improved.

Sir Frederick Bruce's first fifteen months in the United States had witnessed dramatic changes. President Lincoln was dead and his successor greatly at odds with Congress and much of the Northern electorate. The end of the Civil War had seemingly raised as many uncertainties as it had resolved. The economic and political status of the Negro was precarious at best, and it took several constitutional amendments to force some semblance of compliance to the new laws defining freedom and citizenship. America had weathered its internal strife and was now reasserting herself in matters of foreign affairs. Just how obstreperous the United States would be in her quest for her Manifest Destiny remained to be seen.

16

Preoccupation with Domestic Affairs, July 1866–September 1867

Sir Frederick Bruce addressed his first private letter to Lord Stanley on 26 July 1866. At forty years old, the new foreign secretary was well connected with the government, being the eldest son of the new prime minister, the fourteenth earl of Derby. Stanley had attended Rugby School and Trinity College, Cambridge, before setting off on extensive travels to the United States, the West Indies, and parts of Latin America from 1848 to 1850. In 1852 he made his way to Bengal before taking up later that year the appointment of undersecretary for foreign affairs. During these years (1848–69), Stanley also represented King's Lynn in Parliament and secured a cabinet post in 1858 as colonial secretary and secretary for India. That lasted only a year when the Liberals acquired power and the Conservatives languished until the summer of 1866. Edward Henry Stanley was foreign secretary until the Conservatives went out of office in 1868, and a year later, upon the death of his father, he became fifteenth earl of Derby.[1]

I trust you will allow me to communicate my impressions upon events which take place here, and upon the fluctuations of public opinion in the shape of private letters, as I have hitherto been in the habit of doing. — In official correspondence I wish to confine myself as much as possible to the bare recital of facts, which will not compromise or irritate anyone. I should incur the risk of weakening the influence of, or indisposing, persons who are or may be pacifically disposed, were I to comment in despatches which may see the light on their languages and acts at this moment. At present foreign questions of interest are dealt with almost exclusively with a view to the way in which they will influence votes in the forthcoming elections. The issue of the struggle between the President and the extreme Northern party is very uncertain, and as the Irish vote is considerable, each party is doing its best to conciliate it. Unfortunately professions of sympathy for the cause of Irish independence, and hostility to England, are the two topics most popular with the Irish, and as I pointed out in my despatches nos. 149, 205, 211, and 229 (to which I beg to refer), the wish to gain Irish support, and the aid of the Democratic party, is likely to drive this government to renew the controversy with Great Britain on the points on which the two governments are at issue.

The distrust felt here as to the course the Emperor of the French will pursue in Mexico, and the disjointed state of the Union, have hitherto kept the questions with us in the background, but the feeling of irritation against us is little diminished, and I am anxious to warn Her Majesty's Government not to assume too hastily that there is any permanent improvement in our relations with this country.

The President and his Cabinet, after encouraging by their silence the Fenian organization, did undoubtedly exhibit vigour and address in preventing aid and supplies from being forwarded to the filibusters who had crossed the frontier into Canada. The Fenians complain bitterly of these proceedings. They attack the President and Seward as having played them false. They say their schemes were openly avowed, that they were allowed to purchase arms, ammunition, and war-material at government sales in furtherance of their plans, which were thus tacitly acquiesced in,—that they were allowed to invade Canada where several remain as prisoners, and that after they had thus committed themselves, their property was seized, their brethren left to be dealt with by the British Authorities, and their leaders indicted for breach of the Neutrality Laws.

The extreme Republican Party hope, by profession of sympathy with their Fenian complaints, to gain the Irish vote at the forthcoming elections, which have hitherto belonged to the Democratic Party. The Democrats on the other hand are put in a great difficulty between their anxiety not to lose it, and their wish to support the President. The resolutions to call for the release of the prisoners in Canada, and to drop the prosecutions against the Fenian leaders in the United States, as well as Banks' bill to alter the Neutrality Laws, met with no opposition in the House of Representatives. It was known that the Senate would not act upon them, and no member was willing to oppose resolutions which might deprive him of votes of any section of his constituents. Even in the Senate the resolution to lend a public building for the Fenian meeting, which was couched in terms gratuitously offensive to Great Britain, only found seven votes against it, and one member, Mr. Reverdy Johnson,[2] who was courageous enough to characterize it as it deserved.

The policy, which these events will probably compel their President to adopt, it is not too difficult to foresee. You will find in the claims against Great Britain arising out of the Civil War, the means of satisfying both the feeling of national animosity, which is so widely spread, and of insuring the support of the Irish by holding out to them the prospect of the aid of the American people in their views. The Americans, as a body, do not wish to be the instruments of the Irish, but they will be glad to use the Irish as their tools.

By the time Congress meets in December, the course of the Emperor in Mexico will probably be clearly ascertained. If it is clear that the French troops are being withdrawn, and that Maximilian is to be left to himself, no anxiety will be felt in that quarter.[3] Mexico will be allowed to remain to fall to pieces of itself, and to be swallowed up piece-meal as time and opportunity may dictate. France will have submitted to a humiliation which will increase the self-confidence of this nation; and no foreign question will remain to divert public attention and Congress from the favourite scheme of striking a blow at England. . . .

I do not think Mr. Seward inclined to war; on the contrary he would gladly accept any reasonable compromise which would meet him half way—but his position is sadly weakened, and he clings desperately to any chance of recovering his popularity. He will go with the stream wherever it may land him, and indeed his actions and opinions are chiefly valuable as indications of the turn which he believes public sentiment is about to take. . . .

Unfortunately though the disadvantages of having open questions with this government are sufficiently evident to any person who is acquainted with the history of the past and who appreciates the great difficulty of dealing with a democracy, it is by no means certain that the feeling of hostility to England, and the Fenian agitation, will be allayed by any course however conciliatory that we may pursue. The depredations of the "Alabama" and her consorts have added material loss to the sense of injury—but the feeling of dislike to England is of more ancient date, and this people have been taught by their leaders to attribute the duration of the Civil War to our recognition of the Confederates as belligerants, and to the extent to which blockade running was carried on from our ports. No argument makes any impression upon them, and if through Fenianism or any other instrumentality we could be made to suffer in the same way, the feeling of satisfaction would be universal.

Following riots in Memphis in late April and in New Orleans at the end of July 1866, during which some fifty blacks in all were killed, many Northerners were convinced that stronger measuers must be taken to guarantee the rights of the freedmen.[4]

The riots at Memphis and New Orleans show the violence of the passions which divide society in the South and reveal the fact that the war has broken up the harmony which previously existed; and has divided the White population into two camps, one Union and the other Rebel, of which the former, being the numerically weaker, seeks to control its rival by invoking the assistance of the Negro. In this course the Unionists of the South will be supported by the Radical Republicans of the North, and indeed there is little doubt that the attempt to call together the Union Convention of 1864 at New Orleans, was made with the advice or at least with the consent of the Radical leaders in Congress.[5] The effort to form a new party in favour of the President's policy, by calling together delegates from the North and South to meet on the 14th instant in Convention at Philadelphia,[6] occupies public attention. If it results in a meeting confined exclusively to the Democrats and the Southern secessionists, it will confirm and embitter the rupture between the President's and the Republican party. If on the other hand it embraces a considerable section of the moderate Republicans, it may exercise a great influence on the elections in favour of the President. The discipline however of party organization in this country is very vigorous, and the leaders of the Republican party have set their faces against the movement. They are not at all inclined to share with the Democrats the spoils of victory, and it is very doubtful whether they will be abandoned by those who have hitherto supported them. If the President is defeated and the Southern States are treated as a conquest, the powers of the Central Government will be increased at the expense of the rights of the States. This will be the commencement of a change, the end and effects of which no one can pretend to foresee.

The recent Fenian raid into Canada only heightened British concern over her North American provinces and their ability to withstand pressure from the United States. On 13 August Bruce sent his third private letter to Lord Stanley.[7]

I cannot blind myself to the fact that the non-completion of the Inter-Continental railway and the imperfect union of the Provinces, leave us but ill-prepared for a contest with this country in the Canadian frontier. How far the discontent in Ireland would seriously affect our strength I do not know, but it does not admit of a doubt that the condition of that country, and the necessity of continuing the suspension of the Habeas Corpus Act, do operate powerfully in this United States in favour of the War party, and give to the interference of this people a certain justification which in their eyes excuses in some degree the violation of their international obligations.

On 9 September, Bruce voiced his thoughts about the evolution of the British empire and how a colonial possession like Canada could be strengthened if granted a greater measure of autonomy.[8]

In my opinion nothing should be omitted which can appeal to their interest, and can create in them a feeling of national pride. For it is of great importance that they should exchange their Colonial status for independence not for annexation [by America]. Pecuniary sacrifices to that end will have the truest economy. The United States are prepared to lend them credit for the public works necessary to her development, and we ought not to be behind-hand in similar offers.

Hitherto the colonies have been to us rather a source of weakness than strength. In the meantime other states are widening their territories and increasing their power; and I do not see how England is to retain her relative rank among nations, unless she is made the centre of a Confederation of which her great Colonial possessions would be members. I do not see the impossibility of such a constitution with steam and electric telegraphs. If a council or some such body with representatives from the Colonies was formed in England, not only would emigration be more largely directed to our own possessions, but the leading men of the Colonies would be imbued with Imperial ideas, and would take larger views of their own interests and destinies than they do at present. It is a very different and more seductive object of ambition, to be an active member of an Empire which extends over the world, than to be a mere local legislator excluded from all participation in the higher sphere of national life. The statesman who can work out this idea will be the true founder of the English Empire.

By 22 October, Bruce returned to what was becoming a dominant theme in his letters: the political and constitutional gulf between President Johnson and the Republican majority in Congress.[9]

Looking at the internal questions here solely as bearing upon our interests, I do not think that the success of the President's policy is to be desired. The Republican party is more thorough and less compromising in its views of internal policy. As a party it has never coquetted with the Irish element as the Democrats have, nor has it sought to divert attention from home questions by foreign quarrels. It is driven to coquette with the Irish for the present elections but at heart their sympathies are Saxon and not Celtic. The Germans support them in their views about the Negro, and are forming an important counter-poise to the Irish element. Their strength lies in the new North Western states, whereas that of the Irish is in New York and the other large towns of the East. When the new distribution of members consequent upon the census of 1870 comes into play, the North Western deputation will be far more powerful in the House of Representatives and the German element will be strong. The Irish do not agree with it or with the native American more than they do the Saxon at home, and I am in hopes that their influence in elections will be thereby diminished. Unfortunately this result demands time, and at present all parties are exasperated with us; the country at large attributed to our blockade-runners the prolongation of the War, and the shipping interests are smarting from the injuries inflicted by cruisers; the "Alabama" ought to have been detained, as they think, and the "Shenandoah" etc. which escaped from our ports ought not to have been admitted into our Colonial ports.

American political passions, especially in New York State, were inflamed at the end of October and beginning of November 1866 by the trials of the captured Fenian raiders in Canada. Some capital sentences were imposed, but Bruce was assured by the Canadian authorities that these would eventually be commuted. Meanwhile, American politicians courted the Irish vote by every possible means.[10]

As proofs of the importance attached to the Irish vote, I may mention that Sweeny[11] has been re-installed in the United States army; that Dart,[12] the District Attorney of the Buffalo district, has been removed; and the Fenian arms restored to them. These steps are taken in order to conciliate the Irish, and as the Presidential election[13] will be the next great object, as the Irish vote will tell equally in it, and as hostility to England is the topic acceptable to the Irish, I feel little probability of the questions with us disappearing from the platforms of political parties. . . .

The November elections of 1866 were a crushing repudiation of President Johnson. The Republicans controlled all the legislatures and gubernatorial offices of the Northern states, as well as a two-thirds majority in both houses of Congress.[14]

The elections have proved that the West is entirely in the hands of the Radicals, and that the South can look for no support from that quarter. The Constitutional Amendment[15] of last session was a compromise assented to by the extreme Radicals, who did not feel sure of having the country with them. Stevens,[16] the leader, has already drawn up a resolution for a joint Committee to inquire into the conduct of the President, and it will depend upon his influence how far Congress will go in that direction. If he can carry the Republican party with him, it will go hard with the President, but it is not likely the Radicals will allow themselves to be thrown off the scent by foreign questions.

The South are so entirely crushed that they must submit to any conditions the majority of Congress choose to impose, and if they try to resist, the only effect will be that they will be crushed out altogether. There is no doubt they are more alienated than ever, but this feeling can only lead to the destruction of the leading Southerners, which is the real wish of the extreme Republicans. The struggle will be to manage the electoral conditions of the South in such a way as to insure the preponderance of the Union sentiment, if the Southern states are allowed to vote in the next Presidential election. The North does not believe in the bona fide conversion of the South, and will consequently endeavour to render it powerless. It is confident in its strength to carry out any policy Congress may adopt, and I have no doubt its leaders are right. They would not hesitate to divide the lands of the Southern proprietors among the Negroes.

I am very glad to see that you are impressed with the importance of the relations with this country. No policy is sound which deals with it as it is at present, and which does not take into account what it will be in all probability twenty years hence. Whatever becomes of the South, the North and West will constitute an enormous power with which we by our North American possessions and our commerce will be brought into constant rivalry. Our real object ought to be to build up a friendly Power in the North and a counter-poise to this Republic. No such counter-poise can be made to the South with the whites enervated by climate and the Negro and hybrid Mexican. They are a weakness rather than strength, but it would be far different with the hardy Canadians, and the sea-faring population of the Maritime Provinces. They have the elements of a powerful community, if time is given for their development and consolidation.

On 26 November Bruce recounted a conversation he had had with Ulysses S. Grant about the pending Fourteenth Amendment and other current issues.[17]

General Grant is, true, entirely in favour of the Constitutional Amendment. He says the people have decided the question, and their decision ought to be accepted as final by the President. Of him he talked, as a man who is not practical, who is only capable of seeing one thing, and who "mistakes obstinacy for firmness". That at his [Grant's] instigation had gone to argue with the President, and though he did not state it positively I gathered that their efforts had not been successful. That these were the difficulties that arose out of their form of government, and that they would have to put up with them for the Presidential term. He thinks it unfortunate for the South, for had the Administration not made common cause with the Democrats and Copperheads of the North, Johnson's influence would have been sufficient to obtain the acceptance of the Constitutional Amendment, and that Congress would have then passed a resolution of complete amnesty, excepting only the actual leaders of the rebellion from their enjoyment of political privileges. That the delay of a settlement will probably lead to more severe conditions, as the law declaring confiscation of their property, and liability to be treated as traitors remains unrepealed. That the South are misled by the support of the government, and look to it and their alliance with the Democrats to recover their political power, which the mass of the North will not submit to. That the effect of the admission of the South with reduced power would lead to new party combinations and to the obliteration of purely sectional issues. He is confident all will come right—but that the course of the President will make the settlement more difficult and more slow of accomplishment. General Grant has great weight with the Republican party, and I was glad to find his opinions so moderate.

He told me that at the time of the Fenian raid, the government would give no instructions and that the course pursued by General Meade and the other officers was dictated by him. That he had urged the government weeks before to active measures—but without success. This I know to be the case.

He said he had been at first against Sweeny's restoration to the army, but that he thinks now it was judicious. That Sweeny expresses his regret at having had anything to do with the Fenian movement, and declares he thought he was acting according to the wishes of the government and he agreed with me that hanging the Fenian prisoners would do more harm than good, but added that the United States had no right to interfere, whatever we chose to do with them.

It is refreshing after the reticence and evocation of politicians in this country to meet with a man so direct and frank in expressing himself as General Grant.

In Canada the authorities were still holding the Fenian prisoners, some of whom were under sentence of death. Bruce thought that the whole affair might have been handled differently.[18]

> The taking of prisoners was a complete mistake. It has given a false colour of belligerency to what ought to have been treated as a murderous assault, and which ought to have been repressed by shooting the leaders, and by driving back their ragged followers. And the Canadians will only expose themselves to annoyance, and to attempts at rescue, if these prisoners are kept in the country at all. Lord Monck[19] can inform Your Lordship better than I can about the feeling in Canada on the subject. As to this country I feel assured that the true policy toward the prisoners is to get rid of them, to deal with them as men mislead by the equivocal attitude of the United States government, and by the encouragement of politicians; and to be prepared to deal with any future attempt on the spot with the greatest severity and support the Canadians whatever be the consequences. Nothing would be better for us in point of policy than to have a war, if war we must have arising out of the defence of the interest and honour of the Canadians—and I am disposed to believe that if the United States were indiscreet enough to accept such an issue as a cause for War, we should put a sea of blood between them and the Provinces which would be fatal to any ideas of peaceful annexation—or if they declined it, that Fenianism would receive a heavy blow. . . . It certainly strikes me, that there is a deeper question at issue than that of reconstruction. That the power of the Executive increased enormously during the war, and that Congress [was now] determined to assert its power as against him. Johnson's error was in exciting their jealousy, and by proceeding to deal with the South after the conclusion of the War, without calling together and consulting the Legislature. Had he done so they would have made large sacrifices to his views to have avoided the conflict; but now they must assert a superiority over him, or lose their prestige in the country. This is a great constitutional struggle and may have very important results on the future political conditions of the United States. It is not simply State rights as against Federal rights, it is the Presidential power against the authority of Congress. In countries inhabited by our race, that contest has always terminated in one way—and the struggle is more than usually disadvantageous to the "one-man power" on account of the power exercised by the Senate according to the Constitution in matters which in monarchial countries are reserved to the Executive exclusively.

Bruce drew upon his considerable experience in China to draw a comparison with the ever-sprawling and fragmented American empire.[20]

> I have received your letter of the 1st instant. I fully agree in your remark that no Empire so vast as this has held together among Western races. In the East we have an example in China, in which a common language, stereotyped education and habits, and a combination of the provincial authority appointed by a central and despotic power, guided and controlled in its action by public opinion, succeeded amid numerous revolutions in preserving its political unity. But considerations of race, and isolation, make it inapplicable.

I should hesitate in predicting what will be the ultimate destiny of the United States in this respect. But I think it may be safely assumed that nothing is so likely to prevent disunion or consolidate the country as foreign War. It has been the fashion to criticize the forebearing and patient policy of England in her relations with the United States during the last thirty years. The effect however was to concentrate the attention of the people on internal questions, and to give full scope to the antagonism of interests and feelings which culminated in the Civil War. The South and the Northern Democrats would readily at any period have accepted a foreign war, for the sake of avoiding the domestic issue.

I have just had with me an Irishman of Londonderry who has given me information, on which I am disposed to rely, of the proceedings of the Roberts'[21] wing of the Fenians. He says they have $100,000 in their Treasury together with arms and equipment to a considerable amount and that Roberts has from 60 to 80,000 men enrolled. They have within the last fortnight bought overcoats, saddles, etc. at some of the public sales—he has no doubt they intend making a fresh attack on Canada, that they have appointed as yet no military chiefs, and are proceeding with more caution than heretofore. My informant laughs at Stephens' project[22] but considers the proceedings of Roberts as more dangerous. He asserts that the leaders both of the Republican and Democratic party encourage Roberts and his party, not from a sympathy with them, but for electioneering purposes. Of course his information is indirect and the intimacy of Roberts with political men may be exaggerated. But at any rate it is an indication of what is believed among the Irish, and it shows that the course pursued by this Government since the raid, is taken as a proof that there is not much disposition in any quarter to interfere with them. I know from undoubted authority that when Swann,[23] the Governor of Maryland, came here a short time since to recommend a person as consul at some place in Ireland, Seward told him that he could not appoint anyone without consulting the Fenians, as they had proved so loyal to the administration during the election. Swann's remark afterwards was that Seward was either mad or drunk. Johnson could afford now less than ever to quarrel with the Fenians who constitute the Strength of the Democrats. The Irish exercise a most fatal effect on the relations of this country with Great Britain. I should not be sorry to see negro suffrage carried, as the Irish and the Negros hate each other, and the vote of the latter will counterbalance the vote of the former.

From time to time, an envoy like Bruce might be called upon to employ informants or incur other extraordinary expenses. On such occasions he might draw upon the so-called secret service funds under the ultimate authority of the foreign secretary. The Fenian machinations provided ample opportunity for disaffected members to come forward and offer their assistance to the British.[24]

I have received a letter of which I enclose a copy. The writer was Sweeny's and Roberts' adjutant-general[25] during the raid and while it was being organized. The military-correspondence of the Fenian War Department was carried on by him, as I know from the register which is in my possession. He prepared for Sweeny, who is a man of nobility, all of his plans of campaign, etc. He is a man of education, whom it is desirable on every account to detach from the Fenians.

I have written him the enclosed reply, and if we come to terms I shall set him to work at once, to find out what truth there is in the reports of preparations against Canada.

Another man called Delany,[26] the chief of the organization in Connecticut, is here. He is a Stephens man, and addressed a meeting of the circle in this place, declaring Stephens to be the real head of the Fenians, and stating that the idea of attacking England by way of Canada has been abandoned.

This man has been in correspondence with me and offered to go to Ireland and deliver up Stephens, and he has come to Washington to see me on the subject. He was to have called yesterday, but it is possible that he was too much surrounded by his brother Fenians. An Englishman resident at Connecticut, who has given me information from patriotic motives, has told me that this man may be very useful to H.M. Government if properly handled. He [Delany] is connected intimately with Stephens, and acquainted with his plans, and is I apprehend quite prepared to make a good thing for himself out of the business. If I can come to terms with another of these men I will not hesitate to close it. There is no doubt as to their ability to serve us, from their acquaintance with the schemes of the leaders. In general the informers who come forward, are men who have no access to the secret plans of the leaders.

The fact of such men abandoning the cause is in itself a proof of diminished confidence in its success, and if it is found out that we have secret sources of information, it will tend to breed distrust among the conspirators.

In his letter of 24 December, Bruce enclosed a copy of one from the Fenian adjutant general, written to Bruce four days before.[27]

I have the honour to acknowledge the receipt of your note of the 16th inst. this morning.

I was officially connected with the F.B. [Fenian Brotherhood] for many months, as Adjt. Gen'l., etc., and very thoroughly acquainted with every detail of their organization. I have reason to be dissatisfied with their behaviour towards me, and withdrew voluntarily from any official connection with their association. Of late overtures have been made to me by some of their leading men to take an active part in their present preparations: I have no sympathy with the movement and they owe me money. These are the motives which have induced me to address Your Excellency.

The detectives hitherto employed by His Majesty's Government are unable to obtain full and accurate data, on which to work, from their inability to mingle freely among the circles, where many are personally known to the members, and where the presence of any stranger always excites suspicion. I would propose my services regularly as an agent of the Government, and can assure Your Excellency that every step taken by the F.B. will be regularly reported. The best guarantee which I can offer for my verity is *this* communication which, if known to the society, would entail very serious consequences on myself.

In this capacity, and were a fixed remuneration to cover all the expenses incident upon necessitated journeys to New York, Boston and other places, where the expedition is at present organizing, I should be most happy to place myself at your orders.

If my offer be refused, I trust that you will destroy this letter and forget that any such communication has ever been addressed to you by Your Obedient Servant.

Also in his letter of 24 December, Bruce alluded to an individual from Connecticut who wished to aid the British in their efforts to thwart the Fenians. A copy of his letter, dated 10 December, was also sent to Lord Stanley.[28]

As a subject of Great Britain I cannot feel otherwise than interested in the interests of the country. I notice in all European and American newspapers the sensation that is created in relation to the Fenian movement, and feel it my duty to contribute anything I can towards its suppression. The Fenians of this place and vicinity are very active at present, both raising money and buying arms and ammunition: they have raised $1,100 this last week. They have sent by express eleven boxes of arms last week; William Delany, formerly central organizer, went in charge of them. He is going to Ireland, he is to sail the week after next to join Stephens, the Head One. I have most positive information about the matter for he is a particular friend of mine.

He acknowledges himself that he is going to join *Stephens*—there are five or ten of them going but he is going alone, for I think he will be the bearer of some *important* despatches, and he thinks it will be safer to go alone. He is a very venturesome fellow but smart as steel. He says he does not care a pin whether they are successful or not, that he will have a good time anyway. I am of the opinion that he could be turned to good advantage to His Majesty's Government if handled right, for I am positively sure he will report to Stephens for he went to New York to see Stephens when he went. If there is anything that I can communicate I shall be happy to do it for the Fenians all over here are making active preparations. I should be happy to hear from you in relation to the matter.

Finally, Bruce sent Lord Stanley a copy of his letter to the former Fenian adjutant general, giving the disaffected Irish-American cautious encouragement.[29]

I have received your letter of the 20th inst. I am willing to recommend your employment as agent for the purposes mentioned, and for such a period as circumstances may render necessary. Of course the test of your fitness for the post will be your furnishing information of so secret and important a nature that will enable me to take beforehand proper measures to defeat any attempt on the frontiers of the Provinces, etc.

To obtain such an appointment as you suggest I must have time to communicate with England, and I must be able to state the scale of remuneration you expect.

In the meantime your services may be useful and I am ready to give you a reasonable sum to enable you to commence at once. It is reported that there are plans under consideration with a view to immediate action.

I wish to know what these plans are, and where the arms that are to be used are to be deposited on the frontier.

I have only to add that you will have no reason to complain of illiberal treatment, if you can supply information of use in preserving peace on the frontier.

On Christmas Day, Bruce was able to report on his successful meeting with his potential informant, William Delany.[30]

Delany called upon me yesterday evening. He is a man of about 5 feet 7 or 8 inches high—neither stout nor thin. Regular features on a small scale. Black hair; dark grey eyes. No whiskers or moustache. He talks fluently and has a slight Irish accent. He is not unpleasing, but he is evidently vain and easily worked upon and insecure. His age I should put about 30.

His position he defines thus—He says the Fenian organization originated in a wish to create a strong political power in Ireland which should act by moral force on

Parliament and the Government; that it was to be supported by opinion here, and that in order to excite public opinion here, it was necessary to use very inflammatory language about the wrongs of Ireland, etc.

That Stephens, Roberts, etc., for reasons of their own, have given it a revolutionary character—that men like himself, and many others who joined it with a view to the benefit of Ireland are shocked at the schemes they propound. That at a meeting of the Brotherhood near Boston Stephens avowed that firing the docks in London and Liverpool, and the destruction of English property in all forms, was part of this plan— and that these avowals had revolted a large part of the sympathizers, who looked to the regeneration of the Irish, but not to the injury of England.

He told me that Cullen, MacHale, and others of the Fenian dignitaries[31] have written most strongly deprecating the movement as destructive of the Irish people— that the Fenian commissioners who went over last summer, reported on their return that no man of note would join them—that they had communicated with O'Donoghue[32] who said he would have nothing to do with them, and that they had better try it, if they thought they could raise the country.

He says that the schemes of Stephens for immediate revolt have checked emigration from Ireland; as members of the Fenian organization dare not venture to come here, while this agitation continues—they would be denounced as traitors.

He therefore considers that the arrest of Stephens and of the Irish executive, and their detention or removal, would be a great service to the cause of Ireland, as it would weaken the revolutionary element, and strengthen the efforts of those who seek to improve the condition of Ireland by peaceful agitation. He is willing to lend his aid to effect it.

He is now under orders to proceed to Ireland with despatches for Stephens which he is to deliver to him, or if not, to an agent to be designated either in Dublin or Queenstown. He says that according to the plans Stephens ought to reach Ireland about this time; that the Fenian rendez-vous in Dublin is an hotel in Thomas Street; he wished to be put in communication with *one* high officer in Dublin, who will keep his secret and to whom he can give the necessary information, but he declines having anything to do with detectives. I shall suggest to him Sir Thomas Larcom.[33] He mentioned to me the probable departure next week of a man called Tresilian,[34] an engineer officer in Gen. Logan's[35] division during the Civil War. He represents him as an able, and desperate man. He is to telegraph to me the name of the steamer by which he sails and I will let Your Lordship know by cable.

He informed me that 2,000 muskets and 10,000 rounds of ammunition were being forwarded by the Fenian circles here to New York for the same purpose including the arms collected for the former raid on Canada. I told him that in no way would the cause of humanity be more effectually served, and less objectionably, than by information which would lead to the seizure of these arms either on landing in Ireland or England, and that I was authorized to state that half the value of the arms will be given to the informer. I have little doubt he will communicate to me what he can find out about this transmission.

He doubts Roberts being sincere in his proposals to invade Canada. He believes that he is aiming at a seat in Congress, and that he hopes to effect it by the support of the Irish population.

True, he [Delany] is a needy and a vain man. I had to pay the expenses of his journey here. It is not unlikely that he has been carried away by his Irish and Roman Catholic sympathies, and by the love of the applause which he found he could secure by his fluency on the subject of Irish wrongs. How far he is really shocked by the extreme proposals of Stephens, how far he is guided by a wish to make money, I do not know—

but I took care to flatter his vanity by treating him as a man who honestly wished to save the people of Ireland from a cruel disaster. I will write as soon as I hear further from him.

As the New Year 1867 got underway, debate in Canada and in Great Britain grew more heated over whether or not the North American provinces would federate and achieve a large measure of autonomy from the mother country.[36]

Altogether I think the Brotherhood is on the wane. There is less bitterness against England, and a greater desire to settle pacifically outstanding difficulties.

I have just had a visit from Mr. Taylor[37] of Minnesota, the gentleman who advocates strongly free trade with the Provinces and the improvement of communications across British America with the Pacific. Singularly enough he has been urging very strongly the incorporation of the British Provinces with England, and their representation in Parliament. He used the same arguments which I have presented at different times on this, as the only method of maintaining permanently their connection with the Mother-Country, and of developing their resources by doing here what is being done in India. In confess I believe that this idea ought at all events to be brought forward as a matter of speculation, were it only for the effect it would have in obviating bad effects produced in the provinces by the language of "The Times" on confederation. The Provinces resent the idea that Confederation is advocated as a means of getting rid of them, and I cannot understand the poverty and bitterness of views of the future of England, which is implied in a policy which contemplates as desirable a diminution of her territory and influence.

He dwelt strongly on the necessity of carrying out the implements required for the accommodation of the growing West, as indispensable if we are to prevent a feeling in favour of annexation from growing up. I am convinced that there is no question more worthy of the attention of British statesmen, and that the pecuniary burdens it might entail will be found the cheapest way to secure us, and to curb the United States.

He tells me that New England and the frontier Northwestern states are all showing a strong opposition to the heavy duties imposed on coal, lumber and other produce of the Provinces, and that this subject cannot fail to be taken up, as soon as their own revenue system is arranged on a permanent footing. It is very desirable that in the meantime, the Fishery question, and the navigation of the Lakes and St. Lawrence, should be allowed to remain in abeyance, as our best hope for a reasonable adjustment is to be found in taking them up together.

As the French government rapidly withdrew its troops from Mexico, the position of Maximilian's empire appeared precarious indeed.[38]

The United States Government persists in recognizing Juarez as legitimate President, and in ignoring the Emperor Maximilian. They will agree to nothing which would tend on that way to modify the reaction against the Imperialists, which will probably then break out. This will certainly not improve the relations between France and the United States. . . . The impeachment does not make progress,[39] and the scheme for reducing the Southern states to territories excites much opposition. The President is entirely unmoved, and, as he told me a few days ago, he will stand by the Constitution in the hope of public opinion changing in his favour, to whatever extremes the majority proceed. He said I represent the real majority of the people of the United States, and the present dominant party are driven to revolutionary measures in order to prolong their rule which is that of a minority. I do not think that Congress during its present session will be able to do anything against him; but unfortunately the next Congress[40] which meets on the 4th of March will even be more hostile to him than the present, and there are indications that they intend to proceed at once to business.

With impeachment proceedings against the president a possibility and with Southern states uncertain of their future, the United States Constitution and government seemed very much in flux. This was especially the case as the Fortieth Congress opened its first session on 4 March 1867.[41]

The future alone can decide, for the Constitution of the United States is itself undergoing a change, the end of which cannot be foreseen. A strong feeling prevails in favour of a centralized power, and though at present the disposition is to lodge that power in the hands of Congress, it seems impossible that it can be permanently exercised by so fluctuating a body. This may turn in favour of a more permanent Executive with a more direct participation on the part of Congress in the administration. Hitherto, Congress has exercised no such power, and the struggle of the last two sessions in the present incomplete state of the representation shows how difficult it is to impose on the President a different policy from the one he is inclined to pursue. In act, Congress was intended to legislate and tax, but not to govern, and the device of stopping supplies to bring about a change of administration is totally unknown in the history of the United States. The theory of this government is, the separation of the Executive, Legislative, and Judicial powers, as the President has stated in his Veto of the Tenure of Office Bill[42] and if, as seems probable, our legislature is to become more democratic, and is to be the organ of public opinion, whether than subject to and controlled by it, the power of the Executive ought to be increased, if the example of the United States is to be followed as a precedent.

Despite the convening of the Fortieth Congress, seven Northern states had still not elected their representatives, so that the sentiment for or against the impeachment of the president was ambiguous, to say the least.[43]

Impeachment has lost ground, and if Congress adjourns till December, it may be considered as dropped. I think that the Republican party are satisfied with having carried the Reconstruction Bill, and the more politic among them argue that it is better to have a hostile President on whose shoulders they can throw the blame of failure if anything goes wrong. No one knows how it will work in the South, or who will gain command of the Negro vote.

Although President Johnson personally pardoned thousands of former rebels, he was reluctant to rehabilitate notorious Confederate leaders like Jefferson Davis. Instead, he threatened them with trials for treason, but after two years had elapsed, less harsh penalties seemed appropriate.[44]

Jefferson Davis has been admitted to bail, which I think is a first step to dropping proceedings against him, if the Reconstruction of the South works smoothly. Every day's delay will make it more difficult to obtain a conviction before a Southern jury, unless it is packed, for juries here are more guided by their sympathies and by the opinion of their district than with us. I do not envy the future lot of a juryman in Virginia who should find a verdict of guilty against Davis.

The acts of some of the generals in the South interfering with the freedom of the press, with the delivery of lectures by ex-rebels, and ordering the display of the flag of the United States in local processions, with public marks of respect, are much criticized by the Northern newspapers. Northern sentiment will support all measures required to organize the Southern states on Union principles, but it is averse to acts which inflict useless humiliation on the population of that region. The registration of voters will offer many questions of difficulty. The Attorney-General[45] is occupied in preparing a code of instructions for the guidance of the officers in this delicate matter. It will be conceived in a liberal spirit by him, but his views will probably meet with opposition in the Cabinet.

Bruce's first and perhaps only allusion to physical indisposition came on 3 June, but anyone familiar with the Washington climate would not find that surprising. Bruce's predecessor, Lord Lyons, spent years suffering and, as we have seen, finally had to escape the United States precipitately.[46]

The disposition of this country is ambitious and unscrupulous in the extreme, and this spirit is fostered and pandered to by the leaders of all parties. But they do not contemplate war at present, and it may do good to show them that we are prepared for the consequences, if they persist in a course which is inconsistent with peaceful relations.

The reprieve of the Fenian convicts has had a good effect here and I think will lead to the abandonment of any attempt on Canada this summer. Roberts, I hear, is about to embark for Europe to solicit the aid of the French Government in an attack on Canada, so he tells his adherents. I should not be surprised if this Government has hinted to him that no raid will be permitted, and that he takes this pretext for stopping it.

The longer Bruce resided in America, the more insufferable he found politicians like Seward. Bruce felt that the United States in 1867 was a poor testimonial to the blessings of democracy.[47]

He is the type of the American politician, and when I see what an unscrupulous, arrogant, and aggressive character it is, I confess I am not reassured as to the future the spread of democracy has in store for Europe.

I am very glad Bourke[48] is not hanged. This execution would have encouraged Fenianism here, and would have been a good theme for declaimers where with to empty fresh packets and fill their exchequer. As long as there is discontent on a large scale in Ireland, there will not be wanting fanatics and desperate adventurers in the United States to promote, and join in, insurrection. I am in hopes Canada will be left in peace this year, though drilling, etc., still go on among the Fenians at Portland and other Northeastern towns.

The radical party are preaching agrarianism to the Southern Negros, as the only means of securing their oaths. Secret societies are spreading among them and it seems to me that party considerations will render hopeless the attempt to produce harmony between the Negro labourer and the white proprietors. Were it to exist, the South should be anti-Republican and the Radicals would rather see the Negro exterminated than be driven from power by the union of the South and the Democratic Party in the North.

On 17 June Bruce described his recent conversation with Secretary of State Seward, soon after the latter had returned from a trip to North Carolina.[49]

The Negros and Whites would get on smoothly, if left alone. But it is essential to the success of the Radicals, that antagonism should exist between the former Slave and his Master. Agrarianism, social equality, etc., are preached as a means of attaining that end. If by these means the Negro vote is carried, the Whites will make common cause against him, and the end will certainly be destruction of the Negro and probably anarchy in the South.

This is the conclusion he draws from what he sees and hears. He finds consolation in general reflection—that in the natural course of events excitement is diminishing, and extreme parties on both sides are losing ground. But he seemed to me to express rather a hope than a belief, and he has so completely miscalculated opinion during the last two years, that I confess my faith in his political prescience is much shaken.

From the confident tone in which he stated that the Fenians would remain quiet on the Canadian frontier, I am led to infer that this Government has taken steps to make the leaders understand that their enterprise will not be tolerated. If so, the result is undoubtedly due to the capital sentences in Ireland not having been carried out. The attempt to get up a fresh agitation a fortnight ago seems to have failed.

During my visit to the President, his manner to Mr. Seward did not seem to me very cordial. After we had taken our leave the President sent for me back to say he wished me to come and see him quietly and informally. He said nothing about it while Seward was in the room, which struck me as remarkable.

Writing from New York on 24 June, Bruce recounted a conversation he had recently with President Johnson.[50]

I stopped for an hour with the President alone the evening previous to my departure. He is absorbed by the question that has arisen on the relation between civil and military authority in the Southern states. His views are diametrically opposed to those of Congress. He talked of Sheridan's removal of the Governor of Louisiana, as monstrous, and as an invasion of sovereignty of the State.[51] This view is quite irreconcilable with the Military Bill, which proceeds on the assumption that the Southern States are not in possession of their political rights, and their government provisional only. He would have stood better if he had confined himself to claiming the right to supervise and over-rule the action of the General. But he really appears to court political martyrdom on behalf of his constitutional views, though his Northern friends object to his course, and the South are aware that the result of a fresh contest with Congress will be the tightening of their fetters. The South beg to be left alone, and not made the battle field for Republicans and Democrats. They are now conscious that neither party is guided by a sincere desire to promote their interests, and therefore they would prefer a consistent policy, however harsh. In the North the question is one of political supremacy; in the South it is a question of life and death. Capital and labour are required to enable them to escape from ruin and starvation, and political uncertainty and agitation drive them away. The President put his views clearly and ably, but I do not think his views are sufficiently broad and comprehensive for the crisis.

He spoke a little of Mexico, of the bad prospects of that country; and his hope that Maximilian will escape.

Ordinarily the first session of the Fortieth Congress would have run until April or May and then not convened again until December. The Radical Republicans, however, were intent upon pursuing their policies and scheduled an extra session for July, to the considerable apprehension of the administration. Nevertheless, that did not prevent both Seward and Bruce escaping from Washington for a time, as Bruce mentioned in his letter of 6 August.[52]

I passed the week with Mr. Seward at Auburn,[53] his country residence. His tone is much more conciliatory with respect to England, and he seems convinced that the first foreign question that will be taken up is that of Mexico. But he is of opinion that the prospects of the South are the reverse of encouraging. He hoped that a reaction will take place in the North against the extreme Radicals. But admitting this to be the case, the Tennessee election shows that the Radicals by means of the Negro are likely to carry the Southern states, and thus control the moderate men of the North by means of the Southern delegations. This will be a singular inversion of the relative situation of the two sections.

On my return I called on the President and had a long informal conversation with him en tête à tête. He looked to a war of races in the South as probable, and thinks a difficulty with Mexico imminent, as the popular feeling there is more critical; more excited against the Yankees than any other class of foreigners. . . .

The most salient point I can observe, is the growing conviction that the state of the South becomes worse instead of better. Two gentlemen, Southern proprietors, and Union men, called upon me last week to ascertain what encouragement they would meet in our Colonies. Both agreed as to the inevitable war of races, and as to the increasing disaffection of the South, which now extends to those who are opposed to secession. They said loyal and disloyal were alike ruined, and that the policy pursued by Congress made recovery impossible.— That a different policy at the close of the war would have rallied the Southern states to the Union—and they added what is remarkable and no doubt correct, that the proprietary classes, whom the Radicals treat as special enemies, were against secession, but were overpowered by the votes of the mean whites stirred by discontented politicians, and by lawyers and doctors without practice.

As the material interests and future of these gentlemen and of their families are at stake, their views of the condition of the country are not likely to be the result of any political bias. They are agreed to the letter with the gloomy foreboding of the President and his friends. . . .

I did not allude [in conversation with President Johnson] to the late address of Mr. Seward,[54] who, considering the position he occupies in the Government, has shown himself a more unscrupulous panderer to the cupidity of this people than any of his compeers. In nothing are the dangerous effects of extreme democracy more visible than the language held by public men in the United States on questions of foreign policy. The masses are sufficiently educated to appreciate the material advantages held out to excite their acquisitiveness, but they are not sufficiently enlightened to understand how much of utility and benefit is bound up in the observance of the principles of justice and good faith, and how much danger there is in incorporating into their political system populations that are disaffected and uncivilized. They are bred up in a blind unreasoning confidence in their destiny, which enables unscrupulous demagogues to overpower the warnings of thoughtful and moderate men. The President seems not insensible to this danger.

The President is fond of generalizing, and I am careful in my conversations with him to confine myself to the discussion of principles, and not to treat on specific points on which we are at issue, as the jealousy of Mr. Seward might be aroused. They may suggest topics of reflection which may be of use, and at all events these interviews put him at ease with me, and give some insight into his peculiar turn of thought.

During the spring and summer of 1867 Bruce saw distinct signs that President Johnson was asserting his authority. He had dismissed Edwin M. Stanton from the secretaryship of war, and had replaced General Philip Sheridan with General George H. Thomas. Johnson no doubt hoped that the result of all this would be to weaken Seward's position in the cabinet, since he had often supported Stanton against the president.[55]

The President must feel that his difficulties have been seriously increased by his hesitation in getting rid of his War Minister, and to that hesitation I have little doubt Seward's advice largely contributed. He has now dismissed Sheridan and appointed Gen. Thomas in his place. . . . It is not very clear in a political point of view what the President will gain from these changes, and it is quite uncertain what part Gen. Grant will take in the political questions which will come before him in the Cabinet.

Seward continues to talk vaguely of reaction, and envisions the French Revolution. But he appears to me to confound a legitimate and prudent reaction, which comes in time to prevent evils, with the revulsion which takes place in opinion, after the evils of anarchy and the overthrows of the Constitution have made themselves felt by their effects. This revulsion will doubtless come, but, if he is right in his anticipation of the disastrous consequences of Radical policy in the South, it will come too late for the Conservative party. Whatever may be Seward's convictions he will make no personal sacrifice for them. His line is to hold onto office and wait like Micawber[56] for something to turn up. He has miscalculated public opinion and is now without adherents. But his knowledge of foreign questions is such as to make it difficult to replace him, and his pliability secures the President against any active opposition on his part.

During September Sir Frederick Bruce traveled through New York State and parts of New England. As the following letter indicates, he took suddenly ill and soon died. On 27 September William A. C. Barrington, the third secretary of the British legation in Washington, reported the details of Bruce's death to the British chargé d'affaires, Secretary of Legation Francis C. Ford.[57]

As you are already aware I left this city [Washington] on the evening of the 5th instant for the purpose of getting change of air for a brief period. I reached New York on the morning of the 6th and there found the late Sir Frederick Bruce, who had quit Washington 24 hours before myself. He seemed extremely well both in health and spirits, but alluded cursorily to a feeling of slight disorder of the stomach which he ascribed to the night journey he had made. From subsequent letters to yourself, however, in which he spoke of being much better, I infer that this must have passed off.

Sir Federick Bruce left New York that afternoon for West Point, and I did not again see him nor hear directly of his subsequent movements. . . .

The first person I saw who was able to give me any details of Sir Frederick's short illness was the servant who had been travelling with the deceased. He told me that Sir Frederick had gone on the 12th inst. to Narragansett Beach; that it was very chilly there and Sir Frederick must have taken cold for that on the evening of Saturday the 14th, he complained of an uneasiness in the throat and he also had a slight diarrhea. On the Sunday he was worse, and after the early dinner at the hotel, at which he scarcely ate anything, he retired to his room to lie down and a doctor was sent for. Later he desired his servant to help him to undress and after he was in bed he sent for some tea and toast, but took very little of either. On the following day, the 16th another doctor was sent for, Mr. Hazard,[58] a homeopathic physician of the neighbouring town of Wakefield. Sir Frederick complained to him only of a sore throat and mentioned that during April and May last he had been a good deal troubled with intermittent sore throat which he thought was a bronchial affliction. Dr. Hazard recommended him to leave Narragansett at once as the atmosphere there was likely to prove prejudicial to him, but to this Sir Frederick would not accede as he said he did not wish to alter his plans then. Dr. Hazard accordingly treated him for sore throat and the slight fever which accompanied it, and advised him not to leave his room or speak more than was necessary.

On the Tuesday, Sir Frederick thought he felt rather better, and on Wednesday the 18th, when the doctor called about noon, he found Sir Frederick up. He told the doctor he felt much the same and said he had made up his mind to go to Boston, asking if he was quite fit to undertake the journey. The doctor assured him on this head and it was arranged that he should have the use of the former's carriage to convey him to the railway station at Kingston, which was some few miles distant. During these days the diarrhea of which Dr. Hazard knew nothing had continued, and Sir Frederick had had little or no nourishment, for tea and toast alternating with beef tea were all that was brought to him and these he scarcely touched. He was much weakened in consequence and on leaving his room his steps faltered so much as to induce the servant to assist him. At the foot of the stairs Mr. Gilpin,[59] ex-Governor of Colorado, who was staying in the same house and had been requested by Sir Frederick's friends to accompany the patient to Boston, stepped forward to meet him and held out his hand. Sir Frederick however seemed hardly to recognize him and appeared flustered in manner. This was merely attributed by Mr. Gilpin to the natural effect of the sudden glare of the open air and the dazzling light of the sunshine on the water striking full in the face of a person who had been keeping his room for three days.

Shortly afterwards they started together in the Doctor's carriage for Kingston, Sir Frederick having with him a bottle of claret and water previously mixed by the servant, which he used from time to time as a gargle. During the drive he spoke but little though he indicated by signs whatever interested him on the road. Mr. Gilpin describes his condition then as that of a man weakened by confinement to his room and disinclined to undergo the exertion of conversation.

On arriving at Kingston he got out of the carriage with a little assistance and went into a private waiting room, where there was a lounge on which he lay down, the servant preparing him some pillows. He then asked the servant for a little whiskey and water of which he took a few spoonfuls. Mr. Gilpin then came in to consult him about the train he would take, there being two to choose from, and Sir Frederick expressed his preference for the one which took the most direct line, though he would have to wait some two hours and half for it; and on Mr. Gilpin's alluding to the chances of accommodation, should it be necessary to stop on the road, Sir Frederick said "there is nothing the matter with me." He also gave directions about a note to be left for the messenger who was to have met him at Narragansett but whom he now desired to come to Boston. Nevertheless, he seems to have begun to feel uneasy here, for after being at Kingston a little while, he said he would like to go to bed, a wish which it was impossible to carry out. Later, too, though exactly at what moment I am unable to say, he allowed the servant to telegraph for me, that which he would not consent to when permission had previously been asked more than once at Narragansett. This telegram, as I have since learnt, only reached Washington shortly before the one announcing Sir Frederick's death, nor could it have been delivered in time to have been of any avail.

As the time drew near for leaving Kingston, Mr. Gilpin again left the room to make further inquiries. Sir Frederick seemed to be dozing and the servant accordingly went to purchase the tickets. He had scarcely procured them when he heard a fall. He hurried back and found that Sir Frederick had risen from the lounge and had fallen at a distance of a pace or two from it. Mr. Gilpin also came in and they two gave Sir Frederick the help he needed and got him back on the lounge.

After this, Sir Frederick seemed hardly to have spoken at all, except in monosyllables, though Mr. Gilpin states that there was no sudden excess of weakness consequent upon the fall, which apparently had caused Sir Frederick no pain. His strength seems to have failed by degrees.

As the train drew up, Sir Frederick was placed on a chair on the platform and thus carried to the car. During the journey he was occasionally restless, and once made a great but unavailing effort to say something. He still noticed things but by signs which happened to strike him.

On arriving at Boston, he had to be lifted from the train into a carriage and thence up the stairs into a hotel to his room, which he reached about 9:00 o'clock in the evening.

Dr. Bigelow Senior,[60] the first physician in Boston was at once sent for, but Sir Frederick was unable to speak to him. He understood what was said to him and indicated by a pressure of the hand that some of his acquaintances who might be in town and who were named to him should be fetched. Dr. Bigelow went at once for Mr. Sumner and on his way back called for his son, Dr. H. J. Bigelow,[61] who is also very eminent in his profession at Boston and has made a special study of affections of the throat.

Mr. Sumner reached the hotel at 11:00 P.M. As he entered the bedroom, Sir Frederick seemed to recognize him for he slightly turned his head and smiled. Mr. Sumner sat down by his side and asked him several questions as whether anything could be done, whether any pain was felt, etc. To all of which Sir Frederick replied no, and this the doctors thought was the only word he could say but on Mr. Sumner asking him if he were comfortable, Sir Frederick replied yes.

During this time there was a certain amount of restlessness and movement of the limbs, called by doctors "jactitation". The breathing was very heavy and stertorous, the beating of the heart scarcely perceptible, and that of the pulse very faint and rapid—up to 150 strokes a minute, but the countenance remained clear and unclouded, and the eye full and bright, without a trace of suffering evincing itself in either, nor any sound as of pain coming from the lips.

Two other gentlemen arrived—one a physician, Dr. Hodges,[62] the other, Mr. Bayard,[63] an acquaintance of Sir Frederick. Whether Sir Frederick really recognized the latter or not is impossible to say. Shortly after midnight, there being nothing more to be done, the two doctors Bigelow, who never entertained any hope of recovery, went away after giving some few final instructions to Dr. Hodges, who remained with the other gentlemen to watch the end.

One more attempt was made to administer some nourishment in the shape of beef tea, and also some sherry in water, for which Sir Frederick by pressure of the hand had indicated a wish. But it was no use for all power of swallowing was completely lost and with it all power of articulation. Sir Frederick evidently tried hard to say something but though Mr. Sumner bent his ear close down, he could not catch a single word.

About half an hour before death, the movement of the limbs ceased and the extremities began to lose warmth. All perceptible motion of the heart ceased and the pulse could be barely felt. The inhalations grew lighter, the intervals between them much rarer, till 2:00 in the morning of the 19th, when Sir Frederick drew one more light breath and died quite quietly.

His face, when I saw it for the last time on the 20th, was perfectly placid, not a feature being disturbed.

The remains lay at the hotel until the afternoon of the 19th when, as I have said before, they were removed to the undertakers where they were carefully kept in complete privacy.

The cause of death seemed so entirely uncertain, I found both the medical and the other gentlemen most desirous that a post mortem examination should be made, so that some satisfactory account might be given to the family of the deceased of the disorder which had proved, in so rapid a manner, fatal to their relative. This point being also alluded to in your instruction to Mr. Howard,[64] the necessary arrangements were made and the examination took place on the afternoon of Friday, the 20th instant.

Of the result of the autopsy you are already informed. Nothing whatever was revealed to explain so sudden a death, every organ including the brain being found in a healthy condition. The slight redness of the tonsils was alone apparent, and Dr. Bigelow Jr. afterwards told me that under the microscope he detected a slight disposition to fattiness in a portion of the heart, but so faint as to have been of absolutely no consequence. The only conclusion to be gathered from the statement of the various doctors is that Sir Frederick was not naturally a long-lived man, that he was abnormally weakened by diarrhea and want of nourishment for which sore throat gave him a distaste; vitality rapidly collapsed and death ensued from prostration. It may also be surmised that there was paralysis of the throat and chest, but whether of gradual growth and a cause or the consequence of physical exhaustion cannot be decided. It seems doubtful whether Sir Frederick's mental condition was continuously perfect to the end and whether he was at all aware of the crisis; also whether the latter might have been averted by timely attention or whether the illness was fatal from the first. With those who knew him well, a certain apathy which he apparently exhibited from the first and which was not of his nature might have attracted attention before he sank into the final comatose state, and if so, would have been a symptom to cause some anxiety which was evidently in no way felt by those about him till quite the last. But such speculation is entirely fruitless on my part.

A simple funeral service was held for Sir Frederick Bruce in Boston on 24 September 1867, and his coffin was then placed aboard a Cunard ship, the *China*, which sailed for Liverpool on the twenty-fifth. Bruce's servant accompanied his master back to England.

Appendix: Biographical Directory

ABERDEEN, LORD (1784–1860) George Hamilton Gordon, forth earl Aberdeen, secured his education at Harrow and Cambridge University. He was one of the British diplomatic representatives to the Congress of Vienna in 1814, and in 1828–30 served as British foreign secretary. From 1834 to 1835 he was secretary for war and from 1841 to 1846, foreign secretary. His career culminated in his being prime minister, 1852–55, but popular dissatisfaction with the course of the Crimean War forced him into retirement.

ANDREWS, ISRAEL DeWOLF (1813–71) American consul in New Brunswick in 1849. Secretary of State Clayton appointed him special agent to gather statistics concerning British North America. Released two reports based on his reasearch. He was active in the efforts to create a reciprocity treaty between the United States and Canada. Removed from consulship by Buchanan. Little known before 1849 and after 1856.

ARCHIBALD, CHARLES D. (1802–68) Born in Nova Scotia, and author of *A Look Toward the Future of the British Colonies* (1854).

ARCHIBALD, EDWARD M. (1810–84) Lawyer and eventually (1846) attorney general of Nova Scotia; member of executive and legislative councils of Nova Scotia, 1847–55; British consul in New York, 1857–71.

BARCLAY, ANTHONY (1877) British consul at New York City from December 1842 to May 1856. He was one of the British diplomats asked to leave the United States in the wake of the recruitment dispute.

BENJAMIN, JUDAH P. (1811–84) Admitted to the Louisiana bar, 1832, and practiced in New Orleans for many years. Entered the United States Senate 1853 as a Whig and was reelected as a Democrat in 1859. In February 1861 he left the Senate and became attorney general of a provisional Confederate government. During the Civil War he served as Confederate secretary of war, 1861–62, and Confederate secretary of state, 1862–65. With war's end, he fled to England and was soon admitted to the bar; practiced law in exile for the rest of his life.

BENTON, THOMAS H. (1782–1858) He was admitted to the bar at Nashville, Tennessee, in 1806. When Missouri was admitted as a state (1821), he was elected as a Democratic senator. He was reelected in 1827, 1833, 1839, and 1845. He was unsuccessful in his reelection bid in 1850. Elected as a Missouri Compromise Democratic United States senator in 1853 and served until 1855. He was not reelected in 1854. Unsuccessful gubernatorial candidacy in 1856.

BORLAND, SOLON (1808–64) Practiced medicine in Little Rock, Arkansas. Member of Yell's Arkansas Volunteer Cavalry throughout the Mexican War. Elected as a Democratic senator to fill a vacancy. Served from 1848 to 1853. United States minister to Nicaragua and other Central American countries from 1853 to 1854. Returned to practice medicine in Little Rock until 1861. Raised a brigade of Confederate troops and captured Fort Smith in 1861. Raised Third Regiment, Arkansas Cavalry, and was its colonel. Reached rank of brigadier general in the Confederate army before his death.

BRECKENRIDGE, JOHN C. (1821–75) Born in Kentucky and admitted to the bar in 1840. Rose to the rank of major during the war with Mexico. Entered the Kentucky state legislature in 1849 and the United States House of Representatives (1851–55). As Buchanan's running mate in 1856, he was the youngest candidate to have held the office of vice president. After losing to Lincoln in the presidential election of 1860, he held a seat in the United States Senate (March–December 1861) until being expelled for his Southern sympathies. During the Civil War he rose to the rank of general in the Confederate Army.

BROOKS, PRESTON S. (1819–57) Graduated from the University of South Carolina at Columbia in 1839; admitted to the bar in 1845; served as a captain in the Mexican War; and represented South Carolina in the United States House of Representatives from March 1853 to July 1856. He resigned from Congress following his attack upon Senator Charles Sumner, ran for reelection, and resumed his seat in Congress.

BRUCE, FREDERICK WILLIAM ADOLPHUS (1814–67) He held diplomatic or consular posts in Hong Kong, Nova Scotia, Bolivia, Uruguay, Egypt, and China before taking up his duties in Washington on 1 March 1865. He was the brother of Lord Elgin, who was governor-general of Canada from 1847 to 1854.

BUCHANAN, JAMES (1791–1868) He was admitted to the bar in 1812. Elected as a Federalist to United States Congress in 1820, reelected as a Democrat in 1824. Minister to Russia, 1831. Elected to the United States Senate to complete an unfinished term. Reelected in 1837 and 1843 (from Pennsylvania). Secretary of state in Polk's cabinet (served full term). Helped draw up Ostend Manifesto in 1854. Elected president in 1856. Retired after Lincoln's inauguration.

BULWER, WILLIAM HENRY LYTTON (1801–72) After being educated at Harrow and at Cambridge University, he took up his first diplomatic post at Berlin in 1827. Subsequent assignments took him to Vienna (1829) and The Hague (1830). From 1830 to 1835 he was a member of Parliament, and then returned to a diplomatic career. This took him to Brussels (1835), Constantinople (1837), Paris (1839), Madrid (1843), and Washington (1849). In 1852 he came out of retirement again to become minister to Florence; but his longest tour of duty was as ambassador to Constantinople from 1858 to 1865. In 1868 he reentered Parliament. He was also an author of various historical works.

BUNCH, ROBERT From 1842 to 1845 he was an attaché in Bogotá and Lima; vice-consul in New York, 1848–53; and consul at Charleston, South Carolina, 1853–64. He then was appointed consul general at Havana, Cuba, in 1864.

BUTLER, ANDREW P. (1796–1857) Admitted to the South Carolina bar in 1818, practiced law in Columbia, South Carolina, as well as elsewhere in the state. Appointed and then elected to the United States Senate as a States' Rights Democrat in 1846. Served until his death. As a result of a verbal attack against Butler by Senator Charles Sumner, he (Sumner) was beaten by Preston Brooks.

CALHOUN, JOHN C. (1782–1850) He began practicing law in Abbeville, South Carolina. Elected as a Democratic Republican congressman in 1810. Appointed secretary of war by President Monroe, 1817–25. Elected vice president in 1824, reelected in 1828. Resigned the vice presidency in 1833 and became a senator from South Carolina. Secretary of state under Tyler. Retired from public life until was with Mexico was looming on the horizon.

CAMERON, SIMON (1799–1889) He purchased the *Harrisburg Republican* in 1821, renaming it the *Intelligencer*. Elected to United States Senate to fill a vacancy. Served from 1857 to 1861, when he resigned to become secretary of war, 1861–62. He was appointed minister to Russia in January of 1862, and served until November of that year. Reelected to United States Senate in 1867, served until 1877.

CASS, LEWIS (1782–1866) He was admitted to the Ohio bar in 1802. Rose to the rank of brigadier general while serving in the army (1812–14). Military and civil governor of Michigan Territory from 1813 to 1831. Secretary of war under Jackson, 1831–36. Appointed envoy extraordinary and minister plenipotentiary to France; served in that post from 1836 to 1842. Elected as Democratic senator in 1845 (until 1848). Reelected to United States Senate in 1849 after unsuccessful bid for the presidency; served until 1857. Appointed secretary of state under Buchanan. Served from 1857 to 1860, when he resigned.

CHASE, SALMON P. (1808–73) He was admitted to the Ohio bar in 1829 and started practicing in Cincinnati. Elected to the United States Senate by a combination of Democrats and Free-Soilers, served 1849–55. Elected Free-Soiler governor of Ohio in 1855, reelected in 1857 as a Republican. Elected senator in 1860, but resigned in 1861 to become secretary of the treasury under Lincoln, served until 1864, when he resigned. Appointed chief justice of the Supreme Court in October 1864, presided over President Johnson's impeachment trial.

CLARENDON, LORD (1800–1870) George William Frederick Villiers, Fourth Earl of Clarendon, entered the diplomatic service at age twenty and achieved the ambassadorship to Madrid, 1833–39. Having succeeded to his earldom in 1838, he soon entered the House of Lords and eventually held the cabinet post of secretary of state for foreign affairs during the years 1853–58, 1865–66, and 1868–70.

CLAY, HENRY (1777–1852) Earned his license to practice law in 1797, practiced in Lexington, Kentucky. Member of Kentucky legislature from 1803 to 1806. Became a senator in 1806 to fill a vacancy. Kentucky state Speaker of the House from 1807 to 1809, then returned to the United States Senate. Left the Senate in 1811 to become state Speaker of the House and served until 1814 when he became a member of the peace negotiations at Ghent. Returned to the House and was a member until 1821. Reentered United States Congress in 1824, unsuccessful presidential candidate in that same year. Secretary of state under Adams. Reelected to the United States Senate in 1831, resigned in 1842, and returned in 1849 and served until 1852.

CLAYTON, JOHN M. (1796–1856) Admitted to the Delaware bar in 1819. He was a member of the state House of Representatives in 1824, then secretary of the state of Delaware during 1826–28. Republican senator, 1829–36. Delaware chief justice, 1837–39. Reelected to the United States Senate as a Whig and served 1845–49. Secretary of state under Taylor, 1849–50. Reelected as a Whig senator in 1853 and served until 1856.

COOPER, JAMES (1810–63) He was admitted to the bar and began practicing law in Gettysburg, Pennsylvania, in 1834. Elected as a Whig to United States Congress; served 1839–43. Member of the state House of Representatives, 1843–48. He was attorney general of Pennsylvania when he was elected to the United States Senate in 1849, and served until 1855. Raised a brigade of Maryland loyalists under an order by Lincoln. Reached the rank of brigadier general in the army and was commander of Camp Chase until his death.

CRAMPTON, JOHN F. T. (1805–86) Born and educated in Ireland, Crampton entered upon his diplomatic career in 1844 at Bern. The following year brought him to Washington, where he served as secretary of legation and then minister plenipotentiary for the next decade. The United States expelled him in May 1856 on the grounds that he had violated the American neutrality laws by recruiting soldiers for the Crimean War. His next posting was in Hanover (1857).

CUSHING, CALEB (1800–1879) Admitted to the bar and began practicing law in Newburyport, Massachusetts, in 1823. He was a member of the state legislature (as both a representative and a senator) from 1825 to 1834. Elected to United States Congress as a Whig and served from 1835 to 1843. Appointed envoy extraordinary and minister plenipotentiary to China by Tyler. Served from 1843 until his resignation in 1845. Member of the state House of Representatives, 1845–46. During the Mexican War, he was a colonel in a Massachusetts regiment; appointed brigadier general in 1847. Attorney general of Massachusetts in 1851; attorney general of United States from 1853 until 1857. Envoy extraordinary and Minister plenipotentiary to Spain from 1874 to 1877.

DAVIS, JEFFERSON (1808–89) Graduated from West Point in 1828, served on frontier posts in Wisconsin and Illinois. Elected to United States Congress as a Democrat in 1845 but resigned to command a volunteer regiment during the Mexican War. He became a United States senator in 1847, served until 1851. Secretary of war under Pierce from 1853 to 1857, when he returned to the United States Senate. He withdrew from the Senate when Mississippi seceded. Elected provisional president of the Confederate States in 1861 and served throughout the war. Captured by federal troops 10 May 1865.

DERBY, LORD (1799–1869) As Edward G. G. S. Stanley, he was educated at Eton and Christ Church, Oxford. He first entered Parliament as a Whig in 1822 and remained in the House of Commons until 1844, when he assumed a seat in the Lords. He was prime minister on three occasions: 1852; 1858–59; and 1866–68. It was during this last period that the Second Reform Bill, extending the franchise, was passed into law. By the 1840s and thereafter he had ceased to be a Whig, and became a Conservative in politics.

DOUGLAS, STEPHEN A. (1813–61) He was licensed to practice law in 1834, and elected state's attorney for the first judicial district in less than a year. He was elected to the state legislature and served in various state posts until 1847, when he was appointed to the United States Senate. Reelected senator in 1852, and again in 1858, when he defeated Abraham Lincoln. Left Washington at the beginning of the Civil War on Lincoln's orders to arouse support for the Union in the Northwest; died while on this mission.

ELGIN, LORD (1811–63) As James Bruce, eighth earl Elgin, he received his formal education at Eton and Oxford University. He entered Parliament in 1841, and in 1842 was appointed governor of Jamaica. From 1847 to 1854 he served as governor-general of Canada. In 1857 he became British envoy to China, concluding treaties with both China and Japan the following year. Returning to Britain, he became postmaster general in 1859; returned to China, 1860–61; and then became viceroy of India, 1862.

EVERETT, EDWARD (1794–1865) Independent Congressman from Massachusetts, 1825–35. Whig governor of Massachusetts, 1836–39. He was American minister to the Court of St. James, 1841–45, and United States secretary of state, 1852–53. Elected United States senator in 1853, served until 1854, when he resigned because of the Kansas–Nebraska conflict. Supporter of Lincoln until his death.

FANSHAWE, ARTHUR (1794–1864) He entered the Royal Navy in 1804, rose to the rank of captain in 1816, and took command of the fleet for North America and the West Indies from 1853 to 1856. Meanwhile, in 1851, he had been promoted to rear admiral, in 1857, to vice admiral, and finally to admiral in 1862.

FARRAGUT, DAVID G. (1801–70) He was appointed midshipman in 1810. Taken prisoner in 1814, then served 1815–20. While serving in the West Indies, he was given his first command of a naval vessel, the *Ferret*. Promoted to lieutenant in 1825. He was made Commander in 1841 while on duty in Brazil of the *Decatur*. He was commissioned captain in 1855, took command of the *Brooklyn* in 1859. In 1862, he was appointed commander of the West Gulf Blockading Squadron. After a daring victory during the capture of New Orleans, he was promoted to rear admiral, the first American of this rank. In 1864, he was commissioned a vice admiral, then, in 1866, he was made an admiral, a grade made specially for him. After the war, he commanded the European squadron on a goodwill tour.

FILLMORE, MILLARD (1800–1874) He was admitted to the New York bar in 1823. In 1828, he was elected Anti-Masonic representative to the state legislature. He became a Whig in 1834. Served in United States Congress, 1833–35 and 1837–43. He was elected vice president in 1848. Became president upon Zachary Taylor's death in 1850. He lost the 1852 Whig nomination to General Winfield Scott. Ran third in the 1856 election when nominated by the Know-Nothings.

FORNEY, JOHN W. (1817–81) He was a journalist from Pennsylvania and a long-time supporter of James Buchanan. During the Pierce administration he was a frequent contributor to the *Washington Union*. In 1857 he broke with Buchanan over the issue of Kansas.

FREMONT, JOHN C. (1813-90) During 1837-41 he explored the Cherokee territory and areas of what is now modern-day Iowa, Washington State, Colorado, and Utah. He was exploring in California in 1845 just as war was brewing with Mexico. When Mexican officials ordered him to leave California, he raised the American flag. The Mexicans chased him but he eluded them and took part in the capture of Los Angeles. He conducted two more explorations in the West, one in 1848-49, and one in 1853-54. He served as a United States Senator, 1850-51. He was nominated by the Republicans for president in 1856 but lost to Buchanan. During the Civil War, he was initially a major general in command of the Department of the West. Removed from that post by Lincoln, he was transferred to the Mountain Department in western Virginia. He resigned after being placed under General Pope.

GLADSTONE, THOMAS H. (1804-89) Educated at Eton and at Christ Church, Oxford. Member of Parliament, 1830-42.

GRATTAN, EDMUND A. (1818-90) His diplomatic career included posts as the consul at Boston (1848-58), Antwerp (1858-83), and consul-general of Belgium (1883-88).

GREY, GEORGE (1799-1882) After graduating from Oxford University he studied law and became a barrister in 1826. He served in Parliament from 1832 to 1874. Among the cabinet posts he held were: home secretary, 1846-52, 1855-58, and 1861-66; and colonial secretary, 1854-55.

HEAD, EDMUND W. (1805-68) From 1830 to 1837 he held an academic position at Merton College, Oxford. In 1841 he was appointed a poor law commissioner. In 1847 he became governor of New Brunswick, and from 1854 to 1861 he served as governor-general of Canada.

HENDERSON, WILLIAM W. (?-1854) Joined the Royal Navy in 1799, rose to rank of captain in 1815, and to rear admiral in 1851. Between 1851 and 1854 he commanded a British fleet off the Southeast coast of the United States. He died en route back to England.

HINCKS, FRANCIS (1807-85) He emigrated to Canada in 1831 and became a member of the Liberal party in 1837. He entered the Canadian Parliament in 1842, held various cabinet posts, and was premier, 1851-54. He negotiated the Reciprocity Treaty with the United States in that latter year. From 1855 to 1862 he was governor of Barbados and Windward Islands, and was governor of British Guiana, 1862-69. He was Canadian finance minister, 1869-73.

HISE, ELIJAH (1801-67) He was raised in Kentucky and was a lawyer. During his post as a United States diplomat in Guatemala, he negotiated a controversial canal treaty with Nicaragua.

HOLLINS, GEORGE N. (1799–1878) He was a United States naval officer until 1861, when he resigned to enter the Confederate navy. He commanded the Confederate flotilla at New Orleans in 1861, and all naval forces of the upper Mississippi in 1862.

HOWE, JOSEPH (1804–73) For years member of the Nova Scotia Executive Council; chairman of the Nova Scotia Railway Commission; and governor of Nova Scotia in 1873.

HUNTER, ROBERT M. T. (1809–87) Admitted to the Virginia bar, 1830, and then entered the United States House of Representatives (1837–43 and 1845–47). In March 1847 he took up his seat in the United States Senate, and remained there until the spring of 1861. The impending Civil War induced him to then withdraw from the Senate, and in July of that year became the secretary of state for the Confederacy. Although he stepped down from this post in February 1862, he remained active throughout the Civil War in the Confederate Senate.

JOHNSON, ANDREW (1808–75) In 1835, he was elected to the Tennessee state legislature, then to the state Senate; in 1843, he was elected Democratic congressman and served till 1853. He was governor of Tennessee from 1853–1857. From 1857 to 1862, he was a United States senator. In 1862, Lincoln appointed Johnson military governor of Tennessee. He was nominated to be Lincoln's vice-presidential running mate at the National Union Convention in 1864. He left Office in 1869. He was reelected to the United States Senate in 1874 and served until his death.

JUAREZ, BENITO (1806–72) Opponent of Santa Anna in the mid-1850s. Leader of a liberal faction during the time of the Mexican Civil War (1857–60), and president of the Mexican Republic thereafter. He opposed the tranformation of Mexico into an empire under Maximilian of Austria. Once French troops withdrew from Mexico, Juarez's troops reasserted their power and were responsible for the execution of the new emperor (19 June 1867). Juarez lived out his life trying to maintain himself in power as Mexican president.

LAW, GEORGE (1806–81) During the middle decades of the nineteenth century, he became an American shipping magnate. He ventured into the construction of the Panama Railroad and the New York City horse-drawn streetcars. He was also active in the Know-Nothing Party.

LAWRENCE, ABBOTT (1792–1855) He was elected as a Whig to the United States Congress and served from 1835 to 1837 and 1839 to 1840. He resigned to be appointed a commissioner in 1842 to handle the dispute between the United States and Canada over the northeastern boundary. He was temporarily appointed by Taylor to be United States minister to Great Britain, a post he held from 1849 to 1852 when he resigned.

LOPEZ, NARCISO (1798?–1851) Born in Venezuela, he lived in Cuba from 1841 to 1849. For the next few years thereafter he organized several attempts to stir up revolution in Cuba from a base in the United States. On the third of these attempts, the Spanish authorities in Cuba captured and executed him.

LUMLEY, JOHN S. Entered the British diplomatic service in 1841 and first served in Berlin, then in St. Petersburg, 1849. In 1854 he became secretary of legation in Washington, and following Crampton's expulsion, was chargé d'affaires from May 1856 to January 1857. In February 1858 he went to Madrid.

LYONS, LORD (1817–87) Richard Bickerton Pemell, Second baron and First earl Lyons, was educated at Winchester College and Christ Church, Oxford. He held his first diplomatic post at Athens and in 1852 went to Dresden. The following year he was in Florence, and in 1859 he took up his duties in Washington. In 1865 he became ambassador at Constantinople, and two years later he went to Paris, remaining there as ambassador for the next twenty years.

McLANE, LOUIS (1786–1857) He was a Democratic Republican congressman from 1817 to 1827 and a United States senator from 1827 to 1829. Appointed United States minister to Great Britain in 1829 and served until 1831, when he returned to become United States secretary of the treasury. Became secretary of state in 1833. He resigned in 1843. He again served as minister to Great Britain during 1845–46, when he negotiated the Oregon boundary dispute.

MALMESBURY, LORD (1807–89) Born James Howard Harris, he succeeded to the title of Third Earl of Malmesbury in 1841. During February–December 1852 he was foreign secretary under the Derby government and was again in 1858–59, when Derby was prime minister. He was personally known to, and on good terms with, Napoleon III.

MARCY, WILLIAM L. (1786–1857) He was admitted to the bar in 1811. He was New York State comptroller from 1823 to 1829. He was a justice of the New York State Suprreme Court during 1829–31. He served as a United States senator during 1831–32. From 1833 to 1838 he was governor of New York. He served as a negotiator during the Mexican claims dispute of 1840–42. He served as secretary of war, 1845–49. Appointed secretary of state by Pierce and served 1853–57. Handled the *Black Warrior* affair and was indirectly responsible for the Ostend Manifesto sensation.

MASON, JAMES M. (1798–1871) He was a Democratic congressman, 1837–39, and a United States senator, 1847–61, from Virginia. Drafted the Fugitive Slave Law of 1850. He was appointed Confederate diplomatic commissioner to England in 1861. Along with John Slidell, Mason's capture aboard the *Trent* on the way to England almost precipitated a war between the United States and England.

MASON, JOHN Y. (1799–1859) He was Democratic congressman, 1831–37. Secretary of the navy in 1844 and 1846–49. He was a United States attorney general, 1845–46 and United States minister to France, 1853–59. He was one of the three signers of the Ostend Manifesto.

MATHEW, GEORGE B. Rose to the rank of captain in the British Army during the early 1830s, and then entered Parliament, 1835–41. In 1844 he became governor of the Bahamas, and in March 1850 assumed the duties of consul at Charleston, South Carolina. In July 1853 he became consul at Philadelphia, and in May 1856 he was one of several British diplomats expelled from the United States as a result of the recruitment controversy. He then became consul general at Odessa.

MAXIMILIAN, EMPEROR (1832–67) Younger brother of Francis Joseph, emperor of Austria, and a Hapsburg archduke. Ferdinand Maximilian Joseph became emperor of Mexico in 1864. Following the withdrawal of French troops from Mexico in 1866–67, Maximilian was taken prisoner by the forces of Benito Juarez and executed.

MILNE, ALEXANDER (1806–96) He began his British naval career in 1827 and was stationed in the Western Hemisphere from 1836 to 1841. From 1847 to 1859 he was a junior lord of the admiralty, and then returned to the West Indies and North America in 1860. He again became junior lord of the admiralty, 1866–68 and 1872–76. Between these appointments he was commander-in-chief in the Mediterranean.

MITCHEL, JOHN (1815–75) After attending Trinity College, Dublin, he eventually became a solicitor in 1840. He then threw himself into Irish politics and journalism, culminating in his being found guilty of treason in 1848. His punishment was transportation to Australia, from which he escaped to San Francisco in 1853. During the 1850s and 1860s he was active in American journalism and in Fenian circles. In 1875 he was elected to the British House of Commons but was denied his seat because of his previous record as a felon.

MORESBY, ADMIRAL FAIRFAX (1796–1877) As a career British naval officer, he achieved steady promotion throughout his life, from midshipman (1799);

lieutenant (1806); commander (1811); rear admiral (1849); viceadmiral (1856); admiral (1864); and admiral of the fleet (1870).

MURE, WILLIAM (?-1864) In August 1843 he was appointed British consul at New Orleans, and in 1853 was transferred to Spain. After a brief mission to Cuba in April 1855, he retired to his home in Britain that August of 1855.

NAPIER, LORD (1819-98) Francis (first baron) Napier attended Trinity College, Cambridge, in the mid-1830s, studied privately abroad thereafter, and took up his first diplomatic post in Vienna in 1840. Subsequent appointments included Constantinople (1843); Naples (1846); St. Petersburg (1852); Constantinople (1854); Washington (1857); The Hague (1859); St. Petersburg (1860); and Berlin (1864). From 1866 to 1872 he was governor-general of Madras, India.

NICHOLSON, ALFRED O. P. (1808-76) Born in Tennessee, and entered the bar there in 1831. Soon became a newspaper editor as well, and also a member of the state legislature. From 1840 to 1842 he filled a vacancy in the United States Senate, returned to Tennessee, but came back to Washington , D.C. from 1853 to 1856 as editor of the *Washington Union*. Elected to United States Senate in 1859, but was then expelled in early 1861 for supporting the Confederate cause. From 1870 to 1876 he was Supreme Court justice for the state.

OUSELEY, WILLIAM G. (1797-1866) From 1825 to 1832 he was attached to the British legation in Washington, and in his last year there he published a book entitled *Remarks on the Statistics and Political Institutions of the United States*. There followed long assignments in Brazil (1832-44) and Argentina (1844-47). He then went into retirement, and in October 1857 he was sent on special mission to Central America but delayed his departure from Washington for many months. He returned to Britain in 1860 for retirement.

PAKENHAM, RICHARD (1797-1868) Educated at Trinity College, Dublin, he entered the diplomatic service in 1817. Much of his early career (1826-43) was spent in Mexico, followed by a tour of duty in Washington (1844-47). Returning to Europe, he took early retirement, went back into active service as minister to Lisbon (1851-55), and again returned to his estates in Ireland.

PALMERSTON, LORD (1794-1865) Born Henry John Temple, he succeeded to the title of third Viscount Palmerston on the death of his father in 1802. His education included Harrow, Edinburgh, and Cambridge University. He entered Parliament in 1807 and was secretary for war in 1809. He held various cabinet positions until 1828, was out of office for two years, and then served as foreign secretary from 1830 to 1841. He then went into opposition for five years, resuming the post of foreign secretary for the years 1846–52. He was prime minister almost continuously during the last decade of his life, 1855–65.

PAULDING, HIRAM (1797–1878) He embarked upon a naval career in 1811, and commanded ships thereafter in the Atlantic, Pacific, and the Caribbean. During the Civil War he was preoccupied with the construction of warships for the Union.

PEEL, ROBERT (1788–1850) Following his formal education at Harrow and Christ Church, Oxford, he entered the House of Commons in 1809. Between 1812 and 1818 he was secretary for Ireland, then secretary for the Home Office, 1822–17. In 1828 he again became home secretary as well as Leader of the House of Commons. He was briefly prime minister in 1834–35 and again in 1841–46. He became especially known for free trade legislation and the repeal of the Corn Laws.

PIERCE, FRANKLIN (1804–69) He was elected to the New Hampshire lower house in 1829 and was Speaker from 1831 to 1832. He served in the United States House of Representatives from 1833 to 1837 then in the Senate from 1837 to 1842. From 1842 to 1852, he practiced law. In 1852 he was elected president as a compromise candidate. He made the Gadsden Purchase in 1853. In 1856, he refused renomination.

POLK, JAMES K. (1795–1849) He was admitted to the bar in 1820. He served in the Tennessee State Legislature for three years. He was chief clerk of the state Senate, 1821–23, and a member of the state House of Representatives, 1823–25. He was elected as a Democrat to the United States Senate and served from 1825 to 1839. He did not attempt reelection in 1838 because he had become a gubernatorial candidate. He was Speaker during the Fourteenth and Fifteenth Congresses. He was governor of Tennessee, 1839–41. Elected President in 1844 as a Democrat. He served until 1849 and declined renomination.

PORTER, DAVID D. (1813–91) He became a midshipman in the United States Navy in 1829. From 1849 to 1855 he was a commander of merchant ships. During the Civil War, he reached the rank of rear admiral and commanded a squadron on the Mississippi. He was superintendent of the United States naval Academy, 1865–69.

QUITMAN, JOHN A. (1798–1858) He was active in Mississippi state politics; an ardent advocate of states' rights; a behind-the-scenes promoter of filibustering in Cuba; and a United States congressman from March 1855 to his death.

ROWAN, WILLIAM (1789–1879) He began his military career in 1803 and fought with the British troops at Waterloo. Between 1823 and 1829 he was a military secretary in Canada, returning there from 1849 to 1855 as commander of British forces. In 1862 he was promoted to the rank of general and to field marshal in 1877.

ROWCROFT, CHARLES He served as consul at Cincinnati from July 1852 to May 1856. He was one of several British diplomats asked to leave the United States as a result of the controversy over recruitment.

RUSSELL, LORD (1792–1878) Lord John Russell, first Earl Russell, was the third son of the duke of Bedford. He received his formal education at Westminster School and at Edinburgh University. He entered the House of Commons as a Whig in 1813 and was a consistent advocate of parliamentary electoral reform thereafter. In coming years he held various cabinet offices, including that of home secretary (1835); colonial secretary (1839); prime minister (1846); foreign secretary (1852); foreign secretary (1859); and prime minister (1865).

SANDERS, GEORGE N. (1812–73). He was a speculator, a political agent, and one of the leaders of the Young American party. During 1853–54 he was attached to the American legation in London, at a time when James Buchanan was minister there. He had a reputation for being friendly to European revolutionaries and republicans.

SANTA ANNA, ANTONIO LOPEZ DE (1795?–1876) His activities as a Mexican revolutionary during the 1820s and 1830s culminated in his becoming president, 1833–35. Vainly tried to prevent Texas from breaking away from Mexico (1836). Governed Mexico during latter 1830s and early 1840s and was formally named dictator in 1844. He was ousted in 1845, but then became provisional president in 1846. During this time he commanded the Mexican army in its war with the United States. He was in exile in 1848, but called to be president, 1853–55. Between 1855 and 1874 he lived in Cuba, Venezuela, St. Thomas, and the United States. Shortly before his death, he went back to Mexico.

SEWARD, WILLIAM H. (1801–72) He was admitted to the bar in 1822 and elected to the New York State Senate in 1830. He practiced law until 1839, when he was elected governor of New York, an office he held until 1860. He was appointed secretary of state by Lincoln and held that position until 1868.

SHIELDS, JAMES (1820–79) He was admitted to the Illinois bar in 1832. He became a member of the state House of Representatives in 1836 and held various state positions until 1847. During the Mexican War, he reached the rank of major general and was discharged in 1848. He was elected as a Democrat from

Illinois to the United States Senate in 1848, but the Senate declared him ineligible because he had not been a citizen long enough. He ran again in 1849 and served from 1849 to 1855. He was unsuccessful in his bid for reelection and moved to Minnesota, where he was elected a United States senator when Minnesota was admitted as a state. He served until 1859, when he was not reelected. He moved to California and during the Civil War was a brigadier general in command of a group of volunteers. He resigned in 1863 and moved to Missouri, where he was a member of the state House of Representatives in 1874 and 1879. He was elected to the United States Senate in 1879 to fill a vacancy and served from January to March of that year. He declined renomination after that term was completed.

SICKLES, DANIEL E. (1825–1914) He was active in New York State politics before becoming secretary of legation in London under James Buchanan, 1853–55.

SIMPSON, GEORGE (1792–1860) Most of his life was identified with British North America and with the Hudson's Bay Company. He undertook strenuous treks across Canada and elsewhere throughout the world.

SLIDELL, JOHN (1793–1871) He served in the United States Congress as a Jackson Democrat from Louisiana, 1843–45, when he was appointed United States commissioner to Mexico. He was a United States senator from 1853 to 1861. Slidell represented the Confederacy in France but was distrusted by the other Confederate agents.

SOULÉ, PIERRE (1801–70) He served as a United States Senator from Louisiana, 1847–1853, when he was appointed United States minister to Spain. He resigned in 1854 after the Ostend Manifesto affair. He sided with the Confederacy during the Civil War.

SQUIER, EPHRAIM G. (1821–88) Squier held a number of diplomatic and consular posts throughout his lifetime. In 1848 he was clerk of the Ohio House of Representatives. He was appointed chargé d'affaires to Central America in 1849. He was United States commissioner to Peru from 1863 to 1865. In 1868, he was made consul general of Honduras in New York City. He wrote several books on Central and South America.

STANLEY, EDWARD HENRY (1826–93) He succeeded to his father's title and became fifteenth Earl Derby in 1869. The son of a prime minister, Stanley was destined to an active political career. Over the years he was colonial secretary (1858 and 1882–85), and foreign secretary (1866–68 and 1874–78).

STANTON, EDWIN M. (1814–69) He was admitted to the bar in 1836. In 1858, he was special counsel for the United States government for handling fraudulent land claims in California. In 1860 he was appointed attorney general of the United States. He became secretary of war in 1862. He was dismissed in 1868. In 1869, Grant appointed him to the United States Supreme Court, but he died before he could take office.

STEVENS, THADDEUS (1792–1868) He was elected on the Anti-Masonic ticket to the Pennsylvania House and served from 1833 to 1841. He was elected to the United States Congress as a Whig in 1848 and served until 1853, when he left Congress. He was reelected to Congress in 1858 as a Republican and served until his death.

STUART, WILLIAM (1824–96) He was attaché to the Paris embassy in 1845. He was secretary of legation in Rio de Janeiro in 1858. In 1859, he became secretary of legation at Naples. In 1861, he became secretary of legation at Washington, then chargé d'affaires until 1863. He was secretary of embassy at Constantinople in 1864, then at St. Petersburg in 1866. He was minister plenipotentiary at Buenos Aires in 1868. He was sent on a special mission to Athens in 1870. He became envoy extraordinary and minister plenipotentiary to Greece in 1872, and then held the same post at The Hague in 1877. He was plenipotentiary for the signing of the North Sea fishery convention in 1882.

SUMNER, CHARLES (1811–74) He was elected to the United States Senate from Massachusetts in 1851 by a coalition of Free-Soilers and Democrats. He served until his death except for a period of three and a half years when he was recovering from an attack by Preston S. Brooks.

TAYLOR, ZACHARY (1784–1850) He was appointed first lieutenant in the Seventh Infantry in 1808. He rose to the rank of captain in 1810, and major in 1812. He assisted in the defense of the frontier from Indiana to Missouri during the War of 1812. He was appointed lieutenant colonel of the Fourth Infantry in 1819. He served in the Southwest and Western frontiers until 1832, when he was promoted to colonel and put in command of the First Regiment stationed at Fort Crawford. He was promoted to brigadier general in 1837. From 1840 to 1847 he served in the Southwest. In 1847 he defeated Santa Anna while disobeying orders. In 1848, he was elected president as a Whig. He died while in office in 1850.

TOOMBS, ROBERT (1810–85) A Georgian by birth, he began practicing law there in 1828. After serving in the Georgia State Legislature (1837–44) he entered the United States Senate in March 1845. In February 1861 he withdrew

APPENDIX: BIOGRAPHICAL DIRECTORY

from the Senate and threw in his lot with the Confederacy as a congressman, a secretary of state, and as a brigadier general. For several years after the war he remained in Europe, and then returned to his native Georgia.

TYLER, JOHN (1790–1862) He was elected to the Virginia House of Delegates in 1811 and served until 1816. He was elected as a Democrat to the United States Congress in 1816 and served until 1821. He was governor of Virginia from 1824 to 1827. In 1827 he was elected to the United States Senate as an anti-Jackson Democrat. He resigned from the Senate in 1836. In 1839, he was nominated as vice-presidential running mate to Harrison. He became president in 1840, when Harrison died. He withdrew his name for reelection in 1844. He served in the provisional Congress of the Confederacy and was elected to the Confederate House of Representatives. He died before he could take office.

UPSHUR, ABEL P. (1791–1844) He was a judge of the Virginia Supreme Court, 1826–41. He was United States secretary of the navy from 1841 to 1843, when he succeeded Webster as secretary of state. He was killed when a gun exploded on the *Princeton.*

VANDERBILT, CORNELIUS (1794–1877) As early as 1810 he was operating ferryboats between New York City and Staten Island. During the War of 1812 he amassed a small fleet of river and coastal vessels, eventually (1829) converting from sailing to steam-powered vessels. During the latter 1840s and early 1850s he was a partner in several concerns providing transport across Nicaragua, thus facilitating travel from the East to the West coast of the United States. Later in the decade he tried (without much success) to challenge the Cunard and Collins lines for the transatlantic passenger trade. During the latter 1860s he consolidated several lines into the New York Central Railroad.

WALKER, JOSEPH K. (1818–63) He graduated from Yale in 1838 and then studied law in Memphis. He began practicing law in Memphis but also served as Polk's private secretary during two unsuccessful election attempts. In 1844, he began working as President Polk's private secretary. He stayed in Washington after Polk's term was up and worked as an attorney and claims agent. In 1852 he returned to Memphis to practice law. He was elected as a state senator in 1857. When the Civil War broke out, he sided with the Confederacy and was a colonel in charge of a regiment. He served until his capture; however, Union officers gave him safe passage to Memphis, where he died.

WALKER, ROBERT J. (1801–69) He was admitted to the bar in 1821. He was a United States senator from Mississippi from 1836 to 1845. He was appointed governor of the Kansas Territory from March to December of 1857. He sided with the Union during the Civil War. He is chiefly remembered for being a strong supporter of the annexation of Texas.

WALKER, WILLIAM (1824–60) He was admitted to the bar in New Orleans but moved to practice in California. In 1853, he invaded the province of Lower Mexico and proclaimed himself president of an independent republic there. He was forced to leave, but in 1855 he led another armed group to Nicaragua at the invitation of a revolutionary leader there. He seized control with the help of the Accessory Transit Company and his new government was recognized by the United States government in 1856. With the help of Vanderbilt, a coalition of republics forced him out. In 1857 he attempted to invade Nicaragua but was arrested by Captain Paulding of the United States Navy and sent back to the United States. In 1860, he was arrested by British authorities when he landed in Honduras. He was condemned to death by a court martial of Honduran officers and shot.

WEBSTER, DANIEL (1782–1852) He was admitted to the bar in 1805. He was elected to the United States Congress in 1812 and served until 1816. He returned to Congress and served from 1823 to 1827. He was elected to the United States Senate from Massachusetts in 1827 and served until 1840. He was named secretary of state by Harrison in 1840 and served until he resigned in 1843. He was reelected to the United States Senate in 1845 and served until 1850, when he again became secretary of state, a position he held until his death.

WHITE, JOSEPH L. (?–1861) Born in New York State, admitted to the Indiana State bar, and represented Indiana in the United States House of Representatives, 1841–43. He then practiced law in New York City and became one of the partners along with Cornelius Vanderbilt in the development of a transit route across Nicaragua in the early 1850s.

Notes

Introduction

1. "Memorandum on the Forms to be observed in Official Correspondence with the Department of Her Majesty's Principal Secretary of State for Foreign Affairs," ca. 1850; enclosed with circular letter no. 405. We are much indebted to the Foreign Office and Commonwealth Library for calling our attention to this and other memoranda in connection with the writing of dispatches.

2. Foreign Office and Commonwealth Library, no. 1475; memorandum to consuls, 11 October 1879.

3. Britain had embassies in major European capitals, such as Paris, Berlin, Bern, St. Petersburg, and Constantinople, but maintained legations in most other capitals throughout the world. Washington, D.C., was upgraded from a legation to an embassy in the early 1890s.

4. Crampton to Granville, 28 March 1852, P.R.O. F.O. 5/544, f. 284.

5. *Parliamentary Papers: Reports from Committees*, "Report from the Select Committee on Diplomatic Service," 1861 (459), vol. 10.

6. Ibid, qs. 990, 1773, 2665, and 3501.

7. Ibid.

8. Ibid., qs. 988 and 2662.

9. Ibid., q. 897.

10. Ibid., q. 2348.

11. Ibid., qs. 899, 2351, and 2666–67.

12. Bulwer to Palmerston, 17 June 1850, P.R.O. F.O. 5/513, f. 159.

13. Crampton to Clarendon, 19 May 1856, Bodleian Library, Clarendon Papers, C. 64, f. 96. See also, *Parliamentary Papers*, 1861, q. 2350.

14. Motley to Lowell, 28 August 1864, Houghton Library, B MS Am765 (546).

15. 1861 Select Committee, q. 2350.

16. Bulwer to Palmerston, 12 August 1851, *Palmerston Papers*, Historical Manuscripts Commission, GC/BU/472/4.

17. Crampton to Clarendon, 13 February 1853, Clarendon Papers, C. 11, ff. 23–28.

18. F. Hudson, *Journalism in the United States from 1690–1872* (New York, 1873), p. 481.

19. Crampton to Clarendon, 9 April 1854, 7 May 1854, and 29 March 1856, in Clarendon Papers, C. 24, ff. 235 and 291, and C. 63, f. 192.

20. Moore to Crampton, 14 November 1855, Bodleian Library, Crampton Papers, box A-5, November 1855 folder. For additional information about the activities of T. W. Charles Moore, see J. J. Barnes, *Authors, Publishers and Politicians: The Quest for an Anglo-American Copyright Agreement, 1815–1854* (London and Columbus, 1974), pp. 178–80, 184–85, 214–15, 217, 226–28, 231, and 293–96. For the earlier career of Thomas William Moore, see C. Vaughan to J. Backhouse, 28 August and

27 November 1830; and Moore to Vaughan, 12 August 1830, in P.R.O. F.O. 5/260, ff. 165-78 and 294.

Chapter 1. Sir Richard Pakenham and the Oregon Question, 1843-1846

1. The resulting Webster-Ashburton Treaty, 9 August 1842, dealt only with the northeastern boundary.

2. The key passage in Aberdeen's instructions to Pakenham of 28 December 1843 is reprinted in J. Schafer, "The British Attitude Toward the Oregon Question, 1815-1846," *American Historical Review* 16 (January 1911): 295-96. Much of this same letter but minus the key passage is reprinted in *British and Foreign State Papers, 1845-1846* vol. 34 (London, 1860), 56-57.

3. Aberdeen to Pakenham, 4 March 1844, as reprinted in W. D. Jones, *Lord Aberdeen and the Americas* (Athens, Ga., 1958), pp. 29-30.

4. Pakenham to Aberdeen, 28 March 1844, B.M. Add. MS. 43123, ff. 235-38.

5. Pakenham to Aberdeen, 13 June 1844, Ibid., ff. 239-41.

6. Pakenham to Lord Aberdeen, 29 August 1844, Ibid., ff. 243-46.

7. Reprinted in *British and Foreign State Papers*, 34:61-62.

8. J. D. Richardson, comp., *A Compilation of the Messages and Papers of the Presidents, 1789-1908* vol. 4 (Washington, D.C., 1908), 338.

9. Ibid., 381.

10. Aberdeen to Pakenham, 2 April 1845, B.M. Add. MS. 43123, ff. 247-48.

11. Pakenham to Aberdeen, 28 April 1845, ibid., ff. 253-57.

12. Pakenham to Aberdeen, 13 May 1845, ibid, ff. 259-60.

13. Buchanan's lengthy proposal of 12 July 1845 is reprinted in House Executive Document no. 2, 29th Congress, 1st Session (480). It is also reprinted in *British and Foreign State Papers* 34:93-101.

14. For Pakenham's refusal of 29 July 1845 see *British and Foreign State Papers* 34:101-11.

15. On 30 August 1845 Buchanan formally withdrew his proposal of the previous July. See ibid. 34:110-30.

16. P.R.O. F.O. 5/423, f. 135, no. 64.

17. P.R.O. F.O. 5/429, f. 55, no. 114.

18. Pakenham to Aberdeen, 28 October 1845, B.M. Add. MS. 43123, ff. 264-70.

19. A. H. Gordon, ed., *Selections from the Correspondence of the Earl of Aberdeen*, 14 vols. (London: privately published, 1854-88), vol. for 1845, pp. 141, 328-29. There is a set of these privately printed volumes in the State Paper Room of the British Museum. Aberdeen's private letter of 3 October 1845 is also reprinted in H. Miller, *Treaties and Other International Acts of the United States of America*, vol. 5, *1846-1852* (Washington, D.C., 1937), pp. 39-40.

20. Aberdeen to Pakenham, 3 December 1845, B.M. Add. MS. 43123, ff. 272-73.

21. During the Irish potato famine of 1845-46, the British government sought to alleviate the situation in part by importing large quantities of Indian corn, or maize, from the United States.

22. Pakenham to Aberdeen, 29 December, P.R.O. F.O. 5/430, f. 186, "Separate and Confidential."

23. Richardson, *Messages and Papers of the Presidents* 4:394-95.

24. The extent to which the Polk administration became concerned with the British buildup of military and naval forces is ably discussed in S. Anderson, "British Threats and the Settlement of the Oregon Boundary Dispute," *Pacific Northwest Quarterly* 66 (October 1975): 153–60. See also Miller, *Treaties* 5:57–61.

25. Pakenham to Aberdeen, 26 February 1846, in Gordon, *Correspondence of Aberdeen*, vol. for 1846, PP. 85–86.

26. Aberdeen to Pakenham, 18 May 1846, in Miller, *Treaties* 5:75–78.

27. Ibid., 78–79.

28. Ibid., pp. 79–81. Miller reprints this private letter as well as Aberdeen dispatch no. 18 of the same day, from Gordon, *Correspondence of Aberdeen*, vol. for 1846, pp. 212–21.

29. Pakenham to Aberdeen, 28 May 1846, B.M. Add. MS. 43123, ff. 294–95.

30. Pakenham to Aberdeen, 7 June 1846, in Gordon, *Correspondence of Aberdeen*, vol. for 1846, p. 297.

31. Pakenham to Aberdeen, 13 June 1846, ibid., p. 298.

32. Pakenham to Aberdeen, 13 June 1846, ibid., p. 299.

33. Aberdeen to Pakenham, 30 June 1846, ibid., p. 300.

34. Pakenham to Aberdeen, 27 July 1846, B.M. Add. MS. 43123, ff. 310–11.

35. P.R.O. F.O. 5/430, f. 172, no. 138; F.O. 5/430, f. 186, "Separate and Confidential"; and F.O. 5/446, f. 177, "Separate and Confidential."

Chapter 2. Henry Bulwer and Central America, 1850–1851

1. See the Appendix for biographical details.

2. Ibid.

3. Clayton to Colonel G. W. Hughes, 4 September 1849, quoted in J. Bigelow, *Breaches of Anglo-American Treaties* (New York, 1917), pp. 73–74.

4. On 27 August 1849 David L. White, representing the Ship Canal Company, signed a contract with the Nicaraguan government that was formally ratified on 23 September 1849. The contract is reprinted in *Senate Executive Documents*, 47th Congress 1st Session, vol. 6 (1882), no. 194, pp. 49–55. It is also reprinted in W. R. Manning, comp., *Diplomatic Correspondence of the United States: Inter-American Affairs, 1831–1860* (Washington, D.C., 1933), 3:363–66. In March 1849 the Nicaraguans had signed a tentative agreement with Dr. D. T. Brown, representing a different group of investors, but this earlier contract was repudiated by the Nicaraguans shortly before concluding a contract with D. L. White, see Manning, *Diplomatic Correspondence* 3:334–35 and 348.

5. For background on White, see the Appendix.

6. Bulwer to Palmerston, 6 January 1850, Palmerston Papers, GC/BU/461/1.

7. Bulwer's euphemism alludes to the king of the Mosquito Indians.

8. The allusion was to Abbott Lawrence, American minister to the Court of St. James.

9. The company's headman is presumably Joseph L. White, while it is uncertain as to the identity of Clayton's headman.

10. For a discussion of the British Navigation Acts and their repeal in 1849, and why the British felt the United States should modify the registration of vessels in American ports, see W. S. Lindsay, *History of Merchant Shipping and Ancient Commerce*, 4 vols. (London, 1874–76; reprinted 1965), especially vol. 3.

11. Bulwer to Palmerston, 20 January 1850, Palmerston Papers, Historical Manuscripts Commission GC/BU/462/2.

12. Eventually, Senator Stephen A. Douglas of Illinois became the "patron" and sponsored a reciprocity bill.

13. Bulwer to Palmerston, 3 February 1850, Palmerston Papers, GC/BU/463/3.

14. For the text of this *projet*, see *British and Foreign State Papers, 1850-1851*, vol. 40 (London, 1863), 1008-18; and Bigelow, *Breaches of Treaties*, pp. 79-90. Bigelow compares the *projet* with the provisions of the treaty as it was finally signed on 19 April 1850.

15. The allusion is presumably to Squier's book *Nicaragua: Its People, Scenery, Monuments, and the Proposed Interoceanic Canal* (New York, 1852).

16. During the first six months of 1850, Nicaragua was represented in Washington by Eduardo Carache. For his exchange of correspondence with Clayton, see Manning, *Diplomatic Correspondence* 3:57-59, and 487.

17. Bulwer to Palmerston, 18 February 1850, Palmerston Papers, GC/BU/464/2.

18. The newspaper referred to was the *National Intelligencer*, and its most active editor at this time was William Winston Seaton.

19. Bulwer is apparently alluding to British agents who aided the Mosquito Indians against the encroachments of the Nicaraguans during the 1840s. We are unable to identify Johnson and Smith. Patrick Walker died during one of the skirmishes with the Nicaraguans.

20. Bulwer to Palmerston, 31 March 1850, P.R.O. F.O. 5/512, f. 137.

21. Dispatch 56 is to be found in P.R.O. F.O. 5/512.

22. *British and Foreign State Papers* 40:1024, 1028-30.

23. Bulwer to Palmerston, 28 April 1850, P.R.O. F.O. 5/512, f. 205; and reprinted in *British and Foreign State Papers* 40:1030-32.

24. The "Agent" in London was Don Jose de Marcoleta. In early 1851 he came to Washington as Nicaragua's representative.

25. Bulwer to Palmerston, 6 May 1850, P.R.O. F.O. 5/512, f. 248.

26. Bulwer to Palmerston, 6 May 1850, P.R.O. F.O. 5/512, f. 237.

27. The individuals in question were: Charles S. Todd; John R. Clay; Colin M. Ingersoll; Arthur P. Bagby; Neill S. Brown.

28. Andrew J. Donelson (1799-1871) was accredited to Berlin from 1846 to 1849.

29. Nathan Clifford (1803-81) was sent to Mexico in March 1848 to help negotiate an end to the war.

30. James W. Webb (1802-84), a former general and journalist, was not confirmed as minister to Vienna.

31. Bulwer was correct in anticipating changes in the allowances that Congress allocated to newly appointed diplomats. However, in the case of consuls, the fees that they could charge were reduced, thus making such posts less remunerative. See Acts of 1 March 1875 (*Statutes at Large* 10:619-26); and August 1856 (*Statutes at Large* 11:52-65).

32. *British and Foreign State Papers*, 40:1047-52.

33. Bulwer to Palmerston, 7 October 1850, P.R.O. F.O. 5/515, f. 157.

34. Palmerston's dispatch 117 will be found in P.R.O. F.O. 5/510.

35. Bulwer to Palmerston, 7 October 1850, P.R.O. F.O. 5/515, f. 137.

36. The secretary of the treasury was Thomas Corwin.

37. Bulwer to Palmerston, 27 January 1851, P.R.O. F.O. 5/527, f. 101.

38. Bulwer to Palmerston, 29 July 1851, Palmerston Papers, GC/BU/470/1.

39. Felipe Molina represented both Costa Rica and Guatemala in Washington during the early 1850s.

40. Bigelow, *Breaches of Treaties*, pp. 94–95.
41. J. Bigelow, *Retrospections of an Active Life* (New York, 1909), 2:386–87.

Chapter 3. John F. T. Crampton and the American Political System, 1852–1853

1. Crampton's letters to Lord Malmesbury are to be found in a volume marked "Turkey . . . N. and S. America, 1852." The volume, which has no pagination, is in the possession of the earl of Malmesbury. The first letter quoted is dated 9 August 1852.
2. Marshfield was Webster's farm in Massachusetts.
3. John Davis (1787–1854) of Massachusetts concluded his active political career by serving in the United States Senate 1845–53.
4. Crampton to Malmesbury, 15 August 1852.
5. Crampton to Malmesbury, 12 September 1852, with enclosure from Crampton to Elgin, 3 November 1851.
6. Crampton to Malmesbury, 12 September 1852, dispatch 145, in F.O. 5/547, f. 107.
7. For a fuller discussion of the "Organization" and its membership, see J. J. Barnes, *Authors, Publishers and Politicians* (London and Columbus, Ohio, 1974), chaps. 9–12.
8. The person alluded to was Senator Stephen A. Douglas of Illinois, who in 1851 sponsored a reciprocity bill in Congress.
9. The head of the Organization was Joseph Knox Walker, nephew and private secretary of former President James K. Polk. For further details, see note 7 above.
10. Crampton to Malmesbury, 24 October 1852.
11. The Lobos Islands, off the coast of Peru, were a source of guano. American ships and their captains did not acknowledge Peru's claim to the islands and thus refused to pay duty on the guano.
12. Crampton to Malmesbury, 24 October 1852.
13. Henry Clay had died the previous June of 1852.
14. Crampton's Private and Confidential letters to Lord Clarendon are to be found in the Bodleian Library, Oxford, under MS Clarendon Dep. The letter for 5 February 1853 is in C. 11, ff. 1–4.
15. Abbot Lawrence, former American minister to London, returned to the United States in October 1852 and resumed his business activities in Boston.
16. Crampton to Clarendon, 7 February 1853, C. 11, ff. 5–22.
17. Lewis Cass was a United States senator from Michigan.
18. The Tripartite Convention of 23 April 1852 between Britain, France, and the United States disclaimed "now and for hereafter, all intention to obtain possession of the island of Cuba." The United States, under Secretary of State Edward Everett, refused to ratify the treaty.
19. The Sandwich Islands were what the British called the Hawaiian Islands.
20. The expedition to Japan under the command of Admiral Matthew C. Perry left the United States on 24 November 1852 and reached Japan on 2 July 1853.
21. The Russian agent to the Sandwich Islands was the consul general, Baron Edouard de Stoeckl.
22. Crampton to Clarendon, 21 February 1853, C. 11, ff. 29–34.
23. Crampton to Clarendon, 27 February 1853, C. 11, ff. 38–39.

24. Crampton to Clarendon, 7 March 1853, C. 11, ff. 40–45.

25. Crampton to Clarendon, 13 March 1853, C. 11, ff. 48–49.

26. Crampton to Clarendon, 21 March 1853, C. 11, ff. 55–60.

27. The Anglo-American Claims Convention was signed in London on 8 February 1853 and was ratified by the Senate on 15 March. For further details, see dispatch 69 of 21 March 1853 in F.O. 5/563, ff. 95–98.

28. Concerning the attempt to negotiate and pass an American copyright agreement, see Barnes, *Authors*, pp. 242–61.

29. Crampton to Clarendon, 27 March 1853, C. 11, ff. 61–66. The most comprehensive treatment of the "Coloured Seamen" question is to be found in P. M. Hamer, "Great Britain, the United States, and the Negro Seamen Acts, 1822–1848," and "British Consuls and the Negro Seamen Acts, 1850–1860," *Journal of Southern History* 1 (February and May 1935): 3–28, 138–68. For South Carolina in particular, see M. Wikramanayake, *A World in Shadow: The Free Black in Antebellum South Carolina* (Columbia, S.C., 1973). For official dispatches on the subject, see for example: F.O. 5/565, f. 40, no. 99 (2 May 1853); F.O. 5/561, f. 241, no. 32 (20 May 1853); and F.O. 5/577, f. 113, memorandum (14 June 1853).

30. The Oregon Affair was that of 1845–46, see above, chap. 1.

31. Robert Bunch became British consul at Charleston, South Carolina, in July 1853.

32. Crampton to Clarendon, 4 April 1853, C. 11, ff. 77–84.

33. An allusion to an interminable case before the Court of Chancery in Charles Dickens's *Bleak House*.

34. *Acts . . . of the State of Louisiana* (New Orleans, 1852), 193, which permitted a black seaman to remain onboard ship rather than requiring his imprisonment. The British consul in New Orleans had been instrumental in securing this modification of the law, and that was why the same tactic was tried in other Southern states, with varying degrees of success during the next seven years. Andrew P. Butler was at that time a United States senator from the state of South Carolina.

35. Crampton to Clarendon, 18 April 1853, C. 11, ff. 92–101.

36. On 17 June 1848, Secretary of State James Buchanan instructed Romulus M. Saunders, American minister to Madrid, to offer Spain $100 million for the acquisition of Cuba. The offer was firmly rejected. The dispatch is reprinted in *House Executive Documents* no. 121, 32d Congress, 1st Session, serial 648 (1852), pp. 42–46. Upon the publication of this and other material relating to Cuba, Crampton forwarded a copy to the Foreign Office: dispatch 197 of 29 November 1852, F.O. 5/548, ff. 155–61.

37. For information about Ferencz Pulszky, Ambrosia José Gonzalez, Narciso Lopez, and George Law, see B. Rauch, *American Interest in Cuba, 1848–1855* (New York, 1948; reissued 1974). Lopez was finally executed by the Spanish authorities for attempting to stir up a revolution in Cuba. George Law controlled a line of steamships that competed for the traffic between New York and California.

38. Calderon de la Barca was Spanish minister to the United States.

39. Crampton to Clarendon, 2 May 1853, C. 11, ff. 126–34.

40. An allusion to the revolutions that swept Europe in 1848 but that did not break out in England or Russia.

41. Crampton to Clarendon, 16 May 1853, C. 11, ff. 151–54.

42. Crampton to Clarendon, 5 June 1853, C. 11, ff. 162–65.

43. Crampton to Clarendon, 19 June 1853, C. 11, ff. 177–86. For further details about the Organization, see Barnes, *Authors*, pp. 194–221.

44. Crampton to Clarendon, 27 June 1853, C. 11, ff. 187–90.

45. Crampton's dispatch 129 is in F.O. 5/565, ff. 249–62. The case involved James

Dyson, who claimed to be a British subject and who was accused by the New Orleans authorities of trying to foment a slave uprising in the area.

46. William Mure was British consul at New Orleans.

47. Ruben Roberts was a free black cook on board a British vessel that stopped at Charleston, South Carolina, in May 1852. Roberts was removed and put in jail for eight days, pending the departure of his ship. He was then allowed to depart onboard, all of which was in conformity with state law. It was later decided by the British to test the laws of South Carolina on the subject dating back to 1794 and culminating in that of 1835 before a federal circuit court. The presumption was that the case against the sheriff of Charleston for false imprisonment would lose at this level, which in fact it did in April 1853, but it could then be appealed to the United States Supreme Court. However, that action was not taken in part because of Crampton's doubts on the wisdom of such a course, as expressed in his dispatch 99 of 2 May 1853, in F.O. 5/565, ff. 40–48.

48. Crampton to Clarendon, 25 July 1853, C. 11, ff. 235–38.

49. Crampton to Clarendon, 8 August 1853, C. 11, ff. 245–56.

50. Crampton to Clarendon, 22 August 1853, C. 11, ff. 278–83.

51. As far as one can tell, Gonzalez Bravo did not serve as chargé d'affaires. Instead, the first secretary of the Spanish legation, Don Jose Maria Megallon, assumed that position.

52. Henry S. Fox was British minister to Washington.

53. Crampton to Clarendon, 19 September 1853, C. 11, ff. 339–46.

54. See the Appendix for details of Porter's career.

55. Hincks was Canadian finance minister.

56. Crampton to Clarendon, 25 September 1853, C. 11, ff. 359–65.

57. Everett's rejoinder to Lord John Russell's criticism was dated 17 September 1853. His original rejection of the Tripartite Convention took place on 1 December 1852. Russell's critical comments were made in a dispatch to Crampton on 16 February 1853, which was subsequently shown to Everett.

58. The act alluded to passed during the administration of John Adams.

59. Crampton to Clarendon, 9 October 1853, C. 11, ff. 371–78.

60. George Canning was British foreign secretary from 1822–27.

61. Crampton to Clarendon, 17 October 1853, C. 11, ff. 385–90.

62. C. Edward Lester's first contribution to *The Times* appeared on 18 March 1853.

63. Crampton to Clarendon, 23 October 1853, C. 11, ff. 401–6.

64. The *Daily Union* article that touched off press agitation was in the issue of 20 October 1853. For other articles, see *New York Herald*, 24 October; *Daily Mirror*, 25–28 October; and *National Intelligencer*, 29 October.

65. Crampton to Clarendon, 31 October 1853, C. 11, ff. 422–25.

66. Crampton to Clarendon, 14 November 1853, C. 11, ff. 446–49.

67. *National Intelligencer*, 8 November 1853; *Daily Union*, 9 November and 11 November.

68. Crampton's dispatch 176 of 14 November 1853 is in F.O. 5/567, ff. 79–85.

69. Crampton to Clarendon, 20 November 1853, C. 11, ff. 456–61.

70. John T. Delane was editor of *The Times* of London.

71. Billingsgate was a raucous fish market in the City of London along the Thames.

72. Crampton's dispatch 181 of 20 November 1853 is in F.O. 5/567, ff. 106–13.

73. Crampton to Clarendon, 4 December 1853, C. 11, ff. 473–76.

74. Crampton to Clarendon, 18 December 1853, C. 11, ff. 494–503.

75. A year after the publication of *Uncle Tom's Cabin*, Harriet Beecher Stowe visited England, lectured widely, and was warmly received.

76. Thomas Francis Meagher (1823–67) was convicted of treason in Dublin in 1848, sentenced to transportation for life in 1849, and escaped from Australia several years later, reaching New York in May 1852.

77. Admiral Fairfax Moresby was chief of British naval forces in the Pacific.

Chapter 4. British Preoccupation with the Crimean War, 1854

1. Crampton to Clarendon, 27 February 1854, Bodleian Library, MS Clarendon Dep., C. 24, ff. 116–22.

2. Baron Roenne, Prussian minister to the United States in 1849, was involved in an attempt, on the part of some of the German states, to procure and equip a ship of war for possible use against Denmark in the Schleswig-Holstein affair. Secretary of State John M. Clayton would not permit the vessel to sail until Roenne guaranteed that it would honor the American Neutrality Law of 1818.

3. Gen. Zachary Taylor was president of the United States at the time.

4. Crampton to Clarendon, 2 March 1854, C. 24, ff. 136–42.

5. Clarendon's speech in the House of Lords of 31 January 1854 is in *Parliamentary Debates*, vol. 130, cols. 35–42.

6. Clarendon's dispatch 19 of 2 February 1854 is missing from F.O. 5/590 but may be found in F.O. 115/136, ff. 144–51. Sir Edmund Head was governor of New Brunswick, and Sir Gaspard Le Marchant was lieutenant governor of Nova Scotia.

7. For the earlier discussion of prohibitions against the registering of foreign vessels in America, see chap. 2, note 10.

8. Crampton's dispatch 48 of 2 March 1854 is in F.O. 5/594, ff. 31–31v.

9. The *New York Herald* of 20 February 1854 had claimed that three Russian agents, Grumwald, Fersteine and Lockoloff, had recently arrived in the United States to purchase ships.

10. Crampton to Clarendon, 6 March 1854, C. 24, ff. 169–72.

11. During the 1840s the king of the Mosquito Indians had made large grants of land to two Jamaicans, Peter and Samuel Sheppard, which Nicaragua later disputed.

12. Ruatan was one of the Bay Islands that Britain had declared to be a Crown Colony in 1852 in the face of opposition from Honduras, which also laid claim to them. The Americans regarded the British action as a violation of the Clayton-Bulwer Treaty of 1850.

13. The Kansas-Nebraska Bill tried to resolve the issue of slavery in these territories by permitting the inhabitants to vote for or against free soil upon their admission to statehood. The situation was also complicated by alternative plans for a rail route to the Pacific Coast and the competition these schemes engendered in politicians throughout the country. One proposal would have sent the railroad through the Kansas Territory, while another would have linked New Orleans with the West Coast.

14. Crampton to Clarendon, 20 March 1854, C. 24, ff. 192–99.

15. The Gadsden Treaty was signed in Mexico on 13 December 1853. Its purpose was to facilitate the purchase by the United States of enough land to construct a transcontinental railroad via a southern route to California.

16. The Garay land grant had to do with the possibility of constructing a canal across the Isthmus of Tehuantepec in Mexico. By the 1850s the Mexican government had repudiated the grant, but some Americans persisted in asserting their claim to the land.

17. Crampton to Clarendon, 26 March 1854, C. 24, ff. 208–11.

18. Crampton to Clarendon, 3 April 1854, C. 24, ff. 221–28.

19. Crampton to Clarendon, 9 April 1854, C. 24, ff. 235–44.

20. Campbell's resolution in the House of Representatives was introduced on 3 April 1854. See *Congressional Globe*, vol. 23, 845.

21. A report of Mitchel's proclamation was forwarded by Crampton in his dispatch 89 of 10 April 1854, in F.O. 5/594, ff. 349–60. For background on Mitchel, see the Appendix.

22. Clarendon to Crampton, 24 March 1854, in F.O. 5/590, ff. 126–28, dispatch 66.

23. Crampton to Clarendon, 1 May 1854, C. 24, ff. 281–86.

24. Crampton to Clarendon, 15 May 1854, C. 24, ff. 313–18.

25. Crampton to Clarendon, 29 May 1854, C. 24, ff. 331–40.

26. Crampton is presumably alluding to the article entitled "British and American Slavery," which appeared in the *Southern Quarterly Review* for October 1853, pp. 396–411. Alternatively, he was referring to the article, "Carey on the Slave Trade," in the issue for January 1854, pp. 115–84.

27. Crampton to Clarendon, 12 June 1854, C. 24, ff. 350–59.

28. See note 25 above, Crampton to Clarendon, 29 May 1854.

29. Crampton to Clarendon, 26 June 1854, C. 24, ff. 382–89.

30. The so-called Webster-Ashburton Treaty of 1842.

31. Crampton to Clarendon, 24 July 1854, C. 25, ff. 46–51.

32. Crampton to Clarendon, 31 July 1854, C. 25, ff. 52–61.

33. A town on Sitka Sound on the west coast of Baranof Island, part of the Alexander Archipelago, or "panhandle" of Alaska.

34. G. P. R. James, the novelist, was British consul at Richmond, Virginia.

35. Crampton's dispatch 206 of 31 July is in F.O. 5/598, ff. 42–52.

36. Crampton to Clarendon, 3 August 1854, C. 25, ff. 69–70.

37. Crampton's allusion to the use of the telegraph refers to communication between the United States and Halifax, Nova Scotia, where the message would then be put onboard the next steamship to Liverpool. Regular transatlantic cable service was not successfully established until 1866.

38. Crampton to Clarendon, 7 August 1854, C. 25, ff. 77–84.

39. Crampton's dispatch 214 of 7 August is in F.O. 5/598, ff. 94–140.

40. Joseph W. Fabens was American commercial agent at Greytown.

41. According to the *New York Herald* of 3 August 1854, Dr. Thomas Cottman, formerly a medical doctor and state legislator from Louisiana, went abroad in 1853 to place his daughter in a Paris school. He then traveled extensively in Russia, spending some months in St. Petersburg. Upon his return to the United States, he allegedly tried to negotiate the sale by Russia of part of Alaska to the United States.

42. Crampton to Clarendon, 13 August 1854, C. 25, ff. 94–101.

43. Admiral Fanshawe, commander of the North American squadron, was the person responsible for enforcing the fishing provisions of the new Reciprocity Treaty.

44. Crampton to Clarendon, 10–11 September 1854, C. 25, ff. 125–36.

45. The allusion to Copenhagen refers to the period of the Napoleonic wars. Following Napoleon's imposition of a mercantile blockade of Denmark, the British retaliated by bombarding Copenhagen (8–12 September 1807). The action was taken in part to prevent the Danish fleet from falling into French hands.

46. Warren Hastings (1732–1818) symbolized British rule in India during the eighteenth century, especially arbitrary power exercised by the agent of the East India Company.

47. Crampton's dispatch 224 of 11 September is in F.O. 5/598, ff. 326–33.

48. Crampton to Clarendon, 25 September 1854, C. 25, ff. 146–50.

49. Crampton to Clarendon, 2 October 1854, C. 25, ff. 164–74.

50. Barclay was British consul in New York. According to the first edition of *The Random House Dictionary*, a razee was "a sailing ship, especially a warship, reduced in height by the removal of the upper deck."

51. Charles Morgan was president of the Accessory Transit Company with headquarters in New York City. Details of the Poyais swindle have eluded our inquires.

52. Crampton to Clarendon, 16 October 1854, C. 25, ff. 178–93.

53. Samana Bay is on the north coast of Santo Domingo.

54. The arrival of the *Colossus* and the *Termagant* reinforced the West Indies squadron.

55. Crampton to Clarendon, 6 November 1854, C. 25, ff. 239–48.

56. The allusion is presumably to the Grattan expedition against the Sioux Indians east of Fort Laramie, Wyoming. Lieutenant John L. Grattan and twenty-nine others were killed on 19 August 1854.

57. Crampton to Clarendon, 17 November 1854, C. 25, ff. 280–94.

58. For details concerning the careers of Daniel Sickles and George N. Sanders, see the Appendix. See also Lumley to Clarendon, 28 September 1856 in chap. 6, where Buchanan's political friends are referred to with disparagement.

59. The transcontinental railway was not completed until 1869.

Chapter 5. Recruitment, 1855

1. Mathew to Clarendon, 31 October 1854, Bodleian Library, MS Clarendon Dep., C. 14, f. 515. Portions of this and other letters in this chapter are reprinted in R. Van Alstyne, "John F. Crampton: Conspirator or Dupe?" *American Historical Review*, 41 (April 1936): 492–502. Many of the official dispatches are to be found in: *Parliamentary Papers, Accounts and Papers*, vol. 60 (1856), nos. 2080, 2094, and 2108; and in *Senate Executive Documents*, 34th Congress, 1st Session, serial 859 (1855–56), no. 107.

2. Clarendon to Graham, 16 November, and Graham to Clarendon, 17 November 1854, C. 14, ff. 512–13.

3. Clarendon to Crampton, 17 November 1854, C. 130, ff. 442–52; and Crampton to Clarendon, 4 December 1854, C. 25, ff. 357–75.

4. Crampton to Clarendon, 30 December 1854, C. 25, ff. 405–12.

5. Crampton to Clarendon, 15 January 1855, C. 43, ff. 10–21. The "Act to Permit Foreigners to be Enlisted," was pressed on 23 December 1854 as 18 Vict. C. 2.

6. Captain William Francis Lynch (1801–65) was an American naval commander at the Falkland Islands.

7. *New York Herald*, 13 January 1855.

8. Crampton to Clarendon, 22 January 1855, C. 43, ff. 38–39.

9. Crampton to Clarendon, 28 January 1855, C. 43, ff. 46–55.

10. The Collins and Southampton lines were American owned, and competed with the Cunard steamships for the transatlantic service.

11. The *San Franciso* sailed from New York on 22 December 1853 bound for the West Coast. Two days later it was wrecked by a terrible storm. Of the seven hundred troops onboard, one-third lost their lives.

12. For Clarendon to Crampton of 19 January 1855, see C. 131, ff. 322–25; and for Clarendon to Crampton of 16 February 1855, see *Parliamentary Papers*, no. 2080,

vol. 60, (1856), 364. On the same day, Clarendon also dealt with recruitment in a private letter: C. 131, ff. 514–21.

13. Crampton to Clarendon, 4 February 1855, C. 43, ff. 56–57.

14. Crampton had met with an accident that kept him indoors for several days.

15. Crampton to Clarendon, 12 February 1855, C. 43, ff. 61–64.

16. Crampton to Clarendon, 25 February 1855, C. 43, ff. 93–108.

17. Crampton to Clarendon, 6 March 1855, C. 43, ff. 115–17.

18. Crampton to Clarendon, 12 March 1855, C. 43, ff. 119–22. See also note 20 below.

19. Le Marchant wanted more from the Colonial Office than instructions to examine the feasibility of establishing depots and attracting recruits from the United States.

20. Crampton's dispatch 57 of 12 March is in F.O. 5/620, ff. 33–35. Carlisle's opinion comes on ff. 39–41. See also Crampton to Le Marchant, 11 March, ff. 43–46.

21. For further details about the McDonald handbill, see F.O. 5/620, f. 132.

22. Crampton to Clarendon, 26 March 1855, C. 43, ff. 129–34.

23. The best account of Howe's activities is to be found in J. B. Brebner, "Joseph Howe and the Crimean War Enlistment Controversy between Great Britain and the United States," *Canadian Historical Review* 11 (December 1930): 300–327.

24. Crampton's dispatch 75 of 26 March is in F.O. 5/620, ff. 128–30.

25. Crampton to Clarendon, 9 April 1855, C. 43, ff. 163–74.

26. Toward the end of March and beginning of April 1855, indictments against recruiting agents were brought by the district attorneys of New York and Philadelphia.

27. Emanuel C. Perkins and Henry Hertz were indicted by the federal district attorney, James C. Van Dyke, and bound over for trial before Judge John K. Kane of the circuit court in Philadelphia. Hertz was one of Joseph Howe's original agents, whom Howe found difficult to control.

28. Crampton to Clarendon, 23 April 1855, C. 43, ff. 188–93.

29. Gabriel de Korponay sought to raise six hundred Kentucky riflemen, assemble them in Cincinnati, and secure them rail transport to Canada. However, the recuits were few and were apprehended by the local authorities before they could depart. See Brebner, "Joseph Howe," pp. 317, 319. According to Brebner, Korponay was Hungarian, not Polish.

30. Crampton to Clarendon, 2 May 1855, C. 43, ff. 210–16.

31. Howe had returned to Nova Scotia suddenly in order to defend his seat in the provincial legislature. He lost the election, and by then Crampton was thoroughly disillusioned with him. He was determined not to entrust Howe with any further commissions.

32. Crampton to Clarendon, 3 June 1855, C. 43, ff. 293–310. For some details concerning Judge Kane's decision, see Lumley to Clarendon, dispatch 18 of 29 May in F.O. 5/621, ff. 134–35. For Crampton's own description of his conversations in Canada, see Bodleian Library, MS Clarendon Dep., C. 43, ff. 251–58 (9 May), ff. 265–66 (11 May), and ff. 275–80 (20 May). By mid-May the maritime route to Halifax had yielded only 128 recruits.

33. Crampton to Clarendon, 18 June 1855, C. 43, ff. 317–19.

34. The allusion is presumably to General Charles Stephen Gore (1793–1869). The identity of Lieutenant Preston is unknown.

35. Crampton to Clarendon, 2 July 1855, C. 43, ff. 336–41; for Marcy's 9 June 1855 dispatch to Buchanan, see *Senate Executive Document*, no. 35, 34th Congress, 1st Session, serial 819; and for Clarendon's 22 dispatch to Crampton, see also *Parliamentary Papers*, no. 2080, vol. 60, (1856) 374.

36. Crampton to Clarendon, 16 July 1855, C. 43, ff. 377–90; Clarendon's instructions of 22 June were briefly acknowledged on 10 July, C. 43, f. 362.

37. For the type of evidence which the American government compiled against Joseph Smolenski, see *Senate Executive Documents*, no. 107, 34th Congress, 1st Session, pp. 52–56.

38. Moses H. Perley from New Brunswick had been nominated by the Canadians as their commissioner under the provisions of the Reciprocity Treaty of 1854.

39. The Moloch was a Canaanite idol to which children might be sacrificed.

40. For further details of Rowcroft's arrest in Cincinnati, see Crampton to Clarendon, 16 and 30 July 1855, dispatches 140 and 149 in F.O. 5/622, ff. 37–38 and 91–95. Rowcroft was convinced he had been framed by the testimony of Irish extremists who wished to embarrass Great Britain in the eyes of the American people.

41. Crampton to Clarendon, 30 July 1855, C. 43, ff. 398–414. For Marcy to Buchanan, 15 July, and Clarendon to Buchanan, 16 July 1855, see *Parliamentary Papers*, no. 2080, vol. 60, (1856) 478–79 and 378–79.

42. Crampton to Clarendon, 7 August 1855, C. 43, ff. 429–35.

43. Cushing's report of 9 August 1855 is reprinted in *Parliamentary Papers*, no. 2094, vol. 60, (1856) 690–98, and also in Brebner, "Joseph Howe," p. 325. The quotation from Marcy is contained in his dispatch 113 to Buchanan of 1 October 1855 and can be found in F.O. 5/642, ff. 19v–20. For Crampton's scathing comments on Strobel's use of blackmail and deception, see F.O. 5/641, ff. 92–92v; and F.O. 5/642, ff. 136–40. In Brebner, "Joseph Howe," pp. 317–18, we are told that Strobel eventually received two hundred dollars from Cushing for services rendered.

44. Crampton to Clarendon, 4 September 1855, C. 44, ff. 3–6.

45. Crampton's dispatch 183 of 4 September 1855 is in F.O. 5/622, ff. 263–65.

46. Marcy's note of 5 September and Crampton's reply of 7 September 1855 are reprinted in *Parliamentary Papers*, no. 2080, vol. 60, (1856) 384–87.

47. Crampton to Clarendon, 10 September 1855, C. 44, ff. 19–34.

48. In the autumn of 1849 the United States government asked France to recall its envoy, Guillaume Tell Lavallée Poussin. He was thought to have used insulting diplomatic language over a disputed claim to salvage a French vessel in the Gulf of Mexico. Alden A. M. Jackson was Mexican consul at Pensacola during much of the 1840s.

49. Crampton's request to be recalled was not put on file at the Foreign Office but remained among the private papers of Lord Clarendon: C. 44, ff. 52–53.

50. The play, *Venice Preserved*, by Thomas Otway (1652–85) was first performed in London in February 1682. Pierre was one of the conspirators seeking to undermine the power of the Venetian Senate. Contemporary Englishmen would also have detected in the play echoes of the recent agitation of 1678 in Britain, known as the Popish Plot.

51. John S. Lumley was secretary of legation at Washington.

52. Crampton to Clarendon, 18 September 1855, C. 44, ff. 54–57. For the Kentucky election riots, see Crampton to Clarendon, 13 August 1855, dispatch 169, in F.O. 5/622, ff. 205–07.

53. Irish machinations are referred to in note 45 above. Rowcroft followed up his observations with additional information that Crampton enclosed in his dispatch 216 of 15 October, F.O. 5/623, ff. 128–48.

54. Crampton to Clarendon, 24 September 1855, C. 44, ff. 59–70.

55. Crampton to Clarendon, 2 October 1855, C. 44, ff. 82–95.

56. Colonel Henry L. Kinney reached Greytown in mid-July 1855 with a reported band of followers numbering about twenty-five. He was opposed by an even larger

though ill-disciplined group of retainers hired by the Transit Company to protect its interests. In September, Kinney was briefly chosen to be civil and military governor of Greytown, but his support soon melted away. See Crampton to Clarendon, 7 August 1855, dispatch 165, in F.O. 5/622, ff. 183–84; dispatch 170 of 13 August, ff. 208–9; dispatch 203 of 2 October, F.O. 5/623, ff. 83–86.

57. Ouseley was very much to figure in Anglo-American relations by 1857–58. See chap. 7.

58. Crampton to Clarendon, 15 October 1855, C. 44, ff. 185–96.

59. During the course of the Hertz trial in Philadelphia.

60. Crampton's stringent assessment of Cushing's character and motives is remarkably consistent with the more sympathetic biography by Sister M. M. C. Hodgson, *Caleb Cushing: The Attorney General of the United States, 1853–1857* (Washington D.C., 1955), pp. 190–200.

61. Crampton to Clarendon, 3 November 1855, C. 44, ff. 327–38.

62. Crampton to Clarendon, 3 December 1855, C. 44, ff. 481–90.

63. Crampton to Clarendon, 11 December 1855, C. 44, ff. 491–514.

64. The allusion is to a character in Sheridan's *The Rivals*.

65. The convention of the Irish Emigrant Aid Association in New York City during 4–6 December had representatives from throughout the country. The ostensibly secret sessions were covered by the local press. John McClenahan was editor of the *Citizen*. Rumors had it that the Irish in America planned to raise a force of five thousand to march on Canada. See Crampton to Clarendon, 11 December 1855, dispatch 265, in F.O. 5/624, ff. 223–31.

66. Crampton to Clarendon, 17 December 1855, C. 44, ff. 526–34.

67. See Crampton to Clarendon, 17 December 1855, dispatch 271, in F.O. 5/624, ff. 270–74.

68. The Austrian chargé d'affaires was Chevalier Hulsemann; the Prussian minister was Baron Fr. von Gerolt; the Netherlands chargé d'affaires was Jean Corneille Gevers; the Belgian minister was Guillaume Henri Bosch-Spencer; the Swedish chargé was Chevalier George de Sibbern; the French chargé, Gauldree de Boilleau; and the Danish Torben de Bille.

69. Crampton to Clarendon, 24 December 1855 with postscript of 25 December 1855, C. 44, ff. 544–53.

70. Marcy to Buchanan, 28 December 1855, reprinted in *Parliamentary Papers*, no. 2080, vol. 60, (1856) 493–525.

Chapter 6. Expulsion, Transition, and Restoration: Crampton, Lumley, and Napier, 1856–1857

1. Crampton to Clarendon, 13 January 1856, Bodleian Library, MS Clarendon Dep., C. 63, ff. 7–15.

2. The House of Representatives had not yet succeeded in electing a Speaker.

3. Crampton to Clarendon, 27 January 1856, C. 63, ff. 21–28.

4. For further details see Crampton's dispatch 8 of 14 January and no. 17 of 28 January 1856, in F.O. 5/640, ff. 83–87 and 141–44.

5. Crampton to Clarendon, 11 February 1856, C. 63, ff. 59–69.

6. For the speeches of Seward and Foot see *Congressional Globe*, appendix to vol. 25, pp. 75–80 (31 January 1856) and pp. 81–84 (5 February 1856).

7. George M. Dallas, former vice president of the United States under the Polk administration, was appointed to succeed James Buchanan as American minister to the Court of St. James. Buchanan had returned to America to prepare himself for the presidential campaign of 1856.

8. Rowcroft's inability to secure convictions against alleged Irish revolutionaries is covered in Crampton's dispatch 27 of 11 February 1856, in F.O. 5/640, ff. 177–84.

9. Theobald Wolfe Tone (1763–98) was perhaps the most famous revolutionary of the eighteenth century. During the latter stages of the French Revolution, he attempted an invasion of Ireland, was captured, and was condemned to death. Robert Emmett (1778–1803), a member of the United Irishmen, was hanged during the furor accompanying the Napoleonic Wars and the continuing threat of French invasions.

10. Crampton to Clarendon, 3 March 1856, C. 63, ff. 112–27. Marcy's dispatch to Buchanan of 28 December 1855 was reprinted in *Parliamentary Papers*, no. 2080, vol. 60 (1856), 493–525.

11. John S. Lumley was secretary of the British legation at Washington.

12. Crampton to Clarendon, 9 March 1856, C. 63, ff. 149–60.

13. Crampton to Clarendon, 17 March 1856, C. 63, ff. 181–89.

14. For further details concerning such legislation, see Crampton's dispatch 67 of 17 March and no. 69 of 18 March 1856, in F.O. 5/642, ff. 50–52, 61–63.

15. The speeches of Iverson and Brown are to be found in the *Congressional Globe*, vol. 25 (10 March 1856), 623–26; and appendix to vol. 25 (11 March 1856), 234–35, 238–42

16. Crampton to Clarendon, 7 April 1856, C. 63, ff. 202–11.

17. Since the Napoleonic Wars the United States had claimed damages from the French government for "spoliation" of private American shipping and property, but the French government steadfastly refused compensation deemed adequate by President Andrew Jackson.

18. Crampton to Clarendon, 14 April 1856, C. 63, ff. 223–30.

19. Molina was the envoy from Costa Rica in Washington. For further details about the concerted attack against Walker, see Crampton's dispatch 90 of 15 April in F.O. 5/642, ff. 155–73.

20. Crampton to Clarendon, 20 April 1856, C. 63, ff. 234–45.

21. Crampton to Clarendon, 5 May 1856, C. 64, ff. 1–7.

22. For Douglas's speech see Crampton's dispatch 113 of 5 May 1856, in F.O. 5/643, ff. 27–42; *Congressional Globe*, vol. 25 (1 May 1856), 1071–72.

23. Father Augustine Vigil was reputed to be a Nicaraguan Catholic priest.

24. Lord Clarendon's dispatches 85 and 89 of 17–18 April 1856 are in F.O. 5/638, ff. 95–96, 203–4.

25. Crampton to Clarendon, 12 May 1856, C. 64, ff. 17–32.

26. Crampton's dispatch 118 of 12 May is in F.O. 5/643, ff. 90–119.

27. On 16 April 1856 the American ship *Orizaba*, commanded by Captain Edward Tinklepaugh, arrived in Greytown, but before her passengers could disembark, they were scrutinized by Captain Tarleton to determine whether anyone was a recruit for General Walker's army.

28. Crampton to Clarendon, 19 May 1856, C. 64, ff. 97–104.

29. Crampton to Clarendon, 26 May 1856, C. 64, ff. 123–36.

30. Preston Smith Brooks (1819–57) was elected to the U.S. House of Representatives from the state of South Carolina in 1852. A few days before Brooks attacked Sumner, the latter had made a highly critical speech about Brooks's uncle, Senator Andrew Pickens Butler of South Carolina. By way of revenge, Brooks exacted retribution in the chamber of the Senate on 22 May, assisted by Lawrence M. Keitt

(1824–64), a fellow congressman from South Carolina who entered the House of Representatives the same year he had. In the uproar that followed, both Brooks and Keitt resigned their congressional seats but regained them in the next election.

31. Messrs. George B. Mathew, Anthony Barclay, and Charles Rowcroft.

32. C. D. Archibald to Clarendon, 29 August 1856, C. 65, ff. 44–51.

33. Joseph R. Ingersoll of Pennsylvania assumed his duties as American minister to Britain in October 1852, and was replaced by Buchanan the following August.

34. On 17 September 1856, the remnants of the Whig party chose Millard Fillmore to be their Pennsylvania candidate.

35. In fact, a nobleman in the person of Lord Napier was eventually chosen as the next minister to the United States.

36. Grattan to Clarendon, 7 September 1856, C. 65, ff. 52–57.

37. General John W. Geary was acting governor of Kansas and Major General P. F. Smith was commander of United States troops in the territory.

38. Senate Henry Wilson's speech is to be found in the *Congressional Globe*, appendix to vol. 25 (7 August 1856), 1101–3.

39. Grattan to Clarendon, 23 September 1856, C. 65, ff. 63–66.

40. Lumley to Clarendon, 28 September 1856, C. 65, ff. 69–80.

41. For background on the individuals, see the Appendix.

42. Robbles was Mexican minister to the United States. John E. Ward (1814–1902) was active in Georgia state politics, and in 1856 served as president of the Democratic convention at Cincinnati, which nominated Buchanan for the presidency of the United States.

43. John C. Fremont, the "Pathfinder," was the presidential candidate of the newly formed Republican party.

44. For Bartlett's experiment with a pro-British newspaper in North America, see J. J. and P. P. Barnes, "A British Venture into North American Journalism," *Canadian Review of American Studies* 18 (Summer 1987): 197–208.

45. Lumley to Clarendon, 14 October 1856, with an enclosure of a printed memorandum submitted by J. S. Bartlett, C. 65, ff. 96–101.

46. Sir Charles Elliott (1801–75) was chargé d'affaires in Texas from 1842 to 1846. Previous to that, he had attained the rank of captain in the Royal Navy and then served as British agent in China in the years leading up to the Opium War of 1839.

47. Sir Dominick Daly (1798–1868) was appointed lieutenant governor of Prince Edward Island in 1854, was knighted in 1856, and served as governor of South Australia from 1862 until his death. Sir Francis Hincks (1807–85) was premier of Canada during the 1850s and was the first colonial statesman to be made governor of a British colony, namely Barbados, from 1855 to 1862. He was knighted in 1869.

48. Sir Allan Napier McNab (1798–1862) was knighted in 1838 in recognition of his role in helping to put down the revolution of the previous year. He became one of the leading conservative politicians of his day. Sir John Beverley Robinson (1791–1863) became chief justice of Upper Canada in 1829 and was made a baronet in 1854.

49. Lumley to Clarendon, 11 November 1856, C. 65, ff. 115–27.

50. Bunch to Clarendon, 25 September 1856, C: unnumbered dispatch in F.O. 5/649, ff. 93–95.

51. The allusion is to Queen Victoria's week-long visit to Paris in August 1855.

52. The waterfalls of Schaffhausen are on the Rhine River in Switzerland and represent the farthest point of navigation.

53. Lumley to Clarendon, 17 November 1856, C. 65, ff. 141–47.

54. Burrowes Willcocks Arthur Sleigh (1821–69) was born in Montreal and spent

many years in North America, including tours of duty in the colonial military service, 1842–52. This inspired his venture into periodical publication, the *British Army Dispatch*. After selling this, he ran unsuccessfully in several parliamentary elections, and eventually returned to journalism. On 29 June 1855 he began publishing the *Daily Telegraph* in London, which he retained for several years and then sold. It was the first penny daily newspaper to be published in London.

55. See chap. 4 above.

56. Lumley to Clarendon, 24 November 1856, C. 65, ff. 176–85.

57. Lumley to Clarendon, 30 November 1856, C. 65, ff. 204–16.

58. John Addison Thomas (1811–58) was a graduate of West Point and for many years a career army officer. He then took up the practice of law and in November 1855 was appointed an assistant secretary of state. He retained that position until April 1857.

59. Archibald to Clarendon, 5 December 1856, C. 65, ff. 231–34.

60. Lumley to Clarendon, 7 December 1856, C. 65, ff. 239–48.

61. The so-called vigilante committees.

62. Thomas H. Gladstone of Stockwell Lodge, Surrey, had letters to *The Times* published on 11 October, 22 October, 5 November, and 10 November 1856. See the Appendix for further details about Gladstone.

63. The election riots in Baltimore began on 4 November between the Know-Nothings of the Seventh Ward and the Irish of the Eighth Ward. An estimated twenty-five people were killed and a further one hundred wounded. See Lumley's dispatch 105 of 11 November in F.O. 5/646, ff. 153–62.

64. *National Intelligencer*, 4 November 1856.

65. *New York Herald*, 29 July 1856. Philemon T. Herbert had been refused service for breakfast because of the lateness of the hour. A jury eventually acquitted him.

66. *Baltimore Sun*, 18 November 1856.

67. *Washington Star*, 3 December 1856.

68. The Russian secretary of legation was M. Cramer.

69. *Baltimore Sun*, 2 December 1856.

70. These enclosures are not clearly identified on f. 252 of C. 65.

71. Lumley to Clarendon, 7 January 1857, C. 81, ff. 1–10. Lord Clarendon's dispatch 36 of 18 December 1856 is in F.O. 5/639, ff. 223–24.

72. Henry Wheaton (1785–1848) and James Kent (1763–1847) were two of America's leading legal authorities.

73. Lumley to Clarendon, 19 January 1857, C. 81, ff. 26–33.

74. Lumley is alluding to an episode that took place on 16 November 1856, when the American sloop of war *Portsmouth*, under Commander Andrew H. Foote, bombarded the forts guarding Canton. This was in retaliation for the Chinese refusal to guarantee the safety of American citizens in Canton and the Chinese firing upon Foote's launch. In the ensuing days, the remaining Cantonese forts were destroyed by an American landing party, at which point the Chinese authorities agreed to respect the American flag and to restore friendly relations between the two nations. See J. W. Pratt, "Our first 'War' in China," *American Historical Review* 53 (July 1948); 776–86.

75. Chusan is an island near one of the mouths of the Yangtze River.

76. Basic biographical information about Lord Napier may be found in the Appendix. Napier's acceptance of the American ministerial appointment is in a private letter to Lord Clarendon of 24 December 1856, C, 65, ff. 287–88.

77. Napier to Clarendon, 31 March 1857, C. 81, ff. 87–90.

78. Napier to Clarendon, 14 April 1857, C. 81, ff. 108–12.

79. Lewis Cass had become secretary of state under the Buchanan administration.

80. Sir Edward Coke (1552–1634), British legal authority, member of Parliament, chief justice of the Court of Common Pleas (1606), chief justice of the Court of King's Bench (1613).

81. Sydney Smith (1771–1845), English essayist, lecturer, and canon of St. Paul's. The "Noodle Oration" appeared in the *Edinburgh Review* for August 1825. It satirized those who resisted all constitutional reform.

82. Buchanan was born in 1791 and Cass in 1782.

83. Crampton had also dealt with this question of free navigation of the Amazon. See for example his private letter of 8 August 1853 in chap. 3 above.

84. As newly appointed envoy extraordinary and minister plenipotentiary to China, William B. Reed received his instructions on 30 May 1857. His grandfather, Joseph Reed (1741–85), was military secretary to General Washington in 1775 and later adjutant general of the Continental Army.

85. Napier to Clarendon, 20 May 1857, C. 81, ff. 177–78.

86. Napier's dispatch 80 of 20 May is in F.O. 5/671, ff. 181–205.

87. Napier to Clarendon, 8 June 1857, C. 81, ff. 193–96.

88. The marquis de Lafayette and the comte de Rochambeau commanded French troops in North America during the American Revolution.

89. For the American reaction to Lord Clarendon's proposal, see Napier's dispatch 90 or 7 June 1857 in F.O. 5/672, ff. 13–62. John Appleton (1815–64) was appointed assistant secretary of state on 4 April 1857. Previously he had been a United States congressman and, briefly, secretary of Legation in London under Buchanan. He remained at the State Department until 8 June 1860.

90. William Hogarth (1697–1776), painter and engraver, and Tobias Smollett (1721–71), novelist.

91. Napier to Clarendon, 14 June 1857, C. 81, ff. 197–201.

92. Although domestic literary copyright was well established in Britain and America, there was no Anglo-American copyright treaty, and each country could freely pirate the publications of the other.

93. Napier to Clarendon, 19 June 1857, C. 81, ff. 204–5.

94. Napier to Clarendon, 23 June 1857, C. 81, ff. 208–11.

95. Britain claimed that it was eventually prepared to cede the Bay Islands to Honduras.

96. Napier to Clarendon, 29 June 1857, C. 81, ff. 212–13.

97. Napier to Clarendon, 12 July 1857, C. 81, ff. 219–24.

98. Buchanan was a bachelor and so his niece, Harriet Lane, took charge of all official entertaining at the White House.

99. Napier to Clarendon, 18 July 1857, C. 81, ff. 229–30.

100. Between 1846 and 1849 Edward Everett was president of Harvard College.

101. Henry W. Longfellow, the poet, and William H. Prescott, the historian.

102. Napier to Clarendon, 26 July 1857, C. 81, ff. 246–49.

103. The East India Company.

104. Edward Law, first earl Ellenborough (1790–1871), governor-general of India, 1841–44; Sir Charles James Napier (1782–1853), conqueror and governor of Sind, 1843–46; Sir William Francis Patrick Napier (1785–1860), brother of Sir Charles, published several historical works on the conquest and administration of Sind.

Chapter 7. Napier and Ouseley: A Conflict of Personalities, 1857–1859

1. Aberdeen to Clarendon, 25 February 1853, Bodleian Library, MS Clarendon Dep., C. 4, f. 3.

2. Ouseley to Clarendon, 24 November 1857, C. 81, ff. 381–85.

3. The treaty with Nicaragua was signed on 16 November 1857. For Napier's assessment and a copy of it, see dispatch 247 (16 November) in F.O. 5/674, ff. 304–9; and dispatch 260 (24 November) in F.O. 5/675, ff. 64–89.

4. Napier to Clarendon, 30 November 1857, C. 81, ff. 403–8.

5. Napier to Clarendon, 14 December 1857, C. 81, ff. 423–28.

6. Napier's prediction that Kansas would be admitted as a free state came true in 1859.

7. Daniel O'Connell (1775–1847) was the leading Irish politician of the first half of the nineteenth century.

8. Lord Derby (1799–1869) was one of the leading Tories and several times prime minister.

9. James Whiteside (1804–76) was a Conservative member of Parliament, 1851–66, and appointed chief justice of the Court of Queen's Bench, 1866.

10. Jefferson Davis, senator from Mississippi, and Robert Toombs, senator from Georgia.

11. Ouseley to Clarendon, 14 December 1857, C. 81, ff. 419–22.

12. Ouseley to Clarendon, 22 December 1857, C. 81, ff. 429–30.

13. Ouseley to Clarendon, 28 December 1857, C. 81, ff. 438–41.

14. Napier to Clarendon, 5 January 1858, C. 83, ff. 271–75.

15. Ouseley to Clarendon, 9 January 1858, C. 83, ff. 350–53.

16. Napier to Clarendon, 11 January 1858, C. 83, ff. 276–81.

17. Sir Charles L. Wyke (1815–97) was consul general for Central America, 1852; chargé d'affaires in Guatemala, 1854; envoy extraordinary to Central America, 1859; and minister plenipotentiary to Mexico, 1860–61.

18. Ouseley to Clarendon, 12 January 1858, C. 83, ff. 355–56.

19. Henry Peter Brougham (1778–1868), Baron Brougham and Vaux, member of Parliament and lord chancellor.

20. Napier to Clarendon, 19 January 1858, C. 83, ff. 282–84.

21. Ouseley to Clarendon, 19 January 1858, C. 83, ff. 357–60.

22. The Princess Royal was Queen Victoria's eldest daughter, "Vicky," who married Prince Frederick William of Prussia, the future though short-lived Frederick III of Germany.

23. In the wings of a theater.

24. Ouseley to Clarendon, 20 January 1858, C. 83, ff. 363–66. Walker carried on his filibustering activities until he was executed by the Honduras government in 1860.

25. Ouseley to Clarendon, 22 January 1858, C. 83, ff. 367–69.

26. Thomas Carlyle (1795–1881), British essayist and historian.

27. Ouseley to Clarendon, 23 January 1858, C. 83, ff. 371–74.

28. General Winfield Scott.

29. Ouseley's dispatch 14 of 25 January 1858 is in F.O. 15/98, ff. 36–39.

30. It was opened in 1869.

31. Greek for the "great or important people."

32. Napier to Clarendon, 25 January 1858, C. 83, ff. 295–98.

33. The British and French claimed that Mexico should indemnify these nations for wrongs committed against them, but successive Mexican governments refused to acknowledge these debts.

34. Napier to Clarendon, 2 February 1858, C. 83, ff. 300–304.

35. Napier to Clarendon, 9 February 1858, C. 83, ff. 307–12.

36. Lawrence M. Keitt (1824–64) of South Carolina and Galusha A. Grow (1822–1907) of Pennsylvania were well known for their political antipathy to one another and their readiness for brawling. For additional background on Keitt, see note 30 of chap. 6.

37. Ouseley to Clarendon, 15 February 1858, C. 83, ff. 385–88.

38. Napier to Clarendon, 15 February 1858, C. 83, ff. 313–16.

39. Napier to Clarendon, 22 February 1858, C. 83, ff. 317–21

40. Napier to Clarendon, 2 March 1858, C. 83, ff. 322–26.

41. Napier to Clarendon, 8 March 1858, C. 83, ff. 327–31.

42. For background on Judah P. Benjamin see the Appendix.

43. William Hope was attached to the British legation in Washington from 14 September 1857 to 21 January 1859.

44. See the Appendix for further details.

45. Ibid.

46. Felice Orsini (1819–58) was executed by the French authorities on 13 March 1858.

47. Napier to Malmesbury, 16 March 1858, C. 83, ff. 333–35; and Ouseley to Malmesbury, 16 March 1858, Malmesbury Papers, volume marked "N. and S. America, 1858," f. 8, in the possession of the earl of Malmesbury.

48. Napier to Malmesbury, 22 March 1858, f. 10.

49. Ouseley to Malmesbury, 22 March 1858, f. 11.

50. While living in England, Orsini had procured the bomb that he eventually threw at the emperor, thus giving rise to bitter French resentment against the permissive British attitude toward political exiles.

51. Ouseley to Clarendon, 30 March 1858, C. 83, ff. 402–3.

52. Napier to Malmesbury, 30 March 1858, volume marked "N. and S. America, 1858," f. 15.

53. See the Appendix.

54. Napier to Malmesbury, 5 April 1858, f. 18.

55. Ouseley to Malmesbury, 12 April 1858, f. 20.

56. Napier to Malmesbury, 13 April 1858, f. 19.

57. Napier to Malmesbury, 3 May 1858, f. 36.

58. Napier to Malmesbury, 31 May 1858, f. 41.

59. The allusions to embarrassments refer to the aftermath of the mutiny in India and the Orsini Affair in France.

60. Napier to Malmesbury, 8 June 1858, f. 52.

61. Ouseley to Malmesbury, 6 July 1858, f. 71

62. John Arthur Roebuck (1801–79) was a barrister and member of Parliament.

63. Ouseley to Malmesbury, 27 July 1858; filed out of order in the Malmesbury papers in the volume for 1859, "N. and S. America," f. 20.

64. Derby to Malmesbury, 20 August 1858, in volume of Malmesbury Papers marked "Private Correspondence, Lord Derby, etc.," 1858–59, no pagination.

65. Napier to Malmesbury, 20 September 1858, volume for "N. and S. America, 1858," f. 112.

66. See the Appendix for further details.

67. Ibid.

68. Ibid.

69. Ouseley to Malmesbury, 5 September 1858, f. 113.

70. Charles Frederick Henningsen (1815–77) was a British subject who during the 1830s and 1840s was a kind of soldier of fortune in Spain, Russia, and Hungary. When the Hungarian revolutionary exile Kossuth visited America in 1851–52, Henningsen served as private secretary. Thereafter he took up residence in the United States, married a Southerner, and became a champion of Southern rights. In 1856–57 he supported William Walker's regime in Nicaragua. The American Civil War found him serving in the Confederate Army.

71. Ouseley to Malmesbury, 26 September 1858, f. 114.

72. Ouseley to Malmesbury, 11 October 1858, f. 123.

73. Derby to Malmesbury, 11 October 1858, in volume marked "Private Correspondence, Lord Derby, etc." 1858–59, no pagination.

74. Napier to Malmesbury, 26 October 1858, volume for "N. and S. America, 1858," f. 141.

75. John Arthur Douglas Bloomfield, second baron Bloomfield (1802–79), was appointed minister plenipotentiary to Berlin in 1851.

76. Erminia Frezzolini (1818–84) was an Italian operatic soprano who toured America in 1857–58. Maurice Strakosch (1825–87) was a musician and impresario in New York City from 1848 to 1860. Henri Francois Joseph Vieuxtemps (1820–81) and Sigismund Thalberg (1812–71).

77. Napier to Malmesbury, 9 November 1858, f. 143.

78. Napier to Malmesbury, 15 November 1858, f. 145.

79. Napier's dispatch 265 of 14 November is in F.O. 5/694, ff. 237–82.

80. Lyons to Malmesbury, 15 and 22 November 1858, ff. 146, 149.

81. Napier to Malmesbury, 13 December 1858, f. 160.

82. David Teniers (1582–1649) and David Teniers (1610–90) were Flemish painters.

83. Charles Hope, Lord Granton (1763–1851), became lord justice clerk in 1804. His father was John Hope (1739–85). William Pitt "the Younger" (1759–1806) was prime minister, 1783–1801 and 1804–6. William Dundas (1762–1845) was a member of Parliament and secretary-at-war, 1804–6.

84. Napier to Malmesbury, 4 January 1859, volume marked" N. and S. America, 1859, f. 8.

85. Napier is presumably alluding to dispatch 6 of 8 January 1859, F.O. 5/711, ff. 17–20.

86. Loftus Charles Otway was secretary of legation at Madrid in the 1850s prior to his appointment on 19 February 1858 as minister plenipotentiary to the Mexican Republic.

87. During the latter 1850s a state of virtual civil war existed in Mexico, with conservative proclerical elements seeking to defend themselves against the nominally progressive and anticlerical forces of Benito Pablo Juarez (1806–72). In 1855 he became minister of justice and in 1857 minister of the interior. Soon thereafter he declared himself provisional president, a position that he successfully maintained throughout much of Mexico during the next few years. See also note 91 below.

88. Napier to Malmesbury, 10 January 1859, f. 11.

89. Commodore Charles Wise (1810–77) was in command of the British West African squadron from June 1857 to August 1859.

90. The Webster-Ashburton Treaty to 1842.

91. Felix Zuloaga (1814–76) supported the Comonfort administration, 1855–57, but then acquired power for himself in Mexico City and proclaimed that he was president, January 1858. At this time Juarez was unable to exercise control over Mexico City.

92. Ouseley to Malmesbury, 8 January 1859, f. 29.

93. Napier to Malmesbury, 21 February 1859, f. 34.

94. Napier to Malmesbury, 18 April 1859, f. 57.

95. Ouseley to Malmesbury, 22 May 1859, f. 70.

96. Ouseley to Malmesbury, 24 May 1859, f. 73.

97. Edward Ellice (1781–1863) was a former member of Parliament and Hudson's Bay Company director. Richard Cobden and John Bright were two of the best-known British parliamentarians of the mid–nineteenth century.

98. Thomas Milner-Gibson (1806–84) was a member of Parliament.

Chapter 8. Lord Lyons and the Buchanan Administration, 1859–1860

1. Lyons to Malmesbury, 12 April 1859, f. 56, in volume marked "N. and S. America, 1859" in the possession of the earl of Malmesbury.

2. The Ouseley treaty of commerce with Nicaragua was signed on 18 January 1859. See F.O. 5/708, dispatch 8 from Malmesbury to Lyons, 31 March 1859.

3. Frederick Richard Warre received his appointment to Washington on 13 December 1858.

4. Lyons to Malmesbury, 18 April 1859, f. 58.

5. Lyons's dispatch 13 of 18 April 1859 is in F.O. 5/713, ff. 15–20.

6. Lyons to Malmesbury, 24 May 1859, f. 72.

7. Lord Napier had been mildly reprimanded by Lord Malmesbury for his illegible dispatches.

8. Lyons to Malmesbury, 21 June 1859, f. 98.

9. Edmund John Monson had been transferred from Paris to Washington at the end of 1858 and became Lord Lyons's private secretary in June 1859.

10. William Douglas Irvine was appointed secretary of legation at Washington on 24 December 1858.

11. Lyons to Russell, 11 July 1859. Lord John Russell's private papers are deposited in the Public Record Office. This letter can be found in P.R.O. 30/22/34, ff. 1–4.

12. Lyons's dispatch 100 of 5 July is in F.O. 5/714, ff. 150–57.

13. Lyons to Russell, 19 July 1859, P.R.O. 30/22/34, ff. 6–12.

14. Lyons's dispatch 112, confidential, of 19 July is in F.O. 5/714, ff. 197–212.

15. Lyons to Russell, 22 August 1859, P.R.O. 30/22/34, f. 21.

16. Lyons to Russell, 11 October 1859, P.R.O. 30/22/34, ff. 29–32.

17. Lyons to Russell, 25 October 1859, P.R.O. 30/22/34, ff. 38–41.

18. Lyons to Russell, 8 November 1859, P.R.O. 30/22/34, ff. 42–44.

19. Russell's dispatch 26 of 4 August is in F.O. 5/710, ff. 3–6.

20. Concerning the deputy collector of customs, see Lyons's dispatch 252 of 8 November in F.O. 5/716, ff. 224–42.

21. Lyons to Russell, 22 November 1859, P.R.O. 30/22/34, ff. 49–50.

22. Lyons to Russell, 22 November 1859, P.R.O. 30/22/34, ff. 52–57.

23. Lyons to Russell, 28 November 1859, P.R.O. 30/22/34, ff. 58–61.

24. Robert M. McLane (1815–98) was active in Maryland state politics, a member of the United States Congress, 1847–51, American commissioner to China, 1853–54, and minister to the Juarez government at Vera Cruz, 1859.

25. Lyons to Russell, 6 December 1859, P.R.O. 30/22/34, ff. 62–67.

26. Lyons's dispatch 279 of 6 December is in F.O. 5/716, ff. 348–49.

27. Lyons to Russell, 12 December 1859, P.R.O. 30/22/34, ff. 68–72.

28. Lyons to Russell, 20 December 1859, P.R.O. 30/22/34, ff. 74–75.

29. Lyons to Russell, 26 December 1859, P.R.O. 30/22/34, ff. 77–86.

30. In 1849 the French had sent troops to Rome to defeat the Republic established by Mazzini and Garibaldi and to restore the pope. Although the troops were withdrawn temporarily during the 1860s, the disturbed international situation induced Napoleon III to send them back again. There they remained until France had sudden need of them in 1870, during the Franco-Prussian War. The five years to which Lyons alludes were 1853–58.

31. Lyons to Russell, 3 January 1860, P.R.O. 30/22/34, ff. 90–95.

32. For Buchanan's message to Congress delivered on December 19, 1859, see Richardson, *Messages and Papers of the Presidents*, 5:552–576.

33. Wyke, the British minister to Central America, had concluded a treaty with Honduras in November 1859 which Lyons communicated to Cass in December. See Lyons's dispatch 302 of 26 December in F.O. 5/716, ff. 445–49.

34. In the autumn of 1859 it looked as though General William S. Harney (1800–1889) would refuse to withdraw his troops from the island of San Juan. Buchanan therefore sent a senior general, Winfield Scott, to supercede Harney, thus defusing the situation pending its diplomatic resolution.

35. Lyons to Russell, 23 January 1860, P.R.O. 30/22/34, ff. 99–101.

36. Lyons to Russell, 6 February, 1860, P.R.O. 30/22/34, ff. 103–15.

37. Lyons to Russell, 5 March 1860, P.R.O. 30/22/34, ff. 117–19.

38. Mure's dispatch 5 of 16 February is in F.O. 5/744, ff. 15–20. Mure succeeded in persuading the chief of police in New Orleans to allow blacks to remain aboard ship to avoid being jailed while their ships were in port.

39. Lyons to Russell, 2 April 1860, P.R.O. 30/22/34, ff. 121–25.

40. Following a skirmish off the coast of Vera Cruz on 6 March 1860, the American ships captured two of the Mexican steamers. In retaliation, the Miramón regime in Mexico City threatened to seize property belonging to American citizens in the capital. See Lyons's dispatch 122 of 2 April 1860 in F.O. 5/736, ff. 65–71; and dispatches 159 and 160 of 23 April in F.O. 5/736, ff. 316–99, 400–433.

41. Lyons to Russell, 10 April 1860, P.R.O. 30/22/34, ff. 126–29.

42. Lyons's dispatch 8 has been removed from F.O. 5/734.

43. Lyons to Russell, 10 April 1860, P.R.O. 30/22/34, ff. 130–33.

44. Lyons to Russell, 30 April 1860, P.R.O. 30/22/34, ff. 135–36.

45. Although nominally outlawed, prizefighting attracted great interest in England throughout the nineteenth century. During the 1850s the acknowledged British champion was Tom Sayers (1826–65), whose unofficial title was challenged by John C. Heenan (1835–73), an American called "Benicia Boy." Their fight in 1860 was stopped before either had a clear victory and was declared a draw, and each was granted recognition as a world champion.

46. Lyons to Russell, 8 May 1860, P.R.O. 30/22/34, ff. 138–41.

47. Bunch's dispatch on the Charleston convention is missing from both the consular reports and Lyons's dispatches.

48. Lyons to Russell, 22 May 1860, P.R.O. 30/22/34, ff. 149–50.

49. Lyons to Russell, 19 June 1860, P.R.O. 30/22/34, ff. 167–70.

50. Lyons to Russell, 23 July 1860, P.R.O. 30/22/34, ff. 183–90.

51. John Bell (1797–1869) had formerly been a United States Senator from Tennessee and was the nominee of the Constitutional Union party.

52. Joseph Lane (1801–81) was governor of the Oregon Territory, 1849–50, represented the territory in Congress, 1851–59, and served in the United States Senate, 1859–61.

53. Lyons to Russell, 22 October 1860, P.R.O. 30/22/34, ff. 204–09.

54. Lyons to Russell, 12 November 1860, P.R.O. 30/22/34, ff. 218–21.

55. Lyons to Russell, 25 November 1860, P.R.O. 30/22/34, ff. 229–34.

56. William Shaw Lindsay (1816–77) was founder of the large shipping firm of W. S. Lindsay and Co.; member of Parliament, 1854–65; and author of *History of Merchant Shipping and Commerce* (London, 1874–76).

Chapter 9. Prelude to Civil War, 1861

1. Lyons to Russell, 7 January 1861, P.R.O. 30/22/35, ff. 1–4.

2. Jeremiah Sullivan Black (1810–83) had been attorney general during the Buchanan administration.

3. Lyons to Russell, 4 February 1861, P.R.O. 30/22/35, ff. 12–15.

4. Lyons's dispatch 40 of 4 February is in F.O. 5/760, ff. 28–35.

5. Lyons to Russell, 12 February 1861, P.R.O. 30/22/35, ff. 16–19.

6. Henry Pelham Fiennes Pelham Clinton, fifth duke of Newcastle (1811–64), was colonial secretary from 1859 to his death.

7. Many observers, including Lyons, assumed that when Lincoln took office in

March 1861 Seward would dominate the administration and become a kind of prime minister because it was thought that Lincoln was too inexperienced and weak to assert himself as chief executive.

8. Lyons to Russell, 26 March 1861, P.R.O. 30/22/35, ff. 24–35.

9. Lyons to Russell, 29 March 1861, P.R.O. 30/22/35, ff. 36–37.

10. Lyons to Russell, 1 April 1861, P.R.O. 30/22/35, ff. 38–40.

11. Lyons's dispatch 129 of 1 April is in F.O. 5/762, ff. 197–208. However, the dispatch in question is no. 125, confidential.

12. Lyons to Russell, 12 April 1861, P.R.O. 30/22/35, ff. 47–49.

13. Tennessee, West Virginia, Kentucky, and Arkansas were still uncommitted.

14. The city of Washington was peculiarly vulnerable to potential Southern attack because it closely bordered on the state of Virginia.

15. Lyons to Russell, 15 April 1861, P.R.O. 30/22/35, ff. 50–54.

16. Lyons to Russell, 23 April 1861, P.R.O. 30/22/35, ff. 55–58.

17. Robert E. Lee was the most important of these Virginia officers.

18. Lyons to Russell, 27 April 1861, P.R.O. 30/22/35, ff. 59–64.

19. The Conference of Paris in 1856 formulated rules governing the use of blockades and the rights of neutrals during time of war, but the United States had not signed this convention.

20. Edward Mortimer Archibald was British consul at New York.

21. Admiral Alexander Milne (1806–96) was the commander of the West Indian and North American squadrons of the British Navy.

22. Lyons to Russell, 14 June 1861, P.R.O. 30/22/35, ff. 109–17.

23. Russell's reply to Sir John Ramsden in the House of Commons comes in *Parliamentary Debates*, vol. 162 (2 May 1861), 1378–79.

24. Lyons to Russell, 18 June 1861, P.R.O. 30/22/35, ff. 119–24.

25. William Lewis Dayton (1807–64) was a candidate for vice president in 1856 and the American minister to France from 1861 until his death.

26. A special session of Congress was called to deal with this emergency.

27. General Winfield Scott assumed the duties of commander-in-chief of the Union Army when he was in his midseventies, but military reverses led to his resignation in August 1861.

28. Lyons to Russell, 24 June 1861, P.R.O. 30/22/35, ff. 131–40.

29. Lyons's dispatch 209 of 23 May is in F.O. 5/764, ff. 76–83. Charles Sumner, chairman of the Senate Foreign Relations Committee, was the person who informed Lyons of Seward's instruction to Adams and the way in which Lincoln had softened the strident tone used by the American secretary of state. While not requiring Seward to alter his words, Lincoln insisted that his diapatches not be "read or shown to the British Secretary of State." For a recent account of this episode and Seward's instructions of 21 May 1861 to Adams, see Brain Jenkins, *Britain and the War for the Union*, vol. 1 (Montreal, 1974), p. 104.

30. The Reciprocity Treaty of 1854 reduced tariffs between Canada and the United States.

31. Lyons's dispatch 282 of 17 June is in F.O. 5/766, ff. 124–38.

32. Lyons to Russell, 2 July 1861, P.R.O. 30/22/35, ff. 141–49.

33. Lyons to Russell, 16 July 1861, P.R.O. 30/22/35, ff. 155–56.

34. Lyons to Russell, 19 July 1861, P.R.O. 30/22/35, f. 157.

35. This battle took place at Manassas Junction, Virginia, and was called the First Battle of Bull Run.

36. Lyons to Russell, 20 July 1861, P.R.O. 30/22/35, ff. 161–70.

37. Seward was raising the spectre of war in the event that the Northern blockade of Southern ports was ignored by one or more European powers.

38. Lyons to Russell, 22 July 1861, P.R.O. 30/22/35, ff. 171–72. Jackson's stand at this battle earned him the nickname "Stonewall."

Chapter 10. The *Trent* Affair

1. Lyons to Russell, 30 July 1861, Russell Papers, P.R.O. 30/22/35, ff. 176–77.
2. Lyons to Russell, 2 August 1861, P.R.O. 30/22/35, ff. 178–83.
3. Lyons to Russell, 2 August 1861, P.R.O. 30/22/35, ff. 185–86.
4. Lyons to Russell, 5 August 1861, P.R.O. 30/22/35, ff. 187–89.
5. Lyons to Russell, 13 August 1861, P.R.O. 30/22/35, ff. 191–94.
6. The secretary of the treasury was Salmon P. Chase (1808–73).
7. Prince Napoleon was the cousin of Napoleon III.
8. Charles James Faulkner of Virginia became United States minister to France in February 1860 but requested to be relieved of his position as the Civil War became inevitable. His request was not granted, however, and he was kept in Paris until May 1861. Upon arriving in the United States, he was arrested and charged with treason.
9. George Brinton McClellan (1826–85) was a West Point graduate who was commissioned a major general at the beginning of the Civil War. Following the North's defeat at Bull Run, he was given the task of reorganizing the Union Army and providing for the defense of Washington.
10. Lyons to Russell, 16 August 1861, P.R.O. 30/22/35, ff. 195–98.
11. Nathaniel Lyon (1818–61) was commander of the United States troops at St. Louis, Missouri. At the battle of Wilson's Creek, Lyon forced his way out of a Confederate encirclement, but only by sacrificing large numbers of Union soldiers. After the battle, that portion of the state south of the Missouri River remained in the hands of the Confederacy.
12. Fremont was General Lyon's commanding officer in his capacity of commander of the Department of the West, which had its headquarters at St. Louis.
13. Admiral Alexander Milne (1806–96) commanded the West Indian and North American squadrons of the British Navy, and each time the Palmerston government felt that the North was becoming too hostile to Britain, it reinforced Milne's squadrons or increased the number of British troops stationed in Canada.
14. Lyons to Russell, 23 August 1861, P.R.O. 30/22/35, ff. 199–205.
15. Major General Nathaniel Prentiss Banks (1816–94) was governor of Massachusetts for three years before the outbreak of the Civil War.
16. Lyons to Russell, 27 August 1861, P.R.O. 30/22/35, ff. 207–10.
17. Lyons to Russell, 30 August 1861, P.R.O. 30/22/35, ff. 211–16.
18. Lyons to Russell, 6 September 1861, P.R.O. 30/22/35, ff. 229–40.
19. Lyons to Russell, 30 September 1861, P.R.O. 30/22/35, ff. 260–61.
20. Lyons to Russell, 4 October 1861, P.R.O. 30/22/35, ff. 263–78.
21. Lyons to Russell, 14 October 1861, P.R.O. 30/22/35, ff. 279–90.
22. Lyons to Russell, 28 October 1861, P.R.O. 30/22/35, ff. 301–6.
23. In fact, Bunch was ultimately allowed to stay on at Charleston, South Carolina.
24. Lyons to Russell, 19 November 1861, P.R.O. 30/22/35, ff. 315–16.
25. Lyons to Russell, 22 November 1861, P.R.O. 30/22/35, ff. 327–23.
26. When in the autumn of 1861 the Juarez regime declared its intention to suspend

interest payments on government bonds, the reaction among European bondholders was swift and decisive. In the London convention of 31 October, Britain, France, and Spain agreed to occupy certain Mexican ports in order to collect customs revenues until the Mexican government resumed its debt obligations. The three powers disclaimed any wish to acquire territory or interfere in the internal affairs of Mexico.

27. Fort Beaufort was one of a number of Confederate outposts along the coast of North and South Carolina. Its capture by daring though ill-organized Union raids was one of the few successes in an otherwise gloomy Northern military record.

28. The Morrill Tariff, named after Congressman Justin Smith Morrill (1810–98) was passed in 1861 and symbolized the Republican party's policy of protectionism.

29. Lyons to Russell, 25 November 1861, P.R.O. 30/22/35, ff. 326–28.

30. Lyons to Russell, 29 November 1861, P.R.O. 30/22/35, ff. 330–34.

31. In fact, that is exactly what Lincoln did.

32. Donald McNeill Fairfax (1821–94).

33. Lyons to Russell, 6 December 1861, P.R.O. 30/22/35, ff. 340–43.

34. Alexander Tilloch Galt (1817–93) was the Canadian inspector general. When he arrived in Washington in early December he was greatly perturbed by the inadequacy of Canadian military defenses in the event of a threat from the United States.

35. Lyons to Russell, 19 December 1861, P.R.O. 30/22/35, ff. 347–50.

36. Edouard Antoine Thouvenel was French foreign minister under Napoleon III.

37. Lyons to Russell, 23 December 1861 P.R.O. 30/22/35, ff. 359–68.

38. Lyons to Russell, 31 December 1861, P.R.O. 30/22/35, ff. 381–86.

39. "Prisoners" refers to Mason and Slidell.

Chapter 11. Decisive Victory Eludes the North, January– June 1862

1. Lyons to Russell, 11 January 1862, Russell papers, P.R.O. 30/22/36, ff. 5–10.

2. Ambrose Edward Burnside (1824–81) was a graduate of West Point and was commissioned a brigadier general at the beginning of the Civil War.

3. The Revolutionary party refers to a group of Radical Republicans led by Senators Benjamin F. Wade (Ohio, 1800–1878), and Zachariah Chandler (Michigan, 1813–79), and Representative Thaddeus Stevens (Pennsylvania, 1792–1868).

4. Congress, dominated by Radical Republicans, appointed a Joint Committee on the Conduct of the War because it resented that Lincoln and Seward often dictated policy without consulting Congress.

5. Lyons to Russell, 20 January 1862, P.R.O. 30/22/36, ff. 11–18.

6. The capital of the Confederacy was moved from Montgomery, Alabama, to Richmond, Virginia, in June 1861. The initial strategy of each side was to surround and lay siege to the other's capital.

7. Port Royal at Annapolis, Maryland, had been captured by the North in November 1861.

8. Some regarded emancipation as an effective way to disrupt the Southern economy. Freeing slaves was used as a threat in several edicts. Lincoln signed the first Confiscation Act on 6 August, 1861, freeing slaves employed or used by Confederates in arms or labor against the United States. On 30 August 1861, Major General John Charles Fremont personally extended this in Missouri, where he also declared martial law. The Second Confiscation Act was passed on 17 July 1862, and included a provision for

sending "persons of the African race" to colonize "some tropical country beyond the limits of the United States," as well as a clause giving representatives of the Union the right to "employ" freed blacks to help in suppressing the rebellion.

9. Contre-Admiral Aime-Felix-Saint-Elme Reynaud was French commander-in-chief of the Naval Division of the Gulf and North America.

10. Lyons to Russell, 28 January 1862, P.R.O. 30/22/36, ff. 19–22.

11. George H. Thomas (1816–70) was a Virginian who graduated from West Point but chose to side with the North. He was appointed a brigadier general at the outset of the war.

12. The victory at Mill Spring enabled General Ulysses S. Grant to advance upon the Mississippi, Cumberland, and Tennessee rivers.

13. William T. Sherman (1820–91) was a West Point graduate from Ohio who was commander of the Department of the Cumberland in November 1861 when Port Royal was captured. Soon thereafter he had a nervous breakdown and was replaced by Don Carlos Buell.

14. This is an allusion to a commercial treaty of 1854 between Canada and the United States, which was due to expire after ten years.

15. Lyons to Russell, 7 February 1862, P.R.O. 30/22/36, ff. 35–40.

16. Lyons to Russell, 11 February 1862, P.R.O. 30/22/36, ff. 41–42.

17. Fort Henry, on the Tennessee River, surrendered to the federal forces on 6 February 1862. On 8 February, federal troops under General Burnside defeated the Confederate garrison on Roanoke Island, off the coast of North Carolina.

18. Lyons to Russell, 21 February 1862, P.R.O. 30/22/36, ff. 47–50.

19. Lyons's dispatch 118 of 17 February 1862 is in F.O. 5/825, ff. 108–19.

20. Edwin M. Stanton (1814–69) was a lawyer from Ohio who held the post of United States attorney general from 1860 to 1861, and secretary of war from 1862 to 1868.

21. Lyons to Russell, 31 March 1862, P.R.O. 30/22/36, ff. 58–62. The Mutual Search Treaty was approved by the Senate in executive session in April.

22. A Confederate battery on Island No. 10 impeded the advance of federal troops southward toward New Madrid, Missouri. However, by 14 March 1862 the Northern Army had captured New Madrid. David Glasgow Farragut was the commander of the West Gulf Blockading Squadron, which had orders to open the Mississippi River and attack New Orleans. In recognition of his victory over the Confederate fleet in April, he was commissioned a rear admiral.

23. Lyons's dispatch 132 of 21 February 1862 and dispatch 177 of 10 March are in F.O. 5/825, ff. 243–51 and F.O. 5/826, ff. 140–50.

24. Lyons to Russell, 8 April 1862, P.R.O. 30/22/36, ff. 63–67. McClellan preferred an advance by way of the peninsula between the James and York rivers, whereas Lincoln had advocated a front assault on Richmond from Washington.

25. The Battle of Shiloh took place 6–7 April, and news of its outcome was anxiously being awaited.

26. John Pope (1822–92) was a graduate of West Point and was commissioned a brigadier general at the beginning of the Civil War. He assumed command of the Army of the Mississippi in February 1862.

27. Lyons to Russell, 25 April 1862, P.R.O. 30/22/36, ff. 74–84.

28. Pittsburg Landing was south of Savannah, Tennessee, where General Grant had his headquarters. It was the site of Battle of Shiloh.

29. The U.S.S. *Merrimac* became the first Confederate "ironclad" ship by virtue of being in port at Norfolk at the outbreak of the war. It was subsequently commissioned the C.S.S. *Virginia* by the South and destroyed several Union frigates before being routed by the U.S.S. *Monitor* in a five-hour battle on the James River in March 1862.

When Norfolk fell on 10 May, the Confederates burned her to keep her from falling into Union hands.

30. Fort Jackson and Fort St. Phillip guarded the mouth of the Mississippi River and access to the port of New Orleans.

31. Lyons to Russell, 2 May 1862, P.R.O. 30/22/36, ff. 85–86.

32. Lyons to Russell, 6 May 1862, P.R.O. 30/22/36, ff. 87–90.

33. Lyons accompanied the Prince of Wales during the summer of 1860.

34. Lyons to Russell, 16 May 1862, P.R.O. 30/22/36, ff. 91–94.

35. When it became apparent that France intended to do more in Mexico than merely send a punitive expedition to collect bad debts, Britain withdrew its support.

36. Reference here is probably being made to the anticipated end of the Peninsula campaign.

37. Lyons to Russell, 23 May 1862, P.R.O. 30/22/36, ff. 95–99.

38. George Coppell was acting British consul at New Orleans from September 1861 to February 1865.

39. John Vincent Crawford was acting British consul general at Havana.

40. Lyons to Russell, 6 June 1862, P.R.O. 30/22/36, ff. 102–7.

41. Henry W. Halleck (1815–72) was appointed a major general in 1861 and succeeded General Fremont as commander of the Department of Missouri that November.

42. Lyons to Russell, 9 June 1862, P.R.O. 30/22/36, ff. 116–18.

43. Lyons to Russell, 13 June 1862, P.R.O. 30/22/36, ff. 119–20.

Chapter 12. William Stuart and the Interventionist Crisis, June–November 1862

1. Stuart to Russell, 23 June 1862, Russell Papers, P.R.O. 30/22/36, ff. 121–26.

2. Stuart to Russell, 1 July 1862, P.R.O. 30/22/36, ff. 136–38.

3. Thomas J. ("Stonewall") Jackson (1824–63) had already distinguished himself in the Shenandoah Campaign of 1862.

4. Stuart to Russell, 4 July 1862, P.R.O. 30/22/36, ff. 139–42.

5. At the conclusion of the Battle of Seven Pines, 31 May–1 June, (Fair Oaks, Virginia), Robert E. Lee was given command of the Army of Virginia.

6. On 26 June Lee attacked McClellan's right flank at Mechanicsville, Virginia.

7. Frank Vizetelly (1830–83) was an artist who edited *Le Monde Illustre* in Paris from 1857 to 1859, afterward serving until his death as a war correspondent for the *Illustrated London News*.

8. Stuart to Russell, 7 July 1862, P.R.O. 30/22/36, ff. 143–45.

9. Stuart to Russell, 15 July 1862, P.R.O. 30/22/36, ff. 149–54.

10. A second Confiscation Act was reluctantly approved by Lincoln on 17 July 1862. It paved the way for the federal government to confiscate the property of Confederate officeholders and others in rebellion. Any slaves who successfully ran away and came under federal jurisdiction would be guaranteed their freedom.

11. Benjamin F. Butler (1818–93) took part in the capture of New Orleans, and for six months thereafter was military governor of that port. His exercise of authority there was highly controversial and drew complaints from both Northerners and Southerners.

12. Stuart to Russell, 21 July 1862, P.R.O. 30/22/36, ff. 155–57.

13. Stuart to Russell, 29 July 1862, P.R.O. 30/22/36, ff. 158–61.

14. General George F. Shepley (1819–78) became military governor of Louisiana in June 1862. Two years later he became commander of the East Virginia Military District, and by war's end was military governor of Richmond.

15. See note 11 above.

16. Stuart to Russell, 12 August 1862, P.R.O. 30/22/36, ff. 170–74.

17. Henry Percy Anderson was a B.A. from Christ Church College, Oxford, who became a clerk in the Foreign Office in 1854. He was second secretary of the British legation in Washington from August 1861 until the autumn of 1863.

18. Stuart to Russell, 22 August 1862, P.R.O. 30/22/36, ff. 179–81.

19. Gebhard Leberecht von Bluecher (1742–1819) was generally credited with arriving at the Battle of Waterloo just in time to turn the tide against Napoleon.

20. While at a meeting of the cabinet on 22 July, Lincoln unexpectedly broached the subject of freeing all slaves throughout the South. Among others, Seward advocated postponing such a decision, which Lincoln did, awaiting what he and others regarded as a more propitious moment. Thurlow Weed (1797–1882) was a leading New York politician and a major figure in the Whig party during the 1840s. In the 1850s he became a strong supporter of the Republicans, and Lincoln held him in high regard throughout the Civil War.

21. Cassius Marcellus Clay (1810–1903) had earned a reputation for strong abolitionist feeling prior to the War. During 1861–62 he served as American minister to Russia, a post that he resumed from 1863 to 1869.

22. Stuart to Russell, 1 September 1862, P.R.O. 30/22/36, ff. 187–91.

23. Stuart to Russell, 9 September 1862, P.R.O. 30/22/36, ff. 196–202.

24. Stuart to Russell, 15 September 1862, P.R.O. 30/22/36, ff. 202–7.

25. Pierre Gustave Toutant Beauregard (1818–93) was a native of Louisiana, a graduate of West Point, and commander of the batteries that fired on Fort Sumter in April 1861.

26. Samuel R. Curtis (1805–66) was for many years an army engineer and later became a politician in Iowa. In August 1861 he was appointed brigadier general and was one of the commanders at the successful battle of Pea Ridge, Arkansas, in March 1862. Later that year he was promoted to major general and put in charge of the Department of the Missouri, but Lincoln relieved him of this command following persistent quarreling with its governor.

27. Stuart to Russell, 19 September 1862, P.R.O. 30/22/36, ff. 208–11.

28. Stuart to Russell, 23 September 1862, P.R.O. 30/22/36, ff. 212–18.

29. Stuart to Russell, 26 September 1862, P.R.O. 30/22/36, ff. 219–225.

30. Stuart to Russell, 29 September 1862, P.R.O. 30/22/36, ff. 225–26.

31. For further details of this proposal, see chap. 13.

32. Salmon Portland Chase became secretary of the treasury on 4 March, 1861. The "orders about cotton" refers to strict enforcement of federal laws which stipulated that those purchasing cotton, including foreigners, had to faithfully observe the naval blockade or have their ships confiscated.

33. Stuart to Russell, 7 October 1862, P.R.O. 30/22/36, ff. 230–34.

34. James S. Wadsworth (1807–64) was a brigadier general charged with the defense of Washington, D.C., in 1862. He was defeated in the forthcoming election.

35. "The Edict" refers to the Emancipation Proclamation, and the "Black Flag" probably alludes to the element of piracy involved by the South's commissioning of the C.S.S. *Alabama* to be built in Liverpool, England, and then becoming a major threat to Northern shipping along the Atlantic seaboard.

36. At times during 1862 Seward considered permitting cotton to be exported from Southern ports that were under federal jurisdiction.

37. Joseph E. Hooker (1814–79), nicknamed "Fighting Joe," was wounded at Antietam, promoted to brigadier general, and in January 1863 succeeded Burnside as commander of the Army of the Potomac.

38. Stuart to Russell, 17 October 1862, P.R.O. 30/22/36, ff. 240–45.

39. During the latter half of September, General Ulysses S. Grant achieved his victory at Corinth, Mississippi.

40. Stuart to Russell, 26 October 1862, P.R.O. 30/22/36, ff. 254–60.

41. Horatio Seymour (1810–86) was Democratic governor of New York State, 1853–55 and 1863–65.

42. Stuart to Russell, 31 October 1862, P.R.O. 30/22/36, ff. 268–71.

43. John McNeil (1813–91) commanded Union troops under Fremont at St. Louis and elsewhere in Missouri. He was promoted to brigadier general in November 1862.

44. Stuart to Russell, 4 November 1862, P.R.O. 30/22/36, ff. 271–73.

45. The allusion to a Confederate invasion of England presumably refers to the failure of Southern envoys like J. M. Mason to persuade Britain to recognize the independence of the Confederacy.

46. Stuart to Russell, 7 November 1862, P.R.O. 30/22/36, ff. 273–76. A very useful discussion of the official British attitude toward mediation is N. A. Graebner, "European Interventionism and the Crisis of 1862," *Journal of the Illinois State Historical Society*, 68 (February 1976): pp. 35–45.

47. Eduard Drouyn de Lhuys (1805–81) had served several French governments as foreign minister since 1848. In November 1862 he urged France, Russia, and Britain to act jointly and offer mediation, hoping that this would force an end to the Civil War.

Chapter 13. Mediation and Domestic Emancipation, November 1862–June 1863

1. Lyons to Russell, 11 November 1862, Russell Papers, P.R.O. 30/22/36, ff. 281–90.

2. John Van Buren (1810–66) was a strong critic of Lincoln's wartime policies. He was a staunch admirer of General McClellan and supported Seymour for governor of New York State in 1862.

3. Lyons to Russell, 14 November 1862, P.R.O. 30/22/36, ff. 291–300.

4. The duke of Newcastle was colonial secretary in the British cabinet.

5. Lyons to Russell, 21 November 1862, P.R.O. 30/22/36, ff. 303–5.

6. Lyons to Russell, 24 November 1862, P.R.O. 30/22/36 ff. 306–9.

7. Lyons to Russell, 2 December 1862, P.R.O. 30/22/36, ff. 312–15.

8. Lyons to Russell, 5 December 1862, P.R.O. 30/22/36, ff. 316–19.

9. Lyons to Russell, 19 December 1862, P.R.O. 30/22/36, ff. 324–26.

10. Lyons to Russell, 22 December 1862, P.R.O. 30/22/36, ff. 327–30.

11. Lyons to Russell, 30 December 1862, P.R.O. 30/22/36, ff. 333–36.

12. Lyons to Russell, 2 January 1863, Russell Papers, P.R.O. 30/22/36, ff. 1–3.

13. Lyons to Russell, 5 January 1863, P.R.O. 30/22/37, ff. 4–6.

14. James Magee was acting British consul at Mobile, Alabama, March 1861 to March 1863.

15. The *Alabama* was a steam-powered cruiser that the Confederates clandestinely had built in Enlgand. Despite protests from the American minister to London, Charles Francis Adams, the ship was allowed to depart, on the grounds that it was unarmed,

its ownership was ostensibly neutral, and its links with the Confederacy were unproved. Once at sea, it was fitted out with guns and proved to be a highly effective raider of Northern commerce.

16. Lyons to Russell, 9 January 1863, P.R.O. 30/22/37, ff. 7–8.

17. Lyons to Russell, 23 January 1863, P.R.O. 30/22/37, ff. 9–12.

18. The "plan" may be an allusion to assisting unemployed British textile workers to emigrate to the colonies. However, there was the chance that it might be modified in terms of facilitating American slaves to escape from the South and find refuge somewhere in the possessions of the British Empire.

19. In 1862, Lincoln appointed the Revolution James Mitchell to be the new commissioner of emigration, who would aid former slaves to resettle in America or elsewhere.

20. Lyons to Russell, 2 February 1863, P.R.O. 30/22/37, ff. 13–16.

21. Lyons to Russell, 6 February 1863, P.R.O. 30/22/37, ff. 17–18.

22. Lyons to Russell, 10 February 1863, P.R.O. 30/22/37, ff. 19–22.

23. Lyons to Russell, 24 February 1863, P.R.O. 30/22/37, ff. 29–30.

24. Letters of marque and reprisal were the traditional means by which privateers could be authorized to attack an enemy's merchant shipping. In 1863, many Northerners pointed out that such letters were unnecessary since the Confederacy had no merchant fleet to intercept. Advocates of the bill in Congress contended that the measure was in partial retaliation for the British construction of Confederate commerce raiders like the *Alabama*. The clear implication was that the North might be induced to revive the use of privateers against British merchant ships, as had been done during the War of 1812, if the British continued to permit their shipyards to build Confederate vessels. The whole issue also reflected Northern frustration over the number of British merchant ships successfully running the blockade of Southern ports.

25. Lyons to Russell, 2 March 1863, P.R.O. 30/22/37, ff. 31–34.

26. Lyons to Russell, 10 March 1863, P.R.O. 30/22/37, ff. 35–37.

27. Lyons to Russell, 24 March 1863, P.R.O. 30/22/37, ff. 38–41.

28. Lyons to Russell, 7 April 1863 P.R.O. 30/22/37, ff. 42–44. The allusion to Lyons's dispatch is presumably to that of 8 December 1862, published in a Blue Book of 19 March 1863; in *Parliamentary Papers*, vol. 72, no. 3119, (1864) p. 137.

29. Lyons to Russell, 13 April 1863, P.R.O. 30/22/37, ff. 45–46.

30. Lyons to Russell, 17 April 1863, P.R.O. 30/22/37, ff. 47–50.

31. Lyons to Russell, 24 April 1863, P.R.O. 30/22/37, ff. 55–56.

32. Lyons to Russell, 5 May 1863, P.R.O. 30/22/37, ff. 57–60.

33. Gideon Welles (1802–78) was secretary of the navy from 1861 to 1869. The *Peterhoff* was a British merchant vessel bound for Mexico. Rear Admiral Charles Wilkes, responsible for the *Trent Affair* ordered the search and seizure of the *Peterhoff* off the coast of St. Thomas in the West Indies, on the pretext that its cargo was destined ultimately for the Confederacy via neutral Mexico.

34. Lyons to Russell, 8 May 1863, P.R.O. 30/22/37, ff. 61–62.

35. At Chancellorsville.

36. Lyons to Russell, 11 May 1863, P.R.O. 30/22/37, ff. 63–64.

37. Lyons to Russell, 2 June 1863, P.R.O. 30/22/37, ff. 73–74.

38. Lyons to Russell, 8 June 1863, P.R.O. 30/22/37, ff. 75–77.

39. Lyons to Russell, 12 June 1863, P.R.O. 30/22/37, ff. 78–80.

40. Charles Stanley, first baron Monck (1819–94), had been appointed governor-general of Canada in 1861.

41. Sir Alexander Milne (1806–96) was commander of the British fleet in the West Indies and North America.

42. Lyons to Russell, 19 June 1863, P.R.O. 30/22/37, ff. 84–86.
43. John Hodge was an agent for the British Honduras Company. See the letter from J. P. Usher to Hodge, 11 May 1863, in *Senate Executive Documents*, no. 55, serial 1238, 39th Congress, 1st Session, 1865–66, p. 33.
44. Lyons to Russell, 26 June 1863, P.R.O. 30/22/37, ff. 89–92.
45. Lyons to Russell, 30 June 1863, P.R.O. 30/22/37, ff. 93–95.

Chapter 14. From Gettysburg to President Lincoln's Reelection, July 1863–December 1864

1. Lyons to Russell, 3 July 1863, Russell Papers, P.R.O. 30/22/37, ff. 96–97.
2. Lyons to Russell, 6 July 1863, P.R.O. 30/22/37, ff. 98–99.
3. Lyons to Russell, 10 July 1863, P.R.O. 30/22/37, ff. 101–6.
4. Port Hudson was some 150 miles south of Vicksburg on the Mississippi River.
5. General Meade had assumed command of the Army of the Potomac shortly before the battle of Gettysburg, and it was his task to follow up this victory by pursuing the forces of Robert E. Lee.
6. Lyons to Russell, 14 July 1863, P.R.O. 30/22/37, ff. 107–10.
7. General Pierre Gustave Toutant Beauregard (1818–93) was in charge of the defense of the coastline along Georgia and South Carolina during 1863–64.
8. Edward Mortimer Archibald was British consul at New York.
9. Lyons to Russell, 17 July 1863, P.R.O. 30/22/37, ff. 111–13.
10. See below, note 16.
11. Lyons to Russell, 20 July 1863, P.R.O. 30/22/37, ff. 114–15.
12. In New York City the rioters not only attacked public officials but hapless black bystanders.
13. Lyons to Russell, 24 July 1863, P.R.O. 30/22/37, ff. 117–20.
14. Lyons to Russell, 28 July 1863, P.R.O. 30/22/37, ff. 121–29.
15. General John Hunt Morgan (1825–64) invaded Kentucky on 2 July with a force of 2,500 cavalry. Consternation spread as Morgan's Raiders moved into Indiana and then Ohio. Fresh volunteers enlisted to help thwart such inroads and to discourage Southern sympathizers. Finally, on 26 July the remnants of the Raiders, along with their commander, were captured near the Ohio-Pennsylvania border. After creating such panic in its early stages, the foray produced negligible results and wasted precious Confederate cavalry.
16. Viscount Jules Treilhard had served as chargé d'affaires of the French legation in Washington prior to Mercier's arrival and resumed these duties whenever the minister was absent from the capital.
17. Lyons to Russell, 14 August 1863, P.R.O. 30/22/37, ff. 143–46.
18. Lyons to Russell, 2 September 1863, P.R.O. 30/22/37, ff. 147–59.
19. Stuart to Russell, 18 September 1863, P.R.O. 30/22/37, ff. 170–73.
20. Congressional Act of 3 March 1863.
21. Stuart to Russell, 18 September 1863, P.R.O. 30/22/37, ff. 174–75.
22. Frederick Bernal had been British consul in Baltimore since January 1861.
23. Lord Monck was British governor-general of Canada.
24. Stuart to Russell, 22 September 1863, P.R.O. 30/22/37, ff. 178–82.
25. Salmon P. Chase (1808–73) was secretary of the treasury, 1861–64.
26. Edwin M. Stanton (1814–69) served as secretary of war, 1862–68.

27. Stuart to Russell, 28 September 1863, P.R.O. 30/22/37, ff. 183–87.

28. William S. Rosecrans (1819–98) was at this time commander of the Army of the Cumberland.

29. Braxton Bragg (1817–76) commanded the Army of the Tennessee.

30. George H. Thomas (1816–70) earned the epithet the "Rock of Chickamauga" by his crucial defensive role.

31. Ambrose E. Burnside (1824–81).

32. At the Laird shipyard in Liverpool two ironclads were nearing completion, and in early October 1863 the British government made certain that the vessels would not slip away by stationing marines aboard them.

33. Lyons to Russell, 29 September 1863, P.R.O. 30/22/37, ff. 188–92.

34. Lyons to Russell, 16 October 1863, P.R.O. 30/22/37, ff. 203–8.

35. Lyons to Russell, 20 October 1863, P.R.O. 30/22/37, ff. 209–12.

36. Lyons to Russell, 6 November 1863, P.R.O. 30/22/37, ff. 227–30.

37. Benjamin F. Butler (1818–93) earned an unenviable reputation for harshness and corruption in connection with the occupation of New Orleans in 1862.

38. Lyons to Russell, 23 November 1863, P.R.O. 30/22/37, ff. 247–50.

39. Montgomery Blair (1813–83) was Lincoln's postmaster general until forced to resign because of Radical Republican pressure in 1864. He had formerly been a member of the Democratic party.

40. Edwin M. Stanton: see above, note 26.

41. Lyons to Russell, 7 December 1863, P.R.O. 30/22/37, ff. 253–54.

42. Lyons to Russell, 21 December 1863, P.R.O. 30/22/37, ff. 259–60.

43. Charles Hastings Doyle (1805–83) was commander of British forces in Nova Scotia. He later became Nova Scotia's lieutenant governor.

44. Lyons to Russell, 24 December 1863, P.R.O. 30/22/37, ff. 261–62.

45. Thomas Corwin (1794–1865) was American minister to Mexico, 1861–64.

46. As it turned out, Mercier did leave the United States for good in December 1863. In the autumn of 1864 he became French ambassador to Spain.

47. Lyons to Russell, 29 December 1863, P.R.O. 30/22/37, ff. 263–66.

48. Lyons to Russell, 12 January 1864, Russell Papers, P.R.O. 30/22/38, ff. 1–4.

49. Charles Francis Adams (1807–86) was American minister to the Court of St. James 1861–68.

50. On 12 January 1864 federal troops landed at Matamoros, in the mouth of the Rio Grande, to rescue an American consul trapped in the midst of Mexican warring factions.

51. Admiral Alexander Milne commanded British naval forces in North America and the West Indies.

52. Lyons to Russell, 26 January 1864, P.R.O. 30/22/38, ff. 7–8.

53. Lyons to Russell, 9 February 1864, P.R.O. 30/22/38, ff. 12–15.

54. Lyons to Russell, 4 March 1864, P.R.O. 30/22/38, ff. 19–20.

55. William Tecumseh Sherman (1820–91) commanded the Army of the Tennessee.

56. Hugh Judson Kilpatrick (1836–81), with a force of about 3,500 cavalry, had tried to penetrate the defenses around Richmond in order to free Northern prisoners but found the city's perimeter too well guarded.

57. Lyons to Russell, 19 April 1864, P.R.O. 30/22/38, ff. 39–40.

58. Henry James Alderson (1834–1909) had seen action in the Crimean War prior to his assignment to the United States in 1864. Thomas Lionel Gallwey (1821–1906) grew up in Ireland, and in the years prior to his being posted to the United States, served with the Royal Engineers in the West Indies, Canada, and Gibraltar. The third name is hard to read, but appears to be Gore Browne. Unfortunately, he does not show up in the Navy list.

59. Lyons to Russell, 9 May 1864, P.R.O. 30/22/38, ff. 44–45.

60. Lyons is alluding to the efforts in Congress to terminate the Reciprocity Treaty with the Canadian provinces.

61. Lyons to Russell, 17 May 1864, P.R.O. 30/22/38, ff. 46–49.

62. Edmund Hammond (1802–90) was permanent undersecretary of the Foreign Office from 1854 to 1873.

63. Lyons to Russell, 23 May 1864, P.R.O. 30/22/38, ff. 51–52.

64. Fort Lafayette was in New York.

65. Lyons to Russell, 17 June 1864, P.R.O. 30/22/38, ff. 60–63.

66. Lyons to Russell, 12 July 1864, P.R.O. 30/22/38, ff. 64–65.

67. Lyons to Russell, 13 July 1864, P.R.O. 30/22/38, ff. 66–67.

68. During May–July, Grant's army laid siege to Petersburg on the James River south of Richmond.

69. Lyons to Russell, 15 July 1864, P.R.O. 30/22/38, ff. 70–71.

70. Joseph Hume Burnley was on the point of taking up his post at Copenhagen when he was suddenly transferred to Washington. This change of assignment reflected Lord Lyons's desperate need for assistance at the legation.

71. Francis Ottiwell Adams was serving for a few months at the Foreign Office in London before being reassigned to Washington.

72. Lyons to Russell, 22 July 1864, P.R.O. 30/22/38, ff. 74–77.

73. Lyons to Russell, 9 August 1864, P.R.O. 30/22/38, ff. 85–90.

74. Burnley was chargé d'affaires during Lyons's absence.

75. Lyons to Russell, 15 August 1864, P.R.O. 30/22/38, ff. 91–93.

76. Lyons to Russell, 23 August 1864, P.R.O. 30/22/38, ff. 95–97.

77. Lyons to Russell, 30 August 1864, P.R.O. 30/22/38, ff. 98–101.

78. Fort Morgan guarded Mobile Bay in Alabama and capitulated to the federal troops on 23 August 1854.

79. George B. McClellan (1826–85) had been relieved of his command of the Army of the Potomac in November 1862 and was not reappointed thereafter.

80. Lyons to Russell, 16 September 1864, P.R.O. 30/22/38, ff. 107–9.

81. Atlanta, Georgia, capitulated on 1 September 1864.

82. William Pitt Fessenden (1806–69) was appointed secretary of the treasury on 1 July 1864.

83. Lyons to Russell, 24 October 1864, P.R.O. 30/22/38, ff. 117–18.

84. Lyons to Russell, 1 November 1864, P.R.O. 30/22/38, ff. 123–24.

85. Lyons to Russell, 1 November 1864, P.R.O. 30/22/38, ff. 126–33.

86. Lyons to Russell, 5 December 1864, P.R.O. 30/22/38, ff. 135–36.

Chapter 15. Sir Frederick Bruce and the Opening Stages of American Reconstruction, April 1865–July 1866

1. Bruce to Russell, 27 February 1865, Russell Papers, P.R.O. 30/22/38, ff. 158–59.

2. Bruce to Russell, 8 April 1865, P.R.O. 30/22/38, ff. 170–71.

3. On 25 March 1865 a Confederate raid from Petersburg momentarily dislodged the federal garrison at Fort Stedman, but by the end of the day, the attackers were forced to withdraw after sustaining heavy casualties.

4. Joseph Eggleston Johnston (1807–91).

5. Edward Mortimer Archibald was British consul at New York.

6. Bruce to Russell, 14 April 1865, P.R.O. 30/22/38, ff. 172–74.

7. Bruce to Russell, 18 April 1865, P.R.O. 30/22/38, ff. 176–81.

8. On the same evening that Lincoln was killed, Seward was badly wounded by one of the conspirators, Lewis Payne.

9. French troops were still propping up the shaky empire of Maximilian.

10. Rudolph Waldemar Raasloff was Danish chargé d'affaires in Washington, 1857–62. He then went on special mission to China before returning to the United States.

11. John Archibald Campbell (1811–89) had been appointed a United States Supreme Court justice in 1853, opposed secession in 1861 but sided with the Confederacy, and served as Confederate assistant secretary of war, 1862–65.

12. Godfrey Weitzel (1835–84) was the major general in charge of occupying Richmond on 3 April 1865.

13. In 1865 Major General Edward Otho Cresap Ord (1818–83) was commander of the Army of the James River.

14. Bruce to Russell, 20 April 1865, P.R.O. 30/22/38, ff. 183–84.

15. Bruce to Russell, 20 April 1865, P.R.O. 30/22/38, ff. 186–89.

16. Bruce to Russell, 24 April 1865, P.R.O. 30/22/38, ff. 190–95.

17. Dispatch 251 of 23 April 1865 is in F.O. 5/1017, ff. 215–18. President Johnson's speech was made to a delegation from Indiana on 21 April.

18. On 17–18 April 1865, Johnston and Sherman negotiated terms for the surrender of various Confederate forces, while George Stoneman (1822–94) carried on operations in North Carolina.

19. President Johnson repudiated Sherman's agreement with Johnston (see note 18).

20. Bruce to Russell, 27 April 1865, P.R.O. 30/22/38, ff. 198–99.

21. Bruce to Russell, 5 May 1865, P.R.O. 30/22/38, ff. 201–2.

22. As early as 2 May, Davis was still urging the South to keep on fighting. During these days, he headed farther south through South Carolina to Georgia, where he was apprehended and imprisoned by federal troops on 10 May.

23. Bruce to Russell, 6 May 1865, P.R.O. 30/22/38, ff. 204–10.

24. Salmon P. Chase (1808–73) became chief justice of the Supreme Court in October 1864.

25. Bruce to Russell, 10 May 1865, P.R.O. 30/22/38, ff. 214–19.

26. Bruce to Russell, 16 May 1865, P.R.O. 30/22/38, ff. 221–22.

27. Bruce to Russell, 19 May 1865, P.R.O. 30/22/38, ff. 224–29.

28. Bruce to Russell, 22 May 1865, P.R.O. 30/22/38, ff. 236–41.

29. Jefferson Davis (1808–89) spent the next two years imprisoned at Fort Monroe in Virginia. He was never brought to trial.

30. Edwin M. Stanton (1814–69) remained as secretary of war following Lincoln's assassination.

31. Edmund Kirby-Smith (1824–93) commanded the Confederate forces west of the Mississippi River and was the last general to surrender to the federal authorities, provisionally on 26 May and definitively on 2 June 1865.

32. The Confederate raider *Stonewall* reached Havana on 11 May and surrendered to the Spanish authorities on 19 May.

33. Bruce to Russell, 26 May 1865, P.R.O. 30/22/38, ff. 242–46.

34. Philip Henry Sheridan (1831–88) took charge of the Army of the Shenandoah in 1864, played a key role in harassing Lee's army thereafter, and at the end of the war administered the states along the Gulf of Mexico.

35. Bruce to Russell, 1 June 1865, P.R.O. 30/22/38, ff. 252–59.

36. Bruce to Russell, 18 June 1865, P.R.O. 30/22/38, ff. 277–88.

37. Dispatch 352 of 19 June 1865 is in F.O. 5/1019, ff. 130–34. Bruce enclosed a newspaper cutting describing how police and troops in Richmond harassed newly freed blacks, restricting their movements, requiring them to carry identity cards, and jailing them arbitrarily.

38. Bruce to Russell, 17 July 1865, P.R.O. 30/22/38, ff. 313-16.

39. Bruce to Russell, 18 September 1865, P.R.O. 30/22/38, ff. 355–60.

40. Anson Burlingame (1820–70) had been a United States congressman from Massachusetts (1855-60) and American minister to China (1861–67). During part of 1865–66 he was back in the United States. Bruce had presumably first met him when they both were in China.

41. General Benjamin Franklin Butler was generally a supporter of the Radical Republicans.

42. In 1861 the term "copperhead" was applied to those Northern Democrats who wished to negotiate a settlement with the Confederacy rather than prosecuting the war to the bitter end.

43. Bruce to Clarendon, 24 November 1865, Bodleian Library, Clarendon Papers, MS Clar. Dep., C. 90, ff. 3–5.

44. An allusion to the thirty-six states then making up the Union.

45. Bruce to Clarendon, 4 December 1865, ff. 14–20.

46. Bruce to Clarendon, 2 December 1865, ff. 21–27.

47. Andrew Johnson's first annual message to Congress was delivered on 4 December 1865.

48. Charles Sumner of Massachusetts.

49. Nathaniel Prentiss Banks (1816–94) was a lawyer from Massachusetts, a governor of that state, 1858–61, a major general of volunteers during the war, and served in the United States House of Representatives, 1853–57 and 1865–73.

50. Charles Francis Adams was still American minister to Great Britain.

51. Thaddeus Stevens (1792–1868) was a representative from Pennsylvania and one of the leaders of the Radical Republicans in Congress.

52. Bruce to Clarendon, 18 December 1865, ff. 29–35.

53. Hugh McCulloch (1808–95) was secretary of the treasury from 1865 to 1869.

54. Bruce to Clarendon, 14 January 1866, ff. 58–62.

55. Bruce to Clarendon, 29 January 1866, ff. 75–82.

56. Henry J. Raymond (1820-69) was elected to the House of Representatives in 1864 and served only one term.

57. Bruce to Clarendon, 5 February 1866, ff. 93–100.

58. Myers had been British vice-consul in Norfolk, Virginia, since 1856.

59. Bruce to Clarendon, 9 February 1866, ff. 103–9.

60. The Freedmen's Bureau was a government agency established by act of Congress on 3 March 1865. Its intention was to assist blacks in their transition from slavery to citizenship. Local agents were empowered to dispense food and clothing, help blacks find work or occasionally settle on government land, and provide for education or training.

61. Bruce to Clarendon, 27 February 1866, ff. 142–44.

62. An allusion to two fifth century B.C. Athenian leaders. Cleon was the more demagogic.

63. Bruce to Clarendon, 10 March 1866, ff. 156–66.

64. Bruce to Clarendon, 16 March 1866, ff. 175–87.

65. John O'Mahony (1816–77) left Ireland in 1848, settled in the United States in 1853, helped found the Fenian Brotherhood in 1858, and headed its American branch until 1866.

66. Toward the end of 1865 the Fenian Brotherhood split over the question of short- and long-term goals. O'Mahony felt that all efforts should be directed to the fomenting of revolution in Ireland, while two of his lieutenants, Thomas William Sweeny (1820–92) and William R. Roberts (1830–97), insisted upon the immediate invasion of Canada. Their notion was that Great Britain would become so involved with disturbances in North America that she would be unable to contain any uprising in Ireland. Thus, in 1866 Roberts replaced O'Mahony as President of the Brotherhood in America, while Sweeny retained his post as Fenian secretary of war. He seemed eminently well qualified since he had been a brigadier general in the Union army during the Civil War.

67. Bruce to Clarendon, 20 March 1866, ff. 188–92.

68. Gleeson: we are unable to identify him further.

69. Bruce to Clarendon, 26 March 1866, ff. 194–98.

70. Bruce to Clarendon, 29 March 1866, ff. 199–204.

71. Bruce to Clarendon, 3 April 1866, ff. 207–12.

72. F.O. 5/1064, ff. 94–97, dispatch 117 of 3 April 1866. President Johnson's proclamation of 2 April declared that the insurrection in the South was over except for in the state of Texas.

73. Bruce to Clarendon, 29 April 1866, ff. 256–60.

74. George Gordon Meade (1815–72) was commander of the Military Division of the Atlantic.

75. Bruce to Clarendon, 6 May 1866, ff. 265–72.

76. Bruce to Clarendon, 15 May 1866, ff. 274–77.

77. Lewis Davis Campbell (1811–82) represented Ohio as a Whig in the United States Congress from 1849 to 1858, served as a colonel in the Union army, and resigned from his post as minister to Mexico on 16 June 1867.

78. Allen Granberry Thurman (1813–95) was among the leaders of the "Peace Democrats" in the North during the Civil War and served as a Democrat from Ohio in the Senate from 1867 to 1879.

79. John Albion Andrew (1818–67) established his reputation before the Civil War as an ardent abolitionist and served as governor of Massachusetts from 1860 to 1866.

80. Sonora was a state in northwestern Mexico.

81. Robert Cumming Schenck (1809–90) was a major general in the early years of the Civil War and then entered the House of Representatives in early 1863. He continued to represent Ohio until 1871 and during those years became an outspoken opponent of President Johnson.

82. Seward's wish soon came true, for the Seven Weeks War between Austria and Prussia broke out a month later.

83. Russell's cabinet resigned in mid-June to be succeeded by the earl of Derby's third ministry.

84. Bruce to Clarendon, 4 June 1866, ff. 297–98.

85. B. Doran Killian was a Fenian lawyer who had vaguely sounded out Seward in 1865 on the probable reaction that the United States government would have to a raid upon Canada.

86. Bruce to Clarendon, 10 June 1866, ff. 299–308.

87. When Earl Russell succeeded Viscount Palmerston in October 1865, it was anticipated that the new cabinet would seek to broaden the franchise.

88. The allusion is Congressional and state elections set for November 1866.

89. Bruce to Clarendon, 18 June 1866, ff. 314-19.

90. Bruce to Clarendon, 15 July 1866, ff. 328-31.

91. William Dennison (1815–82) was a former governor of Ohio, 1859-61, and United States postmaster general, 1864-69.

92. James Speed (1812–87) of Kentucky had been Lincoln's attorney general in 1864 but proved antipathetic to President Johnson and resigned in mid-July 1866.

93. James Harlan (1820–99) of Iowa served as secretary of the interior from May 1865 to August 1866.

94. Bruce to Clarendon, 22 July 1866, ff. 332–35.

Chapter 16. Preoccupation with Domestic Affairs, July 1866–September 1867

1. Bruce to Stanley, 26 July 1866, Brown Library, Liverpool, Derby Papers, volume marked "United States: Sir F. Bruce," vol. 1, f. 1.

2. Reverdy Johnson (1796–1876) had served as a Whig from Maryland in the United States Senate, 1845–49, and as a Democrat, 1863–68.

3. Napoleon III reluctantly ordered the withdrawal of French troops from Mexico, to be carried out in stages during 1866–67.

4. Bruce to Stanley, 7 August 1866 , f. 2.

5. The constitutional convention of April 1864 had abolished slavery in Louisiana. In late July 1866 some argued that this earlier convention should be reconvened in order to enfranchise certain of the blacks.

6. The Philadelphia convention was President Johnson's attempt to create a new political party of moderate Northern Democrats and rehabilitate Southerners to offset the power of the Radical Republicans.

7. Bruce to Stanley, 13 August 1866. f. 3.

8. Bruce to Stanley, 9 September 1866, f. 5.

9. Bruce to Stanley, 22 October 1866, f. 10.

10. Bruce to Stanley, 5 November 1866, f. 12.

11. See chap. 15 above for Thomas Sweeny's role in the Fenian movement.

12. William A. Dart had succeeded in intercepting some of the Fenians trying to invade Canada and had brought indictments against them. His removal from office was clearly motivated by a wish to placate the Irish vote in New York State.

13. Scheduled for November 1866.

14. Bruce to Stanley, 19 November 1866, f. 15.

15. The Fourteenth Amendment was submitted to the states for ratification on 16 June 1866.

16. Thaddeus Stevens (1792–1868) served in Congress for the state of Pennsylvania from 1848 to 1853 and 1859 until his death. As a Republican, he was an uncompromising foe of slavery, headed the powerful congressional Ways and Means Committee during the Civil War, and became an implacable opponent of Andrew Johnson's Reconstruction policy.

17. Bruce to Stanley, 26 November 1866, f. 16.

18. Bruce to Stanley, 11 December 1866, f. 17.

19. Lord Monck was governor-general of Canada.

20. Bruce to Stanley, 17 December 1866, f. 18.

21. For the role of William R. Roberts, see chap. 15 above.

22. James Stephens (1825–1901) was one of the founders of the Fenian Brotherhood; he visited America in 1858 and 1864 to raise funds, but felt the American branch should concentrate on revolution in Ireland and not on raids upon Canada. In 1866 he was living in France while trying to convince his followers that he would soon return to Ireland. In fact, he postponed that for twenty years and settled peacefully in Dublin.

23. Thomas Swann (1806–83) had been president of the Baltimore and Ohio Railroad, 1848–53, then mayor of Baltimore, 1856–60, and finally governor of Maryland, 1866–68.

24. Bruce to Stanley, 24 December 1866, f. 19.

25. Which was presumably Charles C. Tevis, who had been appointed adjutant general by the Brotherhood's cofounder, O'Mahony.

26. For more about William Delany, see below, under dates of 10 and 25 December 1866.

27. Letter of former Fenian adjutant general to Bruce, 20 December 1866, f. 19.

28. Letter of unidentified Englishman to Bruce, 10 December 1866, f. 19.

29. Bruce to former Fenian adjutant general, 22 December 1866, f. 19.

30. Bruce to Stanley, 25 December 1866, f. 20.

31. Paul Cullen (1803–78) was archbishop of Dublin and cardinal-priest; John MacHale (1791–1881) was an archbishop and Greek scholar.

32. The allusion could refer to several individuals but most likely meant Daniel O'Donoghue.

33. Sir Thomas Larcom (1801–79) was undersecretary for Ireland.

34. In May 1867 Colonel S. R. Tresilian was one of the leaders of an abortive invasion off the coast of Donegal.

35. John Alexander Logan (1826–86) rose to the rank of major general and in 1864 commanded the Army of the Tennessee.

36. Bruce to Stanley, 8 January 1867, f. 22.

37. James Wickes Taylor (1819–93) was a journalist in Ohio before opening a law office in St. Paul, Minnesota, in 1856. There he took an active interest in railroads, Minnesota's relations with Canada, and doing special commercial reports for the United States Treasury Department.

38. Bruce to Stanley, 22 January 1867, f. 23.

39. During the latter months of 1866 and the whole of 1867, there was a growing sentiment among the Republicans to bring impeachment proceedings against the president. These culminated in the formal trial of March–April 1868.

40. Those elected to Congress in November 1866 were due to take up their seats with the opening of the first session of the Fortieth Congress on 4 March 1867.

41. Bruce to Stanley, 4 March 1867, f. 30.

42. The Tenure of Office bill prevented the president from dismissing officials without the assent of the Senate, provided such appointment had originally required senatorial confirmation. It was designed to impose cabinet officials like Stanton on President Johnson. On 2 March 1867 Congress overrode the president's veto.

43. Bruce to Stanley, 25 March 1867, f. 31.

44. Bruce to Stanley, 14 May 1867, f. 36.

45. Henry Stanbery (1803–81) from Ohio was attorney general from July 1866–March 1868.

46. Bruce to Stanley, 3 June 1867, f. 37.

47. Bruce to Stanley, 11 June 1867, f. 38.

48. In the spring of 1867, Thomas F. Bourke was tried and found guilty of treason. As one of the Irish-Americans who had served in the Union Army during the American Civil War, Bourke was well known to the American press and his death sentence met with much protest in the United States. Scheduled to be hanged on 29 May, his reprieve was granted the day before.

49. Bruce to Stanley, 17 June 1867, f. 39.

50. Bruce to Stanley, 24 June 1867, f. 40.

51. During the first half of 1867, General Philip Sheridan (1831–88) was military administrator of Louisiana and Texas. The governor whom Sheridan dismissed was

James Madison Wells (1808–99), who had served since 1865. Sheridan himself was relieved of his command in July 1867 by President Johnson.

52. Bruce to Stanley, 6 August 1867, f. 45.

53. In the state of New York.

54. In July, Seward had forecast America's geographical destiny as stretching along the Pacific coast from Mexico to the North Pole. This was not surprising, since the treaty concluding America's purchase of Alaska from Russia was publicly announced on 20 June 1867.

55. Bruce to Stanley, 20 August 1867, f. 46.

56. Mr. Micawber was a character in Charles Dickens's *David Copperfield*.

57. Barrington to Ford, 27 September 1867, f. 50.

58. The doctor alluded to was presumably Dr. William Henry Hazard, who began fifty years of practice in Wakefield about 1830.

59. William Gilpin (1813–94) was the first territorial governor of Colorado, 1861–62.

60. Jacob Bigelow (1787–1879) received his medical degree from the University of Pennsylvania in 1810, taught medicine at Harvard University, and was a leading author on various diseases.

61. The allusion is presumably to Senator Charles Sumner. Henry Jacob Bigelow (1818–90) had studied medicine under his father and also practiced in Boston.

62. The allusion is presumably to Dr. Richard M. Hodges of Boston, author of several medical texts.

63. The person in question is probably Thomas Francis Bayard (1828–98).

64. Henry Howard was an attaché at the British legation in Washington from March 1866 to February 1869.

Index

463